THE MUSIC SOLUTION

Every 4LTR Press solution includes:

| Visually Engaging Textbook | + | Online Study Tools | + | Tear-out Review Cards | + | Interactive eBook | **Heading Numbers Connect Print & eBook** |

STUDENT RESOURCES:

- Interactive eBook
- Active Listening Guides
- Streaming Music
- Auto-Graded Quizzes
- Flashcards
- Audio Study Tools
- Review Cards
- OPTIONAL: Upgrade to Include Music Downloads

Students sign in at **www.cengagebrain.com**

INSTRUCTOR RESOURCES:

- All Student Resources
- Engagement Tracker
- LMS Integration
- Instructor's Manual
- Test Bank
- PowerPoint® Slides
- Instructor Prep Cards

Instructors sign in at **www.cengage.com/login**

> "Like a good recipe, you simply can't alter things that are already great. Love this layout and the study tools provided online are fantastic!"
>
> — **Amanda Brenek**, Student, *The University of Texas at San Antonio*

Engagement Tracker launches, giving faculty a window into student usage of digital tools.

4LTR Press adds eBooks in response to a 10% uptick in digital learning preferences.

AUGUST 2010

1 out of every 3 (1,400) schools has adopted a 4LTR Press solution.

NOVEMBER 2010

750,000 students are IN.

 A+

Third party research confirms that 4LTR Press digital solutions improve retention and outcomes.

IN 2011

60 unique solutions across multiple course areas validates the 4LTR Press concept.

CourseMate

Students access the 4LTR Press website at 4x's the industry average.

IN 2011

APRIL 2011

1 out of every 2 (2,000) schools has a 4LTR Press adoption.

2,000

AUGUST 2011

Over 1 million students are IN.

We're always evolving. Join the 4LTR Press In-Crowd on Facebook at www.facebook.com/4ltrpress

2013 AND BEYOND

MUSIC, Second Edition
Michael Campbell

Product Director: Monica Eckman

Product Manager: Sharon Adams Poore

Senior Content Developer: Sue Gleason Wade

Product Assistant: Rachael Bailey

Media Developer: Chad Kirchner

Associate Media Developer: Elizabeth Newell

Marketing Manager: Jillian Borden

Senior Content Project Manager: Lianne Ames

Art Director: Faith Brosnan

Manufacturing Planner: Julio Esperas

Rights Acquisition Specialist: Jessica Elias

Production Service: MPS Limited

Text Designer: Jeanne Calabrese

Cover Designer: Melissa Welch/Studio Montage

Cover Image: Gary Cralle/Stone/Getty Images

Compositor: MPS Limited

For product information and technology assistance, contact us at **Cengage Learning Customer & Sales Support, 1-800-354-9706**

For permission to use material from this text or product, submit all requests online at **www.cengage.com/permissions** Further permissions questions can be emailed to **permissionrequest@cengage.com**

Library of Congress Control Number: 2013938462

ISBN-13: 978-1-285-45405-4

ISBN-10: 1-285-45405-7

Cengage Learning
200 First Stamford Place, 4th Floor
Stamford, CT 06902
USA

Cengage Learning is a leading provider of customized learning solutions with office locations around the globe, including Singapore, the United Kingdom, Australia, Mexico, Brazil and Japan. Locate your local office at **international.cengage.com/region**

Cengage Learning products are represented in Canada by Nelson Education, Ltd.

For your course and learning solutions, visit **www.cengage.com**

Purchase any of our products at your local college store or at our preferred online store **www.cengagebrain.com**

Instructors: Please visit **login.cengage.com** and log in to access instructor-specific resources.

Printed in the United States of America
1 2 3 4 5 6 7 17 16 15 14 13

Brief Contents

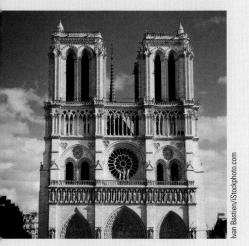

Nick Schlax/iStockphoto.com

Ivan Bastien/iStockphoto.com

Artemiy Bogdanoff/Shutterstock.com

Boston Globe/Getty Images

James Steidl/Shutterstock.com

Contents

Juan Oliver/The Bridgeman Art Library/Getty

Banner images left to right: Kickers/iStockphoto.com; SuperStock/Getty Images; Peter Macdiarmid/Getty Images News /Getty Images; Beatriz Schiller/Time Life Pictures/Getty Images; © Mats/ShutterStock.com

cenap refik ONGAN/iStockphoto.com

Apic/Hulton Archive/Getty Images

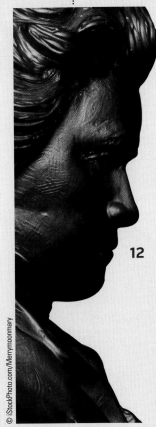

© iStockPhoto.com/Merrymoonmary

© Igor Bulgarin/ShutterStock.com

© auremar /ShutterStock.com

Constance Bannister Corp/Hulton Archive/Getty Images

© iStockPhoto.com/MarsBars

© Hung Chung Chih/ShutterStock.com

A custom edition of *MUSIC2* can be created including supplementary chapters
on the following topics from the first edition:

Vernacular Music before 1700

Eighteenth-Century Vernacular and Light Classical Music

Nineteenth-Century Vernacular and Light Classical Music

Twentieth-Century Black Voices

From Vernacular to Art

Twentieth-Century Latin Music

Contact your Cengage Learning representative for ordering information.

LEARNING OUTCOMES

After studying this chapter, you will be able to do the following:

1-1 Describe and recognize the basic properties of musical sound, relating them to the elements of music.

1-2 Define dynamics in detail.

1-3 In the context of understanding timbre and instrumentation, compare the tone color of a piano with that of an orchestra.

1-4 Learn the musical meanings of *rhythm, beat, tempo,* and *meter.*

On August 29, 1952, pianist David Tudor walked onstage at the Maverick Concert Hall in Woodstock, New York, sat down at a grand piano, placed a musical score on the piano rack, and pulled out a stopwatch. He started the watch, then closed the lid to cover the piano keys. After thirty seconds, he raised the lid. He closed it again and then lifted it two minutes and twenty-three seconds later. He closed the lid a third time and lifted it for the last time after one minute and forty seconds. During the intervals between lowering and raising the lid, Tudor sat quietly, moving only to shift pages in the music. After lifting the lid over the keys for the third time, Tudor stopped the watch, then stood up to signal the end of the work.

Most of the audience were outraged. Some left before the end of the performance. For them, Tudor had violated the most basic assumption about musical composition and performance: that musicians actually do something with sound in performance—that they make sounds with intention. To the audience, it must have seemed like a musical emperor's new clothes.

Tudor's performance was the premiere of *4'33",* a composition by the American composer and thinker John Cage (1912–1992). Cage called it his "silent piece," but he composed *4'33"* to demonstrate that no environment is truly silent. In this respect, Woodstock's Maverick Concert Hall, the back of which was open to the forest, was an ideal venue. The audience at the first performance could have heard wind rustling through the trees and rain splattering on the roof if they hadn't been so irritated at Cage's seeming violation of musical sensibility. They missed the point. Cage's composition *4'33"* was—and is—an invitation to tune in to the surrounding sound world with heightened awareness and without judgment.

Music is about structuring sound and silence in particular ways. The traditional definition of **music** is the organization of sound in time. The composition *4'33"* represents one extreme of the musical experience—unstructured ambient sound within Cage's temporal frame. We will hear music at the other extreme—music that is completely unvarying—toward the end of our survey. However, most of the music that we will encounter lies in a more familiar middle ground such as that occupied by Beethoven's Fifth Symphony.

By 1807, the year that he began work on his Fifth Symphony, Ludwig van Beethoven (1770–1827) had accepted that his deafness was irreversible. We don't know exactly when the deterioration of his hearing began, but we have correspondence from 1801 and 1802 in which he describes his symptoms and bemoans his fate. He contemplates suicide, but elects to live and to compose.

For a musician, there is no more devastating affliction than deafness. For Beethoven, it meant the end of his career as a performer. He would hear the music that he created only inside his head. He turned inward professionally and socially; visitors used notebooks to communicate with him. That Beethoven was one of the truly great composers of any era puts him in select company. That he not only continued to compose but also created his greatest works after losing his hearing makes his achievement unique.

Beethoven's Fifth Symphony is his most autobiographical work: it is the story of his triumph over adversity. The evidence is in the music; it gives some credence to an apparently fabricated anecdote that Beethoven told his secretary Anton Schindler that the famous opening motive is "fate knocking at the door." Among the most compelling moments in Beethoven's musical account is the passage that connects the third and fourth major sections of the work, or movements (see Music Concept Check: Musical Expression). This passage depicts Beethoven's deafness and his determination to triumph over it.

🛜 Music Concept Check: Musical Expression

Listen to Beethoven, Symphony No. 5, third and fourth movements, in CourseMate or your eBook. ●

The excerpt begins with the oboe and the plucked (pizzicato) violins reprising a modified version of the melody heard earlier in the movement, at that time blared out by horns. Here, the dramatic drop in volume is Beethoven's way of communicating that he can no longer hear. As the movement draws to a close, the music continues to disintegrate, until we are left with only a sustained chord and the soft tap on a kettledrum. After a few seconds, the violins begin to noodle in a seemingly aimless way with a fragment of melody. The music gradually grows louder as the full orchestra joins in. Suddenly, the orchestra blasts out a stirring melody, with the trumpets leading the charge. Within seconds, we have our bearings: music we don't have to strain to hear, the blare of brass instruments, a steady beat, and a tune we can easily remember. With these familiar sounds, Beethoven completes his journey from darkness to light: he refuses to let deafness stifle his creative spirit.

This excerpt highlights our most familiar ways of responding to a musical experience: hearing how loud it is, recognizing the sounds we hear, locating the beat, memorizing the tune. It also demonstrates how great musicians can shape these most fundamental musical qualities to convey deep feeling with enormous power. The beginning of the fourth movement of this symphony is stirring enough on its own, but it gains even more impact because it contrasts so dramatically with what preceded it: from soft to loud, from unusual (plucked strings, drums playing a "melody") to familiar sounds, from ambiguous rhythms to a strong pulse, from seemingly tuneless tones to tuneful melody.

LEARNING OUTCOME 1-1

Describe and recognize the basic properties of musical sound, relating them to the elements of music.

1-1 Properties of Musical Sound

The four entry points just listed—volume, sounds, beat, and tune—grow out of the properties of musical sound. They are the most accessible manifestations of the four properties of musical sound:

1. How loud the sound is
2. How long it lasts
3. How high or low it is
4. Its distinctive tonal quality

1-1A Dynamics

We use the word **dynamics** to refer to the relative loudness or softness of musical sound. We measure the volume of sound in **decibels (dB)**, units that range from 0 dB (the minimum that you can hear) to 60 dB (the ordinary speaking voice),

music Organization of sound in time

dynamics Relative loudness or softness of musical sound

decibel (dB) Unit that measures the volume of sound

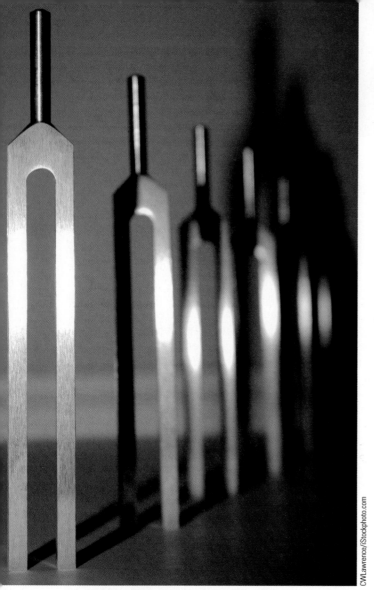

A tuning fork that vibrates at 440 cycles per second produces a definite pitch in the midrange of a woman's voice.

CWLawrence/iStockphoto.com

to 110 dB (heard at the front rows at a rock concert), to 130 dB (the pain threshold), to 160 dB (resulting in a perforated eardrum). However, in musical contexts we typically describe dynamics in more general terms: very loud, very soft, or somewhere in between.

1-1B Duration

We use the word duration to refer to the length of time that a musical sound or silence lasts. In many instances, we measure the duration of a sound or intended silence simply by noting when it begins and when it ends. However, when we encounter a series of sounds separated by silence, such as the audible space between strokes in a drum solo, we tend to measure the duration of the sound as the length of time between one impact and the next rather than the actual duration of the sound, which dies away quickly.

duration The length of time that a musical sound or silence lasts
pitch The relative highness or lowness of a sound
timbre The distinctive tonal properties of a sound
elements of music Dynamics, rhythm, timbre, melody, harmony, texture, and form

1-1C Pitch

We use the word pitch to refer to the relative highness or lowness of a sound. The pitch of a sound is determined by its frequency, which is measured as the number of vibrations or cycles per second. The highest-pitched string of a conventionally tuned guitar vibrates at 330 cycles per second, whereas the lowest-pitched string vibrates at one-fourth of that speed, 82.5 cycles per second. We typically use words like *high* and *low* to describe the speed of the vibration: for example, we would say that the top string of the guitar (the one closest to the performer's leg) produces a higher pitch than the bottom string does. We also distinguish between sounds with definite pitch, because they have a consistent frequency, and sounds with indefinite pitch, which do not. Many percussion sounds, including those made on a drum set, convey only a general sense of high and low. Sounds such as the crash of a cymbal or the white noise (the complete range of audible frequencies heard at the same time) heard between radio stations may have duration, but because they have no consistent frequency, they lack definite pitch.

1-1D Timbre

We use the word timbre (TAM-ber) to refer to the distinctive tonal properties of a sound. When we distinguish the sound of your voice from the sound of a friend's and, in music, the sound of an electric guitar from the sound of a violin, we are responding to differences in timbre. Timbre is the only property of musical sound that does not fall on a continuum. Differences in dynamics, duration, and pitch do, because they involve matters of degree: louder or softer, longer or shorter, higher or lower. By contrast, distinctions in timbre are not measurable by degree but by the shapes and frequencies of the sound waves produced by a voice or instrument. A single instrument playing a single tone creates a complex and distinctive waveform. Why? Because almost all musical sounds contain several frequencies sounding simultaneously. When you hear a tone, one frequency dominates, but the tone also contains other frequencies vibrating faster, and sometimes slower, in varying strengths. The resulting waveform—a synthesis of these various frequencies—produces the distinctive timbre of a musical sound. The timbre of a piano is different from the timbre of a flute or a violin because the combinations of frequencies represented by their waveforms are different.

1-1E The Elements of Music

The properties of sound are the four qualities from which the elements of music emerge. Dynamics describes levels and fluctuations in loudness. Timbre is at the heart of *instrumentation*—the selection and combination of instruments and voices used and the manner in which they are performed. *Rhythm* is the product of the durational patterns created by voices and instruments. Successions and combinations of pitches become *melody* and *harmony*. From timbre, rhythm, melody, and harmony comes *texture*, the fabric of sound created by the interaction of all the parts of a musical performance. From the sequence of events, as shaped by all of these elements, comes *form*—the organization of music in time. We discuss each element in turn in this and the next chapter.

1-2 Dynamics

On our recording of Beethoven's symphony by the Cleveland Symphony Orchestra (see Music Concept Check: Musical Expression), more than sixty string players sound out the stirring melody that begins the fourth movement and the harmony that supports it. At the same time, only seven members of the orchestra's brass section play the same melody and harmony. Despite their disadvantage in numbers, the brass instruments dominate, while the other instruments remain in the background.

This stunning discrepancy between sheer numbers and power demonstrates that how an instrument is designed and the manner in which it is played are linked to how loud it sounds. Accordingly, in this chapter we consider dynamics and timbre together and experience them as well in a contrast between the sounds of the solo piano and the full symphony orchestra.

Terms associated with dynamics (see The Language of Music: Dynamics) describe either a level of loudness or a change in loudness. Dynamics is the easiest element to discern: no specialized musical training is needed to hear contrasts between loud and soft or even to hear loud gradually becoming soft or vice versa.

Dynamics, more immediately than any other element, can help communicate the character of a musical work or of a section within a work. Before we process anything else in a piece of music—the shape of the melody, the rhythm, the instruments—we respond to its dynamic level. We are most responsive to dynamics when the dynamic levels approach the extreme in either direction or when there are strong contrasts, either sudden or gradual. The ear-splitting loudness of heavy-metal groups is a big part of their musical message; conversely, the gentle synthesizer sounds of New Age music are integral to its message.

🛜 Music Concept Check: Dynamics

In your eBook, view a demonstration of dynamics. ●

1-3 Timbre and Instrumentation

Timbre is most fundamentally realized in instrumentation, the selection and combination of instruments and voices used in the performance of a musical work. A performance may require only singers, only instruments, or singers and instruments together. It may require only a single musician, such as a pianist—even no musician at all, as is the case in purely electronic compositions—or it may require the massed resources of a 100-member orchestra and a 200-voice choir.

In the course of our survey, you will hear instruments from many times and places, from medieval rebecs and recorders to the rhythm instruments of rock bands. In this chapter, we introduce the symphony orchestra to present many of the instruments that you will hear in the musical examples and to explore the expressive potential of tone color.

1-3A The Symphony Orchestra

The most established and iconic instrumental ensemble in Western culture is the symphony orchestra (see Fig. 1.1). Many major cities in the world have a resident symphony orchestra. Enjoying more widespread support than any other musical group, orchestras perform the most familiar instrumental music in the classical tradition, accompany operas and musicals, and have become a popular medium for film scores, such as John Williams's music for the *Star Wars* series. A large symphony orchestra, such as the Chicago Symphony Orchestra or the New York Philharmonic, has a roster of about a hundred musicians. Among common large instrumental ensembles, only a university marching band is likely to be larger than a modern symphony orchestra.

Today's orchestra is built around four major sections, or families, of instruments: bowed strings, woodwinds, brass, and percussion.

1-3B String Instruments

The bowed string family, or strings, is the core of the orchestra. There are four orchestral string instruments: the violin, the viola, the violoncello (or simply cello), and the double bass. The violin is the highest-pitched member of the string family, and it has the most brilliant sound. The viola is slightly larger and proportionally wider than the violin.

instrumentation Selection and combination of instruments and voices used in the performance of a musical work

symphony orchestra Large (often 100 musicians or more) musical ensemble containing strings, woodwinds, brass, and percussion

strings Musical instruments that produce sound when the musician draws a bow across or plucks the strings

THE language OF MUSIC

Dynamics

In part because the composer's practice of indicating dynamics in a musical score began in Italy, the terms commonly used for dynamics are Italian. The two basic terms for indicating dynamic levels are the Italian words for loud and soft: *forte* (FOR-tay) means "loud," and *piano* (pee-AH-noh) means "soft." By attaching the superlative suffix –*issimo* (EE-see-moh) or adding the word *mezzo* (MEHD-soh), which means "middle" or "medium," composers could easily indicate six levels of dynamics. Here are the terms for the six most commonly used dynamic levels, from loudest to softest, along with their abbreviations:

fortissimo, *ff* (for-TEE-see-moh)	the superlative of forte: very loud
forte, *f* (FOR-tay)	loud
mezzo forte, *mf* (MEHD-soh FOR-tay)	medium loud: softer than forte but louder than mezzo piano
mezzo piano, *mp* (MEHD-soh pee-AH-noh)	medium soft: louder than piano but softer than mezzo forte
piano, *p* (pee-AH-noh)	soft
pianissimo, *pp* (pee-ah-NEE-see-moh)	very soft

Just as the ups and downs of inflection are intrinsic to speech, dynamic change—raising or lowering the level of sound—occurs in music making. Here, too, musicians use Italian words to describe dynamic change. Here are the most common:

crescendo, ◁ (creh-SHEN-doh)	growing louder
decrescendo or diminuendo, ▷ (dih-min-yoo-EN-doh)	growing softer
sforzando, *sf* (ssfort-SAHN-doh)	a strong accent on a single note or chord

Dynamic indications like the abbreviations shown here began to appear in musical scores around 1600. However, it wasn't until the late eighteenth century that dynamic indications appeared routinely in composers' scores and that the markings indicated both dynamic level and dynamic change.

It is somewhat lower in range and has a richer, mellower sound. In orchestral playing, both the violin and the viola are played by placing the instrument under the chin so that the left hand is free to move up and down the neck of the instrument and the right hand can draw the bow across the strings.

The cello is significantly larger than the viola and is tuned lower. The double bass, or simply bass, is the largest and lowest pitched of the four orchestral strings.

In a modern major symphony orchestra, the strings comprise almost two-thirds of the entire roster (see Music Concept Check: Strings). Even though there are four different string instruments that make up the string section of the symphony orchestra, as described above, there are five string sections, each with multiple players. The violins are divided into two sections: first violins and second violins. Usually there are sixteen to nineteen first violins, thirteen to

fortissimo, *ff* Very loud
forte, *f* Loud
mezzo forte, *mf* Medium loud
mezzo piano, *mp* Medium soft
piano, *p* Soft
pianissimo, *pp* Very soft
crescendo, ◁ Growing louder
decrescendo (diminuendo), ▷ Growing softer
sforzando, *sf* Strong accent on a single note or chord

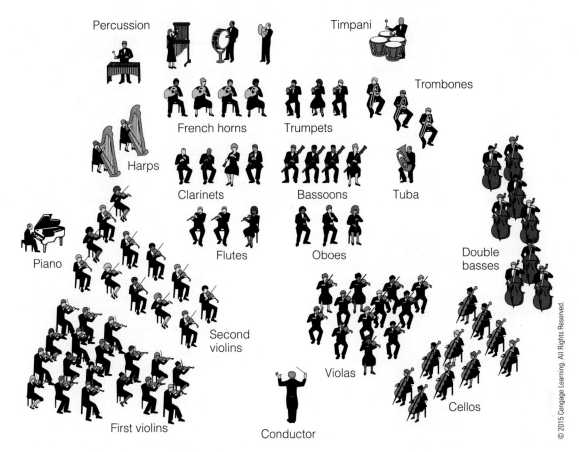

Figure 1.1 Layout of a symphony orchestra

The family of string instruments. These musicians represent the relative sizes of some of the string sections of the orchestra. From left to right: viola, first and second violins, and cello. Note the pronounced difference in size between the cello and the other three instruments, and that the viola is slightly larger and wider than the violin.

sixteen second violins, eleven or twelve violas, ten or eleven cellos, and eight or nine basses. Typically, all of the players within a section play the same part: the first violinists play the first violin part; the second violinists, the second violin part; and so on. The most common exception to this is the bass part, which often **doubles** (plays the same part as) the cello part, an octave lower. Multiple performers on each string part are necessary in most of the orchestral repertoire to create a rich string sound and to balance the power and brilliance of the rest of the orchestra, particularly the brass and percussion instruments.

Music Concept Check: Strings

In your eBook, hear the orchestral strings enter in Beethoven's Fifth Symphony, third movement, from low to high: first low strings, with the basses doubling the cellos, and then violas, second violins, and first violins. •

In orchestral music, the most common way of producing sound on a string instrument is to draw a bow across a string, which is stretched over the *bridge*, a small piece of wood held in place on the instrument's body by the tension of the strings themselves. Skilled performers can use the bow to produce a remarkable range of sounds, from melodies that flow smoothly to sharp, clipped notes. A common alternative

double Having the same line of music played by more than one instrument simultaneously

timbre and instrumentation | **7**

playing technique is pizzicato, in which the performer plucks the string instead of bowing it (Music Concept Check: Pizzicato). In both cases, the resulting vibrations are transmitted to a resonating cavity, then out through sound holes carved in the front of the instrument.

Music Concept Check: Pizzicato

In your eBook, hear pizzicato violins (and bassoon) in the third movement of Beethoven's Symphony No. 5. •

1-3C Woodwind Instruments

There are four woodwind sections in all major orchestras: flutes (piccolo, flute); oboes (oboe, English horn); clarinets (clarinet, bass clarinet); and bassoons (bassoon, contrabassoon) (see Music Concept Check: Woodwinds). Each group of instruments has a distinctive shape and method of tone production. Indeed, the flute is no longer made of wood, although it once was; today it is usually made from precious metals. However, it is still considered a woodwind instrument.

Flutists (sometimes referred to as flautists) produce sound by blowing across a mouth hole; they hold the instrument horizontally. Oboists blow into a double reed, two slightly curved pieces of cane that have been bound together and scraped to almost nothing at the tip. Oboists hold the instrument out from their body. Clarinetists attach a reed made from a single piece of cane to a mouthpiece that connects to the body of the instrument. They

also hold the instrument out from their body. Bassoonists also use a double reed attached to a long, thin tube, which connects to the body of the instrument. They usually play sitting down. Due to the length of the bassoon, performers must hold the instrument out to the right side of their body.

The other instruments in each section, such as the piccolo and English horn, are similar enough in shape and playing technique that performers can move between them much more easily than they could move between instruments in different groups. A flutist playing the piccolo need only adapt her basic technique to a smaller instrument; a flutist attempting to play the oboe would have to learn an entirely new instrument.

Not surprisingly, these instruments have quite distinct timbres, which nineteenth-century French composer Hector Berlioz described vividly in *Grand Traité d'Instrumentation et d'Orchestration Modernes*, his landmark treatise on orchestration.

> The flute: The sonority of this instrument is gentle in the middle range, fairly penetrating in the upper range.
>
> The oboe: The oboe is principally a melodic instrument; it has a rustic character, full of tenderness, I would say even of shyness.
>
> The clarinet: The clarinet is . . . an epic instrument. . . . It is the voice of heroic love.

The woodwind quintet, the most established woodwind chamber ensemble, includes the four main orchestral woodwinds and the French horn. From left to right: flute, clarinet, French horn, bassoon, and oboe. Performers: the Camerata Woodwind Quintet of Western Illinois University.

The brass quintet, the major brass-only chamber group, features the four main orchestral brass instruments. From left to right: trumpets, French horn, tuba, and trombone. Performers: the Lamoine Brass Quintet of Western Illinois University.

The bassoon: The bassoon . . . has a propensity towards the grotesque . . . [its] upper notes have a somewhat painful and suffering character, I might call it almost pitiful.

If you listen to the woodwinds one after the other, you will hear sharp timbral contrasts; by contrast, the members of the string family provide a relatively smooth timbral continuum.

🛜 Music Concept Check: Woodwinds

In your eBook, hear a pair of flutes, in Dvořák's Slavonic Dance in G minor.

Listen to an oboe solo in the first movement of Beethoven's Symphony No. 5.

Hear the clarinet, in Berlioz's *Symphonie fantastique*, fifth movement.

Listen to the bassoon, at first alone and then joined by clarinets, at the beginning of Stravinsky's ballet *The Rite of Spring*. ●

1-3D Brass Instruments

Brass instruments (see Music Concept Check: Brass Section) produce sound when musicians' lips vibrate against a mouthpiece that has been inserted into a coiled metal tube ending in a flared bell. The most widely used brass instruments in a modern symphony orchestra are, from highest to lowest pitched, the trumpet, horn (also called the French horn), trombone, and tuba. All four descend from ancient trumpets, which were also long, conical metal tubes with a mouthpiece at one end and a bell at the other.

Like the modern-day bugle, these early instruments were limited to only a few notes due to the fixed length of the tube. So, instrument makers later developed mechanisms that enabled brass instruments to play all of the available pitches over the range of the instrument. The trombone was the first to assume its modern form. The slide, which enables trombonists to change pitch by temporarily lengthening the tubing, first appeared in the fifteenth century in the sackbut, an antecedent of the modern trombone. Valves and pistons first appeared around 1800 on trumpets and horns. The tuba is a much more modern instrument, invented during the 1830s.

The most characteristic sound of brass instruments is produced with an open bell. However, brass players occasionally change the timbre of their instruments by inserting a **mute** in the bell. A mute for brass instruments is any device placed in the bell of the brass instrument that alters the character of the sound produced. It is

pizzicato Technique of plucking a string instead of bowing it
woodwind Musical instrument that produces sound by blowing air through a reed or across an open hole causing air to vibrate within a tube
brass Musical instrument that produces sound when the musician's lips vibrate against a mouthpiece that has been inserted into a coiled tube ending in a flared bell
mute Device that can change the timbre of an instrument when it is inserted in or applied to the instrument; instruments that most frequently use mutes are those of the brass and string families

typically a hollow, conical-shaped device made of metal, cardboard, fiberboard, wood, or similar material.

 Music Concept Check: Brass Section

In your eBook, hear the brass section, with trumpets dominant, in the second movement of Beethoven's Symphony No. 5.

Listen to horns, in the third movement of Beethoven's Symphony No. 5. •

1-3E Percussion Instruments

The percussion family is potentially the largest and most diverse family of orchestral instruments. Their common feature is the method of sound production: percussionists play their instruments by striking one object against another—for example, a drumstick against a cymbal or drum, or mallets against the bars of a xylophone.

Percussion instruments are distinguished by two criteria. One pertains to the final result: percussion instruments that produce definite pitches, such as timpani and xylophones, and those that produce indefinite pitches, such as cymbals and drums. The other pertains to the part of the instrument that is struck: some instruments, such as drums and timpani, have a membrane made of animal skin or synthetic material, which is stretched over a frame; others feature thicker materials such as metal (cymbals, triangle, xylophone) or wood (marimba, wood block).

The extensive use of percussion in orchestral composition is a relatively recent development. During the eighteenth century, the only frequently used percussion instrument in symphonic music was the timpani. Drums, triangle, and cymbals, used occasionally in the eighteenth century, became more common in the nineteenth. Xylophones, marimbas, and other similar instruments were still a novelty in the nineteenth century but became more widely used in the twentieth. Twentieth-century orchestral music generally features percussion, including ethnic percussion instruments, such as the maracas, more prominently than did early orchestral pieces.

1-3F Other Instruments

A few instruments, most commonly the harp, piano, organ, and saxophone, are used infrequently in the symphony orchestra and thus are not discussed in detail here. The harp has the longest orchestral history (and the longest history overall). Mozart composed a concerto for flute and harp, and his contemporaries occasionally used it in opera orchestras. The harp was used more frequently in the nineteenth century, especially in ballet music. The piano has been used as an orchestral instrument mostly in the twentieth century. The pipe organ has been a less popular member of the orchestra because many concert halls do not have one installed.

The saxophone, a member of the woodwind family, is more common in jazz ensembles than in the symphony orchestra. It has a mouthpiece onto which a single reed is attached, similar to the clarinet. But unlike most woodwinds, the saxophone is—and always has been—made of metal.

Cymbals

bikeriderlondon/shutterstock.com

Xylophone

M.M.I/Shutterstock.com

Timpani

Vhsrt-just /iStockphoto.com

Snare drum

Pixhook/iStockphoto.com

🛜 Music Concept Check: Orchestra Tour

In CourseMate and your eBook, hear and see all the sections of the orchestra and a complete performance of Benjamin Britten's *Young Person's Guide to the Orchestra.* •

1-3G Orchestration

In the 1980s, Ted Turner scandalized the film establishment by adding color to old black-and-white films. An analogous practice in music—arranging works originally composed for piano or organ to be played by a symphony orchestra—was well established. We use the term orchestration to identify the technique and artistry of assigning musical parts for instruments in various combinations. Although orchestration typically refers to the symphony orchestra, the term applies to assigning musical parts for combinations of instruments found in any instrumental ensemble.

One purpose of orchestration is to add a variety of timbres, or tone colors. If we compare the timbre of a work for a single instrument, such as the piano, with a black-and-white film, then arranging that work for an orchestra, with its dozens of timbres and countless timbral combinations, is akin to "colorizing" it. We illustrate this point by presenting a hybrid version of Wolfgang Amadeus Mozart's (1756–1791) variations on a theme composed earlier by Christoph Willibald Gluck (1714–1787): "Unser dummer Pöbel meint" (see Music Concept Check: Timbral Contrast). Mozart originally composed his version of the work for piano. In 1887, about a century later, the Russian composer Pyotr Ilyich Tchaikovsky (chy-KOFF-skee; 1840–1893), a lifelong admirer of Mozart's music, arranged it for full orchestra as part of his *Mozartiana* suite.

In a conventional piano performance of Mozart's original work, one hears almost every section twice. In our sampling from both works, we have replaced the repetition of each section on the piano with Tchaikovsky's orchestral remake so that you can hear piano and orchestral versions of the same material, one after the other.

This hybrid example illustrates how orchestral timbres can transform the sound of a musical work. The personalities of the many instruments in effect reshape the work. Tchaikovsky's orchestration of Mozart's sparkling variations enriches them with tone color. Instead of using the sound of only one instrument—the piano—Tchaikovsky drew on the varied timbres of a full orchestra: combinations of strings, woodwinds, and brass, along with a battery of percussion instruments. Tchaikovsky varies both instrument choice and the number of instruments as a way of highlighting differences in dynamics and providing timbral interest.

The two versions acquaint us with two of the important sound worlds of classical music: the piano and the orchestra, a single instrument versus a hundred. It is important to keep in mind that although the timbral variety of Tchaikovsky's orchestration adds immediate appeal, more tone color isn't necessarily better; it's just different. For listeners, it isn't as much about choosing one over the other as it is about appreciating what both versions have to offer.

🛜 Music Concept Check: Timbral Contrast

In your eBook, hear the contrast between "black-and-white" piano timbre and the "colors" of the orchestra in Mozart/ Tchaikovsky, hybrid compilation of "Unser dummer Pöbel meint" and *Mozartiana.* •

LEARNING OUTCOME 1-4

Learn the musical meanings of *rhythm, beat, tempo,* and *meter.*

1-4 Rhythm, Beat, Tempo, and Meter

Rhythm is the time dimension of music. It grows out of the patterns of musical movement in time. Every musical event that happens in time contributes to the rhythm of a musical work. The overall impression of rhythm can be simple or complex, fast or slow, measured or unmeasured.

We will encounter a broad range of rhythmic approaches in our survey, from a chant that does not have a steady beat and an electronic composition without a steady beat to the propulsive rhythms heard in music by J. S. Bach, Béla Bartók, and Chuck Berry.

1-4A Beat

Our most familiar and accessible experiences with rhythm—in life as well as in music—typically occur when events—our heartbeat, the clickety-clack of the train on the tracks, the rhythms in a dance track or a Bach concerto—establish and maintain regular patterns. We call the regular rhythm that mostly easily connects our movements to the music the beat. It is most often our point of entry into rhythm.

percussion instrument Musical instrument that produces sound by striking one object against another
orchestration The craft and artistry of assigning musical parts for instruments in various combinations
tone color A distinctive timbre
rhythm Pattern or patterns of musical movement in time

Poco_bw /iStockphoto.com

Rhythm is that irresistible element of music that makes you want to move in time to the beat.

In most situations, what we call the beat is the regular, recurring pulse at a speed that matches up with large-scale physical movement: walking, running, marching, dancing, exercising, tapping our foot, or conducting an orchestra. We most easily sense the beat through some combination of accent and pattern, such as the OOM-pah rhythm in the accompaniment of a march or a rag (see Music Concept Check: Sensing the Beat). By contrast, the absence of regular accent and pattern makes the beat hard or even impossible to discern.

 Music Concept Check: Sensing the Beat

In your eBook, listen to an easily found beat created by the regular OOM-pah pattern in the accompaniment of Scott Joplin's "The Entertainer."

In an excerpt from Berlioz, *Symphonie fantastique*, the beat is difficult to hear because there is no consistent rhythmic pattern or regular accent. •

1-4B Tempo

We use the word tempo (see The Language of Music: Tempo) to describe the speed of the beat—fast, slow, or somewhere in between—and we measure it in beats per minute. Typically, the tempo of a musical work falls somewhere between 70 and 140 beats per minute. For example, a march and a disco song typically have a fast tempo—about 120 beats per minute—energetic enough that you can march or dance in time to the music, but not so fast that you're exhausted after a few minutes.

Tempo can contribute significantly to the mood of a musical composition, in part because we can so easily relate it to such basic pulses as our heartbeat and the speed at which we walk. This is especially the case at the upper and lower boundaries of our comfort zone. For example, the supercharged tempos of a punk song or a circus march convey manic energy, whereas the extremely slow tempo of a funeral march—so slow that we have to hesitate between steps—helps convey the solemnity of the occasion.

1-4C Meter

Meter is the framework for rhythmic organization, created by the grouping and division of beats. We label meters both by the grouping of beats into slower rhythms and by the characteristic division of the beat. However, in this chapter, we are concerned almost exclusively with the grouping of beats and the terminology associated with it.

A meter in which the beats are grouped by twos is a duple meter. "Twinkle, Twinkle, Little Star" is an obvious and familiar example. A meter in

beat Regularly recurring pulse associated with music

tempo Speed of the beat in a piece of music

meter Framework for rhythmic organization, created by the grouping and division of beats

duple meter Meter whose beats are grouped by two

triple meter Meter whose beats are grouped by three

quadruple meter Meter whose beats are grouped by four

measure (bar) Consistent grouping of beats in a work

accent *More* of some musical element

The supercharged tempo of a punk song helps convey manic energy.

which beats are grouped by threes is a triple meter. "The Star-Spangled Banner" has a clear triple meter. A meter in which the beats are grouped by fours is a quadruple meter. The Christmas carol "Hark! The Herald Angels Sing" is in quadruple meter.

1-4D Recognizing Meter

We recognize the meter of a musical work mainly through two rhythmic features: pattern repetition and accent. Patterns can be regular or irregular, but the *repetition* of the pattern must be regular enough in order to confirm the meter.

Accent most often involves *more* of some musical element: a sound is accented if it is louder, longer, higher, thicker (a chord versus a single note), or more prominent in any way. The two most common forms of accent are loudness and duration. As the excerpts cited here and countless other musical works evidence, accent and pattern generally work together to establish meter. It is possible to have accents and patterns that do not line up with the metrical structure; we will encounter examples shortly. But accent and pattern must consistently confirm the metrical structure if it is to be projected clearly and unambiguously.

1-4E Rhythm and Meter

In most of the music that we encounter, meter is the framework for rhythm (see The Language of Music: Notating Rhythm). Meter is like a hierarchical grid drawn in time rather than space. Meter is necessarily generic and simplified. There are countless compositions in duple meter and countless more in triple meter, for instance. Rhythm is the specific design etched on the grid. It is, or can be, more individual and particular. By way of example: the fourth, fifth, and sixth variations from Mozart's twelve variations on "Twinkle, Twinkle, Little Star" (which he knew as the French song "Ah, vous dirai-je, Maman") are all in duple *meter*. But, even though they move at the same tempo and use the same melody, their *rhythm* is discernibly different in part because the beat is divided into four, three, and two equal parts, respectively (see Music Concept Check: Beat Division).

THE language OF MUSIC

Tempo

Like dynamic markings, the most widely used tempo indications are in Italian. Although there is general agreement as to their relative speeds—presto is faster than allegro; largo is slower than adagio—none represents a specific range of speeds measured in beats per minute. Here are the eight most common terms with their English translations, ordered from fast to slow:

presto	(PRESS-toe): very fast
vivace	(vih-VAH-chay): lively and fast
allegro	(ah-LEG-grow): cheerful, lively
moderato	(mod-air-AH-toe): moderate
andante	(ahn-DAHN-tay): walking speed
adagio	(ah-DAH-gee-oh): slow and stately
lento	(LEN-toe): very slow
largo	(LAR-go): broad

Interestingly, only moderato and lento refer specifically to tempo. The others originally indicated the character of the work rather than a specific speed. Two additional notes: First, like dynamic markings, these eight tempo markings are occasionally modified by superlatives (*-issimo*) and diminutives (*-etto; -ino*). Second, tempo indications were often modified with further clues to the character of the work: "allegro con brio," Beethoven's tempo indication for the first movement of his Fifth Symphony, translates as "cheerfully lively with brilliance."

🛜 Music Concept Check: Beat Division

In your eBook, compare the different rhythms of Variations 4, 5, and 6, all of which have the same tempo and meter, in an excerpt from Mozart's twelve variations on "Ah, vous dirai-je, Maman." ●

The degree to which rhythmic events line up with the meter often depends on the function of the music. Music intended for movement—marching, dancing, aerobicizing—typically marks beat clearly. Anyone who has spent time in a club has probably experienced the relentless thump of a synthesized bass drum marking the beat. By contrast, in music intended for listening, meter may recede into the background; the Berlioz excerpt cited above is an extreme example.

A comparison of the theme of Mozart's variation set (which you will certainly recognize as a version of "Twinkle, Twinkle, Little Star") and the elegant eleventh variation highlights the varying relationship between meter and rhythm. The simple theme could easily be a primer on meter: the rhythm of the melody marks the beat; the rhythm of note change in the melody (a change every two notes) establishes a duple meter. It's hard to imagine a more straightforward instance of duple meter (see Music Concept Check).

🛜 Music Concept Check: Meter and Rhythm

In your eBook, hear an instance of a close relationship between meter and rhythm in the theme of Mozart's twelve variations "Ah, vous dirai-je, Maman." ●

In the first ten variations, Mozart maintains the tempo and clarity of meter while adding rhythmic variety. However, in the eleventh variation, he abruptly downshifts to a slower tempo and makes use of several rhythmic strategies that play off our expectations regarding beat and meter (see Music Concept Checks on rhythm that follow).

Anyone who has spent time in a club has probably experienced the relentless thump of a synthesized bass drum marking the beat.

THE language OF MUSIC

The most common symbols for notating rhythm serve one of four functions:
1. Indicate the duration of sound
2. Indicate the duration of silence
3. Identify or clarify the meter
4. Indicate tempo

The notation of duration begins with a set of symbols that shows rhythmic relationships in a 2:1 ratio. This durational pyramid shows the relative durations of the most commonly used durational values.

The symbols in the pyramid indicate the duration of sound. A comparable set of symbols exists to notate silences within a musical work. These symbols, called rests, are shown here, on the right, with their sound equivalents.

The time (meter) signature (see below), which appears at the beginning of a musical score (or at any point in the score where the meter changes), identifies the meter. The top number tells the user that there are two beats per measure (duple meter); the bottom number indicates that the quarter note is assigned to represent the beat. Barlines mark off measures or bars with a vertical line. The line runs from the top to the bottom of the staff, the set of five horizontal lines.

Since the early 1800s, composers have had the option of including a metronome marking to indicate the tempo, or speed of the beat. The marking is written as: (duration representing the beat) = (speed of the beat in beats per minute). In this illustration, the beat is represented by the quarter note, and the tempo is 120 beats per minute.

The Pyramid of Halfs

Each line represents one bar of 4/4 time

One whole note

Two half notes

Four quarter notes

Eight eighth notes

Sixteen sixteenth notes

Name	Note	Rest
Whole note		
Half note		
Quarter note		
Eighth note		
Sixteenth note		

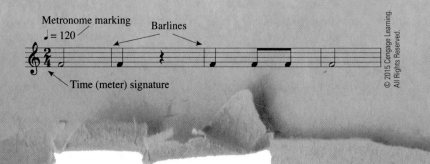

Metronome marking ♩ = 120

Barlines

Time (meter) signature

🛜 Music Concept Check: Rhythmic Play

In your eBook, hear Mozart's multiple strategies for playing off the meter in the eleventh of his twelve variations on "Ah, vous dirai-je, Maman." •

Here are Mozart's strategies in order of appearance in the eleventh variation:

1. A tempo outside the "comfort zone" of the beat. The tempo of the slow eleventh variation is less than half the speed of the preceding variations. The slower tempo invests the music with a sense of dignity: it's as if royalty suddenly entered the room.

2. Irregular division of the beat. Unlike the theme (and the preceding variations), which feature mostly even division of the beat, the slow variations offer strong contrasts between long and short durations and irregular alternations between silence and sound. This rhythmic approach gives the rhythmic flow a more distinctive profile.

🛜 Music Concept Check: Rhythmic Contrast

In your eBook, hear a decided contrast between short and long, and sound and silence. •

3. Syncopation. A syncopation is an accent that conflicts with the beat or meter instead of confirming it. In this variation, the syncopations are long notes that come between beats instead of aligning with the beat. Here, they give the rhythmic flow a gentle lift. Syncopation is one of the most common forms of rhythmic play in most of the music that we will encounter.

🛜 Music Concept Check: Syncopation

In your eBook, hear syncopations shortly after the variation begins; the melody becomes syncopated when the lower part enters. •

4. Held notes and pauses that interrupt the pulse. Throughout much of the variation, the music proceeds steadily, if slowly. However, just before the return of the opening material, Mozart arrests the rhythmic flow, first with a high note that the performer can hold longer than its notated value, then with a silence whose length is also at the discretion of the performer. In this instance, the purpose of the pause is to delay the inevitable. Listeners expect the return of the opening, but the performer controls when the return occurs.

🛜 Music Concept Check: Rhythmic Suspense

Toward the end of this section, Mozart directs the performer to hold a note and a rest longer than normal, which interrupts the steady flow of the rhythm. •

All four strategies create rhythmic play by using the meter as a springboard for a distinctive design. These varying forms of play make the rhythms of a musical work interesting and inviting. By transcending the meter, they help elevate the music from nursery song to art. In the course of our survey, we will hear the extraordinarily varied ways in which the relationship between rhythm and meter has been realized over the centuries.

Looking Back, Looking Ahead

In this chapter, we identified the four properties of musical sound: loudness, duration, pitch, and timbre. We linked these properties to the elements of music that grow out of them: loudness into dynamics, timbre into instrumentation, duration into rhythm, pitch into melody and harmony, and all of these properties into texture and form. We introduced key terms and concepts for dynamics, instrumentation, and rhythm.

We continue our introduction to the elements by considering, in the next chapter, how pitch develops into both melody and harmony.

time (meter) signature Notational device indicating number of beats per measure and note value that is assigned to represent the beat

syncopation Accent that conflicts with the beat or meter instead of confirming it

 study tools 1

Elements of Music: Melody, Harmony, Texture, Form, and Style

LEARNING OUTCOMES

After studying this chapter, you will be able to do the following:

2-1 Define *melody* and describe how melodies are constructed of pitches and intervals.

2-2 Understand the terms *scale*, *key*, and *tonality*.

2-3 Understand harmony as the complement of melody; describe a chord progression; and discuss the meaning and function of a cadence.

2-4 Define *texture* and the roles of part, line, and voice in texture; and distinguish between density and independence in texture.

2-5 Define *musical form*; describe how we recognize musical form through musical punctuation (cadences) and pattern; and differentiate some basic musical forms.

2-6 Describe what we mean by *musical style* and important considerations in identifying it.

study tools

After you read this chapter, go to the Study Tools at the end of the chapter, page 31.

Volume, sound, and duration are present in all musical events—even Cage's "silent piece" referred to in Chapter 1. Pitch, or at least definite pitch, may not be. Music, especially twentieth-century music, may use nonpitched sounds and instruments extensively or even exclusively. Edgard Varèse's 1931 composition *Ionisation* requires thirteen percussion instruments (we'll hear another ground-breaking work by Varèse in Chapter 23); a rock or jazz drummer may use that many during an extended solo.

However, most of us subsist on a musical diet with pitch. Pitch brings specificity and structure to music, and is the primary source of the expressive messages in so much of the music that we will encounter. Pitch is the only property that generates two elements of music—melody and harmony—and it also plays the dominant role in shaping the remaining two elements—texture and form.

In their purest form, melody and harmony are complementary. A melody is a series of pitches; it unfolds in time. By contrast, a harmony is a group of pitches sounding all at the same time. Texture and form

leoks/shutterstock.com

are musical elements that grow out of the interaction of other elements. Both are centered on pitch. Texture describes the relationship of the various parts—melodies, harmonies, and occasionally nonpitched sounds—in musical space, through blocks of time. Form describes the relationship of musical events as they happen in time. In most of the music that we will encounter, harmony gives form its structural underpinning, and melody gives it its face. Here we introduce, then compare, these pitch-oriented elements, beginning with melody.

LEARNING OUTCOME 2-1

Define *melody* and describe how melodies are constructed of pitches and intervals.

2-1 Melody

A melody is an organized succession of pitches that presents a complete musical idea. In a melody, we expect to hear the pitches one after the other—that is, in a series. It is important that the pitch series hangs together coherently, though. We don't generally consider a random string of notes, such as those produced by a toddler plunking away on a piano, to be a melody. We expect an organized melody to have a beginning, an end, and a middle connecting the two. And we expect it to have a rhythm and contour (pattern of rise and fall) that make it distinctive. We describe the contour of a melody in terms of intervals.

In the moments before the beginning of an orchestral concert, the musicians begin to come on stage, warm up, make sure they have all of their music, get accustomed to the hall, and perhaps just focus. Soon, all but one of the musicians are on stage, ready to perform. The concertmaster (the leader of the first violins and the last of the musicians to enter) walks to his or her seat, then turns to cue the first oboist to sound an A, a pitch that vibrates at 440 cycles per second. Quickly, many of the other musicians play the A's on their instrument, adjusting as necessary to match the oboist's A so that they will be playing in tune when the concert gets under way. However, instruments in a lower range, such as the cellos and bassoons, will play a different A, one that vibrates at 220 cycles per second, or half as fast.

We call the distance between the two A's an octave. The octave is an instance of an interval. An interval is the distance between two pitches; we measure it by comparing the frequencies at which the pitches vibrate. With its 2:1 ratio between frequencies, the octave is the purest interval between two different pitches. It is so fundamental to music making that pitches that are an octave apart are identified with the same letter—such as the A to which the orchestra tunes. The octave is the only interval that you will be expected to identify specifically. If you can imagine the first two pitches of "Take me out to the ball game" or "Somewhere, over the rainbow," you know the sound of an octave. The octave is a large interval; most of the other intervals heard in melodies are smaller.

In describing all other intervals in this text, we differentiate only between steps and leaps (see Fig. 2.1). A step is a small interval between two pitches. A leap is anything larger: it can range from just a bit bigger than a step to the distance between the lowest and highest audible pitches (although it is very unlikely that we would find such a large leap in any melody). In the opening phrase of "Twinkle, Twinkle, Little Star"/"Ah, vous dirai-je, maman," only the first interval (from the first "twinkle" to the second) is a leap; the others are steps.

Melody is most obvious when it is sung, or at least singable—as is the case with "Twinkle." However, a series of pitches doesn't *have* to be singable to be a melody. Some of the melodies that we will encounter have wide ranges, fast rhythms, or active contours. They are played on instruments, rather than sung, and their combination of speed, range, and contour may make them difficult—even impossible—to sing. Nevertheless, they are melodies for these reasons:

- They have a beginning, middle, and end.
- They unfold as a series of pitches, one after the other.
- They are the most interesting, prominent, and appealing of the several parts heard at that time.

Two short excerpts from the second movement of the "Surprise" symphony by Mozart's contemporary Joseph Haydn (1732–1809) highlight the contrast between vocal and instrumental melody and underscore their common qualities (see Music Concept Check: Types of Melody).

> We don't generally consider a random string of notes to be a melody.

melody Organized succession of pitches that presents a complete musical idea

contour Pattern of rise and fall in a melody

interval Distance between two pitches

octave Relationship between two pitches that vibrate in a 2:1 ratio, with the higher pitch vibrating twice as fast as the lower; notes that are an octave apart share the same note name

step A small interval between two pitches

leap Any interval larger than a step

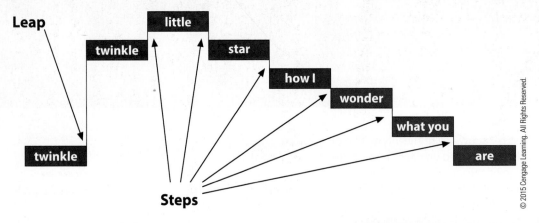

Leap

little

twinkle · star

how I

wonder

what you

twinkle

are

Steps

Figure 2.1 Steps and a leap

🌐 Music Concept Check: Types of Melody

In your eBook, hear the contrast between vocal- and instrumental-style melodic writing in Haydn's Symphony No. 94, second movement. In the second excerpt, vocal and instrumental melodies are heard simultaneously. •

The second movement is a theme and variations, similar in general approach to the hybrid Mozart/Tchaikovsky variations. The first excerpt is the beginning of the movement, which presents the simple melody of the first half of the theme. The violins play this simple melody, which is certainly singable, even if it not sung here. Indeed, it has acquired several sets of lyrics over the years. The second excerpt, which follows immediately afterward, is the beginning of the fourth variation. In this second excerpt, you will hear two competing melodies: the theme, played by winds and brass, and a variation of the melody played by the violins. The theme remains singable, but it would take an agile vocalist to sing the violin part because it moves rapidly, skips around, and covers a wide range. The important point is that both the familiar theme and the varied version of it played by the violins are melodies.

Scales are the raw materials of melody, serving as pitch banks on which musicians draw to create melodies.

2-2 Scales, Key, and Tonality

Much of the music that we will encounter in this survey draws on a familiar group of pitches: a specific series of steps called a scale. Scales are the raw materials of melody. They serve as a pitch bank on which musicians draw to create melodies.

2-2A Scales

The word *scale* comes from the Latin word *scala*, meaning "stairs" or "ladder." Accordingly, scales are a series of steps. These steps come in two sizes, half and whole. A half-step is the smallest interval in common use. You can hear and visualize a half-step by playing any two adjacent keys on a keyboard instrument or by playing notes on adjacent frets on a guitar or other fretted instrument. A whole step is twice as big as a half-step.

Two familiar images, the guitar fretboard and the piano keyboard, provide ways to visualize whole and half-steps. On the guitar fretboard, each fret marks off a half-step; the white dots span a whole step (two frets). The blue dots on the piano keyboard mark off half-steps. A half-step is the interval between two adjacent keys, white or black. The orange dots mark off whole steps: in each case, there is a key between adjacent dots.

Most scales are unique arrangements of whole and half-steps within an octave (a few scales also include small leaps of three half-steps). The pattern of whole and half-steps is understood in relation to a focal pitch, most often called the tonic or keynote: Mozart's variations on "Twinkle" begin and end on the tonic pitch. Most of the scales that we will encounter are diatonic scales, scales with seven notes per octave.

2-2B Major and Minor Scales

The scale that we hear in the themes of the Mozart variation sets is a major scale. A major scale is a diatonic scale with half-steps only between its third and fourth, and seventh and eighth notes. (The eighth note is an octave higher than the tonic.) Major scales are often contrasted with minor scales. The minor scale is also a diatonic scale, but it has a different arrangement of the seven tones. Melodies derived from the major scale are said to be in *major mode*; melodies derived from the minor scale are said to be in *minor mode*.

Since the time of ancient Greece, musicians and commentators have presumed a connection between mode and mood. In the *Republic*, Plato advised soldiers to listen to music using certain modes to gain strength and to avoid other modes that caused weakness. Ancient Greek music made use of several modes; so did European music during the Middle Ages and the Renaissance. By the eighteenth century, however, most composers used only two modes: major and minor. As in ancient Greece, there was a strong connection with mood. During the eighteenth and nineteenth centuries, when composers wanted to write a work that conveyed an upbeat, happy message, they generally used

Plato advised soldiers to listen to music using certain modes to gain strength and to avoid other modes that caused weakness.

Like a boomerang or a roller coaster, a melody often has a point of both departure and return: the tonic.

major mode. When they wanted to convey sadness, sorrow, anxiety, and other similar emotions, they most often used minor mode (Music Concept Check: Major and Minor).

Music Concept Check: Major and Minor

In your eBook, hear how Purcell uses minor mode to help convey Dido's unbearable sadness, in "When I am laid in earth," from *Dido and Aeneas*.

Hear how Mozart uses major mode to help Don Giovanni feign innocence as he tries to seduce Zerlina, in his opera *Don Giovanni*. ●

2-2C Other Scales

Although we encounter major and minor scales more frequently than any others, they are far from the only possible scales. Other diatonic scales, called modes or modal scales, predate the major and minor scales by several centuries. There are also scales containing five pitches per octave (pentatonic scales), which come down to us mainly in folk music. A scale containing all twelve possible pitches within the octave is called a chromatic scale; other scales are also possible. We will discuss these in more detail as we encounter them.

half-step The smallest interval possible between any two pitches (immediately adjacent keys) on a piano

scales Unique arrangement of whole and half-steps within an octave

tonic (keynote) Focal pitch of a scale, to which the other pitches are related

diatonic scale Specific sequence of seven pitches per octave

major scale A diatonic scale with half-steps between the third and fourth notes, and seventh and eighth notes of the scale

minor scale A family of three diatonic scales, all of which have a half-step between the second and third notes of the scale

mode (modal scale) A diatonic scale that predates major and minor scales

pentatonic scale Scale containing five pitches per octave

chromatic scale Scale containing all twelve possible pitches within the octave

THE language OF MUSIC

Pitch Notation

The most widely used method for identifying pitch typically involves just ten specific labels: the first seven letters of the alphabet (A to G) and three modifiers—sharp, flat, and natural. The pitches A through G account for seven of the twelve pitches within each octave; they correspond to the white keys on a piano keyboard and are identified as natural notes. If we **sharp** a letter-name pitch, we raise it one half-step: an F sharp is a half-step above the note F (natural). Similarly, if we **flat** a pitch, we lower it one half-step: an F flat is a half-step below F. By using sharps and flats we are able to account for all twelve pitches within an octave. Pitches an octave apart use the same letter name. So, on a conventional piano keyboard, which contains eighty-eight pitches, there are more than seven complete octaves.

The system of pitch notation, developed over almost a millennium, enables musicians to notate all eighty-eight pitches on a piano (and more) by using a relatively small set of symbols. Here are the most common, and most essential. The common feature of the symbols used to notate duration is the *note head*. It can be open or closed and with or without a stem and other components. The note head is placed on, above, or below a **staff** (Fig. 2.2) with a clef to indicate a specific pitch.

Figure 2.2 The staff is a set of five horizontal lines used for music notation.

2-2D Scale and Key

When a scale has a tonic pitch or keynote, we say that it is in the **key** of that pitch. A tonic pitch, or keynote, is the principal tone of a scale. Almost all of the music that we will hear has a tonic pitch. The scales that surround a given tonic may differ, but the fact that each scale's tones relate in a specific way to a tonic pitch (either higher or lower) is constant. The tonic can be any one of the twelve pitches within an octave.

In the same way that we label a pitch (see The Language of Music: Pitch Notation), we label a key by keynote: the alphabetic symbol plus sharp or flat as needed: A, B♭, C♯, and so on. For example, if we say a melody is in the key of E major, we mean that it is using a major scale that has E as the tonic pitch.

Music can be in any key. We stay in the key by preserving the relationship of all the other pitches to the keynote. Some music stays in one key throughout. More extended works often begin in one key and move to others before returning to the initial key.

sharp (♯) Musical symbol that raises a pitch by a half-step

flat (♭) Musical symbol that lowers a pitch by a half-step

staff Set of five horizontal lines used for music notation

key The pitch that serves as the central reference point for pitch organization in a scale

tonal Used to describe music that uses one note of the scale as a reference pitch

atonal Used to describe music that does not use one pitch as a reference point

2-2E Tonal Music

The idea of using a tonic pitch as the primary point of reference is central to the music of many cultures. In European culture, it dates back to the very first preserved examples. Music that uses one note of a scale as a reference pitch is said to be **tonal**. Most of the music that we will hear is tonal.

It is also possible to compose **atonal** music, that is, music that does not use one pitch as a reference point with the other pitches arranged hierarchically around it. However, the fact that there is neither a tonic pitch nor a scale related to that tonic typically makes the music more difficult to process (Music Concept Check: Melody and Scale).

Scales such as the major scale have familiar sounds—sounds that we have heard in countless musical examples. When we hear a new melody formed from the notes of a scale that we know, we are often able to grasp it more easily because we hear its close relationship with the scale. Your experience with the Mozart variations and the opening melody of the fourth movement of Beethoven's symphony (which you heard in Chapter 1) should bear this out.

🔊 Music Concept Check: Melody and Scale

Both Webern's Concerto for Nine Instruments and Brahms's Symphony No. 2 have slow-moving melodies, but you will probably find the second excerpt in your eBook, from Brahms, easier to process because it draws its notes from a tonal major scale, whereas the first excerpt, from Webern, draws its melodic material from a unique, atonal sequence of pitches. ●

Pitches are notated on both the lines of the staff and the spaces between the lines. However, a plain staff, such as the one pictured here, cannot be used to indicate specific pitches because there is no symbol to indicate what pitch a particular line or space represents. To use the staff to indicate a specific range of pitches, musicians use **clefs** (Fig. 2.3).

Each designates a series of midrange pitches. The shape of the clef sign and its placement on the staff designate a specific pitch. The treble clef is also called a G clef because the inner curl circles the second line up from the bottom of the staff, which is a G.

Similarly, the bass clef is also known as an F clef because the symbol begins on the fourth line and the two dots to the right of the curved line are on each side of the fourth line, which is F.

Figure 2.4 shows an octave's worth of pitches in both treble and bass clef. Each pitch is assigned a particular place on, above, or below the staff. *Ledger lines* are note-specific extensions of the staff, to notate pitches that lie beyond the range of the staff. The highest of the four A's (notated at the far right) requires a ledger line.

The symbols for sharps (♯) and flats (♭) are placed to the left of the note head (Fig. 2.5).

Note: We use the words *high* and *low* to describe pitch relationships. For instance, we might say that the second pair of pitches in "Twinkle, Twinkle" is higher than the first pair. Technically, this means that the second pair is at a faster frequency than the first. Notation reinforces the impression of high and low: higher pitches above lower pitches in the same clef, and clefs specifying a higher range of pitches, generally appear above those spanning a lower range.

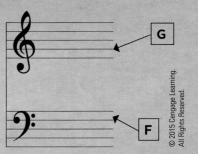

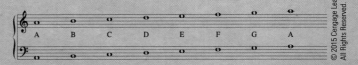

Figure 2.3 The two most common clef symbols are the *treble clef* (top) and the *bass clef* (bottom).

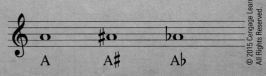

Figure 2.4 Pitches on the staff

Figure 2.5 Sharps and flats

2-3 Harmony

As the second movement of Haydn's Symphony No. 94 begins, the focus is squarely on the melody. The only accompaniment is a single note in the lower strings every two beats. That lasts through the entire first section. When the violins repeat the section even more softly, the rest of the strings pluck a series of chords in the same deliberate rhythm. It's almost like a soundtrack for an old cartoon: one can imagine a character sneaking up on someone, then popping a paper bag or setting off a firecracker just as the full orchestra sounds the "surprise." The loud sound certainly must have surprised the audience at the premiere of the symphony—and maybe you, if you're hearing it for the first time (Music Concept Check: Chords).

Haydn's "surprise" chord explodes at the end of the first phrase when heard the second time.

🌐 Music Concept Check: Chords

Hear the surprising chord in Haydn's Symphony No. 94, second movement, in your eBook. •

Haydn's surprise is a crystal-clear example of a **chord**: several notes sounding together. Chords are most easily recognized and identified when all the pitches in the chord are sounding at the same time. In this case, it's unmistakable.

However, in much of the music that we will encounter, we will hear chords presented in other, less obvious ways. Among the most common is a chord whose notes are heard in a series rather than all at once. A chord in this form is an **arpeggio**, also called a **broken chord**. Because the pitches of chords can sound simultaneously or in a series, we use the term **block chord** to refer to chords where all the pitches sound at once and *arpeggio* for chords where the pitches are heard one after the other (Fig. 2.6).

clef Symbol placed on a staff to indicate specific pitches, treble and bass clefs being the two most common

chord Several notes sounding together

arpeggio (broken chord) Chord whose notes are presented separately, in a series

block chord Chord whose notes are sounded simultaneously

Block chord   Arpeggio

Figure 2.6 Block chord and arpeggio

In music, the term harmony has two common meanings. Musicians might use it as a synonym for *chord*, as in the phrase "an exquisite harmony." It can also be used as an umbrella term that encompasses all aspects of chords, including how they follow one another, mark the musical flow of a piece, and play a key role in outlining the overall form of a musical work. We explore both of these meanings next.

2-3A Listening for Harmony

We listen for harmony differently from the way we listen to melody. When we listen to the melody, we are usually hearing the music from the top, in that the melody is most often the highest part. By contrast, when we listen for harmony, we start with the lowest pitch—the bass note—and work our way up. When we listen in this way, we can more easily identify individual harmonies, or chords, and hear when they change.

Listening for harmony by way of the bass line is an acquired skill. It doesn't come as naturally as listening for—and singing along with—melody, if only because bass lines are typically not as distinctive as melodies. They are buried at the bottom instead of riding along the top. To help hear bass lines and the harmony that they support more clearly, please view the video referenced in Music Concept Check: Hearing Harmony. It contains three musical segments, all based on the theme from Haydn's "Surprise" symphony (No. 94). The first is the bass line of the theme alone. The second is the recording of the theme reinforced by a synthesized bass line, and the third is the recording as you previously heard it. As you move from one to the next, you should get a clear sense of how the bass line undergirds the harmony beneath the melody.

Music Concept Check: Hearing Harmony

In your eBook, see and hear bass lines and harmony in a video demonstration of Haydn's theme from the second movement. •

harmony A synonym for *chord*; also an umbrella term that encompasses all aspects of chords

chord progression Series of chords that proceed toward a harmonic goal

tonic chord The single chord that represents the definite center or "home" in relationship to other chords that are used in the composition

cadence A short series of chords (typically two or three) that defines and achieves a harmonic goal

2-3B Chord Progressions

The bass-line video in your eBook illustrates two key features of harmony: chord progressions and cadences. A chord progression is a series of chords that proceeds—or progresses—toward a harmonic goal. In the sense that we will use the term here, a chord progression not only progresses toward a goal—for example, toward the tonic chord (the single chord that represents the definite center or "home" in relationship to other chords that are used in the composition)—but often does so by following well-traveled paths. Progressions often end their journey along these familiar paths with a cadence.

2-3C Cadences

A cadence is a short series of chords (typically three or four) that signals the arrival at a harmonic goal. Because they define intermediate and final goals, cadences come at the ends of progressions. Cadences punctuate the musical flow, much as commas and periods punctuate the flow of words in sentences. To emphasize a cadence, composers often coordinate reaching the harmonic goal with a lull in activity. This slowdown helps signal arrival at a cadence; the particular chord progression determines the degree to which the cadence punctuates the musical flow. (The expectation of a drop in activity is one important reason that the "surprise" chord is so surprising!)

A progression that ends decisively on the tonic chord functions like a red light. It brings the music to a complete stop, thus delineating a complete musical statement. By contrast, cadences that don't end decisively on the tonic function more like yellow lights, in that they arrest the musical flow momentarily but don't bring it to a final stop.

We also note that the first cadence in Haydn's second movement is comma-like because it does not end on the tonic chord, whereas the second cadence functions like a period because it does end on the tonic (Music Concept Check: Cadences). It is precisely this capability—to determine through chord choice how emphatically a cadence punctuates the musical flow—that makes possible the large-scale hierarchical organization heard in the concertos of Mozart, the symphonies of Beethoven, and virtually all of the music of the eighteenth and nineteenth centuries.

Some cadences are yellow lights or red lights; some are commas, semicolons, or periods.

Music Concept Check: Cadences

In your eBook, hear a comma-like cadence in Haydn's second movement.

Hear a musical "period" at the end of the second cadence. ●

2-3D Harmony and Key

Harmony enables us to hear the key even more strongly than melody does, for two reasons. First, the tonic chord confirms the tonic note as the focal pitch. Second, chord progressions that depart from and ultimately return to the tonic chord by a predictable path create a sense of expectation, which is fulfilled upon arrival at the tonic chord. The path may include one or more intermediate stops but ultimately completes the round trip from tonic to tonic.

2-3E Chords as Harmony, Chords in Melody

The straightforward example above helps us perceive three important points about the relationship between harmony and melody.

- *Melody and harmony.* In most of our musical examples that include harmony, the composers have typically derived both melody and harmony from the same set of pitches.
- *Melody versus harmony.* Although it is easy to distinguish harmony from melody when we hear harmony as block chords and melodies as individual pitches, the boundary becomes fuzzier when we hear the pitches of a chord one after the other. In composing his theme, Haydn had to tweak the rhythm only a little to turn a simple arpeggio into the beginning of his melody.
- *Melody or harmony.* Whether we hear a series of pitches as melody or harmony depends on what we are listening for. If we listen for the contour and rhythm of an arpeggio, then we are hearing it melodically. However, if we group each oscillation of the contour into the chord that it is outlining, then we are hearing harmonically. Whether we decide to listen for melody or for harmony will probably depend on the source of the musical interest: a simply oscillating arpeggio does not make for a very interesting melody. The important point, however, is that we have the option.

LEARNING OUTCOME 2-4

Define *texture* and the roles of part, line, and voice in texture; and distinguish between density and independence in texture.

2-4 Texture

Texture is the fabric of sound created by the interaction of all the parts of a piece of music. When we listen for texture, we observe everything that is going on—melody, harmony, and rhythm—and consider how the separate strands of activity relate to one another.

Earlier, we suggested that melody was the face of music, its most distinctive feature. In discussing texture, we can extend that metaphor by describing texture as the body connected to the face. For melody, texture is "the rest of the story" with regard to overall musical activity, just as harmony is the rest of the story with regard to pitch organization.

2-4A Parts

Our point of reference in hearing and describing texture is the *part*. We seek to discover how many parts there are, what their roles are (melody, accompaniment, rhythmic support), and how they interrelate.

Part refers to the music that an individual performer sings or plays. (We also use line or voice to refer to much the same thing.) For example, we can speak of flute and oboe doubling (sharing the same part with) the violins.

For voices and most instruments, a part unfolds one pitch or note at a time. For this reason, we can associate a part—for example, the melody—with a single voice or instrument, as in "the soprano part" or "the flute part." When we cannot make the association, as in the case of instruments that are capable of playing more than one pitch at a time, we identify the part by referring to the sequence of pitches that belong together—a melody line or part of an accompaniment—as the *melody line* or *upper part*, and the *bass line* or *lower part*.

In observing texture, we consider two aspects of the relationship between two or more parts: the *density* of the texture and the *independence* of the parts. Although both contribute to our impression of texture, density and independence are largely independent of each other.

2-4B Density

Density refers to the thickness of the texture. Our impression of textural density emerges mainly from the interrelationship of three variables:

1. The *number* of parts
2. The *spacing* of the parts (how widely separated they are from each other)
3. The *register*, or range of pitches lowest to highest, in which the parts operate

We will hear a denser texture if there are more rather than fewer instruments or voices, if the parts are closely spaced rather than widely separated, and if the parts lie in a low rather than a high register. In general, we use descriptive words to characterize textural density: *thick* or

texture The fabric of sound created by the interaction of all the parts of a piece of music

part (line; voice) Music that an individual performer sings or plays

doubling Two or more instruments sharing the same line or part

density A measure of the thickness of texture

thin, *dense* or *transparent*, and other words that evoke strongly contrasting sound images.

2-4C Textural Independence

Textural independence measures the degree to which a musical line stands apart from those around it. We observe textural independence by considering two criteria:

1. How *different* a part is from those around it in melodic contour and rhythm
2. How *distinctive* and *memorable*, or melody-like, it is

Typically, we use the melody—generally the most dominant line—as our primary point of reference. There are good reasons for this. Our ear tends to go to the melody first, and the style of the melody (simple or elaborate, vocal or instrumental) provides a useful benchmark for observing the other parts.

Textural independence can range from completely dependent to completely independent. A part is *completely dependent* when it follows the contour and rhythm of another part, such as the melody. At the other end of the spectrum are textures whose every part has a distinctive rhythm and contour, and all parts are of comparable melodic interest. Texture is where we encounter one of the miraculous features of music. When several people with different things to say talk at the same time, the result is gibberish. But in music, several interesting and intelligible lines can weave together and make perfect sense.

2-4D Describing Textural Independence

We can view textural independence on a continuum. On one end of the continuum is the simplest texture of all: a single line, or **monophonic** (meaning "one voice") texture. At the other end of the continuum is a multipart texture in which every part is of comparable interest and moves with distinct rhythm and contour. We call such textures polyphonic (meaning "many voices") or contrapuntal (based on the term *counterpoint*—literally, "point against point"). We can easily move from one extreme to the other by starting a song such as "Frère Jacques" together, then continuing as a round (staggered entrances of a melody by different voices or instruments at predetermined points in a composition). It is monophonic when everyone sings the melody at the same time; it becomes polyphonic when sung as a round, with three entrances of the melody.

Most textures that we encounter lie between these two extremes. Commentators who talk or write about music often use the term **homophonic** (meaning "same or similar voice") and **melody and accompaniment** more or less interchangeably to describe the wide range of textures that include more than one part, with one part a clearly dominant melody and the others subordinate. This is by far the most common and most variable range of textures. For example, almost all of the variations we have heard are homophonic, although there are considerable differences from one to the next. For this reason, we will use "homophonic" more often to refer to those textures in which the parts move in the same rhythm (as in a hymn) or when the rhythm of the subordinate parts is less active than the melody, and "melody and accompaniment" more frequently to refer to those textures in which the subordinate parts are more active.

Haydn's slow second movement features a variety of textures. Music Concept Check: Texture includes six excerpts, arranged from least to most independent, from completely homophonic to contrapuntal.

🎵 Music Concept Check: Texture

In your eBook, watch or listen to different textures in six excerpts from Haydn, Symphony No. 94, second movement.

1. Effectively monophonic: the melody line doubled above and below.

2. Homophonic; melody supported by chords most of the time; accompaniment mainly chords supporting the melody, little independence.

3. Melody with an active accompaniment.

4. Two versions of the melody, both interesting, supported by chordal accompaniment. The first violin part begins as an elaborate instrumental-style melody line that is a variation of the theme. Toward the end, it diverges from echoing the melody.

5. Melody, countermelody, and simple chordal accompaniment. First violins, then first violins and flute answer the theme with a contrasting melody with a more varied contour and rhythm.

6. A contrapuntal texture: upper strings play rapid scales and figuration, while lower strings play fragments of the theme and winds sustain chords. This is also the densest texture because of the number and spacing of the parts. ●

We may often find that although melody draws us into a musical work, texture helps us keep listening. The variations demonstrate this convincingly. They begin with a tuneful melody that catches our ear. However, in the variations that follow, the main source of interest is texture because it is the source of the greatest contrasts and variety. No other aspect of the music changes as clearly and decisively within and between variations.

textural independence Degree to which a musical line stands apart from those around it

monophonic (n. monophony) Used to describe texture with a single line, or voice

polyphonic (n. polyphony), contrapuntal (n. counterpoint) Used to describe multipart texture in which every part is of comparable interest and moves with distinct rhythm and contour

round Staggered entrances of a melody by different voices or instruments at predetermined points in a composition

homophonic (melody and accompaniment n. homophony) Used to describe a wide range of textures that include more than one part, with one part a clearly dominant melody and the others subordinate

LEARNING OUTCOME 2-5

Define *musical form*; describe how we recognize musical form through musical punctuation (cadences) and pattern; and differentiate some basic musical forms.

2-5 Form

Music unfolds in time. New events continually replace old; we hear something, and then it is gone. Listening to a live performance of a musical work, we can't absorb it all at once or even examine it at our own pace, as we can a painting or sculpture. For this reason, most successful composers have provided musical cues that help listeners hear a work as a single coherent statement. These cues help us assemble the stream of sounds that we hear into larger segments, which can ultimately evolve into a pattern that we can understand as a unified whole. We refer to such patterns as the form of a musical work.

Form is the organization of musical elements in time. It is concerned principally with the structure and coherence of a musical work. *Structure* in this sense means the relationship of various sections of a musical work to one another. *Coherence* refers to those qualities that make a musical work a purposefully unified creative effort rather than a random assemblage of sounds. That has been the case with all of the music discussed in these opening chapters—even Cage's "silent piece," if only because Cage imposed a time frame on the ambient sounds—and it will be our experience in virtually all of the music that we will listen to from this point on. The first goal in our discussion of form is to identify the kinds of musical cues that enable us to recognize the boundaries of and relationships among forms.

2-5A Recognizing Form

We can usually recognize the form of a musical work by following a three-step process. The first step is to identify the sectional boundaries within the work. The second is to compare the music on either side of these boundaries. The third is to recognize the relationships between sections as a larger pattern. We begin this process at a local level, then assemble the work into progressively larger sections until we can grasp it in its entirety. We locate boundaries by listening for musical punctuation.

2-5B Punctuation and Formal Boundaries

Punctuation in music is a decisive change in the musical flow that marks a boundary between two sections of music. Typically, punctuation results from a reduction of musical activity or an interruption of the musical flow. The drop in musical activity can—and usually does—come from coordinated change in several elements; for instance, a long note and a melodic descent to the tonic, confirmed by a cadence. We hear these

Listening to a live performance of a musical work, we can't absorb it all at once or even examine it at our own pace, as we can a painting or sculpture.

changes as a decisive punctuation, like the period at the end of a sentence, because several elements send much the same signal: stop. Some musical signals are more or less universal: the descent of the melody or a long note following shorter notes. (These are like the drop in your voice at the end of a declarative sentence and the short pause you take before continuing.) Others are specific to the pitch organization: a cadence on the tonic may define a complete musical unit. (This parallels completing the grammatical requirements for a complete sentence.) All work together to punctuate the musical flow.

Our impression of the strength of a musical punctuation comes both from the events that lead up to the punctuation and from what follows. As a rule, the greater the contrast between sections, the more decisive the punctuation seems to be. Typically, there is a correlation between the strength of the punctuation and the amount of music that it marks off: the stronger the punctuation, the more music it delineates.

Punctuations outline the shape of the musical work in time. The musical material between punctuations fills in the outline. We explore this aspect of form next.

2-5C Sectional Relationships

The relationship between two sections of music falls somewhere on a continuum that ranges from literal repetition to strong contrast. In its purest form, **repetition** is exactly that: an exact restatement of something heard earlier in the work. **Contrast** involves substantial

form Organization of musical elements in time; concerned principally with the structure and coherence of a musical work
repetition Literal restatement of something heard earlier in a work
contrast Substantial change in a work, usually in more than one element

change, usually in more than one element. For example, dynamics could change from soft to loud; harmony could shift to a new key or mode; rhythm could become more or less active; or register could shift from low to high. Our sense of contrast grows out of three variables: the number of elements that change, the degree of change in each element, and the prominence of the elements that are changed. The greater the cumulative change, the stronger the contrast. Musical works seldom have complete contrast—that is, completely new rhythms, meters, instruments, themes, tempos, and the like—because some element of connection is necessary to lend coherence to the work. Still, strong contrasts are possible, particularly between major sections. Repetition and contrast are at the two ends of the continuum. Between them lies variation. Variation involves a balanced mix of continuity and change in the work. It is the compositional technique of applying changes to one or more elements of a musical work. The varied material is enough like material in an earlier section that we hear a clear connection, but altered enough that we hear a discernible difference between them.

Form is hierarchical. Formal organization happens on multiple levels, from brief musical ideas lasting only a few notes to the entire work. So, we'll consider form at two levels: that of individual musical ideas, or themes, and that of larger forms.

2-5D Building a Theme: Motive, Phrase, and Period

Phrase is among the most loosely used musical terms. *Grove Music Online*, the most authoritative English reference work on music, defines phrase in this way:

> A term adopted from linguistic syntax and used for short musical units of various lengths; a phrase is generally regarded as longer than a motive but shorter than a period.

By contrast, the terms *motive* and *period* are relatively easy to define. A motive is a short musical idea used as a building block, both in melodies and throughout the texture. Arguably, the most famous motive in music is the one that begins Beethoven's Fifth Symphony. We hear it twice in isolation in Music Concept Check: Motive and Phrase, then hear it several times as it is used to construct three phrases ending in a cadence. That's one extreme.

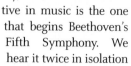

A motive is a short musical idea used as a building block.

🔊 Music Concept Check: Motive and Phrase

In your eBook, hear how Beethoven uses a motive to build a series of phrases. ●

At the other end of the extreme is the period. A period is a complete musical statement made up of two or more phrases; two is by far the most common option. Each phrase ends in a cadence. The first cadence typically ends on a chord other than the tonic; in this respect, it is like a question that requires an answer. The final phrase ends on the tonic; the cadence in the home key functions much like a period. We hear the short and the long of it in music by Mozart and Chopin, in Music Concept Check: Two-Phrase Period.

🔊 Music Concept Check: Two-Phrase Period

In your eBook, hear a brief two-phrase period, sung first by Don Giovanni, then by Zerlina, the peasant girl he is trying to seduce. Mozart hints at her reluctance by extending the second phrase in her restatement of the melody.

Chopin's prelude consists of a two-phrase period that serves as a complete work. Listen to it in your eBook. ●

In both the Mozart and the Chopin examples, the two phrases begin with the same melodic material. Periods in which phrases begin identically are parallel periods.

Between motives and periods, statements substantial enough to form a major section, or even a complete work, are phrases. We can understand why the definition of *phrase* is so inclusive (and so dependent on the terms *motive* and *period*) when we listen to another two-phrase period: the theme of Haydn's variation set (Music Concept Check: Phrase). The first half of the theme (the part before the "surprise" chord) consists of four short musical segments, each punctuated by a long note. The third segment, a repetition of the first segment, suggests retrospectively that the first two segments form a larger formal unit. A stronger punctuation at the end of the fourth segment confirms the hierarchical organization: four segments, grouped first by twos, then into one longer segment. Is each segment a phrase? Are the two-segment pairs phrases? Is the four-segment unit that is repeated also a phrase? According to the definition above, and the prevailing understanding of the term, the answer to all is "yes."

🔊 Music Concept Check: Phrase

In your eBook, watch and listen to the theme from Haydn, Symphony No. 94, second movement. ●

Haydn's theme and the two-phrase periods by Mozart and Chopin make apparent how broad a range of melodic material the term *phrase* includes and, because of this, why the term eludes a more precise definition. Chopin's phrases last half a work; Haydn's shortest phrases (which some commentators label "subphrases") last only four beats.

What is also clear, especially in the Haydn theme, is the hierarchical structuring of phrases in music of this type. In particular, Haydn's theme suggests the role that harmony plays in shaping form. The cadence at the end of each long phrase provides more emphatic punctuation than the long notes at the end of each segment. Harmony plays an even more crucial role in shaping larger forms.

2-5E Larger Forms: Strophic, Variation, Binary, Ternary

The Chopin prelude is the exception to the rule. A period generally comprises part of a work, not the complete work. As compositions develop from motives, phrases, and periods into major sections and complete compositions, the shape of the form typically relies not only on melody, but also on the other elements. In much of the music that we will encounter, there is coordination between length and difference: the larger the time span, the more comprehensively variation and contrast are defined.

The most enduring forms grow out of the common options for continuation: repetition, variation, and contrast. Strophic form, a vocal-only form, is based on musical repetition. Variation form is, of course, based on variation. Binary form uses a different approach to variation, while ternary form relies on strong contrast to define its three sections. We consider each in turn.

Strophic Form. You've probably known the words to the first stanza of "Twinkle, Twinkle, Little Star" most of your life. However, one version of the original lyrics for "Twinkle, Twinkle," written by Jane Taylor in 1806, contains not one stanza, but three.

> Twinkle, twinkle, little star,
> How I wonder what you are.
> Up above the world so high,
> Like a diamond in the sky.
> Twinkle, twinkle, little star,
> How I wonder what you are!
>
> When the blazing sun is gone,
> When he nothing shines upon,
> Then you show your little light,
> Twinkle, twinkle, all the night.
> Twinkle, twinkle, little star,
> How I wonder what you are!
>
> Then the traveler in the dark
> Thanks you for your tiny spark;
> He could not see which way to go,
> If you did not twinkle so.
> Twinkle, twinkle, little star,
> How I wonder what you are!

We would sing the now mostly forgotten second and third stanzas to the same melody as the first stanza. The melody would remain unchanged, but the words vary with each restatement of the melody. We call a vocal form in

Comstock/photos.com

Strophic form is common in church hymns.

which different lyrics are sung to each repetition of the same melody strophic form. Strophic form is common in "people's music": not only children's songs but also church hymns, popular songs (especially from the nineteenth and early twentieth century), and folk songs of many kinds, including blues, ballads, and other story-telling song genres.

Variation Form. Variation form is, of course, all about variation. Variation form (also known as theme and variations) typically begins with a theme, and the rest of the work is some number of variations on the theme. Mozart's "Twinkle" variations, the hybrid variations by Mozart and Tchaikovsky, and Haydn's second movement all demonstrate this form. As these examples show, variation form typically begins with the statement of a theme that is simple, which invites variation of many kinds.

Typically, the foundation of variation form—the basic outline of the theme and the main harmonies that support it—is not substantially varied. This framework provides continuity from variation to variation and helps unify the work. It also serves as the springboard for performers' and composers' imagination. What *is* varied can range from simple melodic elaboration to thorough transformation of several elements. Haydn's slow movement spotlights a range of nonmelodic alternatives because he continues to repeat the melody in every variation (Music Concept Check: Variation Form).

variation The compositional technique of applying changes to one or more elements of a musical work
phrase Short musical unit of varying length
motive Short musical idea used as a building block
period Complete musical statement made up of two or more phrases
parallel periods Complete musical statements made up of two or more phrases that begin identically
strophic form A vocal form in which different lyrics are sung to each repetition of the same melody
variation form (theme and variations) Form that typically begins with a theme; the rest of the work is some number of variations on the theme

In your eBook, listen to Variation 1: Texture. Haydn enriches the texture by adding a second more active melodic line in the first violins.

Listen to Variation 2: Harmony, melody, dynamics, texture. Switch to minor mode; new melodic material; strong and sudden contrasts between very loud and very soft; a range of textures, from the melody doubled by the full orchestra to a dense, more contrapuntal texture, with sustained winds, racing violins, and lower strings fragmenting the melody.

Listen to Variation 3: Melody, texture. First, a more active version of the melody with a similarly active accompaniment, then just melodies without accompaniment.

Listen to Variation 4 (which is effectively two variations in one, because the repetition of each half is different from the initial version): Melody, dynamics, texture. First, melody in the winds plus an elaborated version of the melody in the violins, all very loud; then another variation of the melody played softly and accompanied by offbeat chords. ●

FMNG/istockphoto.com

Binary form is a two-part form.

The extension of the final variation underscores a key point about both variation and strophic form: both are modular. In a strophic song, the lyric determines the overall length. The melody is repeated until all stanzas have been sung. In a variation set, there is no set number of variations, and the theme and individual variations seldom give any sense of the overall length of the entire work. Nor does the typical succession of variations impose a larger structure in which individual variations group into larger units. Haydn addresses this matter in two ways. First, he places the minor mode variation in the middle, to provide dramatic contrast with the pairs of variations on either side. And to bring closure to the movement, he significantly extends the final variation.

Other common forms often project the large-scale design of a composition as they unfold. The next work features two of them.

Binary and Ternary Form. Binary form is a two-part form in which both parts are usually repeated. Ternary form is a three-part form. In binary form, the second part typically contains varied versions of the music in the first part. The texture remains much the same and the melodic material is similar. Ternary form highlights contrast: typically the outer sections are identical or similar, while the middle section contrasts. We hear both forms (Music Concept Check: Binary and Ternary) in a short piano piece by Beethoven entitled *Lustig und traurig* (*Happy and Sad*).

binary form Two-part form in which both parts are usually repeated
ternary (ABA) form Three-part form in which the outer sections are typically identical or similar, while the middle section contrasts
rounded binary form Two-part form in which the opening material returns in the second part

In your eBook, watch and listen to Beethoven's short piano piece *Lustig und traurig* (*Happy and Sad*). ●

In its overall design, *Happy and Sad* offers a straightforward version of ternary form. The piece contains three distinct, self-contained sections. The first and last are identical. The middle section contrasts with the outer sections in virtually every respect. To convey this relationship succinctly, we can indicate the form as ABA, where A designates the opening section and any repetition of it and B is a contrasting statement.

Both A and B sections here are themselves in binary form. The A section of this ternary form is a small binary section: like Haydn's theme, it is a two-phrase period in which both parts are repeated. The B section is a more expanded version of binary form, because the second part is somewhat extended. The second part of the B section includes a reprise of the melodic idea that opens the section. We use the term rounded binary form to describe works or sections in

Lori Martin/iStockphoto.com

In ternary form, the outer sections are similar, while the middle contrasts.

binary form in which the opening material returns in the second part, usually somewhat varied. Both Mozart variation themes are also in rounded binary form.

Taken together, the music presented in this chapter reveals several key features about form.

1. We grasp form first by observing punctuation, then comparing the sections outlined by the punctuations.
2. Form takes shape through patterns involving repetition, variation, and contrast. Collectively, these fall on a continuum from completely the same in every respect to substantially different.
3. Form is hierarchical. Smaller formal units are typically nested inside larger ones, as in the case of binary sections within a large-scale ternary design.
4. Form is extensible. It can be expanded modularly, as in strophic or variation form. Or it can be expanded from within, as in the Chopin prelude or the second part of the B section of *Happy and Sad*. As a result, the difference between small- and large-scale forms is often a matter of degree—shorter versus longer—rather than a difference in kind.

Almost all of the music that we will encounter in our survey uses the same basic principles of formal organization, and much of it uses some kind of formal template, such as variation form or ternary form. Any formal template is necessarily reductive. There are countless compositions that can be labeled ABA form, but the label can't begin to account for the extraordinary diversity of these compositions. We can use the formal template as a point of reference in becoming familiar with a work, then come to appreciate the distinctive ways in which inspired musicians express themselves within the bounds of form.

LEARNING OUTCOME 2-6
Describe what we mean by *musical style* and important considerations in identifying it.

2-6 Style

In the 2003 film *School of Rock*, Dewey Finn (Jack Black), an unemployed rock-guitarist-turned-teacher at an exclusive private school, gives his class a crash course in rock appreciation. Filling the blackboard with little boxes containing words like *punk, soul,* and *grunge,* as well as a host of band names and lines connecting the various boxes, he takes his students on a whirlwind tour of fifty years of rock.

As he points to the boxes, Finn relies on his students to make connections between the boxed words and the music that they have heard. This pedagogical approach is a frenetic version of one strategy for introducing students to music: play examples of different kinds of music and link them to words that represent the style of each example.

Jack Black as Dewey Finn in *School of Rock* (2003).

Punk, soul, and *grunge* are style labels. In a single word, a style label evokes the common features of similar musical works. For instance, we expect a punk song to be loud and fast, and have an insistent rhythm, distorted guitar sounds, screamed vocals, and confrontational lyrics. In its ability to convey information succinctly, a style label functions much like *house* or *car,* labels that identify an object and lead us to expect that object to have certain features.

Style labels in music work only to the extent that they call to mind a set of criteria in one or more musical elements. Whether it is Baroque or blues, hip-hop or bebop, Romantic or rock, a label is meaningful only if it evokes sound images that are representative of the style.

We can define **style** in music, then, as a consistent and comprehensive set of characteristics that define a body of music from a time, place, culture, or creative entity (a composer, performer, or group). The characteristics aren't requirements, but they must be at least likely. For example, classic rock songs likely have a rock beat; before the 1950s, no songs had a rock beat. Many early eighteenth-century compositions feature a strong, continuous bass line, played by both a bass-range instrument like the cello, and a chord instrument like the harpsichord; by the end of the century, however, the bass line was not a continuous stream, as we heard in Haydn's variation theme.

2-6A Style and the Elements of Music

Style emerges from common and consistent ways of handling the musical elements. In some cases, certain elements may be more prominent, or more indicative of the style, by either their presence or their absence. Still, no single element defines style. The cumulative impression gathered from all of the elements does.

Two examples illustrate this point. If we compare the examples by Mozart, Haydn, Beethoven, and Chopin discussed in this chapter, we might conclude that the Mozart, Haydn, and Beethoven examples are stylistically similar

style A consistent and comprehensive set of characteristics that define a body of music from a time, place, culture, or creative entity (a composer, performer, or group) because all of them feature frequent punctuation and relatively routine homophonic accompaniment, whereas the Chopin piece represents a different style because of its long phrases and distinctive slithering chordal accompaniment.

The hybrid Mozart and Tchaikovsky variations from the previous chapter provide a vivid illustration of why style involves a consistent and comprehensive *set* of choices. By examining *all* of the elements we can understand why a work whose pitches and rhythms are borrowed almost note for note from Mozart still sounds like Tchaikovsky. Recall that the Haydn variations featured a relatively small orchestra in which the violins were the dominant melody instrument. This is typical of late eighteenth-century orchestral music. However, Tchaikovsky's orchestration, completed almost a century later, features winds prominently in most of the variations, and it uses percussion instruments like the cymbals in the second variation and bells in the last variation. The prominent role of winds and the occasional use of a variety of percussion instruments is characteristic of his music and far more common in the late nineteenth century than a century earlier: percussion instruments other than timpani were seldom used before 1800 in orchestral music. By employing nineteenth-century practice in the choice and use of orchestral instruments, Tchaikovsky brings an eighteenth-century work a century into the future.

2-6B Listening for Style

For us, perhaps the most important question about style is this: *Why* listen for style? After all, isn't it enough simply to let the music wash over us? Here's an answer. We study style because style is a gateway to understanding a work, its creator, and the culture from which it comes. Listening for style is valuable for all the music that you encounter, in and outside of class. Keep in mind that this is something you already do. Our hope is that by listening comprehensively and systematically, your awareness of style will become sharper—the aural equivalent of moving from conventional to high-def TV.

LISTEN UP!

TOTAL TIME: 1:48

Hildegard of Bingen, "Nunc aperuit nobis" (ca. 1150)

TAKEAWAY POINT: Long, flowing melodic lines without a steady beat

STYLE: Chant

FORM: Through-composed

GENRE: Antiphon

INSTRUMENTS: Female voices

CONTEXT: Song for worship in a monastery

SECTION 1

0:00   Smoothly flowing melodies moving mainly by step, with long melismas

Nunc aperuit nobis clausa porta	Now a door long shut has opened [to show us]

SECTION 2

0:42   The use of a modal scale is most evident just before cadences, when the melody drops below the drone.

quod serpens in muliere suffocavit	what the serpent choked in the woman.

SECTION 3

1:04   Notice the free rhythm throughout, with the fastest-moving notes in the middle of sections.

Unde lucet in aurora	And so there shines brightly in the dawn
flos de Virgine Maria.	the flower of the Virgin Mary.

 Listen to this selection streaming or in an Active Listening Guide at CourseMate or in the eBook.

2-6C Listening Guides

The text includes "Listen Up!" listening guides that walk you, minute by minute, through each piece of music. The listening guide for that first selection in Chapter 3 appears here (see Listen Up!).

To assist you in listening for style in another way, we provide, in CourseMate and the eBook, an Active Listening Guide for each example (Fig. 2.7). Each Active Listening Guide has several components:

- *Background information* on the musical example and the musicians responsible for it
- An Active Listening *timeline* that highlights noteworthy events in the recording, as it plays
- A *Profile* that describes the characteristic handling of each element
- Several *Key Points* about style, meaning, and the connection between the music and the culture that nurtured it
- A *quiz* to test your familiarity with the example

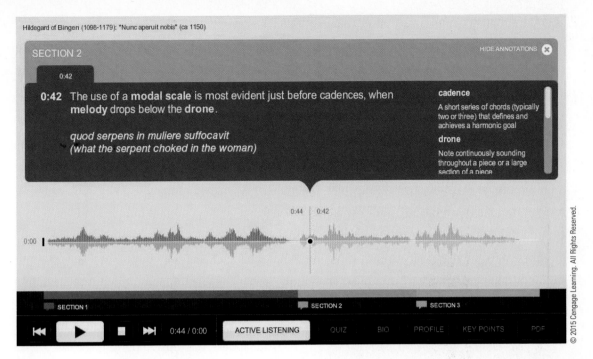

Hildegard of Bingen (1098-1179): "Nunc aperuit nobis" (ca 1150)

SECTION 2   HIDE ANNOTATIONS ✕

0:42

0:42 The use of a **modal scale** is most evident just before cadences, when **melody** drops below the **drone**.

quod serpens in muliere suffocavit
(what the serpent choked in the woman)

cadence

A short series of chords (typically two or three) that defines and achieves a harmonic goal

drone

Note continuously sounding throughout a piece or a large section of a piece

0:44 | 0:42

0:00

SECTION 1 | SECTION 2 | SECTION 3

▶ ■ ▶▶ 0:44 / 0:00 **ACTIVE LISTENING** QUIZ BIO PROFILE KEY POINTS PDF

Figure 2.7 Active Listening Guide

Looking Back, Looking Ahead

These two chapters have given you a foundation for style-based listening. The Listen Up! guides and Active Listening Guides will help you identify salient characteristics of each style. As you progress through the course, you should find that listening comprehensively for style becomes a matter of habit, not only in the musical examples discussed in this book but also in the music you encounter outside class. That is one of the lasting benefits of a music appreciation course.

 study tools 2

Ready to study?
In the book you can:

- Review Learning Outcome answers and Glossary terms with the tear-out Chapter Review card.

Or you can go online to CourseMate, at www.cengagebrain.com, for these resources:

- Chapter Quizzes to prepare for tests

- Interactive flashcards of all Glossary terms

- Active Listening Guides, streaming music, and YouTube playlists

- An eBook with live links to all web resources

Medieval Music

LEARNING OUTCOMES

After studying this chapter, you will be able to do the following:

3-1 Describe monastic life in the Middle Ages.

3-2 Define *chant* and its three forms of text setting.

3-3 Recognize the style of an antiphon through Hildegard of Bingen's "Nunc aperuit nobis."

3-4 Become familiar with the emergence of secular culture in France during the late Middle Ages.

3-5 Understand more about minstrels and troubadours, the most important secular musicians of the time.

3-6 Describe the life, poetry, and music of Guillaume de Machaut, an important fourteenth-century composer.

3-7 Analyze an example of the earliest dance music that has come down to us.

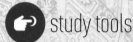 study tools

After you read this chapter, go to the Study Tools at the end of the chapter, page 44.

A thousand years from now, historians with access to today's artifacts will be able to reconstruct musical life in our time with considerable precision and in excruciating detail. They will hear music exactly as its creators intended, and they will be able to disassemble recordings to better understand the creative and production processes. They will experience music in performance, via video recordings. They will read writings about music, from fan magazines and blogs to scholarly commentary. They will sift through data concerning sales, distribution, audience share, artist compensation, profits and losses, and other matters related to the music business. Their biggest problem may be simply managing the enormous amount of information available to them.

Those who study musical life at the beginning of the previous millennium have the opposite problem. There is almost no documentary evidence of the music being made in Europe around the year 1000. Moreover, what has survived is in a form impossible to decode with certainty, and what it does convey provides us with only the sketchiest information about the sound of the music. We do know that music manuscripts came from monasteries scattered throughout Europe and that monks created this music for use in daily worship. And we believe that it was a monophonic vocal music with free rhythm.

We begin our survey of musical life in the twelfth century with a late instance of this monophonic vocal music: a chant by the remarkable Hildegard of Bingen. We end this first chapter two centuries later with a French **secular** (nonsacred) song and one of the first dances to be preserved in notation. This admittedly minuscule sample of three centuries of European music nevertheless highlights several important aspects of musical life in the medieval era (ca. 100–1450 C.E.). Among the most significant are the central role of the Catholic church in the creation and preservation of music, the gradual development of harmony and the concurrent development of a means of writing it down, and the gradual emergence of notated secular music.

Tomas Navratil/iStockphoto.com

LEARNING OUTCOME 3-1
Describe monastic life in the Middle Ages.

3-1 Monastic Life in the Middle Ages

Monasteries, convents, and abbeys are places where monks and nuns live, work, and pray. In our secular, fast-paced society, few choose to retreat from the world to devote their life to prayer and work. Although almost 68 million Catholics live in the United States, there are only about 135 monasteries and convents, and most of these religious communities are small.

Monastic life was much more popular in the Middle Ages, for both spiritual and secular reasons. For those living in medieval Europe, the central fact of life was the afterlife. Life on earth was the prelude to eternity; how you lived it determined whether you would spend that eternity in heaven or hell. For many, the best route to heaven was to live apart from the world in a community devoted in principle to poverty, chastity, and obedience. Members of a monastic community followed a particular *rule*, a stringent set of guidelines drawn up by the founder of the order; the monks of Santo Domingo de Silos still follow the rule of St. Benedict of Nursia (ca. 480–543), established

1,500 years ago. Strict adherence to the rule not only made earthly life more fulfilling but also virtually guaranteed entrance into God's heavenly kingdom.

There were also more mundane reasons for joining a monastery, which date from the fall of the Roman Empire. After the collapse of the empire, the Catholic Church gradually became the dominant institution in Europe. It was the universal religion and the main—almost exclusive—repository of learning. Until the fourteenth century, cathedral schools, monasteries, and convents were the only places where a young person could receive an education.

The Catholic Church was an institution whose wealth grew through such revenue sources as landholdings, donations, dowries, and fees for joining the clergy or a religious order. It also became a political force to be reckoned with, through its links with rulers throughout Europe and through the moral authority that it wielded, often for nonspiritual reasons.

secular Nonsacred

33

THE language OF MUSIC

Evolution of Musical Notation

In Chapter 2, The Language of Music: Pitch Notation, we introduced the notational system used to preserve and disseminate most of the music we hear. Between 1000 and 1700, this system evolved gradually from a system of vague reminders for performers who knew the music to a system for rendering instrumentation, pitch, rhythm, and dynamics with considerable accuracy. The following images highlight important stages in the evolution of this system.

WHAT'S NEW: (1) Four-line staff. (2) Clef sign. The staff and the clef sign enabled composers to specify exact pitches. (3) Rectangular noteheads to indicate specific pitches. Groups of notes linked together are sung to a single syllable.

Chant notation, thirteenth century

Very early (ca. 900 C.E.) example of musical notation

WHAT'S NEW: The fact of it, the notation itself. But note the absence of lines: staff lines to indicate pitch, bar lines to indicate measures, stems and beams to indicate the duration of individual notes. We are unable to say with any certainty what the notational symbols mean.

Work by Guillaume de Machaut, fourteenth century: early mensural notation (system for notating measured rhythm)

WHAT'S NEW: Early attempt at notating rhythm. Note the different notehead shapes and the use of stems. Still, there is no meter signature, and there are no barlines.

If there was one moment that symbolized the rise in power of the church, it came on Christmas Day in 800. On that day, Pope Leo III crowned Charlemagne (742–814), who had conquered, then reunited, much of the old Roman Empire, as Holy Roman Emperor. For the rest of his reign, Charlemagne was the secular counterpart to the pope; his empire was a single political entity with a single religion. Although it did not remain united under one ruler after his death, the Holy Roman Empire would last for a millennium. The pope's coronation of Charlemagne highlights the near-indivisible bond between church and state at that time and the rarely questioned authority of the church.

Passage from Monteverdi's opera Orfeo, early seventeenth century

WHAT'S NEW: The notation of rhythm is much closer to modern notation: there are barlines, a time signature, and a wider range of durations, including notes with flags and dots. In addition, in Monteverdi's early orchestral scores (not shown here), all parts lined up, and all instruments were specified, showing, for instance, five trumpet parts.

First edition of Chopin's Funeral March (mid-nineteenth century)

WHAT'S NEW: This is the manuscript of a modern score. The notation of rhythm and pitch is identical to that in current practice. New features include a tempo indication at the top left, articulation indications (the slurs—long curved lines covering several notes that instruct the performer to play as connectedly as possible), and dynamic markings (the *f* at the end).

Members of the clergy enjoyed a social standing comparable to that of nobility; both were well above peasant, artisan, or tradesman status. For many, entering the clergy meant maintaining or elevating one's social status, getting an education, and living within a relatively stable, well-protected community. For noble families, a religious vocation often helped resolve inheritance issues: there was one fewer heir to share the estate. And there were few career options during the Middle Ages. As a result, many joined the clergy, though not all were fully committed to the religious life.

Still, in those monasteries where the rule was carefully observed, life centered on God. The daily routine

For scribes, copying books and music was both an art and a tedious task.

British Library/Robana via Getty Images

alternated between prayer—eight times a day, in addition to Mass—and work. The periods of daily prayer, called the Divine Office, occurred at regular intervals of the day, from sunrise to after sunset. Following the maxim of St. Augustine "to sing is to pray twice," prayers were sung as well as spoken. Among the sung prayers were parts of the Mass, psalms, and prayers that commented on the psalms, such as the antiphon discussed later.

Among the most important work of religious orders was copying books and music; for scribes, this was both an art and a tedious task. Monasteries typically included a library and a *scriptorium*, a room where monks or nuns would copy documents for the library. Monastery libraries have been our main source of chant and other medieval sacred music.

Divine Office Periods of daily prayer in monasteries, which occurred at regular intervals in the day, from sunrise to after sunset

chant (plainchant) Monophonic vocal music in a free rhythm, used in both the Mass and the Divine Office

Gregorian chant The most widely used chant in western Europe

syllabic Used to describe chant text setting having one note per syllable of text

neumatic Used to describe chant text setting that generally has two to four notes per syllable

melismatic Used to describe the most elaborate form of text setting, in which a single syllable may be sustained for many notes

3-2 Chant

The music used in both the Mass and the Divine Office was chant, or plainchant. Several distinct chant practices developed in both western and eastern Europe during the early Christian era. However, after Charlemagne's father, King Pippen, ordered that liturgical practice follow the Roman model—an initiative that Charlemagne continued—Gregorian chant became the most widely used chant in western Europe. There is still debate about whether the Gregory of Gregorian chant is Pope Gregory I (Gregory the Great, 590–604) or Gregory II (715–731); despite the confusion, the name remains in common use.

Most Gregorian chant was created between the eighth and eleventh centuries. It survived only in oral tradition until the ninth century, when scribes began to notate it. We surmise that the first efforts at notation were simply reminders for those who were still learning the chants by ear. By the eleventh century, however, the notation of chant had become precise enough for modern-day scholars to reconstruct its pitches, if not its rhythms, with some accuracy, and by this time the basic chant repertory was in place. Later chants, such as those of Hildegard, serve as fresh commentary on the established texts and chants.

Chant is pure melody. It is a single stream of pitches sung by an individual singer or group. Most often, it is sung without accompaniment; if there is any other part, it will be a single pitch sustained by singers or instruments. Its rhythm is free; the notes of the melody do not line up with a steady beat. Because it is a single, rhythmically free melodic line, we can sense in it the close connection between speech and song.

The setting of the text generally takes one of three forms. The simplest is syllabic, or one note per syllable of text. A neumatic text setting generally has two to four notes per syllable. The most elaborate form of text setting is melismatic, in which a single syllable may be sustained for many notes—sometimes as many as fifty or seventy-five notes. Our example of chant features several melismatic passages.

3-3 Hildegard of Bingen

Hildegard of Bingen (1098–1179)  was one of the most extraordinary women of the Middle Ages. When she was eight, her parents promised her to the church, and she entered a Benedictine abbey when she was fourteen. Eventually, she became the prioress, the nun in charge of a priory or ranking next below the abbess of an abbey, then left to found her own convent around 1150. She had an extraordinary range of talents. Her work includes volumes on science, lives of the saints, poetry, artwork, and songs. Toward the end of her life, she corresponded with both popes and princes.

Ecstatic visions, which she had experienced since the age of five, informed much of her work. She captured their essence in her poetry and music, as we hear in "Nunc aperuit nobis," an antiphon, a chant with prose, not poetic, text, sung before and sometimes after a psalm. It is one of seventy-seven works collected in a volume entitled *Symphonia Harmonie Celestium Revelationum (Symphony of Harmony of Heavenly Revelations)*. See Listen Up!

3-3A Melody in Chant

In the performance discussed here, the chant melody soars above a drone, a note continuously sounding throughout the piece or a large section of the piece, similar to the sound you would hear listening to music played on bagpipes. Although the chant melody occasionally dips below the drone, it never stays there for long. The melodic movement is mostly by step, with few skips to high notes. In effect, this mostly stepwise movement is speech inflection, magnified so enormously that it has taken on an identity of its own. One can almost imagine Hildegard needing to set her words to music because the words as spoken cannot project the power of her vision. Especially if we take into account the use of symbolism in medieval art, we might suggest that the drone is earthly reality, and the chant melody represents Hildegard's ecstatic state during her vision, which the text reflects.

It is the text that determines the pacing of the chant; the melody comes to rest at the ends of words and, more decisively, at the ends of phrases. The absence of a steady pulse directs our attention to the pacing of the text, where we frequently hear key syllables extended by melismas. The melismas magnify the rhythm of the text as spoken, much as the melodic flourishes magnify its inflection. Together, they project the ecstasy of Hildegard's mystical experiences.

Hildegard's antiphon, and chant in general, underscores both the close connection between speech and "pure" melody, and the notion that chant, as song, transcends speech. In this context, it is intended to open the door to the divine.

3-3B Key, Scale, and Mode

As we listen to Hildegard's antiphon, we notice that the sustained tone acts as a home base for pitch. It is the

LISTEN UP!

TOTAL TIME: 1:48

Hildegard of Bingen, "Nunc aperuit nobis" (ca. 1150)

TAKEAWAY POINT: Long, flowing melodic lines without a steady beat

STYLE: Chant

FORM: Through-composed

GENRE: Antiphon

INSTRUMENTS: Female voices

CONTEXT: Song for worship in a monastery

SECTION 1

0:00 Smoothly flowing melodies, moving mainly by step, with long melismas

| *Nunc aperuit nobis clausa porta* | Now a door long shut has opened [to show us] |

SECTION 2

0:42 The use of a modal scale is most evident just before cadences, when the melody drops below the drone.

| *quod serpens in muliere suffocavit* | what the serpent choked in the woman. |

SECTION 3

1:04 Notice the free rhythm throughout, with the fastest-moving notes in the middle of sections.

| *Unde lucet in aurora* | And so there shines brightly in the dawn |
| *flos de Virgine Maria.* | the flower of the Virgin Mary. |

 Listen to this selection streaming or in an Active Listening Guide at CourseMate or in the eBook.

starting note of the melody and of several phrases, and it is always the ending note of a phrase. The melody soars above it and swoops below it but always comes to rest on it. Because this sustained tone serves as a point of orientation for every other note in the melody—a point of departure and, even more, a point of return—we can say that in the broadest, most modern sense this music is tonal. In this general way, *tonal* means that the other notes of the melody are understood in terms of a single referential pitch. This sense of a home tone is explicit in "Nunc aperuit nobis" because of the sustained tone; in chant with only one line, it is also present, but not as persistent.

However, the chant is not tonal in the more specific modern sense of being constructed from the major or minor scale or using the chord progressions associated with it. It does use a seven-note scale identical to the major

antiphon Chant with prose (not poetic) text, sung before and sometimes after a psalm

drone Note continuously sounding throughout a piece or a large section of a piece

FAST FACTS

- Dates: 1098–1179
- Place: Today's western Germany
- Reasons to remember: Most famous female composer of chants; a gifted "woman of letters"; works include volumes on science, lives of the saints, poetry, art-work, and songs, much of it informed by ecstatic visions

German School/The Bridgeman Art Library/ Getty Images

Hildegard of Bingen receives one of her visions as the monk Voldmar peers in at her, in awe.

scale at the outset. However, at cadences, such as the one on the word "nobis," Hildegard makes use of a different arrangement of the seven scale tones. We refer to such alternate arrangements of seven-note (diatonic) scales as *modes*. At the time Hildegard composed this chant, eight modes were in use: two variants each of four basic modes. These modes gradually gave way to the major/minor system of tonality during the late sixteenth and early seventeenth centuries. Over time, only two of the original eight modes survived in common use. The Ionian and Aeolian modes, also known as our modern major and minor scales, are still the basis for the vast majority of musical works in both Western art music and popular music.

3-3C The Significance of Chant

Hildegard's antiphon has introduced us to chant, the monophonic vocal music used in the Catholic liturgy. We have encountered its salient features: free rhythm, melismatic passages, absence of harmony, and text-dictated form. We have also considered the function of chant: to bridge the gap between human and divine. In this respect, we can understand the soaring phrases of Hildegard's chant as ecstatic communion with the divine. Moreover, the fact that chant and chant-derived music were virtually the only music preserved during Hildegard's lifetime strongly suggests the central place of religion in daily life through the twelfth century.

Almost from the start of recorded musical history, chant provided the foundation for polyphonic (i.e., music for more than one part) sacred music. Simple two-part compositions are among the earliest examples of notated music. By the fourteenth century, the important compositions of sacred music were polyphonic. Of necessity, this music had measured rhythm—performers had to coordinate their parts, but chant shaped this music in numerous ways. Most central was

the use of a dramatically slowed-down presentation of a chant melody as the backbone of the composition; other parts wove around it. And often these parts were chant-like: florid, melismatic lines moving much faster than the underlying chant melody.

Secular song and dance followed a parallel path from monophonic to polyphonic during the Medieval era. However, the musical results were typically quite different, because they were based on movement, not speech.

LEARNING OUTCOME 3-4

Become familiar with the emergence of secular culture in France during the late Middle Ages.

3-4 Secular Culture in France

Secular culture in what is now France emerged gradually within the rigid constraints of feudalism in the first four centuries of the new millennium. Feudalism organized society around land and war. The feudal arrangement—land from a lord in exchange for loyalty from a vassal—began as a response to the devastating invasions of the Vikings and Goths after the fall of the Roman Empire. Over time, the invasions stopped, but the wars didn't. The most drawn out was the Hundred Years' War (1337–1453), an on-again, off-again series of battles involving squabbles over property rights between nobles in England and France that dated from the twelfth century.

Feudal society calcified as those who had power worked hard to hold on to it. The nobility closed ranks; it was rare for a commoner to attain noble status. Members of the nobility preserved their power and wealth through inheritance, which presented complex, even insoluble, problems for noble fathers. It was customary for land and the wealth associated with it to pass from father to firstborn son. For daughters and remaining sons, the options were often less appealing. Some, like Hildegard, entered the clergy or joined a religious order. Noble families arranged marriages; the package included not only a bride but also a dowry. All of this complicated landholdings, as did the hierarchical structure of feudal allegiances.

Feudalism created a privileged class with time and money and made possible a new culture distinct from both the church and peasant life. One dimension of this culture was chivalry, the code of behavior expected of the noble class. Although certainly shaped by church teachings, chivalry represented a set of values independent of church authority. As such, it is a sign of the gradual emergence of secular culture.

The other major factor in the secularization of European culture was a series of crusades to the Holy Land, which began in the eleventh century and would continue through the end of the thirteenth century. Their intended goal was to reclaim Jerusalem for Christianity;

in this respect, they were a failure. However, they dramatically increased trade, which brought wealth back home and opened new perspectives on the world for those who ventured abroad. Ironically, the Crusades, although undertaken at the urging of the pope, helped undermine church authority by making people more aware of the material world.

3-4A Love and Marriage in the Middle Ages

It may seem obvious to us that a couple decides to marry because they believe they are in love. So it may be surprising to discover that marrying for love is a relatively recent development, particularly for the upper classes. Keep in mind that Cinderella is a fairy tale; for royalty, the reality has been closer to the sad tale of Edward VIII of England, who reigned for less than a year in 1936 before abdicating the throne so that he could marry Wallis Warfield Simpson, a divorced American commoner. The class boundaries that prohibited Edward from marrying Mrs. Simpson and retaining his throne date from the late Middle Ages. In medieval times, a relationship based on love, especially among the nobility, was more often a happy accident than a likely outcome. Political and social constraints presented almost insurmountable obstacles to love and its expression.

Arranged Marriages. During the Middle Ages, marriage among the nobility typically had much more to do with family and power than it did with love. In a society where land was the basis of wealth, marriages were used to consolidate landholdings.

The poster woman for this kind of arrangement was Eleanor of Aquitaine (1122–1204), the daughter of Duke William X of Aquitaine, whose domain was larger than that of the king of France. At fifteen, she inherited his duchy and immediately married the heir to the throne of France; two years later he became Louis VII. Their relationship was one-sided: he apparently adored her, and she apparently considered him a wimp. In 1152, she traded him in for a stronger man, Henry Plantagenet, who became Henry II of England two years later. She bore him eight children (five sons and three daughters); she had had two daughters with Louis. One of the sons became known as Richard the Lion Hearted. Other children married into families that controlled parts of modern-day Germany, Italy, and Spain. Eleanor spent much of her later years taking sides in disputes between her husband and her sons, for which she was imprisoned, and between various children and grandchildren.

Eleanor was, by all accounts, both beautiful and promiscuous. Bernart de Ventadorn, a troubadour employed at Eleanor's court and allegedly her lover, reputedly wrote a poem that obliquely expressed his disappointment after, while hiding in a closet, he had witnessed Eleanor's amorous encounter with another man. If love was for pleasure for Eleanor, marriage

Universal History Archive/Getty Images

In medieval times, a relationship based on love, especially among the nobility, was more often a happy accident than a likely outcome.

was business: for her and her children, it was about preserving and augmenting power and influence.

Social Barriers. Bernart's plight points up the disadvantageous position of commoners. A few might, through some special talent—in arms, music, verse, or dancing—come to the attention of a noblewoman. They might even gain her favor and occasionally enjoy the pleasures of her intimate company, if she were so inclined. But troubadours like Bernart, even those of noble birth, were forced to conduct their affairs in secret, or only in their head, because an open relationship was not possible. The almost unbearable conflict between passion and decorum gave rise to courtly love, a look-but-don't-touch protocol regarding the relationship between men and women, and a new way of expressing it—the poetry of the troubadours. The poems were not in Latin, but in the vernacular—that is, the everyday language of a particular region.

3-4B Vernacular Language and Secular Culture

The writing of poetry in vernacular was a clear indication of the reemergence of secular culture. For centuries, Latin had been the official language of the church.

chivalry Code of behavior expected of the medieval noble class
courtly love Rigid medieval social protocol in which a man could imagine an adulterous relationship with a woman but could not consummate it
vernacular Everyday language of a particular region

(It would remain so until Vatican II, which opened in 1962.) There were symbolic and practical reasons for this. The use of Latin in church affairs fostered the connection with the past, which was a central component of the church's authority. Because it was not an everyday language, it helped preserve an elite status for those who communicated with it, both in and outside religious orders. Moreover, it was a crucial unifying element for the church. Mass would sound much the same in any part of western and central Europe, and it provided a common language for conducting church affairs. Having a "universal" language was especially appropriate because so many more languages and dialects existed in Europe than do now. In France alone, three language families were used during the Middle Ages: the Romance languages (Parisian French, Occitan/Provencal), Germanic (Burgundian), and Celtic (Breton). These subdivided into numerous local dialects, most of which have been lost.

Because of the influence of the church in secular civil affairs, Latin was also the language of scholarship, law, and politics. It was used in universities, monastery schools and cathedral schools, and in serious discourse: a relevant example is that music treatises of the Middle Ages were written in Latin. In both sacred and secular domains, Latin was a church-imposed element of control.

In this context, we can see the use of the vernacular to express intimate and personal feelings as a bold if inevitable step in the emancipation of secular culture. It would lead to a flowering of literature in the fourteenth century, notably Dante's *Divine Comedy*, Chaucer's *Canterbury Tales*, and Boccaccio's *Decameron*.

3-5 Minstrels and Troubadours

The music of the emerging secular culture included both songs and dances. The musicians most responsible for this new secular music were minstrels and troubadours. When we think of minstrels, we may recollect—with a cringe—the blackface entertainers so popular in America (and Europe) during much of the nineteenth century. And when we conjure up the image of a troubadour, we may call to mind a happy-go-lucky songster, a fellow who travels around singing his own poetry to music. For the forerunners of these more contemporary entertainers, life and work were quite different.

3-5A The Minstrel

During much of the Middle Ages, minstrels were multifaceted entertainers. They might sing or play an instrument, recite poems and tell stories, dance, juggle, do acrobatic routines, and more; many were skilled in more than one area. However, by the thirteenth century, "minstrel" had acquired a more specific connotation: it typically referred to an instrumentalist attached to a court. Among their numerous duties, minstrels played for dancing and often accompanied singers.

Early in their recorded history, minstrels lived on the fringes of society. Unlike serfs and vassals, clergy and the religious, they were not bound to a higher authority. They were often itinerant—the legendary "wandering minstrels." They moved from place to place in response to the demand for their services. Church authorities routinely condemned them and the music that they produced. Over time, however, many minstrels found steady employment as part of the court retinue; they essentially became the house band for a particular noble. Like the cooks and grooms, they were servants, usually paid accordingly, but some enjoyed the favor of their masters. Their more elevated status parallels the greater value placed on secular music.

Minstrels were multifaceted entertainers.

Bibliotheque Nationale, Paris, France/Flammarion/The Bridgeman Art Library

3-5B The Troubadour

The original troubadours, poets who wrote and sang about courtly love, lived throughout France—especially Provence, in southern France—and came from both upper and lower classes. The man generally regarded as the first troubadour was William IX of Aquitaine, a duke and the grandfather of Eleanor. By contrast, Bernart de Ventadorn, generally regarded as the finest of the troubadour poets, was reputedly the son of a castle baker. Regardless of their station, troubadours needed to cultivate refinement, courtesy, and skill to obtain success.

The troubadours put women on a pedestal, an unaccustomed height for them prior to this time. This went beyond the idealized portraits of women in the poems; troubadour poetry gave expression to the atmosphere of cultivation and grace that became an essential aspect of courtly life during the latter part of the Middle Ages. This newfound attention to women, especially those of noble birth, emerged as the invasions from the north, east, and south tapered off. With survival no longer such a pressing issue, court members had leisure time, and the dynamics of courtly love helped regulate social interactions.

Troubadour poems typically portray the agonies and ecstasies of an idealized love. They are concerned above all with the sensations of romantic love—infatuation, despair, sublimation—and absolute fidelity, regardless of the circumstances. The affair that the poet describes and longs for may never take place; the entire relationship may take place at a distance. Indeed, one famous, if fictional, account of the life and sweet death of the troubadour Jaufre Rudel tells how Rudel fell in love with a countess after hearing of her from pilgrims. He journeyed to her, became mortally ill on the trip, and died in her arms.

We can see troubadour poetry as a response to the influence of the church and the realities of the social world of the nobility. In its emphasis on romantic, even erotic, love, it seems at odds with the emphasis on chastity and the denial of the body that was central to official church doctrine. Yet, in content and tone troubadour poems run parallel to the love of the Virgin Mary portrayed in devotional writings around the same time. Troubadour poetry also afforded those who wrote it and those who read it a way to come to terms with the fact that a real relationship with a desirable woman was often not possible.

Troubadour poetry would influence lyric poetry and the music that accompanied it for generations. Among those it strongly influenced was the fourteenth-century poet-composer Guillaume de Machaut.

LEARNING OUTCOME 3-6

Describe the life, poetry, and music of Guillaume de Machaut, an important fourteenth-century composer.

3-6 Guillaume de Machaut and Secular Song

For the last half of the twentieth century or so, it has been almost an article of faith that musicians deliver a complete package: they write the words and the song, then perform it, either individually or as part of a group. However, only a very few of these singer-songwriters have enjoyed comparable acclaim as poet and musician: Leonard Cohen, Joni Mitchell, and—above all—Bob Dylan stand out in this regard. In classical music, it is the rare composer who sets his own words; most successful song composers use preexisting poems rather than their own words as inspiration. It is with this frame of reference that we view the unique career of Guillaume de Machaut.

3-6A Life

We know little of the early life of Guillaume de Machaut (ca. 1300–1377) ♪. We do know that he became a priest and spent his life in service, first to King John of Luxembourg through John's death in battle in 1346, then to the cathedral at Reims. Although attached to the cathedral, he was largely free of everyday priestly responsibilities, so he was able to write

▶Guillaume de Machaut

FAST FACTS

- Dates: ca. 1300–1377
- Place: France
- Reasons to remember: Equally renowned as a poet and a composer; one of the first singer-songwriters and the most esteemed composer in France during the fourteenth century; the first musician identified as the composer of a complete mass, the *Mass of Notre Dame*

Ivan Bastien/iStockphoto.com

and compose. By this time, he had acquired an extensive list of patrons.

Machaut stands apart from every other musician of the time, for several reasons. He was equally renowned as a poet and a composer; indeed, much of his work consists of poems without music. He was the first musician identified as the composer of a complete mass, the *Mass of Notre Dame*. Machaut is among the first composers for whom we have a substantial record of composition; he spent much of his later years preparing definitive versions of his music. And we know him better than other composers of the time because his writings contain personal commentary.

Although the age of the troubadours had passed by the time Machaut was born, the idea of courtly love was still very much in the air. The majority of his poems and compositions, including the rondeau that we hear next, express the refined sensibility that we associate with courtly love.

3-6B The Rondeau

The rondeau was the oldest of the song forms popular in fourteenth-century France. Its roots date from dance songs from the twelfth and thirteenth centuries. Machaut revised the rondeau to become a multipart song with a recurrent refrain. These songs had vernacular texts that described some aspect of love. In the rondeau presented here, the poet-admirer bemoans his fate, maintaining his fidelity to a woman who is so indifferent to him that she does not remember who he is.

Machaut's song underscores the different paths of sacred and secular vocal music during medieval times. Contrasts between Machaut's "Puis qu'en oubli" (see Listen Up!) and Hildegard's chant involve most

minstrel Multifaceted entertainer who, by the thirteenth century, was typically an instrumentalist attached to a court
troubadour Poet-musician who wrote and sang about courtly love
rondeau Multipart song with a recurrent refrain

Guillaume de Machaut, "Puis qu'en oubli" (mid-14th century)

TAKEAWAY POINT: Melody made up of several short phrases, with homophonic accompaniment

STYLE: Late medieval

FORM: Modified strophic form

GENRE: Rondeau

INSTRUMENTS: Voice and viols

CONTEXT: Song for the court expressing courtly love

STATEMENT 1

0:00 Notice four-part question-and-answer relationship between phrases of refrain.

Puis qu'en oubli sui de vous dous amis	Since I am forgotten by you, sweet friend,
Vie amoureuse et joie a dieu commant.	I say farewell to joy and to a life of love.

STATEMENT 2

0:22 The melody is always dominant, but the accompaniment varied. Initially, lower parts move in same rhythm as melody.

Mar vi le jour que m'amour en vous mis	Ill-fated was the day I placed my love in you

0:33 Lower parts gain more rhythmic independence during descending phrases and in first phrase of last line.

Puis qu'en oubli sui de vous dous amis.	Since I am forgotten by you, sweet friend.
Mais ce tenray que je vous ay promis	But what I have promised you I will maintain,
C'est que jamais n'aray mul autre amant.	which is that I shall never have any other lover.

REPEAT OF STATEMENT 1

1:08 Accompaniment presents series of chords: complete triads and a chord progression.

Puis qu'en oubli sui de vous dous amis	Since I am forgotten by you, sweet friend,
Vie amoureuse et joie a dieu commant.	I say farewell to joy and to a life of love.

 Listen to this selection streaming or in an Active Listening Guide at CourseMate or in the eBook.

---

of the musical elements: voices alone versus voices and instruments; long, flowing phrases versus short melodic statements; unmeasured rhythms versus rhythms with a clear beat; a melody over a drone versus multiple parts moving in synch; no chords versus chords; nonrepetitive versus repetitive form.

LEARNING OUTCOME 3-7
Anaylize an example of the earliest dance music that has come down to us.

3-7 The Emergence of Instrumental Music

Dancing seems to be about as ancient as singing. Both the Bible and the writings of Homer make reference to it. In ancient Greece and Rome, it became not only an elegant art but also an elaborate, often erotic entertainment for all social classes. We know that such dances typically had instrumental accompaniment, but we know virtually nothing about either the dance or the music for it. The same holds true for dance in the Middle Ages. Folk dancing almost certainly remained a part of life for serfs. Eventually, it also became part of court life; the most compelling evidence is the preservation of dances in manuscripts, beginning around 1250. These dances are the first notated instrumental music.

3-7A Dance Music

Although we are glad to have these earliest examples of dance music, we have only a sketchy picture of what the dances looked like and at best an imperfect understanding of the way the music for them sounded. The first treatises on dance did not appear until the fifteenth century, and the notated music typically has only a single line. There are no clues to instrumentation, tempo, dynamics, texture, and other features; there is just the melody.

Mensural Notation. Almost all of the early dance pieces make use of mensural notation, that is, notation that indicates specific rhythmic relationships as well as pitch. Mensural notation was a thirteenth-century innovation used to write down dances as well more complex polyphonic music. In the case of dance music, it was absolutely necessary because the dances have a strong, definite rhythm.

Reconstructing Dance Music. In the absence of notated instructions for performance beyond the melody, performers of this music must try to infer its sound from extramusical sources. These sources are as diverse as paintings and illustrations, poetry and literature, treatises, and court records, which tell us, for instance, how many musicians were engaged for a particular social function. The musicians on the recording used here surrounded the melody with other compatible and appropriate sounds.

The Estampie. The estampie was a dance popular in France and Italy from the twelfth through the fourteenth centuries. In aristocratic circles, it was probably a couples dance. We can only speculate about the steps and the origin of the name; scholars offer several possibilities. We do know that it is the first dance identified by name in musical sources.

Like other medieval dances, the estampie appeared first as a sung poem; the earliest examples have words, but not music. There are two possible interpretations

for this: the poems were set to preexisting estampies known only in oral tradition, or the sung estampies eventually became dance tunes. Both were likely, because at least one troubadour song was set to an existing estampie, and documentary evidence suggests that the songs of Machaut and others were also performed as instrumental pieces.

The earliest estampies were lively dances in a fast, simple triple meter. Their melodies comprised several groups of short phrases. Typically, each phrase group is heard twice, and each group ends with a refrain, a device related to both sacred and secular song. We hear the last of a set of eight estampies included in a late thirteenth-century manuscript, whose title (*Manuscrit du roi, or The King's Manuscript*) denotes its noble origins. See Listen Up!

This medieval dance sounds both strange and familiar at the same time. The sounds of authentic instruments date the style to the Middle Ages; so does the style of the melody—fairly quick notes moving mainly

mensural notation Notation developed in the mid-thirteenth century that, for the first time, indicated specific rhythmic relationships as well as pitch

estampie Dance for couples, popular in France and Italy from the twelfth through the fourteenth centuries

Juan Oliver/The Bridgeman Art Library/Getty

French School/The Bridgeman Art Library/Getty Images

by step in a narrow range. However, the practice of building dance music from short segments and linking them with a refrain is still a common practice in contemporary dance music. And we can view the tabor (drum) accompaniment as an early ancestor of the contemporary rhythm section.

Although it is one of only a few examples, this estampie conveys in notation what was almost certainly the case in oral tradition: the presence of vigorous dance music in the courts of the twelfth and thirteenth centuries. The fact that it was notated underscores the growing independence of secular culture from church control.

Looking Back, Looking Ahead

Because they are so far removed in time from us, the three musical examples discussed here invite consideration from two perspectives. We can view the Middle Ages as a musical world quite different from our own, but we can also view it as the starting point of a long evolutionary path that has led to the familiar music of our time.

When we compare the two secular examples with Hildegard's chant, we can first sense the vast gulf that separated sacred and secular music during the late Middle Ages. Hildegard's chant—streams of melody spinning out over a drone—seems to want to escape the world. The estampie, with its strong, definite rhythms, is very much of this world; we can imagine nobles of both sexes taking a turn on the dance floor. We can hear the influence of dance music in the subtler but still definite

rhythms of Machaut's rondeau. We are aware from the lyric that the song is about love, the most compelling of earthly experiences, and we find the lyric set to a tuneful melody with a simple, clearly outlined form.

As we listen to this music with twenty-first-century ears, we may be struck by how different it is from the music that typically surrounds us. The chant is timeless; it is an artifact of a different age and culture. But the two secular works are more connected to our present. In a typical modern performance of the estampie, the kinship of this medieval dance with Celtic music becomes evident in the instrumentation—melody instruments, drone, percussion, simultaneous versions of the melody, simple rhythms creating a strong beat at a bright tempo, and short phrases repeated numerous times.

The Machaut song offers the strongest connection to the central element of the rich European musical tradition that is the primary focus of this survey. In the composer's careful choice of consonant chords, we get a foretaste of the tonal harmony that would provide the structural underpinning for the concertos of Vivaldi and Bach, the operas of Mozart and Rossini, the symphonies of Beethoven and Brahms, and so much more great music.

Tonal harmony is unique to European music and one of its cultural achievements. It has its roots in polyphonic sacred music, with the earliest surviving polyphonic compositions dating from the ninth century. By the fourteenth century, it had also filtered into secular song, such as the one heard here. Machaut and several other leading composers of the time wrote for both church and court. We encounter harmony in sacred music in the next chapter.

 study tools 3

Medieval Music

 ## KEY CONCEPTS

1. **Multiple styles.** Medieval music is not one style, but several. Sacred music, secular vocal music, and secular instrumental music are decidedly different from each other. Medieval sacred and instrumental music are opposites in some respects: free-flowing melody versus short phrases with a definite, repetitive rhythm. These differences diminish by the end of the era, but the divisions between sacred and secular, and vocal and instrumental, are still evident.

2. **Multiple centuries.** Our overview of medieval music effectively covers over three centuries, from the 1100s to the 1400s. During this time, both sacred and secular music evolved considerably, from monophonic chant and secular song through sophisticated counterpoint and harmony.

3. **Multiple performance possibilities.** Surviving medieval musical scores offer only the sketchiest clues to such details of performance as instrumentation, dynamics, tempo and rhythmic nuance, and performing style. As a result, performers of early music try to reconstruct performance traditions from a variety of indirect sources, such as paintings, documents, and instruments. Their interpretations may lead to widely divergent versions of the same material.

 ## KEY FEATURES

1. **Ad hoc instrumentation.** About the closest thing to a constant in medieval instrumentation is that vocalists sing the most prominent part in vocal music. Other parts could be sung or played by any instrument. Instruments could be added to provide a drone or rhythmic support.

2. **Modal music.** Sacred and secular music use modes, seven-note scales in which the order of half- and whole steps differs from that heard in major and minor scales.

3. **Every part for itself.** Polyphonic medieval music followed several paths: elaborate parts in free or measured rhythm over a slow-moving tenor; parts moving in the same rhythm; and one active part, with the rest in simpler rhythms. In all options, there is often the sense that the parts were conceived layer by layer. The parts are generally consonant on the beats and follow predictable cadences, but there is little exchange between parts until the end of the era.

4. **Restricted rhythmic options.** The most common rhythmic options are either the largely undifferentiated but unmeasured flow of chant, or measured rhythm typically formed by simple, repetitive rhythmic patterns.

 ## KEY COMPOSERS

Hildegard of Bingen (1098–1179)
Guillaume de Machaut (ca. 1300–1377)

Music Concept Check

To assist you in recognizing its distinctive features, we present an interactive demo of medieval music in CourseMate and the eBook.

SuperStock/Getty Images

LEARNING OUTCOMES

After studying this chapter, you will be able to do the following:

4-1 Understand the significance of "L'homme armé," a popular song from the fifteenth century.

4-2 Recognize the main features and functions of Renaissance polyphony, and hear a Catholic Mass movement set by Josquin des Prez.

4-3 Describe the madrigal, its history in Italy and England, its sound, and its social function.

4-4 Understand Elizabethan solo song, the instrument that typically accompanied it, and the use of song in theatrical productions.

4-5 Identify the sounds of Renaissance instruments and their roles within a chamber ensemble.

 study tools

After you read this chapter, go to the Study Tools at the end of the chapter, page 60.

n 1501, the Italian printer Ottaviano Petrucci published *Harmonice Musices Odhecaton*. Both the fact of its publication—*Harmonice Musices Odhecaton* was the first polyphonic music printed with moveable type—and the type of music published—French secular songs—signaled far-reaching changes in musical life during the sixteenth century. Printing made music far more accessible, and the ratio of secular to sacred compositions increased dramatically. Both the technological breakthrough and the choice of printing secular music showed the impact of the Renaissance on musical life.

As **Renaissance** values, particularly the rediscovery of classical Greek and Roman civilization and the use of vernacular languages, took hold in western Europe during the fifteenth and sixteenth centuries (between roughly 1450 and 1600), the influence of secular culture on musical life grew significantly. Secular vocal music intended for amateur performance flourished during the sixteenth century. This vocal music ranged from solo songs and simple homophonic settings of songs for several voices to Italian and English madrigals, which often featured contrapuntal textures and expressive text settings of highly regarded poetry.

More subtle was the integration of secular material into sacred compositions and the blurring of the stylistic boundary between sacred and secular. This integration occurred in both sophisticated and simple music. Secular songs, especially those by masterful composers, became more contrapuntal (like sacred compositions), and sacred compositions began to include more homophonic passages (like secular songs). And, as we will hear shortly, even the most high-minded composers occasionally quoted a secular song in a sacred composition. More accessibly, Martin Luther (1483–1546), the architect of the Protestant Reformation, reintroduced congregational singing into services and composed several well-known hymns, many of which were inspired or even borrowed from the secular songs of the day. Congregational singing would become common practice in virtually all Protestant denominations, in sharp contrast to the complex polyphonic vocal works that trained choirs sang at Catholic churches and cathedrals.

The church remained the most important patron and employer of musicians during the early Renaissance and through much of the sixteenth century in Catholic Europe. Still, the musical examples discussed in this chapter—the greatest hit of the fifteenth century and a mass movement that quotes it; a madrigal and two versions of a secular song, both from Elizabethan England—hint at the gradual erosion of the church's influence on musical life, much as it diminished in other domains.

4-1 "L'homme armé"

In our world of instant classics, the average stay on the top of the pop charts is less than a month; the majority of pop hits last only a week or two at number one, and only a small percentage survive even a generation. So, it may be hard to imagine a song staying current for almost two centuries. However, that was the case with "L'homme armé."

As its title and opening words suggest, "L'homme armé" is a French secular song (chanson) about an armed man. We don't know who composed it, and we aren't sure of the date of its earliest use in a composed work. We do know that sometime after 1450 it began to appear in masses by numerous composers as a cantus firmus—a preexisting melody serving as the starting point for polyphonic compositions. It is likely that

the song predates its earliest use by at least a few decades, because its popularity was one of the key reasons for quoting it, and in that era it would have taken some time for a song to become popular. It appeared around 1475 as an independent work in a collection of secular songs. Composers continued to use it for more than a century; it appeared in over thirty-five masses composed in the fifteenth and sixteenth centuries. The fact that composers used secular melodies in sacred music was not in itself unusual; early Renaissance composers occasionally wove popular melodies into their masses. However, "L'homme armé" occurs almost ten times more frequently than any other popular tune of the time. Its popularity had less to do with its inherent musical interest than with its significance as a musical symbol.

4-1A "L'homme armé": Words and Music

"L'homme armé" (see Listen Up!) has survived in several forms: woven into extensive and elaborate polyphonic settings; highlighted in the three-voice setting found in the first existing secular version of the song; and as a monophonic song, the way people would have most often heard it during the fifteenth and sixteenth centuries.

Its lyric consists of a single stanza:

The man, the man, the armed man:
the armed man is to be feared.

Everywhere the cry has gone out.
Everyone should arm himself with
a breastplate of iron.

The man, the man, the armed man:
the armed man is to be feared.

"The man, the man, the armed man: the armed man is to be feared."

Sakala/Shutterstock.com

Renaissance Era between roughly 1450 and 1600 in which there were a rediscovery of classical Greek and Roman civilization, a rebirth of humanistic values, and more widespread use of vernacular languages. In music, the era was characterized by such features as seamless, imitative polyphony; rapid growth in quantity and quality of secular music; and the increasing use of instruments

chanson Secular French song of the fifteenth and sixteenth centuries

cantus firmus Preexisting melody that serves as the starting point for a polyphonic composition

LISTEN UP!

TOTAL TIME: 0:26

Anonymous, "L'homme armé" (early fifteenth century?)

TAKEAWAY POINT: Vigorous melody supporting martial lyric

STYLE: Late medieval /early Renaissance

FORM: ABA form (three-part form featuring an opening section, a contrasting middle section, and the repetition of the opening section)

GENRE: Chanson

INSTRUMENTS: Male voices

CONTEXT: Aural symbol of the Christian warrior

OPENING (A)

0:00   The vigorous, straightforward rhythm and brisk tempo match the character of the lyric.

L'homme, l'homme, l'homme armé,	The man, the man, the armed man,
L'homme armé, l'homme armé	The man, the man, the armed man
doibt on doubter, doibt on doubter.	The armed man is to be feared.

CONTRASTING SECTION (B)

0:09   Contrasting section in a higher range

On a fait partout crier	Everywhere the cry has gone out
Que chascun se veigne armer	Everyone should arm himself
d'un haubregon de fer.	with a breastplate of iron.

REPRISE OF OPENING (A)

0:17   The reprise of the opening section is slightly truncated.

L'homme, l'homme, l'homme armé,	The man, the man, the armed man,
L'homme armé, l'homme armé	The man, the man, the armed man,
doibt on doubter.	the armed man is to be feared.

 Listen to this selection streaming or in an Active Listening Guide at CourseMate or in the eBook.

The words simply make a statement; this is no time to tell a long, drawn-out story. The vigorous, tuneful melody supports the song's martial theme, one familiar to people in a society where war was a constant. The style of the melody would also have been familiar to fifteenth-century folk; one can imagine men belting it out in a tavern or singing it while going off to battle.

Why does a song about battle find its way into so many sacred compositions? In *The Maze and the Warrior*, a fascinating study of symbols in medieval and Renaissance Europe, music scholar Craig Wright offers a compelling explanation: the song became a symbol of the Christian warrior.

ABA form Three-part form featuring an opening section, a contrasting middle section, and the repetition of the opening section

4-1B Melody as Symbol

Melody is typically the most distinctive feature of a musical work. For this reason, memorable melodic material can acquire extramusical associations. We experience this in advertising jingles and television theme music, church hymns, and national anthems. The melody may be appropriate to its symbolic purpose, as is the case with "God Save the King," the British national anthem. Or it may not: the tune for the American national anthem, "The Star-Spangled Banner," was originally a drinking song. In either case, the symbolic meaning comes from its function, not from its inherent musical qualities.

4-1C Holy Wars and Holy Warriors

In a country that has insisted on the strict separation of church and state, the notion of a holy war often seems to be literally a foreign concept, seen from a distance in the constant turmoil between Muslims and Jews in the Middle East and the ongoing clashes between Protestants and Catholics in Ireland. But none of this is comparable to the holy wars of the eight crusades undertaken between 1095 and 1272.

In 1095, the pope proclaimed a holy war—a crusade—to reclaim Jerusalem from the Muslims. Christians recaptured Jerusalem in 1099 but could not maintain control. Seven subsequent crusades over the next two centuries also ended in failure, as Muslims reclaimed Christian territories. The fall of Constantinople, the center of eastern Christendom, to the Turks in 1453 added insult to injury. Although the Crusades failed to achieve their goal, they nourished the idea of the righteous warrior.

The era of the Crusades was also the era of *chivalry*, a term that derives from the French *cheval*, meaning "horse." Originally it identified knights—mounted men-at-arms—as opposed to the foot soldiers recruited from the peasantry. By the twelfth century, the term referred not only to the knight but also to the honorable and courteous conduct expected of a knight of the noble class. At least in ideal circumstances, nobility referred to both a social class and a set of values. The chivalrous code of conduct helped the nobility justify endless wars, either against the Muslims or against one another. Those who followed the code could place themselves above those who raped and pillaged the conquered.

Given the active role of the church in both the Crusades and numerous territorial disputes, it is not surprising that the noble knight would gain a spiritual analogue: the Christian warrior. The spiritual counterpart

In the religious art of the period—paintings, stained glass, altars, illuminations, even musical manuscripts—we find St. Michael, the personification of the Christian warrior, protected by a breastplate of iron, or Christ offering bread and wine to a fully armed man.

to the holy wars was the war between good and evil. Good Christians might enlist the aid of the archangel St. Michael, the leader of the heavenly hosts and protector of both Jews and Christians, or even of Christ himself, in their battles against Satan.

In the Middle Ages, the most powerful symbol of the warrior was his armor. It covered him from head to toe—the breastplate of iron mentioned in the lyric was just one of his many pieces of equipment. As the militant and the spiritual merged during the Middle Ages, armor came to identify both the knight and the Christian soldier.

"L'homme armé" became a musical symbol of the Christian man-at-arms, familiar and potent enough to be meaningful even when stripped of its lyrics and placed in a radically new context. We hear a radically altered fragment of the melody in a movement from a mass by the early Renaissance composer Josquin des Prez.

LEARNING OUTCOME 4-2

Recognize the main features and functions of Renaissance polyphony, and hear a Catholic Mass movement set by Josquin des Prez.

4-2 Josquin des Prez and Renaissance Polyphony

Meet Josquin des Prez (1445?–1521) ♪, the most famous composer that you've probably never heard of. But music scholars, students of sacred music, and fans of

Josquin des Prez
FAST FACTS
- Dates: 1445?–1521
- Place: Burgundy (now northeastern France)
- Reasons to remember: The most esteemed composer of the early sixteenth century and a master of Renaissance polyphony

IOSQVINVS PRATENSIS.

Hulton Archive/Getty Images

early music certainly know of Josquin, perhaps the most respected composer of the fifteenth and sixteenth centuries. Although born somewhere in Burgundy (now northeastern France), Josquin was an international figure who held positions in France and Italy, including an extended stay at the papal chapel (ca. 1489–1495). He enjoyed the admiration of his peers, and his music was well known and highly regarded by musicians and commentators, both during his lifetime and for more than a century after.

4-2A Renaissance Polyphony

Josquin's music epitomizes Renaissance polyphony, a style of composition that flourished throughout most of the fifteenth and sixteenth centuries, and throughout much of Europe. Notable composers in this style include several from what is now the Flemish part of Belgium—Josquin, his contemporary Heinrich Isaac (ca. 1450–1517, and Orlande de Lassus (1530/1532–1594); the Italians Giovanni Pierluigi de Palestrina (1525/1524–1594) and Giovanni Gabrieli (ca. 1554–1612), whose music bridged Renaissance and Baroque; and the Englishman William Byrd (1540–1623).

Renaissance polyphony represents a high point in the evolution of contrapuntal writing, which had begun at least 500 years earlier with simple drones set against a chant melody, as in Hildegard's antiphon. The majority of Renaissance polyphonic music was composed for liturgical use in the Mass and other religious celebrations. In this chapter, we briefly trace the early evolution of polyphony, speculate about why it developed only in Catholic Europe, and consider the Kyrie from a mass by Josquin that incorporates the "L'homme armé" tune.

The word *polyphony*, first introduced in Chapter 2, comes from two Greek roots: poly, "many" (as in *polygon*, a many-sided geometric shape), and *phonos*, "sound" or "voice" (as in *phonograph*). The word *counterpoint* comes from two Latin words: *contra*, "against" (as in *contrary*), and *punctus*, "point," a word used in medieval times to identify musical notes. Counterpoint thus means literally "note against note."

Polyphonic can denote any texture with more than one voice—as opposed to the monophonic (single-voiced) texture of music like "L'homme armé." However, as it is most widely used now, *polyphonic* identifies textures in which two or more parts have comparable melodic independence and interest. By this definition, none of the four previous examples qualifies as polyphonic, even though all but "L'homme armé" have more than one part, because the supporting parts are not particularly interesting or independent but are mainly drones (Hildegard's antiphon and the estampie) or slow-moving harmonies (Machaut's rondeau).

Counterpoint is the practice of combining melodically interesting parts. This is often done according to well-established practice; aspiring composers often study sixteenth- and eighteenth-century counterpoint for this reason. We might describe the relationship between counterpoint and polyphony this way: Counterpoint is the compositional procedure; polyphony is the result.

> ⌈Counterpoint is the compositional procedure; polyphony is the result.⌋

4-2B Early Counterpoint

The making of music in parts began simply. The first notated efforts at combining voices, which date from the ninth century, generally took one of two forms: a drone added to a chant melody, as in Hildegard's chant, or voices moving in parallel motion, as we hear today in rock guitar riffs harmonized with power chords. In either case, the subordinate voices have no rhythmic interest or independence. The first steps toward truly independent voices took two forms: parts with different melodic contours but identical rhythms; or an embellished, often melismatic, part against a slower-moving one. In either case, the rhythm was unmeasured, that is, without a steady and predictable beat, as in chant.

By the twelfth century, composers had begun to notate measured rhythms. Multipart music included not only works like Machaut's rondeau, in which one part is dominant, but also two-, three-, and four-voice works in which each voice had a different melodic shape and a

The making of music in parts began simply.

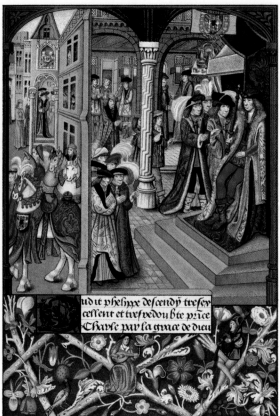

The medieval practice of manuscript illumination parallels early counterpoint, in that both involved the elaborate decoration of an enormously distended sacred text. In music, the sacred text was the chant found in the tenor part; each note of the tenor was prolonged, while one or more parts wove decoratively around it. In art, the sacred text was scripture: the first letter of the passage was drawn much larger than the subsequent letters, and it was colored and typically surrounded with images and other decoration.

different—occasionally *quite* different—rhythm. Often, one voice—the tenor (which derives from the Latin word *tenere*, "to hold")—would move in slow values while the other voices danced around it at a much quicker pace. In the music of the thirteenth and fourteenth centuries, rhythm distinguished one part from its neighbors, either because it moved at a much different pace or because different parts used different rhythmic patterns. Although the harmonies created when the parts lined up rhythmically were almost always consonant, there was often little sense that the parts blended together. Indeed, in numerous instances not only did each part have its own text but the texts were also in different languages! That would change in the fifteenth century.

4-2C The Innovations of Renaissance Polyphony

The use of two distinctly different approaches in early polyphonic composition underscores the challenge faced by composers of sacred music: how to translate the flow of monophonic chant into music for two or more parts while maintaining the rhythmic and harmonic coordination necessary for effective performance. The decorative elaborations of a slow-moving chant melody maintained the rhythmic flexibility of chant but made more than the most rudimentary coordination between parts almost impossible. More measured rhythms make possible more intricate coordination among the parts but sacrifice the rhythmic suppleness of chant. Not until the early Renaissance did composers find ways to merge these contrasting approaches.

A major innovation in Renaissance polyphony was the distribution of rhythmically and melodically distinctive material among all of the parts. This is most obvious in the use of imitation, where other parts restate—imitate—a melodic idea soon after its first presentation. (If you've ever sung a round, like "Frère Jacques" or "Row, Row, Row Your Boat," you've experienced a very specific kind of imitation.) However, even when imitation is not used, there is a consistency in the melodic material among the parts. The effect is of voices weaving together to produce a rich tapestry of sound. They mesh into beautiful harmonies yet flow seamlessly, without the obvious marking of time in at least one part. It was as if Renaissance composers had created the earthly counterpart to the celestial harmonies of choirs of angels, which figured so prominently in medieval Christian theology. We hear these sounds in a movement from a mass setting by Josquin that quotes "L'homme armé."

> The effect is of voices weaving together to produce a rich tapestry of sound.

4-2D Music for the Catholic Mass

The listening example for this chapter is the Kyrie from Josquin's mass *Missa l'homme armé sexti toni* (*Mass of the Armed Man in the Sixth Tone*). The mass is one of two in which Josquin quoted the famous "L'homme armé" tune. The Kyrie is one of five movements included in a complete setting of the mass.

The Mass. The heart of the Catholic liturgy is the Mass (the word *mass* comes from *missa*, the Latin word for "dismissal"; the celebrant said or sang the phrase "Ite, missa est" to mark the end of the service). The Mass consists of two parts: the liturgy of the word, which consists mainly of readings from scripture; and the liturgy of the Eucharist, in which the celebrant and the congregation symbolically relive Christ's death and resurrection. In both the liturgy of the word and the liturgy of the Eucharist, there are parts that change daily (Mass is said every day in most parishes) and parts

The heart of the mass is the transubstantiation.

that do not change. The proper comprises the changing parts of the Mass; the ordinary comprises the unchanging parts.

The Five Mass Movements. The five parts of the Mass used in musical settings are the Kyrie, Gloria, Credo, Sanctus, and Agnus Dei. All come from the ordinary, and each takes its name from the first words of the text used in the Mass: *Kyrie eleison* (Greek for "Lord have mercy"); *Gloria in excelsis Deo* ("Glory to God in the highest"); *Credo in unum deum* ("I believe in one God"); *Sanctus, Sanctus, Sanctus* ("Holy, Holy, Holy"); and *Agnus Dei* ("Lamb of God"). The Kyrie and Gloria belong to the liturgy of the word. The Credo is the bridge between the liturgy of the word and the liturgy of the Eucharist, and the Sanctus and Agnus Dei occur shortly before communion, the part of the Mass when celebrant and congregation partake of the bread and wine.

The texts vary widely in length and content. The Kyrie is the shortest: three 2-word phrases. The Credo, which is a profession of the central tenets of Catholicism, is the longest—over 160 words in Latin. The Gloria, a hymn of praise, is the next longest. The Agnus Dei also contains just three phrases—each begins with the phrase "Lamb of God, who takes away the sins of the world." The Sanctus is also a hymn of praise but not as lengthy as the Gloria.

Symbolism in Music for the Mass. The heart of the Mass is the transubstantiation. Shortly before communion, the celebrant performs a highly ritualized ceremony, transubstantiation, in which Catholics believe the bread and wine are literally transformed into the body and blood of Christ. That the transubstantiation occurs is a central article of faith for Catholics. It must be an act of faith because the outward

imitation Polyphonic technique in which other parts restate—imitate—a melodic idea soon after its first presentation
proper Parts of the Mass that change from day to day
ordinary Unchanging parts of the Mass

LISTEN UP!

TOTAL TIME: 3:35

Josquin des Prez, Kyrie, from *Missa l'homme armé sexti toni*

TAKEAWAY POINT: Rich polyphony floating over a gentle pulse

STYLE: Renaissance

FORM: Multisectional: **ABC form** (three-part form in which each section is different)

GENRE: Mass

INSTRUMENTS: Voice

CONTEXT: Music to be sung during the celebration of the Mass

A

0:00   We hear the "L'homme armé" melody quoted at the beginning in all four voices—much slower and more dignified than in its original form.

   Kyrie eleison   Lord have mercy

B

1:01   More chordal texture at the outset and in general not as contrapuntal as the previous section

   Christe eleison   Christ have mercy

C

2:25   A new third section, despite repetition of text

   Kyrie eleison   Lord have mercy

 Listen to this selection streaming or in an Active Listening Guide at Course-Mate or in the eBook.

4-2E Kyrie, from *Missa L'homme armé sexti toni*

Josquin's mass movement (see Listen Up!) exemplifies the culmination of five centuries of musical evolution. From the simplest of beginnings—drones and parallel motion—polyphonic composition evolved into the richly woven tapestries of sound characteristic of Renaissance polyphony. In the compositions of Josquin and his contemporaries, music for the Catholic liturgy reaches a pinnacle. Arguably, no music before or since better expresses the Catholic understanding of the divine.

Josquin began his Kyrie by quoting the familiar "L'homme armé" melody, which served simultaneously as a melodic hook (because his listeners would recognize the melody) and as a symbol (because the words of the melody would call to mind the Christian warrior). By transforming it so drastically, Josquin essentially converted mundane musical material into sacred sounds.

That sacred compositions such as Josquin's *Mass in the Sixth Tone* would quote familiar melodies hints at a key feature of sacred polyphony: *the style is also a symbol*. The overall sound is quite consistent from work to work; the tunes that composers quoted helped distinguish one from the next. Imparting an individual character to a particular work is, at best, a secondary concern. The overriding objective is to present the text of the Mass ordinary in elevated musical language. In this respect, Renaissance polyphony is the multivoice analogue to chant. Both use singing to transcend the limitations of speech; in polyphony, it assumes a far richer and more complex form.

Josquin probably composed this mass at the end of the fifteenth century, during his service at the Papal Chapel. For the next three examples, we travel about 900 miles northwest and a century ahead in time.

appearance of the bread (the host) and wine does not change.

The challenge for composers like Josquin was to create music that conveyed a comparable message. As in the Mass, they could begin with everyday materials, in this case a popular tune of the day. And they could, through divinely inspired art, transubstantiate it into heavenly music. The tune they used most frequently was "L'homme armé."

"L'homme armé" fused into a single symbol the two most pervasive facts of life in the Middle Ages: religion and war. Recall that both were constants, and both often came together, most notably in the Crusades. The image of the Christian warrior was among the most powerful symbols of the era, especially because the constant wars on earth mirrored the more important and even more constant war between good and evil, heaven and hell.

Setting this song within a polyphonic mass movement, a sound and style that strives to connect with celestial music, in effect transubstantiates the song into a spiritual symbol. We hear this in the Kyrie from Josquin's *Mass in the Sixth Tone* next.

ABC form Three-part form in which each section is different

LEARNING OUTCOME 4-3

Describe the madrigal, its history in Italy and England, its sound, and its social function.

4-3 The Madrigal

One can convincingly argue that the most memorable era in British music has been the last half century. From The Beatles to Radiohead, it's been an incredible run. Never in its history has British music enjoyed greater popularity, prestige, or influence. One can also argue that the most glorious era in English music prior to the rock era occurred around four centuries ago, during the reign of Elizabeth I, the first Queen Elizabeth.

Dutch painter Frans Hals's famous portrait of a clown (1638) reminds us that playing the lute was one of the skills expected of court jesters.

Five madrigal singers sitting around a table, reading from their respective partbooks (1568).

Ayres, or airs, solo songs with lute accompaniment—were popular, and so were sacred music for Anglican and Catholic worship, imported and domestic madrigals, a wealth of keyboard music, and songs and instrumental music for music making at home. In this and the following section, we hear examples of two kinds of vocal music, a madrigal and an accompanied song as well as an instrumental version of the song.

In 1588, Nicholas Yonge, an enthusiastic English singer, published *Musica Transalpina* (*Music across the Alps*), a collection of fifty-seven Italian madrigals with texts translated into English. Yonge's volume must certainly have been a labor of love as well as a good business proposition: in the preface to the volume, Yonge mentions that a "great number of gentlemen and merchants of good account" gather daily at his house to sing madrigals, which were "yearly sent me out of Italy and other places."

Yonge's anthology whetted England's already healthy appetite for Italian madrigals and helped inspire English composers to compose their own. It soon bore fruit. In 1601, Thomas Morley, an enthusiastic admirer of Italian music in general and of the madrigal in particular, published a volume of twenty-five madrigals by twenty-three different English composers. Entitled *The Triumphes of Oriana*, it was Morley's tribute to Queen Elizabeth I, who had supported his work by giving him a monopoly on printing music. ("Oriana" referred to Queen Elizabeth I; all of the madrigals ended with the refrain "Long live fair Oriana.")

The madrigals composed in the sixteenth and early seventeenth centuries were polyphonic settings of secular poems. The settings generally contain four to six parts, and they were typically performed a cappella (without instrumental accompaniment), with each singer reading his or her part from a "partbook." The poems were generally of high quality: the first published collection (1530) to use the word *madrigal* for such settings included several texts by Francesco Petrarch, whose poetry was very fashionable during the early sixteenth century.

The impulse to set the text polyphonically reflects composers' newfound awareness of the quality of secular texts. They seemed to think that good poetry demanded a more substantial approach than the simple homophonic settings used in lighter song genres. The polyphony of the madrigal trickled down from the imitative polyphony used in sacred music, such as the Josquin mass movement; it is a similar approach, but not as complex. The influence of sacred polyphony on the madrigal is not surprising, because many of the first composers of madrigals were, like Josquin, northern European composers working in Italy.

4-3A The Madrigal in Italy

The madrigal had emerged in Italy during the 1520s and flourished in many of the major Italian cities—Rome, Venice, and Florence, the home of the Medicis. Madrigals provided entertainment for aristocrats—either at court or in academies formed to perform this music. Many madrigals,

ayre (air) Elizabethan solo song with lute accompaniment
madrigal Polyphonic setting of a secular poem, composed in the sixteenth and early seventeenth centuries
a cappella Without instrumental accompaniment

the madrigal | **53**

- Dates: ca. 1574–1638
- Place: England
- Reasons to remember: One of England's most important composers of madrigals

especially those written in the middle of the century, were intended for amateur performance. However, others were composed for more elaborate entertainments—for example, as intermission pieces between acts of a play, which sometimes upstaged the main attraction, and for festive occasions.

During the second half of the sixteenth century, the madrigal became the most popular form of aristocratic musical entertainment in Italy and ultimately throughout most of Europe. Among the most popular and prolific madrigalists was Luca Marenzio (1553–1599), who had ten volumes of madrigals published during his lifetime.

The madrigal flourished during a century-long gap between the advent of music printing and the widespread adoption of keyboards and stringed instruments. Printing had made music much more widely available, much less expensive, and much more quickly disseminated. By contrast, the core instruments of the seventeenth century—the violin family and the harpsichord—were still in the early stages of their evolution during the sixteenth century; during the sixteenth century, the lute was far more popular. The musical environment was ideal for madrigals to blossom.

4-3B The Madrigal in England

The madrigal was the first Italian genre to enjoy popularity throughout Europe. (Opera and the concerto would follow in the seventeenth century.) Among the most enthusiastic admirers of the Italian madrigal were the English "gentlemen . . . of good account" mentioned in Yonge's preface. Madrigal singing enjoyed great popularity in England during the reign of Elizabeth I (r. 1558–1603), who was herself a skilled musician. Inspired by the availability of the madrigals in translation and the emergence of major English poets such as Edmund Spenser and Sir Philip Sidney, composers created an English madrigal school. Some composers, such as John Wilbye, are known mainly for their madrigals. Others, such as Thomas Morley and Thomas Weelkes, composed madrigals as well as music in many other genres.

By the time English composers began composing madrigals, it was

text painting (word painting) Strategy to highlight meaning in a text with striking musical gestures: a melodic inflection, a bold harmony, a quick change of rhythmic pace

a well-established genre. Its social functions were well defined, and its musical conventions were in place. For English composers, it was mainly a matter of language: composing to English rather than Italian texts. In either language, the challenge for madrigal composers was to integrate words and music—to have the music enhance the message of the words.

4-3C The Madrigal: Words and Music

The madrigal featured two major innovations: musical settings that responded to the text, and the use of imitative polyphony in a secular style. At first glance, these innovations might seem to be working at cross-purposes. It would seem that the first requirement for expressing a text is to present it intelligibly—it is more challenging for listeners to sense the connection between words and music if they can't understand the words. Imitative polyphony complicates that because all parts share text as well as melodic material. This isn't as big a problem in sacred polyphony, especially in settings where the text is familiar. Josquin could assume that everyone who heard one of his masses would have the text firmly in mind. (For other genres, it was such a problem that members of the Catholic hierarchy tried to ban polyphonic music during the Counter-Reformation because it was supposedly unintelligible.) Rendering the text intelligible was an issue in madrigal composition, even in those works where the text was familiar—as it was in the writings of Petrarch. Madrigal composers found solutions to this problem, as we'll discover shortly.

> The challenge for madrigal composers was to integrate words and music—to have the music enhance the message of the words.

In addition, composers sought to find ways to amplify the meaning of the text in music. Typically, they used two strategies, one general and one specific. The general strategy was to establish a musical mood consonant with the overall sense of the text: a somber mood for a sad poem or a bright mood for more lighthearted verse. The specific strategy, which came to be called text painting or word painting, was to highlight meaning in the text—even a single word—with striking musical gestures, such as a melodic inflection, a bold harmony, or a quick change of rhythmic pace. For instance, sadness came to be conveyed by descending tones. We hear examples of many of these text/music relationships in John Wilbye's "Adew, Sweet Amarillis" ("Adieu, Sweet Amaryllis").

4-3D John Wilbye, Madrigalist

John Wilbye (1574–1638) ▲ remains one of the most highly regarded English madrigal composers active around 1600. Wilbye grew up in Suffolk, in the eastern part of England,

and spent most of his career in the service of a local landowner who valued his services. Wilbye was not a prolific composer. He composed mostly madrigals, and only sixty-six have survived. Almost all appeared in two volumes, published in 1598 and 1609. Wilbye set poems by Sydney and Spenser; he also wrote his own, including "Adew, Sweet Amarillis" (see Listen Up!).

Wilbye's poem is a lover's brief but heartfelt lament on the end of his relationship: "Breaking Up Is Hard to Do" circa 1600. Amarillis (now usually spelled Amaryllis) was a beautiful shepherdess mentioned by the Roman poet Virgil in his *Eclogues*; given the time and place—Renaissance Europe—the classical allusion should not surprise us. Here is the text of the poem:

> Adew, sweet Amarillis:
> For since to part your will is,
> O heavy tyding,
> Here is for mee no biding:
> Yet once againe ere that I part with you,
> Amarillis, sweet Adew.

The overriding theme is resignation leading to acceptance, a quality that Wilbye emphasizes in the music. The poet has been rejected by Amaryllis. Her decision is bad news for him ("O heavy tyding"), and they will not meet again ("here is for mee no biding") before going their separate ways.

Wilbye enhances the dark mood of the poem by opting for minor mode

Wilbye's poem is a lover's brief but heartfelt lament on the end of his relationship.

LISTEN UP!

TOTAL TIME: 2:35

Wilbye, "Adew, Sweet Amarillis" (1609)

TAKEAWAY POINT: Conversational exchanges among four singers

STYLE: Late Renaissance

FORM: Through-composed

GENRE: Madrigal

INSTRUMENTS: Four mixed voices

CONTEXT: Song for recreational singing among skilled men and women of "good account"

SECTION 1

0:00   Music conveys message of title phrase: imitative texture, minor mode all suggest protagonist's agitation at losing Amarillis.

Adew, sweet Amarillis

Adew, sweet Amarillis

0:27   Note shift to more chordal texture.

For since to part your will is.

SECTION 1 REPEATED

0:44   Adieu, sweet Amarillis

Adieu, sweet Amarillis

1:07   For since to part your will is.

SECTION 2

1:24   Emotional crux of the madrigal—beginning slowly, with long values suggesting the weight of bad news

O heavy tyding

Here is for mee no biding.

ENDING

1:41   Then reaching a climax in the final phrase and retreating from it through a long descent, as the poet's feelings change from the agitated despair of the opening to acceptance

Amarillis, sweet Adew.

Adieu, sweet Amarillis.

Listen to this selection streaming or in an Active Listening Guide at CourseMate or in the eBook.

throughout most of the madrigal; the shift to major toward the end, combined with the good-bye ("adew") in the text, suggests a kind of resignation and acceptance. Wilbye presents the text clearly. The setting of the title phrase, which we hear several times, has the most imitative texture. The other lines of the poem have a more chordal setting.

4-3E The Madrigal and Musical Meaning

In the madrigal, more than any other Renaissance genre, we begin to hear a transformation in how music becomes an active interpretive partner in realizing the meaning of the words. Machaut's rondeau is pleasing to the ear, but we are hard pressed to connect its words and music, to find in the music features that enhance the meaning of the text.

By contrast, Wilbye's madrigal seems much more specifically connected to the text, in its general character and in the shift in mood from section to section. There are numerous instances of text painting. For example, the phrase "O heavy tyding" is set to sustained harmonies, as if a heavy weight makes it impossible to move quickly. The phrase "yet once againe" is set to a melodic figure that descends slowly after reaching a peak, to help convey sadness leading to acceptance. And the switch of the opening material from minor to major completely changes the expressive message, from despair to acceptance. Here, it is the music, not the words (which are the same), that tells us of the protagonist's change of heart. In these musical gestures, we hear composers trying to resonate with life experience, for example, by slowing down or speeding up the rhythm, or shaping melodic contour to amplify the rise and fall of speech.

The idea that music can convey a specific mood—that it can communicate meaning through the interaction of several elements—was an enormous change in attitude. Indeed, some music historians have argued that it is the most significant change in the history of Western art music. We will hear such changes even more clearly in opera, and by the eighteenth century, in instrumental music as well. The beginning of this shift is most clearly evident in the madrigal.

LEARNING OUTCOME 4-4
Understand Elizabethan solo song, the instrument that typically accompanied it, and the use of song in theatrical productions.

4-4 Solo Song in Elizabethan England

The madrigal and the accompanied solo song are siblings. Both surfaced around the same time, in the second quarter of the sixteenth century. Both were concerned with presenting the text clearly and in a way that approaches the rhythm and pacing of the words as they might be spoken. Both typically featured texts about love—as is true of "O Mistresse Mine," Wilbye's madrigal, and hundreds of other works. The most significant differences between madrigal and song have to do with the tone of the texts—more serious in the madrigal versus lighter in the song; the complexity of the texture—imitative counterpoint in madrigal versus melody plus chordal accompaniment in song; and a setting for several voices in madrigal versus one voice and instrument in song. But even here, the rules are not hard and fast. Many sixteenth-century madrigals and songs were published in two versions: for voices alone and for solo voice with instrumental accompaniment.

The sound of the accompanied solo song should resonate well with contemporary

course On a lute, a pair of strings tuned to the same pitch
strophic song Song in which the same melody sets two or more stanzas of text
obbligato Second melody playing under a main melody

listeners: it is the Renaissance forerunner of songs by rock-era folksingers and singer-songwriters. It typically features a singer whose theme is the ups and downs of love, supported by a plucked string instrument—in our time, the guitar; in Elizabethan England, the lute.

Lute

4-4A The Lute

The lute's closest cousin in the guitar family might well be the twelve-string guitar, because lutes, like twelve-string guitars, typically had two strings per pitch. (Pairs of strings tuned to the same pitch are called courses.) Like the modern guitar, the Renaissance lute typically had strings tuned to six different pitches, although lutes with seven courses were also common, especially toward the end of the sixteenth century.

The most obvious differences between the modern guitar and the lute are the shape of the body and the shape of the neck. The body of the lute is flat on the front (the side next to the strings) and rounded in the back—much the same shape as half a pear cut lengthwise. The neck, upon which the strings are stretched, has a pronounced bend at the end of the fingerboard.

The lute evolved from an ancient Middle Eastern instrument called the *oud*, which was brought to Spain by the Moors and known in Europe by the ninth century. Evidence of the lute—especially from paintings and illustrations, treatises, and other writings—dates from the fifteenth century. During the sixteenth century, the lute became the dominant household instrument for well-to-do families and the most popular solo instrument among professional musicians. The quantity of music composed for lute far exceeded that composed for harpsichord or any other instrument.

4-4B The Strophic Song

A strophic song is one in which the same melody sets two or more stanzas of text. "O Mistresse Mine," the song to be discussed next, uses a single five-phrase melody to set four stanzas. Declamation of the text—matching the inflection of the text with the music—is more difficult because the same music must serve multiple texts. In this situation, the composer responds most directly to the rhythm of the words. Specific responses to particular words or phrases of the text, such as those we heard in Wilbye's madrigal, are simply not possible in a strophic song.

4-4C Chordal Harmony

In songs like "O Mistresse Mine," the distinction between melody and harmony is about as clear as it can be: the singer sings the melody, while the lutenist plucks chords that follow the rhythm of the melody. Only occasionally does the lutenist play a melody-like obbligato, a second melody playing under the main melody. The idea of chordal accompaniment of a melody wasn't new with the solo song. Recall that we heard this texture at times in the Machaut rondeau and in parts of Josquin's Kyrie and Wilbye's madrigal. However, here it is consistent throughout.

Precisely for this reason, we can hear even more clearly than in the Wilbye madrigal how harmony had evolved into chord sequences that closely resemble common practice harmony. What makes this development significant is the fact that harmony already plays such a key role in organizing musical thought. Chord progressions (introduced in Chapter 2) help define musical phrases and sentences; chord choice at cadences determines the decisiveness of the musical punctuation—a period versus a comma. In this instance, the most decisive punctuation in the melody is the last one, in large part because it is supported by a chord progression that signals a strong close. This song is our first encounter with purposeful harmony—a preview of what we will hear in the next century.

4-4D "O Mistresse Mine"

Early in the second act of Shakespeare's comedy *Twelfth Night*, Sir Toby Belch and Sir Andrew Aguecheek ask Feste, the clown, to sing a love song. Feste obliges them with "O Mistresse Mine," a song often attributed to Thomas Morley (1557/8?–1602) ♪. Robert Armin, a member of Shakespeare's troupe who often played clown roles and was apparently a fine singer, performed the song in the first productions of the play, probably accompanying himself on the lute.

Music was an important component of Elizabethan drama—and indeed, Renaissance drama in general. Music was performed before plays began, between acts, and oftentimes within the act, as part of the drama, as was the case in *Twelfth Night*. We also know that Shakespeare

▶Thomas Morley
FAST FACTS

- Dates: 1557/8?–1602
- Place: England
- Reasons to remember: A true "Renaissance man"— composer, performer, publisher, teacher, promoter— in Renaissance England

cenap refik ONGAN/iStockphoto.com

drew on sources and resources from all strata of society. So it is likely that "O Mistresse Mine" was a popular song known only in oral tradition before Morley's arrangement of it. It's all but certain that Shakespeare kept the tune and the title but added his own words to make the lyric connect to the plot: it contains lines that allude to characters and events in *Twelfth Night*. For example, the first stanza identifies a "true love" that "can sing both high and low." Many commentators view this as a reference to Viola, a woman who presents herself throughout much of the play as a man.

Songs like "O Mistresse Mine" (see Listen Up!) blur the boundary between popular and art music. As we hear it, it is an elegant lament. But its uncertain lineage suggests that it began as a popular song; so do its accessible melody and simple form. As other British songwriters would show about 360 years later, it *is* possible to create artful music in a popular style.

LEARNING OUTCOME 4-5
Identify the sounds of Renaissance instruments and their roles within a chamber ensemble.

4-5 Composing for Instruments

The most direct connection between Thomas Morley and "O Mistresse Mine" comes from his 1599 publication *The First Booke of Consort Lessons*, which contained settings of songs

A small consort showing two flute/recorders and viol

Lebrecht/TL/Lebrecht Music & Arts

LISTEN UP!

TOTAL LENGTH: 1:35

Morley (attributed), "O Mistresse Mine" (ca. 1599)

TAKEAWAY POINT: Gently elaborated version of the melody, with other lines swirling around it

STYLE: Late Renaissance

FORM: Variation (one statement of the melody, with varied repeats)

GENRE: Consort music

INSTRUMENTS: Viol, lute, recorder

CONTEXT: Instrumental music for amateur music making

STANZA 1

0:00   The melody consists of five short, well-articulated phrases. The first two are identical in words and music.

O mistress mine! where are you roaming? (2×)

0:13   The third and fourth phrases share the same text, but the melody of the fourth phrase is a more elaborate variant of the third.

O! stay and hear; your true love's coming, (2×)

0:26   The fifth phrase stands alone.

That can sing both high and low.

STANZA 2

0:30   Modification of conventional strophic form, with three lines of text set to the last three phrases of the melody; no text repetition

Trip no further, pretty sweeting;

Journeys end in lovers meeting,

Every wise man's son doth know.

STANZA 3

0:48   Accompaniment takes its rhythm from the melody, which it supports with chords.

What is love? 'tis not hereafter; (2×)

Present mirth hath present laughter; (2×)

What's to come is still unsure.

STANZA 4

1:16   Again, just the last three lines of the melody, with a few embellishments

In delay there lies no plenty;

Then come kiss me, sweet and twenty,

Youth's a stuff will not endure.

Adieu, sweet Amarillis.

🔊 Listen to this selection streaming or in an Active Listening Guide at CourseMate or in the eBook.

> Thomas Morley was a one-man music industry: composer, performer, publisher, teacher, and promoter.

were arranged for "6 Instruments to play together, the Treble Lute, the Pandora, the Cittern, the Base-Violl, the Flute & Treble Violl." It wasn't the first such publication, but it did signal an important new trend in music: composition specifically for instrumental ensembles.

4-5A The Instrumentation of the Consort

Consort is a term used in England during the sixteenth and seventeenth centuries to identify a small group of diverse instruments. The term is related to *concert*, in the sense of playing together; it came into use toward the end of sixteenth century, during the Elizabethan era, and remained in use for much of the next century.

Although the instrumentation of a consort could vary in number and type, it was generally agreed that certain combinations of instruments sounded better together. The six instruments mentioned by Morley formed an ideal consort. At its heart was the viol. Its most compatible partners were what Morley called the flute (we now call them recorders) and lutelike instruments.

These instruments, all mentioned in Morley's consort book, were especially popular in Elizabethan England. They represent three families of instruments. Viols are bowed stringed instruments; the flute/recorder is a gentle wind instrument; and the lute, pandora, and cittern are similar plucked instruments. As is typical of the era, all three instrument types came in several sizes, to correspond roughly to the ranges of the human voice. Thus, Morley recommends a treble (high range) and bass (low range) viol; plus three lutelike instruments in high, middle, and low ranges; and a flute, which also comes in several ranges (in this version of "O Mistresse Mine," the recorder is in a soprano range). (See Listen Up!)

and dances by "divers exquisite Authors," including Morley himself. (Morley was a one-man music industry: composer, performer, publisher, teacher, and promoter. He was involved in just about every aspect of musical life in Elizabethan England.) The pieces in the collection

consort Small group of diverse instruments in Elizabethan England

If you crossed a cello or violin with a guitar, you'd get a viol. Like the cello, the viol has a curved front, and the performer produces sound by bowing it. Like the guitar, it has a flat back, six strings, and frets. When played well, it produces a sweet, somewhat nasal sound—stronger than that of an acoustic guitar, but not as powerful as that of a violin or cello. The viol is also called a viola da gamba (viol of the knee), because it rests on the lap or between the legs of the performer rather than under the chin. It was an especially popular instrument among music amateurs from the sixteenth through the early eighteenth centuries.

Elizabethan consort music was published with wealthy amateur performers in mind, and it is thought that Bach composed the viola da gamba part in his sixth Brandenburg Concerto for Prince Leopold, his employer at the time. Then as now, instruments had differing social status. Viols, because of their delicate sound and relatively comfortable playing technique, were high on the list. By contrast, wind instruments like the shawm, a predecessor of the oboe, were usually left to professionals or lower-class amateurs because they had an abrasive sound and required that the player contort his face when playing it. (It may be for this reason that women seldom played the shawm.)

You will notice that on this recording, viols play the two most prominent parts, the melody and the bass line, both of which are considerably simpler than the lute part. This is consistent with the place of the viol in the consort, and in society: amateurs of modest skill could play the prominent parts, whereas a more skilled lutenist, perhaps a musician in the service of an aristocrat, would play the more intricate running figures in the background.

4-5B Composing for Instruments

Morley's *First Booke of Consort Lessons* specifies the instruments to be used, as we have noted. In indicating the instrumentation, at least in general terms, Morley was following the practice of the time: such indications were common in mixed consort music. As such, they represent an important innovation in instrumental music.

Most medieval and Renaissance music that made use of instruments did not indicate specific instruments—in many cases even whether instruments were to be used at all. These were decisions left to the performers. As a result, we must infer an appropriate instrumentation from such features as the notation (such as the special notation used for the lute) or the context in which the composition might be heard (a church versus a court setting).

By contrast, Morley narrows the choices considerably. By specifying the instruments to be used, he virtually guarantees that they will blend well together. This narrowing of instrument choice can be understood as an important intermediate step between the almost complete freedom of earlier practice and the more contemporary practice of specifying instrumentation precisely.

4-5C Style and Form in Instrumental Composition

Our inclusion of both a vocal and an instrumental version of "O Mistresse Mine" enables us to explore two questions about composing for instruments. The first has to do with the difference between writing for voice and writing for instruments. The second has to do with the form of instrumental compositions.

Idiomatic composition for an instrument—that is, composing in a way that makes use of its distinctive sounds and capabilities—goes hand in hand with designating a particular instrument for a specific part. In this recording, the viols play the melody and the bass, the two parts that require a sustained sound. The recorder plays a subordinate role. The lute, which can be played with speed and delicacy, has a running line in the background.

idiomatic composition Composing in a way that makes use of an instrument's distinctive sounds and capabilities

Both of the viol parts are singable. There are a few embellishments of the melody that would require some vocal agility. Otherwise, the melody is much as it is in the vocal version. By contrast, the lute part is constantly active, running up and down scales for the most part. In this context, this kind of part works best on the lute—although any of the instruments could play it—because it enriches the texture without covering the melody.

In effect, this version is a variation on "O Mistresse Mine," for instruments. As we mentioned in the discussion of Mozart's variations, variation is one of the easiest ways to create an instrumental composition: simply take a familiar tune and play it several times, each time changing some aspect of it. The form is essentially a strophic form for instruments: melodic and textural embellishment substitute for variety in the text. In this version, we hear only one statement of the melody, but the setting as a whole is richer and more elaborate than the setting for voice and lute heard previously.

Although this version of "O Mistresse Mine" is brief, it is rich in information. We hear some of the most characteristic instrumental sounds of the late Renaissance. We also get strong hints of three important developments during the years around 1600. One is writing specifically and idiomatically for instruments. Another is the gradual shift from the more balanced imitative polyphony of the Renaissance (Josquin, Wilbye) to a texture in which melody and bass are most prominent and are connected by chords. The third is the use of variation procedures to convert a song into an instrumental piece. This practice became fashionable in both solo and consort music around this time.

Looking Back, Looking Ahead

The Renaissance was a glorious time for singing. A wealth of great vocal music came from all over western Europe. Polyphonic motets and settings of the Catholic Mass stand out as a high point in contrapuntal composition, and hymns for congregational singing spawned a new tradition of religious song. The madrigal represented a new kind of secular polyphonic vocal music, one in which the music often responded specifically to poetry of high quality. Simpler but appealing songs with lute accompaniment also appeared toward the end of the sixteenth century, as well as instrumental settings of them. Music printing, a sixteenth-century innovation, made all of this music much more accessible.

If we compare the composed examples in this chapter with those in the previous chapter, we get some sense of the thorough transformation of musical life over three centuries. Hildegard's antiphon and Josquin's mass movement frame the evolution of Catholic sacred music from monophonic melody to rich polyphonic textures. Similarly, Wilbye's madrigal, when compared with Machaut's song, shows not only the evolution of polyphonic composition but also the adaptation of contrapuntal techniques used in the composition of sacred music. What most immediately distinguishes "O Mistresse Mine" from "L'homme armé" is the lute accompaniment; what distinguishes the instrumental version from the estampie is the polyphonic setting of the melody and the fact that all of the parts are composed.

Josquin's mass movement represents the culmination of a cappella Catholic sacred music. Composers continued to create unaccompanied polyphonic masses and motets throughout the sixteenth century, but the tradition all but vanished after 1600. By contrast, our small sample of Elizabethan music provides a foretaste of major new directions in music. In the madrigal, we heard the text painting and other effects designed to make music specifically expressive: to convey in music the emotions behind a word or line of text, and in the instrumental setting of "O Mistresse Mine" we encounter our first example of idiomatic instrumental composition. We hear radical reconceptions of both practices in our initial encounter with Baroque music.

 study tools 4

Renaissance Music

 KEY CONCEPTS

Integration. If there is an all-encompassing trend whose multiple realizations distinguish Renaissance from medieval music, it might well be integration. Integration is evident in several important parameters: voices and instruments, sacred and secular, and the relationship between parts.

 KEY FEATURES

1. **Imitation.** In Renaissance polyphonic music, the sharing of melodic material among two or more parts became commonplace, in both sacred and secular music. Typically, one voice would present a melodic idea, and other voices would enter soon after with the same melodic material.
2. **Full harmonies.** Typically, the harmonies in both polyphonic and homophonic passages are complete triads rather than the emptier sounding harmonies of medieval music. They flow smoothly in sequences that anticipate, but do not consistently follow, the progressions of common practice harmony.
3. **Instruments on their own.** During the Renaissance, composers began to write more specifically and idiomatically for instruments: solo music for keyboard instruments and lute, music for instrumental groups, and instrumental accompaniments and obbligato parts for vocal music. Instruments also continued to substitute for voices in polyphonic works.
4. **Rhythmic flexibility.** In both sacred and secular music, there is greater rhythmic variety and contrast: for example, slow-moving parts in some voices versus faster moving lines in polyphonic music; rhythms that declaim the text in homophonic music; fast-moving instrumental lines versus slower vocal lines. The resulting rhythms may flow with a subtly measured pulse or move along with a sharply defined beat.
5. **Textural contrasts.** Contrasts between imitative counterpoint and more homophonic textures are common in both sacred and secular vocal music. Also common are numerous gradations between these extremes, such as a pair of faster moving voices against more sustained sounds.

 KEY COMPOSERS

Josquin des Prez (1445?–1521)
Heinrich Isaac (1450–1517)
Orlande de Lassus (1530/1532–1594)
Giovanni Pierluigi de Palestrina (1525/1526–1594)
Giovanni Gabrieli (ca. 1554–1612)
William Byrd (1540–1623).
Luca Marenzio (1553–1599)
Thomas Morley (1557/8?–1602)
John Wilbye (ca. 1574–1638)
Thomas Weelkes (1576–1623)

Music Concept Check

To assist you in recognizing their distinctive features, we present an interactive comparison of medieval and Renaissance music in CourseMate and the eBook.

De Agostini Picture Library/Getty Images

LEARNING OUTCOMES

After studying this chapter, you will be able to do the following:

5-1 Describe the characteristics of the Baroque era in music.

5-2 Understand what opera is and the revolutionary impact of the first operas in Europe.

5-3 Recognize the importance of Claudio Monteverdi and the sound and vocal style of his opera *Orfeo*.

5-4 Understand the growth of opera, including musical and dramatic changes, during the seventeenth century.

5-5 Recognize an early example of the use of recitative and aria, as well as the expressive capabilities of common practice harmony, in Henry Purcell's "Dido's Lament."

5-6 Understand the changes in Baroque opera from Monteverdi to Handel, through an examination of Handel's *Giulio Cesare*.

study tools

After you read this chapter, go to the Study Tools at the end of the chapter, page 77.

Toward the end of the sixteenth century, a group of artistically minded Florentine aristocrats and artists gathered regularly at the home of Giovanni de' Bardi, a Florentine nobleman who was also a skilled musician. Following the lead of Girolamo Mei, an Italian historian who produced the first serious study of Greek music, they attempted to revive classical Greek drama. Because Mei proposed that all Greek drama was sung, not spoken, Bardi's circle, later to be known as the Camerata, developed a text-centered approach to vocal writing that stripped away the polyphony customary in sixteenth-century vocal music and replaced it with free, sung text, supported by a truly bare-bones accompaniment. By the end of the century, the musical efforts of the Camerata led directly to the first operas. Jacopo Peri's *L'Euridice*, produced in 1600 for the wedding of Marie de' Medici and King Henri IV of France, is the first such complete opera to survive to our time.

Opera was a revolutionary new genre that precipitated a revolution in musical style: we date the beginning of the Baroque era to the production of the first operas. Opera quickly moved away from its original form, as Baroque music itself changed. High-minded members of the Camerata might have been either horrified at the opera composed later in the century—or perhaps succumbed to its beautiful melodies and enjoyed it as a kind of forbidden fruit. We introduce Baroque music and sample more than a century of Baroque opera in this chapter.

5-1 The Baroque Era

The Baroque era in music spans the century and a half between 1600 and 1750, encompassing almost all of the concert music of the seventeenth and early eighteenth century. The term *baroque* originally referred to an irregularly shaped pearl or a convoluted thought process. It came into use to describe the new art and architecture that emerged in the late sixteenth century and continued through the early eighteenth century, which some critics found bizarre, even grotesque. *Baroque* gradually lost its pejorative connotation among art historians and came to designate simply the art of the period. However, not until the middle of the twentieth century did music historians consistently apply the term to the music of this era. As used in music, it describes the style of the era; there is no strong connection between the term and the aesthetic of the period, as there is with Classicism or Romanticism.

There are innovations in early Baroque music that differentiate it from the music of the Renaissance and that endure throughout the era. Still, from our twenty-first-century perspective, one central fact about the Baroque era is that late Baroque music is likely to be familiar to us, whereas early Baroque music is not. One is most likely to hear music of Claudio Monteverdi and his contemporaries only in recordings and in concerts by early music ensembles. By contrast, the music of Bach, Handel, Vivaldi, and other late Baroque composers is heard not only in concert but also as background music in many situations: while on hold during a phone call, in stores and restaurants, on realtors' websites, and as music that young children study and perform. Vivaldi's *Four Seasons* is a favorite. In this chapter, we trace the evolution of Baroque music, from the unfamiliar to the familiar, through opera, one of the most significant developments of the era.

ollo/E+/Getty Images

The ceiling and altar of Peterskirche in Vienna, Austria, captures the excess that characterized Baroque aesthetics.

And it wasn't just the music that evolved during the Baroque era; so did the industry that supported it. At the beginning of the seventeenth century, opera was a private entertainment subsidized by the wealthy. However, by mid-century it had become a public entertainment in Venice. Italian opera soon spread through much of Europe. Throughout the early eighteenth century, opera was prestigious and popular. George Frideric Handel, for example, came first to England in 1711 as an opera composer; in 1719, he was appointed music director of the Royal Academy of Music, a commercial opera company. Opera was also ripe for parody: John Gay's and Christopher Pepusch's *The Beggar's Opera* (1728) lampooned behind-the-scene friction at Handel's company.

Paid public performance was a new

Baroque Era in music spanning the century and a half between 1600 and 1750

commercial enterprise of the Baroque era, part of a substantial expansion of the music industry. Music publishing of all genres—sacred music, opera and secular song, instrumental music, and much more—catered to church, court, and a growing middle class. Writing about music was directed to professionals and amateurs. Instrument making reached new heights of craftsmanship.

All of this commercial activity supported major new musical genres, which in turn explored new possibilities for musical communication, not only in opera but also in instrumental music. Opera by its very nature virtually demanded that music respond to the emotional message of the text. Instrumental music soon followed suit: composers felt that they could communicate an emotional state, or *affect*, without the aid of a text. By the middle of the seventeenth century, the prevailing practice in both vocal and instrumental music was to establish and maintain a single emotional state through an entire movement or, in a longer work, a major section. The idea that music could convey a wide range of emotions—with or without the aid of text—was a profound change in the perception of music as an expressive art. Nowhere was this potential more fully realized than in opera.

Baroque-era opera, or prospect, glass, designed for viewing the stage from afar.

LEARNING OUTCOME 5-2

Understand what opera is and the revolutionary impact of the first operas in Europe.

5-2 Baroque Opera

For the better part of four centuries, opera has been the most spectacular and lavish form of stage entertainment in Western culture. It can offer timeless stories, powerful drama, memorable music, expressive dance, evocative scenery, and marvelous stage effects. Although it began as an intellectual exercise within a small circle of Italian aristocrats, it soon attracted a large following that included not only aristocrats but also urban audiences of all classes. By the mid-seventeenth century, kings and other royalty emptied their state treasuries to underwrite opera productions. During the same time, opera became the first commercial music: by the 1640s, opera houses in Venice, then in other Italian cities, offered public performances, which anyone who could afford or cadge a ticket for could attend.

Opera's prestige and popularity continue into our own time, as an art and a benchmark for those who aspire to artistic status. No form of live entertainment has enjoyed greater prestige, from the time it was conceived to the present, than opera. In this chapter, we consider the defining characteristics of opera and explore the beginnings of this all-encompassing art.

opera Drama, either tragic or comic, in which all dialogue is sung

recitative Section of an opera that generally contains dialogue to further the action; features text delivered in a rhythm approximating speech, often with strings of repeated notes

aria Accompanied solo operatic melody

5-2A Opera Is . . .

Opera is drama in which all dialogue is sung. This distinguishes it from other kinds of sung stage entertainment, such as musicals, in which much of the dialogue is spoken. The music to be sung may be a kind of sung speech (recitative, a section of an opera that generally contains dialogue to further the action and features text delivered in a rhythm approximating speech); a fully developed melody (performed in a chorus, duet, trio, other combinations, or as an aria—accompanied solo operatic melody); or something in between. Typically, however, *all* of the text is sung. From the start, this has been the closest thing to a constant in opera.

There is usually much more to opera than constant singing, especially as we might experience it in the early twenty-first century. If we were to attend an opera performance at New York's Metropolitan Opera House, we would expect a production on a grand scale. The opera would have a serious subject, perhaps drawn from mythology or history, or adapted from a literary work of distinction (there have been many operas based on Shakespeare); it might treat a comic subject with sophistication. It would require tremendous resources: elaborate sets, star singers dressed in appropriate costumes, a chorus, a full orchestra, and a setting that can accommodate all of this. It is entertainment at its most lavish. Opera didn't begin this way, but it quickly evolved into a grand spectacle.

One can understand the enthusiasm for a genre that integrates drama and music (and often dance and much more). Still, there is a contradiction inherent in the full integration of drama and music. It lies at the heart of opera, and it has challenged composers from Monteverdi to the present.

5-2B The Paradox of Opera

Opera is an art form based on a fascinating paradox: it is a form of drama that is, on the surface, not dramatically credible. If we attend a theater production or view a film, we are aware that what we're seeing and hearing is not "real." At the same time, however, it is often only a small step to imagine that what we're seeing and hearing is, in fact, real—we could say the lines spoken by the members of the cast and connect to the emotions that they project as if it were our own experience.

It is a much bigger step to project ourselves into characters' roles when all of the dialogue is sung. It isn't just that we don't regularly converse in song. Nor is it only a question of intelligibility: today's opera houses often provide supertitles (the text being sung is projected on a display placed above the stage), even when the opera is in English. It also grows out of the fact that we process music more slowly than we process words; music usually unfolds more slowly and requires more repetition before it sinks in. As a result, during many of the most musically memorable moments of an opera, the dramatic action slows down, or even grinds to a halt. Despite this, opera *can* work dramatically, but only if the music enables us to engage with the plot. We suspend our disbelief and allow ourselves to let both words and music tell us the story.

5-2C Opera and Musical Expression

Musicians are accustomed to giving, and we are accustomed to listening for, musical gestures that imply or evoke a specific emotion or image. We find such musical clues in film soundtracks, television commercials, or orchestral works such as those of Hector Berlioz (as we will discover in Chapter 18). However, what is commonplace today was still a novel idea four hundred years ago. Composers were just coming to grips with the evocative capabilities of music. Opera would accelerate that process.

In order for music to work dramatically, it had to become a more specifically expressive art. Composers had to be able to compose music tailored to particular dramatic situations (danger, duplicity, jealousy) or expressive of particular emotions (joy, sorrow, serenity). We noted in the discussion of

Beatriz Schiller/Time Life Pictures/Getty Images

. . . music tailored to particular dramatic situations (danger, duplicity, jealousy)

Wilbye's madrigal (Chapter 6) that expression of emotions was an innovation heard in much of the modern music of the late sixteenth century. In opera, however, it occurred on a much grander scale and often involved the music given both to singers and to the orchestra. In writing opera, composers developed or adapted musical devices that both musicians and audiences found evocative.

5-2D The Beginnings of Opera

Opera began as the last and ultimately the grandest effort to revive classical Greek drama during the Renaissance. Especially when compared to what would soon develop, these first operas were musically simple in the extreme: they consisted mainly of dramatic text sung in a speechlike rhythm with sparse accompaniment from bass and chord-producing instruments. At the same time, composers sought to exploit the expressive potential of the human voice. Giulio Caccini (1558–1618), an important member of the Camerata and a contributor to the production of *Euridice*, published a volume of songs in 1601, which he called *Le nuove musiche* (*The New Music*). The preface to the songs was part manifesto and part method; Caccini supplied a detailed description of melodic ornamentation within a discussion of both aesthetics and practice. In part because of these vocal techniques, opera soon became a much more elaborate entertainment. These and other developments, including the extensive use of instruments, set the stage for a thorough transformation of musical life in Europe.

5-2E Opera and a Musical Revolution

Opera was at the heart of a seventeenth-century musical revolution—the kind that comes along once every couple of centuries. It profoundly affected every aspect of musical life: who made the music, how it sounded, who listened to it, and who organized it. It was warmly embraced by some and denigrated by others.

The revolution occurred in northern Italy four hundred years ago. At our distance from it in time and space, and with limited contact with the music and the culture that produced it, we may have difficulty appreciating how radical a revolution it was. However, by relating to the most recent musical revolution of comparable impact—the one that produced rock in the 1950s and 1960s—we can understand the extent to which this seventeenth-century revolution transformed musical life, first in Italy, then throughout Europe. Here are some interesting comparisons:

1. *A change in attitude, toward a more deeply felt music.* Rock proclaimed that it was "real," that it confronted life as it really is right now. Caccini claimed that the "new music" composed by him and other like-minded composers should "move the affect [i.e., emotion] of the soul" and "delight the senses." It, too, represented a much stronger appeal to feelings.

FAST FACTS

- Dates: 1567–1643
- Place: Italy
- Reason to remember: The first important composer of opera and a key figure in the transition between Renaissance and Baroque music

Imagno/ Hulton Archive/Getty Images

2. *Star power.* Rock icons like Elvis and The Beatles were music stars, and they enjoyed an unprecedented degree of adulation. Opera quickly developed a similar star system; the top singers were perhaps music's first real celebrities.

3. *A generation gap.* Frank Sinatra, arguably the biggest pop singer of the 1950s and early 1960s, called rock and roll "the most brutal, ugly, desperate, vicious form of expression it has been my misfortune to hear." The old guard of composers and critics prior to the seventeenth-century musical revolution similarly attacked those who created and promoted the new music.

4. *Radical musical change.* Rock gave popular music a new beat and new vocal and instrumental sounds; it also emphasized an integrated, interdependent group conception over a solo-oriented approach, which influenced both melody and texture. The new music of the seventeenth century put the spotlight on the soloist instead of diffusing interest throughout the ensemble; it presented new textures, a more flexible approach to rhythm, and new ways of integrating voices and instruments.

> The old guard attacks those who create and promote new music.

5. *New kinds of virtuosity.* In the 1960s and early 1970s, rock's guitar gods and R&B's inventive bass players went beyond technical mastery to add an astonishing variety of sounds. Their seventeenth-century counterparts were the solo singers, who introduced a dazzling array of new vocal sounds seemingly overnight; there is no account of such techniques prior to the end of the sixteenth century, nor are there musical styles that would seem to demand them.

These parallels give us some perspective on the far-reaching musical changes that emerged with early opera. There are, of course, obvious differences. One important difference is that opera began as an exercise for cultivated aristocrats and the musicians in their employ; rock is a grassroots music, although some of its top acts quickly developed artistic aspirations. Still, the many similarities between the two may help give us a clearer sense of the revolutionary impact of Monteverdi's opera.

LEARNING OUTCOME 5-3

Recognize the importance of Claudio Monteverdi and the sound and vocal style of his opera *Orfeo*.

5-3 Monteverdi's *Orfeo*

A significant percentage of the most celebrated and influential musicians in Western culture belongs to one of three groups. One group includes innovators such as Franz Joseph Haydn, Claude Debussy, Louis Armstrong, and The Beatles. These musicians appear at the beginning of an era; they help shape the new style and introduce a new aesthetic. Another group is their complement, those who come at the end of an era and who summarize it in a highly personal way. We will meet several of them: J. S. Bach, George Frideric Handel, and Johannes Brahms. The most exclusive group includes those musicians whose music simultaneously summarizes the prevailing style and decisively influences the music of the next generation. One such musician is a household name: Ludwig van Beethoven. Another member of this group is the Italian composer Claudio Monteverdi.

5-3A Claudio Monteverdi

Claudio Monteverdi ◀ came of age at the end of the Renaissance. He spent the first part of his life in Cremona, where he began composing at an early age: his first works were published when he was only fifteen. Like most musicians of his time, Monteverdi was a composer and a performer. He was apparently a skilled vocalist (subsequently, he taught voice) and violinist (not surprising, since he grew up in Cremona, then center of fine violin making). Such versatility was expected of professional musicians of this time—and for the next two centuries. It would profoundly affect his compositions.

In 1590, Monteverdi took a position as a court musician for the duke of Mantua. There he came in contact with some of the most forward-thinking musicians of the era. Building on their work, he transformed the madrigal into an even more expressive genre and composed the first significant operas. Both earned him an international reputation. In 1613, frustrated at what he considered inferior pay and difficult working conditions, he took a position as the director of music at St. Mark's Basilica in Venice, where he spent the rest of his career.

Monteverdi composed mainly according to the requirements of his position, or for those situations that promised the possibility of remuneration or recognition. He composed madrigals, then operas and other large-scale entertainments, as part of his duties in Mantua, and then a good deal of church music for his position at St. Mark's. When opera houses opened in Venice in 1637, he revived his career as an opera composer, turning out three works for Venetian audiences that were quite different from his earlier operas.

By the time he composed the opera *Orfeo* in 1607, Monteverdi was already a highly esteemed composer. He had published five books of madrigals, some of which had been published outside Italy. The modern elements in his madrigals made him the target of Giovanni Artusi, a conservative musical theorist. Monteverdi responded to Artusi's attacks by pointing out that there were two "practices," by which he meant ways of composing, and that the second practice, which he used, allowed for more expressive responses to text. Still, Monteverdi's innovations were occurring in a genre that was on the wane; his eight books of madrigals represent the final significant contribution to the genre. His significance as a composer rests more substantially in his operas, the genre that he helped bring to life.

5-3B *Orfeo*

It was all but inevitable that the first operas, the first dramas in music, would take a classic Greek story about the power of music as their subject. Their composers chose the most famous musical story of all, the legend of Orpheus and Eurydice. Here is the most familiar version: Orpheus is the son of a king and one of the Muses. He has supernormal musical abilities. His singing and playing of the lyre, a harplike instrument, are of such surpassing beauty that he can charm anything that he encounters: gods, people, animals—even plants and rocks. After returning from a voyage, Orpheus marries Eurydice, a beautiful mortal, who dies from snakebite shortly after they marry. What happens next is the crux of the story, at least for Monteverdi: Orpheus, although distraught at the death of Eurydice, resolves to go to the underworld to rescue her. He lulls Charon, who ferries souls across the River Styx, and his dog, Cerberus, to sleep by singing and then playing the lyre; when they are asleep, he steals the ferry to enter the underworld. Orpheus serenades Hades, the king of the underworld; his music so moves Hades that he agrees to let Eurydice return from the dead, on the condition that neither Orpheus nor Eurydice looks back. When Orpheus sees the sun again, he looks back to Eurydice, who then vanishes. There are several different endings to the legend; the most powerful has Orpheus being killed by women belonging to the cult of Dionysus, the rival of Apollo.

It is easy to understand the appeal of the Orpheus legend to Peri (recall that his setting of the legend in 1600 is the first complete opera that has come down to us), to Monteverdi, and to their audience. It is a timeless story with a direct connection to classical Greek culture, and it virtually demands that music

When Orpheus sees the sun again, he looks back to Eurydice, who then vanishes.

play both a symbolic and a dramatic role. Indeed, music makes the main dramatic events of the story possible. Without music, the decisive events of the story—Orpheus's entry into the underworld and his rescue of Eurydice—cannot happen. Monteverdi underscores this by placing the first of these encounters at the midpoint of the opera. It is as if the fate of Eurydice depends on the musical skills of Orpheus, as indeed it does. Orpheus's encounter with Charon comes in the third of five acts, in the aria "Possente spirto" (poe-SEN-tay SPEER-toe).

5-3C "Possente spirto"

For Monteverdi, it seems, the demand for "supernatural" music—spectacular music suitable for a demigod—offered an opportunity to showcase a new and blatantly virtuosic kind of solo singing. We surmise that the virtuosic element was vitally important to Monteverdi because he supplied two versions of the melody of "Possente spirto," the aria discussed here, in the published **score** (a notated musical document that contains every part to be performed) of the opera. One is an absolutely bare-bones version of the melody; the other is the lavishly ornamented version

> **score** Notated musical document that contains every part to be performed

THE language OF MUSIC

One of the major innovations of Baroque music and a defining feature of Baroque style is **basso continuo**, or continuous bass. As the term implies, basso continuo is a continuous bass line, as well as harmony built on the bass, in support of the melody. Because the continuo roles were generally played by some combination of bass and chord-producing instruments, **continuo** also refers to the group of instruments that supports the melody with bass line and chords. Continuo instruments used in "Possente spirto" include the organ and a low-pitched strummed instrument.

we hear. This second version guides those performers not prepared to provide their own ornamentation; it is an insurance policy of sorts, guaranteeing that no performance will lack the impact that such ornamentation provides.

Orpheus's singing is the most dramatically potent new element in Monteverdi's opera, but there is another novel feature of this aria: the interplay between voice and instruments. To this point in our survey of early music, we've heard voices alone, instruments alone, and—in the lute song—instruments in a subordinate role. This aria offers yet another kind of relationship: one in which voice and melody instruments alternate, each performing in a manner idiomatic to the instrument: vocal acrobatics versus darting scales from the violins, fanfare-like figures from the trumpets, high and low scales from the harps.

This way of combining instruments and voice was an important innovation. Although the practice was already in existence in 1607, the particular form it took in *Orfeo*—a sort of vocal-instrumental interplay—was without significant precedent. In this respect, Monteverdi's way of combining voice and instruments points toward the future, not only to his later operas but also to all of opera as a genre. The use of instruments, both in the supportive role heard during the vocal sections and as alternative melody instruments, certainly expands the composer's sound palette. But there's more to it than just the inherent musical interest in this kind of variety. We can understand Monteverdi's vocal-instrumental interplay in the service of the most fundamental goal of opera: to convey drama through music. Subsequently,

basso continuo Continuous bass line, as well as harmony built on the bass, in support of the melody

continuo An innovation of Baroque music, a group of both bass and chord-producing instruments, providing a strong bass line and continuous harmonic support

opera composers would take the lead in expanding the expressive possibilities of instruments as well as voices as a means to achieve this goal.

5-3D *Dramma per musica*

"Possente spirto" (see Listen Up!) gives us the opportunity to explore the question "How can music work dramatically?" As the aria begins, the stage is set. We (and Monteverdi's audience, who knew the story well) are aware that we've reached a crucial point in the plot: if Orpheus can't convince Charon to let him cross the river, then the story ends. We know that Orpheus will use music to try to persuade Charon to help him. But we don't know *how* Orpheus will charm Charon. Monteverdi conveys the dramatic urgency of the situation through two complementary strategies: he composes an extraordinarily virtuosic vocal line (remember that the score contains the outline and Monteverdi's elaboration), and he builds toward the end, reaching a climax on the last line of the third stanza.

In our discussion of chant, we made the point that song derives much of its power by transcending speech; it begins where speech ends. Imagine, then, Orpheus's impact during this aria: the vocal techniques that Monteverdi requires go so far beyond everyday singing that they must have dazzled his audience. At the time of the premiere of *Orfeo*, these striking effects were still brand-new; it's likely that many of those who attended the premiere hadn't heard anything like them before. Most were accustomed to the more conventional singing heard in solo songs and madrigals, so this kind of singing might well have come as a delightful shock.

This is functional virtuosity, virtuosity with a purpose beyond showing off. Here, Orpheus must sound extraordinary, because he is Orpheus and because the dramatic situation requires that he use all his powers. And it is the sheer brilliance of Orpheus's singing

LISTEN UP!

Monteverdi, "Possente spirto," *Orfeo* (1607)

TAKEAWAY POINT: Dazzling vocal display with orchestral accompaniment and interplay

STYLE: Early Baroque

FORM: Strophic, with variation

GENRE: Opera aria

INSTRUMENTS: Voice, continuo, violins, trumpets, harp

CONTEXT: Brilliant vocal writing charms Charon so that Orpheus can enter the underworld

STANZA 1

0:00   Simple melodic outline, with spectacular vocal embellishments: machine gun–like bursts, rapid scales and trills

Possente spirto e formidabil nume,	Mighty spirit and fearsome deity,
senza cui far passaggio a l'altra riva	without whom no soul separated from its body
alma da corpo sciolta in van presume.	Can presume to gain passage to the other shore.

1:30   Instrumental interlude: pair of violins plays melody.

STANZA 2

1:55   In all three stanzas, instruments—here, a pair of cornettos (a cross between trumpet and flute)—punctuate each line.

Non viv'io, no,	I am not living, no,
che poi di vita è priva mia cara sposa,	for since my dear wife is deprived of life,
il cor non è più meco,	my heart no longer remains with me,
e senza cor com'esser può ch'io viva?	and without a heart, how can it be that I am alive?

3:02   Instrumental interlude: different instruments, different melody

STANZA 3

3:22   In each stanza, the music starts relatively simply and builds to a climax on the last line. The music becomes more intense as Orpheus presses his case with Charon.

A lei volt'ò 'l camin per l'aër cieco,	To her I have made my way through the turbid air,

4:05   The climax comes on the very last line, with "tanta bellezza … ."

a l'inferno non già,	yet not to Hades,
ch'ovunque stasis tanta bellezza	for wherever such beauty is found
il paradiso à seco.	has paradise in it.

 Listen to this selection streaming or in an Active Listening Guide at CourseMate or in the eBook.

that makes the scene dramatically credible. It helps us immerse ourselves in the drama and connect with Orpheus emotionally as he tells his sad tale to Charon. It is only through music that this scene works dramatically. The text certainly lays out the situation for Charon, but it does nothing special to persuade him to let Orpheus cross the river. You or I could do the same. The dazzling elaborations of the aria and the phrases that build to the climax on "tanta bellezza" make Orpheus's plea extraordinarily compelling. The fact that the plea is ultimately unsuccessful does not detract from its dramatic impact, on Monteverdi's audience and on us.

5-3E The Orchestra

In the course of *Orfeo*, Monteverdi requires forty-two instruments, including five trumpets and five trombones (more than in a modern orchestra), plus recorders, violins, and other strings, as well as a large array of continuo instruments. Performances almost certainly did not require forty-two musicians, because there is no one section within the opera where all of the instruments are playing at the same time. More typical is the arrangement heard in "Possente spirto," where we hear continuo plus a few other instruments in support of the voice. Moreover, most musicians of Monteverdi's era, including Monteverdi himself, played more than one instrument. Still, by early seventeenth-century standards, it is a massive ensemble; in its size and variety, we can see the beginnings of the modern symphony orchestra. The ensemble is not an orchestra in the modern sense, but it is an orchestra in concept and spirit.

With size comes the matter of managing it. In this respect, Monteverdi's score is unusually detailed: in many (but not all) of the numbers, Monteverdi specifies particular combinations of instruments. (This was the case in "Possente spirto"; there is an organ continuo as well as the three sets of melody instruments.) Monteverdi was an innovator here as well; specifying the instrumentation of a composition was still a relatively new practice in 1605.

5-3F The Significance of *Orfeo*

Orfeo is the first significant opera. As such, it was the catalyst for a revolution in music. Its impact reverberated throughout the musical world of the upper and middle classes, especially those living in cities. Many of the revolutionary changes were already in the air, but *Orfeo* helped bring them together, harness them, and provide a springboard for further change—more than any other single development of the period. These are among the most influential and far-reaching consequences of *Orfeo*:

1. The integration of drama and music
2. A major step in the transformation of opera from a small-scale private entertainment into a grand spectacle
3. The formation of an orchestra, along with the use of orchestral effects and some attention to idiomatic instrumental writing
4. The creation of textures that focus attention on the star
5. Flamboyant vocal devices that gave audiences a reason to focus on the star
6. The integration of song and dance within a musical drama
7. Above all, the development of a language that can convey expressive meaning through musical gesture

We will hear these reverberate throughout the music of the next several centuries.

Ironically, despite its long-lasting impact, Orfeo was also the last important opera to subscribe to the Camerata's vision of a *dramma per musica*. The free rhythm of the vocal lines and spare setting in "Possente spirto" soon gave way to more tuneful melodies with a steadier pulse and richer accompaniment. We will hear mature examples of this in opera arias by Purcell and Handel.

5-4 The Growth of Opera

During the middle of the seventeenth century, opera became a business. By the early 1640s, four theaters sponsored by the leading Venetian families were competing for the patronage of a ticket-buying audience. The season was short: just the six-week Carnival season that preceded Lent. Opera soon became a major cultural export from Venice as troupes toured throughout Italy and into France and German-speaking Europe. Characteristically, the culturally and politically independent and powerful French court of Louis XIV developed its own operatic tradition in reaction to the Italian model, although an Italian-born musician, Jean-Baptiste Lully, played the principal role in formulating it. English audiences warmed up to opera slowly. Because there was relatively little demand for opera in England, Henry Purcell (1658/9?–1695), the leading English composer of his day, composed only one, *Dido and Aeneas* (uh-NEE-us), and none of his important contemporaries were active in the genre.

Throughout the seventeenth century, opera continued to be identified as *dramma per musica*; this inscription appeared frequently on the front page of librettos (the texts to be sung in operas). The plots, adapted mainly from mythology, epics, and ancient history, quickly assumed a conventional structure featuring noble lovers, with comic servants providing intermittent relief from the tragedy that almost invariably ensued. Operatic plots typically unfolded over three acts. Then as now, singers were the star attraction, and composers quickly modified the aria to showcase their voices.

Because opera began with a new premise—effectively, to sing drama with a spare accompaniment rather than speak it—it differed fundamentally from much other vocal music of the time, such as the Elizabethan music heard in the previous chapter. "Possente spirto" heightened the speech with elaborate vocal flourishes and interpolated instrumental interludes, but still took its rhythm and form from the text. However, as opera became a commercial entertainment, composers replaced these speech-governed arias with more song-like melodies. These arias typically had a steady pulse, a full instrumental accompaniment rather than just continuo, and clearly articulated phrases. This shifted the balance between words and music: music now governed the flow of the text.

For each opera, composers wrote a lot of arias, to give all of the leading singers opportunities to display their vocal prowess. Many were lullabies, mad scenes, or laments. Virtuoso passages could serve a dramatic purpose, as they did in "Possente spirto," but they were

	Recitative	Aria
Function	Move the plot along	Express intense emotion through music
Text/Setting	Large amounts of text, set syllabically, and with no repetition	Not much text, with both syllabic and melismatic settings, and frequent repetition of phrases
Melody	Irregular phrases and contours, often with several repetitions of a single pitch	Regular phrases that coalesce into sections
Rhythm	Intermittent, unmeasured rhythm approximating the rhythm of speech	A steady if sometimes subtle pulse, with occasional slowing down for expressive purposes
Instrumentation	Just continuo instruments: chordal instrument, bass instrument	Full orchestra: at least strings, and sometimes winds and brass, plus continuo
Form	Through-composed	Da capo aria or other well-defined formal stereotype

Table 5.1 Recitative or Aria?

simply a way for singers to thrill audiences with their artistry and technical mastery.

With these changes, aria and recitative assumed different functions, which corresponded to their musical features. Recitative told the story; the focus was on the words. By contrast, arias offered characters moments of reflection, where they could express their feelings. Operas typically proceeded in recitative/aria (or recitative/duet) pairs: their alternation gave the drama a start/stop rhythm.

By the late seventeenth century, musical differences between recitative and aria were clear (see Table 5.1).

To illustrate the emergence of the aria and to exemplify the differences between aria and recitative, we consider the recitative "Thy Hand, Belinda" and the aria "When I Am Laid in Earth," familiarly known as "Dido's Lament," from Henry Purcell's opera *Dido and Aeneas*.

5-5 Henry Purcell's *Dido and Aeneas*

For Henry Purcell ♦, *Dido and Aeneas* was an anomaly. The work was his only opera, and he apparently composed it in the mid-1680s, well before he began

◆Henry Purcell
FAST FACTS
- Dates: 1658/9?–1695
- Place: England
- Reason to remember: The most important English-born composer of the Baroque era

Johan. Closterman/ The Bridgeman Art Library/Getty Images

to compose extensively for the stage. The only known performance of *Dido and Aeneas* took place at a girls' boarding school, probably in 1689. Scholars speculate that it had previously been staged at court, but there is no record of that.

Purcell was the most eminent British composer of his time and one of the most distinguished British composers of any era. For most of his career, Purcell was a court musician, the "composer-in-ordinary" to a succession of kings, and the organist at Westminster Abbey and the Chapel Royal. The majority of his important works were composed as part of his duties; they include anthems and odes to celebrate important occasions. His most substantial output for the stage was a series of semi-operas, works in which the main characters speak and minor characters sing and dance. This genre flourished in England during the latter stages of Purcell's career.

5-5A *Dido and Aeneas*

Although it became the quintessential musical product of the Baroque era, opera was a product of Renaissance culture. This is clearly evident in the plots, which were almost always drawn from antiquity. Our three examples of Baroque opera feature librettos based on a Greek myth (Orpheus and Eurydice), a Roman epic poem (the *Aeneid*), and history—the complicated romance of *Caesar and Cleopatra* (see Section 5-6).

There were compelling reasons for basing plots on the classics. The stories would be familiar because classical learning was part of every cultured person's education. There was honor by association; entertainment suitable for an aristocratic audience should feature principal characters of even more esteemed social status: noble heroes and heroines, gods and demigods. And the enduring stories from classical civilization often contained moral conflicts with tragic consequences, whose resolution was supposed to edify the audience. In the case of *Dido and Aeneas*, the conflict is between duty and love for both Dido and Aeneas.

librettos Text to be sung in an opera
semi-operas Work in which the main characters speak and minor characters sing and dance

Purcell's opera is based on the tragic meeting of Dido and Aeneas, which occurs in the first part of Virgil's *Aeneid*. Aeneas is a Trojan hero, the son of a prince and the goddess Venus, and one of the few survivors of the fall of Troy. His ultimate destiny is to found the city of Rome; the *Aeneid* recounts his roundabout route there from Asia Minor to Italy. In Purcell's opera, Aeneas meets, woos, and then abandons Dido, the recently widowed queen of Carthage.

The opera begins with Dido entertaining Aeneas and his fellow travelers. Through the intercession of Cupid, Dido submits to Aeneas, much to the delight of her courtiers. In a famous scene that happens offstage, the couple goes off to a cave, where they presumably consummate their relationship. Meanwhile, a sorceress and her cronies plot Dido's death. Dido is expecting that their night of love has persuaded Aeneas to marry her. However, one of the witches impersonates Mercury, the messenger god, who commands that Aeneas instead sail away. (In Virgil's version, Aeneas is simply reminded of his destiny and departs.) When Dido discovers that Aeneas is leaving, she confronts him, and they have a bitter exchange, but nothing changes; Aeneas still plans to leave. Distraught, Dido decides that she must die. It is at this point that she sings the famous lament, one of the most moving scenes in all opera.

The plot machinations, shaped by gods, demigods, witches, and other supernatural creatures, must have strained the credulity of its audience, just as it does ours. But Dido's distress rings true, and it is this deep emotion that Purcell captures so poignantly in the lament.

The Death of Dido, depicted in characteristically overwrought Baroque style by French artist Antoine Coypel

DeAgostini/A. Dagli orti/Getty Images

ground Continuous bass line that is recycled without interruption throughout a work; also called **ground bass** or **basso ostinato**

5-5B Common Practice Harmony and Musical Expression

"When I Am Laid in Earth" is the emotional high point of *Dido and Aeneas*; it is the most tragic moment in this tragic opera (see Listen Up!). To convey Dido's grief, Purcell shapes several musical elements to resonate with painful life experience: a slow tempo, labored rhythms, and the interplay between the relentlessly descending bass line and a melody that fights against it. In addition, he uses the structural and expressive capabilities of common practice harmony, a relatively recent musical development, in a way that adds power and nuance to his poignant melody.

The melody is laid over a ground. Ground (or ground bass) is the English term for basso ostinato (obstinate bass). Both terms identify a bass line that is recycled without interruption through the entire composition. The practice of composing extended works over a basso ostinato developed in the early seventeenth century and remained popular through the end of the Baroque era. Composers would establish the bass pattern, then create varied melodic (and sometimes harmonic) material over it. The pattern used in "Dido's Lament" was a cliché in Venetian opera, but Purcell found new magic in this well-worn device.

Purcell's ground sends musical messages at two different levels. The most direct is the slow but inexorable descent through each iteration; every statement of the ground starts high and ends an octave lower. Its persistent measured descent exerts a gravitational pull on Dido's melody. Its implicit, impersonal message is that Dido cannot escape her fate, no matter how much she tries. Its specific design animates her struggle.

There is also an expressive message in the pitches of the ground. It contains ten notes that span an octave, divided into two segments. The first six notes descend by half-step; the last four progress conventionally to a cadence. The first segment is harmonic free fall; it could end anywhere,

David Farrell/Lebrecht Music and Arts Photo Library

⌐Dido cannot escape her fate, no matter how much she tries.⌐

although it always ends in the same place. And because the harmonic destination is momentarily in doubt, Dido's fate—at least in her mind—is also momentarily in doubt. By contrast, the second segment is almost predictable. Because it is so conventional, it reinforces the sense of inevitability.

Purcell uses the oscillation between harmonic instability and harmonic inevitability to dramatize Dido's conflicting emotions as she prepares to die, and he magnifies and personalizes them in the melody. In those passages set over the first segment, we hear Dido fight against her fate: her melody resists the gravitational pull of the ground. Conversely, we sense her resignation most clearly in the second segments, when the melody line descends or she doesn't sing at all. When she is silent during the last statement of the ground, we know musically that the end has come. Dido knows that she is going to die, and so do we. Purcell's music enables us to feel her anguish.

On the strength of this single work, Purcell was the most important opera composer in England during

Tyler Stalman/iStockphoto.com

┌ . . . a slow but inexorable descent . . . ┐

LISTEN UP!

Purcell, "Thy Hand, Belinda"/"When I Am Laid in Earth," *Dido and Aeneas* (1689?)

TAKEAWAY POINT: Anguished melody over ground bass

STYLE: Middle Baroque

FORM: Through-composed/variation

GENRE: Opera recitative and aria

INSTRUMENTS: Voice, strings, and organ

CONTEXT: Dido, brokenhearted because of Aeneas's departure, sings this lament to convey sadness so deep that she cannot continue to live

RECITATIVE

0:00 Slowly descending vocal line in free rhythm determined mainly by pacing of words

Thy hand, Belinda! Darkness shades me; on thy bosom let me rest.

0:29 Slow descent continues.

More I would, but Death invades me: Death is now a welcome guest.

ARIA

Dido's final aria consists of two long melodic statements, both repeated and both unfolding over two statements of the ground, with its inexorable descent. The effect is as if Dido is pulled down to her death by fate, represented by the ground.

0:55 Instrumental; simple statement of ground by the continuo

1:07 Aria begins.

When I am laid, am laid in earth, may my wrongs create no trouble, no trouble in thy breast.

1:40 Repetition of first phrase: note that vocal line ends before cadence, which suggests her distress.

When I am laid, am laid in earth, may my wrongs create no trouble, no trouble in thy breast.

2:15 Phrase begins with repeated notes separated by long pauses, another musical sign of Dido's distress, before peaking on final "Remember me" and slowly descending.

Remember me, remember me, but, ah, forget my fate. Remember me but, ah, forget my fate.

2:53 Repetition of previous phrase, for emphasis

Remember me, remember me, but, ah, forget my fate. Remember me, but, ah, forget my fate.

3:28 Instrumental postlude, consisting mainly of musical sighs (similar to sigh heard on "am laid" in first phrase of vocal line), which gives Dido the opportunity to die with dignity

 Listen to this selection streaming or in an Active Listening Guide at CourseMate or in the eBook.

his lifetime. The most important opera composer in England during the early eighteenth century was George Frideric Handel, a German composer who received his training in Italy.

henry purcell's *dido and aeneas* | **73**

LEARNING OUTCOME 5-6

Understand the changes in Baroque opera from Monteverdi to Handel, through an examination of Handel's *Giulio Cesare*.

5-6 Late Baroque Opera

Prima donna is Italian for "first lady." The *Oxford American Dictionary* gives two definitions of the term: (1) the chief female singer in an opera or opera company and (2) a very temperamental person with an inflated view of his or her own talent or importance. The two meanings often coexist in one individual, as Handel knew all too well.

In 1719, a group of English noblemen formed an opera company, the Royal Academy of Music, and engaged Handel as music director. Four years later, the Academy engaged Francesca Cuzzoni, one of the leading sopranos of the day. During the rehearsal of her first role for the Academy, Cuzzoni refused to sing an aria because she believed that it was intended for another soprano. According to a contemporary historian, Handel confronted her, saying, "Oh! Madame, I know well that you are a real she-devil, but I hereby give you notice, me, that I am Beelzebub, the Chief of Devils." He then threatened to pick her up and throw her out of the window if she persisted in her refusal. She sang the aria, with great success, and soon became a favorite of London audiences. She would create many of the leading female roles in Handel's operas, among them Cleopatra in *Giulio Cesare in Egitto* (*Julius Caesar in Egypt*).

Not long after, the Academy engaged Faustina Bordoni, the most celebrated singer on the Continent. After protracted negotiations, Faustina made her debut in January 1726. A fierce rivalry quickly developed among the supporters of the two *prime donne*. In May 1726, it spilled onto the stage. During a performance of the Italian opera *Astinatte*, hissing, catcalling, and fighting in the audience apparently led to a spat onstage, where, according to the *British Journal*, "coiffures were clawed, [and] vulgar words escaped those lips which moments before had ravished the ears with trills and divisions." The ensuing scandal brought the season to a premature close. In spite (or because) of diversions like the fight between the rival *prime donne*, opera in London was a grand spectacle during the early eighteenth century.

When Handel arrived in England for the first time in 1711, he brought with him a newly revamped form of opera from Italy, where he had been working, and it would soon be called *opera seria*.

opera seria Form of more serious dramatic opera, based mainly on classical mythology, historical figures, and classic literature, that thrived during most of the eighteenth century

da capo aria Aria with three sections: an opening section (A), a contrasting section (B), and a reprise of the opening section (A) in which singers were expected to embellish the opening melody

5-6A *Opera Seria*

About a century after the Camerata first formulated the idea of opera, the Arcadian Academy, another group of Italian aristocrats, took it upon themselves to reform opera. Their primary goal was to elevate its dramatic content, in both subject and style. Plots became more coherent and slightly more credible, and comic episodes disappeared—at least from this new, nobler form of opera. Replacing them were skillfully constructed libretti, based mainly on classical mythology, historical figures, and classic literature. This new kind of opera was known as *opera seria*. It was the most prestigious form of musical expression through the end of the Baroque Era in mid-century.

5-6B The Da Capo Aria

During the early eighteenth century, the most common aria type was the da capo aria. *Capo* means "head" in Italian, and *da capo* means literally "from the head," or "return to the beginning." A da capo aria has three sections: an opening section (A), a contrasting section (B), and a reprise of the opening section (A). The singer would express one emotion in the first A section, perhaps change emotions in the middle, then return to the initial emotion in the reprise of the A section.

In practice, da capo aria form was a vehicle for vocal display. Singers would sing the first A section and the B section much as the composer notated them. However, in the reprise of the A section, singers were expected to embellish the melody; the taste and virtuosity with which they did this was one measure of their art. Unlike today, this was considered an essential part of the singer's art and was the aspect of opera that most thrilled audiences: it wasn't just that the melody was elaborated; there was also an element of surprise, because singers improvised their embellishments, or at least prepared them in secret.

5-6C Handel and Baroque Opera

George Frideric Handel's ♪ compositional gifts were ideally suited to opera; he could spin out gorgeous melodies and compose powerfully dramatic and evocative music. He composed more than forty operas, the most successful of which was *Giulio Cesare in Egitto*.

George Frideric Handel. Handel was the most cosmopolitan composer of the early eighteenth century. He was born in Halle, a city in what is now east-central Germany. After training in Hamburg, he went to Italy for three years to gain more experience composing opera. Encouraged by the warm reception given his opera *Rinaldo* in 1711, he made several trips to England during the decade, finally settling there in 1715. For the greater part of two decades, he devoted most of his energy to composing and producing opera. Between 1718 and 1734, he was the major composer for, and musical director of, two opera companies. Both enjoyed some success but ultimately failed after several years. After the failure of the second company, he turned his attention to writing oratorios. The most successful of these was *Messiah*, but there were many others, including *Israel in Egypt* and *Judas Maccabeus*.

Handel composed in almost every current genre. His output included operas, oratorios, and other smaller-scale vocal works, as well as concertos and suites for orchestra, solo and trio sonatas for several different instruments, and keyboard works.

Handel's legacy is full of ironies. He was a German composer strongly influenced by Italian music who is remembered mainly for vocal music in English, a language he apparently spoke with a thick accent. He was the most versatile composer of his time, yet his enduring fame is linked securely to a single work. He was the greatest opera composer of the era, an era when opera was the most prestigious musical genre, yet his operas remain obscure, not because of their inferior quality (they contain some splendid music) but because of flaws inherent in the genre. At the time of his death, he was widely acknowledged as the finest composer of his era; through his oratorios, he would become the first "classical" composer.

Giulio Cesare in Egitto.

Giulio Cesare in Egitto was first staged in 1724, revived again and again over the next eight years, and performed in Europe during that same time.

The opera has all the ingredients of effective drama—it featured a scenario worthy of soap opera on the grandest scale. The plot revolves around one of the great love affairs in history, that of Caesar and Cleopatra. It includes physical lust and lust for power, betrayal, murder, intrigue, and despair, counterbalanced by honor, fidelity, love, and ultimately a happy ending. Handel and his librettists exercised dramatic license with history, keeping only the basic outline of Caesar's time in Egypt and fictionalizing it as necessary to make the story more sensational.

The plot is complex. The main characters include Cleopatra and her brother Ptolemy, engaged in a power struggle for the throne of Egypt; Pompey and Caesar, Roman generals engaged in a civil war that is resolved in Egypt in the most drastic manner possible, when Ptolemy brings the head of Pompey to Caesar at the beginning of the opera; and other subordinate characters, including Cornelia and Sextus, the wife and son of Pompey.

The recitative and aria presented here (see Listen Up!) come from Act III. Cleopatra has been imprisoned by Ptolemy. As the scene begins, she stands alone with the guards. In the recitative, she despairs that Caesar is dead (he isn't, but she doesn't know that) and bemoans

▶George Frideric Handel
FAST FACTS

- Dates: 1685–1759
- Place: Germany/Italy/England
- Reasons to remember: One of the great composers of the late Baroque era and the premier composer of Italian Baroque opera

DEA/G. DAGLI ORTI/De Agostini/Getty Images

the fact that Cornelia and Sextus cannot come to her aid. She fears that all is lost. In the aria, she expresses her grief in the A section, swears to "torment the tyrant" in the B section, then returns to her state of grief in the reprise of the A section. Handel's aria vividly projects her shifts in mood.

Handel's audiences must have been extremely gullible or attending the opera simply to hear his glorious music. It's hard to imagine Cleopatra, the beautiful seductress, and Caesar, the noble, ardent lover, played by two more unlikely principals. Francesca Cuzzoni may have sung beautifully, but she was no beauty. Charles Burney, a reliable commentator on eighteenth-century musical life, described her as "short and squat, with a doughy cross face, but fine complexion." Burney went on to note that she was not a good actress, dressed poorly, and "was silly and fantastical." Caesar was played by Senesino, one of the most famous castrati singers in Europe. Castration prior to puberty preserved the castrato singer's voice in the female range. Needless to say, manliness was not one of Senesino's attributes.

Abigail Lebrecht/Colouriser/Lebrecht Music and Arts Photo Library

Lebrecht/ColouriserAL

It's hard to imagine Cleopatra and Caesar played by this unlikely couple: Senesino (left) and Cuzzoni (right).

castrato Male singer castrated prior to puberty to preserve the singer's voice in the female range

Handel, "E pur così" and "Piangeró," *Giulio Cesare in Egitto* (1724)

TAKEAWAY POINT: Stellar example of the Baroque da capo aria

STYLE: Late Baroque

FORM: Ternary: ABA

GENRE: Opera aria

INSTRUMENTS: Voice and small orchestra

CONTEXT: Solo vocal number in a dramatic setting, designed to move the story along and express the character's feelings

RECITATIVE

0:00   The recitative is accompanied only by lute at the outset.

E pur così in un giorno	Thus, in a single day,
perdo fasti e grandezze?	must I lose ceremony and greatness?
Ahi fato rio!	Alas, wicked fate!
Cesare, il mio bel nume, è forse estinto;	Caesar, my godlike beloved, is probably dead;
Cornelia e Sesto inermi son,	Cornelia and Sextus are defenseless
né sanno darmi soccorso.	and cannot come to my aid.

0:32   Two-chord instrumental cadence, followed by viola da gamba joining the lute for extra support

O dio!	O gods!
Non resta alcuna speme al viver mio.	There is no hope left to my life.

ARIA

In aria, Handel adds upper strings and reinforces the bass.

A

1:00   Slow tempo, dialogue between violins and voice sharing the melody, and simple, sustained accompaniment

Piangerò la sorte mia,	I shall lament my fate,

1:23   Notice how Handel spins out the melody by varying, then continuing from the simple three-note melodic gesture that begins the aria.

sì crudele e tanto ria,	so cruel and so pitiless,
finché vita in petto avrò.	as long as I have breath in my breast.
Piangerò la sorte mia,	I shall lament my fate,
sì crudele e tanto ria,	so cruel and so pitiless,
finché vita in petto avrò.	as long as I have breath in my breast.

3:14   Orchestral epilogue

B

3:33   Sudden jump to a faster tempo, switch to minor mode, more active vocal line, busy strings conveying the torment Cleopatra will inflict on Ptolemy

Ma poi morta d'ogn'intorno	But when I am dead my ghost will, wherever he may be,
il tiranno e notte e giorno fatta spettro agiterò.	torment the tyrant by night and by day.

4:12   Pause, then decisive cadence

DA CAPO

4:23   Reprise of A section; ornamentation in this recording confined mainly to cadences

Piangerò . . .	I shall . . .

🔊 Listen to this selection streaming or in an Active Listening Guide at CourseMate or in the eBook.

Looking Back, Looking Ahead

The casting for the premiere of *Giulio Cesare in Egitto* demonstrates how opera had been turned on its head during the Baroque era. Recall that opera had begun as a principled attempt to reconstruct Greek drama. The function of the music was to enhance the drama, not overshadow it. *Orfeo*'s vocal display thus makes dramatic sense. However, in Handel's opera, and in Baroque *opera seria* in general, the drama has become only scaffolding for glorious music. The choice of a homely opera singer to portray a mythical beauty simply because she has a beautiful voice certainly—and justifiably—places musical requirements first. But the choice of a castrato as her partner shows a total disregard for dramatic credibility and definitely emphasizes the music. Apparently, singing that combined the power of a man with the range of a woman was irresistible to Baroque era audiences.

More generally, the structure of Baroque *opera seria* virtually ruled out effective drama. The primary musical building block was the recitative/aria pair: the recitative advanced the plot, while the aria allowed the singer to reflect on recent events. In Dido's aria, it worked flawlessly, in part because the aria was the expressive high point of the opera and in part because Purcell built the aria over a ground, which worked dramatically as well as musically. By contrast, the da capo aria is a form designed for musical display rather than dramatic effectiveness: the reprise of the opening section is fine for showcasing the singer's artistry, but it brings the progress of the drama to a standstill. Handel provides a glorious melody in the A section and sharp contrast in the B section but is hamstrung dramatically by the conventions of the genre during the Baroque era. The dramatic limitations of the genre—and the difficulty of finding men who sing really high—explain why the arias are heard in concert far more often than they are on stage.

Handel's aria also highlights another inversion of previous practice. Throughout the Renaissance, instruments often substituted for voices in polyphonic vocal compositions. Compositions that exploited the particular capabilities of an instrument were rare. By the eighteenth century, the relationship was reversed: vocal lines emulated Baroque instrumental writing, as the active melismatic passages of the B section demonstrate.

To begin where we started: Why does late Baroque music—here, the music by Purcell and Handel—sound more familiar to contemporary audiences than music from the early Baroque? It is because the later composers used common practice harmony. It became common practice in musical life around the time that Purcell composed his opera and is still in widespread use. We hear its central role in shaping *instrumental* music in the next chapter.

 study tools 5

Ready to study?
In the book you can:

- Review Learning Outcome answers and Glossary terms with the tear-out Chapter Review card.

Or you can go online to CourseMate, at www.cengagebrain.com, for these resources:

- Chapter Quizzes to prepare for tests

- Interactive flashcards of all Glossary terms

- Active Listening Guides, streaming music, and YouTube playlists

- An eBook with live links to all web resources

6 Late Baroque Instrumental Music

LEARNING OUTCOMES

After studying this chapter, you will be able to do the following:

6-1 Understand the fugue and fugal composition through an early Bach fugue.

6-2 Understand Baroque instruments, ensembles, and orchestra.

6-3 Recognize the sound of the Baroque sonata through the music of Arcangelo Corelli.

6-4 Become familiar with the Baroque suite through the music of J. S. Bach.

6-5 Review the prevailing Baroque musical aesthetic and style.

6-6 Become acquainted with the Baroque concerto through Vivaldi's *The Four Seasons* and Bach's Brandenburg Concertos.

 study tools

After you read this chapter, go to the Study Tools at the end of the chapter, page 95.

Monteverdi's *Orfeo* was a milestone for instrumental as well as vocal music. The use of a large orchestra-like ensemble, idiomatic writing for instruments, the notation of a complete score, and independent numbers for instruments alone were all evidence of the increased importance of instruments and instrumental music in seventeenth-century musical life.

Still, much of the instrumental music before 1700 was functional: either for a church service (for example, organ preludes) or for dancing, onstage or for social occasions. There are sonatas, concertos, suites, and other music just for listening that date from the early 1600s, but it took almost a century for these forms to become well established. However, once that happened, the stream of instrumental works became a flood. Tens of thousands of concertos, sonatas, and suites, genres that we will soon experience, were composed in the first part of the eighteenth century.

Instrumental music in the late seventeenth and early eighteenth centuries had a decidedly national character. Italy was home to the sonata for small ensembles and the concerto for orchestra. From

France came the suite, a collection of dances. There were suites for solo instruments, chamber groups, and orchestras. The most distinctively German music came from the Lutheran north. These were works for organ or harpsichord—typically, free-form compositions such as the prelude, fantasia, or toccata, followed by a fugue, which was always a contrapuntal composition. In this chapter, we sample four genres from two countries: a fugue for organ from Germany, a violin sonata from Italy, a dance from an orchestral suite from Germany, and concerto movements from Germany and Italy.

travellinglight/iStockphoto.com

LEARNING OUTCOME 6-1
Understand the fugue and fugal composition through an early Bach fugue.

6-1 Bach and the Fugue

The final work composed by Johann Sebastian Bach was *The Art of the Fugue (Der Kunst der Fuge)*. Like several other works that he composed during the last two decades of his life, *The Art of the Fugue* is a summary statement for a particular genre: the fugue. Here he explores in great depth the possibilities of contrapuntal composition. He did not live to complete the work.

Bach notated *The Art of the Fugue* in a way that left the instrumentation unclear. As a result, the work has been performed and recorded using a variety of instrumental combinations. However, the prevailing view among scholars is that Bach wrote the work for keyboard. Although he was a capable performer on several instruments and had a lifelong curiosity about them, Bach was best known in his own time as an organist, as well as a consultant on organ construction. It's not difficult to imagine why Bach preferred the organ: he thought contrapuntally, and the organ provided keyboards and pedals for him to weave line against line. We get to know this great composer and experience his organ music and his approach to the fugue through one of his earliest compositions.

6-1A Johann Sebastian Bach

On March 11, 1829, Felix Mendelssohn (1809–1847), already an acclaimed composer, conducted a performance of J. S. Bach's *St. Matthew Passion* at the Berlin Singakademie. The performance, a milestone in the revival of Bach's music, brought Bach's music to the attention of scholars and audiences, and helped raise him from relative obscurity to his current stature as one of the greatest composers of any era.

Today, Johann Sebastian Bach is a household name. Along with Beethoven and Brahms, he is one of the "three B's" and among that handful of composers whose name recognition extends well beyond the classical music world. We hear his music everywhere—not only in the concert hall but also on radio and TV, in stores, even on the telephone as we wait on hold. Keyboard students encounter his music early in their training; a steady diet of Bach is essential for their development.

It wasn't always so. Bach was born in Eisenach, a town in what is now Germany. At ten, he was orphaned and went to live with his older brother. Bach never left Germany. He spent most of his professional life as a music minister for Lutheran churches in out-of-the-way cities in the heart of Germany: Arnstadt, Mühlhausen, Weimar, and Leipzig. His one secular post, in the service of Prince Leopold of Cöthen, spanned the six years between 1717 and 1723. Despite this isolation, Bach was able to familiarize himself with the main musical trends of the eighteenth century, which he integrated into the Lutheran musical world in which he worked for most of his life.

Bach was remarkable for his thoroughness. Despite time-consuming duties at his several posts and a large family (twenty children, of whom ten survived to maturity), Bach produced an astonishing amount of music. He had a passion for taking on—and completing—enormous projects: for example, a five-year cycle of cantatas for church services—about three hundred in all—composed during his first years in Leipzig; and two sets of preludes and fugues for keyboard, in all twenty-four keys, entitled *The Well-Tempered Clavier*. And that's

▶Johann Sebastian Bach

FAST FACTS

- Dates: 1685–1750

- Place: Germany

- Reason to remember: One of the greatest composers of the Baroque era, a composer whose music has influenced every subsequent generation, and the last of the great contrapuntal composers of sacred music

the tip of the iceberg: Bach wrote extensively in every major genre except opera.

In the history of classical music, Bach is the bridge between old and new. He was the last of the significant Lutheran composers and, more important, the last of the great contrapuntal composers of sacred music, a tradition that extended back centuries. He was a profoundly spiritual man, living at a time when secular values were in the ascendancy.

Although his music brings a centuries-old tradition to a close, Bach also influenced important music of every subsequent generation. For the first seventy-five years after his death, Bach and his music were little known to anyone but musicians; Haydn, Mozart, and Beethoven learned from his music. After Mendelssohn's performance of Bach's *St. Matthew Passion*, those influenced by his music included not only such distinguished composers as Chopin, Brahms, Debussy, and Stravinsky but also leading jazz and rock musicians. He was even indirectly responsible for the first big electronic music hit: Walter/Wendy Carlos's *Switched-on Bach*.

6-1B The Organ

For much of its long history, the organ has been an instrument with three essential components: one or more sets of pipes, a mechanism to pump air through the pipes, and a keyboard or other device to dictate which pipes are to be sounded. Organs have ranged in size from instruments small enough to be carried, with one hand operating a bellows and the other fingering the keys (portative organs), to grand instruments whose pipes fill an entire wall of a spacious church.

The organ is among the most ancient instruments. Accounts of organ-like instruments appear in writings from classical Greece. It became a fixture in churches during the Middle Ages and has maintained this position to the present. Because an organ with a full complement of stops is a massive instrument, it must be installed in a building large enough to accommodate

1746 Hildebrandt organ at the Wenzelskirche (St. Wenzel's Church), Naumburg, Germany, one of the best extant German Baroque organs. Bach helped design the organ and tested it after it was built, and would have played instruments like this one.

it and justify the expense of acquiring it. As a result, the most likely locations for organs outside of churches are concert halls in major cities and at educational institutions.

Until the end of the nineteenth century, the organ was a purely mechanical instrument. Even small organs required at least two people: the organist and someone to pump the bellows that provided air to the pipes. Soon thereafter, though, organ builders began to use electricity to connect the keyboard to the pipes and to stream air through them by means of a fan. The Hammond organ, which was first offered for sale in 1935, replaced pipes with electronic tone-wheels. In the wake of the new instrument's popularity, it became necessary to distinguish between pipe organs and electronic organs. Toward the end of the twentieth century, digital keyboards that replicated the sounds of both instruments came into increasingly widespread use.

The pipe organ, like the harpsichord (discussed below) and unlike the piano, uses keys only to start and stop the sound. Organ keyboards are not touch sensitive; the force with which the organist depresses the key has no bearing on the volume of sound produced. However, large pipe organs, such as those on which Bach performed, have an extraordinary dynamic and timbral range. That is because they have an array of **stops**, or rows of pipes designed to produce a specific timbre. Depending on the pipes, the sounds produced can range from abrasive and loud to soft and mellow, with considerable variety in between. The Hildebrandt organ shown here has fifty-two stops.

To move between them, organists pull out stops, either singly or in combination. (The expression "pull out all the stops"—make the greatest possible effort—derives from doing exactly that on an organ.) Organs with a wide array of stops generally have more than one keyboard; each keyboard can be preset with a particular set of stops so that the organist can switch timbres without having to interrupt the performance. The console of the Hildebrandt organ has three keyboards, called **manuals**, plus a pedal board. With the capability of playing as many as twelve pitches simultaneously (ten fingers, two feet) and a broad palette of timbres and dynamic levels, organists have a veritable orchestra of sound at their hands and feet. Small wonder that Bach, whose longstanding curiosity in instrumental sound is evident in the unusual instruments called for in his cantatas, and who seemingly composed and improvised contrapuntal music with unparalleled ease and sophistication, would be drawn to the organ. Among his numerous works for the instrument were fugues,

either as stand-alone works or in combination with a free-form piece—prelude, toccata, or fantasia.

6-1C The Fugue

A **fugue** is a composition in which several parts—usually three or four, but (rarely) as few as two and as many as five or six—enter one by one and continue until the end. It is among the most contrapuntal of genres. Its roots go back to the late medieval era, and its imitative counterpoint, where several voices trade musical material back and forth, harks back to Renaissance polyphony, such as that heard in the Josquin mass movement.

The fugue is a compositional procedure as much as a genre. Sonatas and other independent instrumental works may have **fugal passages**—that is, sections that feature imitative counterpoint much as is heard in a fugue. Fugal passages within other genres generally stand out because of their contrapuntal texture. By contrast, fugues are relentlessly contrapuntal from beginning to end.

The opening section of a fugue, called the **fugal exposition**, generally proceeds as follows:

- The first part enters with complete statement of the opening melodic idea, or **subject**, heard without accompaniment.
- The second part enters with a complete statement of the **answer**, a version of the subject that has been altered or moved to a different pitch level. The first part continues with new melodic material in counterpoint to the answer.
- The remaining parts enter in sequence: odd-numbered parts will enter with the subject; even-numbered parts enter with the answer. Some or all of the parts continue so that by the time the final voice enters, the texture is rich with contrapuntal lines.
- The exposition ends when the final part completes its statement of the subject or answer.

Fugue is a genre and a compositional technique, but it is not a form. There is no "fugue form" analogous to variation form for variations, nor is there a formal stereotype associated with the fugue, analogous to the ABA form associated with the da capo aria. Only the exposition follows a largely predictable sequence of events. The only certainty is that the subject will return, either fully or partially and in one or more voices, at various points during the remainder of the fugue. However,

Some of the 108 labeled organ stops from the organ at St. Paul's Cathedral in London

stop Row of pipes in an organ, designed to produce a specific timbre

manual Organ keyboard

fugue Composition in which several parts—usually three or four, but (rarely) as few as two and as many as five or six—enter one by one and continue until the end

fugal passage Section that features imitative counterpoint, much as is heard in a fugue

fugal exposition Opening section of a fugue, in which the subject is presented in all voices through a series of entries

subject Opening melodic idea in a fugue

answer A version of the fugue subject that has been altered or moved to a different pitch level

 **LISTEN UP!**

Johann Sebastian Bach, "Little" Fugue in G minor (1703–1707)

TAKEAWAY POINT: An accessible and appealing introduction to the fugue and to Bach's music

STYLE: Late Baroque

FORM: Through-composed: exposition, plus a series of episodes and statements of the subject

GENRE: Fugue

INSTRUMENT: Organ

CONTEXT: Nonliturgical music for performance in a church

EXPOSITION

0:00   Subject, by itself

0:13   Answer, with same melody, but lower. First voice continues with new material in counterpoint with the answer.

0:29   Third voice enters with subject restated an octave lower. One of the other two voices is active.

0:41   Fourth voice enters: the second answer, played on the pedal board. Only two other voices in counterpoint; third voice is now silent.

REST OF FUGUE

0:52   Episode. These and other episodes connect statements of the subject with **sequences**: passages that consist of several short segments that repeat the same melodic material at higher or lower pitches.

1:00   Statement of the subject in the home key

1:13   Two episode/statement pairs, all in a new major key

1:50   An episode that modulates to a new key, followed by the subject (2:03) in a minor key different from the home key

2:13   A long episode containing three sequences. This episode brings the fugue back to the home key.

2:34   Final statement of subject

 Listen to this selection streaming or in an Active Listening Guide at CourseMate or in the eBook.

there is no set plan regarding the number, key, and timing of these returns, nor is there any correlation between the length of the exposition and the fugue as a whole.

Bach's "Little" Fugue in G minor, presented in this chapter, features one of his most common and straightforward options: a series of episodes, sections that state neither the subject nor the answer, alternating with statements of the subject in one voice. The fugue is one of his first, dating from between 1703 and 1707, when he was in Arnstadt.

The glory years of fugal composition began in Lutheran Germany during the late seventeenth century and continued through Bach's lifetime, until 1750. For all intents and purposes, Bach's *The Art of the Fugue* was the last word on the fugue as a genre. By the time he began work on it, the genre was out of date and mid-eighteenth-century composers were moving decisively away from contrapuntal music. Although major composers since Bach have occasionally composed fugues and incorporated fugal passages in their works, Bach's fugal compositions, and more generally his contrapuntal music of all kinds, effectively brought to a close a centuries-old tradition of contrapuntal composition.

sequence Fugue passage consisting of several short segments that repeat the same melodic material at higher or lower pitches

episode Fugue section that states neither the fugue subject nor the fugue answer

LEARNING OUTCOME 6-2

Understand Baroque instruments, ensembles, and orchestra.

6-2 Baroque Instruments

In addition to the organ, the core instruments of Baroque music are the harpsichord and members of the string family, especially the violin and cello. Harpsichords and violin-family stringed instruments were not new even in 1600. What changed during the course of the seventeenth century were the quality of the instruments, the ways in which composers and performers exploited the capabilities of these instruments, and the roles played by the various instruments within an ensemble.

6-2A The Violin Family

By the time Corelli composed his violin sonatas at the end of the seventeenth century, the violin family had for the most part assumed its modern form. The bows of the modern violin family have a different shape and are held differently than earlier ones. The necks of the instruments are a little longer, and the strings are made of metal or gut wound with metal rather than just gut. But the instruments are substantially the same now as they were three hundred or more years ago.

The violin was the most widely used melody instrument of the Baroque era, and the cello was the preferred bass instrument. String instruments were equally at home in small groups and large ensembles and were suitable for use in church and chamber settings, as well as in orchestra pits and outdoors.

6-2B The Harpsichord

The harpsichord is a keyboard instrument in which depressing a key causes a plectrum, a plucking device made of quill (the hard shaft of a bird feather), to pluck one or more strings. The sound produced by this plucking has a sharp attack followed by a ringing tone that decays quickly. Although the harpsichord is a pitched instrument, the overall effect is quite percussive: in an ensemble, one often hears the rhythm of the harpsichord part much more clearly than its pitches (hence the identification of the harpsichord as a percussion instrument in a Baroque "rhythm section").

Unlike the piano, but like the organ, the harpsichord is not a touch-sensitive instrument. There is virtually no correlation between the force with which the player pushes down the key and the amount of sound produced. To introduce sound variety, harpsichord makers typically created several sets of strings for each key. These could be coupled together: that is, depressing a key would cause two or more strings to be plucked; they might be the same pitch or an octave apart. More elaborate harpsichords typically had two keyboards, or manuals, one low and toward the performer, the other higher and farther away. This enabled performers to use different sets of strings for each manual.

In the Baroque era, the harpsichord was a popular solo instrument; it was also the preferred chord-producing instrument in chamber ensembles and orchestras performing secular music. Many surviving harpsichords from this era have beautifully

French harpsichord with two manuals

crafted and decorated cases. They are seldom used in performance, however; most reside in museums or private instrument collections. Contemporary harpsichordists typically perform on modern reproductions of earlier instruments.

6-2C Basso Continuo: The Baroque Rhythm Section

Basso continuo, or continuous bass, is a bass line that typically continues steadily throughout a musical work or extended section within the work. The bass line and the chords that complement it can be sustained, slowly changing, or active. But it is almost always there in Baroque music: in ensemble music—vocal and instrumental—the characteristic Baroque texture is one or more melodic parts at the top, a steady basso continuo on the bottom, and keyboard chords filling in the space between top and bottom.

Continuo also refers to the instrumental combination playing the bass line and enriching it with

harpsichord Keyboard instrument in which depressing a key causes a plectrum to pluck one or more strings

plectrum Harpsichord plucking device originally made from a quill (the hard shaft of a bird feather)

continuo Instrumental combination playing chords and a bass line: typically a bass instrument, such as the cello, and a chord-producing instrument, such as the harpsichord

harmony: typically a bass instrument, such as the cello, and a chord-producing instrument, such as the harpsichord. We can think of the continuo instruments as a Baroque-era rhythm section: like the modern rhythm section of drum kit, bass, and rhythm guitar, for instance, they supply a bass line, harmony, and steady underlying rhythm.

The unique texture and sound of the continuo are among the defining features of Baroque music. The continuo was not heard in Renaissance music, and both the harpsichord and the consistent, steady movement of the bass disappeared from the sound world of concert music in the latter part of the eighteenth century. Indeed, the sound of an active, continuous bass does not return as a style-defining feature until the 1930s, in the music of the swing era.

6-2D The Orchestra during the Baroque Era

During the seventeenth century, the orchestra evolved from a large but somewhat random collection of instruments into a more standardized ensemble, which closely resembles the heart of the modern orchestra. Among the most significant developments were these:

- Building the orchestra around bowed stringed instruments and standardizing the string section
- Scoring for specific instruments, with each instrument or instrument section typically having its own part
- Composing independent orchestral works as well as orchestral accompaniments to operas, ballets, and sacred music

LEARNING OUTCOME 6-3

Recognize the sound of the Baroque sonata through the music of Arcangelo Corelli.

6-3 The Baroque Sonata

What does a Baroque chamber music ensemble have in common with a jazz combo or a classic rock band? Quite a bit—despite the obvious differences in time, place, genre, and audience. The similarity begins with instrumental roles. All three groups typically have the features noted in Table 6.1.

In addition, all the textures are similar, featuring a prominent melody supported by a strong, active bass line, and with chord-producing instruments supplying harmony between melody and bass.

chamber music ensemble A group of several musicians, at least two and usually no more than ten, with each musician playing a different part

canzona Italian instrumental genre derived from polyphonic vocal music

sonata By the middle of the seventeenth century, the term of choice in Italy for solo and small-group instrumental compositions; by the early eighteenth century, a three- or four-movement work whose movements have alternately slow and fast tempos

movement Self-contained section of a larger work, typically separated from adjacent movements by silence and distinguished by tempo, meter, and occasionally key

	Baroque Chamber Ensemble	Jazz Combo	Rock Band
One or two melody instruments	Violin, flute	Saxophone, trumpet	Lead guitar(s)
A chord-producing instrument	Harpsichord or organ	Piano or guitar	Rhythm guitar
A bass instrument	Cello or bassoon	String bass	Electric bass
One or more percussion instruments	Harpsichord (see later discussion on the harpsichord)	Drum kit	Drum kit

Table 6.1 Features of Ensembles

But the kinship among genres goes beyond the similarities in roles and texture. In each case, the particular combination of instruments was novel—indeed, the electric bass was just over a decade old when the first British rock bands invaded America. And in each case musicians developed new sounds and new ways of playing, which often exploited the capabilities of the instruments. Our first encounter with the distinctive texture of Baroque instrumental music will be in a violin sonata by the Italian composer Arcangelo Corelli.

Sonata is the Italian word for "sounded." It came into use toward the end of the sixteenth century to identify an instrumental composition not derived from dance. The style of the sonata derived most directly from the canzona, an Italian instrumental genre itself derived from polyphonic vocal music. By the middle of the seventeenth century, sonata was the term of choice in Italy for solo and small-group instrumental compositions. By the early eighteenth century, the sonata had taken on the shape it would assume for the next several decades: an instrumental work in three or four separate movements. A movement is a self-contained section of a larger work, typically separated from adjacent movements by silence and distinguished from them by tempo, meter, and occasionally key.

6-3A Corelli and the Baroque Sonata

If there was one musician working in 1700 who could be considered a legend in his own time, it would be the violinist and composer Arcangelo Corelli ♪, one of the finest violinists of his era and the most influential teacher. He worked in Rome under a series of patrons: Queen Christina of Sweden and two cardinals. Because this support put him in a relatively comfortable financial situation—almost uniquely so for composers of his era—Corelli could afford to be particular about the music he made available to the public.

During his lifetime, Corelli published only six sets of works: four sets of what were termed trio sonatas, a set of solo sonatas, and a set of concertos, for strings and continuo. These works were, by the standards of the time, exceedingly popular throughout western Europe. They were reprinted many times during Corelli's lifetime and after his death, and were the most widely circulated models of all three genres. The six sets of works helped to solidify Corelli's reputation; he was the first composer to make a name for himself strictly as a composer of instrumental music.

6-3B Solo and Trio Sonatas

Corelli's sonata sets played a key role in establishing the function, form, and instrumentation of the sonata. The church sonata *(sonata da chiesa)*, a four-movement sonata, often served as music for the mass; the chamber sonata *(sonata da camera)*, a secular sonata in three or more movements, entertained the aristocratic audiences that supported his music.

Baroque composers like Corelli were somewhat inconsistent in their terminology but not as mathematically challenged as it might seem at first glance. Solo sonatas typically require three players: one playing a featured melodic instrument, such as a violin, and two playing chord-producing and bass instruments (the continuo). Here "solo" refers simply to the spotlighted instrument. A trio sonata typically calls for four performers: two playing melodic instruments and two others playing the continuo. In this case, "trio" refers to the three independent lines: two treble and one bass.

Solo or trio, the sonata was a multimovement work. Typically, there were four movements, in a slow-fast-slow-fast sequence, although this could vary. Church sonatas followed this pattern more consistently than chamber sonatas.

6-3C The Ritornello

The typically fast second movement introduces us to a distinctively Baroque formal device: the ritornello. Ritornello (Italian for "little return") refers to a melodic idea that is introduced at the beginning of a movement and returns periodically, often in different keys, as a kind of musical milestone. *Ritornello* also refers to a form that uses this device.

6-3D The Sound of the Baroque Violin Sonata

Corelli's sonata (see Listen Up! and The Language of Music: Opus) exemplifies several characteristic features of late Baroque music for instrumental ensembles. Running throughout both movements is the melody/continuo texture played on the core instruments: violin (melody), harpsichord (chords, obbligato lines, bass line), and cello (bass). Rhythmically, there is consistency in approach within each movement: the first features alternating sustained and rapid rhythms over a steady bass; the second has mostly fast-moving

▸Arcangelo Corelli
FAST FACTS
- Dates: 1653—1713
- Place: Rome, Italy
- Reason to remember: One of the finest violinists and most influential instrumental composers of his era

Universal History Archive/Universal Images Group/Getty Images

patterns at a brisk tempo. There is little melodic repetition in the first movement, but a consistency in melodic style. In the second movement, Corelli periodically brings back the opening melodic idea—the ritornello. All of these features are in the service of the dominant Baroque aesthetic, which called for one mood, or "affect," per movement (see discussion in Section 6-5).

Composing for Orchestral Instruments: A Baroque Innovation. The demands of the solo line, most notably the elaborate figuration in the first movement and the arpeggiated chords in the second, evidence Corelli's expertise as a violinist. These melodic figures are distinctively instrumental and also especially suited to the violin.

By 1700, the practice of composing idiomatically for the string and wind instruments used in Baroque orchestras and chamber music was so well established that the relationship between vocal and instrumental composition had been reversed: now vocal lines often featured instrumental-style figuration. Because we have grown up hearing instruments played in idiomatic ways, it may be difficult to appreciate how radical a development this was.

To get some idea of the impact of idiomatic composition and performance, imagine that Jimi Hendrix and Eddie Van Halen had limited their guitar lines to what they could do vocally. Their solos would have had none of the brilliant virtuosity or special effects for which their playing is famous. But that was how almost all composers wrote for orchestral instruments prior to 1600.

church sonata (*sonata da chiesa*) Four-movement sonata, which often served as music for the Mass

chamber sonata (*sonata da camera*) Secular sonata in three or more movements

solo sonata Instrumental composition that typically requires three players: one playing a melodic featured instrument, such as a violin, plus continuo (chord-producing and bass instruments)

trio sonata Instrumental composition that typically calls for four performers: two playing melodic instruments and two others playing the continuo

ritornello Melodic idea that is introduced at the beginning of a movement and returns periodically, often in different keys, as a kind of musical milestone; form that uses this device

THE language OF MUSIC

Opus

You'll notice in the Listen Up! for Corelli's sonata that the title of the work contains the following information: the genre (sonata), its key (C major), and the abbreviation "Op. 5, No. 3." This abbreviation reads as "Opus 5, Number 3." *Opus* is the Latin word for "work." In music, **opus** refers to a musical composition or, in this case, a set of musical compositions; here, "No. 3" identifies the third sonata in the set. Composers began to use the word *opus* around this time to identify a set of pieces, usually in the same genre, of sufficiently high quality to merit publication. This designation enabled those who bought the music to distinguish one set of works from another. In the Baroque era, opus numbers provide some sense of chronology because we generally have publication dates. However, a set of works, such as Corelli's sonatas, may have been composed over a period of several years prior to publication; the numbering within a set is not a reliable guide to the date of composition. Beginning with Beethoven's works, opus numbers begin to provide a fairly reliable guide to the date of composition.

Composition and Improvisation. If you've taken music lessons or played in a band or orchestra, you're used to playing what someone else wrote. By contrast, if you're part of a rock band or jazz combo, you may well be playing your own material, which may be partially written down or worked out without notated music.

Corelli's original version of the sonata—especially the first movement—falls somewhere between these two extremes, especially for the harpsichordist and the violinist. The harpsichordist uses the bass line and a series of numerical symbols (called **figured bass**) as a shorthand system for indicating the notes and chords to be played. Figured bass is the Baroque equivalent of the chord changes used in jazz and some rock. In the first movement, the violinist starts with a bare-bones outline and is then expected to add lavish ornamentation to it.

All of this was, or could be, done in the moment (improvised). The keyboardist and the violinist created music on the spot, much like an improvising jazz or rock musician would today. This ability was a skill expected of any accomplished musician. In this respect, skilled musicians in Corelli's time were more like today's rock and jazz musicians than like many of today's classically trained musicians. They were well-rounded musicians who composed, improvised, and performed their own compositions and occasionally those of others. They also had big hair, although it was store bought.

opus In the eighteenth century, a term usually followed by a number, used to identify a musical composition or (more often) a group of compositions in a particular genre deemed worthy of publication

figured bass Bass line and series of numerical symbols used by Baroque musicians as an abbreviated system that indicates specific notes and chords to be played by a keyboard player

David Becker/Getty Images Entertainment/Getty Images

In their ability to improvise, skilled musicians in Corelli's time were more like today's rock and jazz musicians than like many of today's classically trained musicians.

 **LISTEN UP!**

Corelli, Sonata in C major, Op. 5, No. 3, 1st and 2nd movements (1700)

TAKEAWAY POINT: Characteristically Baroque sound and texture: melody + continuo

STYLE: Baroque

FORM: Through-composed (without repetitions) first movement; ritornello-like form in second movement

GENRE: Solo chamber sonata

INSTRUMENTS: Violin, harpsichord, cello

CONTEXT: Instrumental music for the entertainment of elite audiences

MOVEMENT 1: ADAGIO (SLOW)

0:00　Slowly descending vocal line in free rhythm determined mainly by pacing of words. Note lavish ornamentation of violin part over steady support of continuo.

0:29　Next phrase, but higher. Hear the Baroque texture: melody in the highest part, strong bass reinforced by cello and harpsichord, and harpsichord filling in harmony between melody and bass.

1:07　New melody, ending with cadence. Cadential progressions clearly define ends of phrases.

1:28　Another new melody

1:46　More new material: top performers were expected to improvise these running scales and trills. Editions with ornamentation were for those not yet capable of improvising embellishments.

2:15　Return to home key, followed by final melodic phrase

MOVEMENT 2: ALLEGRO (QUICK)

2:51　Opening theme (ritornello), first in violin, then in bass. Returns of ritornello serve as milestones in the path through the movement.

3:24　Ritornello returns in new key after active figuration.

3:40　New section: spotlight on solo instrument, with more virtuosic writing for the violin. Note how the continuo plays intermittently to shift the focus even more to the violin.

4:03　Ritornello again, but with different continuation. The ritornello statement reaffirms the home key but does not reprise the opening material.

4:30　Spotlight on violin again in **cadenza**—a virtuosic solo passage with little or no accompaniment

 Listen to this selection streaming or in an Active Listening Guide at CourseMate or in the eBook.

LEARNING OUTCOME 6-4
Become familiar with the Baroque suite through the music of J. S. Bach.

6-4 The Baroque Suite

A **suite** is a collection of dances linked by key and sometimes by melodic material. The practice of grouping dances in this way dates from the fourteenth century but didn't become widespread until the late sixteenth century. The first common groupings were pairs of dances, such as the courtly pavane and galliard. By the middle of the seventeenth century, dance pairs had grown into a suite of several dances, first in France, then elsewhere in Europe.

6-4A The "Classic" Baroque Suite

Within a Baroque suite, the number and sequence of dances were infinitely variable. However, for about a century—circa 1640 to 1740—the heart of the suite consisted of four dances. In typical order of appearance, they were the allemande, courante, sarabande, and gigue. Suites typically included other popular dances, such as the minuet and the gavotte, and larger-scale suites often began with a prelude, overture, or other grand movement.

The suite is the most important French

cadenza Virtuosic solo passage with little or no accompaniment
suite Collection of dances linked by key and sometimes by melodic material

In France, enthusiasm for dance started at the top. Louis XIV (the "Sun King"), firmly ensconced on the French throne, is outfitted here as Apollo for a court ballet performance.

Baroque composers composed suites for solo instruments, chamber ensembles, and orchestras. In the first part of the seventeenth century, the lute was by far the most common solo instrument. However, by the end of the century the harpsichord had supplanted the lute as the favored solo instrument and would remain dominant during the rest of the Baroque era. The suite for solo instrument was far more common than any other kind. Suites for small ensembles were much less common, although individual dance movements appeared frequently in sonatas. Orchestral suites often required large ensembles, with strings, winds, brass, and percussion. The use of winds, brass, and percussion instruments suggests that such works were often performed outdoors, where the sound of these instruments carried well.

6-4B Bach and the Suite

Bach's numerous and diverse suites provide a unique perspective on his compositional personality. In them, we can hear Bach summarize one of the important genres of the Baroque era and use it as a springboard for his imagination and a means to apply his personal stamp.

Bach composed more than thirty suites. Over half of them are for keyboard, including three sets of six suites, but there are also suites for solo violin, cello, flute, and lute, and four suites for orchestra. Like most composers of his time, Bach wrote most of his music for specific purposes and occasions. Not surprisingly, he composed the majority of his suites during his six-year tenure at Cöthen. However, the genre continued to interest him after he moved to Leipzig: he composed the six partitas (his last set of suites), the four orchestral suites, and his last and largest keyboard suite, the Overture in the French Style, while there.

As the title of his last suite suggests, Bach regarded the suite as a distinctively French genre. He drew inspiration from the French composers Jean-Baptiste Lully and François Couperin as well as German composers from previous generations, most notably Johann Froberger and Dietrich Buxtehude. By way of example, the opening movements of several larger suites, including the four orchestral suites, use Lully's overtures as a model. At the same time, Bach freely mixed and matched French-inspired music with other national styles. The opening movements of an earlier set of suites (the so-called English Suites) resemble concerto movements, and the famous air from the third orchestral suite evokes an Italian aria. Here we hear Bach's connection with French tradition and key features of his musical personality in a gigue, the final movement of his third orchestral suite (see Listen Up!).

6-4C Bach's Gigue and the Suite

Bach's gigue has introduced us to one of the most popular genres of the Baroque era, the suite. Although it is only one movement of several—Bach's suites typically have five or more—it does show key features of the genre: the connection with dance, the use of binary form, and the consistency of rhythm and melody throughout.

contribution to Baroque instrumental music, so it is curious that its four central dances have such an international flavor. Allemande is the French word for "German"; in this case, it means a German dance. Typically, it was in quadruple meter and had a moderate tempo. The courante (the French word for "running") is a French dance, but it has an Italian counterpart, the *corrente* (the Italian word for "running"). Both are in triple meter; the Italian version typically has a faster tempo. The first sarabandes were hot-blooded dances brought to Spain from the New World, and so racy that they were banned in certain quarters. However, by the time it surfaced in the suite, the sarabande had become a slow, stately dance in triple meter, with a characteristic short–long rhythm in the melody. Gigue is a cognate for the English *jig*. Like the jig, the gigue is typically in compound duple meter (two beats per measure; beats divided into three equal parts). The main dances thus come from four different points of the compass—a pleasing symmetry.

allemande German dance, typically in quadruple meter with a moderate tempo

courante French dance with an Italian counterpart, the *corrente*; both in triple meter, but the Italian version typically has a faster tempo

sarabande Slow, stately dance of Spanish origin, in triple meter, with a characteristic short–long rhythm in the melody

gigue Dance, typically in compound duple meter, inspired by the jig; customarily the last movement of a suite

 **LISTEN UP!**

J. S. Bach, Gigue, from Orchestral Suite No. 3 in D major (1731)

TAKEAWAY POINT: From jig to gigue: a rich, contrapuntal setting of this lively dance

STYLE: Baroque

FORM: Binary

GENRE: Suite

INSTRUMENTS: Strings, harpsichord, trumpets, timpani, oboes, bassoon

CONTEXT: Dance-inspired music for the enjoyment of those in Bach's circle in Leipzig

PART 1

0:00   Melody spins out from the simple three-note pattern at the outset.

0:10   A series of sequences, a common Baroque-era strategy for changing key

0:28   Repetition of first part of form. Notice consistent rhythmic movement throughout the section and movement as a whole.

PART 2

0:56   Second section begins a restatement of the opening idea in the new key.

1:11   Again, a series of sequences, this time to enable return to the home key

1:25   Variant of opening idea highlights return to home key. But return is short-lived, as another series of sequential patterns leads ultimately to the final cadence.

1:53   Repetition of second part of form. Notice that the second part of the binary form is longer than the first, to accommodate the return to the home key and the continued development after the return.

 Listen to this selection streaming or in an Active Listening Guide at CourseMate or in the eBook.

We get a taste of Bach's art in the gigue. It is evident in such features as the counterpoint, which enriches rather than impedes the bright mood projected in the theme—it's as if everyone joins in the music making—and in his ability to introduce variety into the basic melodic material, even as he sustains rhythmic momentum throughout each section.

LEARNING OUTCOME 6-5
Review the prevailing Baroque musical aesthetic and style.

6-5 Baroque Aesthetics and Style in Instrumental Music

The sonata and the suite signaled both the increased popularity of instrumental composition and its rise in status. The sonata (and the concerto) *began* as an elite music, serving church and court. Of the dances that merged into the Baroque suite, almost all had humble origins but *became* an elite music. Instrumental music was not as esteemed as opera and other vocal music during the early eighteenth century, but it was far more important in musical life than it had been at the beginning of the seventeenth century.

In our discussion of "Possente spirto" in Chapter 5, we highlighted the profound shift in musical values that took place around 1600: for Monteverdi and like-minded composers, musical gestures could now convey expressive meaning. In vocal music where the composer tries to convey specific emotions and moods, the text typically served as a moment-to-moment guide to the meaning. That was not the case in instrumental music, although composers may have given their works descriptive titles or even indicated in the score what a passage depicted (we hear this in Vivaldi's "Spring" below).

Nevertheless, by the early eighteenth century, composers felt that their music—even instrumental music—could communicate quite specific emotional states, such as joy, languor, or melancholy. Some writers went so far as to link moods with particular dances. Writers on music described such moods as "affects" or "affections." This aesthetic principle thus became known as the **Doctrine of Affections**.

Doctrine of Affections Baroque aesthetic principle holding that music could communicate quite specific emotional states, such as joy, languor, or melancholy, through entire movements or complete works

To communicate a particular affect or emotion, a composer would establish the mood at the outset of a movement, then sustain it throughout. Interest came mainly from varying the material; new musical ideas generally amplified or elaborated upon the original idea. The effect is akin to seeing an object from different perspectives: the object remains the same, but the view is constantly changing.

The three movements considered here approach, in different ways, the "one movement = one affect" idea that is so central to Baroque music. In the first movement of his sonata, Corelli sustains the mood by spinning out the melody and keeping the texture consistent. In the second, he reuses the opening idea throughout the movement. Bach establishes and maintains a relentless rhythmic flow, interrupted only by the cadence at the midpoint. Variety comes from the addition and subtraction of parts and the many permutations of the musical material.

The rise of instrumental music exemplified by Corelli's sonata movements and Bach's gigue—an infinitesimally small sample of the prodigious output of Baroque composers—represents the second and final stage of the musical revolution begun a century earlier. Purely instrumental music was now a suitable vehicle for expressive musical communication. Composers and performers believed this to be true—to the extent that they occasionally noted the affect in the title. This in turn depended on two key developments of the seventeenth and early eighteenth centuries: idiomatic composition for instruments and common practice harmony. Both were securely in place by 1700. We hear further examples of their realization in the following discussion of the concerto.

LEARNING OUTCOME 6-6
Become acquainted with the Baroque concerto through Vivaldi's *The Four Seasons* and Bach's Brandenburg Concertos.

6-6 The Baroque Concerto

You hear them in restaurants, in upscale stores, on hold on the telephone, on the radio, and in commercials. Even if you don't know these works by name, chances are you'll recognize the movements from them that we will discuss in this chapter. What are they? Vivaldi's *The Four Seasons* and Bach's Brandenburg Concertos. These are among the most familiar examples of the Baroque concerto, the most popular orchestral genre of the early eighteenth century.

In the late Baroque era, the concerto was the dominant orchestral genre. It was especially popular in Italy, its home, and spread throughout much of western Europe, although France resisted it until the 1730s. In this and other respects, the concerto was the large-scale instrumental counterpart to the sonata.

The most distinctive feature of the concerto was the contrast between large and small: an orchestra made up of strings along with one or more spotlighted instruments. The number of spotlighted instruments determined the type of concerto. A concerto that features a single solo instrument, such as a violin or flute, is called, appropriately enough, a solo concerto. A concerto that features a small group of soloists (the concertino) is called a concerto grosso. The classic concertino is two violins and cello—in effect, the instrumentation of a trio sonata embedded in an orchestral setting. Other concertinos were possible; they could be formed from virtually any combination of instruments.

The relationship between orchestra and soloists was both collegial and competitive. Sometimes they worked together; at other times, they were in opposition. The presence of larger and smaller groups made it possible for composers to create contrasting sound masses. Tutti passages, in which everyone played (*tutti* means "all" in Italian), alternated with passages in which just the soloists and the continuo played, or at least were prominently featured.

This relationship between orchestra and soloists was still relatively new in 1700. However, the term *concerto* had already been in use for almost two centuries. It first surfaced in the sixteenth century as an all-purpose term for a composition with voices and instruments. Not until the end of the seventeenth century did it acquire the more specific meaning that it has today: an orchestral work that features one or more soloists.

6-6A The Design of the Baroque Concerto

Late Baroque concertos, especially those modeled after Vivaldi's concertos, typically have three movements: the first is fast, the middle is slow, and the third is again fast, although not necessarily in the same tempo (or meter) as the first movement.

The outer movements typically begin with an emphatic statement that sets the character of the movement. Composers used two approaches to give weight to the opening statement. The more contrapuntal way was to have the parts enter one by one playing the main melodic idea, as in a fugue. In that way, listeners would hear the melody three or four times, each time with the support of an additional voice. (After a part played the melody, it would slip into more of a background role.) This is the approach Corelli used in the second movement of the sonata heard in the previous chapter, but on a much grander scale.

concerto Dominant orchestral genre of the late Baroque, featuring contrast between large and small; orchestra made up of strings along with one or more spotlighted instruments

solo concerto Concerto that features a single solo instrument, such as a violin or flute

concertino Small group of soloists featured in a concerto grosso

concerto grosso Concerto that features a small group of soloists (the concertino)

tutti Referring to passages in which everyone plays

The other approach was to have all the instruments play at the same time. Some would play the main melodic idea; the others would support this melody with harmony or other lines. The opening tutti statement is called the ritornello, because it returns, sometimes in fragments (the little return), or in complete statements.

The movement grows out of the opening ritornello. The role of the soloists is to elaborate on the basic character of the movement. Periodically, the orchestra interjects a fragment of the ritornello to reaffirm the affect presented at the outset and mark an intermediate destination on the harmonic round trip from tonic to tonic. Often the movement ends with another complete—or nearly complete—statement of the ritornello.

The two approaches achieved much the same result by different means: in either case, the listener would know the basic character of the movement from the outset. As the movement progressed, there would be contrast in sound (more instruments/fewer instruments) and activity (the solo sections were often busier), but the character remained relatively consistent throughout the movement.

6-6B Vivaldi's *The Four Seasons*

Google "Italian Baroque concertos" and you'll get dozens of composers whose names end in *i*—from Albinoni and Corelli to Locatelli and Torelli. However, the name that appears most often is that of the Venetian composer Antonio Vivaldi. ◗

Vivaldi was a prolific composer. He published thirteen sets of sonatas and concertos during his lifetime and composed hundreds more, including over five hundred concertos. Many feature instruments other than strings: he composed concertos for oboe, bassoon, and even mandolin. Some were composed in great haste to fulfill an immediate need. As a result, the quality is uneven, but the best of them rank with the finest and most influential examples of the genre.

Willi Schmitz/iStockphoto

Vivaldi's practice was to give his sets of concertos distinctive titles. He called his first set of twelve concertos, published in 1711 as Opus 3, *L'estro armonico*, which translates loosely as *Harmonic Fancy*. However, in his Opus 8, which he entitled *Il Cimento dell'armonia e dell'inventione* (*The Contest of Harmony and Invention*), he went a step further. He designated the first four concertos of the set *The Four Seasons*; each depicts a season of the year, beginning with spring. They are the most famous early example of program music.

Program Music. Program music is instrumental music in which a composer depicts an extramusical inspiration, such as a scene, a story, or an idea, or the experience or feeling that the inspiration arouses. As explained by Franz Liszt, the famous nineteenth-century composer and pianist who brought the term into use, the program—a poem or perhaps just a few words of description—serves as a preface to the composition in order to "direct [the listener's] attention to the poetical idea." The idea of composing programmatic music was fashionable throughout the nineteenth century, from Beethoven's "Pastoral" symphony through the tone poems of Liszt, Richard Strauss, and others. Liszt's description summarized prevailing practice even as it guided both future composers and listeners.

The first programmatic works date from the sixteenth century—a noteworthy example is "Battell" music by the English composer William Byrd's—and by 1700, there were numerous works with clear programs, most notably a set of six biblical sonatas by Johann Kuhnau, Bach's predecessor in Leipzig. Opera, particularly French opera with its extensive dance scenes, also required descriptive music. But no work composed before 1800 has matched the fame of Vivaldi's *The Four Seasons*, and few match Vivaldi's skill in depicting the program.

"Spring." "Spring" (see Listen Up!) is a solo concerto: the featured instrument is the violin. In the first movement, Vivaldi harnesses the tutti/solo dynamic of concerto form to express and elaborate on the affect of the movement. The ritornello suggests the joy of spring, at the outset and every time it returns. The solo episodes amplify and clarify the springlike mood by translating sounds of spring—bird calls, a babbling brook, and a thunderstorm—into music.

Vivaldi's aural evocations of nature do not replicate the actual sounds. But they approximate them closely enough

program music Instrumental music in which a composer depicts an extramusical inspiration, such as a scene, story, or idea, or the experience or feeling that the inspiration arouses

 **LISTEN UP!**

Vivaldi, Violin Concerto in E major ("Spring," from *The Four Seasons*), 1st movement (1723)

TAKEAWAY POINT: Baroque-era program music at its finest

STYLE: Baroque

FORM: Ritornello

GENRE: Solo concerto

INSTRUMENTS: Solo violin; orchestral strings (violin, viola, cello, bass) and keyboard

CONTEXT: Music appropriate for public or private, and sacred or secular,
performance in multiple venues: church, theater, large rooms

RITORNELLO

0:00   First part of ritornello: "Springtime is upon us." The full orchestra

0:21   Second part of ritornello

SOLO

0:37   Episode 1: "The birds celebrate her return with festive song." The violins imitate bird sounds.

RITORNELLO

1:12   A "little return": the second part of the ritornello

SOLO

1:20   Episode 2: "Murmuring streams are softly caressed by the breezes." We hear the murmurs first in the violins, then in the lower strings.

RITORNELLO

1:44   The second part of the ritornello, in a new key

SOLO

1:52   Episode 3: "Thunderstorms, those heralds of Spring, roar, casting their dark mantle over heaven." Storm in the violins first, then orchestral violins and solo violin in alternation (thunder and lightning)

RITORNELLO

2:21   The second part of the ritornello, in still another new key

SOLO

2:30   Episode 4: "Then they die away to silence, and the birds take up their charming songs once more"

RITORNELLO

2:49   Variant of the first part of the ritornello

SOLO

3:01   Episode 5

RITORNELLO

3:17   Final ritornello

 Listen to this selection streaming or in an Active Listening Guide at CourseMate or in the eBook.

that listeners can make the association with written descriptions, which Vivaldi provided in the score and to which concertgoers might have access.

"Spring" introduces us to the Baroque orchestra, the Baroque concerto, and program music. Because there's such a clear delineation between solo and tutti, we can hear not only the composition of the orchestra—strings plus keyboard—but also the specific roles assigned to each instrument. The frequent contrasts between orchestra and soloist present the prevailing mood from different perspectives. And in this movement, idiomatic composition is harnessed to the program: the dazzling effects—effectively playable only on the violin—serve the expressive goal of portraying springtime in sound.

Vivaldi's music was a significant influence on J. S. Bach, who went so far as to arrange several of Vivaldi's concertos for other instruments. In section 6-4, we considered how Bach borrowed from the French. In this next example, we explore how he transformed the Italian concerto.

6-6C Bach's Brandenburg Concertos

A Pepsi commercial for the 2004 Super Bowl featured a young Jimi Hendrix trying to decide whether to buy a Pepsi or a Coke. Both soda machines stand in front of music stores: the Pepsi machine in front of a pawnshop selling an electric guitar, the Coke machine in front of Bob's Accordion World. As the eleven-year-old Hendrix opts for Pepsi, we hear strains of "Purple Haze." As the camera pans over to Bob's Accordions and the Coke machine, we hear the opening guitar riff of the song played on an accordion, as the commercial announces, "Whew . . . that was a close one."

What does this commercial have to do with Bach's Brandenburg Concertos? Both are demonstrations of the significance of instrument choice. The commercial is a warning about the dire consequences of choosing the wrong instrument. Bach's concertos are the flip side: they show the enormous appeal of instrumental variety.

Instrumental sounds were as important to Bach as they would become to Hendrix. Bach had a fascination with instruments and instrumental sounds throughout his life. He was the leading consultant on organ construction in Germany during his lifetime. His cantatas require instruments that were obscure in his own time and obsolete now. His estate contained, among other items, eight keyboard instruments and ten stringed instruments.

With the Brandenburg Concertos, Bach took advantage of the musicians available to him to create the most diverse set of concertos produced by him or any of his contemporaries. Each concerto has a decidedly different instrumentation: a large orchestra in one; a high trumpet in another; all strings in a third; recorders in a fourth; a solo group of harpsichord, violin, and flute in the fifth; and no violins in the sixth. Moreover, each concerto has a unique relationship between solo and tutti. This diverse instrumentation sets these works apart from not only Bach's other concertos but also the concertos of his contemporaries. There's no other set quite like it.

Bach's Different Path. How can we account for the uniqueness of the Brandenburg Concertos? We can perhaps understand them as a response to the varied instrumental resources available to the composer. But Bach's mixing of instruments goes well beyond what other composers of the time did, and there are other aspects of the concertos that set them apart, as we will discover. It may be presumptuous to try to establish a causal connection between character and composition—especially in Bach's case, because we have so little firsthand information about him. Still, we can perhaps infer, from the study of his career as a musician and the amount and kinds of music that he composed, something of his character.

Whether he undertook a project in fulfillment of his professional duties; to meet an immediate need for, say, teaching pieces for his children and other pupils; or simply for its own sake, Bach seemed to compose from an overpowering inner need. He composed prodigiously, often far beyond what was needed to satisfy the demands of a particular responsibility. There was little financial incentive to compose: he received no royalties from his works and obtained few commissions. For Bach, it seems, the quality and nature of his work were far more important than recognition or financial gain.

Both his music and certain incidents in his life suggest a strongly independent character. We can sense it from the time that he spent in prison, the result of a conflict between him and the duke who employed him in Weimar, and his occasionally contentious relationship with the town councilors in Leipzig. We can also infer it from certain aspects of his compositions, such as the choice of projects—the Goldberg Variations and the Mass in B minor, both monumental works with virtually no prospects for performance in major venues—and his adherence to a contrapuntal style, even as it grew increasingly out of fashion. Indeed, he composed *The Art of the Fugue* to leave the last word on

LISTEN UP!

TOTAL TIME: 5:52

Bach, Brandenburg Concerto No. 3, 1st movement (1721)

TAKEAWAY POINT: A unique version of the Baroque concerto for strings

STYLE: Baroque

FORM: Ritornello

GENRE: Hybrid concerto

INSTRUMENTS: Three violins, three violas, three cellos, and continuo

CONTEXT: Music for court, to fulfill a request from a potential patron

RITORNELLO
0:00   Opening ritornello

SOLO
0:21   Episode 1: Orchestra breaks into choirs; each player has a separate part

RITORNELLO
0:46   Supporting line becomes main theme in a new key
1:17   Ritornello fragment, in another new key

SOLO
1:54   Episode 2: New melodic idea, in home key

RITORNELLO
2:11   Ritornello in yet another new key
2:51   Ritornello fragment in a different key

SOLO
3:11   Episode 3: Another new melodic idea (solo violin), again in home key

RITORNELLO
4:08   Ritornello fragment in fifth new key
4:50   Modified ritornello fragment after long buildup
5:07   Final ritornello, the same as opening ritornello with an extension

🔊 Listen to this selection streaming or in an Active Listening Guide at CourseMate or in the eBook.

What makes it different is the number of strings: three violins, three violas, three cellos, and continuo of double bass and harpsichord. By specifying precisely the number of string players and assigning each performer a distinct part, Bach created a chamber music work that verges on being orchestral. In some sections, such as the opening ritornello, each group of three strings plays the same part, as in an orchestra. In other passages, each group of strings breaks into close harmony, as in the first episode. And there are passages where a single instrument is in the spotlight, with other instruments in an accompanying role, as in a solo concerto. Indeed, Bach presents so many instrument combinations that it is as if he has upgraded from the stark black and white of the solo/tutti format to gray scale.

As in the Vivaldi concerto, the entire movement grows out of the opening ritornello. But whereas Vivaldi begins with short, clearly articulated phrases, which he repeats, Bach begins at a more molecular level. The concerto opens with a three-note motive, a simple, generic musical idea. The opening ritornello spins out from this very basic idea in three interlocked installments, each of which presents a new perspective on the motive.

© Levent Abdurrahman Cagin/iStockphoto.com

counterpoint before he died, even as the most fashionable music of the day moved toward a lighter, more accessible style.

These observations and inferences may help us understand the uniqueness of the Brandenburg Concertos as a set and so many of the distinctive features of the individual works. Bach would place on them the unmistakable stamp of his personality.

Bach's Third Brandenburg Concerto. In terms of instrument choice, it would seem the third concerto (see Listen Up!) is the most conventional of the six: the orchestra is just strings, as it was for Vivaldi.

Bach and Baroque Style. We've heard four Baroque instrumental works to this point: two by Italian composers and two by Bach. If we compare the Italian sonata and concerto to the two pieces by Bach, we can surmise that Bach's music is distinguished in part by these characteristics:

1. It tends to be denser and more contrapuntal.
2. It is more consistent in its rhythmic flow.
3. Melody is generated by permutations of an opening idea; multiple different melodic ideas are less likely.
4. Bach's instrumentation is more inventive.
5. Bach's music is likely to be more expansive: the first movement of his concerto is almost twice as long as the first movement of Vivaldi's "Spring."

Looking Back, Looking Ahead

In the first part of the eighteenth century, the courts and churches of western Europe enjoyed a deluge of instrumental music. Italy was the primary center of creative activity: sonatas and concertos composed by Italians were performed and emulated throughout Europe. French composers championed dance music; their suites achieved wide currency elsewhere, especially Germany and England. German composers used Italian and French works as models for their own sonatas, suites, and concertos. England imported composers as well as music. The most notable was George Frideric Handel, who composed prolifically in virtually all genres, vocal and instrumental, while residing there. All of this music far exceeded in quantity and quality that which had been produced in the previous century.

There are both extramusical and musical reasons for this profusion of instrumental music. In an increasingly secular Europe, patrons required more instrumental music for their entertainment. A famous example: Handel composed his "Water Music," a series of three suites, at the request of King George I of England, for a concert on the Thames River in which the royal party and the musicians were on separate barges. The growing music publishing industry also catered to this enthusiasm for instrumental music among both the aristocracy and the middle class. One indication of its increasing popularity and rising social status was the widespread use of opus numbers after 1700, particularly in Italy. Craftsmen continued to improve instruments, particularly strings: the violin-family instruments built in Cremona, Italy, by the Stradivari and Guarneri families remain some of the most prized (and expensive) instruments in the world. Musicians increasingly developed performing skills that could not be replicated by singers—even though composers wrote instrument-like melodic lines, as we heard in Handel's opera aria. To cite one spectacular example: Bach's contrapuntal improvisations would have been impossible to replicate by voices, and then as now, audiences admired virtuosity.

However, the most significant musical reason for the growth of instrumental music was the almost universal acceptance of tonal harmony. Tonal harmony was, if anything, more important to instrumental than to vocal composition because it gave composers the ability to project the formal organization of the work without recourse to a text. Devices like the ritornello, used in conjunction with an increasingly familiar harmonic organization, gave instrumental works coherence; audiences could follow the progress of the music and recognize formal milestones. It is no coincidence that the rapid growth and greater prestige of instrumental music occurred after 1680, as tonal harmony became common practice.

Instrumental music would become even more popular and prestigious later in the eighteenth century. We will encounter even more expansive and varied instrumental music by Haydn and Mozart after a brief survey of Baroque sacred vocal music.

 study tools 6

7 Late Baroque Sacred Vocal Music: Chorale, Cantata, and Oratorio

LEARNING OUTCOMES

After studying this chapter, you will be able to do the following:

7-1 Understand the Lutheran chorale as the point of departure for Bach's sacred vocal music.

7-2 Recognize the relationship between the chorale and the cantata through an exploration of Bach's Cantata No. 80.

7-3 Get acquainted with the Baroque oratorio, its importance to Handel's career, and Handel's most successful oratorio, *Messiah*.

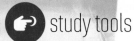 study tools

After you read this chapter, go to the Study Tools at the end of the chapter, page 104.

Productive contemporary artists typically put out an album every year or two. They may spend months in the studio to produce about an hour of music. For example, Radiohead, among the most acclaimed bands of the last two decades, released seven studio albums over a fifteen-year span, from *Pablo Honey* (1993) to *In Rainbows* (2007), the famous pay-what-you-want album.

By contrast, George Frideric Handel composed *Messiah* and eighteen other oratorios (large-scale compositions for chorus, vocal soloists, and orchestra) between 1739 and 1749. Recorded performances of these works would consume about forty CDs. But Handel's impressive accomplishment pales next to J. S. Bach's prodigious output in his first years at Leipzig. Upon assuming his duties as cantor of Thomaskirche (St. Thomas Church), Bach began composing cantatas, vocal music for the Lutheran church year, which amounted to all fifty-two Sundays plus numerous holy days. Between 1723 and 1729—five calendar years—Bach produced five such cycles, plus at least two settings of the Passion of Christ—easily sixty CDs of music. While composing his massive five-year cantata cycle, Bach also taught school; directed a boys' choir; rehearsed his music; raised a large family (and mourned the deaths of the three children who died at birth or in infancy during this time); taught his own children and others; composed other music; played organ for services, weddings, funerals, and other occasions (to make some extra money); and pursued assorted other activities. Bach's industry was mind boggling.

Handel and Bach undertook these tasks for different reasons. After making and losing a fortune with his two opera academies, Handel turned to oratorio, which involved less risk and greater reward. For Bach, the new position in Leipzig enabled him to fulfill his grandest professional ambition: to create a "well regulated church music."

Their respective genres of choice, the church cantata and the sacred oratorio, flourished during the Baroque era and reached an artistic pinnacle in their compositions. Both cantata and oratorio represent in different ways the culmination of a long period of musical evolution and new syntheses of sacred and secular traditions.

ray roper/iStockphoto.com

crixtina/Shutterstock.com

Martin Luther took advantage of the invention of the printing press to advocate that scripture be read in local vernacular languages like German and English rather than Latin.

7-1 Luther and the Chorale

Martin Luther (1483–1546) was the father of both the Reformation—the Protestant reform movement that swept across northern Europe during the sixteenth century—and Protestant congregational singing. Luther, like almost everyone in western Europe at the time, was raised Catholic. He would have grown up hearing the Mass said or sung in Latin, not in the language of the congregation. Especially in the major churches, singing would be the work of a trained choir, and the music that they sang was richly contrapuntal: the Josquin mass movement is a splendid example.

Luther sought to close the distance between those who said or sang the Mass and those who heard it. He did so by encouraging monophonic hymn singing in the vernacular and by composing hymns and hymn tunes himself. Several, including "Ein' feste Burg ist unser Gott" ("A Mighty Fortress Is Our God"), are still familiar.

Luther was especially well qualified to bring a new kind of music into his liturgical reforms. As a boy, he sang well enough to earn free room and board at school. He was apparently a skilled performer on both the flute and the lute, and had some knowledge of music theory. During his formative years, he heard and admired the music of Renaissance polyphonists, including Josquin des Prez, whose music he described as "free as the song of the finch." However, in composing music for his newly reformed liturgy, he turned to secular song for inspiration. Indeed, it is likely that he used or adapted secular songs of the day. Some scholars think that Luther's hymn "Ein feste Burg" (the hymn discussed in this chapter) was inspired by one of the most famous melodies of Hans Sachs, a *Meistersinger* (German lyric poet) and Luther's contemporary. Luther's insistence on integrating congregational singing may have been novel, but his musical models were familiar and well established.

Luther wasn't the first reformer to encourage vernacular hymn singing by the congregation—that honor belongs to the followers of the fifteenth-century Czech reformer Jan Hus. But Luther's central role in the Reformation and his activity as a composer of hymns make him the key figure in bringing music making to the congregation.

Hymn singing had theological and practical benefits for Luther. At the heart of his reforms was the idea that the most direct way to know God was through scripture rather than through church teaching. Hymns, many of which served as commentary on scripture, gave him a powerful way to get the important points in the scripture reading across to the congregation in an accessible way: "Ein' feste Burg" is based on Psalm 46. Moreover, singing in the vernacular made worship services more appealing.

7-1A "Ein' feste Burg ist unser Gott"

Luther's "Ein' feste Burg" (see Listen Up!) is a chorale, a Lutheran hymn designed for congregational singing. Luther's first version was monophonic—just the melody. In this form, the distinctive features of a Lutheran hymn are

Meistersinger German lyric poet of the fourteenth through sixteenth centuries

chorale Lutheran hymn designed for congregational singing

 **LISTEN UP!**

Luther/Walter, "Ein' feste Burg ist unser Gott" (ca. 1525)

TAKEAWAY POINT: Singable melody with short phrases and even rhythm setting text syllabically

STYLE: Renaissance—Baroque

FORM: Strophic

GENRE: Chorale (monophonic/polyphonic/homophonic)

INSTRUMENTS: Mixed voices (plus instruments in Bach)

CONTEXT: Liturgical music based on tuneful secular song to encourage congregational singing; a key component of the Protestant Reformation

LUTHER

0:00   Syllabic text setting to a melody that moves mainly by step in an even rhythm with occasional syncopation

Ein' feste Burg ist unser Gott,	A mighty fortress is our God,
ein gute Wehr und Waffen;	a bulwark never failing;
Er hilfft uns frey aus aller Not,	Our helper He, amid the flood
die uns jetzt hat betroffen.	of mortal ills prevailing.
Der alt' böse Feind mit Ernst ers jetzt meint,	For still our ancient foe doth seek
gros Macht und viel List,	to work us woe,
Sein grausam Rüstung ist,	His craft and power are great,
auf Erd ist nicht seins gleichen.	and, armed with cruel hate, on earth is not his equal.

WALTER

0:55   Walter's setting surrounds the melody with three active parts; the upper line is not the melody. Occasional melismas enrich the texture.

BACH

2:07   Bach's setting evens out the rhythm and adds a homophonic accompaniment.

Das Wort sie sollen lassen stahn,	The Word they still shall let remain
und kein Danck dazu heben,	nor any thanks have for it,
Er ist bei uns wol auf dem Plan	He's by our side upon the plain
mit seinem Geist und Gaben.	with His good gifts and Spirit.
Nemen sie uns den Leib,	And take they our life,
Gut Eher, Kindt und Weib,	goods, fame, child and wife,
Las faren dahin, Sie habens kein Gewin;	Let these all be gone, they yet have nothing won;
das Reich muss uns doch bleiben.	the Kingdom ours remaineth.)

 Listen to this selection streaming or in an Active Listening Guide at CourseMate or in the eBook.

---

evident: a melody that moves in mostly even values, with gently changing contours; syllabic setting of the text; frequent pauses after each line of text; and strophic form. Almost immediately, it appeared in a four-voice setting by Johann Walter (1496–1570), Luther's frequent collaborator and the other key figure in the rise of Lutheran hymns. Walter's polyphonic setting of the chorale was at odds with Luther's quest for accessibility. Subsequent settings, most notably by Bach, are more homophonic and rhythmically regular than Walter's version. We hear one stanza of each setting, although a complete performance would include four stanzas.

It may seem counterintuitive that Bach, the most esteemed contrapuntal composer in the history of music, would compose a more homophonic setting of this same chorale than Walther. However, for Bach, the chorale was one component of a large multimovement composition. Bach would save his polyphony for the instruments.

7-2 Bach and the Church Cantata

Cantata means "sung" in Italian; *sonata* means "sounded." So, one could say that "cantata" is to singing as "sonata" is to playing an instrument. But the parallels go beyond analogy. Like the sonata, the cantata is a genre that emerged in Italy during the early seventeenth century, then flourished throughout Europe during the early eighteenth century. Both began as intimate forms of secular entertainment: the Italian cantata of the seventeenth century typically featured a series of contrasting sections requiring a solo voice and continuo, which grew into distinct movements by the eighteenth century. And both were exceedingly popular.

In Lutheran Germany, the cantata served a different function and assumed a different form. For German composers, especially Bach, the cantata was most often liturgical music. Cantatas were an integral component of Sunday services at churches such as St. Thomas's, as crucial to worship as the pastor's sermon, and they delivered parallel messages. At the heart of each cantata was a hymn, or chorale, a simple melody whose text was drawn from scripture.

Bach's church cantatas typically included three kinds of music: a setting of a chorale for congregational singing, a series of recitative/aria pairs, and one or more choruses. All were connected to the scripture readings of the day. The chorale derived directly from scripture: recall that "Ein' feste Burg" is based on Psalm 46. The recitative/aria pairs set contemporary commentaries on the scripture readings. Choruses were large-scale works for chorus and orchestra. In them, Bach surrounded the chorale melody with a rich polyphonic texture performed by the orchestra. (Note that the term *chorus* in this context refers to the work itself, not to the group singing it.)

7-2A Chorus from Cantata No. 80

Bach composed Cantata No. 80, which is based on the chorale "Ein' feste Burg," for a festival celebrating the Protestant Reformation. This cantata contains eight movements: two choruses, an aria with chorale, two recitatives, a solo aria and a duet, and a setting of Luther's chorale for congregational singing. The five stanzas of Luther's chorale are dispersed among the movements; the opening chorus features the first stanza. The second movement, the aria with chorale, features an instrumental-style vocal line woven around the second verse of the chorale. The fifth movement, also a chorus, embeds the third stanza of the chorale in a rich instrumental accompaniment. The final two stanzas are the simple four-part chorale harmonization, to be sung and played by musicians and the congregation.

In setting the third stanza of Luther's chorale "Und wenn die Welt voll Teufel wär" ("And Though This World Was Filled with Devils"; see Listen Up!), Bach adapted a time-honored strategy to his particular circumstances. Among the earliest kinds of polyphonic music was organum, which featured a slow-moving chant part and one or more other parts weaving actively around it.

In his cantata choruses, Bach often used the chorale melody as the cantus firmus (see Chapter 4). Because both words and melody were so familiar to the congregations in Leipzig, they in effect served as the Bible passages on which Bach would sermonize. The use of familiar chorales gave Bach's congregation a head start in understanding the message in his music. By surrounding the chorale melody with much richer music that has a clear affect, Bach could convey his interpretation of the message expressed in the lyrics of the chorale. It is as if he were giving a homily in music even as the scriptures were being read. He effectively fused the expressive power of Baroque style with the familiar message of the chorale.

To present his message in large movements like the chorus, Bach transformed ritornello form by inverting the relationship between solo and tutti. Recall that in a Baroque concerto, the ritornello contained the main musical message, and the solo episodes elaborated on it. Here the main message is in the chorale tune; the ritornello is essentially a musical commentary on the chorale text. Compositionally, however, nothing has changed. The instrumental statements are like bearing walls: they support the form, even as they reinforce Bach's musical message.

Bach's choruses represent an imaginative synthesis of two conflicting musical trends in Lutheran Germany. Luther's goal of returning singing to the congregation required simple musical settings for his hymns rather than polyphonic settings of the liturgy, however beautiful they might be. However, during the Baroque era, the most polyphonic music came from Germany, and especially from Bach's pen: the fugue flourished there, as we noted in the previous chapter. In choruses such as the one heard here, Bach effectively has his cake and eats it. He preserves the directness of the hymn in the vocal part of the texture, even as he enriches its message with the rich, concerto-like polyphonic instrumental accompaniment.

7-2B Bach: The End and the Beginning

Johann Christian Bach, the youngest son of J. S. Bach, considered his father old-fashioned. While composers such as Vivaldi and Handel were moving toward a more transparent and melodic style, the older Bach continued to compose music rich with

cantata Church or secular vocal composition; Bach's church cantatas typically include one or more choruses, a series of recitative/aria pairs, and a setting of a chorale

church cantata Cantata written for church use. Bach's church cantatas typically include one or more choruses, a series of recitative/aria pairs, and a setting of a chorale

chorus In a Bach cantata, a large-scale work for chorus (choir) and orchestra that is built around the chorale for a church service

 **LISTEN UP!**

Bach, "Und wenn die Welt voll Teufel wär," from Cantata No. 80, *Ein' feste Burg ist unser* Gott (1724)

TAKEAWAY POINT: Bach's chorus as a musical sermon on Luther's chorale

STYLE: Baroque

FORM: Ritornello

GENRE: Church cantata

INSTRUMENTS: Choir plus orchestra consisting of oboes, strings, and continuo

CONTEXT: Music for a Lutheran church service

0:00	Opening ritornello; this material returns throughout, sometimes complete, sometimes fragmented, progressively more varied.

0:19   Ritornello material continues under chorale melody.

Und wenn die Welt voll Teufel wär	And though this world, with devils filled
Und wollt' uns gar verschlingen,	Should threaten to undo us,

0:40   Opening ritornello returns.

1:01	*So fürchten wir uns nicht so sehr*	We will not fear, for God hath willed
	Es soll uns doch gelingen.	His truth to triumph through us.

1:22   Altered version of ritornello

1:41   The darkest part of the stanza—where the faithful confront the devil. Bach symbolizes this by shifting to a minor key, including more syncopations in the violin parts, and making the bass more active.

Der Fürst dieser Welt	The Prince of Darkness grim
Wie sau'r er sich stellt,	We tremble not for him,
Tut er uns doch nicht	His rage we can endure

2:24   This interlude and the following are the most intense of the chorus.

Das macht, er ist gericht't,	For lo, his doom is sure,

22:39   Return to major and a smoother flow, just in time for the devil's doom

Ein Wörtlein kann ihn fallen.	One little word shall fell him.

2:49   Final restatement of opening ritornello

 Listen to this selection streaming or in an Active Listening Guide at CourseMate or in the eBook.

counterpoint. By contrast, J. C. Bach's music was simpler and more decorative—high-class aural wallpaper for aristocrats. It was, for the eighteenth century, an up-to-date sound and a major influence on Mozart.

J. S. Bach and his music effectively ended several musical eras—in particular the glory years of Lutheran church music. In his sacred vocal music—especially the cantatas and passion settings—and his organ music, no Lutheran church composer after him came close to his achievements.

Because Bach came at the end of the Baroque era, his music summarizes his understanding of Baroque style. There is in much of it a sense of wrapping things up, of having the final say. That is certainly the case with the cantatas and the Catholic mass that he composed; with works like *The Well-Tempered Clavier* and the four volumes of keyboard music that he published himself; and with contrapuntal works composed at the end of his life, including *The Musical Offering* and *The Art of the Fugue.*

Yet Bach's music has influenced major composers from Mozart and Beethoven through Romantics such as Schumann and Chopin, to twentieth-century masters such as Debussy, Stravinsky, and Bartók, as well as

Bach, seemingly behind the times in his own lifetime, has spoken to every generation of musicians that followed.

generations of jazz and rock musicians. There is a poetic justice in all of this: Bach, seemingly behind the times in his own lifetime, has spoken to every generation of musicians that followed him, whereas those who dismissed his work as old-fashioned—we have record of one particularly malicious attack on Bach by a young man named Scheibe, an important critic in his time—are now footnotes to history.

LEARNING OUTCOME 7-3

Get acquainted with the Baroque oratorio, its importance to Handel's career, and Handel's most successful oratorio, *Messiah*.

7-3 Handel and the Baroque Oratorio

"Haaaaaaaaal-le-luu-jaah!" The four-note motive that sets this word rivals the opening of Beethoven's Symphony No. 5 as the most popular four notes in history. We hear it at Christmas, in television commercials, on cell phones, and in a host of other places. People may not know about Handel, but there's a good chance they know this motive. But there's more to the Hallelujah Chorus than the opening motive, more to *Messiah* than the Hallelujah Chorus, and more to Handel's music than *Messiah*.

7-3A Handel and Oratorio

In Handel's time, opera and oratorio were cousins. Both told a story through music, using various forms of recitative, arias, and ensemble numbers (duets, choruses, and the like). In Handel's vocal music, there are two major differences: the subject and its presentation. His operas took their plots from history, particularly ancient history, as was the case with *Giulio Cesare*. By contrast, almost all of Handel's oratorios are based on religious subjects. Many are from the Old Testament, although *Messiah*, the most famous, draws from both Old and New Testaments. Moreover, unlike opera, oratorio is not staged; it is simply presented in concert. There is no action or scenery; words and music carry the story along without visual aids.

Oratorio, and especially *Messiah*, turned out to be a much better proposition for Handel than opera, although it didn't seem that way at first. The Bishop of London prohibited the 1732 performance of Handel's oratorio *Esther* in a theater. He felt that presenting religious material in a secular setting was inappropriate. His position was soon reversed, and by the 1740s, Handel's oratorios had become not only an extremely popular genre in England but also a force for morality and religious feeling.

Handel's oratorios were even more successful than his operas, for several reasons. One was the cost factor: it was far less expensive to present an oratorio than to mount an opera production. No scenery had to be built, no costumes had to be sewn, and far fewer stagehands were needed. (One happy result of these savings seems to have been the expansion

oratorio A genre performed in a concert setting that tells a story through music, using various forms of recitative, arias, and ensemble numbers

Handel, Hallelujah Chorus, from *Messiah* (1742)

TAKEAWAY POINT: A triumphant musical statement, and one of the most famous compositions of all time

STYLE: Late Baroque

FORM: Through-composed

GENRE: Oratorio

INSTRUMENTS: Choir plus orchestra of strings, winds, brass (especially trumpet), and timpani

CONTEXT: A sacred subject in a secular concert setting

0:00   Instrumental ritornello

0:06   The famous opening motive/phrase
       Hallelujah! Hallelujah!

0:23   New melodic idea with all parts doubling the melody
       For the Lord God Omnipotent reigneth.

0:44   More contrapuntal accompaniment of the same melody; "Hallelujah" motive appears in counterpoint to main melody.
       For the Lord God Omnipotent reigneth.

1:09   The melody derived from a scale, with a hymn-like setting
       The kingdom of this world is become the kingdom of our Lord, and of His Christ;

1:27   Angular melody, contrapuntal setting
       And He shall reign forever and ever.

1:48   The melody is simply a repeated note; "Hallelujah" motive used in response.
       King of Kings, and Lord of Lords.

2:28   Contrapuntal again
       And He shall reign forever and ever.

2:39   As before
       King of Kings, and Lord of Lords.

3:10   Final "Hallelujahs"

 Listen to this selection streaming or in an Active Listening Guide at CourseMate or in the eBook.

of the orchestra. *Messiah* is more richly scored than many of Handel's operas; the orchestra contains strings, organ, harpsichord, oboes, bassoons, trumpets, horns, and timpani.)

Another was the change in subject: although a good eighteenth-century education included classical languages, literature, and history, scripture was even more familiar, at least to churchgoers. Even more important was the use of English instead of Italian. Audiences knew the text immediately; they no longer had to wonder what the characters were saying. In the case of *Messiah*, following the narrative presented no problem;

no biblical account was more familiar to audiences than the life of Christ. It was like a favorite movie that they had seen fifty or a hundred times. They knew how the story would end, as well as all the lines. Its familiarity was certainly one component of its success.

> For Handel and his audience, the libretto of *Messiah* was like a favorite movie that they had seen fifty or a hundred times.

7-3B *Messiah*

Handel composed *Messiah* at a critical point in his career. Although he was the most famous and respected composer in England, he felt uncertain enough about his future to travel to Germany, to tour as an organist, and perhaps to entertain an offer of employment from Frederick the Great, king of Prussia and himself a serious musician. Whatever his plans, we do know that he gave a "farewell concert" in London in the spring of 1741. At about this time, he received an invitation to provide a work for Dublin charities. The project, which became *Messiah*, reinvigorated him and kept him in England. He finished the massive work in approximately three weeks.

Messiah is the best known of Handel's several collaborations with Charles Jennens, a rich landowner, literate man, and devout Christian. He greatly admired Handel's music and had previously supplied him with English texts to set to music.

After its London premiere in 1742, *Messiah* was performed annually, just as it is in our time. Among the most significant of these annual performances were those mounted to support the Foundling Hospital, from 1750 through 1754.

7-3C The Hallelujah Chorus and Handel's Style

In the context of Baroque style, the most striking feature of the Hallelujah Chorus is the contrast from phrase to phrase. In the course of the movement, we hear the bouncy rhythm of the opening phrase; a declamatory "for the Lord God"; a second statement of the text and melody, now enhanced by "Hallelujahs" coming from chorus and orchestra; a suddenly serene "The Kingdom of this World" followed by an emphatic restatement of the same phrase; an abrupt contrast in both melody (the jagged rise and fall) and texture (contrapuntal instead of hymnlike) in the setting of "and He shall reign"; another declamatory phrase "King of Kings"; followed by glorious combinations of many of the earlier motives; and after a dramatic pause, the final, "amen" "Hallelujah."

Still, Handel sustains a single affect even as he creates bold contrasts on several different levels. How? The text helps, of course. So do the quick "Hallelujahs," which are in effect a more insistent and penetrating ritornello. There is the triumphant character of the chorus, underscored orchestrally by the trumpets, horns, and timpani. And there is tremendous momentum, as each phrase spills into the next, spurred on by the repetitions of the refrain-like "Hallelujah." All of these qualities combine to project an integrated whole, despite dramatic changes between and even within sections.

Contrast and continuity are opposites. One requires difference; the other requires similarity. In the music of Handel's time, their use was most often an either/or proposition. What Handel did better than any other composer of his time was to integrate contrast into continuity. He was able to maintain a consistent affect even as he incorporated bold contrasts in detail. This is one of the hallmarks of his musical style, and an important source of its power, as the Hallelujah Chorus shows in such a spectacular way.

7-3D The Enduring Appeal of Handel's Music

From his time to ours, Handel's music has retained its appeal because it is both accessible and artful. That it is both makes it unusual. Artistry and accessibility have been opposing tendencies in music, as in all art. One promises sophistication; the other, simplicity.

Handel's music contains elements that draw us in: the melodic hooks ("Hallelujah"), the trumpet flourishes, the strong melodic and textural contrasts—all stand out. And there are other features that sustain our interest even through repeated hearings, such as inventive accompaniments and busy counterpoint. Handel's ability to combine immediate appeal and continuing interest demonstrates his ability to embrace and integrate opposing tendencies. Here it happens at the highest level. It is a quality evident in so much of the great music of every era—from Mozart to Motown, from Beethoven to The Beatles. And it is a useful lesson for all aspiring musicians: find something to bring your audience in, and find something else to keep them coming back.

Handel's oratorios occupy a special place in the history of music. They were the first "classical music": music from an earlier generation that never went out of fashion and that was acknowledged as "classic"—that is, the epitome of a particular genre—by the music world of the late eighteenth century and beyond.

Looking Back, Looking Ahead

Bach's cantatas and Handel's oratorios highlight two significant and seemingly irreversible changes in the relationship between sacred and secular music: the extensive use of instruments and the blurring of the boundary between sacred and secular styles. In addition, Handel's oratorios demonstrate the divorce of sacred music from liturgical function.

Sacred music remained almost exclusively vocal music through the end of the sixteenth century, in Catholic and even in some Protestant churches. That began to change in the early Baroque era, and by the early eighteenth century, large-scale sacred works, such as Bach's cantatas and Handel's oratorios, featured full orchestral accompaniment.

Hand in hand with the use of instruments came the blurring of the stylistic boundary between sacred and secular. Flash back to the compositions by Josquin and Wilbye, and consider how different those works are, even though both are Renaissance-era polyphonic works for voices, without accompaniment. By contrast, Bach's instrumental commentary on Luther's chorale speaks the same musical language as his gigue and concerto movement, and in much the same dialect. His "spiritual jig" retains the character of its secular model.

Like Bach, Handel makes little fundamental distinction between sacred and secular style: we hear tuneful melodies supported by strong bass lines in both his opera aria (Chapter 5) and the chorus, and more fundamentally, the sustaining of a single affect through entire sections of music. The most obvious differences are solo voice versus chorus, the expansion of the orchestra, and the form—ABA form in the aria versus the largely through-composed form of the chorus. In both works, Handel vividly paints the message of the text in sound. However, in the Hallelujah Chorus it seems that he is liberated from the formal restraints of the da capo aria; he can respond to the text line by line, without having to tailor the design to a rigid formal model. As with Bach, the musical tone is elevated, but there is no sharp musical distinction between sacred and secular.

Handel's oratorios go even further in blurring the boundary between sacred and secular by bringing the secular into the sacred world and by bringing the sacred into the secular world. Performances of Messiah and other oratorios in concert venues in effect deinstitutionalized the sacred: one could experience the word of God via scripture directly—apart from an official worship service of an organized religion.

In different ways, Bach and Handel set the tone for the relationship between sacred and secular music for subsequent generations. Handel's oratorios have remained popular since their composition, equally at home in church and concert venues, and the Bach revival of the early nineteenth century effectively divorced his sacred music from its original context. We are now much more likely to hear a Bach cantata in a concert hall than at a Lutheran church service. Partly because of these developments, composers since Bach and Handel have almost always scored large-scale sacred compositions, such as masses, requiems, and oratorios, for voices and orchestra. The boundaries between the two worlds that seemed so firm in the sixteenth century had dissolved by the end of the eighteenth century and have remained so into our time.

 study tools 7

Baroque Style

 ## KEY CONCEPTS

1. **One mood per movement (or other complete musical statement).** Mood is accomplished musically by creating it at the outset and sustaining it throughout the work. Melodic and rhythmic consistency help maintain the mood throughout the movement. Contrasting material generally comments upon or amplifies the basic mood.

KEY FEATURES

1. **Basso continuo.** Basso continuo, or simply continuo, is the instrumental, harmonic, and rhythmic foundation of Baroque ensemble music. It comprises a bass instrument (usually cello) and a chord-producing instrument (harpsichord or organ).
2. **Blocks of sound.** Sections within a movement typically maintain a consistent dynamic level, texture, and instrumentation. Changes between sections typically involve sudden changes in all three elements.
3. **Steady rhythms.** Particularly in medium- and fast-paced movements, Baroque rhythms generally maintain a consistent level of activity. Often, composers use a particular rhythmic pattern as a unifying device.
4. **Melodic consistency.** The opening material establishes the mood. Subsequent melodic material helps sustain the mood by spinning the melody out from the opening idea or periodically returning to the opening idea (or a variant of it) after contrasting material.
5. **Melody instrument.** The characteristic sound of the Baroque is the steady support for a mid- or high-range melody instrument: voice, violin, flute, oboe.

KEY COMPOSERS

Giulio Caccini (1558–1618)
Claudio Monteverdi (1567–1643)
Jean-Baptiste Lully (1632–1687)
Arcangelo Corelli (1653–1713)
Henry Purcell (1658/9?–1695)
François Couperin (1668–1733)
John Gay (1685–1732)
Antonio Vivaldi (1678–1741)
Johann Sebastian Bach (1685–1750)
George Frideric Handel (1685–1759)

Music Concept Check

To assist you in recognizing their distinctive features, we present an interactive comparison of Renaissance and Baroque style in CourseMate and the eBook

The Classical Style

Offscreen/Shutterstock

For about thirty years, from 1761 to 1790, Franz Joseph Haydn (1732–1809) was the composer in residence for the Esterházy family. At first, he lived and worked in Eisenstadt, near Vienna, Austria, where the Esterházy family had their winter home. Beginning in 1766, he spent most of his time at Eszterháza, the Esterházy family's sumptuous estate near the town of Fertod, Hungary, about halfway between Vienna and Budapest.

It's only about 70 miles from Vienna to Eszterháza, but it might as well have been 700 or 7,000. Eszterháza was a self-contained community—the palace was large enough to have its own vast concert hall, along with countless salons and bedrooms. Haydn stayed busy with his numerous commitments there, composing an enormous amount of music during his time there, even by eighteenth-century standards. Between his duties and the relative isolation of Eszterháza, Haydn had relatively little contact with musicians in Vienna and other cultural centers.

At Eszterháza, Haydn was a servant. Early on, he slept in the stable while composing the symphonies and string quartets that we still hear today. When his patron, Duke Nikolaus Esterházy, died in 1790, Haydn received a pension and release from his duties. In the interim, he had become one of the most esteemed composers in Europe, due in large part to the publication of his music in both authorized and unauthorized editions.

8-1 Musical Life in Late Eighteenth-Century Europe

Haydn's career was unique, but its transition from patronage to independence was evidence of a major shift in the musical landscape. A century earlier, he would have enjoyed neither the esteem nor the income that came his way after he left Esterháza. As the audience for music expanded beyond church and court to include a rapidly growing middle class, public performance, publishing royalties, and private instruction supplemented—and in some cases replaced—patronage as sources of income for musicians.

8-1A The Spread of Music Making

Music making in the home, both vocal and instrumental, and by both professionals and amateurs, grew significantly during the latter half of the century. An increasingly literate musical public demanded those goods and services that supported their music making. Professional musicians supplemented their income through teaching. Music publishers brought out a wide range of music—from simple airs (songs) to sonatas that still challenge professionals. A clear sign of the times: Carl Philipp Emanuel Bach, J. S. Bach's second surviving son and an important influence on Haydn, published six sets of keyboard pieces "für Kenner und Liebhaber" (for connoisseurs and amateurs) between 1779 and 1787. Both the target audience and the fact of publication (apparently, C. P. E. Bach published only music that he expected would sell well) are evidence of an expanded marketplace for music. Booksellers offered instructional methods and guides to performance: among the several important eighteenth-century treatises are those by C. P. E. Bach on keyboard playing and by Wolfgang Amadeus Mozart's father, Leopold, on violin playing.

8-1B Vienna

Through the first part of the eighteenth century, French and Italian music was by far the most influential

Brian Douglas Knox/Shutterstock.com

During the last quarter of the century, Vienna became the main center of musical activity and influence.

throughout Europe: Handel and Bach composed sonatas, suites, and concertos, and Handel also composed Italian operas for English audiences. However, by the end of the century, the influence of the two countries on musical life had waned. Italy trained a century of opera composers from other countries, from Handel to Mozart, but by the end of the century Italian composers like Mozart's rival Salieri (the villain of the film *Amadeus*) found better job prospects outside of Italy. France was embroiled in a revolution. During the last quarter of the century, Vienna became the main center of musical activity and influence. Haydn, Mozart, and Beethoven all settled there—Haydn after his lengthy service to the Esterházy family; Mozart after growing up in Salzburg, Germany (and throughout Europe, where the child prodigy spent much of his youth touring from city to city); and Beethoven, who left Bonn, Germany, in 1792 to seek fame, fortune, and instruction from Haydn.

8-1C Mozart

In 1785, Haydn told Leopold Mozart "Before God and as an honest man I tell you that your son is the greatest composer known to me either in person or by name; he has taste, and, furthermore, the most profound knowledge of composition." Haydn and Mozart formed a mutual admiration society: each respected the other's genius. Indeed, the occasion for Haydn's remark was an evening of chamber music in which Haydn had heard three string quartets that Mozart had dedicated to him.

◂Wolfgang Amadeus
Mozart

FAST FACTS

- Dates: 1756–1791

- Place: Salzburg/Vienna,
  Austria

- Reason to remember:
  One of the two greatest
  composers in the Classical style

Nicku/Shutterstock.com

Imagno/Hulton Archive/Getty Images

Mozart with his father, Leopold, and his sister, Nannerl,
at the beginning of their grand tour of Europe

If ever someone was born to be a musical genius, it was Haydn's younger contemporary, Wolfgang Amadeus Mozart (1756–1791) ◂. Mozart's father, Leopold, a court musician in Salzburg, Austria, and a famous and respected teacher, recognized his son's aptitude when Wolfgang was three. Leopold had begun piano lessons with Wolfgang's older sister, Nännerl, and discovered his son imitating her. He soon shifted his responsibilities to dedicate himself to the musical training of his children, especially his son.

When young Wolfgang was seven, the Mozart family left their home in Salzburg and began a three-year tour of Europe, which took them to England, France, Belgium, the Netherlands, and Germany. At each stop, Wolfgang played for heads of state and their courts, and in many locations gave public concerts. Audiences were amazed at the extraordinary ability of the child, whose hands were barely able to span five keys, to play his own difficult music and improvise everything from a set of variations to an opera aria. Six years after the first tour, the Mozart family toured Italy for two years, where the boy made an even more powerful impression.

After returning home, Mozart spent a few unhappy years in Salzburg working for the court; he found both his duties and the environment oppressive. He then returned for another extended stay in Paris, where he could act more independently. He left his home base in Salzburg for good in 1780, relocating to Vienna, where he would remain for the rest of his short life. By that time, Mozart enjoyed an international reputation as a superb composer and one of the finest keyboard players in Europe. During his Vienna years, he was a freelance musician, earning substantial fees as a performer, composer (through commissions and publications), and teacher. He died a pauper because, as his sister noted, he could not manage money.

Mozart understood the dramatic potential of the Classical style more clearly than any of his contemporaries, including Haydn. This is most apparent in his operas, which remain among the most treasured and frequently performed works in the genre. His sense of drama is also evident in his instrumental works, especially his later piano concertos. Mozart was at home in every genre: not only operas and concertos, but also symphonies; a wide range of chamber music for strings, piano, and winds; and sonatas and other solo keyboard works. Singers and a broad range of instrumentalists today are grateful for his substantial compositional legacy.

LEARNING OUTCOME 8-2

Contrast the two main styles of eighteenth-century music:
Baroque and Classical.

8-2 The Classical Style

In the last quarter of the eighteenth century, several diverse trends would coalesce into what came to be called the Classical style. Its home was Vienna, and its two leading proponents were Haydn and Mozart. The music of these composers and their contemporaries included new genres, most notably the symphony

Thomas Jefferson's mansion in Virginia—Monticello (completed 1772)—epitomized the clean, balanced classical lines of the new eighteenth-century style.

and the string quartet, and radically new approaches to existing genres, including opera, the concerto, and the sonata. The composers employed new resources: orchestras expanded to include winds, brass, and percussion consistently, and the piano replaced the harpsichord as the keyboard instrument of choice during the 1770s. Their music was performed in public concerts for paying audiences as well as in the salons of the aristocracy.

8-2A From Baroque to Classical

We refer to the music of the latter part of the eighteenth century as Classical. The Classical style in music took shape in tandem with a neoclassical movement in architecture and the visual arts, and shared many of the same values. However, the term *Classical*, as applied to music, has more to do with the growing historical consciousness of nineteenth-century musicians and commentators. As they preserved, published, and performed the music of the past, they referred to the music of Haydn, Mozart, and Beethoven as "classical" in its more general sense, to designate exemplary artifacts of a particular genre, or simply work of supremely high quality.

Over time, the meaning of the term *Classical* has expanded to refer to the prevailing concert music of the late eighteenth century—not just the music of Haydn,

Mozart, and Beethoven (the Classical *style*)—and more generally to the large body of concert music of the last millennium (classical *music*).

They shared the same century and musical language, but late Baroque music and Classical music grew out of distinctly different aesthetics. The Classical style introduced a new aesthetic based on conflict, contrast, and resolution rather than consistency of mood. The expressive goal of late Baroque music was to establish and maintain a single affect throughout an entire work, or at least a major section of it. However, by the last two decades of the century, composers had developed another approach. In their works, musical events followed one another like a rational argument that presented, then reconciled, contrasting musical materials. Indeed, music theorists of the time frequently compared music and rhetoric. This method of musical discourse can be understood as the quintessential musical expression of the Enlightenment—that eighteenth-century period in Western culture when reason and the scientific method replaced heredity as the main sources of legitimacy for authority.

The shift in aesthetic from Baroque to Classical was a gradual process, which occupied the middle

Enlightenment Eighteenth-century period in Western culture when reason and the scientific method replaced heredity as the main sources of legitimacy for authority

decades of the eighteenth century. It was a period of transition and considerable experimentation. There were distinguished and influential musicians active in the middle of the century. Christoph Willibald Gluck (1714–1787) led a reform of opera, and Johann Stamitz (1717–1757), based in Mannheim, Germany, played a key role in the development of the orchestra. Two sons of J. S. Bach were trend setters. Carl Philipp Emanuel Bach (1714–1788) cultivated a style with heightened expression (the German word is *Empfindsamkeit*), and his younger brother Johann Christian Bach (1735–1782) developed a style that sought to be pleasant and elegant (*galant*). Both Bach sons were among the most famous musicians of their time; they were far better known during their lifetimes than their father was during his. Today, however, almost all the music by these composers is far less familiar than the music that came before and after.

8-2B The Emergence of the Classical Style

By the 1770s, the new style that we now call the Classical style had taken shape. The music featured stronger and more frequent contrasts within movements, and greater length. The contrasts touched every element: for example, dramatic shifts between loud and soft, varied melodic material, homophonic versus contrapuntal textures, and slow versus fast rhythms. The consistent, comfortable rhythm of the continuo was now an anachronism. Moreover, these contrasts almost demanded greater length, to present and ultimately reconcile more diverse material. As a result, movements in genres inherited from the Baroque era, such as the concerto, were up to four times longer.

The resources required to perform this music also changed. If listeners from the early eighteenth century could have been transported to concert venues in late eighteenth-century London or Vienna, they would have been surprised to hear a full symphony orchestra performing Haydn's "Surprise" symphony or accompanying Mozart as he performed one of his piano concertos. By the 1780s, the size and instrumentation of the orchestra had grown considerably, with winds, brass, and percussion becoming regular members, and additional strings balancing these instruments. Moreover, orchestras performed in public concerts for paying customers as well as in the homes of aristocrats.

Classical style In music, a term that identifies the concert music of the late eighteenth century; Classical composers sought to create musical tension, typically through contrasts, then to resolve the tension.

sonata form The most characteristic form of first movements (and occasionally other movements) in instrumental compositions of the Classical era; contains three major sections: exposition, development, and recapitulation, and sometimes an introduction and coda; an expansion of rounded binary form

introduction Optional introductory section of sonata form in slow tempo; common in Classical symphonies

8-3 Sonata Form and Classical Style

To shape varied materials into more expansive and coherent statements, Classical composers gradually developed a set of procedures that were consistent in principle yet remarkably varied in their realizations. Typically, these procedures were used most extensively and expansively in the first movements of instrumental compositions: sonatas, quartets, symphonies, concertos, and the like. The organizational principle that informs these procedures in these movements came to be known as "sonata form."

8-3A Sonata Form

If you had asked Mozart about his approach to sonata form in one of his string quartets, he wouldn't have understood what you were asking because he wouldn't have recognized the term. For Mozart, Haydn, and their contemporaries, the sequence of events in what we now call sonata form was simply the way it was done; they didn't give the resulting form a specific name, such as "minuet and trio" or "rondo." Not until 1793, two years after Mozart's death, did the composer-theorist H. C. Koch publish a comprehensive and accurate description of the form—as an expansion of the minuet. The term *sonata form* and the terminology to describe it didn't come into use until the 1840s, when theorists coined them in an effort to describe the first movements in Beethoven sonatas.

The sonata and "sonata form" are two entirely different entities. In the Classical era, the sonata is a multimovement work for one or two instruments. Sonata form is an enormous and comprehensive expansion of the rounded binary form used in minuets and variation forms. Not surprisingly, there is considerable variation in the way sonata form is realized in different compositions. To provide a frame of reference for sonata-form movements, let's review a basic template of the form.

Movements written in sonata form contain at least three large sections: exposition, development, and recapitulation. An introduction in a slow tempo occasionally precedes the exposition, to convey a greater sense of importance. Introductions are relatively common in late Classical symphonies but rare in other genres. And a concluding coda may follow the recapitulation, to bring the movement to an even more emphatic close.

Within these broad, large-scale guidelines, there is virtually unlimited flexibility, in thematic content, connections and contrasts, and proportions. The following detailed descriptions of each section highlight typical features.

crats.

Establishes	Implies
Key	Length
Meter	Mood
Tempo	
Melodic material	

Table 8.1 Typical Features of a First Theme in Sonata Form

8-3B Exposition

The **exposition** serves two main purposes: to establish the basic character of the movement and to present the musical ideas that are to be worked out in the rest of the movement. It does so through a predictable sequence of musical gestures, each of which has a different function.

First Theme. The purpose of the first theme is to set the basic parameters of the movement. Accordingly, the movement typically begins with a complete musical statement that establishes or implies six features (see Table 8.1).

Key, meter, and tempo are relatively generic, because there are so few choices and so many works. For example, the Mozart piano sonata discussed presently is in F major, has a 3/4 meter, and proceeds at a fast tempo; so do many other sonatas, including another by Mozart. The other features are specific to the work. Although it may resemble other melodies, the opening theme is unique to the movement and is often its most distinctive feature. The length of the first theme generally previews the overall length of the movement. Melody and accompaniment set the mood, which usually reverberates throughout the rest of the movement. In the sonata that we will hear shortly, Mozart creates a pastoral feeling from the outset.

Transition. The **transition** section has two functions: to move to a new key and to make that move seem like a big deal. Moving from the tonic to a new key is strictly a harmonic procedure. In most sonata-form movements, it can be accomplished with only three chords and can sound bland when presented simply. However, the opposition of the tonic and the new key is the structural basis of the musical tension characteristic of the form. Accordingly, the other function of the transition is to dramatize the move to the new key. Typically, composers draw on tension-increasing strategies in several elements to highlight the change of key. These may include more active and syncopated rhythms, more contrapuntal textures, irregular phrases, an overall rise in register, and predominantly rising melodic lines. The transition typically concludes with a decisive cadence that prepares the new key.

Second Theme. To highlight arrival in the new key, composers typically present memorable, accessible me-

lodic material. Among the most common options are a new melody that is tuneful, even singable, or a literal or modified restatement of the first theme in the new key. Because the music before and after the second theme is typically more active, the second theme stands out as a moment of relative calm as well as a milestone in the progress of the form.

The first theme and the second theme are the two places in the exposition that confirm a key: the tonic and the contrasting key. The use of memorable melodies at these two points in the movement puts a distinctive face on the otherwise generic opposition of the two keys.

Closing Section. The main function of the music that concludes the exposition is to reinforce the new key. This material can be brief or extensive; it is generally far more active than the second theme, and it ends with a decisive cadence.

Taken as a whole, the exposition sets up an enormous imbalance. Only the very opening—usually less than one-quarter of the exposition—is in the home, or tonic, key. The remainder is either moving to a different key or confirming the new key. As a result, the decisive cadence at the end of the exposition doesn't sound like the end of the movement. Instead, the exposition ends with considerable unresolved tension, despite the strong cadence.

It is customary to repeat the exposition in performance. This has the dual function of reinforcing the sense of imbalance within the exposition and making the events in the subsequent development section even more surprising.

8-3C Development

The function of the **development** section is to further increase the musical tension created in the exposition. It fulfills this function through the extensive use of developmental procedures and the presentation of unstable new material.

To "develop" musical material is to modify it in ways that change important features: for example, compressing the rhythm, fragmenting the melody, changing the harmony, making the texture richer and more complex. Such modifications make the music less predictable and more unsettled. In a

exposition Section of sonata form that serves two main purposes: to establish the basic character of the movement and to present the musical ideas that are to be worked out in the rest of the movement

transition Portion of the exposition in sonata form that moves decisively to a new key and highlights the move; in the recapitulation, the transition is modified so that the second theme enters in the tonic.

development Section of sonata form where material from the exposition (and occasionally new material) is developed, or manipulated through fragmentation and alteration, to project great instability

It is as if you return home from your next-door neighbor's by first heading off in the opposite direction, then wandering around before arriving back at your doorstep.

sonata-form movement, development of musical material can occur in any section, and it is almost always heard in transition sections. It unfailingly occurs in the development section, however.

Not surprisingly, the events in a development section are mostly unpredictable. Unlike the exposition and recapitulation, there is no established sequence of events. The development may feature reworked versions of previously presented material and—less commonly—brand-new material. About the only constant feature is preparation for a return to the home key at the very end.

In most sonata-form movements in the Classical era, the return to the home key from the contrasting key can be as simple as a two-chord progression. The development section resists this simple return; instead, it purposely modulates (changes key) away from the tonic so that when the music ultimately returns to the home key in the recapitulation that follows, it is a much more striking event. It is as if you return home from your next-door neighbor's by first heading

modulation Harmonic procedure that produces a smooth change from one key to another

recapitulation Mostly literal restatement of sonata form's exposition, but with all the material in the contrasting key restated in the home key

coda Optional section of sonata form that follows the recapitulation

off in the opposite direction, then wandering around for a while before finally arriving back at your doorstep.

8-3D Recapitulation

Capo is the Italian word for "head"; to *recapitulate* means "to go to the beginning"—in this case, the beginning of the exposition. The return of the opening theme in the tonic key is the most important point of arrival within the movement. The arrival at the tonic, after the circuitous harmonic path through exposition and development, releases the harmonic tension accumulated since the beginning of the transition; the return of the opening theme highlights the return in the most emphatic possible way.

The recapitulation is a mostly literal restatement of the exposition, with one major difference: the second theme and other material that was stated in the new key in the exposition are now restated in the *home* key. The restatement of previously presented material in the home key stabilizes and balances the movement harmonically and structurally. Only the transition section is likely to be substantially different, as the composer must reroute the harmony so that it cadences in the home key rather than the new one. Mozart and Haydn delighted in presenting surprising twists and turns in the transition section of the recapitulation to inject excitement into a passage that begins and ends in the same place harmonically.

8-3E Coda

A movement in sonata form can conclude at the end of the recapitulation, when the material that ended the exposition in the contrasting key is heard in the home key. However, to counterbalance the tension created in the exposition and development, and make the ending even more emphatic, composers may extend the movement beyond this obvious ending point. The term coda identifies the section of music that comes after the end of the recapitulation. It is optional but not uncommon.

See Figure 8.1 for an outline of a typical movement in sonata form. This description of sonata form is abstract at this point, and necessarily so. Sonata form is the most complex and most variable form that we will encounter. We can generally predict the broad outline of a sonata-form movement, and we can identify the milestones and the activity in between that make them significant. We cannot be more prescriptive than that. In this chapter, we hear both the consistent elements of and variable paths through sonata form in movements from a piano sonata by Mozart and a string quartet by Haydn.

Introduction	Exposition (may repeat)				Development	Recapitulation				Coda
Optional	1st theme	Transition	2nd theme	Closing Section	Working over of musical ideas; moves away from new key *and* tonic key	1st theme	Transition	2nd theme	Transition	Optional; in tonic key
	In tonic key	Moves to new key	In new key			Return to tonic key				

Figure 8.1 Sonata form.

8-4 Mozart and the Piano Sonata

The sonata at the end of the eighteenth century was a radically different genre from the early eighteenth-century sonata. Only the name remained the same. The differences began with the number of instruments: Baroque sonatas typically required three or four musicians. By contrast, during the latter half of the century, *sonata* almost always referred to an independent, multimovement composition, either for keyboard alone or for keyboard and a melody instrument, usually violin. One finds keyboard sonatas and sonatas for violin (or flute or oboe or any number of popular instruments of the time) and piano listed in publishers' announcements beginning in the 1760s.

Differences between Baroque and Classical sonatas are also evident in other large-scale features, such as the number and sequence of movements and the characteristic forms of these movements. During the late eighteenth century, sonatas usually had three movements. Typically, the first movement had a lively tempo, the second was slower, and the final movement was again fast. The forms of the individual movements were more variable than the tempo sequence.

At the center of this new kind of sonata was the piano, an instrument still in the mind of its inventor, Bartolomeo Cristofori, when Corelli composed his solo and trio sonatas in the Baroque style.

8-4A The Piano

The full name of the instrument we call the piano is *pianoforte*. Its name comes from two Italian words, *piano* and *forte*, the terms for "soft" and "loud." The name of the instrument celebrates the feature that most distinguishes it from the harpsichord, the instrument it would replace: the ability to control dynamic level through touch. On the harpsichord, depressing a key causes a plectrum to pluck a string (or several strings). The action is like an on/off switch: the same amount of sound comes out whether you depress the key gently or firmly. By contrast, the action of the piano is more like a volume control. Depressing a key causes a hammer to strike strings. The speed of the key's descent determines the speed at which the

Eighteenth-century piano. Note that the keyboard spans only five octaves, about two-thirds the span of the modern piano.

hammer strikes the strings: the faster the descent, the louder the sound.

Bartolomeo Cristofori, the instrument keeper for the Medici family, invented the piano. He began work on it about 1700; by 1726, he had resolved many of the mechanical issues. Over the next several decades, other manufacturers, especially in England and German-speaking Europe, made improvements to Cristofori's instrument. By 1780, the piano had almost completely supplanted the harpsichord as the keyboard instrument of choice.

Because of its more sustained tone and capability of note-to-note nuance, the piano assumed a more varied and prominent role in music making, especially in ensemble music. In Baroque ensembles, the harpsichordist generally filled the gap between melody and bass, much like a good rhythm guitarist does in a rock band. By contrast, the pianist could balance other instruments or support them. As a result, it became the preferred solo instrument in concertos, an equal partner in chamber music, and the only accompanying instrument in solo song, a genre that emerged in the late eighteenth century in large part because of the piano. Composers such as Mozart also exploited the distinctive capabilities of the piano in solo literature, most notably in the piano sonata.

Lebrecht Music and Arts Photo Library/Alamy

8-4B Mozart's Sonata in F Major

Mozart composed his Sonata in F major, K. 332, sometime in the early 1780s, around the time he also composed his variations on "Ah, vous dirai-je, Maman." (K. in the titles of Mozart compositions stands for Köchel, the man who attempted to arrange all of Mozart's known works in chronological order.) This sonata and the Haydn string quartet discussed later are among the first works to display those features we associate with the mature Classical style.

The sonata has three movements, in the customary fast-slow-fast sequence. All three make use of the procedures that characterize sonata form; the first movement is the most characteristic realization of the form. In it we hear Mozart evoking a clearly pastoral mood.

The salient features of sonata form, particularly the instability of the transition and development sections, the arrival at the new key with the second theme, and the return to the home key at the beginning of the recapitulation, are clearly evident in this movement. The Listen Up! describes these features in greater detail.

This opening movement of Mozart's piano sonata is about as close to a textbook example of sonata form as one is likely to find. The next example, the first movement of Haydn's String Quartet in C major, resembles the Mozart in its overall design. In other respects, such as the character of the musical material, the proportions between and within sections, there are discernible differences. Comparing them gives us insight into both the fundamental impulses behind sonata form and the variety in its realization.

LEARNING OUTCOME 8-5

Discover the sound of the string quartet, the main chamber ensemble of the Classical era, through a string quartet by Franz Joseph Haydn.

8-5 Haydn and the String Quartet

The string quartet is a chamber ensemble consisting of two violinists, a violist, and a cellist. It is also a work composed for this ensemble. The string quartet was a product of the new sensibility that ultimately shaped the Classical style. It has no direct ancestors of any note. The first quartets date from around 1760, around the time the Classical style began to take shape.

K. Abbreviation in the titles of Mozart compositions that stands for **Köchel**, the man who attempted to arrange all of Mozart's known works in chronological order

string quartet Chamber ensemble consisting of two violinists, a violist, and a cellist; also, a work composed for this ensemble

8-5A Timbre and Texture in the String Quartet

The sound of the string quartet is different from that of any other small-ensemble instrumental music that we have heard because all the instruments share the same basic timbre. For example, in Corelli's solo sonata, the sound of the harpsichord contrasts with the sounds of the violin and cello. Before 1760, this mixing of sounds was virtually universal. There are isolated instances of small-ensemble compositions with instruments whose timbres match, but the norm was an ensemble with mixed timbres. What separated the string quartet (and other all-string chamber groups) from even these isolated examples of matched sound was the fact that composers like Haydn and Mozart composed specifically for the ensemble; string quartets sound best when played by stringed instruments rather than by winds, brass, or keyboards.

The matched timbres of the string quartet opened up a significantly new way of thinking for composers. They could conceive of the string quartet as a single instrument capable of playing four (or more) pitches simultaneously, much like the piano. And as with the piano, it is possible to fine-tune dynamics within the string quartet, not only in shaping a melodic line but also in balancing notes sounding at the same time. So in a homophonic texture, the melody could be loud while the accompanying parts were soft. By contrast, in a more contrapuntal texture, all the parts could operate at about the same dynamic level. The possibility of four musicians playing as if they were a single instrument also gave composers unprecedented flexibility in shaping textures: one could add or subtract instruments, distribute the melody among the various instruments, give each instrument a distinct role, or . . . the possibilities seemed limitless.

> Listeners could conceive of the string quartet as a single instrument capable of playing four (or more) pitches simultaneously, much like the piano.

8-5B Franz Joseph Haydn

Franz Joseph Haydn ♦ is remembered as the father of the symphony and the string quartet. He composed prolifically in both genres: 104 symphonies and sixty-eight quartets.

Haydn was born in Rohrau, a small village about twenty-five miles east of Vienna. As a boy, he sang in the choir at St. Stephen's Cathedral. He left the choir school shortly after his voice broke, then worked as a freelance musician in Vienna until accepting positions with nobility. The first position lasted only a short while. The second, with the Esterházy family, lasted almost thirty years. Duke Nikolaus, Haydn's employer, was wealthy enough to have an orchestra that eventually numbered around twenty musicians. Most of them

 **LISTEN UP!**

Mozart, Sonata in F major, K. 332, 1st movement (early 1780s)

TAKEAWAY POINT: A clear example of sonata form

STYLE: Classical

FORM: Sonata form

GENRE: Piano sonata

INSTRUMENT: Piano

CONTEXT: A composition for professionals and skilled amateurs

EXPOSITION

0:00 *Theme 1:* Three distinct melodic phrases and textures, integrated into one complete statement. Graceful flow and repeated bass note hint at pastoral character.

0:15 *Transition, part 1:* Still in home key, but with new melody. More pastoral hints: hornlike sounds, simple tune, and shepherd falling asleep. The calm before the storm.

0:27 *Transition, part 2:* Abrupt change of key, faster rhythms, rising gestures. Abrupt end followed by pause, all highlighting move to new key. The storm.

0:49 *Theme 2:* Simple tune, with two phrases, confirming the new key. Tune and regular phrase structure help listeners get their bearings.

1:08 "Mystery" section. More material in new key. Syncopation, unsettled harmony, and accents suggest disorientation: perhaps a walk in deep woods?

1:25 Still more material in new key. Another tuneful melody: into the sun again?

1:38 Active, stable material; three short flourishes

EXPOSITION REPEATED

1:53 Graceful theme sets home key and mood.

2:19 "Storm" signals move away from home key.

2:41 Another tuneful melody, but in new key

3:30 Rush to end of section

DEVELOPMENT

3:45 New, lyric theme. Unusual, but not surprising, given the lyric character of opening melody and contrast within first theme.

4:05 Development of "mystery" section. This version is longer, more agitated, and more harmonically unstable. It ends well away from home key.

4:22 Continuation of "mystery" section

4:28 Surprise twist (played loudly) directs the movement to the home key.

RECAPITULATION

4:37 Theme 1

4:51 Transition, part 1

5:04 Transition, part 2

5:31 Theme 2, now in home key

5:49 "Mystery," now framed by music in home key

6:07 Final tuneful melody, also in home key

6:20 Closing section ends movement.

 Listen to this selection streaming or in an Active Listening Guide at CourseMate or in the eBook.

▶Franz Joseph Haydn
FAST FACTS

- Dates: 1732–1809
- Place: Vienna, Austria
- Reason to remember: One of the two greatest composers in the Classical style; father of the symphony and the string quartet

Italian School/The Bridgeman Art Library/Getty Images

had transformed the symphony and string quartet from light entertainment into substantial instrumental genres and elevated his reputation to one of the most distinguished composers in Europe. Upon the death of the duke, Haydn moved to Vienna, where he remained for the rest of his life, except for two visits to London.

Haydn is remembered mainly for his symphonies and quartets. However, he also composed oratorios, masses, operas, concertos, piano sonatas and trios, and many other works. With Mozart, he is considered an exemplar of the Classical style. Although Haydn was old enough to be Mozart's father and they were in quite different professional circumstances—Haydn ensconced at Esterháza, Mozart all over the continent—both seemed to find a new level of mastery around 1780, in much the same way.

had other responsibilities, but one of their main duties was to serve as the court orchestra, either to play concerts or to accompany the operas staged in the palace theater.

The combination of a supportive patron and an in-house orchestra created a laboratory-like environment for Haydn. He was free to experiment and did so, even as other composers throughout Europe were also composing thousands of orchestral works. Although during his tenure, Haydn seldom left Esterháza, his music did. Haydn's reputation grew during the decades he spent there. By the time the duke died in 1790, Haydn

8-5C Haydn's String Quartets

Haydn's compositions seem to fall into two groups: those he composed because he had to, and those he composed because he wanted to. In the first group are works such as his operas and baryton trios (the baryton is a complicated bowed string instrument; Duke Nikolaus played it recreationally), both composed to please his patron. In the latter group are the

Esterháza—often called the Hungarian Versailles—is a magnificent palace containing 126 rooms, including a 400-seat theater.

Maran Garai/Shutterstock.com

symphonies and string quartets; these he composed throughout his career.

Haydn was the musician most responsible for establishing the string quartet as an important genre. He virtually invented the genre; a set of six quartets was his first work and among the very first quartets of which we have record. He returned to the genre on a regular basis throughout most of his career; his last two quartets date from 1799. The quartet that we hear comes from a set of six published as Opus 33 in 1782, around the midpoint of Haydn's career. Haydn saw the quartets as a turning point: he claimed that he had composed them "in a quite new, special manner." He did not specify what was so new or special about them, but a comparison with his earlier quartets suggests that they are simultaneously more sophisticated and more accessible.

8-5D Haydn's Humor

Haydn's compositions seem to attract nicknames, in part because of the vivid sound images that he created and in part because he cracked musical jokes. This third quartet of the set is nicknamed the "Bird"; the second is called the "Joke"; the symphony that we hear in the next chapter is the "Surprise."

Haydn is the funniest "serious composer" in Classical music. No composer was more consistently funny, and no composer found more ways to be funny. Haydn's comic repertoire ranged from musical sleight of hand that would bring a knowing smile to the face of a connoisseur to slapstick effects and barnyard humor.

> Haydn, the funniest "serious composer" in Classical music.

Comedy depends a great deal on surprise and timing. Both depend on expectation. The clarity of Classical style, the product of such features as frequent, decisive punctuation, well-articulated melodies, and predictable harmony, made it possible for listeners to track musical events in a composition and anticipate what might come next. This in turn enabled composers to play with these expectations, often as a matter of course. Sometimes the comic elements are obvious, such as the bird chirps extracted from the first theme. Other times, they are more like inside jokes for musicians.

This isn't to say that the style is only comic. Haydn's music could also be serious, sublime, simple, or spiritual, when his mood or the situation warranted. Rather, it is that the comic has been added to the range of moods and character available to composers such as Haydn and Mozart. There are dark moments in the movement discussed here; part of the magic is that Haydn is able to shift through so many moods in such a short time and that the shifts are not governed by formal conventions. The capability of shifting moods at will is one of the hallmarks of Classical style; it is one of the qualities that make it so thoroughly human. It isn't surprising that Haydn, by all accounts a man of good humor and very much down to earth even though he had become the most distinguished composer in Europe by the 1790s, would play a key role in shaping the style.

In the "Bird" quartet (see Listen Up!), Haydn's humor is evident from the outset. The movement begins tentatively, with neither melody nor bass, and as soon as the key is established, the musicians stop, then resume with the same material but on a different chord. They stop again, only to resume yet again on a harmony that is even farther removed from the key of the movement. In this third try, Haydn finally cadences in the home key and simultaneously sets off on the transition.

Later in the movement, Haydn turns this comic molehill into a mountain. After getting completely lost harmonically during the development—and highlighting it with music that sounds even more indecisive—he begins the recapitulation on a harmony other than the tonic. Only when the cello enters does he present the home chord.

Why would eighteenth-century audiences have found this humorous? There are five structural milestones in a sonata-form movement: establishing the tonic at the outset, establishing the new key later in the exposition, returning to the home key at the beginning of the recapitulation, repeating the second theme in the tonic, and closing the movement with a decisive cadence. Of these, the most dramatic is the coincidence of opening theme and opening harmony at the beginning of the recapitulation.

Return after contrast or development occurs in any movement or movement section in rounded binary form: variation themes, minuets and trios, and the like. Eighteenth-century audiences would have heard this pattern thousands of times. "Sonatafying" this familiar pattern—by expanding the form, adding contrasting material, and making the route back to the home key more tortuous—typically makes the reprise a grander event.

By beginning tentatively and returning even more tentatively, Haydn undermines listeners' expectations for this pattern. It is not slapstick humor, although Haydn's music has some of that. But it probably would have brought a smile to the faces of attentive members of the audience. The larger point is that humor is possible in the Classical style to a far greater degree than in any previous style because the sense of expectation is so strong, so composers such as Haydn and Mozart could subvert these expectations for comic effect.

 **LISTEN UP!**

Haydn, String Quartet in C major ("Bird"), 1st movement (1782)

TAKEAWAY POINT: A good-humored sonata-form movement in a new genre

STYLE: Classical

FORM: Sonata form

GENRE: String quartet

INSTRUMENTS: Two violins, viola, and cello

CONTEXT: A new kind of music for the salon, for professionals or skilled amateurs

EXPOSITION

0:00   *Theme 1:* Three phrases in home key

0:30   *Transition, part 1:* Still in home key. Suddenly more contrapuntal and dense; listen to lower strings.

0:47   *Transition, part 2:* Suddenly in new key, switching between major and minor. Everything is in a higher register. Bird chirps come at 0:58, followed by a strong push to the cadence.

1:15   *Theme 2:* Theme in new, contrasting key.

     A Haydn trademark: this theme is based on the first theme (but more compressed) but follows a different path. As a result, it connects and contrasts at the same time.

1:40   Closing section: active, stable material. A slithery scale slinks down from instrument to instrument.

EXPOSITION REPEATED

1:47   As you listen to the exposition again, notice the flow: first, the start and stop of the first theme

1:57   Then the twofold injection of energy in the transition—first more contrapuntal, then higher, busier, and flirting with a new key and both major and minor

2:33   The more stable second theme, with its recollection of the opening to mark the arrival at a major goal within the exposition

3:02   The shift in character in the closing section

DEVELOPMENT

3:34   *Theme 1:* We can hear in this section what is meant by "development." The raw material is drawn from the exposition—especially the "bird" idea—but recast to make its path far less predictable.

3:59   *Theme 2:* Second theme, but in minor and incomplete, followed by sudden change of texture

4:27   Second theme fragment developed, over and around a cushion of string sound, in minor

4:49   More from transition, still far away from home key; this leads to a back-door return to the first theme in the home key.

RECAPITULATION

5:10   Theme 1, slightly rewritten and cut short

5:38   *Transition, part 2:* All firmly in home key. The transition is typically the most intense part of the exposition, because it is where the change of key takes place. In the recapitulation, there is no change of key, so Haydn truncates it.

6:02   Second theme, now in the home key. Toward the end, Haydn breaks away from literal repetition.

CODA

6:25   Recall that recapitulation usually repeats virtually all of exposition, but with new key material (from second theme to closing section) in home key. Here Haydn deletes the closing section, replacing it with a far more extended ending.

6:46   Surprise ending: return of opening and abrupt stop. This is Haydn's final humorous moment.

 Listen to this selection streaming or in an Active Listening Guide at CourseMate or in the eBook.

Looking Back, Looking Ahead

Our encounter with sonata form and Classical style in two different settings—piano sonata and string quartet—has given us a three-dimensional perspective on both. By comparing the two movements, we can get a workable first impression of both form and style. Two things are evident about sonata form. First, it is not genre dependent; that is, its essential qualities are not dependent on particular combinations of voices and instruments. Second, its basic architecture and the procedures used to animate it remain consistent from work to work, but they can be realized in infinitely varied ways.

Among the salient characteristics of Classical style that emerge from the two musical examples are frequent contrast, typically articulated by decisive punctuation, and a strong sense of moving toward goals. This is apparent on the smallest and largest scales. Sections generally contain multiple melodic ideas, varied rhythms, frequent changes in texture, dynamic contrast, and gradual change, and activity generally increases as the music approaches a cadence. The two strongest gestures in a sonata-form movement are the transition, which signals the move to the new key, and the development, which leads the music back to the home key via a circuitous route.

We next add new dimensions to our understanding of both sonata form and Classical style through two orchestral genres, the symphony and the piano concerto.

 study tools 8

LEARNING OUTCOMES

After studying this chapter, you will be able to do the following:

9-1 Describe the instruments and orchestration of the Classical orchestra.

9-2 Be familiar with the Classical symphony, as exemplified by Haydn's Symphony No. 94.

9-3 Understand the form and style of the Classical piano concerto.

9-4 Explore the first movement of a Mozart piano concerto in detail.

 study tools

After you read this chapter, go to the Study Tools at the end of the chapter, page 133.

Shortly after Haydn relocated to Vienna in 1790, Johann Peter Salomon, a composer, violinist, and concert promoter, came to Vienna to personally invite Haydn to England, where he already enjoyed an enthusiastic following. Haydn accepted Salomon's invitation, which included lucrative guarantees for several works, including six symphonies. Haydn arrived in England for the first time on January 2, 1791, and stayed through the following year. The visit was successful enough that he returned in 1794 for another visit, once again producing six new symphonies.

9-1 The Orchestra in the Classical Era

London, then as now, was a great place to hear orchestral music. The orchestra that Salomon made available to Haydn for his first visit included about forty musicians. By the time of his second visit, it had grown to about sixty. Salomon's London orchestras suggest the extent to which the orchestra grew in size during the eighteenth century. Much of the growth was due to the addition of string players. However, the most significant change in the orchestra was the permanent addition of woodwind, brass, and percussion instruments.

9-1A The Instruments of the Classical Orchestra

The six symphonies that Haydn composed for his first visit to London require not only a good-sized string section but also pairs of flutes, oboes, bassoons, trumpets, horns, and timpani—all of which had been in use throughout the eighteenth century. Those he composed for his second visit included all of the above instruments plus a pair of clarinets.

The major difference between early and late eighteenth-century orchestras was that these new instruments were no longer optional. In the latter half of the century, compositions that required an orchestra—symphonies, concertos, operas, and sacred choral works—were scored for strings and most or all of these woodwind, brass, and percussion instruments, and occasionally even more. Woodwinds became permanent parts of the orchestra in stages: first oboes, then flutes and bassoons, and finally clarinets. Horns were the first brass instrument to become a permanent part of the orchestra; they were part of the orchestra in the most of the early Classical symphonies. Trumpets and timpani were used intermittently during the last quarter of the century but did not become fixtures in the symphonic orchestra until the 1790s.

The woodwinds of the late eighteenth century are fundamentally similar to their modern counterparts. They lack the keys found on contemporary instruments but were capable of playing all the notes in all keys throughout the range of the instrument. By contrast, the brass instruments of the late eighteenth century did not have the valves or pistons that enabled performers to easily play all the notes of the scale. Hornists developed

Wind, brass, and percussion were permanently added to the orchestra in the Classical era.

techniques that enabled them to play most notes of a scale. By contrast, late eighteenth-century trumpets could play far fewer, so their role was more limited. Timpani of the era were limited to one note per drum, because they could not be tuned easily once a work was under way; the mechanical device that allows rapid tuning of the drum had not been invented. As a result, a timpanist typically had two or three timpani at his disposal.

Salomon's orchestra is the core of the modern symphony orchestra. Other wind, brass, and percussion instruments would be added in subsequent generations, but the main instruments within each section of the orchestra were already present. This is one important reason why contemporary symphony orchestras perform Mozart and Haydn far more frequently than they do Bach and Handel.

9-1B Orchestrating the Classical Symphony

The addition of winds, brass, and percussion added a wealth of tone color and greatly expanded the opportunity for timbral, dynamic, and textural contrast. Winds, brass, even percussion could share the solo spotlight with strings, and the dynamic range grew significantly—from one or two instruments alone to the massed orchestra. Even more striking are the new textures made possible by the choir of winds plus trumpets, horns, and timpani.

Frequent and vivid contrasts in timbre, dynamics, and texture are one quality that distinguishes the Classical symphony from earlier orchestral music. We consider other distinguishing features in a brief introduction to the *symphony*, that long, multimovement work for symphony orchestra.

9-2 The Classical Symphony

Haydn arrived in London as a celebrity. He was received by royalty, granted an honorary doctorate at Oxford, and attended numerous events, including concerts at Westminster Abbey (where he heard Handel's oratorios performed). Although his contract with Salomon included the six symphonies as well as an opera and twenty other compositions, the symphonies were clearly the centerpiece of the contract. They were the highlight of the concerts in which they were presented; unlike contemporary orchestra concerts, these also included a fair amount of non-orchestral music. Critics couldn't find enough good things to say about Haydn's music.

These circumstances—Haydn's visit, the active concert scene in London, Salomon's administrative and musical skill, the receptiveness of the London audience and critics—all point to a dramatic shift in urban musical life. Vocal music—opera and oratorio—was no longer preeminent in public performance. Instrumental music, and the symphony in particular, had grown in prestige during the eighteenth century; by the end of the century, some even considered it equal or superior to vocal music as a form of musical expression.

9-2A Haydn's Late Symphonies

The large-scale organization of Haydn's London symphonies follows a well-established plan. Typically, a symphony had four movements. The first movement might begin at a fast tempo, or it might have a slow introduction. In either event, the fast part would be cast in sonata form. The second movement was slow and could take almost any form, from a trimmed-down sonata form to simple variations. The third movement was either a minuet, a popular eighteenth-century dance in triple meter, or a scherzo, a playful, more high-spirited alternative. Although both minuet and scherzo derived from dance music, neither was music for dancing. The last movement was typically a rondo, a form in which a tuneful and simple opening theme returns again and again.

In the Classical symphony, this sequence of movements was front weighted. That is, the forms that require more attention from the audience occur earlier; those that were easier to follow come later. This is in part a response to the relative complexity of sonata form. The increased length of the movements is also a likely factor: by way of example, a performance of all three movements of Vivaldi's "Spring" takes less time than a performance of the first movement of the "Surprise" symphony.

9-2B Haydn's Symphony No. 94, First Movement

As we noted in Chapter 2, Haydn's Symphony No. 94 owes its nickname—the "Surprise" symphony—to the loud chords that periodically disrupt the soft statement of the simple melody that opens the second movement. However, the entire symphony is full of surprises, although the others are more subtle and sophisticated than the famous chords.

In the first movement (see Listen Up!), Haydn's surprises have to do with the expectations for sonata form. By the time of the work's premiere in 1792, he had composed hundreds of works in which he employed sonata form, and he evidently assumed that his London audiences were familiar with the form, through listening and performance.

For listeners, it is the outlining features—decisive punctuations and memorable themes marking the main structural goals—that most clearly mark the progress through a movement in sonata form, while the ebb and flow of activity that leads to and continues from major landmarks give shape to the form. In the first movement, Haydn deliberately subverts these expectations: the most decisive and memorable melodic material is displaced; it does not line up with the important structural goals. He uses the introduction to set up these surprises.

In general, the primary function of the introduction is to convey a sense of solemnity and importance—to let the audience know that something significant is under way. The clearest clue is the stately tempo, but the character of the melodic material typically contributes as well. As a rule, introductions simply precede the main part of the movement; it is rare that musical material from the introduction returns later in the movement in its original form. But that is the case here.

However, the introduction in this symphony seems to set off a chain reaction. Because it begins with a simple tuneful melody that immediately locks in the home key, the introduction seems to absolve Haydn of the need to use the first and second themes to orient the listener. As a result, the first theme is just a wisp of a melody that begins far away from the home key; it lasts only a few

symphony An extended work for orchestra that typically contains four movements: a first movement in sonata form, a slow movement, a minuet or scherzo, and a finale

scherzo Playful, high-spirited third movement of a four-movement instrumental composition, such as a symphony or string quartet

LISTEN UP!

Haydn, Symphony No. 94 in G major (the "Surprise"), 1st movement (1792)

TAKEAWAY POINT: The sound of the Classical orchestra in a high-spirited and good-humored symphony

STYLE: Classical

FORM: Sonata form

GENRE: Symphony

INSTRUMENTS: Symphony orchestra: full string section plus flutes, oboes, bassoons, horns, trumpets, and timpani

CONTEXT: A work composed for Haydn's first visit to London

INTRODUCTION

0:00   Tuneful melody, in four clearly defined phrases. Dialogue between winds (oboe prominent) and strings.

0:31   Repeated notes, unsettled harmony replace simple, stable melody of opening. No real melody; lower parts more active. Helps convey sense of mystery.

0:54   Gradually stabilizes, preparing the fast part of the movement. Violins take over, gradually settling in on chord that prepares the home key.

EXPOSITION

1:15   *Theme 1:* Short, tuneful phrase, followed by vigorous new music in home key. We hear the same pattern three times: soft wisp of a theme, followed by loud, active material that firmly establishes the key.

1:47   *Transition, part 1:* Tuneful melody again, followed by transition material that moves to new key

2:10   *Transition, part 2:* Opening melody in another key, signaling a turbulent section that ends up preparing the contrasting key used for theme 2

2:27   *Theme 2:* Single note, repeated several times in syncopated rhythm, gradually giving way to more active rhythms, all leading to a cadence

2:47   More lyric theme with rich accompaniment, in new key. Stated twice, the second time extended. The most relaxed section of exposition.

3:18   Busy closing material, but in the new key. Ends with a repeated note rather than a strong cadence. The first time it leads smoothly back to the first theme.

EXPOSITION REPEATED

3:31   *Theme 1:* Short, tuneful phrase, followed immediately by vigorous new music

4:03   *Transition, part 1:* Tuneful melody again, followed by transition material that moves to new key

4:26   *Transition, part 2:* Opening melody yet again, signaling a turbulent section that ends up preparing the new key

4:44   *Theme 2:* Single note, in syncopated rhythm gradually giving way to more active rhythms, all leading to a cadence

5:03   More lyric theme

5:34   Busy closing material, but in the new key. This time it leads to the new version of the theme that begins the development.

DEVELOPMENT

5:47   Immediate variation on first theme: new key, expanded melodic curve, fragmentation of melody

Sunny beginning to the development, but gradually clouding over

6:11   Stormy section: loud, with sharp contrasts, quick exchanges, key shifts

The "storm" leaves us completely disoriented.

6:48   Stabilizes on a chord, then a single note, which leads back to the first theme.

The storm subsides—is it a momentary lull? We wonder as we listen to the repeated note.

Continued

RECAPITULATION

6:57   First theme, as before

       The biggest surprise in the movement: unobtrusive return of opening theme. Haydn omits the transition section that effects the change of key, instead pretending to move by developing earlier material, but "staying home."

7:29   More development of the end of the previous section, instead of return to the main theme

7:39   Syncopated melody and accompaniment again, now in home key

7:59   Opening theme again, this time in lower strings, and developed

       Yet another surprise: instead of simply repeating last part of exposition in new key, Haydn plays with opening theme, expanding it and grounding it firmly in home key.

8:31   Opening theme again, but grounded in the home key and featuring woodwinds

8:49   Lyric theme from exposition, but in the home key

9:20   Closing material, with added emphasis to bring the movement to a close

 Listen to this selection streaming or in an Active Listening Guide at CourseMate or in the eBook.

seconds before being overrun by a vigorous new section. The remainder of the movement takes its cue from the first theme: the other most surprising moments occur at those points in the form where we expect the greatest clarity: the entrance of the second theme, the end of the exposition, and the beginning of the recapitulation. In each case, we expect a decisive punctuation and a memorable melody. But in this symphony, these junctures seem to whiz by; we discover only after the fact that we have passed a major point of arrival in the form. It is the material that comes later that seems to best fit our expectations for first- and second-theme material. These are the most apparent of numerous surprises throughout the movement, from the "mystery" section in the introduction to the pseudo-development and the restatement of the opening theme by the lower strings in the recapitulation. Haydn's London audience certainly would have heard it as "something new."

9-2C **Second Movement**

In Classical instrumental compositions, the second movement is the only movement that does *not* have a characteristic form. In this particular case, Haydn opts for the most accessible of all instrumental forms, theme and variations (see Listen Up!).

    The second movement of Haydn's symphony gives us a new perspective on variation form and his sense of humor. Unlike the piano variations we've heard earlier, Haydn's variation movement was conceived from the start as a composed work for orchestra rather than an improvised set of variations for a solo instrument. This may account for the nature of the variations—far greater emphasis on variation in texture, timbre, and dynamics than on melodic embellishment. Indeed, the theme is present throughout most of the variations but is overlaid with other melodic parts. Good humor is most evident in the theme, but it is marbled through the entire movement. There are other funny moments right up through the buildup to the cadenza that never happens. Such passages contain some of the most obvious humor in the symphony.

9-2D **Third Movement**

During the eighteenth century, the minuet was an elegant court dance. It is in a simple triple meter, most

The minuet began as an elegant court dance in which dancers usually moved apart from one another.

minuet Dance in triple meter, the most popular dance of the eighteenth century among the aristocracy; often the third movement of a four-movement instrumental composition

Haydn, Symphony No. 94 in G major (the "Surprise"), 2nd movement (1792)

TAKEAWAY POINT: The sound of the Classical orchestra in a high-spirited and good-humored symphony

STYLE: Classical

FORM: Theme and variations

GENRE: Symphony

INSTRUMENTS: Symphony orchestra: full string section plus flutes, oboes, bassoons, horns, trumpets, and timpani

CONTEXT: A work composed for Haydn's first visit to London

THEME

0:00   First part of theme. An extremely simple melody, which Haydn presents innocently. This sets up the surprise at the end of the first part, when it's repeated.

0:17   First part, repeated

0:34   Second part of theme. Now that the surprise has passed, Haydn continues with a more elaborate melody and richer accompaniment.

VARIATION 1: TEXTURAL

1:07   Theme in middle strings; countermelody in first violins. This variation makes clear that Haydn is taking a different approach to variation form. The theme is still heard, like a cantus firmus, and Haydn varies the texture by adding a countermelody rather than varying the melody. Notice another wakeup chord at the beginning of the repeat of the first part.

1:25   Repeat of first phrase, as before

1:41   Second phrase: same plan—first violin countermelody; melody in second violins

1:57   Repeat of second phrase, as before

VARIATION 2: DEVELOPMENTAL

2:14   Switch to minor mode. The melody begins much like the original theme but turns in a new direction around the halfway point. The first part uses a typical Haydn melodic strategy: use a recognizable version of the first part of a melody as the starting point for a new melody.

The development-like section that substitutes for the second part breaks up the regular rhythm of the form.

2:30   First part repeated

2:46   Agitated development-like section replaces second half of melody; gentle return to major theme.

VARIATION 3: TIMBRAL

3:22   Simple oboe variation on main theme. This variation is a showcase for the winds.

3:38   Repeat of first phrase, with new variation/orchestration: strings have melody; flutes play countermelody.

3:55   Second phrase of melody, continuing flute/violin orchestration

4:12   Repeat of second phrase: sustained bass note (pedal tone) added, then rising horns

VARIATION 4: DYNAMICS

4:29   Full orchestra: melody in winds; figuration in strings for first phrase. This is, in effect, two variations in one: the outer sections feature full orchestra, thick texture; contrasting inner sections are soft, with a variation of the melody and a much thinner texture.

4:46   Repeat: soft, melodic variation, played by violins

5:02   Second part continues melodic variation, played by violins.

5:19   Return to opening full orchestra sound and texture; theme in the melody

CODA

5:37   Blustery passage, followed by a simple melodic fragment borrowed from the theme

This passage is another connoisseur's joke: the orchestra plays the kind of music that precedes a concerto cadenza, the part where the soloist shows off. But this is not a concerto, and the music continues as simply as possible. All this turns out to be much ado about very little.

5:55   Final version of first phrase, this time in home key. Bass note, played by low strings and timpani (fast repeated note) also grounds the movement in the home key. Gentle ending.

 Listen to this selection streaming or in an Active Listening Guide at CourseMate or in the eBook.

often at a moderate or slow tempo, which allowed for dignified and graceful movement. Dancers followed a strict protocol in performing the minuet. Couples took turns on the dance floor as the other members of the aristocracy in attendance watched. They followed a thoroughly worked-out choreography consisting mainly of small steps, usually tracing a "Z" across the dance floor. The dancers usually moved apart from one another, though occasionally they met and held hands.

From the start, the minuet enjoyed a life apart from the dance floor. In the first part of the century, it was one of the optional dances in the Baroque suite, as well as a popular independent piece. There are thousands of keyboard minuets from Bach's time; then as now, they made good teaching pieces. The minuet remained popular in the latter part of the century as a social dance and a dance-based independent instrumental piece—most of Mozart's first compositions were minuets for keyboard. More important, it served as a movement in sonatas, symphonies, and other multimovement compositions. In the symphony, it was the third of four movements, after the slow second movement and before the finale. Indeed, the minuet was only one of the early eighteenth-century dances to flourish in the latter part of the century.

The Form of Minuets. A minuet movement usually includes three independent musical units: minuet, trio, and a reprise of the minuet. As a rule, minuet and trio are complete musical units; typically each could stand alone as an independent piece. Most often, minuet and trio contrast in mood, and the trio is not as expansive as the minuet. That is the case here.

The rounded binary form that we hear in both minuets is different from the rounded binary form of the variation themes used by Mozart or the binary form of the theme of the second movement. In the first part, Haydn moves away from the home key; the cadence at the end of the first part is in a new key. The music that begins the second part starts in the new key and returns to the home key after a fairly long digression. Earlier, we noted that sonata form is rounded binary form greatly expanded. The rounded binary form used in both minuets is closer to sonata form, in size and harmonic plan, than the earlier examples.

Haydn's Minuet. Haydn's minuet begins as a heavy-footed peasant dance, rather than an elegant accompaniment for aristocrats. The gentler continuation and the flourish that ends the first part move the music up both the social and the musical scale. In the second part of the minuet, Haydn goes to the other extreme as the second part begins, writing first a contrapuntal passage, then a passage that passes through several keys. The rest of the second part gives further evidence of the range of Haydn's art—more buffoonery plus magical compositional tricks. These are noted in the Listen Up! As is the norm, the trio is contrasting in mood and more modest in its dimensions.

Haydn's minuet uses the dance as a point of departure. However, the numerous contrasts in character, the comic gestures, the developmental passages, and the irregular phrase structure show that the movement is much more closely aligned with the first two movements than it is with music for dancing. Title to the contrary, this is dance-inspired concert music, not music for dancing. In its journey from the ballroom to the concert hall, the minuet grew in size and scope and moved away from its roots in dance.

9-2E Fourth Movement

The fourth movement is a rondo. A **rondo** is a form in which a tuneful and simple opening theme returns again and again, but only after alternating with one or more contrasting themes, much as a chorus does in vocal music. And like the chorus, the rondo theme serves as a formal anchor, the spot where we can get our bearings. By contrast, what happens between statements of the rondo theme is completely variable. It can be a succession of new ideas, or other material presented earlier can return.

Sometimes, we hear the entire theme; on other occasions, we may hear just a section of it. In this respect, it is very much like ritornello form. There are, however, several differences between the ritornello form of the Baroque **concerto** and Classical rondo form. Two stand out: First, the Classical rondo theme is a self-contained unit—a complete musical sentence that could stand alone if necessary. The other is that the material between statements of this rondo theme *contrasts* with it instead of amplifying the basic message, as is the case in a Baroque concerto, say, in the "spring" themes throughout Vivaldi's concerto.

In this movement, we can get a sense of how what was subsequently called "sonata form" was for Haydn and his contemporaries a common compositional process that could be used and adapted to other forms. The sequence of events outlined in the Listen Up! highlights the unmistakable parallel with first-movement sonata form. Virtually all of the material that contrasts with the rondo theme functions like its sonata-form counterparts: transition, second theme, closing material, development.

Still, there is a crucial difference: the numerous restatements of the rondo theme. This familiar theme signals the periodic returns to the home key. These returns release any accumulated musical tension rather than continuing and intensifying it by moving further away from the home key. That is one reason why a rondo, even a "sonata-form rondo," has a much higher comfort level than a movement in sonata form.

rondo Form in which a tuneful and simple opening theme returns again and again but only after alternating with one or more contrasting themes

concerto In the Classical era, a work for solo instrument and orchestra in which the soloist counterbalances the greater numbers of the orchestra through virtuosity, harmonic ingenuity, and lyricism

Haydn, Symphony No. 94 in G major (the "Surprise"), 3rd movement (1792)

TAKEAWAY POINT: The sound of the Classical orchestra in a high-spirited and good-humored symphony

STYLE: Classical

FORM: Minuet and trio

GENRE: Symphony

INSTRUMENTS: Symphony orchestra: full string section, plus flutes, oboes, bassoons, horns, trumpets, and timpani

CONTEXT: A work composed for Haydn's first visit to London

MINUET

0:00   First section: two phrases—the first rustic and the second refined. Notice the very end of the first part, right after the scale in the violins. This becomes the material that is developed in the next section.

0:18   First phrase, repeated

0:36   Developmental section: Haydn moves effortlessly from high art to low humor in this section. He begins the second part by treating the last phrase of the first part contrapuntally, then takes a fragment of it and runs it through several keys. As he prepares the return to the home key, he uses the little three-note scale fragment with which the movement began. We hear it three times in the orchestra—at which point the return could begin. Instead, Haydn interpolates two more, the first with the flute, then—upside down—with the bassoon, often regarded as the buffoon of the orchestra. This is clearly comic.

1:21   Developmental section again

1:43   Return

TRIO

2:09   First phrase: The trio is much shorter and more regular: the first part is two 4-measure phrases.

2:17   First phrase, repeated

2:26   Development of first phrase: Some gentle humor from Haydn: the developmental section of the second part breaks up the regular rhythm of the first part to make the timing of the return of the beginning a surprise. We know it's coming, but Haydn makes *when* a guess—the spinning around in the melody just before the return underscores this point.

2:38   Return of the first phrase, but redirected to the home key

2:46   Development, repeated

2:58   Return of the modified first phrase, repeated

MINUET, WITHOUT REPEATS

3:07   First part, as before

3:23   Development, as before

4:17   Return, as before

 Listen to this selection streaming or in an Active Listening Guide at CourseMate or in the eBook.

Judging by the evidence of thousands of compositions, Classical composers usually wanted to end larger works in an upbeat mood. Rondo form was the most popular choice because of two features of the form: the periodic return of the opening theme and the timing of the return. The frequent return of the rondo theme after an excursion into a new key releases any musical tension that has built up. And because the returns are easily anticipated, composers can tease their audience by delaying the return or avoiding it altogether by heading off on a different tangent. In combination, these features make rondo form an ideal vehicle for a fun, high-spirited, and comfortable movement.

9-2F Haydn, the Symphony, and Classical Style: Something for Everyone

Haydn's "Surprise" symphony has been a favorite of audiences for over two hundred years. Audiences loved this symphony in 1792, and they love it now. One reason is that there's something for everyone. The musical

 **LISTEN UP!**

Haydn, Symphony No. 94 in G major (the "Surprise"), 4th movement (1792)

TAKEAWAY POINT: The sound of the Classical orchestra in a high-spirited and good-humored symphony

STYLE: Classical

FORM: Rondo

GENRE: Symphony

INSTRUMENTS: Symphony orchestra: full string section plus flutes, oboes, bassoons, horns, trumpets, and timpani

CONTEXT: A work composed for Haydn's first visit to London

A: RONDO THEME

0:00   Four sections: The first two are identical, the third contrasts, and the fourth is a varied version of the first.

0:31   Transition-like material

B: CONTRASTING THEME

1:02   Contrasting theme

1:13   Closing material, followed by a little transition that leads back to the rondo theme

A: RONDO THEME

1:27   Rondo theme fragment—just the first phrase

C: "DEVELOPMENT," PART 1

1:33   Development-like section

A: RONDO THEME

2:02   Rondo theme

C: "DEVELOPMENT," PART 2

2:09   Another developmental section, this time beginning in minor mode

A: RONDO THEME

2:32   Rondo theme—the first part plus the contrasting section of the second part

2:47   Surprise! An early transition. Instead of restating the last part of the theme, Haydn develops it.

B: CONTRASTING THEME

2:57   Contrasting theme, in the home key

A: RONDO THEME

3:11   Rondo theme—or so it seems: it begins to disintegrate. Instead of the closing material, Haydn quotes the beginning of the rondo theme.

3:15   Timpani wakeup call: detour, then closing material

3:41   The last laugh. Typically, the work would remain strong and forceful to the very end. The meek little woodwind toots here show Haydn's sense of humor carrying through to the end.

 Listen to this selection streaming or in an Active Listening Guide at CourseMate or in the eBook.

events cross class boundaries; they range from folklike materials to passages of great sophistication. His audience may have been dazzled by the first movement, but after the first performance they probably left the theater humming the tune of the second movement.

The mix of art and accessibility was the norm during the latter half of the eighteenth century. But Haydn's music is both more accessible and more artful than that of any other composer of his time, with the exception of Mozart.

9-3 The Classical Concerto

You're at a symphony orchestra concert. The program includes an overture to Verdi's opera *La forza del destino*, Mozart's Concerto in C minor for piano (the work discussed later), and Tchaikovsky's Fourth Symphony. The members of the orchestra gradually take their places. The concertmaster comes onstage; the oboist plays an A, the note to which the rest of the orchestra will tune. The musicians tune, then become quiet. So does the audience, in anticipation of the conductor's entrance. The conductor walks onstage, acknowledges the audience with a generous bow, then takes his place at the podium. He raises his baton and with a bold gesture commands the brass players to intone their solemn call. Although this is an overture for an opera, there are no sets, nor are there singers. This is an in-concert performance of part of an opera that is strictly orchestral. The overture concludes with a flourish, led by brass and timpani. The conductor turns to the audience, thanks them with a bow, steps down from the podium, and walks offstage.

> Mozart's late concertos, especially those he composed for his own use, were instrumental dramas in which he was not only the star but also the only main character.

The musicians stand up as stagehands move their chairs to clear a space at the front of the stage. Some of the musicians leave because they will not be needed in the next work. In a few minutes, a grand piano—nine feet in length—is situated in front of the podium, the stage is rearranged, and the musicians have returned to their seats. The concertmaster stands up, walks over to the piano, and plays the tuning note. The orchestra tunes to the A from the piano, then grows quiet once again; so does the audience. The conductor comes onstage once again, but this time he is preceded by a young Asian woman, the soloist in the Mozart concerto. She is elegantly dressed in a long sleeveless gown that allows complete freedom of movement in her arms. She and the conductor acknowledge the applause of the audience; she takes her seat at the piano while the conductor steps up on the podium. Once in place, he turns to the soloist, as if to ask, "Are you ready?" She answers with an affirmative nod. Again he raises his baton, but this time he begins with a subtle gesture, to express the soft, suspenseful beginning of the concerto. The young pianist sits quietly at the piano for over two minutes, while the orchestra plays the first part of the concerto.

Stuart Monk/Shutterstock.com

They conclude, and she begins to play a mournful melody. For almost half a minute, there is no orchestral accompaniment; it is as if Mozart is shining a spotlight on the piano. Then the orchestra enters again, and the interplay between soloist and orchestra begins.

The concert that you're attending is an orchestral concert, not an opera. But the influence of opera pervades the first half of the program. It is explicit in the Verdi overture and implicit in Mozart's concerto. Indeed, Mozart's late piano concertos are the closest that instrumental music has come to opera-like drama. The only thing that could make the drama more evident would be to have the soloist walk on after the orchestra has begun to play, arriving at the piano just in time to play—much like a leading character in an opera making a grand entrance.

9-3A The Concerto in Late Eighteenth-Century Cultural Life

Quick question: What are the names of the four Beatles? It's a good bet that you know, and if you don't, it's an even better bet that your parents—and grandparents—do. It seems to be a basic urge, at least in our culture, to relate to individuals, to single them out even when they're part of a group. This impulse helps explain the transformation of the Baroque concerto, a genre in which the soloist emerges from the orchestra, into the Classical concerto, in which the soloist is set off against the orchestra.

This transformation was a consequence of several major changes in musical life during the latter part of the eighteenth century: the continued growth of instrumental music, major improvements in the piano, the emergence of instrumental stars, and the increasing frequency of public concerts. These circumstances created an ideal breeding ground for a new kind of concerto. Hundreds of composers began turning out thousands of concertos, for keyboard and most orchestral instruments. The most familiar concertos of the Classical era are those of Mozart, who understood the dramatic potential of the genre far better than any of his contemporaries.

Mozart frequently performed his concertos in public concerts. These public concerts were far different from contemporary orchestral concerts. The music was new—in Mozart's case, so new at times that the ink was barely dry—and the programs were far more diverse. They were showcases for a particular composer rather than the revival of traditional repertoire. And they were usually ad hoc affairs; resident orchestras, concert series, and other institutions found in contemporary musical life did not exist.

Public concerts did not replace private engagements before royalty and in the homes of the aristocracy. But they did add an important new outlet and source of income for musicians, especially those with an entrepreneurial bent.

9-3B Mozart and the Classical Concerto

The concertos of Mozart, especially the keyboard concertos, are the only eighteenth-century concertos that routinely appear on the concert programs of contemporary symphony orchestras. There are practical reasons for this: the late keyboard concertos typically have full wind sections (that is the case here), so more of the orchestra is used. There are aesthetic reasons as well: Mozart's concertos are marvelous works. They strike an ideal balance between solo and orchestra. Still another reason is that they are the first concertos that truly embody our contemporary understanding of the concerto and concerto performance: the soloist is a star; the orchestra can be a partner, an adversary, a support system, or occasionally just a bystander.

For many of the later concertos, Mozart himself was the star performer. These concertos, including the Concerto in C minor discussed presently, received their first performances at concerts of his music, which might also include a symphony, vocal music, and improvisations. Mozart's concertos introduce a new relationship between soloist and orchestra, one that is fundamentally different from that heard in Baroque concertos.

9-3C The Concerto, from Baroque to Classical

Recall that the concerto movements by Vivaldi and Bach open with an orchestral ritornello. Solo passages, no matter how brilliant, expanded on the character of the ritornello. In the sense that the music played by the orchestra determined the fundamental character of the movement, the orchestra was in charge.

By contrast, in the Classical concerto, the soloist is heard *in opposition to* the orchestra rather than as an extension of it. The idea of opposition and its harmonious resolution is inherent in the Classical style. In instrumental music, this dialectic is realized most powerfully in the concerto, in part because composers can put a face on it: soloist versus orchestra, more than soloist with orchestra, or orchestra with soloists. This is apparent visually and aurally—in performance one hears and sees the contrast between solo and orchestra, when that is the intent of the composer.

9-3D The Keyboard Concerto

Piano concertos are different in kind from all other solo concertos because the piano is a self-sufficient solo instrument. That is, pianists can play both melody and harmony, with as many parts as necessary to create a complete texture, as we heard in Mozart's piano sonata. It was—and is—customary to compose for piano alone, in ways that are not possible on the violin, bassoon, horn, or any other orchestral instrument.

The harpsichord has the same capability, but it does not have the capacity for the expressive nuance that was so important to post-Baroque composers. For this reason, composers wrote far more flute and violin concertos than keyboard concertos in the 1750s and 1760s. However, as the piano replaced the harpsichord as the keyboard instrument of choice in the 1770s, piano concertos appeared on concert programs far more frequently. Mozart's piano concertos, most of which were composed after 1780, far outnumber his concertos for all other instruments combined.

A piano concerto is—or can be—an unequal contest among equals. Piano and orchestra are equal in the sense that both can provide complete textures: melody, accompaniment, even countermelody. The pianist can play alone for extended stretches or exchange musical ideas back and forth with the orchestra without the feeling that something is missing. However, in terms of forces, it's David versus Goliath: one modestly loud instrument versus an orchestra of thirty or more musicians. No one understood the dramatic potential of this dynamic better than Mozart, and no one surpassed his strategy for bringing this inequality into balance.

9-3E Mozart and the Keyboard Concerto

Of the twenty-seven concertos typically attributed to Mozart, only the last eighteen are customarily played. These eighteen concertos (seventeen for one piano, and one for two pianos) fall into two groups: those he composed for others, most notably his student Barbara Ployer, and those he composed for his own use. Many of those he composed for himself are identifiable by what they lack: notes in the solo part. (Mozart knew in general what he wanted to play, so at times he left just enough information to reconstruct his part in performance or outline a passage that he would improvise.)

We know that Mozart had an unsurpassed affinity for drama through music. So it is only a small step to understand Mozart's late concertos, especially those he composed for his own use, as instrumental dramas, dramas in which he was not only the star but also the only main character. It is from this perspective that we consider the first movement of his Concerto in C minor (see Listen Up!).

Mozart, Concerto in C minor, 1st movement (1786)

TAKEAWAY POINT: Instrumental music as tragic drama

STYLE: Classical

FORM: Classical concerto form (expansion of sonata form)

GENRE: Concerto

INSTRUMENTS: Piano and symphony orchestra with strings, winds, brass, and timpani

CONTEXT: Mozart showcases himself in public performance as a composer, pianist, and improviser

FULL EXPOSITION

0:00   *Theme 1*: The opening theme is deliberately unsettling, evident in immediate move away from tonic and dramatic syncopations.

0:17   *Transition, part 1*: Opening theme, this time very loud. Restatement of theme is open ended, leading to the next section without a cadence on the tonic.

0:37   *Transition, part 2*: This kind of activity normally signals the move to a new key, but Mozart never leaves the tonic.

0:47   *Transition, part 3*: More development of a motive from opening theme, featuring winds

0:59   *Theme 2*: Winds in lyric moments. Not complete melodies, but melody-like fragments. Notice that they mainly descend, lending an air of sadness.

1:26   *Theme 1*: Opening theme returns.

1:40   More lyric moments; dialogue between warm strings and cool winds.

2:05   Closing-type material: a severe sound. Long–short rhythm and descending melodic lines reinforce dark mood.

SOLO EXPOSITION

2:18   Soloist alone, playing lyric melody. Operatic influence is evident in character of soloist's first entrance: his first responsibility is to "sing," or play a singable melody.

2:45   Orchestra reenters with opening theme, but piano takes over. In this passage, the soloist in effect shows the orchestra how to move to a new key. He ends with a flourish: rapid figuration that highlights his facility.

3:24   New melody in new key, played first by piano and then by winds. To signal change of key, Mozart gives soloist a new and expressive melodic line. However, like the earlier melodic lines, it isn't really a complete, self-sufficient melody.

3:48   Piano figuration, supported by sustained chords and melodic fragments in winds. Another demonstration of soloist's virtuosity. Notice that there are several different patterns, including one with a more singable melodic part.

4:33   Another lyric moment, featuring oboe, strings, piano. Contest between pianist and orchestra is even enough that orchestra can introduce another lyric melody. You can clearly hear contrast between coolness of winds and warmth of strings.

5:01   Main theme in new key; flute has melody, piano accompanies with arpeggios. Return of opening theme disrupts the calm of the preceding section. A new role for the soloist: an intricate accompaniment for the melody.

5:28   More figuration with piano in spotlight. Mozart's invention isn't limited to melody. Running passages are as varied as themes. This section makes a big push to a cadence that marks the beginning of an extended orchestral statement.

TUTTI/DEVELOPMENT

5:59   Central tutti: strong orchestral statement, with melody from opening theme. This section functions much like a major mid-movement ritornello in a Baroque concerto, reasserting the primacy of the orchestra.

6:23   Singing theme returns, leading to development. Piano answers by returning to singing melodic line of its first entrance. As in exposition, the solo leads the way in exploring new keys.

6:50   Opening theme again, developed; beginning of the most unstable section of a very unsettled piece

7:27   Rapid exchanges between orchestra and soloist. Power versus brilliance: strong orchestral statements answered by rocketing soloist arpeggios.

7:47   Another turbulent passage, leading back to main theme. Notice especially the rich texture: sustained strings, active wind lines, rapid scales in piano.

RECAPITULATION

8:08   Opening theme, orchestra, and then piano almost immediately, as in solo exposition. This version of opening theme wanders even farther away from home key.

Continued

8:34	Pianist takes over material from first exposition.
8:48	The last lyric melody of the solo exposition: oboe, then strings and piano, with piano version in a higher key.
9:16	Pianist's second theme melody. It was in major in exposition, and sunny. Here it's in minor, and heartbreakingly sad, as if all hope is lost.
9:39	Figuration from solo exposition; much more condensed, because there are so many themes to bring back.
9:50	Orchestra themes. Varied interplay between winds and piano. Piano overlays wind melody with scales and busy accompaniment.
10:26	Final figuration: again, much briefer than earlier

CODA

10:40	Opening theme, again played by orchestra. Begins like final ritornello in a Baroque concerto. It ends by moving away from the original version, then stopping on a suspenseful chord.
11:01	*Cadenza*: This is the final and most dramatic stage in the soloist's quest for equal standing, the chord on which the orchestra pauses demands that the soloist continue on to the tonic.
12:03	Themes from the end of the orchestral exposition. This is material not presented in the recapitulation, so it is introduced here.
12:34	Sustained chords in winds; piano figuration. No melody; simply fading away. A bleak ending to a bleak movement.

 Listen to this selection streaming or in an Active Listening Guide at CourseMate or in the eBook.

LEARNING OUTCOME 9-4
Explore the first movement of a Mozart piano concerto in detail.

9-4 Mozart's Concerto in C Minor

A sense of balance is integral to the Classical style, and especially to the music of Mozart. It is a balance created by complementary energies, like purposely holding one's breath, then exhaling vigorously. This would seem to be at odds with the idea of a piano concerto because its defining feature is the apparent imbalance between orchestra and soloist. This imbalance is evident at the outset, both visually (many against one) and aurally (the orchestra throws down the gauntlet, with a long opening statement). Mozart's self-imposed challenge was to bring them into some kind of parity by the end of the movement.

Mozart's strategy was to counterbalance the power of the orchestra with solo-only features and opportunities. To portray the conflict and resolution of these opposing forces on the grandest scale, Mozart expanded and modified the sonata-form model found in sonatas, chamber music, and symphonies. First movements in the later Mozart piano concertos typically follow this sequence of events:

The Orchestral Exposition. The concerto opens with a long orchestral statement. It presents melodic material that returns later in the movement, and it features frequent contrasts in activity, dynamics, texture, and instrumentation. In these respects, it sounds like an exposition. But it is harmonically static; it remains in the same key throughout. The structural tension between contrasting keys that underpins all of the events in the movement has been postponed.

cadenza Virtuosic and rhapsodic improvisation of variable length that typically occurs close to the end of each of the outer movements of a concerto

Solo Exposition. The key events in this second and different exposition are designed to empower the soloist:

- The soloist's entrance, with little or no accompaniment, playing tuneful music—either the orchestral first theme, if it is lyrical, or new material that precedes the restatement of the first theme if it is not
- A transition to the new key, usually highlighted by brilliant figuration
- A *new* second theme to spotlight the arrival in the new key, which confirms that only the soloist has the power to initiate harmonic change
- More brilliant figuration leading to a decisive cadence that closes the solo exposition.

Development Section. The typical sequence of events within the development section includes the central tutti, an extended statement by the orchestra; rapid, often argumentative dialogue between soloist and orchestra that wanders far afield harmonically; and a long preparation for the return of the opening theme.

Recapitulation. The recapitulation merges the orchestral and solo exposition, as if to signal that the soloist and orchestra are now on an equal footing. Mozart does not include all the material from both expositions; themes from the two expositions not used in the recapitulation almost always appear in the development or coda.

Coda. The coda, like the development, begins with a big orchestral statement and then pauses at a point of great harmonic tension. At this point, the soloist plays a **cadenza**, a rhapsodic and virtuosic improvisation of variable length. This final moment or two in the spotlight cements the soloist's status as an equal partner. It ends with the soloist leading the orchestra back to the tonic key. The orchestra brings the movement to a close; the pianist may join in but seldom does.

9-4A Mozart's Music as Drama and a Preview of Romanticism?

Concerto movements like this are the most first-person music of the era. In performance—the only way Mozart's audience would have encountered it—we can hear and see the interaction of one against many. But the concerto is far more than soloist versus orchestra. The drama is in the dynamic relationship between soloist and orchestra: it changes during the course of the movement. Mozart's gifts to the soloist—harmonic ingenuity, lyrical lines, brilliant figuration, and the cadenza where they all come together—bring the soloist and orchestra into balance by the end of the movement.

The ease with which we can link the solo part to the composer historically and the inherently dramatic nature of the concerto and Mozart's music may prompt us to consider to what extent the concerto is autobiographical. This is a provocative inquiry because the movement (and the concerto as a whole) is an uncharacteristically dark piece. The vast majority of Classical-era compositions, by Mozart and his contemporaries, are brighter in mood: they are in major mode and generally more optimistic in tone. This movement is gloomy from the foreboding opening theme to the enigmatic ending, in which soloist and orchestra fade away rather than finish triumphantly. We know that Mozart was, by late eighteenth-century standards, a free spirit—not to the extent that he is portrayed in *Amadeus* perhaps, but certainly not the solid citizen that Haydn was. Could this concerto be Mozart's way of expressing his struggle with authority?

Autobiographical or not (and we will never know), this concerto certainly explains why Mozart's contemporaries considered him a Romantic. It is a highly personal work, and it is emotionally charged.

The Romantic generation, inspired by Beethoven—who himself was deeply inspired by Mozart and this particular concerto, which served as a model for his third piano concerto—would focus on the personal feeling to a far greater degree than eighteenth-century composers did. We get a foretaste of it in this concerto.

Looking Back, Looking Ahead

The orchestral music discussed in this chapter demonstrates several salient features of Classical style even more powerfully than the solo and chamber music heard in Chapter 8, in large part because the resources are so much more substantial. Both the piano and the string quartet present an essentially homogenous sound. By contrast, the late eighteenth-century symphony orchestra features a range of contrasting timbres, and the keyboard concerto offers a further level of contrast because it pits the orchestra against an instrument that was not part of the orchestra. As a result, the contrasts are more vivid and more varied because they are colored by different timbres.

The greater breadth of late Classical music is also evident. The length grows out of the need to first create the comprehensive oppositions in melody, harmony, dynamics and timbre, develop them, and bring them into balance.

The Classical style is dynamic: frequent and comprehensive change keeps the music moving toward well-defined goals, and the oppositions created by multilayered contrasts enable greater control of the tension and resolution that is at the heart of drama. It's evident in Haydn's symphony, in a good-natured way, and it is central to the pathos that pervades Mozart's concerto. We hear how the dynamic nature of the Classical style transformed opera in the next chapter.

 study tools 9

LEARNING OUTCOMES

After reading this chapter, you will be able to do the following:

10-1 Describe the changes in opera during the late eighteenth century.

10-2 Recognize Mozart's opera *Don Giovanni* as an example of a successful eighteenth-century opera that also reflected the significant weakening of aristocratic control of culture and society.

10-3 Understand the dramatic power of Mozart's music and opera through a comparison of two scenes from *Don Giovanni*.

☞ study tools

After you read this chapter, go to the Study Tools at the end of the chapter, page 143.

⎮magine a production with an absolutely unscrupulous, sex-crazed leading man; a string of scorned women; murder; spectacular special effects; and a spine-chilling ending. The latest TV mini-series? Perhaps. But a surer candidate is Mozart's magnificent opera *Don Giovanni*.

More than any other opera of the eighteenth century, *Don Giovanni*, an operatic setting of the legend of Don Juan, not only shows the changes in operatic style during the era but also reflects—more than any other single musical work of the era—the significant changes in European society. We outline the story and sample the music as we explore why *Don Giovanni* has been held in such high regard since its premiere.

10-1 Opera during the Late Eighteenth Century: From Reform to Reconception

Don Giovanni would have shocked early eighteenth-century audiences, especially the aristocracy. The idea that a nobleman—one of their own—was being portrayed as ignoble in his dealings with women would have offended them. They probably wouldn't have known what to make of it and almost certainly would have tried to get it banned.

One can use opera as a barometer of social change in eighteenth-century Europe. At the beginning of the century, *opera seria* reigned supreme; so did the absolute monarchs, like Louis XIV, who supported it. The connection between court and plot went deeper: although it wasn't made explicit, there was a presumption that the ruler who sponsored a particular opera identified with the noble mythical or historical hero.

However, after mid-century, "lighter" forms of music and theatrical entertainment became popular. Their rise in popularity coincided with drastic changes in the social order. The premiere of *Don Giovanni* came about a decade after the American Revolution and two years before the start of the French Revolution. In *Don Giovanni*, it is quite clear that the aristocracy is no longer being viewed through rose-colored glasses. *Don Giovanni* is the notorious Don Juan, a Spanish nobleman who is anything but noble. In Mozart's opera he is an antihero.

The radical transformation of opera during the latter part of the eighteenth century grew out of three interrelated developments: the growing popularity and sophistication of new, lighter forms of stage entertainment; the reform of serious opera; and the dramatic change in musical style. Collectively, they reshaped opera into a more flexible and more dramatically credible genre.

10-1A New Operatic Genres

Even as *opera seria* reigned triumphant in England, a new genre, the ballad opera, emerged to lampoon and subvert it. Handel's *Julius Caesar* premiered in 1724; John Gay's *The Beggar's Opera* was staged four years

later. As its title implies, Gay's ballad opera was a much humbler genre. Spoken dialogue replaced recitative, and Gay's musical collaborator, Christopher Pepusch, gathered music from all strata of society, from jigs and ballads to parodies of opera arias.

The ballad opera would help shape new, more comic genres on the continent. By mid-century, one could hear French *opéra comique* and Italian *opera buffa* (both terms translate as "comic opera") not only in their home countries but also all over Europe. Their German counterpart was the *Singspiel*. Mozart's first great stage success was the *Singspiel Die Entführung aus dem Serail* (*The Abduction from the Seraglio* [a *seraglio* is a harem]).

Distinctions between the genres were often a matter of language. Gluck's *Die Pilgrime von Mekka*, the *Singspiel* from which Mozart took "Unser dummer Pöbel meint," was originally produced as an opéra comique: *La Rencontre imprévue*. (*Opéra comique* had a substantial following in Vienna.) The version in German appeared somewhat later.

These lighter operatic forms were less bound by convention. Spoken dialogue often replaced recitative, as in the ballad opera. They were often comic in spirit (as opposed to *opera seria*) and topical in subject matter, with an undertone of social commentary—sometimes overt, other times thinly disguised. Over time, both drama and music became more sophisticated: *Don Giovanni* was identified as an *opera buffa*, although it ends about as seriously as one can imagine. This contributed to the blurring of boundaries among the several types of musical stage entertainment at the time.

10-1B The Reform of *Opera Seria*

Throughout almost the entire history of opera there has been a tension between drama and music. Recall that opera was originally conceived of as "drama through music." The pendulum quickly swung the other way: the plot became scaffolding for a series of arias—an excuse to enjoy singing and singers. The reform movement of the Arcadian Academy led to the more noble operas of Handel and other

ballad opera British stage entertainment, popular through most of the eighteenth century, that mixed spoken dialogue with popular and traditional songs

opéra comique Humorous French stage entertainment that blends spoken dialogue with song

opera buffa In the 1700s, Italian comic opera, often with contemporary everyday characters instead of gods and historical heroes

Singspiel Literally "song/play"; lighthearted stage entertainment in German that, like *opéra comique*, combines spoken dialogue with song

Baroque-era composers. But infighting among singers helped undermine efforts of librettists and composers to create dramatically cogent opera. The two most flagrant musical abuses were the demands for equal time in the spotlight—if singer X gets three arias, then so should singer Y—and the retention of the da capo aria, in order to allow singers to display their virtuosity and inventiveness. Add backstage bickering, which often reached scandalous proportions, and plots that were literally incredible, and one finds that opera had strayed far from the high-minded ideals of its founders and was in serious need of yet another reform. That would come in mid-century.

The musician most responsible for the reform of serious opera was the German composer Christoph Willibald Gluck. Gluck composed mainly for the theater: not only lighter entertainment such as *Die Pilgrime von Mekka* but also ballets and *opera seria*, including another famous version of the Orpheus legend, entitled *Orfeo ed Euridice*, the first of Gluck's three reform operas. In his preface to *Alceste*, the second of the reform operas, Gluck issued a reform manifesto. In bold language, he outlines the abuses that cripple *opera seria*. He targeted singers, whose "mistaken vanity" causes them to stifle dramatic action with a "useless superfluity of ornaments." He asserted that his goal was simply "to restrict music to its true office of serving poetry by means of expression and by following the situations of the story." To do this, Gluck put aside many of the rigid conventions that had hamstrung Baroque opera.

Despite these reforms, *opera seria* lost its dominant position in the operatic world. There was still an audience for it during Mozart's lifetime—*La Clemenza di Tito*, an *opera seria*, was Mozart's last opera—but *opera buffa* and *Singspiel* by Mozart and his contemporaries were more popular.

A third reason for the ascendancy of *opera buffa* was that it grew up with the new Classical style. This style allowed for frequent and dramatic contrast, which enabled composers to respond more flexibly to dramatic demands. We will hear Mozart's skill in this regard in the two selections from *Don Giovanni* discussed presently.

10-2 Mozart, Opera, and *Don Giovanni*

Although Mozart composed masterfully in every genre, he is perhaps most esteemed for his operas. Virtually since their composition, Mozart's best operas have been regarded by many as not only his supreme achievements—if only because of their magnitude and complexity—but also the most successful operas of any era.

Mozart began composing for the stage at age ten and produced works in practically every fashionable genre, from *opera seria* to *Singspiel*. However, the works

for which he is best remembered are four late comic operas—*The Marriage of Figaro*, *Don Giovanni*, *Cosi fan tutte*, and *The Magic Flute*. Critics have praised them for the beauty of the music and their dramatic power.

10-2A *Don Giovanni*

Mozart composed *Don Giovanni* in 1787 for a performance in Prague. *The Marriage of Figaro*, which premiered the previous year, had been exceptionally well received and resulted in a commission for the new opera.

Don Giovanni, with a libretto by Lorenzo da Ponte, tells the tale of Don Giovanni (Don Juan), a Spanish nobleman and the most notorious womanizer in Europe. (Even today, "Don Juan" is a term for a man who lives to seduce women; he woos one, then quickly drops her to pursue a new conquest.) Although Leporello, his manservant, reminds us periodically that his conquests number in the thousands, the plot concerns mainly his amorous relations with three women: Donna Anna, Donna Elvira, and Zerlina. Don Giovanni tries to seduce Donna Anna early in the opera. He fails, is discovered, and then is challenged to a duel by her elderly father, the Commandant, whom he kills. Donna Anna swears revenge. Donna Elvira is an earlier conquest who, with exquisitely bad timing, has resurfaced in Seville. She is the archetypal jilted lover. Zerlina is a peasant girl who is about to be married; Don Giovanni spies her as he escapes from an encounter with Elvira and tries to seduce her right under the nose of her soon-to-be husband.

Patrick Riviere/Getty Images

Leporello (left), Don Giovanni's faithful if timid sidekick, offers comic relief in an often deadly serious story.

The plot grows out of the complications ensuing from Don Giovanni's pursuit of these women. By the second act, Giovanni has men and women alike after him—the men trying to kill him and Donna Elvira trying to reform him.

The plot sends a host of conflicting signals about Don Giovanni. He is, by Leporello's account, an incorrigible rake. But he not only fails to bed any of the women during the course of the opera but also bungles every attempt to do so. He runs away from each of the women at different points in the opera but stands up to the statue of the dead Commandant that comes to life at the end, despite the threat of damnation. Does his lack of repentance express the courage of his convictions or arrogance so overwhelming that he is blind to its consequences?

In its grand scheme, *Don Giovanni* is a comic opera with a tragic ending. There are laughs throughout, but the end is a graphic reminder that immorality leads to damnation. Don Giovanni is the hero or, more properly, the antihero. He and Leporello are the focus of the plot; it is their antics that entertain the audience. Yet the subtitle of the opera is *Il dissoluto punito* (*The Rake Punished*), and after Don Giovanni goes up in flames on his way down to hell, the rest of the cast comes onstage to wag their collective finger and warn the audience that evildoers will always be punished.

The composition and production of *Don Giovanni* clearly signaled that aristocratic control of culture and society had weakened significantly. The heart of the plot of *Don Giovanni*—a murdered man returns as a statue, invites his murderer to dinner, and casts him into hell—is a legend that dates from the Middle Ages. Da Ponte, the librettist, drew on *Dom Juan*, a setting of the story by the seventeenth-century French playwright Molière that scandalized French authorities and was effectively banned during Molière's lifetime. Da Ponte and Mozart present Don Giovanni as an ignoble nobleman, a complex and substantially evil character, a rake, a buffoon, yet a man unafraid of death. This more realistic and far less flattering portrait of a member of the nobility would have been at odds with the honorable heroes presented in opera seria and a far cry from the image that the nobility sought to project to the masses.

We can hear how Mozart characterizes Don Giovanni's wooing and Zerlina's reluctance.

the second is *Don Giovanni's* final scene, "A cenar teco" ("To Dine with You").

10-3A "Là ci darem la mano"

The duet (see Listen Up!) occurs early in the opera, but Don Giovanni has already tried to seduce Donna Anna, killed her father, and encountered Donna Elvira, a former conquest who refuses to take no for an answer. After he eludes Donna Elvira, Don Giovanni goes on the hunt again and comes upon a wedding of two peasants, Zerlina and Masetto. He is attracted to the bride-to-be, so he invites Masetto and the rest of the wedding party to his estate so that he can make his move on Zerlina. In the course of the duet, he converts her from a girl who can say no to another potential notch on his belt by promising to marry her, even though her wedding to Masetto is imminent.

How does Mozart help Don Giovanni seduce Zerlina? The melody that Don Giovanni sings sends two strong signals: it is simple, and it is irresistible. In the context of the opera, the duet requires simple music because Zerlina is a peasant, albeit a beautiful one. So Mozart simplifies his musical language (compared to that in the rest of the opera) so that it reaches Zerlina (and everyone else) directly. Then the pure loveliness of the melody takes

10-3 Mozart's Music for *Don Giovanni*

Without question, the legend of Don Juan was a terrific point of departure for an opera, but it was Mozart who transformed it into one of the great operas of all time. We get some sense of the range and dramatic power of his music through a comparison of two scenes. The first is a duet, "Là ci darem la mano" ("Give Me Your Hand");

LISTEN UP!

Mozart, "Là ci darem la mano," *Don Giovanni* (1787)

TAKEAWAY POINT: Simple, spellbinding music for a seduction in song

STYLE: Classical

FORM: AA'BA'' with extensions and a coda

GENRE: Opera

INSTRUMENTS: Voices with orchestral accompaniment

CONTEXT: A simple, irresistible melody for a simple peasant girl

A

0:00 Don Giovanni begins to make his case with a tender, tuneful melody with light string accompaniment.

Don Giovanni

Là ci darem la mano	Give me your hand, o fairest,
là mi dirai di sì.	whisper a gentle "yes."
Vedi, non e lontano:	See, it's not far:
partiam, ben mio, da qui.	let's go, my love.

A'

0:17 Zerlina is clearly dazzled by his attentions but has her doubts, highlighted musically by the extension of the last phrase of the melody.

Zerlina

Vorrei, e non vorrei,	I'd like to but yet I would not.
mi trema un poco il cor;	My heart will not be still.
felice, e ver, sarei,	'Tis true I would be happy,
ma puo burlarmi ancor.	yet he may deceive me still.

B

0:40 Don Giovanni becomes more ardent in his seduction; a new, more active phrase in a new key and richer orchestration. Zerlina resists at first, but then weakens.

Don Giovanni

Vieni, mio bel diletto!	Come with me, my pretty!

0:44 **Zerlina**

Mi fa pieta Masetto!	May Masetto take pity!

Don Giovanni

Io cangiero tua sorte!	I will change your fate!

0:53 **Zerlina**

Presto, non son piu forte.	Quick then, I can no longer resist.

Don Giovanni

Vieni, vieni!	Come, come!

A''

1:05 Don Giovanni and Zerlina reprise opening melody, but now they trade phrases. This seems to be a musical signal that Don Giovanni has just about broken through Zerlina's resistance.

1:29 Mozart extends the reprise of the opening phrase to support Don Giovanni's increasingly ardent pursuit of Zerlina, and her increasing reluctance before giving in.

2:03 Don Giovanni and Zerlina sing as a pair, to a new melody in a more sprightly tempo.

Andiam, andiam mio bene,	Let's go, let's go, my treasure,
a ristorar le pene	to soothe the pangs
d'un innocente amor!	of innocent love!

 Listen to this selection streaming or in an Active Listening Guide at CourseMate or in the eBook.

over. Could anyone singing a melody so sweet be a bad guy? The answer is yes, of course, but Zerlina doesn't know that; she is momentarily spellbound.

Mozart's setting of the melody certainly heightens the mood. Among the details are the simple accompaniment at the beginning, underscoring the simplicity of the melody, and the quickening rhythm of exchange—he sings and she sings at increasingly shorter intervals until they go off together. And there are parts of the melody where Mozart guides the action. In the contrasting section ("Vieni, mio bel diletto!"), we can hear how Mozart characterizes Don Giovanni's increasingly ardent wooing and Zerlina's steadily decreasing reluctance.

Nevertheless, at the heart of it all is Mozart's simple and charming melody. It draws us in, it makes sense apart from the words, and it also makes dramatic sense. It is an invitation to love, specifically for Don Giovanni's seduction of a peasant girl.

"Là ci darem la mano" shows one aspect of Mozart's art, the ability to compose captivating melodies that function flawlessly in a dramatic context. Such a beautiful melody would be horribly out of place in the next scene, in which Don Giovanni literally goes down in flames. Instead, we hear what may well be the most terrifying music of the eighteenth century.

10-3B "A cenar teco"

"A cenar teco" (see Listen Up!) takes place in the scene in which Don Giovanni meets his fate. Shortly before, Don Giovanni and Leporello are trading their cloaks, which they had exchanged earlier so that Don Giovanni could pass himself off as a servant. They are in a cemetery, near a statue of the Commandant. As Don Giovanni brags about his flirtation with Elvira's maid, they hear a sepulchral voice telling them that Don Giovanni will stop laughing before morning. The voice comes from the statue. Leporello is appropriately terrified, but Don Giovanni impudently invites the voice to supper.

Later, as Don Giovanni is eating, the Commandant—in statue form—arrives at his castle. As Leporello

cowers under the dining table, Don Giovanni invites the statue to join him for dinner. The Commandant declines, instead inviting Don Giovanni to dine with *him*. He takes Don Giovanni's hand and asks him to repent. As the Commandant does so, Don Giovanni discovers that the hand is very cold and begins to realize that something is gravely amiss. When Don Giovanni refuses the Commandant's invitation, he is engulfed in flames. Voices from below direct him to the hell where he will spend eternity.

If taken literally, the plot is simply not believable: a statue comes alive to become the agent of Don Giovanni's immolation. It is Mozart's music that can get us beneath the story: it enables us to experience this final scene emotionally, as if it were true. The orchestral accompaniment, from the first terrifying chord to the final push to the end, lets us know that Don Giovanni's end is near. There are clues everywhere: swirling violins, voice-of-doom trombones, relentless rhythms. The vocal lines of the three characters match their personalities. The wide intervals and downward thrust of the Commandant's melodic material depict the voice of doom; Leporello's chattering underscores his cowardice; Don Giovanni's answers resonate with defiance.

Beatriz Schiller/Time Life Pictures/Getty Images

A creative staging of the final scene of Don Giovanni, when the Don literally goes down in flames.

Mozart, "A cenar teco," *Don Giovanni* (1787)

TAKEAWAY POINT: Terrifying music for a terrible moment

STYLE: Classical

FORM: Through-composed

GENRE: Opera

INSTRUMENTS: Voices with orchestral accompaniment

CONTEXT: Don Giovanni being damned to hell: just deserts for an immoral life

0:00   Two bold chords announce the stone guest, who has come to punish Don Giovanni. Notice full orchestra, martial rhythms in stately tempo, dramatic leaps in vocal line of statue, and boldness and rapidity of Don Giovanni's responses.

0:08   **The Statue**

Don Giovanni, a cenar teco	Don Giovanni, you invited me to dinner,
m'invitasti e son venuto!	and I have come!

0:26   **Don Giovanni**

Non l'avrei giammai creduto;	I never would have believed it,
ma farò quel che potrò.	but I will do what I can.
Leporello, un altra cena	Leporello, see to it that another dinner
fa che subito si porti!	is served at once!

0:38   **Leporello** (peeping out from under the table)

Ah padron! Siam tutti morti.	Ah, master, we are lost.

0:42   **Don Giovanni**

Vanne dico!	Go, I said!

0:44   **The Statue**

Ferma un po'!	Wait a moment!
Non si pasce di cibo mortale	He who dines on heavenly food
chi si pasce di cibo celeste;	has no need for the food of mortals!
Altra cure più gravi di queste,	Other more serious considerations
altra brama quaggiù mi guidò!	have caused me to come here!

1:24   Action picks up, Leporello mumbles underneath, and exchanges between statue and Don Giovanni become sharper.

Leporello

La terzana d'avere mi sembra	I feel as if I have a fever,
e le membra fermar più non so.	for I cannot control my limbs.

Don Giovanni

Parla dunque! Che chiedi! Che vuoi?	Speak then! What do you ask? What do you wish?

1:32   **The Statue**

Parlo; ascolta! Più tempo non ho!	I will speak. Listen! My time is short!

Don Giovanni

Parla, parla, ascoltandoti sto.	Speak then, for I am listening.

The Statue

Parlo; ascolta! Più tempo non ho!	I will speak. Listen! My time is short!

Don Giovanni

Parla, parla, ascoltandoti sto.	Speak then, for I am listening.

2:02   With a bold chord comes the event that spells Don Giovanni's doom: an offer sealed with a handshake.

The Statue

Tu m'invitasti a cena,   You invited me to dinner,

il tuo dover or sai.   now you know your duty.

Rispondimi: verrai tu a cenar meco?   Answer me: Will you come to dine with me?

2:35   **Leporello**

Oibò; tempo non ha, scusate.   Oh my! Excuse him, but he hasn't time.

2:41   **Don Giovanni**

A torto di viltate tacciato mai sarò.   No one will ever say of me that I have ever been afraid.

2:49   **The Statue**

Risolvi!   Make up your mind!

Don Giovanni

Ho già risolto!   I have done so already.

The Statue

Verrai?   You will come?

Leporello

Dite di no! Dite di no!   Tell him no! Tell him no!

Don Giovanni

Ho fermo il cuore in petto.   My heart beats firmly.

Non ho timor: verrò!   I'm not afraid: I'll come!

The Statue

Dammi la mano in pegno!   Give me your hand upon it!

Don Giovanni

Eccola! Ohimé!   Here it is! [He gives the Statue his hand.] Oh me!

3:23   Tremolos in strings and violent skips in vocal line signal that the moment has arrived. Again, notice the quickened pace and the suspension of timekeeping.

The Statue

Cos'hai?   What is wrong?

Don Giovanni

Che gelo è questo mai?   What is this deadly chill?

The Statue

Pentiti, cangia vita   Repent! Change your ways,

è l'ultimo momento!   for this is your last hour!

Don Giovanni (trying to free himself)

No, no, ch'io non mi pento,   No, no, I will not repent,

vanne lontan da me!   leave me be!

The Statue

Pentiti, scellerato!   Repent, you scoundrel!

Don Giovanni

No, vecchio infatuato!   No, you old fool!

The Statue

Pentiti!   Repent!

Don Giovanni

No!   No!

Continued

The Statue

Sì!   Yes!

Don Giovanni

No!   No!

3:55   **The Statue**

Ah! tempo più non v'è!   Ah, your time is up!

4:02   The statue disappears. Flames surround Don Giovanni. Everything happens at once: brass, drums, diabolical chorus, Don Giovanni's last words on earth.

Don Giovanni

Da qual tremore insolito   What strange fear

sento assalir gli spiriti!   now assails my soul!

Dond'escono quei vortici   Where do those flames of horror

di foco pien d'orror?   come from?

4:13   **Chorus of Demons**

Tuo a tue colpe è poco!   No horror is too dreadful for you!

Vieni, c'è un mal peggior!   Come, there are worse in store!

4:21   **Don Giovanni**

Chi l'anima mi lacera?   Who lacerates my soul?

Chi m'agita le viscere?   Who torments my body?

Che strazio, ohimè, che smania!   What torment, oh me, what agony!

Che inferno, che terror!   What a Hell! What a terror!

4:25   **Leporello**

Che ceffo disperato!   What a look of desperation!

Che gesti da dannato!   The gestures of the damned!

Che gridi, che lamenti!   What cries, what laments!

Come mi fa terror!   How he makes me afraid!

(The flames engulf Don Giovanni.)

4:51   **Don Giovanni**

Ah!

(Don Giovanni sinks into the earth.)

🔊 Listen to this selection streaming or in an Active Listening Guide at CourseMate or in the eBook.

The scene's music gains power precisely because it is so different from that in "Là ci darem la mano." The contrasts between the two scenes highlight many facets of Don Giovanni's character: charmer, arrogant but gracious host, courageous if foolhardy libertine. The music helps us to identify with him, even as we are repelled by his obsessive need for seduction, which he pursues without regard for the hurt he causes, and to be horrified at his fate.

10-3C Mozart, Classical Music, and Opera as Drama

Numerous commentators have observed that Classical music, both instrumental and vocal, was inherently dramatic because of the underlying patterns of tension and release and the frequent contrast and directional thrust used to animate both tension and its resolution. However, in instrumental music, the dramatic events are often a matter of interpretation. In these two excerpts from *Don Giovanni*, we know from the libretto exactly what the music is supposed to convey. Here we seek to discover how the music works dramatically.

If we compare either of these scenes to Cleopatra's aria in Handel's *Julius Caesar*, we immediately sense a fundamental difference. The Baroque da capo aria is dramatically static, whereas these two scenes are dynamic. In "Piangeró," the plot is essentially in the same place at the end of the aria as it was at the beginning. Cleopatra lets us know that she is distressed, that she will make life a living hell for Ptolemy if she dies, then reminds us that she is indeed distressed. The music is gorgeous and evocative, but there is no *action*. By contrast, Mozart not only helps Don Giovanni seduce Zerlina but also gives us the details: his gentle first step in the simple melody, Zerlina's initial reluctance in the extension of her answer, the Don's more impassioned plea, Zerlina's quick reply, her gradual weakening, then her acquiescence at the shift in tempo. The music not only helps advance the plot but also tells us about both characters. We learn—from the music as well as the libretto—that Don Giovanni is a relentless, unprincipled charmer and that Zerlina is gullible, dazzled by riches and power, and not particularly principled herself.

The final scene is the most dramatic moment in the opera. Mozart invests it with foreboding in the spine-tingling chords that open the scene. He crafts all three vocal lines to match the characters: bold skips in the Commandant's music, Leporello chattering away, and the Don absolutely defiant, especially in the jagged rhythms just before he gives his hand to the Commandant. Underneath, the orchestra is turbulent, violent, agitated, leaving no doubt that Don Giovanni is doomed. Again, the story moves relentlessly toward its denouement: Don Giovanni's bizarre dinner guest (when was the last time you invited a statue to dinner?) sends him to hell.

It is in music like this that we can feel most powerfully the dramatic potential of opera. In both scenes, the music does the dramatic work. The text—and the acting onstage—lets us know what is happening, but it is the music that compels us to feel the drama in a way that is impossible with words alone.

Looking Back, Looking Ahead

The Classical era in music coincided with the Enlightenment's triumph of rationality, and it reflected and expressed its values. European culture in the nineteenth century would turn away from rationality toward emotion. Its manifestation in the arts was labeled Romanticism. The Mozart of the C minor piano concerto and *Don Giovanni* previews the coming Romantic era. Neither work is full of empty decoration and flourishes, as so much late eighteenth-century music was. Instead, both works communicate deep feeling—one with text, the other without—with a mastery and power that was unsurpassed by Mozart's peers.

In the next chapter, we encounter a composer who played the decisive role in the transition from Classical to Romantic.

 study tools 10

Ready to study?
In the book you can:

- Review Learning Outcome answers and Glossary terms with the tear-out Chapter Review card.

Or you can go online to CourseMate, at www.cengagebrain.com, for these resources:

- Chapter Quizzes to prepare for tests

- Interactive flashcards of all Glossary terms

- Active Listening Guides, streaming music, and YouTube playlists

- An eBook with live links to all web resources

Gang Liu/Shutterstock.com

LEARNING OUTCOMES

After reading this chapter, you will be able to do the following:

11-1 Understand the revolutionary qualities in Beethoven's music that set it apart from the music of other composers.

11-2 Describe Beethoven's radically different approach to the piano and the piano sonata.

11-3 Understand Beethoven's conception of a four-movement symphony as an integrated musical statement.

11-4 Grasp the impact of Beethoven and his music.

 study tools

After you read this chapter, go to the Study Tools at the end of the chapter, page 160.

n October 1802, Beethoven wrote to his brothers Carl and Johann a famous letter known as the Heiligenstadt Testament (after the town where he wrote it), in which he reveals his loss of hearing, which had plagued him since 1796. It is impossible to overestimate how cursed Beethoven must have felt—imagine a sculptor who is almost blind. Beethoven would live almost twenty-five more years, and his hearing would deteriorate even further. Yet he would rise from the depths of despair to triumph over his affliction again and again. Remarkably, he composed many of his greatest works after penning this letter. Beethoven's achievements and influence are unmatched by any other composer. He played the leading role in the transformation from Classical to Romantic and in elevating instrumental music to a status higher than that of vocal music. That he was able to compose with his hearing increasingly impaired only makes his achievements more astounding. In this unit, we consider Beethoven's unique place in the history of music and examine two compositions that reveal the qualities that make his music so exceptional.

> "Beethoven was 'more of a Romantic than any composer who has existed.'"
> —E. T. A. Hoffmann

11-1 Beethoven the Revolutionary

Ludwig van Beethoven  was born in Bonn, in what is now west-central Germany. His father, a musician of moderate skill and terrible temper, recognized his son's talent and tried to promote him as Leopold Mozart had done with his son. Beethoven was not a prodigy but became a superb pianist and one of the great innovators in keyboard music.

In the late eighteenth century, Vienna was the musical capital of Europe. Beethoven went there twice—briefly in 1787 and in 1792, when he returned to stay for the rest of his life. When he came back, it was to study composition with Haydn and make a name for himself as a pianist and composer. His relationship with the great composer was both cordial and complicated. He maintained his respect for Haydn as a composer and was grateful for his support, but he apparently told several acquaintances that he felt he learned next to nothing from Haydn during his period of study.

Beethoven made a profound impression as a pianist and gained a reputation as an *enfant terrible* because of his disdain for social conventions, his bad temper, and his relentless assaults on delicate Viennese instruments; he reportedly broke more strings than any other pianist in Vienna. The most

> Beethoven reportedly broke more strings than any other pianist in Vienna.

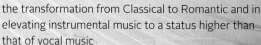

▶ Ludwig van Beethoven
FAST FACTS

- Dates: 1770–1827

- Place: Germany/Vienna

- Reasons to remember: Composer whose achievements and influence are unmatched by any other; played the leading role in the transformation from Classical to Romantic and in elevating instrumental music to a status higher than that of vocal music

sensational parts of his performances were his improvisations. His pupil Carl Czerny noted that they often moved audiences to tears, an observation confirmed by other accounts.

Why did the Viennese lionize Beethoven so? The overriding reason was, of course, Beethoven's inherent genius. In his own time, Beethoven was recognized in Vienna and throughout Europe as not only the greatest living composer but also as a man who was almost single-handedly transforming musical life. The popular novelist and critic E. T. A. Hoffmann, himself a first-generation Romantic, wrote in 1813 that Beethoven was "more of a Romantic than any composer who has existed." However, he also benefited from living in a time when the stature of the artist rose dramatically. This in turn was a product of significant changes in European society.

11-1A Political, Economic, and Social Revolutions

Beethoven's musical revolution echoed the revolutionary changes in European life in the years around 1800. The American and French revolutions took place during Beethoven's youth. Napoleon's rise and fall came during his early maturity; Beethoven initially dedicated his Third Symphony to Napoleon but later retracted the dedication when Napoleon declared himself emperor of France. In the original

manuscript, it can be seen that Beethoven violently scratched out the name "Bonaparte" in a moment of disdain over Napoleon's decision to declare himself emperor. After the retraction he renamed the work "Sinfonia eroica, composta per festeggiare il sovvenire d'un grand'uomo" ("Heroic symphony composed to celebrate the memory of a great man"), now known simply as the "Eroica" Symphony. The realignment of Europe after the Congress of Vienna, for which Beethoven composed an overture, occurred toward the end of his career.

During this same time, the first stage of the Industrial Revolution was under way, first in England, then on the continent and in North America. James Watt patented the first steam engine in 1769, the year before Beethoven's birth; steam power would become a core technology in the development of industry, revolutionizing production and transportation.

These political and economic revolutions helped reshape the structure of European society, tilting political power and social status away from the landed aristocracy and organized religion and toward industrialists, merchants, and the bourgeoisie, whose wealth was usually earned, not inherited. With this shift in ideology and power came the idea that social standing should be based on achievement, not birth. The transformation of cultural life was gradual; the aristocracy fought to preserve their privileges.

However, the two revolutions opened the door to a more egalitarian society, and there was no way for the nobility to close it.

11-1B Beethoven's Revolutionary Spirit

Then as now, the Viennese valued greatness in the arts. This cultural climate, when coupled with the political and social changes that occurred during Beethoven's lifetime, made it possible for Beethoven to earn unprecedented recognition for his achievements. What made this recognition even more remarkable was Beethoven's disregard for courtly protocol; on several occasions, he was more than willing to bite the hand that fed him. His deafness, which began early in his career and worsened incrementally until he was totally deaf for the last decade of his life, only exacerbated his social difficulties. Despite his awkward manners, which at times descended into boorishness, Beethoven gained a loyal following among aristocrats, including three who supported him with an annual stipend that enabled him to concentrate on composing.

Vienna embraced Beethoven as a performer before they enjoyed him as a composer. His Opus 1 (first work), a set of three piano trios, was not published until 1795, three years after his arrival; Opus 2, a set of three piano sonatas, did not appear in print until the following year.

The title page to Beethoven's Third Symphony, with a dedication to Napoleon scratched out

11-2 Beethoven and the Piano Sonata

Long before there were battles of the bands, there were piano playoffs. One of the favorite amusements of Viennese aristocrats during the late eighteenth century was a duel between rival pianists, usually featuring a local favorite versus a touring virtuoso. A noteworthy piano duel, one that was closer to a clash between heavyweight boxers than a contest of keyboard artists, was the "Scene in Wien," a rematch between Daniel Steibelt and Ludwig van Beethoven.

When Steibelt arrived in Vienna in 1800, fresh from successes in Paris and Prague, a duel between him and Beethoven was arranged at the home of Count Fries. Beethoven, by now a fixture in Viennese salons, performed a movement from a recently composed trio: a set of variations on a popular tune. Steibelt then played one of his own compositions, which apparently dazzled the audience. Beethoven refused to play after Steibelt.

Steibelt was easy to dislike. Numerous accounts portray him as extraordinarily egocentric and self-promoting. He was without scruples, often leaving town with a pile of unpaid debts, selling the same music to competing publishers, and claiming others' music as his own. His playing and composing offered more flash than substance. Still, he enjoyed a successful career as both a composer and a pianist, although he often outstayed his welcome and left town before being apprehended by the authorities.

A few weeks later, Count Fries hosted another duel between Steibelt and Beethoven. This time Steibelt went first. To show his disdain, Steibelt and a local string quartet performed his freshly composed quintet for piano and strings on the same theme that Beethoven had used in his trio, much to the delight of the audience. Beethoven responded in kind by walking to the piano, grabbing the cello part from the cellist's music stand on his way, putting it on the piano rack upside down, poking out a theme, then proceeding to improvise on it rhapsodically. The audience was overwhelmed. It would have been a knockout for Beethoven except that a humiliated Steibelt sneaked out before Beethoven finished. Later, Steibelt told people never to invite him if Beethoven was also going to be present.

Contemporary accounts of Beethoven's improvising repeatedly mention the magic in his playing. They suggest that the piano gave Beethoven his most direct way of communicating through music. We cannot reconstruct his improvisations, but we can get some sense of their boldness through his piano sonatas, the genre in which Beethoven gave his imagination the freest rein.

We can sense in his sonatas Beethoven's almost symbiotic relationship with the piano in several ways.

First, he composed far more piano sonatas than symphonies, string quartets, or any other major genre. Second, he single-handedly elevated its status from a part of the education of young women to serious music for public performance. Third, his piano sonatas document his unparalleled growth as a composer more fully than any other single genre in which he worked. And most compellingly, the sonatas were his laboratory—the place where he experimented with bold new approaches and ideas, which he often used subsequently in other genres.

11-2A Transforming the Piano Sonata

In the eighteenth century, the piano was, for the most part, a woman's instrument. Like learning to dance the minuet elegantly, learning to play the piano was part of a well-bred young woman's education. Publishers issued thousands of sonatas, variation sets, and dances for the piano to cater to the demand for new piano music. Most of Haydn's piano sonatas, including his last three, are dedicated to women. Men composed most of this music, and those composers who were fluent pianists, such as Mozart, Clementi, and C. P. E. Bach, certainly performed their own music. But in their dimensions and impact, their sonatas were, with few exceptions, far more modest than their symphonies (which were intended for public performance) or their string quartets (string players were usually men).

With his first set of three sonatas, which he designated Opus 2, Beethoven took the sonata out of the parlor. All three have four movements, like symphonies and string quartets but unlike earlier piano sonatas. In addition, they are bigger in scale and gesture; in all three sonatas, Beethoven uses the entire range of the piano, rather than the middle and upper registers, to a much greater extent than Mozart, Haydn, and their contemporaries. In the process, he raised the piano sonata's stature to a level comparable to that of the string quartet, concerto, and symphony.

In Beethoven's lifetime, the piano sonata was not a genre performed in public concerts nearly to the extent that the symphony or concerto was. Still, one can easily imagine Beethoven playing his sonatas in the salons of the Viennese aristocracy, demanding more of the pianos than they were able to give. In his person and in his playing, power and passion figured much more prominently than refinement and elegance. In that setting, their impact would have been comparable to a symphony heard in a theater.

11-2B The Evolution of Beethoven's Piano Sonatas

Beethoven composed thirty-two piano sonatas with opus numbers over a twenty-five–year period, from about 1793 to 1822. He composed the majority of them before 1807 but returned periodically to the genre at key points in his career. It is not surprising that he composed more sonatas early in his career, because he was active as a pianist at that time. What is more surprising is that he continued to compose boldly experimental sonatas after he stopped performing publicly because of his deafness.

One of the most remarkable aspects of Beethoven's music is its tremendous growth over the course of his career. The changes in his music were so dramatic that commentators, beginning the year after his death, began grouping his works into three periods: early, middle, and late. In the early-period works, Beethoven built on the Classical style as defined by the music of Mozart and Haydn, even as he sought to go beyond its conventions. In the middle-period works, Beethoven clearly straddled the boundary between Classical and Romantic: works such as his Fifth Symphony feature bold contrasts, expansive gestures, and distinctive character that foreshadow Romantic music's emphasis on feeling and individuality. In his late works, Beethoven follows two distinct paths. In his more public music, most notably the Ninth Symphony, he continues his expansion of Classical style: this monumental work would both inspire and intimidate a century of symphonic composers. In music composed for more intimate settings, most notably the string quartets and late piano sonatas, Beethoven drew inspiration from the music of Bach and Handel to chart a future path that only he took. These works are among the most sublime music ever created.

The idea that Beethoven's music falls into three periods has enjoyed broad acceptance since it was proposed. More recently, music scholars have also suggested grouping Beethoven's piano sonatas into five periods, to account for several more experimental sonatas, including the famous "Moonlight" sonata, as well as the distinct differences between the last five sonatas and the four that preceded them.

It is in his piano sonatas that the stages in Beethoven's growth as a composer are most fully documented, for two reasons. First, there are many more of them than there are symphonies, or even string quartets, so there is more evidence. Second, Beethoven often worked out compositional problems in the piano sonatas before working through the same problem in other genres. The two works in C minor discussed in this unit evidence this. Beethoven composed six piano sonatas in minor mode, including the "Pathétique," as he worked out how to compose a work that was both intense and concentrated yet constructed on a large scale. Only after completing the "Appassionata" sonata did he complete his first symphony in minor mode.

Beethoven's piano sonatas are more consistently daring than his compositions in any other genre, as we'll soon discover. We can easily imagine how works like the "Pathétique" sonata, which begins with a loud chord in a low register that is allowed to reverberate for several seconds, or the "Moonlight" sonata, whose opening movement sustains an ethereal mood throughout, must have surprised listeners accustomed to snappy themes in brisk tempos. The experimental quality of so many sonatas is evident in virtually every important aspect of the works: they range from the form and sequence of movements and key relationships to character and mood and the use of the instrument.

11-2c Beethoven's "Pathétique" Sonata

Imagine that you are a mature Viennese aristocrat—say, between forty and fifty years old. Perhaps you have some ability at the piano and have mastered some of the easier sonatas and sonatinas composed by Mozart and his contemporaries. You've heard Mozart perform his sonatas and concertos, and you've heard Beethoven perform several times in the salons of your peers. You have been invited once again to hear Beethoven perform; he will introduce his new sonata in C minor, which he will call the "Pathétique" (see Listen Up!).

You've heard Beethoven play some of his earlier sonatas and are perceptive enough to realize that he has been exploring new directions in his piano music. Still, years of listening to and playing sonatas have accustomed you to expect the sonata to begin with a melody in the high mid-range of the piano, with a discreet accompaniment, and performed at a brisk tempo. Beethoven sits down to play, and the first sound that you hear is a thick chord in the low register of the instrument that seems to last forever—about three or four seconds. As it dies away, other, softer chords follow. Another explosion, this time a little higher, then more chords, then still another explosive chord, followed by more urgent chords, which lead to a single note and a whoosh down the keyboard. You're stunned . . . you've never heard a sonata begin like this.

One problem with listening to music from earlier generations is that it is hard to be as surprised by it as this. In our own time, Elvis sounds tame, but to those who grew up in the 1950s listening to pop crooners and musical theater stars, he was radical indeed. Even acts as deliberately confrontational as the Sex Pistols or Public Enemy lose their shock value when the music becomes familiar. So, it's difficult to put ourselves in the place of those who encountered this sonata soon after Beethoven composed it. But by trying to do so can we gain a sense of how radically innovative Beethoven's music was.

The differences between a more conventional sonata, such as the Mozart sonata discussed in Chapter 8, and Beethoven's radical departure give us insight into Beethoven's genius and appeal and also highlight his role in the transition from Classical to Romantic.

Beethoven's Bold Beginning. The slow introduction is the most distinctive feature of the sonata, first because of its presence, then because of its recurrence. Slow introductions were relatively common in grand orchestral music, such as opera overtures and symphonies. They also occurred occasionally in chamber music: quartets and quintets for strings, and various combinations of

 **LISTEN UP!**

Beethoven, Sonata in C minor ("Pathétique"), 1st movement (1798)

STYLE: Classical to Romantic

FORM: Sonata form with introduction

GENRE: Piano sonata

INSTRUMENT: Piano

CONTEXT: Beethoven liberating the piano sonata from conventional practice and elevating its stature

INTRODUCTION

0:00   Opening motive, stated three times. Each statement is more intense.

0:39   Motive, repeated in new key. Major key, steady accompaniment, soft dynamic level provide momentary relief; bold, loud chords that interrupt statements make clear that relief is only temporary.

1:16   Motive dissolves into a single note; long preparation for return to home key. Here contrast is in rhythm: between long notes and silence on one hand and headlong rush of the final scale on the other.

EXPOSITION

1:28   *Theme 1:* Quick ascent followed by slower fall that descends only halfway. The quickly rising melodic line (not a singable melody) and tremolo accompaniment establish a mood of great agitation.

1:39   *Transition:* Syncopated long notes versus fast drop; then a series of quickly rising gestures. Beethoven ratchets up tension with strong oppositions, then three long rises followed by sudden drops.

1:57   *Theme 2:* Dialogue between low and high; in a new key, but also in minor. This is almost melodrama: low-register motive followed by same motive expanded and higher; one can almost imagine the villain pursuing the heroine.

2:25   *Closing section:* Active, stable material, followed by return of opening theme in new key. Music relaxes harmonically by settling in a major key, but active rhythms undermine any sense of repose.

EXPOSITION REPEATED

3:00   *Theme 1:* Quick ascent followed by slower fall that descends only halfway

3:12   *Transition:* Syncopated long notes versus fast drop; then a series of quickly rising gestures

3:30   *Theme 2:* Dialogue between low and high; in a new key, but also in minor

3:58   *Closing section:* Active, stable material, followed by return of opening theme in new key

DEVELOPMENT

4:34   Reprise of opening motive, in a new key. There are three statements, as before, but the third goes in a new, disorienting, direction.

5:11   Transition theme, developed. Here Beethoven combines the rocket-like transition material with a smoothed-out version of the opening motive from the introduction.

5:33   A long tremolo signals that the recapitulation is coming, but the melody resists with an undulating pattern that alternates with the rocket-like transition material.

RECAPITULATION

5:54   First theme plus transition-like expansion of the melodic idea. Only first phrase of first theme is repeated literally. The restatement is developed, replacing the transition section, which is omitted entirely.

6:13   Second theme, first in new key, then finally on the tonic. By delaying return to home key in second theme, Beethoven sustains tension at a normal point of repose.

6:37   Closing section, now in home key. Minor mode helps give this section a darker, almost fatalistic sound. At the end, Beethoven veers away from a final cadence to a suspenseful return of the introductory material.

CODA

7:13   Intro again. In this final version, we hear only the tail of the motive; the big chords are omitted.

7:42   Final, abbreviated version of first theme. A hectic dash to the end of the movement leaves the tension generated throughout the movement unresolved, despite a strong final cadence.

 Listen to this selection streaming or in an Active Listening Guide at CourseMate or in the eBook.

instruments with piano. However, there is no significant precedent for Beethoven's use of it in a piano sonata; not surprisingly, perhaps, Beethoven's more traditional contemporaries considered it eccentric. What made the appearance of a slow introduction even more striking was its reappearance; this was far rarer in instrumental music of any genre. Its return on two occasions demonstrates its crucial role in the expressive message of the movement.

Individuality and Expansion. The introduction is the first truly bold example of two qualities that would characterize so much of Beethoven's music throughout his career: individuality and expansion. The slow introduction and its recurrence immediately and obviously set the sonata apart from any other piano sonata composed up to that time, by Beethoven or any other composer. Within the framework of late eighteenth-century music, Beethoven could not have found a more powerful way to assert his individuality.

What makes Beethoven's expansion of Classical forms so dramatic is that it is comprehensive: works are longer, the contrasts are deeper, and the expressive range is greater. The impact of the introduction on the overall length of the movement is significant; it accounts for more than one-third the length of the movement. Without it, the movement would be less than four minutes long (without repeating the exposition)—below average length for a late eighteenth-century sonata and much too short for the big sonatas that Beethoven was motivated to compose.

Contrasts. The contrast between slow and fast is the most pronounced of the contrasts that Beethoven creates in this movement. Through this and other strong contrasts—loud versus soft, high versus low—Beethoven paints musical oppositions in broad, bold strokes. Their impact is immediate and unmistakable. Collectively, these contrasts establish and maintain the expressive message of the movement: conflict without resolution.

Innovation. This is the fourth example of sonata form that we have explored: the first three were the opening movements of the Mozart piano sonata, the Haydn quartet, and Haydn's "Surprise" symphony. As we compare it with the other three, and especially Mozart's sonata, we can easily hear how innovative it is. It is most obvious in the introduction, and in its recurrence at the end of the exposition and recapitulation. But there are other features, such as the use of minor mode and remote keys even in normally restful places, such as the second theme, that also deviate from convention.

These innovations are the product of expressive necessity rather than simply a desire for novelty. As is evident from start to finish, the sonata movement is about conflict created by strong oppositions. The most innovative features are in the service of making the oppositions stronger and more obvious to all listeners and sustaining the sense of conflict throughout the movement. We can hear Beethoven literally ripping apart the conventions of Classical style.

Beethoven's "Pathétique" sonata also gives us a hint of the "piano sonata as laboratory." Although the first movement of the Fifth Symphony (Beethoven's only work in C minor that is better known than the "Pathétique") is quite different—from the opening motive to the final chord—they are closely related in mood. Not surprisingly, there are procedures that carry over from this early work to the symphony, written almost a decade later. We consider them next.

LEARNING OUTCOME 11-3
Understand Beethoven's conception of a four-movement symphony as an integrated musical statement.

11-3 Beethoven and the Symphony

On the evening of December 22, 1808, Ludwig van Beethoven presented a benefit concert at the Theater an der Wien. It featured works that were, as an advertisement in the *Wiener Zeitung* stated, "entirely new, and not yet heard in public." The concert was a marathon event that lasted about four hours. The program included the fourth piano concerto; a choral fantasy for piano, orchestra, and chorus; an aria with orchestral accompaniment; three movements from a mass; an improvisation by Beethoven; and the Fifth and Sixth Symphonies. The vast theater was not adequately heated, so patrons sat in bitter cold. A visiting composer made the uncharitable comment that he "experienced the truth that one can easily have too much of a good thing—and still more of a loud."

For the Sixth Symphony, Beethoven provided programmatic descriptions, which he called "recollections of country life," for each of the five movements. For the Fifth Symphony, he provided nothing other than tempo markings. However, Anton Schindler, a close associate of Beethoven during the composer's later years, recalled in the third edition of his biography *Beethoven As I Knew Him* (1860) that the composer allegedly "pointed to the beginning of the first movement [of the Fifth Symphony] and expressed in these words the fundamental idea of his work: 'Thus Fate knocks at the door!'"

> We can hear Beethoven literally ripping apart the conventions of Classical style.

Unfortunately, scholars have discovered that Schindler's testimony about his interactions with Beethoven is so unreliable that nothing he wrote can be assumed to be true unless corroborated by other evidence. However, Beethoven scholar Owen Jander, using Schindler's remark as a point of departure, makes a compelling case that the symphony represents Beethoven's struggle with deafness and his eventual triumph, and that Beethoven goes so far as to embed in the music clues of the symptoms of his deafness. Although Jander's argument must remain speculation, there is little argument that the Fifth Symphony depicts struggle and triumph with unprecedented boldness and originality.

11-3A Beethoven's Symphonies

With the exception of opera, Beethoven transformed every important genre of the Classical era: the piano sonata; chamber music, including duo sonatas for violin or cello and piano, the piano trio, and the string quartet; the concerto; and the overture. But the nine symphonies are the peak of his many achievements. If we listen to them in order, we come away with a sense of Beethoven's enormous growth as a composer: from the first two symphonies, impressive but clearly derived from Classical models, through the next several symphonies—each a powerful statement—and culminating in the Ninth Symphony, this was work of enormous originality and scale. Indeed, with Beethoven, the symphony replaced opera as the most esteemed genre of art music.

Subsequent generations of composers have found Beethoven's symphonies to be inspiring because of their originality, expansion of Classical style, and expressive impact. They also found them intimidating precisely because of these qualities and because they knew that Beethoven's symphonies would be the yardstick by which their own symphonies would be measured. How to account for the unparalleled prestige of Beethoven's symphonies? We can gain some insight into the special qualities of Beethoven's symphonic music through an exploration of his Fifth Symphony.

11-3B Beethoven's Fifth Symphony

The writer E. T. A. Hoffmann, a contemporary of Beethoven and a leading figure in the Romantic movement, claimed that Beethoven's Fifth Symphony not only symbolized the ascendancy of instrumental music but also signaled the full emergence of Romanticism in music. Hoffmann's perceptive observation highlights a unique quality of Beethoven's famous work: its uncanny ability to portray the past, present, and future of music simultaneously. Its link to the Classical past is evident in its overall design and use of formal plans and procedures derived directly from Haydn, Mozart, and their contemporaries. Like the Classical symphonies

of Haydn, Mozart, and others, the work has four movements in the typical sequence—sonata-form first movement, slow second movement, scherzo and trio (updated from minuet and trio) third movement, and brisk final movement. However, Beethoven expands, integrates, and individualizes these procedures in ways that stamp the work as a product of the nineteenth century. His innovations would in turn have a decisive influence on most of the important composers of the 1800s. To gain some sense of the symphony's distinctive place in the orchestral literature, and in the history of music, we focus on three qualities that typify Beethoven's style: his comprehensive expansion of Classical models, his ability to impart a distinctive identity to a musical work, and the power with which he expresses feelings through sound.

11-3C Beethoven's Expansion of Classical Style

In his Fifth Symphony, Beethoven's expansion of Classical style is evident in the length of the work and the resources required to perform it. A sense of increased size comes not only from the overall length of the work but also from the internal proportions and the distribution of length among the movements. The sense of bigness comes in large part from the addition of instruments, especially in the fourth movement, which increases the dynamic range of the orchestra.

Length of the Work. A typical contemporary performance of the symphony lasts about thirty-five minutes—almost ten minutes longer than the average length of one of Haydn's London symphonies. But even this increase is deceptively small because of the distribution of length among the four movements. In eighteenth-century symphonies, the length typically decreased progressively from movement to movement: the first was generally the longest; and the last, the shortest. In historically accurate performances of Beethoven's Fifth Symphony, however, the order is often reversed. In performance, the first is typically the shortest. By contrast, the last is the longest and seems even longer because the third movement leads directly into it without interruption.

More Instruments, More Sounds. The expansion of Classical style extends to the instrumental resources and range. For the last movement, Beethoven adds piccolo and contrabassoon, which extend the range of the woodwind section higher and lower, and three trombones, which reinforce the lower range of the brass section.

Beethoven maximizes the contrast in volume available from these additional resources by calling for dynamic extremes: fortissimo, pianissimo, even pianississimo (almost imperceptibly quiet), occasionally in rapid alternation or succession. These changes give the symphony presence and impact well beyond those of the typical late eighteenth-century symphony.

11-3D Integration and Individualization

The Fifth Symphony is remarkable for its integration and distinct identity—even for Beethoven. Not only the first movement but the entire work reverberates out of the famous opening motive; it is as if the motive is a stone tossed in a pond, and the symphony forms the ripples when the stone hits the water.

Beethoven integrates and individualizes the symphony through a multidimensional strategy. Some aspects are obvious: the unbroken connection between the third and fourth movements, the brief flashback to the third movement midway through the fourth movement, and numerous versions of the four-note motive employed in every movement of the symphony. Others, such as the dramatic reworking of Classical approaches to form and character to serve the immediate expressive needs of the symphony, are more subtle. All work together to create a unified four-movement symphony that progresses from almost unbearable tension to triumph.

First Movement. The beginning of the symphony is one of the extraordinary moments in music history (see Listen Up!). It encapsulates not only one of the most memorable musical ideas of all time but also the transition from the Classical to Romantic era and the impulses that motivated that transition.

The boldness and originality of the opening stem from what it does and what it does not do. What it does is announce in the most emphatic terms, "This is what this piece is about!" Whether this is Schindler's fate knocking at the door or something else known only to Beethoven, it stays in our ear because it is short, distinctive, powerful, and pure—there is no accompaniment.

What it does not do is provide the immediate orientation that opening statements typically provide. It doesn't establish key (it could as easily be in the secondary key as the home key), meter (the short-short-short-long rhythm works as well, if not better, in a compound meter or in a fast triple meter), or tempo (the long unmeasured pauses after each statement of the motive undermine any sense of beat). As a result, the opening projects enormous instability and uneasiness, which resonate through the entire first movement as well as the remaining three movements.

In this opening gesture, Beethoven makes clear that the conventions he inherited from Haydn, Mozart, and their contemporaries are subordinate to the musical message that he intends to communicate. If the message is conveyed more powerfully by deliberately

Kieran Wills/iStockphoto.com

flouting them, then he does so without hesitation. Indeed, much of the expressive power of the opening, both in the moment and retrospectively, derives from its defiance of the normal way of doing things. For Beethoven, conventional practice was a resource and a frame of reference, not a straitjacket.

> "Thus Fate knocks at the door!"
> –Anton Schindler

Beethoven opens the symphony with a motive, not a melody. Because it is short, distinctive, and memorable, Beethoven can and does use it as a building block for other thematic material. Varied versions of the motive permeate and unify the first movement: sections based on this famous motive include the entire first theme, the transition material, the first part of the second theme, and the final closing material. In addition, it occurs throughout developmental passages and as periodic counterpoint to other melodic material. Indeed, one reason the movement sounds so distinctive is that so much of the melodic and accompanying material develop from the famous opening motive rather than more generic material, such as scales, arpeggios, and arpeggiated accompaniment figures.

The movement ends with a dramatic change. The end of the recapitulation, which could easily be

LISTEN UP!

TOTAL TIME: 7:35

Beethoven, Symphony No. 5 in C minor, 1st movement (1808)

TAKEAWAY POINT: The opening movement of perhaps the most famous instrumental composition in the history of music

STYLE: Late Classical/early Romantic

FORM: Sonata form with extended coda

GENRE: Symphony

INSTRUMENTS: Full orchestra

CONTEXT: Beethoven straining against the conventions of Classical style

EXPOSITION

0:00	*Theme 1:* Beethoven begins boldly by presenting the "fate" motive without accompaniment. Note that it doesn't define key, tempo, or meter, as is customary in a sonata movement.
0:06	Continuation, built on motive, quickly rushes to a "question mark" cadence.
0:18	*Transition:* Beethoven ratchets up tension by blasting out fate motive at a higher pitch than the opening.
0:25	The rest of transition rushes to a tonally ambiguous chord that, after a fair amount of commotion, gives way to a new key.
0:44	*Theme 2:* Different version of fate motive announces theme 2, in major.
	Change of mode, extended length of motive, and answering phrase—an elaboration of the long notes of the horn call—hint at a more hopeful outcome for adversity that has befallen Beethoven.
1:16	Fate motive returns to close out the exposition; in this version, it is more affirming, in part because it defines a key in major.

EXPOSITION REPEATED

1:27	*Theme 1:* Return of opening immediately negates any optimism at end of exposition. Here Beethoven uses the almost obligatory exposition repeat for expressive effect.
1:46	*Transition:* Beethoven builds the section from three variants of the fate motive.
2:11	*Theme 2:* Note that the lower strings play a rising version of the fate motive underneath the lyric line of the violins . . .
2:27	. . . and a variant on a single pitch in the more anxious section that follows.
2:44	The long pause after the cadence makes the negation of the positive mood even more powerful.

DEVELOPMENT

2:54	Two unaccompanied statements of fate motive quickly undermine relative stability at end of exposition. Development begins with reworking of first theme through three keys, with question/answer exchanges prominent.
3:17	Altered version of motive, now a rising pattern, leads to climax featuring still another variant of motive, now on a single note, repeated three times without a break. It is as if the music is saying there is no way for Beethoven to escape his fate.
3:30	Development of the horn call at the beginning of the second theme
3:41	Development gradually disintegrates into alternating chords and then single notes. These confirm Beethoven's worst fears: we hear the optimism of the second theme undercut, and then Beethoven almost literally falls apart.
4:03	A momentary interjection of a more positive statement of the fate motive cannot stem the tide. This otherwise confusing passage almost demands an extramusical interpretation.
4:12	A particularly intense presentation of the fate motive, preparing recapitulation

RECAPITULATION

4:17	*Theme 1:* Normal function of recapitulation turned on its head. Because of inherent instability of fate motive and its insistent repetitions before recapitulation, beginning of recap is a moment of great tension, rather than a point when tension is released.

(Continued)

beethoven and the symphony | **153**

the end of the movement, is in major; it seems to be bringing the movement to a close. But Beethoven cuts it off and moves abruptly into a turbulent coda, which seems to give up just before the end, when the first theme returns softly before a series of powerful chords. The silence after the final chord vibrates with unresolved tension; there is clearly unfinished business that must be addressed in the following movements.

Second Movement. The second movement (see Listen Up!) responds to the unreleased tension of the first movement with a more serene and positive mood. To convey this sense of relative repose, Beethoven uses variation form, in many ways the most predictable of all Classical forms. Although the second movement sounds a more optimistic tone, with prominent rising melodic gestures in both the main and contrasting sections, it doesn't completely dissipate the tension. Indeed, the movement—at the center of the symphony—looks to the past and the future, most clearly in the contrasting theme. It connects to the first movement through the use of the rhythm of the opening motive, and it anticipates the final movement because the reshaped motive rises and is played loudly by brass and other instruments.

Third Movement. As in the previous movements, Beethoven uses a conventional form as a point of departure for the third movement (see Listen Up!)—in this case, the scherzo and trio. Typically, scherzo and trio (and its predecessor, minuet and trio) movements are relatively light and lighthearted: *scherzo* is the Italian word for "joke." Beethoven's movement is an "anti-scherzo"; it is somber, with low strings playing a prominent role and an altered version of the "fate" motive—the most obvious reference to the first-movement motive in the last three movements—casting a cloud over the movement. The music fades as if dying away at the end of the movement: pizzicato strings, then the timpanist tapping out the rhythm of the "fate" motive over suspenseful strings.

Beethoven extends the movement from within by repeating the trio, then developing the obligatory restatement of the scherzo. Then, after a long, suspenseful transition, he effectively continues to extend the movement by connecting it directly to the finale; there is no break between movements.

Fourth Movement. In the fourth movement (see Listen Up!), Beethoven again turns Classical convention on its head. Typically, the finale of a symphony or sonata is a short, lighthearted movement, with a form to match—the most common fourth-movement form is the rondo, a form in which a tuneful opening theme

scherzo and trio More modern version of the minuet and trio, typically the third movement in a four-movement instrumental work. In the Classical style, scherzo (minuet) and trio movements almost always have three major sections, in an ABA pattern: the scherzo (or minuet); the trio, which is in a different key; and a repetition of the scherzo. Each major section is most often in rounded binary form. Scherzo originally designated a composition or movement with a playful, high-spirited character. However, with Beethoven the term came to refer more to the form of the work than the character.

 **LISTEN UP!**

Beethoven, Symphony No. 5 in C minor, 2nd movement (1808)

TAKEAWAY POINT: A moment of relative repose between the tension-filled first and third movements

STYLE: Late Classical/early Romantic

FORM: Variation form, with contrasting material and development

GENRE: Symphony

INSTRUMENTS: Full orchestra

CONTEXT: A movement with a distinct identity and range of moods but with strong connections to the other three movements

SECTION 1

0:00   Phrase begins with three-note melodic fragment that becomes the seed for much thematic material in movement. Unusually, melody is in low-middle register played by cellos and violas, like range of average male singer.

0:14   Cadence at end of first phrase begins long string of cadences. Beethoven uses this predictable material to express comfort musically. The series of cadences ends on the tonic.

0:53   Variant of musical seed of movement starts new melodic idea, built mainly from uplifting reworking of fate motive, played more slowly. It leads into a suspenseful segment where harmony is suspended for several beats—a moment of doubt?

1:14   Much bolder restatement of the new melody, now in the key of the triumphant last movement, affirms the good news that must come eventually.

1:30   Like the first version, the restatement ends with a mystery moment, which gives way to an emphatic comma-style cadence that leads directly to the return of the opening material.

SECTION 2

1:57   Opening theme returns, varied; rhythm of melody moves in even values, rather than the long-short rhythm of the original. The even flow of the rhythm suggests Beethoven's growing hope for a positive outcome.

2:11   The restatement of the cadences retains the variant form of the ending of the first phrase, but this segment ends as it did previously.

2:48   As before. This melody embodies a message of hope, despite moments of doubt. It bears repeating, and it helps set up even more affirmative variations of the opening melody.

3:10   As before, bolder restatement of new melody

3:26   As before, except for more active rhythms in lower strings and faster rhythm of winds at the cadence

SECTION 3

3:52   Second variation of opening melody, moving twice as fast as previous variation. The variation, now ending without extended cadences, is heard three times, in middle, high, and low registers: everyone agrees that everything will ultimately be all right.

4:54   Variation of "musical seed" motive, with rhythm evened out; winds take over and simply go up and down scale fragments. Just as the statement of the opening melody is lengthened by restating it three times, so is this section.

5:50   Triumphant second melody, but with the last notes of the fate motive drawn out, to make the statement even more emphatic

6:15   Playing again with the motivic seed. It soon dissolves into simple arpeggiation of a single chord, which normally leads directly back to the tonic. Here, the return is suspended for several seconds, perhaps to suggest doubt or insecurity.

SECTION 4

6:36   The variation theme again, this time in minor mode, treated developmentally, and played softly by winds. The change of mode, soft dynamics, and instability of the developmental process combine to continue the sense of uncertainty.

7:17   Final stirring statement of the melody wipes away doubt.

7:30   The cadences begin by retaining the energy of the theme, but they soon return to the peaceful, reassuring character heard previously.

CODA

8:09   A sprightly version of the opening theme, in an even rhythm and faster tempo, begins a coda-like section. The cadences return at the original tempo; this is the most emphatic version. The theme projects a positive mood.

9:09   Final restatement of motivic seed swells to an arpeggiation of the tonic chord, and then the final statements of the motivic seed. Beethoven's sense of peace is hard earned; it is about to be undermined in the next movement.

 Listen to this selection streaming or in an Active Listening Guide at CourseMate or in the eBook.

 **LISTEN UP!**

Beethoven, Symphony No. 5 in C minor, 3rd movement (1808)

TAKEAWAY POINT: Beethoven's "anti-scherzo": a dark, foreboding movement that leads directly to the finale

STYLE: Late Classical/early Romantic

FORM: Scherzo and trio, expanded and developed

GENRE: Symphony

INSTRUMENTS: Full orchestra

CONTEXT: A return to the mood of the opening, which sets up the triumph of the last movement

SCHERZO

0:00   The sharply rising melodic contour of the opening melody, played softly in a low register; the return to minor mode; and the inconclusive end of the phrase create a pensive mood.

0:19   The horns blare out a varied version of the fate motive, which is developed into a contrasting section. It ends far from the home key.

0:40   Restatement of the opening theme, away from the tonic. The harmonic road back home leads directly into the fate motive.

1:03   Again, contrast with material developed from the new version of the fate motive

1:24   Opening theme emerges tentatively from the end of the previous section. This time, however, it continues much more assertively, only to be cut off by yet another emphatic statement of the fate motive.

TRIO

1:58   Trio features bustling figuration made up mainly of rising scale fragments. Strings treat it imitatively, with each entry higher than the previous one. The shift back to major mode helps give the passage a sunnier mood.

2:14   An almost literal repetition of the section. This is Beethoven regaining his energy.

2:30   Second part of the trio continues the energetic mood. Eventually, the entire orchestra joins in, leading to a rousing ending.

2:58   Repetition begins as before, but the texture thins out, the music grows softer, and the dynamic level drops: a foreshadowing of deafness.

SCHERZO

3:30   Opening theme returns. Its restatement is played with more separation between notes. The loss of resonance is Beethoven's way of conveying the onset of deafness. This worsens as the movement continues to unfold.

3:50   Fate motive returns, played softly and accompanied with pizzicato (plucked) strings

4:12   Opening theme returns again, played softly and with separation. It continues with just violins playing the melody pizzicato, and a spare accompaniment. The fate motive returns; it is almost inaudibly soft.

TRANSITION

4:46   With a surprising harmony sustained by the strings and the timpani lightly tapping out the motive, Beethoven portrays his almost complete deafness and the despair that accompanies it.

5:00   From this low point, Beethoven seems to rise from the ashes. The opening theme comes back but breaks off into fragments, which slowly come together as they gather the momentum to lead into the final movement.

 Listen to this selection streaming or in an Active Listening Guide at CourseMate or in the eBook.

156 | CHAPTER 11 : beethoven

Beethoven, Symphony No. 5 in C minor, 4th movement (1808)

TAKEAWAY POINT: Triumphal conclusion to a remarkable, and remarkably integrated, symphony

STYLE: Late Classical/early Romantic

FORM: Sonata form

GENRE: Symphony

INSTRUMENTS: Full orchestra, with extra high and low winds added

CONTEXT: An emphatically positive ending to a symphony that began with great foreboding

EXPOSITION

0:00 *Theme 1:* In three notes, Beethoven establishes key, tempo, and meter. The theme as a whole communicates a sense of well-being through the sound of the trumpets and the quick rise and smooth descent of the melody.

0:33 *Transition:* The transition modulates simply and effortlessly to the new key while maintaining the upbeat character of the opening. There are no detours or shifts in mood; the music marches straight to the second theme.

0:59 *Theme 2:* Second theme puts a new spin on the fate motive. The da-da-da-dumm rhythm remains, but linked to a rising scale fragment, which is repeated again and again, in numerous forms. The overall good humor takes the sting out of the fate motive.

1:25 Melody built from another scale fragment before final push to end of exposition. Sonata form is typically about the creation and release of musical tension. But in this movement, there is little tension; rather, the entire exposition is exuberant.

DEVELOPMENT

2:00 Second theme provides raw material for development. Begins with restatement of theme in higher key and continues through a number of keys, moving around the orchestra. A four-note motive heard first as a supporting line becomes more prominent.

2:23 Bold new version of second theme, now focusing on the development of four-note motive originally in the accompaniment.

2:31 A brief shift to minor and an expansion of the four-note motive, played by the trombones, continue this relatively turbulent section, which continues to build.

2:45 The trumpets comment behind the strings with a fast version of the fate motive as heard in the third movement.

3:00 The section ends with a long passage almost exclusively on the chord that leads back to the tonic. For about half a minute, it sounds as though the recapitulation is imminent, but Beethoven has one last surprise in store.

3:31 Instead of resolving, the music dies down and Beethoven returns to a subdued version of the fate motive in the third movement.

3:38 Beethoven adds a mournful oboe countermelody—a flashback to the oboe cadenza in the first movement. It is as if Beethoven acknowledges that his deafness is incurable. The preparation for the recap evidences his resolve to triumph over his affliction.

RECAPITULATION

4:09 *Theme 1:* The theme as a whole communicates a sense of well-being through the sound of the trumpets and the quick rise and smooth descent of the melody. The music that follows reinforces the mood.

4:42 *Transition:* An expansion of the transition in the exposition, to create activity before the arrival of the second theme in the home key

5:13 *Theme 2:* The second theme, now in the home key

5:38 The closing theme returns, also in the home key. It leads to an extension of the recapitulation.

6:09 Instead of bringing the movement and the symphony to a close, Beethoven continues by developing the second theme motive. It leads to a big climax, which sounds as if the symphony will end.

(Continued)

6:40   Instead of a final cadence, Beethoven now develops the material from the transition section, then accelerates the tempo into a frantic rush to the end.

7:33   Beethoven builds the final sprint to the end from the closing theme, now at the brisker tempo.

7:48   The first theme returns at a faster tempo that sounds almost like a fanfare. The symphony ends with a seemingly endless string of cadences and finally music that sustains the tonic. In another context, this would have been overkill; here, it is fitting.

 Listen to this selection streaming or in an Active Listening Guide at CourseMate or in the eBook.

returns several times after contrasting material. By contrast, Beethoven's finale is the longest of the four movements. In it, he uses sonata form, the most substantial and serious form in the Classical style.

The sun breaks through at the beginning of the fourth movement, as the brass-led orchestra blasts out an affirmative melody. The mood remains upbeat through most of the movement. The most extended agitation comes in the development section, which ends with a great "wait a minute" moment: first, the orchestra gets stuck on the chord that should lead back to the recapitulation, and then it dissolves into a brief recollection of the third movement. This passage suggests a momentary setback on the inevitable road to triumph.

The fourth movement sprints to the end with a sudden shift to a faster tempo, then concludes with a long string of tonic chords. The ending is the final evidence of Beethoven's conception of the symphony as a multi-movement narrative: the chords are much too emphatic for the close of a movement—even a long movement. But as the conclusion of a symphony that began with such a struggle, it serves as a final affirmation of the triumph of will over fate.

11-3E Sound and Feeling

Beethoven's Fifth Symphony is a powerful statement with a clear emotional message; no discerning listener would likely hear the first movement as happy and serene or the last movement as agitated and somber. Beethoven achieves this expressive power through an approach that is simultaneously direct and subliminal. The directness comes from elemental oppositions—loud/soft, fast/slow, up/down, thick/thin, measured/unmeasured—that are sound-painted in broad strokes and from the opening motive, the musical seed from which the entire symphony grows. The subliminal impact comes from the complex network of associations spawned from the opening motive and Beethoven's forceful bending of customary practice in the search for greater expression.

A large part of Beethoven's genius in this symphony is his ability to put ordinary material in extraordinary settings, to heighten or oppose the unsettled mood of the opening. Beethoven crafts the opening motive from generic materials: two notes of a

chord, a simple rhythm. But because he invests it with such significance by presenting it initially out of time, out of key, and without accompaniment, it immediately becomes specific to the symphony and emotionally charged. And because so much of the remaining thematic material is either an outgrowth of it or a response to it, Beethoven can intensify, shift, or contrast moods while still retaining a sense of identity.

LEARNING OUTCOME 11-4
Grasp the impact of Beethoven and his music.

11-4 Beethoven's Legacy

Beethoven's position in the history of classical music is unique. He and his music were revered during his lifetime and have never gone out of favor. His music—the symphonies and sonatas, concertos and chamber music—has been consistently performed, analyzed, and emulated since its composition. The music that we have heard is over two hundred years old, but it is more familiar to us than it was to people in Beethoven's own time, and far more familiar than any contemporary orchestral or piano music.

Why this unique status? It begins, of course, with the music. Beethoven's important music is big and bold. It has personality: major works sound like Beethoven and no one else, yet each work has a highly individual character. His music evolved over several decades; until his death, Beethoven was searching for new directions. Much of Beethoven's music is at once accessible and sophisticated—it can go straight to the heart and challenge the mind. It is optimistic: even works that begin darkly, like the Fifth and Ninth Symphonies, end in triumph.

Then there is Beethoven the man, the man who lived for his art, who overcame a devastating affliction, and who struggled to transcend the limitations imposed by society and his musical contemporaries. And he also had the good fortune to be born in the right place at the right time. He lived during an era when the centuries-old monarchical tradition was disintegrating, when what you achieved and what you stood for began to matter more than who your parents were. Beethoven's life and work became a symbol of this new order, not only for his time but also for

Nicku/Shutterstock.com

Wolfgang Amade Mozart.

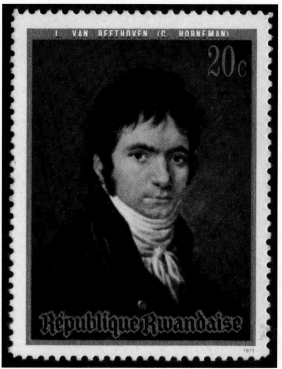

Artemiy Bogdanoff/Shutterstock.com

Beethoven's hair gives us some insight into the changing times and his place in them. From the seventeenth through the early nineteenth centuries, men's wigs were an external symbol of high rank. During the eighteenth century, members of the upper class and those who moved in upper-class circles—such as Bach, Handel, Haydn, and Mozart (left)—routinely wore wigs. By contrast, even the earliest authentic portraits of Beethoven (right) show his hair. These images suggest the power of his personality—his determination to be his own person, his disdain for class standing based on birth rather than achievement.

subsequent generations. He came at a time of musical transition; almost single-handedly, he engineered the shift from Classicism to Romanticism, and the wholesale change of values that went with it. Beethoven was clearly a man for his times.

Moreover, Beethoven elevated the status of the composer from servant to artist. Haydn worked for the Esterházy family. Beethoven demanded a pension from his aristocratic patrons so that he would not have to concern himself with such mundane matters as money. Our modern conception of the musician as artist derives most directly from him.

Beethoven is the quintessential composer. In his music and his life, he epitomizes the composer as artist—as one hyperenthusiastic biographer put it: Beethoven, the Man Who Freed Music. Virtually since his arrival in Vienna, people have responded to the power and boldness of his music and his personal magnetism and, in particular, his struggle with the musician's ultimate adversity: deafness.

We sense in Beethoven's music that he is almost compelled to follow his own path rather than write on demand. No other composer has gone through such a dramatic evolution in style. That he continued to develop as a composer despite the seemingly insurmountable obstacle his deafness imposed makes his

achievement even more compelling. No single person has had a greater impact on musical life in Western civilization than Beethoven.

Looking Back, Looking Ahead

Beethoven cast a long shadow over the nineteenth century, musically and culturally. All felt his presence, and most claimed him as an influence; those few who didn't, such as Chopin, felt compelled to assert that he did *not* influence their work.

Beethoven was indirectly responsible for the idea of classical music as we now understand it. It was only after Beethoven's death that the practice of offering concerts of music by deceased composers really took root. One important reason was to keep alive Beethoven's musical legacy. Franz Liszt, the great nineteenth-century piano virtuoso (and "grand-pupil" of Beethoven, having studied with Carl Czerny, one of Beethoven's piano students), began programming piano recitals that included Beethoven sonatas (and his own piano transcriptions of the symphonies). Newly emerging resident orchestras made his symphonies the cornerstone of their repertoire—as they are now.

In his ability to project strong emotions and moods through his music and to invest compositions with decidedly individual character, Beethoven was in tune with two main currents of Romanticism: the emphasis on feeling and the focus on the individual. The symphony discussed in this chapter stands apart from earlier works in the boldness of its conception and the way it expresses a range of moods so comprehensively and cogently. Add to that the power of Beethoven's personality and his role in elevating the stature of the artist, and we can readily understand why Hoffmann considered Beethoven the ultimate Romantic.

At the same time, Beethoven's music retains the logic and coherence that characterize the best music of the Classical style. The slow introduction to the "Pathétique" and the pure opening motive of the Fifth Symphony are dramatic departures from convention that communicate a sense of breaking free of the constraints imposed by the expectations of Classical style. However, as the movements unfold, we discover that each is a necessary first step in projecting the expressive intent of the movement and that there is an indivisible connection between opening gesture and large-scale conception. In retrospect, we are left with the distinct impression that the movements had to begin as they did; anything less bold would have diluted their expressive message.

Beethoven challenged himself again and again to stretch the boundaries of Classical style without forsaking its integrity. That he succeeded so often is even more shocking than the musical features that so often shocked his audiences.

 study tools 11

Ready to study?
In the book you can:

- Review Learning Outcome answers and Glossary terms with the tear-out Chapter Review card.

Or you can go online to CourseMate, at www.cengagebrain.com, for these resources:

- Chapter Quizzes to prepare for tests

- Interactive flashcards of all Glossary terms

- Active Listening Guides, streaming music, and YouTube playlists

- An eBook with live links to all web resources

Classical Style

 ## KEY CONCEPTS

Drama with or without words. In its most sophisticated and characteristic expressions, the Classical style is inherently dramatic, because composers can create, regulate, and resolve musical tension within a movement or work.

 ## KEY FEATURES

In the Classical style, contrast is comprehensive and frequent. It is often evident in these ways:

1. **Melody plus simple, frequently changing accompaniments.** Accompaniment patterns tend to be simple. They include occasional chords filling out the harmony, repeated chords, and various arpeggiated chord patterns. More contrapuntal textures occur mainly in developmental sections. Frequent change of texture is typical.
2. **Terraced and tapered dynamics.** Dynamic change is frequent. The two most common options are abrupt shifts between loud and soft and crescendos, such as gradual change from soft to loud. Diminuendos (gradual change from loud to soft) are less common.
3. **Varied rhythms.** Rhythmic contrast occurs on both a local and a global scale. It can occur within a melody, typically between phrases, and it almost always occurs between sections. Moreover, rhythms usually accelerate in the approach to structural goals, such as the end of a major section or the end of the movement.
4. **Melodic contrast.** The most pronounced contrasts are those between tuneful melody and figuration or other faster-moving lines. These typically occur between sections but can also occur within a theme. Contrast between different kinds of melodic material within a theme or section, such as a statement and response, also occurs regularly.
5. **Well-articulated forms.** Classical compositions generally feature frequent articulation through decisive cadences and/or sudden shifts in multiple elements.

 ## KEY TERMS

1. **Sonata form.** The most common form in first movements of Classical instrumental compositions. Such movements contain an exposition, development, and recapitulation. Some sonata-form movements also feature an introduction and a coda.
2. **String quartet.** Ensemble featuring two violinists, a violist, and a cellist. Also, the term used for compositions written for this ensemble.
3. **Cadenza.** Rhapsodic and virtuosic passage for the solo instrument in a concerto, characterized by rhythmic freedom and an improvisatory succession of events

 ## KEY COMPOSERS

Christoph Willibald Gluck (1714–1787)
Carl Philipp Emanuel Bach (1714–1788)
Johann Stamitz (1717–1757)
Franz Joseph Haydn (1732–1790)
Wolfgang Amadeus Mozart (1756–1791)
Ludwig van Beethoven (1770–1827)

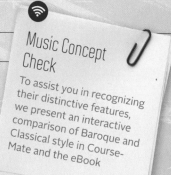

Music Concept Check

To assist you in recognizing their distinctive features, we present an interactive comparison of Baroque and Classical style in Course-Mate and the eBook

LEARNING OUTCOMES

After reading this chapter, you will be able to do the following:

12-1 Chart the development of diverse trends in nineteenth-century musical life: music publishing, music education, musical instruments and technologies, and entertainment.

12-2 Describe the characteristics of Romanticism.

12-3 Discuss the increasing stratification of musical life, particularly in the latter part of the nineteenth century

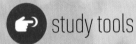 study tools

After you read this chapter, go to the Study Tools at the end of the chapter, page 171.

On March 26, 1827, Ludwig van Beethoven passed away. Three days later, twenty thousand people lined the streets of Vienna to observe his funeral procession. By the time of his death, Beethoven had become a celebrated figure throughout Europe and especially in Vienna, although his deafness had kept him from performing publicly for almost two decades. Contemporary reports suggest that the size of the crowd—over 5 percent of Vienna's population—surpassed that for any previous funeral.

On March 11, 1829, Felix Mendelssohn conducted a performance of J. S. Bach's St. Matthew Passion at the Berlin Singakademie. It was the first public performance of the work since Bach's death, although Mendelssohn's teacher Carl Zelter had rehearsed it privately as early as 1815. The concert, so successful that it was repeated twice within a few weeks, was the catalyst for the resurrection of Bach's music.

The death of one great composer and the resurrection of another highlight profound changes in musical life during the nineteenth century. Beethoven's lionization by the Viennese signaled the ascension of the artist: the musician was no longer a servant; greatness was now measured by achievement, not birth. The Bach revival both stimulated and confirmed interest in music of the past; "classical music"—that is, music from the past worth preserving or reviving—became a significant and regular part of musical life. The corollary to heightened awareness of the past was a vision of the future;

> If the Enlightenment was Western civilization's left brain at work, Romanticism was its right brain.

indeed, one of the important new directions in the latter part of the century was "music of the future." Further, the posthumous veneration of Beethoven and Bach gave nineteenth-century composers hope that future generations would value their music, even if contemporary audiences did not.

LEARNING OUTCOME 12-1

Chart the development of diverse trends in nineteenth-century musical life: music publishing, music education, musical instruments and technologies, and entertainment.

12-1 The Expansion of Musical Life

In the nineteenth century, the erosion of monarchical authority, the decline of the influence of organized religion, economic growth, new technologies, better transportation, and an expanding middle class transformed the music professions from a system that still relied heavily on church and court patronage to one that derived much more of its revenue from the marketplace. Music publishing grew exponentially to cater to increased demand. Writing about music became a profession. Public performance, from operas and orchestral concerts to minstrel shows and band concerts, grew at a comparable rate, and institutions and industries grew up around them. Newly founded conservatories trained professional and amateur performers and composers. Instrument makers applied newly developed manufacturing processes to invent new and to improve existing instruments.

12-1A Music Publishing

Music publishing flourished in the 1800s for several reasons. Most significant was the growth of the middle class; their numbers, added to those of the upper class, greatly expanded the market for secular musical compositions, especially songs and piano music. Both came at several levels of sophistication, from art songs by Schubert and Schumann to minstrel show ditties, from virtuoso pieces to simple dance tunes for one or two players. The market grew for these genres as pianos became less expensive and more readily available.

For most of the nineteenth century, Americans could learn lyrics to the latest songs from published song sheets. These were new songs being sung in music halls or new lyrics to familiar songs, like "Yankee Doodle" or "The Last Rose of Summer." Some of America's most beloved tunes were printed as song sheets, including "The Star-Spangled Banner" and the "Battle Hymn of the Republic."

The growing interest in classical music also contributed to the growth of music publishing. This included both new editions of established repertoire and publication of earlier music previously available only in manuscript. The most notable instance of the latter came about with the formation of the Bach Gesellschaft in 1850 (the centenary of J. S. Bach's death), which had as its main goal the publication of all of Bach's extant music. For much of the century, music publishers' catalogs contained all kinds of music. However, in the last quarter of the century, a few music publishers in New York began issuing only popular songs.

In a time before recordings, radio, and television, many middle-class families made their own music.

This was a crucial step in the formation of a distinct popular music tradition.

12-1B Music and Words

Words and music came together in a multitude of new ways during the nineteenth century. The most prominent was an outpouring of song: sophisticated art songs for sophisticated audiences; simpler songs, many of which were settings of old folk melodies, created mainly for home use; and songs for various kinds of mass public entertainment. There was also music inspired by words: instrumental compositions that used literary works, such as Lenau's *Don Juan*, as a program, as well as programs written by the composer.

12-1C Music Education

With the growth in music publishing and writing came a drive for music education at all levels, from music literacy for everyone to the highest-level training for aspiring professionals. For the general public, vocal-music education became a component of public school instruction in Europe and North America over the course of the nineteenth century.

More specialized musical training had been mainly the province of church schools from medieval times through the eighteenth century. As they closed, conservatories were formed to take their place. Among the first was the Paris Conservatoire, founded in 1795. Other conservatories

musicologist Scholar who researches the history of music

were founded in major European musical centers, such as Vienna and London, throughout the nineteenth century. The first American conservatory was the Peabody Conservatory in Baltimore, founded in 1857 and now part of Johns Hopkins University. Many of these conservatories were formed to train orchestral musicians, who required more rigorous training to meet the demands of increasingly difficult orchestral music in the concert hall and the opera orchestra pit. Conservatories also catered to amateurs; their fees helped make ends meet. Their popularity was one sign of a growing middle class, many of whom had upper-class aspirations. Conservatories also trained singers for opera and oratorio, keyboard performers, and composers.

Academic study of music as an independent scholarly discipline gradually took shape during the nineteenth century, especially in France and German-speaking Europe. The work of pioneering musicologists (scholars who research the history of music) provided essential support for the rediscovery of music of the past—not only Bach and his contemporaries but also medieval and Renaissance composers.

Collectively, these developments put in place the structure of the contemporary classical music world. Many of the major institutions in contemporary musical life have been in place since the latter part of the nineteenth century.

12-1D Musical Instruments and Technology

The technological advances introduced during the nineteenth century had a substantial impact on almost every aspect of musical life, including the size and makeup of audiences, the venues where they heard music, transportation, publishing and dissemination of music, and—toward the end of the century—sound recording. However, the most significant impact was the introduction of manufacturing into the production of musical instruments.

Manufacturing made working with metal easier, more efficient, and more consistent. Accordingly, most of the major innovations in instrument making involved metal. Instrument makers invented dozens of new instruments; most were metal wind instruments. The most famous maker was the Belgian Adolphe Sax, who gave his name to full lines of saxophones and saxhorns.

Of the instruments invented during the nineteenth century, only one, the tuba, has become an integral part of the symphony orchestra. Others, such as the saxhorns and euphonium, found a home in bands. The saxophone eventually became a part-time member of the orchestra, a full-time member of the military band, and since the 1920s, the dominant wind instrument in popular music.

More far-reaching were the modifications of existing instruments, most significantly the piano and the wind, brass, and percussion instruments of the orchestra.

The Piano. Around 1800, the piano was a delicate wood-framed instrument with a range of five octaves. By 1900, it had grown into the concert instrument that we know today. The most significant improvement was the development of a one-piece metal frame by the American piano builder Alpheus Babcock in 1825. This allowed piano makers to string the piano much more tightly, which in turn dramatically increased the amount of sound the instrument could produce. By the 1850s, the metal-frame piano was the norm in the United States and Europe. There were other improvements: a faster, more reliable action and expansion of the range to more than seven octaves. In the latter part of the century, piano manufacturers converted to a factory system, which enabled them to make more instruments less expensively. The piano became the household instrument of choice for middle- and upper-class households, as well as the most popular concert instrument.

Orchestral Instruments. Among woodwinds, the flute underwent the most dramatic change; it became a metal instrument, although it remained part of the woodwind section. All of the woodwinds acquired extra keys for greater fluency. Brass instruments benefited even more from new technology; trumpets and horns acquired valves or pistons, which enabled musicians to play any note in any scale within the range of the instrument. These advances allowed brass instruments to play a more active role in orchestras. Timpani received a similar upgrade through devices that enabled the performer to rapidly change the pitch of the drum.

Sound Recording. In 1877, the great American inventor Thomas Edison successfully captured his voice on a device he called a "phonograph"; the recording medium was a cylinder covered with tinfoil. Eleven years later, he produced and marketed an improved version; so did a company that included Alexander Graham Bell, the inventor of the telephone. By 1890, the record business was up and running. Among the first groups to be recorded was the Sousa band. In 1894, Emile Berliner,

By the turn of the century, concert bands, such as the one led by John Philip Sousa, were the most popular musical ensembles in the United States.

who would eventually found Victor records, began issuing recordings on discs rather than cylinders. His technology would eventually win out and remain in place for the better part of the twentieth century. The most significant fact about these early sound recordings is that they happened. Early acoustic recordings are virtually unlistenable because the fidelity is so poor and the surface noise so disruptive. Still, it was the beginning of a technology that would transform the music industry and transform the listening experience in subsequent generations.

12-1E The Growth of Musical Entertainment

In the nineteenth century, music went public. Musical entertainment—and entertainment in which music is

Descendant of Edison's "phonograph"

Conductors grew in stature to become dictatorial figures.

Among the most significant developments were Richard Wagner's music dramas, which were based on Teutonic myths; nationalistic operas from Bohemia, Russia, and elsewhere; grand and comic opera in France; and Gilbert and Sullivan's operettas in England. Opera singers were among the most celebrated artists in Europe and North America; they enjoyed rock star like celebrity.

During the nineteenth century, orchestras joined opera companies as major cultural institutions. At the beginning of the century, resident civic orchestras did not exist: the orchestra that Salomon assembled for Haydn's visits was an ad hoc ensemble. By the end of the nineteenth century there were resident symphony orchestras in London, Paris, Vienna, Berlin, Amsterdam, and other major European cities, as well as New York, Boston, Chicago, and several other American cities. Most were formed in the latter part of the century; the New York Philharmonic, formed in 1842, was one of the first. Orchestra programs included a mix of well-known standard repertoire and contemporary works.

Among the stars of nineteenth-century musical life were touring soloists and conductors. Audiences flocked to hear singers such as Jenny Lind and instrumentalists such as the violinist Niccolò Paganini and the pianist Franz Liszt. Conductors were the quintessential nineteenth-century musical figures: an individual in charge of a big ensemble. With Felix Mendelssohn in the 1830s, and Berlioz and Wagner in the 1850s, conductors literally grew in stature from first violinists occasionally beating time with their bows to dictatorial figures standing on a podium waving a baton as they led orchestras in their personal interpretation of Beethoven's or—in many cases—their own music.

Ballet went solo during the nineteenth century. For the better part of two centuries, it had been an integral part of opera, especially in France. After 1830, it emerged as an independent expressive art. By the last quarter of the century, it was well established in France and in Russia, where French high culture was dominant. The most important nineteenth-century composer of ballet was Tchaikovsky.

More popular and commercially oriented analogs to these classical genres also took shape during the nineteenth century, especially after 1850. Musical stage entertainment included operettas, popular both

an integral part—grew rapidly in the first half of the century, then mushroomed during the second half. A major reason for this accelerated growth was the rapid increase in mass entertainment. By the end of the century, professional musical entertainment included several well-established genres directed toward a mass audience. In the United States, these ranged from musical comedy, minstrel shows, and vaudeville to concerts by touring concert bands.

The growth of what gradually became classical music was comparably dramatic. Among the most important trends was the institutionalization of classical music: resident opera companies and orchestras in major cities; public concerts by solo performers, especially singers and pianists; and formation of societies for the preservation and exploration of earlier music, like the Berlin Singakademie, where Mendelssohn conducted Bach's *St. Matthew Passion*, and Boston's Handel and Haydn Society, one of America's most venerable musical institutions. Other important developments include the emergence of new music-dependent art forms, most notably ballet.

Opera flourished during the nineteenth century, musically and commercially. Four generations of Italian composers, including the well-known Gioachino Rossini, Giuseppe Verdi, and, at the end of the century, Giacomo Puccini, composed the works that quickly became opera's core repertory. Rossini and Verdi were among the most popular composers of the century; much of their music trickled down into popular culture. Opera further diversified culturally and geographically.

in England and North America and in German-speaking Europe; musical comedy; and the minstrel show, an American entertainment that also became popular in Europe, especially England and France. Bands were the popular counterpart to orchestras; in America, professional concert bands, most notably the one led by John Philip Sousa, were among the top attractions.

Social dancing became a more commercial enterprise that appealed to all classes. Venues ranged from elegant ballrooms to working-class dance halls. Musical accompaniment was similarly varied, from the sophisticated Viennese dance orchestras, most notably those of the Strauss family, to a fiddler or piano player. The waltz, a dance of humble origins, became the most popular social dance of the nineteenth century. Folk dances, especially from exotic locales or subcultures, became popular music for dancing or performing at home. They ranged from "Hungarian" and Slavonic dances to jigs, reels, and cakewalks.

By the end of the century, audiences had many more choices for musical entertainment. Some types—from ballet and traveling opera stars and virtuosi to concert bands and minstrel troupes—were almost unimaginable at the beginning of the century. At the dawn of the twentieth century, musical entertainment was truly a business, and a thriving one.

LEARNING OUTCOME 12-2
Describe the characteristics of Romanticism.

12-2 Romanticism and Nineteenth-Century Music

The 1800s were the Romantic century. They were also a century of industrialization and urbanization, exploration and colonization. Romantic values both resonated with and reacted against tumultuous changes in Western society. Even as they continued the secularization and democratization of society brought about by the Enlightenment and the two major revolutions of the late eighteenth century, they rejected Enlightenment values.

If the Enlightenment was Western civilization's left brain at work, Romanticism was its right brain. The Enlightenment valued rationality and the human's role in society. Romanticism valued subjectivity, feeling, and inspiration, and venerated individuals whose work expressed those values. A Romantic sensibility underpinned many of the significant musical trends during the century. Among them were a focus on individuality, an obsession with size, and a fascination with the exotic. Each found multiple forms of expression during the course of the nineteenth century.

12-2A Individuality

The Romantic emphasis on subjectivity and feeling focused the spotlight on the individual. Among the most significant musical expressions of this tendency were the quest for individuality, the rise of the virtuoso performer, and the growing division between composition and performance.

Personal Styles. The most esteemed Romantic composers cultivated a personal style to a much greater degree than their eighteenth-century predecessors. The differences between Berlioz, Liszt, and Schumann, or Wagner, Brahms, and Tchaikovsky are more pronounced than those between Haydn and Mozart, or Bach and Handel. Composers' individual styles were a product of several cultural forces. Most generally, this involved the elevation in status of the musician, especially the composer, from servant to artistic genius. This dynamic new environment encouraged composers to follow their own path, regardless of where it took them. Another factor was a heightened awareness of the past, particularly of Beethoven, whose music is notable for its individuality, both in general style and from work to work. It is no coincidence that the stylistic contrast from composer to composer increased as the idea of classical music became more entrenched.

Virtuosity. Through Paganini and Liszt, the musical world fell in love with virtuosity, performance skills well beyond the norm. Their breathtakingly brilliant playing mesmerized audiences, who found their seemingly superhuman abilities incredible. It was widely rumored, and apparently often believed, that Paganini had made a pact with the devil in order to achieve his supreme mastery of the violin.

The most obvious compositional evidence of the heightened appreciation for virtuosic performance was the elevation of the etude. An etude—étude is the French word for "study"—is a musical work designed to develop a particular technical skill. In Beethoven's time, these were pieces used to prepare performers for real repertoire. With Liszt, Chopin, and their contemporaries, the etude became concert music. Virtuosity was not confined to the etude; much of the important solo and orchestral literature demanded greater fluency and new techniques. The piano music of, for example, Chopin, Liszt, and Schumann; the concertos of Brahms and Tchaikovsky; and the orchestral music of Wagner and Strauss still challenge today's best musicians.

At its worst, virtuosity is a stunt—an excuse to show off a particular skill. However, for many Romantic composers, virtuosity dramatically extended the range of possibility:

Romanticism Cultural movement of the nineteenth century that valued subjectivity, feeling, and inspiration and venerated individuals whose work expressed those values; a Romantic sensibility that had a focus on individuality, an obsession with size, and a fascination with the exotic

virtuosity Performance skills far beyond the norm; extraordinary technical abilities

etude Musical work designed to develop a particular technical skill

Franz Liszt was the matinee idol of the Romantic era, here shown performing for a crowd of adoring female fans.

A. DAGLI ORTI/De Agostini Picture Library/Getty Images

more elaborate figuration; richer, more florid accompaniments; stunning sounds; and more powerful gestures. Liszt, the king of piano virtuosos, claimed that "virtuosity is not an outgrowth, but an indispensable element of music." For him and many other Romantic composers, it was.

Composers and Performers. In the 1830s and for most of the 1840s, Franz Liszt, perhaps the most celebrated pianist of any era, toured Europe—from Russia to Ireland. He dazzled audiences, broke hearts, composed fiendishly difficult works, arranged the works of other composers for the piano, and generally caused a sensation wherever he played. In 1847, at the urging of his new mistress, Carolyn Sayn-Wittgenstein, he abruptly stopped performing. He settled in Weimar, a small duchy in Germany with a long and rich artistic heritage, where he concentrated on composing, teaching, and conducting the orchestra.

> "Virtuosity is not an outgrowth, but an indispensable element of music."
> —Franz Liszt

It is almost as if Liszt flipped a switch in 1847. Several major composers from the first half of the century—Beethoven, Mendelssohn, Chopin, Liszt—were also outstanding performers; most of the major composers from the latter half—Wagner, Tchaikovsky, Richard Strauss, Dvořák—were not well known as performers, although Brahms toured occasionally as a pianist. Moreover, those composers who focused on opera, most notably, Rossini, Verdi, Wagner, and Puccini, are remembered exclusively for their composing.

The division of musical labor that occurred in the nineteenth century resulted from numerous factors. Among the most significant were the increasing demands of composition and performance. The twin pressures of size and originality made composition a more arduous task, and the increasing difficulty of the music that composers produced compelled performers to devote more time to preparing music for performance.

In the wake of the success of Paganini and Liszt, virtuosi rivaled opera stars as celebrity musicians. Women swooned; men sat in amazement at their skill. They became the object of admiration, especially when they married technical brilliance with expressive artistry. Their popularity, and the popularity of conductors in the latter part of the century, was due not only to musical changes but also to changes within society: the increase in the number of public concerts, the Romantic appreciation of artistic genius, focus on the individual, and sensitivity to feeling. Instrumentalists and conductors personified the music that audiences heard. It is through them that audiences connected to the music. Then as now, they received the lion's share of the attention.

It was still possible to be a successful composer and a successful performer at the end of the nineteenth century. What was seemingly not possible was the pursuit of both activities simultaneously. Mozart's practice of performing a concerto completed the night before was all but inconceivable a century later; the music had become too difficult, and standards in solo and orchestral playing had risen considerably. Those musicians who pursued both careers typically did so in alternation: Gustav Mahler conducted during the concert season, which paralleled the school year, and composed in the summer. The Russian composer/pianist/conductor Sergei Rachmaninoff admitted that he was most comfortable when he could devote his time and energy to only one activity at a time. In general, fewer musicians elected to follow multiple paths.

12-2B Size

The nineteenth century was obsessed with size—from colonial empires, most notably the British, on which the sun never set; to the territorial expansion of the United

View of the Great Coliseum at the World's Peace Jubilee

States and the railroad that spanned it; to rapidly growing cities, many with skyscrapers by the end of the century; to enormous fortunes acquired by captains of industry and the palatial estates on which they spent them; to international expositions in London (1851), Paris (1889), and Chicago (1893). All this and more earned public admiration.

The obsession with bigness carried over into almost every aspect of musical life. Festivals drew huge crowds who heard mammoth ensembles. Among the most spectacular was the World's Peace Jubilee and International Musical Festival, organized by American bandmaster Patrick Gilmore and presented in Boston in 1872; it featured a twenty thousand–voice chorus and a two thousand–member orchestra playing in a newly erected pavilion that held one hundred thousand people.

Stage performances could feature enormous casts and last for hours, or even days. However, the grandest staged music event of the century was Richard Wagner's *Der Ring des Nibelungen*, a cycle of four music dramas that last about fifteen hours. After 1876, one could hear the Ring cycle at the Bayreuth Festspielhaus, the theater constructed specifically for performances of Wagner's works.

Orchestras more than doubled in size during the course of the century, in response to increased demands from composers. Many required much larger brass, wind, and percussion sections, with string sections also expanded to balance the rest of the orchestra. Inspired by Beethoven, who increased the size of the orchestra and lengthened symphonic works, composers such as Berlioz, Bruckner, and Mahler wrote expansive symphonies often lasting more than an hour.

Bigness was even evident in miniatures such as Chopin's preludes, which expanded what would be a short section within a larger work into a stand-alone composition.

12-2c Beyond the Norm

At the beginning of the century, the music business catered mainly to urban upper- and middle-class audiences. From this starting point, nineteenth-century musicians reached out in every direction to expand the musical world that they had inherited. They looked to the past and projected into the future. They looked and listened in the countryside to find inspiration and national identity. They were stimulated by the exotic: faraway places and people. They bypassed established religion to explore the spiritual directly or delve into the diabolical. They sought inspiration from and communion with the other arts: literature, the visual arts, and dance. Their open-mindedness was comprehensive and unprecedented.

Past and Future. In 1860, Richard Wagner published "Zukunftsmusik" ("Music of the Future"). Wagner claimed that the future direction of music was the synthesis of the arts that he championed in his later operas. It wasn't, but Wagner still became the most influential composer of the late nineteenth century.

Wagner's main partner in this musical vanguard was Franz Liszt; each influenced the other significantly. Liszt was not a polemicist, but his later works anticipate important developments in twentieth-century music, including more rigorous adaptations of folk materials, musical impressionism, and atonality (a system of tonal organization in which pitches do not focus around a tonic).

Wagner's pronouncement was the corollary to nineteenth-century musicians' greater awareness of the past (if there's a past, there must also be a future) and, more specifically, the sense, especially among German and German-based musicians, that their music was a continuation of Beethoven's legacy.

More pervasively, the music of previous generations, especially the music of Beethoven, both inspired and intimidated nineteenth-century composers, who typically followed one of three paths: emulate the classics, outdo the classics, or find a completely novel path.

Major instrumental genres—the sonata, the concerto, and especially the symphony—gained in prestige during the course of the century. Most of the important instrumental composers of the century composed some of each, even though the presence of Beethoven loomed over them. No major nineteenth-century composer completed more than nine symphonies, and only a very few of those works were as monumental as Beethoven's own Ninth Symphony. Still, a few composers took established genres beyond what Beethoven and the eighteenth century had done: Chopin's set of twenty-four preludes, Liszt's piano sonata, Brahms's second piano concerto, and Berlioz's *Symphonie fantastique* stand out in this regard. The more common paths toward originality were the creation of new forms and genres, such as the tone poem, and the reinvigoration and expansion of small forms, many of them from dances.

Opera maintained its elite status while embracing a far wider range of subject matter; not surprisingly, the music dramas of Wagner were the most forward looking, even as they reached back into a distant Teutonic past. The most important and innovative vocal genre of the century was the *Lied* (German for "song"; see Chapter 13), which embedded melody in individual, often complex accompaniments and elevated song into a higher artistic statement.

Folk Music, Nature, and National Identity. One consequence of rapid urbanization was a nostalgia for and idealization of the countryside and those who lived there. Nature was a recurrent theme in both vocal and instrumental music; it inspired composers to create evocative effects, especially in orchestral music and music for solo piano. Folk song settings, such as Thomas Moore's ten volumes of *Irish Melodies*, were among the most popular music of the century. Folk dances, especially those with a clear cultural identity, were the instrumental analog to folk song settings: Brahms's *Hungarian Dances* (actually inspired by gypsy music rather than Hungarian peasant music) were among his best-selling compositions. Folk dances also provided a clear musical signal of national identity for expatriates like Chopin and for those on the periphery of Germany. The geographic identity of the waltz, Europe's most popular dance, was even more specific. Its most characteristic version came from Vienna, the capital of the Austrian Empire, the most diffuse and diverse political entity in Europe.

The folk songs and dances presented in middle- and upper-class musical settings were thoroughly cleansed of many of the defining features of authentic folk style. We know this from comparisons of nineteenth-century folk settings with twentieth-century field recordings of folk performers. Still, the best settings captured much of the vitality of the original and merged it with the craft and richness of classical music. Folk music found a more direct route to the stage in the early minstrel show, whose performers portrayed blacks but sounded more like Irish and Scottish folk musicians.

Exoticism. The continued expansion of colonial empires took Europeans to distant lands; international expositions brought the world to Europe, and eventually the United States. Foreign lands—the Orient (Asia), the Near East, Africa, the Americas, even the Iberian Peninsula—inspired nineteenth-century composers as locales for opera and images and sounds for instrumental compositions. The musical settings, which typically filtered any foreign elements through nineteenth-century musical practice, reflected the cultural imperialism of the age. The exploration of the exotic, like the use of folk traditions, represented a far greater willingness to embrace nondominant cultures.

Death and the Dark Side. The Romantic fascination with death and the dark side expressed itself in numerous ways. The most impressive sacred choral works of the century were requiems, musical settings of the Catholic funeral Mass. Those by Berlioz and Verdi were spectacular and decidedly secular; Brahms's was nondenominational. The *Dies irae* (Day of Wrath), the dire plainchant from the Catholic requiem Mass, became the sound symbol of damnation and witches, demons, and devils, and inspired numerous instrumental compositions.

Marriage of the Arts. A dominant theme in innovative Romantic music was a marriage of the arts. It is most evident and pervasive in the coming together of music and literature. Poetry and music merged in the

---

atonality System of tonal organization in which pitches do not focus around a tonic

art songs of Schubert, Schumann, Brahms, and others. Classic and contemporary literature—such as poetry, drama, and novels—inspired instrumental music. Programmatic works appeared far more frequently, and the programs, often drawn from literature, were usually more detailed.

The visual arts also inspired Romantic-era composers: the composer Robert Schumann claimed that "the educated musician will be able to derive as much usefulness from the study of a Madonna by Raphael as will a painter from a Mozart symphony"; six years later, Liszt composed a piano piece about a Raphael painting. Perhaps the best-known visually inspired work of the century was Modest Mussorgsky's piano tableaus *Pictures at an Exhibition.*

Characteristically, Wagner proposed the grandest artistic synthesis of all. In his theoretical writings, he asserted that music, poetry, and dance must be reunited, as they were in ancient Greece; further, artists and architects would contribute to the production of works that brought together the three classical arts. He called such fusions *Gesamtkunstwerk*, total works of art, or works that synthesize all of the arts.

LEARNING OUTCOME 12-3
Discuss the increasing stratification of musical life, particularly in the latter part of the nineteenth century.

12-3 The Stratification of Music and Musical Life

The cumulative effect of these wide-ranging musical developments was the stratification of music and musical life. At one extreme was the idea of "art for art's sake,"

which led to musical styles far removed from everyday musical language and the formation of an artistic elite around the composers of this music. At the other was popular—and often populist—"lowbrow" music, particularly in the United States.

In between were multiple levels of musical discourse. There were art songs for sophisticated salons and sentimental songs for middle-class parlors. There were piano pieces for earnest amateurs, and sonatas, fantasies, and etudes for skilled professionals. There were operas, operettas, and musical comedy; music for and about dancing; symphonic music that drew inspiration from widely different sources, including folk songs and dances of national and ethnic groups; and music for chamber ensembles of varying sizes.

As a result, musical life in the latter part of the century was different from that in previous generations: the musical languages of the past, present, and future were all part of musical life. Moreover, they were heard at varying levels of sophistication, from the most basic common practice harmony found in popular song and dance music to the complex chromatic harmony of elite classical composers. It is from this time that the idea of "heavy" and "light" music—classical versus popular, heavy classics versus light classics—takes shape, in practice, if not in theory.

We touch on all of these trends in the next several chapters.

Gesamtkunstwerk Total work of art, or work that synthesizes all the arts; associated with Richard Wagner

study tools 12

Ready to study?
In the book you can:

• Review Learning Outcome answers and Glossary terms with the tear-out Chapter Review card.

Or you can go online to CourseMate, at www.cengagebrain.com, for these resources:

• Chapter Quizzes to prepare for tests

• Interactive flashcards of all Glossary terms

• Active Listening Guides, streaming music, and YouTube playlists

• An eBook with live links to all web resources

Louis Edmond Pomey/Fine Art Photographic/Getty Images

LEARNING OUTCOMES

After reading this chapter, you will be able to do the following:

13-1 Describe the flowering of song in the nineteenth century.

13-2 Recognize the art song, through the *Lieder* of Franz Schubert.

13-3 Encounter the song cycle through Robert Schumann's *Dichterliebe*.

13-4 Reexamine the musical and social boundaries between sacred and secular, and religious and spiritual, through an exploration of Brahms's *Requiem*.

study tools

After you read this chapter, go to the Study Tools at the end of the chapter, page 187.

After you read this chapter, go to the Study Tools at the end of the chapter, page 187.

The hottest tickets in Boston and New York in the fall of 1850 were those to concerts by Jenny Lind, the "Swedish nightingale." Lind was one of the leading operatic sopranos in Europe during the 1830s and 1840s; wherever she appeared, impresarios raised ticket prices and still sold out theaters. P. T. Barnum, the man who both raised promotion to an art and also gave it a bad name, sent an agent to London to persuade Lind to come to America for a series of up to 150 concerts. Barnum's agent was persuasive; so was a deposit of $187,500 in a London bank (worth about $4.5 million today). With the contract signed and Lind on the way to the United States, Barnum, who had made his reputation promoting midgets, Siamese twins, mermaids, elephants, and other real and fake "oddities," promoted her visit so well that a crowd estimated to be over thirty thousand people was waiting dockside when she arrived in New York. Barnum auctioned off tickets for her opening concerts: the first one sold for $225 (over $5,000 today). The entire nation was gripped in "Jennymania"; her one-person Swedish invasion was even more far reaching than the British rock invasion a century or so later. Barnum sold out theaters wherever she sang and memorabilia as fast as he could produce it. People named children, towns, schools—even clipper ships—after her. Jenny Lind was America's first imported celebrity.

So popular was the "Swedish nightingale" that she graces her homeland's currency (center).

Although Lind had made her reputation as an opera diva, her programs cut across class boundaries: they included acknowledged classics such as arias from operas and oratorios; popular songs intended for a mainly middle-class audience; and even the most respectable kind of song from the minstrel show, a decidedly lowbrow form of entertainment.

13-1 Song and Singing in the Nineteenth Century

The overwhelming success of Lind's American tour highlights the central place of singing and song in nineteenth-century musical life. Seemingly everyone sang, from opera stars like Lind to laborers learning the current favorites or participating in singing clubs. Song with piano accompaniment, a relatively new genre in 1800, flourished as it hadn't before and hasn't since, in all strata of society. Choral music ranged from simple hymn settings to grand works for chorus and orchestra. Music for stage entertainment, from music dramas to minstrel shows, was often disseminated via sheet music in arrangements for voice(s) and piano. Music was available for every taste and almost every occasion.

Among the most significant reasons for the enormous popularity of singing, both amateur and professional, were the following:

- *Publishers.* Music publishing took off in the nineteenth century, with products aimed at all classes: classical choral works and art songs; popular songs published as sheet music and in "songsters," which contain only words; and hymnals, including shape-note hymnals that simplified music reading.
- *Pianos.* Pianos became the accompanying instrument of choice, and piano manufacturing made them affordable for middle-class families and small businesses.
- *Public performances.* Vocal music in performance grew in multiple ways. Music onstage diversified, from music dramas to minstrel shows. Choral societies in Europe and North America, made up of singers from all classes, performed new and classic choral works. Professional singers performed songs—*Lieder,* popular songs of the day, arias, and more—in concert, in theaters, and in salons.
- *Parlors.* A rapidly growing middle class sang at home in their parlors, the middle-class counterpart to the salons of the upper class, and at church; joined choral societies to sing classical choral masterworks; and attended concerts to hear singers like Jenny Lind.

The extraordinary range of nineteenth-century vocal music clearly shows the stratification of music and culture, which grew more pronounced as the century progressed. There was music for the most sophisticated tastes and music directed toward the masses. Still, vocal music and its performance also crossed the seemingly unbridgeable gulf between high and low class, from singing societies that drew their membership from all levels of society to the co-opting of opera by popular songwriters and minstrel show troupes. In this chapter, we focus on two genres with a deep connection to the nineteenth century: the art song, or *Lied,* and the requiem.

13-2 The *Lied*, a Romantic Genre

In October 1814, at the age of seventeen, Franz Schubert composed the song *Gretchen am Spinnrade (Gretchen at the Spinning Wheel).* The following year, he composed *Erlkönig (The Elf King).* The songs were

FAST FACTS

- Dates: 1797–1828
- Place: Vienna, Austria
- Reasons to remember: Composer who almost single-handedly established the art song as a significant and distinctly Romantic musical genre

Nicku/Shutterstock.com

among Schubert's first successes; he would publish them as Op. 2 and Op. 1, respectively, some years later.

Both songs used texts by the renowned German Romantic poet Johann Wolfgang von Goethe. The first sets a heartbreaking scene from Goethe's drama *Faust*; the second is a setting of Goethe's poem *Erlkönig*. During Schubert's brief lifetime, Goethe was the most important literary figure in German-speaking Europe and one of the most influential thinkers of the era.

By contrast, Schubert was virtually unknown when he composed these songs. During his brief career, he lived precariously on the fringes of Viennese society, although he had well-to-do friends who championed his music. He periodically received royalties from the sale of his music, but he spent the money as fast as it came in. He was the stereotypical starving artist to whom widespread recognition comes only posthumously.

Schubert desperately wanted to meet Goethe, so his well-connected friends sent Goethe copies of Schubert's songs that used the poet's texts. Apparently, Goethe wasn't impressed, because he never made an effort to arrange a meeting. He was far more enthusiastic about the songs of his good friend Carl Friedrich Zelter, who set Goethe's poems much more simply. Ironically, Goethe's poems are far better known in Schubert's settings than they are as poetry—at least outside German-speaking Europe.

Schubert's two early songs are harbingers of Romanticism. Both the genre and Schubert's realizations of it helped usher in a new era and turn the page on the Classical style.

13-2A The Aesthetic of the *Lied*

Lied (plural, *Lieder*) is German for "song." Although the term can refer to any song in German, it has also acquired a more specific connotation: nineteenth- and early twentieth-century song (in German) for voice and piano in which both melody and accompaniment amplify dominant

Lied (plural, *Lieder*) In art music, a song for voice and piano in which both melody and accompaniment amplify dominant themes and images in the text

art song Nineteenth- and early twentieth-century song that set poetry to music of comparable quality

themes and images in the text. Romantic *Lieder* were among the first instances of the art song. The goal of the art song was to set poetry with music of comparable quality. This practice took shape first in German-speaking Europe, most decisively and importantly in the *Lieder* of Schubert.

Lieder exemplified many of the qualities and characteristics associated with the early Romantic movement. The *Lied* was, first of all, a marriage of the arts: fine poetry set to beautiful music that brought added depth to the feelings expressed in the text. German *Lieder* form the most substantial and important musical repertoire in service of this goal. The extent to which words and music merged was sometimes evident in the form of a song: the music typically took its formal cue from the poem rather than employing a conventional musical form, such as the da capo aria, that required adaptation of the text. At the simplest level, this might involve the use of strophic form. However, both songs discussed later offer more complex narrative forms.

The use of German also fostered national sentiment on at least three levels. First, it favored the local language over Italian, the de facto international language in secular vocal music through much of the eighteenth century. In this respect, it was the art counterpart to the folk-song settings that were especially popular in the British Isles and elsewhere in the first years of the nineteenth century. Second, it affirmed the importance of the writers whose poetry was set to the music. Among Schubert's most esteemed songs are those using the texts of Goethe, Müller, Schiller, and other leading poets of the era.

Most important, the musical settings in well-composed songs were able to bring out the idiomatic qualities of the language because the composers were responsive to the inflection and rhythm of the text. German is a heavily inflected language, with considerable difference in accentuation between strong and weak syllables. Schubert's settings of Goethe's poems amplify the inflection and rhythm of the text as spoken. The text remains intact and intelligible, even as the melody goes beyond the expressive capabilities of speech.

This sensitivity to the nuances of language is evident in art songs in many languages throughout the nineteenth century and into the twentieth. Some of the musical differences between the *Lieder* of Schubert, Schumann, and Hugo Wolf, and the *chansons* (the French counterparts of the *Lied*) of Fauré and Duparc, are attributable to the differences in inflection between German and French.

13-2B Franz Schubert

The composer most responsible for the emergence of the *Lied* was the Viennese composer Franz Schubert ♪. Schubert was among the first of a new kind of composer.

Puccini's opera *La bohème*—the story of a young poet falling in love with a seamstress afflicted with tuberculosis—romanticized the "bohemian" life.

In 1821, Franz von Schober, one of Franz Schubert's circle of friends, organized at his lodgings the first Schubertiade, an evening of music written and sometimes performed by Schubert.

He was neither a servant, as Haydn had been, nor a gifted performer, as Mozart and Beethoven were. He did not hold a steady job, as Bach had, and he lacked the business instincts of Handel. Through his tragically short life, he lived on the fringes of Viennese society. But he was arguably the most precocious composer of any era. The two extraordinary songs discussed in this chapter were written before his nineteenth birthday. No other composer has created such innovative and mature music at such an early age.

Schubert was born near Vienna into a musical family. He received his musical education at home, then at a school in Vienna, where he studied under Mozart's rival Salieri. After leaving the school, he tried teaching for a while but didn't take to it. Instead, he became the first noteworthy musical bohemian. He developed a loyal circle of friends and professional acquaintances who supported him when he lacked funds or even a place to stay. The group included writers, painters, and others who led a bohemian lifestyle: work in the morning (or not at all), and then spend the afternoon and evening talking, drinking, and generally having a good time in a café. Bohemians were the first counterculture, the underbelly of a new cultural elite. They rejected the values of the bourgeois, who aspired to respectability. They became poets, painters, and musicians rather than bankers, merchants, or civil servants, and they often lived off an inheritance or their friends.

Schubert composed at a feverish pace. Friends described his composing style as virtually unconscious—as if he were a medium channeling inspiration from a higher power. Accurate or not, there's no question that Schubert was extraordinarily prolific. It is hard to imagine anyone creating more music of value in a shorter time. In a career that lasted barely more than a decade, he created an enormous amount of music, despite suffering horribly from syphilis over the last six years of his life. In addition to the songs, he composed several symphonies (although two were left unfinished), a great deal of important chamber music, and music for solo piano and piano duet. Although connected to the Viennese Classical traditions, Schubert's music is Romantic in its emphasis on deep personal feeling expressed in lyric melody, distinctive settings, and adventurous harmonies.

13-2C Schubert's *Lieder*

Schubert's legacy begins with his songs. He composed more than 660 of them, many of which exemplify the very best of the genre. Beginning with *Gretchen am Spinnrade*, Schubert ushered in a new generation of song, one that was fully Romantic in text and music.

Schubert's genius as a composer of songs begins with a sensitivity to the text—its inflection, its rhythms, its meaning. It is expressed most directly through an extraordinary melodic gift: Schubert's melodies are not only intrinsically beautiful but often specifically responsive to the text that they set.

However, Schubert's most significant innovation in song composition was expanding the role of the accompaniment. Compared to earlier songs and contemporaneous folk-song settings, Schubert's accompaniments are typically richer, more individual, and more demanding for the pianist (the accompaniment to Schubert's *Erlkönig* is extraordinarily fatiguing). Moreover, they now not only provide support for the melody but also bring to life a key aspect of the text. In the case of *Gretchen am Spinnrade*, the piano evokes the spinning wheel where Gretchen sits waiting for her lover. In *Erlkönig*, the accompaniment depicts the frantic galloping of the horse as father and son try to elude the evil Elf King.

Schubertiade An evening of music composed by Franz Schubert, often with Schubert as accompanist

Schubert's two songs express some of our deepest emotions, as shown in these nineteenth-century depictions of compelling scenes from them. *Gretchen am Spinnrade* appears on the left; *Erlkönig*, on the right.

13-2D Schubert and the Romantic Sensibility

Schubert's *Lieder* manifest the Romantic ascendancy of feeling over thought. The two songs presented here express some of our deepest emotions: love given and abandoned, and the intrusion of death into life. In *Gretchen am Spinnrade,* Gretchen, pregnant and alone, recalls her lover with desire and anguish. In *Erlkönig,* father and son lose a race with death, personified by the Elf King. In both, the accompaniment evokes a vivid image so that changes in it can signal moments of intense emotion.

Lieder are the most intimately personal first-person music of the Romantic era. Through both words and music, the singer assumes the persona—or personae—depicted in the poem. In convincing performances of *Gretchen am Spinnrade,* we can feel Gretchen's lust and pain as if the singer herself were experiencing it. *Erlkönig* presents a more formidable challenge: the singer must portray not one persona, but four: the narrator, the father, the son, and the Elf King. Whether singers project a character or simply narrate, they sing in the first person.

The circumstances of performance made *Lieder* particularly personal. The venues were intimate. Early performances typically took place in the salons of private homes, where audiences seldom exceeded one hundred. There were no props, no costumes, and only the support of a pianist. *Gretchen am Spinnrade* is exceptional in its reference to a longer narrative; in most cases, the poem is self-contained. The vocal artifice associated with opera and oratorio is largely absent: texts are set syllabically, and melodic elaboration

through-composed form Form in which there is no large-scale formal repetition

is rare. The focus is on the words, the melody, and the person singing them.

Schubert's songs were warmly received in Viennese salons, grand rooms in the mansions of the wealthy, whose diverse audiences were a mix of the aristocratic, the wealthy, the cultured (university professors, professional musicians) and those members of the middle class drawn to the world of high culture, and the artistic, bohemian, and otherwise. The salon remained an important venue for the art song throughout the nineteenth century.

13-2E *Gretchen am Spinnrade, Erlkönig,* and Narrative

In both songs discussed here (see Listen Up! sections), Schubert crafts the form to the story. In *Erlkönig,* he uses through-composed form, which means that there is no large-scale formal repetition. The glue that holds the song together musically is not the melody, but the accompaniment, which hammers away relentlessly—except when the Elf King sings and, devastatingly, when the father discovers that his child has died in his arms.

In *Gretchen am Spinnrade,* Schubert must shift between reality and remembrance. To do so, he adapts a familiar musical device, the refrain. In this song, the refrain depicts Gretchen in the present, with no peace and a heavy heart. As the music wanders away from the refrain, we can almost visualize Gretchen retreating from a dismal present into the erotic memories of her time with Faust. Each time the refrain returns, it brings her abruptly back to reality.

The two songs signal a shift in the expressive intent of form. The Classical conflict and resolution outlined by the opposition of two main keys and filled in by

 **LISTEN UP!**

Schubert, *Erlkönig* (1815)

TAKEAWAY POINT: Dramatic song with vivid piano accompaniment; a tour de force for the skilled vocalist who can portray all four characters

STYLE: Early Romantic

FORM: Through-composed

GENRE: *Lied*

INSTRUMENTS: Voice and piano

CONTEXT: Song for a Schubertiade

0:00   Piano introduction sets the mood with "galloping" accompaniment and ominous low-register growls.

NARRATOR

0:23   The narrator's melody is angular; melody and relentless accompaniment convey urgency.

Wer reitet so spät durch Nacht und Wind?	Who rides so late through night and wind?
Es ist der Vater mit seinem Kind.	It is the father with his child.
Er hat den Knaben wohl in dem Arm,	He holds the boy safe in his arm,
Er fasst ihn sicher, er hält ihn warm.	He holds him tight, he keeps him warm.

FATHER

0:56   Melodic material of father and son responds directly to text: rising during father's question and the distress of the son.

Mein Sohn, was birgst du so bang dein Gesicht?	My son, what makes you hide your face?

SON

1:03 | | |
|---|---|
| *Siehst, Vater, du den Erlkönig nicht?* | Father, don't you see the Elf King? |
| *Den Erlenkönig mit Kron und Schweif?* | The Elf King, with crown and cloak? |

FATHER

1:20   Smooth, lower phrases to soothe the son.

Mein Sohn, es ist ein Nebelstreif.	My son, it is the foggy mist.

ELF KING

1:29   Elf King's pleasant, singsong melody, with which he hopes to entice the child. The lighter accompaniment underscores the shift in mood.

Du liebes Kind, komm, geh' mit mir!	You dear child, come go with me!
Gar schöne Spiele spiel ich mit dir.	What lovely games I'll play with thee.
Manch bunte Blumen sind an dem Strand	Such colorful flowers on the strand,
Meine Mutter hat manch gülden Gewand.	My mother has such golden garb.

SON

1:52   A dramatic shift in mood highlights the son's reaction to the Elf King and the father's attempt to calm him.

Mein Vater, mein Vater, und hörest du nicht	My father, my father, and don't you hear
Was Erlenkönig mir leise verspricht?	What the Elf King is whispering to me?

FATHER

2:04 | | |
|---|---|
| *Sei ruhig, bleibe ruhig, mein Kind.* | Be calm, stay calm, my child. |
| *In dürren Blättern säuselt der Wind.* | The wind is rustling in the dead leaves. |

(Continued)

ELF KING

2:14 Schubert again characterizes the Elf King and his "offer" with a much more pleasant setting in melody and accompaniment.

Willst, feiner Knabe, du mit mir gehn?	Will you go with me, fine lad?
Meine Töchter sollen dich warten schön.	My daughters shall sweetly wait on you.
Meine Töchter führen den nächtlichen Reih'n.	My daughters lead nightly dances.
Und wiegen und tanzen und singen dich ein.	And will rock and dance and sing to you.

SON

2:32 Because the previous section was so light, the sudden shift back to the son's terrified response is even more powerful.

Mein Vater, mein Vater, und siehst du nicht dort	My Father, my father, and can't you see there
Erlkönigs Töchter am düstern Ort?	The Elf King's daughters in that murky place?

FATHER

2:44

Mein Sohn, mein Sohn, ich seh es genau	My son, my son, now I see it
Es scheinen die alten Weiden so grau.	The old willows look grey like that.

ELF KING

3:01 Repeated chord accompaniment suggests Elf King's impatience; if he cannot beguile the child, then he will use force.

Ich liebe dich, mich reizt deine schöne Gestalt	I love you, your lovely form tempts me.
Und bist du nicht willig, so brauch' ich Gewalt!	And if you're not willing, I'll take you by force!

SON

3:12

Mein Vater, mein Vater, jetzt fasst er mich an!	My father, my father, he's seizing me now!
Erlkönig hat mir ein Leids getan!	The Elf King has hurt me!

NARRATOR

3:26 Narrator returns to deliver the tragic ending—set off in the most dramatic way.

Dem Vater grauset's, er reitet geschwind,	The father shudders, he rides like the wind,
Er hält in Armen das ächzende Kind,	He holds the groaning child in his arms,
Erreicht den Hof mit Müh' und Not:	He reaches the inn with toil and dread:
In seinen Armen das Kind war tot.	In his arms the child was dead.

 Listen to this selection streaming or in an Active Listening Guide at CourseMate or in the eBook.

---

frequently contrasting musical materials now belong to the previous generation. In Schubert's songs, harmony is more responsive to the sense of the text. Like the poems, the music tells a story, shifting mood along with the text. The songs evidence how the emphasis on narrative replaced the dramatic tension of Classical music. Narrative, and forms that conveyed it, would become a key feature of Romantic music, both vocal and instrumental.

13-2F Schubert's Influence on the *Lied*

Schubert wasn't the first composer of *Lieder*. Mozart, Haydn, and especially Beethoven composed memorable songs; so did several others, including Goethe's friend Zelter and Johann Zumsteeg, a composer whose songs Schubert especially admired. However, with *Gretchen am Spinnrade*, *Erlkönig*, and the hundreds of songs that followed, Schubert almost single-handedly established the art song as a significant and distinctly Romantic musical genre. Important features of his style—most notably text declamation, distinctive and expressive accompaniments, interplay between voice and piano, and expressive melody that amplifies the inflection and emotions of the text—became both inspiration and model for nineteenth-century song composers in German-speaking Europe and elsewhere. Moreover, those songs published during his lifetime and the first few years after his death became the core repertoire for nineteenth-century art song.

LISTEN UP!

Schubert, *Gretchen am Spinnrade* (1814)

TAKEAWAY POINT: Sensitive, evocative musical setting of a poignant scene from Goethe's *Faust*

STYLE: Early Romantic

FORM: Episodic, with refrain

GENRE: *Lied*

INSTRUMENTS: Voice and piano

CONTEXT: Song for a Schubertiade

0:00   Brief piano introduction evokes spinning wheel; this continues through most of the song.

REFRAIN

0:03   Gretchen is in the painful present in the refrain; it serves as a repeated reality check.

Meine Ruh' ist hin,	My peace is gone,
mein Herz ist schwer;	my heart is heavy;
ich finde sie nimmer und nimmermehr.	I will find it never, never again.

EPISODE

0:23   The first of three reflections on Faust. The music connects present to recent past by beginning as if simply repeating the opening material, then moving in a different, more intense direction.

Wo ich ihn nicht hab' ist mir das Grab,	Where I am not with him I am in my grave,
die ganze Welt ist mir vergällt.	the whole world is bitterness to me.
Mein armer Kopf ist mir verrückt,	My poor head is in a whirl,
mein armer Sinn ist mir zerstückt.	my poor thoughts are distracted.

REFRAIN

0:54   Jarring return to her present circumstances

Meine Ruh' ist hin,	My peace is gone,
mein Herz ist schwer;	my heart is heavy;
ich finde sie nimmer und nimmermehr.	I will find it never, never again.

EPISODE

1:14   A reverie as Faust's image becomes clearer; as she relives their intimate moments, the accompaniment stops, as if Gretchen stops spinning the wheel.

Nach ihm nur schau ich zum Fenster hinaus;	Him alone do I seek when I gaze out the window;
Nach ihm nur geh' ich aus dem Haus.	to him alone do I go on leaving the house.
Sein hoher Gang, sein' edle Gestalt,	His noble gait, his fine build,
seines Mundes Lächeln, seiner Augen Gewalt,	his laughing lips, his powerful eyes,
Und seiner Rede Zauberfluss,	And of his speech the magic glow,
sein Händedruck, und ach, sein Kuss!	the grasp of his hand, and ah, his kiss!

REFRAIN

2:15   We can almost hear her snap out of her reverie in the start and stop of the accompaniment, before it resumes.

Meine Ruh' ist hin,	My peace is gone,
mein Herz ist schwer;	my heart is heavy;
ich finde sie nimmer und nimmermehr.	I will find it never, never again.

(Continued)

EPISODE

EPISODE

2:35   Unlike other episodes, this doesn't begin with refrain fragment. Instead, music continues erotic memory.

Mein Busen drängt sich nach ihm hin.	My breast yearns toward him.
Ach dürft ich fassen und halten ihn,	Ah, could I but seize him and hold him
und küssen ihn, so wie ich wollt,	and kiss him as much as I want,
an seine Küssen vergehen sollt!	beneath his kisses then should I die!
O könnt' ich ihn küssen, so wie ich wollt,	and kiss him as much as I want,
an seinen Küssen vergehen sollt!	beneath his kisses then should I die!
An seine Küssen vergehen sollt!	Beneath his kisses then should I die!

REFRAIN

3:26   Final statement of refrain contains only the first two lines. There is no resolution at the end of the song, just the powerful reminder of Gretchen's grief.

Meine Ruh' ist hin,	My peace is gone,
mein Herz ist schwer;	my heart is heavy;

 Listen to this selection streaming or in an Active Listening Guide at CourseMate or in the eBook.

13-3 Schumann and the Song Cycle

The *Lied* is inherently a small-scale form. At about four minutes, *Erlkönig* is unusually long for a *lied*. Most songs, including the two by Robert Schumann that we are about to discuss, are shorter. But the cultivation of a genre consisting of miniatures was at odds with the Romantic emphasis on bigness. As the *Lied* grew in prestige, Schubert and his contemporaries faced the challenge of creating a big work out of small pieces. Their solution was the song cycle.

13-3A From Song Collection to Song Cycle

Beginning in the late eighteenth century, *Lieder* with piano accompaniment were often published in collections rather than individually. It was a strategy that made sense for everyone. For the composer, it made for a more impressive achievement and potentially a more substantial sale. For the publisher, it resulted in more efficient and economical production and promotion.

In this respect, nineteenth-century music publishing was much like the LP/cassette/CD era in recording, in that collections were much like albums, and individual editions like singles, from both a marketing and musical perspective. The sale of a collection earned a larger sum, and customers might well buy a collection in order to own one or two songs, just as a

song cycle Group of thematically connected poems set as songs that are compiled into a single large-scale work

twentieth-century listener would buy an album for one or two of its tracks.

Musically, collections could, and often did, include simply a group of freshly composed (or at least freshly assembled) songs, with no thematic connection—in effect, a collection of singles. However, a few early composers of *Lieder* composed **song cycles**, groups of thematically connected poems set as songs that are compiled into a single large-scale work. Among the first were those by Zumsteeg; Beethoven's *An die ferne Geliebte* (*To a Distant Beloved*), composed in 1816, was the first important song cycle. Still, it was Schubert who played the key role in establishing the song cycle as the large-scale counterpart to the *Lied*. He composed two major song cycles: *Die schöne Müllerin* (*The Beautiful Miller's Maid*) in 1823 and *Die Winterreise* (*The Winter Journey*) in 1828. *Die Winterreise*'s twenty-four songs is a full evening of music. Schubert's song cycles quickly became the standard for composers in subsequent generations. However, the two major cycles represent only a small fraction of his total *Lieder* output. That was not the case with Robert Schumann.

13-3B Robert Schumann's Song Cycles

1840 was Robert Schumann's "year of song." (You will receive a proper introduction to Robert and his wife, Clara, in Chapter 14.) Most of his songs—well over one hundred—were composed in that single year. About half of them belong to four song cycles.

Schumann had multiple reasons for turning to song. After a long courtship made difficult because of a fractious relationship with his former piano teacher and future father-in-law, Schumann married the concert pianist Clara Wieck in 1840. Clara's father was justifiably concerned that Schumann could not provide for the two of them. Songs promised the largest sales, so it is not unreasonable to assume that Schumann may have focused on this genre to earn money.

There were also musical and aesthetic reasons. After years of composing mainly works for solo piano, Schumann began to go through annual phases: song in 1840, orchestral music in 1841, and chamber music in 1842–1843. More specifically, he was arguably the most literary-minded of the early Romantic composers. His approach to song texts was more high-minded than Schubert's: he chose only poetry that he deemed worthy of an art setting.

Schumann may have been inclined to compose song cycles not only because of the greater breadth that the genre provided but also because of his compositional approach. Several of his early piano works, most famously *Kinderszenen (Scenes from Childhood)*, consist of short pieces that are almost too brief to stand alone but coalesce well into a larger work. Schumann would take a similar approach in *Dichterliebe (The Poet's Love)*, Op. 48, the last of his four song cycles from 1840.

13-3C *Dichterliebe*

Dichterliebe is a cycle of sixteen songs that set poems by the German poet Heinrich Heine. Schumann selected the poems from the sixty-five included in Heine's *Lyrisches Intermezzo*, which was published in 1822–1823. In the course of the song cycle, the poet descends from hope in the first song to the depths of despair in the last, when he buries the pain of his unrequited love in an enormous coffin, which is carried by giants to a watery grave. The protagonist wallows in self-pity throughout the cycle; the obvious exaggerations of the final poem underscore that.

The sixteen (originally twenty) poems that Schumann selected for the cycle comprise a set of verbal snapshots. We learn of the poet's fate through images, not narrative. Most of the poems are short—two or three stanzas—and some are incomplete. Schumann matches the poetic fragments with musical ones. Only at the end do we sense a whole.

The fragmentary nature of the songs is one dimension of Schumann's aesthetic in this cycle. In every significant dimension, it is built on integration, interdependence, and balance: between words and music,

LISTEN UP!

TOTAL TIME: 1:37

Schumann, "Im wunderschönen Monat Mai," from *Dichterliebe* (1840)

TAKEAWAY POINT: Beautifully integrated song cycle; one of the most treasured examples of the genre

STYLE: Early Romantic

FORM: Strophic

GENRE: *Lied*

INSTRUMENTS: Voice and piano

CONTEXT: The peak of Schumann's "year of song"

0:00   Enigmatic piano introduction: keynote not stated and key not established. Leap up anticipates the poet's yearning.

0:16   *Im wunderschönen Monat Mai,*   In the wonderfully fair month of May,
    als alle Knospen sprangen,   as all the flower buds burst,
    da ist in meinem Herzen   then in my heart
    die Liebe aufgegangen.   love arose.

Simple-sounding melodic fragment: not even a complete phrase

0:41   Piano introduction returns as interlude; the high melody note conflicts with the peak note of the vocal line.

0:54   As before, but this time we learn of the poet's yearning.
    Im wunderschönen Monat Mai,   In the wonderfully fair month of May,
    als alle Vögel sangen,   as all the birds were singing,
    da hab' ich ihr gestanden   then I confessed to her
    mein Sehnen und Verlangen.   my yearning and longing.

1:19   Piano introduction returns as postlude; even with the third statement, nothing is resolved.

Listen to this selection streaming or in an Active Listening Guide at CourseMate or in the eBook.

voice and piano, and between seemingly artless simplicity and the subtlety of art. We are introduced to this aesthetic in the first two songs from *Dichterliebe*, "Im wunderschönen Monat Mai" ("In the Wonderful Month of May") and "Aus meinen Tränen spriessen" ("From My Tears Spring") (see Listen Up! sections).

In the first few seconds of the first song, we become aware that Schumann's approach is new and different. The pianist begins not with an accompaniment waiting for the melody to start, but with both melody and accompaniment at once. As is often the case in his music, Schumann begins in the middle of something; the opening statement clouds the key rather than confirming it. Only when the voice enters with a different continuation of the same melodic idea do we get our harmonic bearings. However, the next phrase of the vocal line ends unresolved on "aufgegangen." The pianist immediately "corrects" the high note ("-gang-") by reverting to the opening statement,

 **LISTEN UP!**

Schumann, "Aus meinen Tränen spriessen," from *Dichterliebe* (1840)

TAKEAWAY POINT: Beautifully integrated song cycle; one of the most treasured examples of the genre

STYLE: Early Romantic

FORM: AABA

GENRE: *Lied*

INSTRUMENTS: Voice and piano

CONTEXT: The peak of Schumann's "year of song"

A SECTION

0:00   Again, the vocal line is incomplete; the pianist finishes the phrases in the A sections.

Aus meinen Tränen spriessen	From my tears spring
viel blühende Blumen hervor,	many blooming flowers forth,

A SECTION

0:13   *und meine Seufzer warden*   and my sighs become

       ein Nachtigallenchor,   a nightingale choir,

B SECTION

0:26   *und wenn du mich lieb hast, Kindchen,*   and if you have love for me, little child,

       schenk' ich dir die Blumen all',   I'll give you all the flowers,

A SECTION

0:36   *und vor deinem Fenster soll klingen*   and before your window shall sound

       das Lied der Nachtigall.   the song of the nightingale.

 Listen to this selection streaming or in an Active Listening Guide at CourseMate or in the eBook.

which now serves as an interlude between stanzas. After a restatement of the vocal line, the opening piano returns again, this time ending the song as enigmatically as it began.

The second song continues without a pause. It consists of only four short phrases, in an AABA form, which was widely used during the nineteenth century in popular song and folk-song settings. However, the vocal part of the A section is once again incomplete; each time, the pianist finishes it. The sense of incompleteness extends to the song as a whole; it is so short that we expect additional verses.

In just over two minutes of music, we hear salient features of Schumann's approach to song composition. First, the pianist is not an accompanist, but an equal partner: he or she shares the melody and completes vocal statements. That's the obvious part. As the cycle unfolds, their relationship is dynamic: the pianist comments, completes, contradicts, and contextualizes the vocal line. Their subtle interplay is evident from the outset: the harmonically ambiguous material that frames the vocal line effectively contradicts the seemingly straightforward message of both words and music: things are not as they seem. The poem hints at this with "yearning and longing." The music amplifies and reinforces the words; it foretells that the cycle will not end happily. In the second song, the pianist confirms, rather than contradicts, the vocal part.

Schumann uses this interplay to artfully enrich the seeming simplicity of his setting. It is the vocal line—certainly the prominent element of the texture—that seems simple: mostly syllabic setting of the text, a melody that moves mostly by step with a moderately paced rhythm, and simple forms. In its multiple roles, the piano part adds more subtle layers of meaning. By presenting Heine's poems clearly and comprehensibly, yet with sophistication and understanding, Schumann makes his merger of words and music more than the sum of its parts, just as the cycle is more than the sum of its individual songs.

13-3D The Art Song after Schubert

The success of Schubert's *Lieder* inspired several generations of German-speaking composers, first Schumann and Mendelssohn, then Johannes Brahms, Richard Strauss, and Hugo Wolf. Composers in other countries followed the lead of German *Lieder* composers. Among their most notable works are songs in Russian by Modest Mussorgsky and Pyotr Ilyich Tchaikovsky, songs in Polish by Frédéric Chopin, and songs in French by Gabriel Fauré and Henri Duparc.

The art song was, for the most part, an intimate genre: songs that seldom lasted more than two or three minutes, composed for voice and piano, and performed in a salon. Another popular vocal genre among nineteenth-century composers was the requiem, a work for chorus, soloists, and orchestra for—or at least inspired by—the Catholic Mass for the dead.

LEARNING OUTCOME 13-4
Reexamine the musical and social boundaries between sacred and secular, and religious and spiritual, through an exploration of Brahms's *Requiem*.

13-4 Brahms's *Ein Deutsches Requiem*

On February 2, 1865, Johannes Brahms lost his mother, Christiane. Born in 1789, she had married a much younger man just after turning forty and had given birth to three children in short order. Johannes was her second child and first son; she remained close to him until her death. After she passed away, Brahms composed a large-scale work for chorus, vocal soloists, and orchestra that he would call *Ein deutsches Requiem (A German Requiem)*.

The very title of the work underscores the extent to which spirituality and religion had grown apart by the middle of the nineteenth century. The composition is not in Latin, and it is not a liturgical work. Instead, it is both a personal and a universal affirmation of the spirit. We consider the work in the context of this growing separation.

13-4A Religion, Deism, and Spirituality

In the wake of the Renaissance and the Protestant Reformation came a challenge not only to the Catholic Church but also to the very idea of organized religion. Among European intellectuals, the idea of deism the belief that the divine could be understood through reason alone, took root. Deists proposed that God created the world, then set it in motion and left it alone, and that the existence of God could be discerned by reason

alone. Consequently, there was no need for organized religion to serve as an intermediary.

The movement took shape in England in the seventeenth century and spread to the continent and the colonies during the eighteenth century. But deism did not—could not—attract mass support. The most notorious attempt to impose it on a people came during the French Revolution, when Hébertists, the most radical revolutionaries in France, briefly renamed Notre Dame cathedral "The Temple of Reason" and attempted to transform Catholicism into the "Cult of the Supreme Being." This ended in failure.

Deism's indirect impact on the framers of the Constitution and the Bill of Rights would prove far more influential: many of the founders—among them George Washington, Benjamin Franklin, Thomas Jefferson, John Adams, and Thomas Paine—expressed deistic views in their writing. Their philosophical position fundamentally altered the relationship between religion and politics in the newly formed United States, which in turn served as a model for change in Europe. As a result, societies in France and in Protestant Europe and North America were more open to and tolerant of differing expressions of the relationship between God and humanity at the beginning of the nineteenth century than they had been at the beginning of the eighteenth century.

The separation of religion and spirituality deepened during the nineteenth century, particularly among intellectuals. Among the key factors were extensive contact with the scriptures of Eastern religions, Darwin's theory of evolution, and philosophical writings by Immanuel Kant, George Hegel, Herbert Spencer, and others, which offered historical views of religion, in some cases as an artifact of humanity rather than a divinely ordained phenomenon.

Ein deutsches Requiem is a musical work in step with these progressive developments. It is a requiem only in the broadest sense of the term. It is not a work composed for use in a religious service; its most common venue is the concert hall, not the church. In numerous ways, it reflects the more free-thinking attitudes of many nineteenth-century intellectuals, as we will discover.

13-4B The Requiem in the Nineteenth Century

In Catholic liturgy, a requiem is a Mass offered to honor the dead. The dead may be an individual or a small or large group; many parishes offer Requiem Masses on All Souls' Day, the day in the liturgical year set aside to honor those who passed away during the previous year. The text for a

deism A belief originating in the seventeenth century that asserted that the divine could be understood through reason alone

requiem A Mass offered to honor the dead

Johannes Brahms

FAST FACTS

- Dates: 1833–1897
- Place: Germany
- Reasons to remember: One of the most important and highly regarded German composers of the latter half of the nineteenth century

Neftali/Shutterstock.com

Requiem Mass differs from that for an Ordinary Mass; the term *requiem* comes from the most common form of the opening prayer, which begins "Requiem aeternam dona eis, Domine" ("Eternal rest grant unto them, O Lord").

Musical settings of the Requiem Mass are far more variable than musical settings of the Ordinary Mass. Both the Gloria and the Credo are omitted. Instead, composers choose to set some or all of the customary texts, which include the Kyrie, Sanctus, and Agnus Dei from the Ordinary Mass as well as prayers specific to the requiem service, such as the opening "Requiem," the sequence "Dies irae" ("day of wrath"), and the communion prayer "Lux aeterna" ("eternal light").

Nineteenth-century composers were drawn to the requiem; there are many more settings of the requiem by important composers than there are of the Mass. Among the most admired requiems that set the Catholic liturgy are those by Berlioz, Verdi, Bruckner, Dvořák, and Fauré. This would seem to be one manifestation of the Romantic fascination with death. (We encounter others in upcoming chapters: Verdi's *La traviata* and Bizet's *Carmen* end with the deaths of the leading characters; Berlioz quotes the plainchant setting of "Dies irae" in his *Symphonie fantastique*.)

Although these requiems use liturgical texts, most are not suitable for use in the Mass. In particular, those by Berlioz and Verdi are far too theatrical for liturgical use; they are closer to sacred oratorio than to music for a church service. The premiere of Verdi's *Requiem* took place in the church of San Marco in Milan but was not part of a church service; it was repeated three days later at La Scala, the famous opera house in Milan. Subsequently, it received numerous performances in traditional concert venues rather than churches.

In composing works that use liturgical texts but are not intended for liturgical use, composers such as Berlioz and Verdi were elevating these texts to much the same

Dies irae A section of the Requiem Mass that deals with the Day of Judgment

status as biblical readings. Brahms went well beyond this. For his German requiem, he chose readings from Luther's translation of the Bible from both Old and New Testaments, instead of using liturgical texts. Significantly, none mentioned Christ.

13-4C Johannes Brahms

Brahms seemed destined to compose a large-scale choral work. His first important position included among its responsibilities direction of a choir, and his first position in Vienna was directing the Vienna Singakademie, a concert choir formed in 1858 to perform classic choral literature. And in an 1853 article in the *Neue Zeitschrift für Musik*—the last that he would write for the journal that he had founded—Robert Schumann predicted great success for the twenty-year-old Brahms, "should he direct his magic wand where the massed forces of chorus and orchestra may lend him their power."

Brahms ◀ was born and raised in Hamburg, Germany. His mother was a seamstress, and his father, a versatile musician who played several instruments as a member of symphony orchestras, bands, and popular orchestras. Brahms's first training came as a pianist. His major teacher inculcated a love of Bach, Mozart, and Beethoven—an approach customary in our time but still novel in the 1840s. Brahms regularly gave concerts during the first part of his career and premiered both of his piano concertos himself. However, his early professional experiences were almost as varied as his father's: accompanying theatrical performances, teaching, and playing in working-class but respectable taverns. His first important professional experience came with a Hungarian violinist named Remenyi, who introduced him to gypsy music.

These early experiences shaped two complementary sides of his musical personality. The side influenced by popular and folk music is revealed in tuneful, expressive melodies and accessible, invigorating rhythms, such as those heard in his famous *Hungarian Dances*. On the other side, Brahms's formative piano study fueled a deep interest in and reverence for the music of the past. As a choral conductor, he performed music by Renaissance and Baroque masters, and as a music scholar he helped prepare modern editions of early music. The more learned passages in his works reflect this passion.

After establishing himself in Germany as an important pianist and composer, Brahms moved to Vienna in 1863, following a successful visit the previous year. He would call the city home for the rest of his life, although he would travel extensively, for business and pleasure. There was a practical reason for Brahms's choice of Vienna. The city remained the most vital musical center in German-speaking Europe. Institutions in that city, including the university, a newly formed conservatory, and the *Gesellschaft der Musikfreunde* (Society of Friends of Music), supported his interest in the music of the past. In turn, Vienna's musical world recognized and appreciated his connection to Vienna's musical heritage. Many leading musicians and commentators view him as the most important successor to Mozart and Beethoven.

It is this sense of continuation of a valued legacy that makes Brahms's choice of Vienna seem symbolic as well as practical. Like Beethoven, Brahms came to Vienna from a part of Germany at some distance from the Austrian capital. Clearly, Beethoven was the dominant musical influence on Brahms; his music both inspired and intimidated Brahms. Brahms's first piano sonata is modeled on Beethoven's biggest piano sonata; like Beethoven, Brahms composed a great deal of chamber music and music for piano; he did not complete his first symphony until 1876, after working on it for fourteen years. Brahms eventually became the third "B," after Bach and Beethoven. Their common bonds included not only their German heritage and the initial of their last name but also their predilection for instrumental music and avoidance of opera; like Bach, Brahms never composed an opera, although he composed extensively for voice.

13-4D *Ein deutsches Requiem*

It is this context that we can understand *Ein deutsches Requiem* as a fiercely independent work, for Brahms, for Germans, and for humanity. It is Brahms's biggest work—a typical performance requires about seventy minutes. It is his most distinctive work, unique not only in Brahms's body of work but also in important nineteenth-century music; there is no other piece quite like it.

It is a nationalistic work, although not overtly so. The title *A German Requiem* was Brahms's own: Brahms identified the work in this way in an 1865 letter to Clara Schumann. "German" apparently refers to the choice of language (German, not Latin) rather than a musical statement representative of the German people. Still, it appeared at a time when nationalistic fervor was on the rise in Germany. Otto von Bismarck became minister-president of Prussia, the largest German state, in 1862; he would lead the push toward German unification and autonomy from the Austro-Hungarian Empire in 1871. The fact that Brahms chose to compose a "German" requiem is certainly in step with the mood in what is now Germany. The German character of the requiem, evident not only in the title but also in the use of texts from Luther's translation of the Bible, suggests Beethoven's influence: it was Beethoven who popularized the use of German instead of Italian in musical scores to indicate tempo, character, and other musical information. Other composers, most notably Schumann and Brahms himself, followed his lead.

13-4E "Wie lieblich sind deine Wohnungen"

Brahms composed *Ein deutsches Requiem* in stages. Within months of his mother's passing, he had completed the first, second, and fourth movements. By August 1866, he had completed the third, sixth, and seventh movements. He added the fifth movement in 1868; the premiere performance of the complete work took place in February 1869, four years after the death of his mother. "Wie lieblich sind deine Wohnungen" ("How Lovely Is Thy Dwelling Place"), which sets verses from Psalm 84, is the fourth movement of the work (see Listen Up!).

Brahms's familiarity with the rich sacred choral music tradition is evident throughout the movement. The rich counterpoint and sweeping phrases reach back to the Renaissance and Baroque choral music that Brahms knew so well and evoke them in a contemporary musical language. His consummate craft is evident throughout the movement. It is particularly evident in the expressive setting of the text. The work requires substantial resources: a large, well-trained choir plus a full symphony orchestra (and two soloists in a few of the other movements).

In the fourth movement, Brahms lets the psalm verses guide both form and content. Each verse has a distinct musical identity. The opening verse, which states the overriding theme of the movement, returns periodically as an affirmation of this central message. The verses that Brahms selected use all three persons: *you*, *me*, and *they*. The musical settings of those directed to the Lord Almighty are serene, with seemingly endless melody flowing from the choir over a rich orchestral accompaniment. The shift to the first person—those still on earth—prompts more agitated musical settings, with more active rhythms and a more contrapuntal texture. And when Brahms composes in the third person by depicting those who have already gone to the other side, he pays tribute to J. S. Bach, who composed to praise God, by briefly evoking the rich polyphonic texture so often heard in the choral movements of his cantatas. Throughout, the largely homophonic choral writing emphasizes that the "my" in the psalms is not an individual, but all of humanity "cry[ing] out for the living God."

13-4F Brahms's "Anti-Requiem"

Ein deutsches Requiem is a musical work that is a spiritual response to death; for Brahms, it was solace for the loss of his beloved mother. In that sense, his titling the work *Requiem* is accurate. But in virtually every other way, it is the opposite of a traditional requiem. By using the vernacular language instead of Latin and by selecting texts that scrupulously avoided not only affiliation with a particular denomination but—even more—mention of Christ, Brahms created a musical document whose message transcends any particular religion and

 **LISTEN UP!**

Brahms, "Wie lieblich sind deine Wohnungen," from *Ein deutsches Requiem* (1869)

TAKEAWAY POINT: A unique work for chorus and orchestra that brings together the spiritual and the human without the intercession of organized religion

STYLE: Romantic

FORM: Multisectional, with periodic return of opening material

GENRE: Nondenominational sacred choral work

INSTRUMENTS: Chorus and orchestra

CONTEXT: Music composed to express a deeply personal sadness yet send a universal message

0:00   Orchestral introduction

0:08   *Refrain:* Lush texture, with rich homophonic choral writing and more contrapuntal orchestral accompaniment

Wie lieblich sind deine Wohnungen,   How lovely is your dwelling place,

Herr Zebaoth!   O Lord Almighty!

0:46   *Refrain:* New, more imitative setting of refrain, conveying serenity of Heaven

Wie lieblich sind deine Wohnungen,   How lovely is your dwelling place,

Herr Zebaoth!   O Lord Almighty!

1:26   More agitated, contrapuntal; until "for the courts of the Lord," tension between earthly feelings and heavenly experience

Meine Seele verlanget und sehnet sich   My soul yearns, even faints,

nach den Vorhöfen des Herrn;   for the courts of the Lord;

2:00   Syncopated strings: human feelings = agitation

Mein Leib und Seele freuen sich   My heart and my flesh cry out

in dem lebendigen Gott.   for the living God.

2:40   *Refrain:* Refrain-like return of opening

Wie lieblich sind deine Wohnungen,   How lovely is your dwelling place,

Herr Zebaoth!   O Lord Almighty!

3:19   Transition, leading to . . .

Wohl denen,   Blessed are those

die in deinem Hause wohnen,   who dwell in your house,

3:41   Bach-like passage about praise

die loben dich immerdar.   they are ever praising you.

4:28   *Refrain:* Final statement of refrain

Wie lieblich sind deine Wohnungen,   How lovely is your dwelling place,

Herr Zebaoth!   O Lord Almighty!

 Listen to this selection streaming or in an Active Listening Guide at CourseMate or in the eBook.

even Christianity. Indeed, Brahms wrote to a colleague that he felt that the work was a "human requiem."

In disassociating his requiem both from its Catholic context and from a specifically Christian orientation, Brahms effectively divorced the spiritual from the religious. What little we can infer from available sources about Brahms's religious beliefs suggests that he followed his own path within Lutheran tradition and that he, like other nineteenth-century German liberals, associated Lutheranism with national identity. The *Requiem* conveys much the same impression; so does its customary venue—the concert hall rather than a church. Moreover, the texts for the seven movements reorient the traditional focus of a Requiem Mass. Their function is to comfort those left behind rather than pray for the soul of the deceased.

Thus, in every respect, *Ein deutsches Requiem* blurs boundaries—between religious and spiritual, sacred and secular, personal and universal. It is a monumental work in which we can hear Brahms, speaking for humanity, address the divine directly. In this respect, it stands as a powerful symbol of the new spirituality of the nineteenth century.

Looking Back, Looking Ahead

The music discussed in this chapter offers thoroughly transformed and novel versions of ancient vocal genres. Song dates back to prehistory, but the songs discussed in this chapter represent a genre that could flourish only in the nineteenth century, in large part because of the increased manufacturing of pianos, the continued growth of music publishing, and the spread of music literacy among people of all classes. The requiem dates back to the first preserved music, as you'll discover indirectly in Chapter 16. However, nineteenth-century requiems were grand works for chorus, soloists, and full orchestra. They were at best impractical for liturgical use and, in the case of Brahms's work, not associated with the liturgy.

The works shed light on important trends in nineteenth-century cultural life. Together they express the Romantic fascination with extremes: Schumann's miniatures (which form a substantial whole) at one end of the spectrum and Brahms's massive work at the other. The songs also show contrasting tendencies: the emergence of song as an art genre, separate from but connected to an outpouring of song with piano accompaniment; audiences (in Schubert's case, certainly) that were heterogeneous groups of the rich and not so rich brought together by a love of song. The effective divorce of the requiem from its liturgical function signaled the waning influence of the Catholic church in musical life and hinted at the separation of spirituality from religion, at least in certain circles.

The other major vocal genre in art music was opera. It too would undergo a thorough transformation, as we'll discover in Chapter 15.

 study tools 13

Early Romantic Piano Music

LEARNING OUTCOMES

After reading this chapter, you will be able to do the following:

14-1 Explain how the piano became the most common vehicle for the first generation of star soloists during the nineteenth century.

14-2 Describe the conservative approach of early Romantic piano composers Robert and Clara Schumann and Felix and Fanny Mendelssohn.

14-3 Contrast the conservative approach with the more progressive approach of Paris-based piano composers Frédéric Chopin and Franz Liszt.

👉 study tools

After you read this chapter, go to the Study Tools at the end of the chapter, page 197.

Clara and Robert Schumann ♪, classical music's most famous married couple, had a complex relationship that bore much fruit but ended much too soon—about two months before their six-teenth wedding anniversary. They enjoyed an artis-tic communion unique in the history of Western music: shared diaries and musical explorations, composi-tions undertaken together and inspired by each other, and seemingly unreserved support for each other's work. But throughout their relationship, from the beginning of their courtship through Robert's difficult last years, they faced enormous obstacles, from without and within.

Robert Schumann was almost ten years older than Clara. The son of a publisher and bookseller, he grew up with twin passions in literature and music. In 1828, he went to the university in Leipzig, ostensibly to study law, a discipline that had no appeal for him and to which he devoted almost no effort. Instead, he spent much of his time either reading or at the piano and began to study with Friedrich Wieck, one of Leipzig's most highly regarded piano teachers and, more important, Clara's father. Wieck recognized Robert's potential and took him on as a student. However, Robert permanently injured two fingers on his right hand, which cut short his career as a pianist. He quickly turned to journalism, first writing for an established journal, then in 1834 founding his own, the *Neue Zeitschrift für Musik (New Magazine for Music)*, with a group of like-minded friends. Schumann soon became one of the most respected music critics in Europe. His first published compositions appeared during this time, although by the end of the decade he was still better known as a critic than as a composer.

Meanwhile, Clara Wieck was becoming the darling of the European concert world. She made successful debuts in Leipzig at the age of eleven, Paris at twelve, and Vienna at eighteen. Her programs included not only popular works by other composers but also her own compositions and improvisations. Among her fans were Goethe, Paganini, Mendelssohn, and, of course, Robert, who had watched her mature as a pianist, composer, and woman. They began their courtship around 1835, when she was only fifteen.

Musically, Clara and Robert were a mutual admiration society. Several of Robert's early piano works include references to and even musical quotations from Clara. Clara's early compositions are clearly influenced by Robert and other first-generation Romantic composers, and a few quote themes from Robert's works. Throughout their time together, before and during their marriage, they studied music together and supported each other's work. Among the fruits of their combined efforts was the publication of a joint collection of songs in 1840, the Schumanns' "year of song."

It took Clara and Robert more than five years and a trip to court before they were able to marry. Their adversary was Clara's father, who had apparently hoped that his daughter would find a wealthy husband and had a better opinion of Robert as a musical talent than as a prospective son-in-law. He respected Robert's gifts but also had firsthand knowledge of Robert's lack of discipline and fondness for drink, and he was skeptical about Robert's financial prospects. After a two-year struggle in and out of court, Robert and Clara married the day before her twenty-first birthday.

At the time of their marriage, Clara had a much bigger reputation than her husband's. She was known and admired throughout Europe, whereas her husband was struggling to establish himself as a composer. She had accepted and applied her father's discipline, which served her well. Although she was almost ten years younger than her husband, she seems to have been the one who held the household together. During their relatively brief marriage—effectively about fourteen years, because Robert spent the last two years of his life in a sanatorium after a failed suicide attempt—she gave birth to eight children; provided the bulk of the family

Omikron Omikron/Photo Researchers/ Getty Images

▶Clara and Robert Schumann

FAST FACTS

- Dates: Clara, 1819–1896; Robert, 1810–1856
- Place: Germany (Leipzig)
- Reasons to remember: Premier nineteenth-century piano composers and performers in the Classical style

income through teaching and concert tours, which she booked herself; and dealt with the fearsome mood swings of her husband, who suffered from what seems to have been bipolar disorder throughout his adult life. She continued to compose while Robert was still alive, but shut down after his death. In her forty years of widowhood, she promoted his music through performances and publications but silenced her own muse.

Robert's reputation as a composer grew during their marriage, to the point that there was some reconciliation with his father-in-law. Clara's compositions, well received when she was active as a composer, were largely ignored after Robert's death until the latter part of the twentieth century.

During her widowhood, Clara remained one of the most esteemed pianists in Europe. However, she stood apart from most of her peers because she was a woman and took such a high-minded approach to programming, disdaining flashy showpieces for the music of her husband and the classics. Far more common were flamboyant virtuosos, most notably Franz Liszt.

LEARNING OUTCOME 14-1

Explain how the piano became the most common vehicle for the first generation of star soloists during the nineteenth century.

14-1 Pianists and Pianos in the Nineteenth Century

The Romantic piano virtuosos were the guitar gods of the nineteenth century. They dazzled audiences with their virtuosity and showmanship. And at least a few of them enjoyed celebrity-style perks as some compensation for their rigorous travel schedules and hours of practice. Franz Liszt, the greatest of the virtuoso pianists, allegedly fathered several children out of wedlock, not only with one of his mistresses but also presumably with the many women who threw themselves at his feet after—or even during—his concerts.

14-1A The Virtuoso Pianist

In the 1830s, the piano became the vehicle for the first generation of star soloists. Five necessary components were in place: the instruments, the music, the performers, the venues, and the appeal. For the next quarter century, a new generation of pianist-composers, including, above all, Liszt, Frédéric Chopin, Robert and Clara Schumann, and many others, composed piano music that capitalized on the new capabilities of the piano. Some of their music was flamboyant and virtuosic; other works were more intimate.

Pianists dazzled their audiences with their technical prowess and their artistry. Increasingly, their concerts included not only their own music and that of their contemporaries but also music of earlier generations, especially the sonatas of Beethoven. Liszt reputedly gave the first solo piano recital, toward the end of the 1830s. Prior to this, public concerts typically involved several musicians—singers, pianists, and other instrumentalists. The program was typically a musical potpourri. The solo piano recital included only piano music, of course, but there was already plenty to choose from.

There were numerous advantages to the solo recital. It cost less to put on, because there was only a single performer. It allowed audiences to focus on the performer to an unprecedented degree, and many did. Women swooned and fainted at Liszt's concerts and fought over locks of his hair. There was more to this reaction than Liszt's unsurpassed mastery of the piano. He looked the part: in the portraits we have of him as a young man, he is the match of any matinee idol. However, the reaction was also a sign of the times: the growing stature of the artist and the opportunity to see him display his art in performance, and more generally, the Romantic era's glorification of the individual.

Most of the virtuoso pianists were also composers. Much of their work represented new genres and was intended for audiences ranging from talented amateurs to the most accomplished pianists of the era.

14-1B Romantic Piano Music

Romantic pianist-composers poured out a profusion of piano pieces beginning in the 1830s. They brought a Romantic sensibility to eighteenth-century forms, such as the prelude, sonata, and variation set, and to old and new dances. They invented a host of new forms, some with literary allusions (including ballade, romance, and song without words) and some more visual (nocturne and

Liszt looked every bit the part of a matinee idol.

Olga Popova/Shutterstock.com

barcarolle—an evocation of Venetian gondoliers). And in free-form fantasies and rhapsodies, they abandoned conventional forms altogether. At times, they would infuse their music with patriotic sentiment (the Polish mazurkas and polonaises of Chopin) or explore the exotic (Brahms's Hungarian, or gypsy, dances for piano duet). Some of this piano music was overtly programmatic: Liszt's depictions of his years in Italy and Switzerland, Robert Schumann's descriptively titled piano works. A few works focused on virtuosity: the etude graduated from boring practice-room fare to dazzling concert music. Most of these pieces were short—less than five minutes, as a rule—yet they were usually big in conception.

14-1C Small Forms, Big Gestures

Romantic piano music presents an apparent paradox. Most Romantic piano pieces aren't very long, but they often feature big gestures. This represents a digression from Beethoven's expansion of Classical style, where both size and gesture were grand.

One reason that Romantic piano works often sound "bigger" than their Classical antecedents even when brief is that they start from small forms and expand them. For many shorter Romantic piano works, the comparable Classical formal unit is at most a small movement, such as a minuet and trio—indeed, it may be only a section of a movement or even a simple two-phrase theme. Romantic composers, however, expanded these smaller formal units from within by making phrases and sections longer, and from without by increasing the number of sections. In our survey of Romantic piano music, we hear several different approaches to making a small formal unit sound big.

There were sound commercial reasons as well for composing extensively in smaller forms. Piano works were typically published as parts of larger sets rather than as stand-alone compositions. A set of piano pieces was in some ways the nineteenth-century counterpart to the CD album: in effect, multiple tracks issued in a single package. (In fact, several composers, including Robert Schumann, referred to sets as *Albumblätter*, "album leaves"). Often, one or more pieces were within the capabilities of an amateur pianist with some training: the E minor prelude by Chopin discussed later is a good example. The inclusion of an attractive and pianistically accessible work or two, like the hit single a century or so later, would give the set commercial appeal.

All of the works discussed in this chapter come from sets, as do most of the shorter piano pieces published during the middle of the nineteenth century. Robert Schumann composed several sets, often with fanciful names—*Fantasy Pieces, Scenes from Childhood,*

Forest Scenes. Chopin titled his works by genre—prelude, etude, waltz, mazurka—but all of the shorter works appeared in sets. Among the most popular piano works of the era, especially in Germany and England, were Mendelssohn's *Songs without Words,* published in sets of six pieces.

14-1D Musical Approaches in Romantic Piano Music

The first generation of Romantic composer-pianists, most notably the two Schumanns, Felix Mendelssohn and his sister Fanny, Chopin, and Liszt, brought to the public new kinds of piano music that took advantage of a rapidly evolving instrument. As the instrument became sturdier and more powerful, composers created more sonorous music: soaring, sustained melodies; richer textures; wider registral spans; and more extreme dynamics.

Within this general trend were conservative and progressive tendencies. The more conservative early Romantics were German, most notably Robert and Clara Schumann and the Mendelssohns. Their conservatism is evident in their approach to the piano, which exploited the full range and sonority of the instrument less frequently and less dramatically, closer adherence to established forms, steadier and less contrasting rhythms, thicker textures, and more predictable harmony.

The most important of the more progressive Romantics were two Paris-based expatriates: Chopin came to Paris from Poland; Liszt left Hungary for Paris as an adolescent and used the city as his home base throughout the first part of his career. Their piano music featured more elaborate and wide-ranging figuration and accompaniment patterns; more open textures; greater dynamic range, from thundering octave passages to delicate filigree; more flexibility in tempo; and more adventurous forms and harmonies.

Clara Schumann, Romance in G minor (1855)

TAKEAWAY POINT: A mature, expansive example of German Romantic piano music

STYLE: Romantic

FORM: Ternary

GENRE: Romance

INSTRUMENTS: Piano

CONTEXT: Music composed for the advanced amateur or professional pianist

A SECTION

0:00	No melody, just agitated figuration
0:22	A melody in a new key
0:36	A passionate return to the figuration of the opening, building to the climax of the section
0:58	Reprise of the opening material, but with a different ending

B SECTION

1:26	Change of mode, from minor to major, and change of mood. A tuneful melody replaces the figuration of the opening section.
1:58	Return to the opening melody of the section, leading to new material and a conclusion of the section

A SECTION

2:19	No melody, just agitated figuration
2:40	A melody in a new key
2:54	A passionate return to the figuration of the opening, building to the climax of the section
3:16	Reprise of the opening as before, but with a different ending that returns to the home key
3:41	A brief, coda-like section

 Listen to this selection streaming or in an Active Listening Guide at CourseMate or in the eBook.

LEARNING OUTCOME 14-2

Describe the conservative approach of early Romantic piano composers Robert and Clara Schumann and Felix and Fanny Mendelssohn.

14-2 German Romantic Piano Music: The Schumanns

Robert Schumann composed his eight *Fantasy Pieces,* Op. 12, during the 1830s, relatively early in his career; they were published in 1838 during his courtship of Clara. Clara completed the *Three Romances,* Op. 21, in 1855, after Robert's failed suicide attempt and move to a sanatorium. They would be her last piano works to receive an opus number. These two works offer complementary views of German Romanticism and the Schumanns as composers.

14-2A Clara Schumann's Romance

For Romantics, romance was a generic title with a literary allusion but no specific program. It typically referred to a short, lyrical piano piece. The third of Clara Schumann's late *Three Romances* heard here (see Listen Up!) is exceptional in that regard, in that it is expansive and agitated in the outer sections; it is a big, bold example of the German Romantic piano piece.

romance Short, lyrical piano piece

More generally, however, Clara Schumann's romance provides a helpful introduction to significant features of Romantic piano music. The work is in a large-scale ternary form, a common choice in Romantic piano music. The most direct Classical antecedent is the minuet and trio, and more particularly the third movements of Beethoven's early four-movement sonatas. Compared to these Beethoven movements, the dimensions of Clara Schumann's romance are bigger, the boundaries between and within major sections are less sharply drawn, and the contrast between sections is deeper.

The intricate figuration in the outer sections is characteristic of Romantic style in two important respects. First, the figuration is distinctive and unique to this work. It avoids more generic patterns, such as simple scales or arpeggios, often found in Classical figuration. Second, the figuration/accompaniment texture is maintained for extended stretches rather than quickly moving on to contrasting material. The middle section is comparably expansive and full of harmonic twists and turns.

The tradition of German Romantic piano music exemplified by Clara Schumann's romance began with the late piano pieces of Beethoven and the shorter piano works of Schubert and effectively ended with the late piano pieces of Brahms, composed at the end of the century. By contrast, Robert Schumann cultivated a highly personal, even idiosyncratic style, almost from the outset of his career.

Pefkos/Shutterstock.com

Schumann's notion of a shadow self would take a more personal form.

14-2B Robert Schumann's Fantasy World

In a diary entry on his twenty-first birthday, Robert Schumann described the split between his inner and outer worlds: "as if my objective self wanted to separate itself completely from my subjective self, or as if I stood between my appearance and my actual being, between form and shadow." Jean Paul and E. T. A. Hoffmann, two contemporary novelists whose writings captivated Schumann, undoubtedly influenced his self-reflection. The idea of a doppelgänger, a shadow self, was a recurrent theme in their work.

Schumann's notion of a shadow self would soon take a more personal form. Around the same time, he began giving the members of his circle fanciful names. He himself became first "Florestan the improviser," a projection of his aspirations for a career as a virtuoso pianist. Later, he would add another persona, Eusebius, whom he connected to Saint Eusebius, who was a pope for only sixteen months in 309 and 310. Florestan and Eusebius would come to represent the manic and depressive sides of Schumann's seemingly bipolar condition. He introduced them publicly in several early works, most notably in *Carnaval*, where he identifies them by name and characterizes them musically. Florestan is all energy and passion; Eusebius is dreamy.

Literature fueled Schumann's fantasy world and found expression in his music in numerous ways. Writings of Paul and Hoffmann inspired two important early piano works: *Papillons* and *Kreisleriana*. Literature also helped shape the Davidsbund (League of David), Schumann's partly fictional, partly real group whose purpose was to preserve art from the uncultured. Many of his works have titles that represent characters or moods associated with particular states or situations. Among these works are the eight *Fantasiestücke* (*Fantasy Pieces*), Op. 12.

In "Aufschwung," the second of the eight fantasy pieces (Listen Up!), Florestan is dominant, although there are moments of relative repose. In it, Schumann portrays a dimension of his fantasy world, using devices inspired by his reading. These include an *in medias res*, "start-in-the-middle," beginning and an equally abrupt ending, and a series of contrasting sections that are in various ways fragmentary or at least incomplete.

Unlike eighteenth-century works, which almost always begin by establishing the home key, Schumann's fantasy jumps right in with a chord reverberating with tension, and the first short section ends away from the tonic. This immediate immersion into the work is analogous to the novelist's strategy of beginning the story in the middle of the action.

 **LISTEN UP!**

TOTAL TIME: 3:15

Robert Schumann, "Aufschwung," from *Fantasiestücke* (1837)

TAKEAWAY POINT: An exuberant expression of German Romantic piano music

STYLE: Romantic

FORM: Ternary

GENRE: Character piece

INSTRUMENT: Piano

CONTEXT: Schumann sharing his fantasy world with talented pianists, professional and amateur

A SECTION

0:00   As he often does, Schumann begins as if the piece were already under way, rather than beginning by establishing the key. This opening section ends as abruptly as it began.

0:19   Dramatic change of character—again beginning with short fragments that suggest things are already under way

0:51   A return, then development, of the opening material, which leads smoothly into a new section

B SECTION

1:07   The serene flow of melody and accompaniment contrasts sharply with the turbulent opening section.

1:30   A more animated and humorous section charts a different direction.

1:48   Brief reprise of opening material of B section

1:58   A long transition back to the A section, with the opening motive gradually expanded into the complete phrase

A SECTION

2:23   A slightly varied version of the opening

2:32   The contrasting part of the A section in a new key but otherwise much the same

3:05   The final restatement of the opening, this time with a definitive, if abrupt, ending

 Listen to this selection streaming or in an Active Listening Guide at CourseMate or in the eBook.

The overall design of the piece is ternary on several levels. There are three big sections: energetic outer sections frame a less agitated middle section. But the outer sections also have a ternary design, with a strongly contrasting subsection sandwiched between the opening statement and its reprise. By contrast, the several segments that compose the middle section seem to flow almost imperceptibly from one to the next. With the exception of the final restatement of the opening material, none of the major sections or subsections is a complete musical statement. This fragmentary sectional structure also seems to take its cue from the novel; it is as if the story has several threads and the author/composer moves from one to the next as if shifting scenes.

Schumann delineates the sectional structure with textures that embed or support melody with distinctive, often thickly textured accompaniments in different registers. As in Clara Schumann's romance, there is nothing generic about the musical material.

The piano pieces by the two Schumanns differ fundamentally: one is programmatic; the other is not. Still, both highlight characteristic features of German Romantic piano music—relatively thick texture concentrated in the middle and lower range of the instrument, consistent rhythmic patterns in melody and accompaniment, flexible interpretations of large-scale ternary form. The piano music of Chopin, admired very much by both Schumanns, evidences a different approach to the piano and piano music.

Frédéric Chopin

FAST FACTS

- Dates: 1810–1849
- Place: Poland (near Warsaw)
- Reasons to remember: The poet of the piano. In his numerous compositions, Chopin opened up a new, richer sound world for the piano.

tristan tan/Shutterstock.com

14-3 Chopin's Piano Music

Frédéric Chopin ♠ was the poet of the piano. Although highly regarded as a pianist by those who knew his playing, Chopin did not pursue a concert career. He had neither the inclination nor the stamina to commit himself to the rigors of touring. However, he was committed to the instrument in a way that no other major composer was. All of his music involves the piano. He composed two concertos and other shorter works for piano and orchestra, some chamber music for piano and strings, and a few songs, but the bulk of his work is for solo piano.

14-3A Frédéric Chopin

Chopin was born in a small village about 30 miles west of Warsaw, and received his early musical training in the Polish capital. He received his musical training in his native country, where he was much in demand in the salons of the aristocracy, then left for Vienna in 1830. While Chopin was in Vienna, an armed insurrection against Russian rule failed. Chopin would never return to his homeland; instead, he moved to Paris shortly after learning of the failure of the uprising. Paris would be his home base for the rest of his life; he would express his yearning for Poland in music, through his mazurkas and mature polonaises, which redefined these Polish national dances.

In Paris, Chopin moved easily in the higher social circles, through his expanding contact with Polish émigrés, musicians such as Franz Liszt and Hector Berlioz and others in the arts (he would have a long affair with the novelist George Sand [the pen name for Amantine Dupin]), and the aristocracy and bourgeoisie

who frequented the Parisian salons. His success as a performer in these intimate settings enabled him to charge high fees for teaching. Teaching would be his principal source of income for the rest of his career, although he also earned well from the publication of his compositions.

Chopin was in poor health throughout his too-short life. He was treated for tuberculosis, which was listed as the cause of death, but he suffered other maladies. His fragile constitution certainly contributed to his reluctance to undertake the rigors of a concert career. In a compositional career that spanned less than two decades, he did more to define Romantic piano music and redefine the possibilities of a still-evolving instrument than any other composer.

14-3B Chopin's Innovations

His compositions opened up new sound possibilities: rich figuration, singing melodies, chords and patterns that tapped into the piano's idiomatic resonance. Some works seemed to tell stories without words or paint images in sound—although, unlike many of his contemporaries, Chopin never attached programmatic titles to his pieces.

More significantly, he opened up a completely new, piano-based sound world. In his compositions, he showed how to take advantage of the increased range and power of his rapidly changing instrument (although it should be emphasized that the pianos Chopin played and composed on were still some distance from the modern piano). His music features room-filling cascades of sound and delicate shadings; rich chords and elaborate figuration that take advantage of the damper pedal, which allows pianists to sustain notes after they have finished playing them; melodies that seem to sing yet go beyond what the voice can do. It demands new kinds of skills to produce these new sounds. Quite simply, no composer, before or since, has ever made the piano sound better.

14-3C The Etude

No group of Chopin's early works better shows the interconnection between composer, performer, and instrument than Chopin's Op. 10 etudes. *Étude* is the French word for "study." Before Chopin's etudes, the etude was a teaching piece designed to develop technical facility. Each etude typically focused on a particular difficulty: scales, chords, jumps, and so on. They were usually dry, relatively uninteresting pieces not intended for public performance.

Chopin elevated the status and stature of the etude from practice piece to concert music—an especially challenging concert music. In his etudes, the technical problem is no longer just an end in itself—a difficulty to be mastered—but also the main source

 **LISTEN UP!**

Chopin, Etude in C minor ("Revolutionary"; 1831)

TAKEAWAY POINT: Technical development as virtuoso concert music

STYLE: Romantic

FORM: Enormously expanded two-phrase parallel period

GENRE: Concert etude

INSTRUMENT: Piano

CONTEXT: Virtuoso piano music for a new generation of virtuoso pianists

0:00	Introduction
0:16	Main melodic idea strikes martial air. Combination of surging accompaniment and jagged melodic rhythms helps project "revolutionary" mood.
0:32	Main idea, in a new direction
0:47	New melodic material in new key, like the contrasting section in a binary-form section
1:09	Introduction again
1:25	Main idea, somewhat elaborated
1:42	More elaborate restatement of main idea, which is cut short
1:55	New melodic idea in a distant key eventually leads back to home key.
2:11	Coda

 Listen to this selection streaming or in an Active Listening Guide at CourseMate or in the eBook.

---

of its musical impact. This is virtuosity put to expressive use, as we hear in Chopin's "Revolutionary" etude (Listen Up!).

Chopin's etudes were directed toward serious pianists. They represented a small but significant part of Chopin's music for the piano. Among his other works are larger-scale pieces like the sonatas and ballades; various dance-inspired works—including two Polish dances, the mazurka and the polonaise; melodious, slow-paced works that he called nocturnes; and the twenty-four preludes, a set of miniatures in all keys. Some of these works were accessible to less advanced pianists, including many of his students. We consider two of the preludes next.

14-3D Chopin's Preludes

Among the most familiar sets of short pieces are Chopin's twenty-four preludes. Chopin took his cue from Bach, who had composed two sets of twenty-four preludes and fugues, in each of the twelve major and twelve minor keys. The preludes pay homage to Bach, but Chopin's style is very much up to date.

Regarding the preludes, two qualities stand out: their brevity and their variety. Most of the preludes are very short; several require less than a minute to play.

In the two preludes considered here, Chopin expands a small-format unit—the two-phrase parallel period—into a complete piece. A two-phrase parallel period consists of two phrases that begin the same way and end differently. Typically, the first phrase ends with a comma-style cadence, whereas the second ends with a period-style cadence.

We can gauge Chopin's expansion and transformation of this modestly sized formal unit by comparing the two preludes to an earlier instance of the form. "Là ci darem la mano," Don Giovanni's duet with Zerlina, opens with a simple two-phrase parallel period; it takes about twenty seconds to perform. It is only one segment in the overall form of the duet. In the whirlwind G major prelude (see Listen Up!), Chopin lengthens the gestures, adds a short introduction and coda, and more than doubles the overall length. Partly for this reason, this two-phrase period is no longer a segment of a larger formal unit but a complete, if short, musical statement. The doleful E minor prelude unfolds much more

prelude Originally, a brief introduction to a longer work; a short work for piano

two-phrase parallel period Two phrases that begin the same way and end differently, the first phrase typically ending with a comma-style cadence and the second with a period-style cadence

 **LISTEN UP!**

Chopin, Prelude No. 3 in G major (1838–1839)

TAKEAWAY POINT: Piano miniature with distinctive accompaniment

STYLE: Romantic

FORM: Two-phrase period

GENRE: Prelude

INSTRUMENTS: Piano

CONTEXT: Challenging music for skilled pianists

0:00   *Phrase 1* (with a short introduction): Whirlwind accompaniment pattern, which remains consistent throughout the piece, enables Chopin to write a melody consisting only of fragments.

0:16   *Phrase 2:* Second phrase begins like the first but becomes more expansive and calming as this brief musical statement draws to a close.

0:38   Final flourish, with accompaniment figuration in both hands

 Listen to this selection streaming or in an Active Listening Guide at CourseMate or in the eBook.

 **LISTEN UP!**

Chopin, Prelude No. 4 in E minor (1838)

TAKEAWAY POINT: Poignant piano miniature

STYLE: Romantic

FORM: Two-phrase period

GENRE: Prelude

INSTRUMENT: Piano

CONTEXT: Accessible piano work for able pianists

0:00   *Phrase 1:* Great effort at end of phrase, but it ends where it began.

0:45   *Phrase 2:* The decline of the person/melody speeds up, as the accompaniment descends more quickly. The climax of the prelude is the person's last gasp; at the end, the life force ebbs away, ending abruptly on an unresolved chord.

1:23   Last three chords introduce a new, more solemn sound, like a chorus singing "rest in peace."

 Listen to this selection streaming or in an Active Listening Guide at CourseMate or in the eBook.

slowly. Even more impressively, it is a complete statement; there is nothing ephemeral about it.

The two preludes also showcase the extraordinary variety in Chopin's music. The E minor prelude (see Listen Up!) has a drawn-out melody supported by what seem to be simple repeated chords. But the unpredictable changes of harmony make the accompaniment distinctive, not generic. A more fragmentary melody rides on the wavelike accompaniment of the G major prelude. The contrast between one prelude and the next is striking, because both melody and accompaniment are distinctive and expressive and because the two complement each other in defining the character of the prelude. The distinctive character of both melody and accompaniment is one of the features that most clearly distinguishes Romantic music from Classical.

Looking Back, Looking Ahead

The piano compositions by the Schumanns and Chopin offer comparisons with the past and with each other. In these five Romantic works, we can hear the continued evolution of piano music in the direction charted by Beethoven and made possible by improvements in the instrument: expanded musical gestures, more individuality in musical materials, wider range, and more challenging execution. The five works also exemplify different approaches in Romantic piano music—the rich sounds and regular rhythms of German Romanticism versus Chopin's more sonorous and flexible style. In all of the works, there is evidence of a new aesthetic, one that emphasizes narrative over drama. Explicitly or implicitly, the five works seem to be more about telling a story or painting a scene than conducting a musical argument of the kind heard in the Classical sonata.

Chopin's miniatures represent one extreme in musical Romanticism. In Chapter 16, we encounter its opposite: an extremely large five-movement work for a massive orchestra, composed about the same time as Chopin's preludes.

 study tools 14

Ready to study?
In the book you can:

- Review Learning Outcome answers and Glossary terms with the tear-out Chapter Review card.

Or you can go online to CourseMate, at www.cengagebrain.com, for these resources:

- Chapter Quizzes to prepare for tests

- Interactive flashcards of all Glossary terms

- Active Listening Guides, streaming music, and YouTube playlists

- An eBook with live links to all web resources

LEARNING OUTCOMES

After reading this chapter, you will be able to do the following:

15-1 Understand how Gioachino Rossini inspired a renaissance of Italian opera through his innovative approach to integrating music and drama.

15-2 Describe how Giuseppe Verdi reformed Italian opera.

15-3 Differentiate *opéra comique* from other types of nineteenth-century opera through an understanding of Bizet's *Carmen*.

15-4 Recognize how Richard Wagner changed music and opera.

 study tools

After you read this chapter, go to the Study Tools at the end of the chapter, page 219.

In recent years, the Metropolitan Opera, the most prestigious opera house in the Americas, has presented about thirty operas a season. In a typical season, about two-thirds of the operas date from the nineteenth century, and about half of them are by Italian composers. The only eighteenth-century composer whose operas are routinely performed is Mozart. Core repertoire from the twentieth century is almost as sparse. Giacomo Puccini and Richard Strauss, the composers of the most frequently performed twentieth-century operas, began their careers well before the turn of the century and composed most of their important operas by 1920. No opera by a composer whose career began in the twentieth century has become a staple of the repertoire. Indeed, the core repertoire has remained much the same since the 1930s.

In this chapter, we introduce this core repertoire through excerpts from four operas. Two are from operas by Italian composers, Gioachino Rossini and Giuseppe Verdi. One is the French composer Bizet's *Carmen*, one of the most famous operas of any era. The fourth comes from a cycle of four operas by the German composer Richard Wagner, the most influential composer of the second half of the nineteenth century. Collectively, they help document major developments in nineteenth-century opera and provide insight into the enduring appeal of this repertoire.

LEARNING OUTCOME 15-1

Understand how Gioachino Rossini inspired a renaissance of Italian opera through his innovative approach to integrating music and drama.

15-1 Rossini and the Renaissance of Italian Opera

The Paris Opéra presented the premiere of Gioachino Rossini's final opera *Guillaume Tell (William Tell)* on August 3, 1829. Rossini was thirty-seven at the time and would live almost four decades longer. Although he was planning another opera at the time of the premiere, he abandoned the project soon after. He composed very little after that; he called several of the few works that he did produce the "Sins of Old Age."

Rossini's abrupt retirement is one of the great mysteries in music history. At the time of his retirement, Rossini was perhaps the most esteemed and popular composer in Europe. *William Tell* received glowing reviews in the contemporary press, despite its excessive length (even for Rossini). He must have been exhausted, because he had composed thirty-nine operas in less than two decades. He may have been upset by political turmoil. One of the consequences of the 1830 revolution in France was the termination of his pension from the government. It would take him six years to have it restored. He may have been tired of dealing with the difficult personalities that are a seemingly integral part of operatic life: the first "prima donnas" were female opera stars.

Rossini's motivation for retiring may never be known. What is certain, however, is that he *could* retire with half his life ahead of him. Rossini was arguably the most commercially successful classical composer of all time. He was the antithesis of the starving artist. Photographs taken toward the end of his life reveal a well-fed person, probably from eating numerous helpings of Tournedos Rossini, a steak/butter/paté dish created in his honor by a great chef. The financial security that he enjoyed after retirement was only a dream for virtually every other composer of the era. Rossini's success was the result of a fresh and enormously appealing approach to the use of music in drama. He would play the key role in returning Italy to the center of the operatic world and rise from humble circumstances to great celebrity in the process.

15-1A Gioachino Rossini

Gioachino Rossini ❯ was the only child of musician parents: his father was a hornist, and his mother was a singer.

❯Gioachino Rossini
FAST FACTS

- Dates: 1792–1868

- Place: Italy

- Reasons to remember: Masterful composer of both comic and serious opera; the key figure in the revitalization of Italian opera in the nineteenth century

© rook76/ShutterStock.com

Growing up, he became proficient as a singer, hornist, and harpsichordist (harpsichord was still used to accompany recitative in opera). He was precocious as a composer, completing his first opera at eighteen. Success came early, and in 1815 he signed a contract to produce one opera per year for two venues in Naples. By 1820, he was celebrated throughout Europe. After visits to Vienna (where he met Beethoven) and London, he signed a contract with the French government and relocated to Paris. After retiring, he remained in Paris until 1837, returned to Italy for a difficult two decades—of poor health, friction with fellow Italians after the 1848 revolution, and other troubles—then returned to Paris in 1855, where he enjoyed better health and more gracious living for the rest of his life.

As is the case with the important Italian composers of succeeding generations, Rossini's fame came almost exclusively from his operas. They comprise most of his output and virtually all of his important music. He is best known in our time as a composer of comic opera, but his innovations in serious opera would also prove extremely influential. His best-known opera, and arguably the greatest comic opera of any era, is *The Barber of Seville (Il barbiere di Siviglia)*, which was first produced in 1816.

15-1B The Barber of Seville

The Barber of Seville is a two-act *opera buffa* that received its premiere in 1816. The libretto is based on a play by the French author Pierre Beaumarchais. Beaumarchais's play is the first of a trilogy involving Figaro, a barber and jack-of-all-trades. (The second would become the basis of Mozart's opera *The Marriage of Figaro*.) The plot, set in seventeenth-century Spain, revolves around the romance between Count Almaviva and Rosina, a beautiful young girl who is the ward of Dr. Bartolo, an old man who has his own plans to marry her. Almaviva disguises himself as a poor student to ensure that Rosina loves him for himself rather than for his wealth or position. Through the machinations of Figaro, Almaviva is able to communicate with Rosina, even though Dr. Bartolo keeps her housebound. Eventually they marry, as Dr. Bartolo accepts Rosina's dowry as compensation for agreeing to their marriage. One of the most familiar moments in the opera comes toward the beginning, when Figaro introduces himself to the audience.

Figaro's entrance is one of the great *tours de force* in the opera repertoire because it enables a skilled baritone to show off the full range of his abilities in the service of dramatic characterization. Rossini's dramatic objective is to portray Figaro as a likeable, good-humored, somewhat self-satisfied fellow: someone who by his own account does an important job well and enjoys a good life because of it. This objective guided Rossini's musical decisions.

In previous generations, dramatic and musical conventions often worked at cross-purposes: the da capo aria is exhibit A in this regard, as we heard in Chapter 5. In "Largo al factotum" (see Listen Up!), Rossini liberated the musical setting from formal conventions so that it could more effectively serve dramatic ends. This greater freedom is most obvious in the pacing. The aria begins in high spirits, first in the orchestra, then with Figaro, who enters singing nonsense syllables. But instead of continuing in this same vein, Rossini has Figaro stop rushing to his shop long enough to reflect pleasurably on his good fortune. (Rossini embeds some musical fun here: the musical direction "a piacere"— "at [one's] pleasure"—gives a performer some freedom in determining the rhythm.) In the course of the aria, Figaro abandons the quick, steady rhythm of the orchestral accompaniment two more times. Both interruptions make sense dramatically—first he talks about rubbing shoulders with the upper classes as if he's sharing a secret, then about the constant demands for his attention—while giving him a chance to show off his range and his lightning-quick tongue. All is done in good humor.

At the same time, Rossini's music is immediately accessible. It uses the familiar musical language of the late eighteenth century; during his early training Rossini immersed himself in the orchestral music of Mozart and Haydn. He then parcels it out in easily grasped modules, distributing it flexibly between singer and orchestra according to

Figaro, played here in a Russian production, is a good-humored, self-satisfied fellow.

the dramatic demands of the moment: when it works, the orchestra can maintain the musical momentum. This in turn allows the singer to *act*; in this instance, he becomes a more credible character. The combination of immediately accessible music and ample opportunity for vocal display, all supporting the drama, was enormously appealing at the time; it is still considered the perfect *opera buffa*.

15-1C Rossini and Beethoven

In April 1822, Rossini met Beethoven for the first and only time, in Vienna at a festival of his music. He knew and admired some of Beethoven's music from having studied scores of the works. During his visit, he attended a performance of Beethoven's third symphony, which moved him to such an extent that he persuaded a mutual acquaintance to arrange a visit with the master.

In his account of the visit, Rossini described the squalor of Beethoven's living quarters and recounted Beethoven's backhanded compliment:

> Ah, Rossini. So you're the composer of *The Barber of Seville*. I congratulate you. It will be played as long as Italian opera exists. Never try to write anything else but opera buffa; any other style would do violence to your nature.

Beethoven's remark almost certainly mixes admiration with condescension. In other remarks about Rossini's music, Beethoven clearly regarded it as inferior and lightweight compared to his music and that of his German-speaking contemporaries, but he almost certainly envied Rossini's success.

In retrospect, it is not hard to understand Beethoven's grudging admiration. He had fame, whereas Rossini had both fame and fortune, but their musical values were diametrically opposed. The two composers started from a similar place: wholesale admiration for and thorough study of the music of Haydn and Mozart. However, they ended up far apart in both musical aesthetic and result. Beethoven sought individuality and innovation: his most memorable compositions carve out new musical territory. Rossini developed a repertoire of stock devices, which he used and reused—especially when faced with multiple deadlines, he had no qualms about recycling

 **LISTEN UP!**

Rossini, "Largo al factotum," *The Barber of Seville* (1816)

TAKEAWAY POINT: Good-humored, high-spirited music that deftly portrays a main character in the opera

STYLE: Late Classical/early Romantic

FORM: Aria with recitative-like interruptions; periodic return of earlier material, but not in a predetermined way

GENRE: Early nineteenth-century *opera buffa*

INSTRUMENTS: Baritone and orchestra

CONTEXT: Figaro introduces himself as a man who gets things done.

A

0:00   Orchestral introduction presents the two main up-tempo musical ideas in the aria.

B

0:14   Rossini crescendo (music gets louder and rhythmically more active). Figaro walks in singing nonsense syllables.

A

0:36   Begins with orchestra's opening material but goes out of tempo as Figaro becomes expansive about his good life

Largo al factotum della citta.	Make way for the chief of the city.
Presto a bottega che l'alba e gia.	Off to his shop at break of day.
Ah, che bel vivere, che bel piacere	Ah, such a good life, such a pleasure
per un barbiere di qualita!	for a barber of quality!

1:04   Return to opening material as Figaro affirms his good fortune

Ah, bravo Figaro!	Ah, bravo, Figaro!
Bravo, bravissimo!	Bravo, bravissimo!
Fortunatissimo per verita!	You're the luckiest of guys for sure!

C

1:29   New material in a new key as Figaro provides more detail about his life

Pronto a far tutto,	Ready to do anything,
la notte e il giorno	night and day,
sempre d'intorno in giro sta.	always out and about.
Miglior cuccagna per un barbiere,	A barber couldn't ask for more,
vita piu nobile, no, non si da.	a nobler life couldn't be had.

1:48   Same material in a different, more remote key

1:51
Rasori e pettini	Razors and combs,
lancette e forbici,	lancets and scissors,
al mio comando	at my command
tutto qui sta.	here they all are.

1:59   Cadenza: hobnobbing with the aristocracy. Steady rhythm ceases; music goes out of tempo as Figaro begins to list the important people he serves.

V'e la risorsa,	And all the resources,
poi, de mestiere	then, the craft itself
colla donnetta . . . col cavaliere . . .	with women . . . with gentlemen . . .
per un barbiere di qualita!	for a barber of quality!

(Continued)

B

2:39 Back to B material: "Rossini crescendo" leads to famous display.

Tutti mi chiedono, tutti mi vogliono,	They all ask for me, they all want me,
donne, ragazzi, vecchi, fanciulle:	women, maidens, oldsters, kids;
Qua la parruca . . .	Let's have a wig . . .
Presto la barba . . .	A quick shave . . .
Qua la sanguigna . . .	Let's have a bloodletting . . .
Presto il biglietto . . .	A quick note . . .
Qua la parruca, presto la barba,	Let's have a wig, a quick shave,
Presto il biglietto, ehi!	A quick note, oh my!

2:59 Big moment

Figaro! Figaro! Figaro!	Figaro! Figaro! Figaro!
Ahime, che furia!	Alas, what chaos!
Ahime, che folla!	Alas, what a mob!
Uno alla volta, per carita!	One at a time, I beg of you!

B

3:20 Back to B material again, like a refrain

Figaro! Son qua.	Figaro! Here I am.
Ehi, Figaro! Son qua.	O my, Figaro! Here I am.
Figaro qua, Figaro la,	Figaro here, Figaro there,
Figaro su, Figaro giu,	Figaro up, Figaro down,
Pronto prontissimo son come il fumine:	Faster and faster like lightning:
sono il factotum della citta.	I am the chief of the city.

3:43 Push to the end: tempo suddenly faster

Ah, bravo Figaro! Bravo, bravissimo;	Ah, bravo, Figaro! Bravo, bravissimo;
a te fortuna non manchera.	good fortune can't leave you.
Sono il factotum della citta.	I am the chief of the city.

 Listen to this selection streaming or in an Active Listening Guide at CourseMate or in the eBook.

music from one opera into another. Rossini excelled at opera composition, and especially *opera buffa*. If his legacy were only his nonoperatic works, he would be considered a minor composer. In contrast, Beethoven composed only one opera, *Fidelio*: both its composition and its reception were problematic. His reputation would be considerably diminished if *Fidelio* were at the center of his compositional legacy.

Around the time of their meeting, Beethoven and Rossini were arguably the most famous living composers. Despite the coincidence of time and (briefly) place, it was as if the two composers inhabited different worlds. Their legacies would seem to confirm this view. Beethoven's music would become the model and measure of musical innovation for more than a century, and his symphonies soon became the gold standard in instrumental music. And Rossini understood better than any composer before him how to shape familiar musical materials for dramatic effect. His operas would inspire a renaissance of Italian opera. His operas and those of his successors, most notably Giuseppe Verdi and Giacomo Puccini, have retained their appeal and remained at the heart of the operatic repertory into the twenty-first century. Beethoven's and Rossini's firmest common ground is their importance to nineteenth-century music.

LEARNING OUTCOME 15-2
Describe how Giuseppe Verdi reformed Italian opera.

15-2 Giuseppe Verdi and the Resurgence of Italian Opera

Opera is an Italian art. It began in Italy, and Italian has been its dominant language throughout its history. During the seventeenth and eighteenth centuries, Italian composers produced a prodigious number of operas, and some of these composers, such as Alessandro Scarlatti, Leonardo Vinci, and Giovanni Pergolesi, were particularly influential. But you probably haven't heard of them because very little of their music is performed today, and almost none of it is standard operatic repertoire. Only with Rossini did operas in Italian and by Italians become standard fare.

The first generation of Italian opera composers after Rossini included Vincenzo Bellini and Gaetano Donizetti. Like Rossini, Bellini and Donizetti composed arias in *bel canto* style. **Bel canto**, which means "beautiful singing" in Italian, prizes evenness of sound, vocal agility, and sweetness. These operas have remained in the repertoire mainly because they are vehicles for glorious singing. It was Giuseppe Verdi who would inject opera with an even more substantial dose of reality.

15-2A Giuseppe Verdi

Just as it is possible to imagine young, small-town guitarists who dream of playing to adoring fans in overflowing arenas, so is it possible to imagine a young Giuseppe Verdi ▶ dreaming of succeeding Rossini as Italy's greatest composer. In nineteenth-century Italy, being a great composer meant composing great opera: all of the important composers in this time and place focused on and are remembered for opera. Verdi succeeded, perhaps beyond his wildest dreams. By the end of his career, he was a national hero, more honored than Rossini or any other composer had been.

For Americans, the name Giuseppe Verdi rolls off the tongue impressively. Translated into English, however, it sounds far more humble: Joseph Green. Verdi's early circumstances were comparably humble; he was the son of a village innkeeper. It was a point of pride for him. In 1863, when he was an internationally known celebrity and a national hero, he wrote, "I was, am and always will be a peasant from Roncole."

After early training in the nearby town of Busetto and an apprenticeship with a Milanese opera composer, Verdi got his first opera performed at the famed opera house La Scala in 1839. It led to three more commissions, one of which (*Nabucco*, 1842) established him as Italy's most important composer. For the next three decades, he would be the preeminent opera composer in Europe. The most important phase of his career began with the composition of *Rigoletto* in 1851, followed by *Il trovatore* (produced early in 1853) and *La traviata*. These and the operas that he composed after them are his most frequently performed works. Verdi's final operas, *Otello* (1887) and *Falstaff* (1893), are adapted from plays by Shakespeare; many consider them to be his masterworks.

15-2B Verdi and Realism

In his mature operas, Verdi transformed Italian grand opera from a vehicle for gorgeous singing into true

▶Giuseppe Verdi
FAST FACTS

- Dates: 1813–1901
- Place: Italy
- Reasons to remember: Transformed opera in Europe, Italian opera in particular, with a new focus on realistic characters with real, deep feelings

musical drama by making it more real. Verdi's reforms addressed four crucial aspects of opera: the stories, the musical flow, the use of the orchestra, and the singers.

More Realistic Plots. More than any other composer, Verdi brought opera into the present. In several of his mature operas, including *La traviata*, plots are drawn from contemporary fiction rather than Classical myths and history, and all of them portray characters with real personality and passion. Through them, audiences encountered love and lust, life and death, hate and revenge, honor and dishonor. They empathized with characters such as Violetta, Alfredo, and Giorgio (the principals in *La traviata*) partly because both the characters and their situations were believable and part of the audience's immediate experience.

Flow and Form. However, it is the music that makes opera work, and it is in the music that Verdi's genius comes to the fore. Verdi's operas overflow with gorgeous melodies that begin simply enough for an audience to leave singing snippets of them, yet flower into grand gestures that convey deep emotions and enable great singers to showcase their voices.

But Verdi's achievement went well beyond melody. One magical aspect of Verdi's art was his ability to paint emotions and moods with bold musical strokes and to dovetail one musical

> Verdi's operas overflow with gorgeous melodies that begin simply enough for an audience to leave singing snippets of them, yet flower into grand gestures that convey deep emotions.

bel canto Literally, "beautiful singing" in Italian; a vocal style that prizes evenness of sound, vocal agility, and sweetness

moment into the next in order to highlight the events and emotions taking place onstage. A key element in Verdi's ability to shift emotions so dramatically without losing continuity was his blurring of formal boundaries. He achieved this mainly by making the distinction between recitative and aria less pronounced and by reshaping the formal conventions of the aria to accommodate the dramatic requirements of the scene.

Verdi all but abandoned the rigid alternation between recitative and aria. Arias and duets are discrete enough to stand alone; yet, almost imperceptibly, they emerge from and merge into the music that surrounds them. Verdi's beautiful melodies become moments of emotional expansion and intensification, but they do not disrupt the dramatic momentum of the scene. With Verdi, the stop-and-start rhythm of eighteenth-century opera becomes an ebb and flow.

Verdi and the Orchestra. For Verdi, the orchestra is the ideal complement to the voice: the voices are the emotional focus of the opera; the orchestra is both supporter (behind the singers) and commentator (when they are not singing). Verdi had the ability to change the atmosphere quickly and decisively. As we listen to Verdi's music, we may have to consult the synopsis or the supertitles to learn what events caused the shift in mood, but we have no trouble recognizing that the mood has shifted, and we usually have a pretty good idea what the new mood is. The orchestra is most responsible for these shifts; they take place in the interludes between vocal statements and in the character of the accompaniments. Verdi masterfully exploited the capabilities of the orchestra to enhance and extend the message conveyed in words and melody.

Verdi and His Singers. In writing for the voice, Verdi traded grace for drama. He forsook the flowery, light-voiced style demanded in *bel canto* arias. His vocal writing demanded power and expressive range rather than agility, for both men and women.

In particular, both Verdi and Wagner spearheaded a movement to inject masculinity into male vocal roles. In the first part of the eighteenth century, castrati played many of the lead male roles: in the original productions of Handel's *Giulio Cesare*, Julius Caesar was a castrato. The practice died out toward the end of the century; Mozart's Don Giovanni is a baritone. Most glamorous roles in early nineteenth-century opera belonged to sopranos, who had the vocal agility to sing elaborately ornamented arias. Wagner deemed similar vocal display by men as "unmanly, weak, and lackluster." He and Verdi helped give the leading male roles a more masculine character by requiring more sound and stamina and less ornamentation in tenor roles—Wagner's *Heldentenor* (heroic tenor) and Verdi's *tenore robusto* (robust tenor). Others achieved a similar result by giving lead roles to baritones: Boris Godunov, the central figure in

Mussorgsky's opera of the same name, *Boris Godunov* (1874), is a baritone.

Thus, in the course of a century and a half, the customary range of the leading male operatic roles dropped from unnaturally high (castration left the castrato's voice in the vocal range of a woman's) to high through the use of falsetto, to a midrange much closer to that of the normal male voice. As a result, the main male characters were more believable vocally as well as dramatically.

Taken together, these changes resulted in opera that was dramatically more compelling because it was more musically powerful. We hear and see them in an extended scene from Verdi's *La traviata* (which translates roughly as "the fallen woman").

15-2c *La traviata*

It is a safe bet that Verdi never put himself under greater pressure than he did during the composition of *La traviata*. The premiere of the opera took place on March 6, 1853. Although he had agreed to compose an opera for the Venetian Carnival season (the period immediately preceding Lent) the previous April, he didn't settle on a subject for the opera until November. He and his librettist decided to base the opera on *La Dame aux camélias (The Lady of the Camellias)*, a novel by French author Alexandre Dumas the Younger, which he had adapted into a play early in 1852. Apparently, Verdi did not begin composing in earnest until early in 1853. The premiere went on as scheduled but was not successful. Verdi subsequently revised it and engaged different singers; a production mounted the following year was an unqualified success.

The heroine of *La traviata*, Violetta Valery, is a courtesan, an upper-class call girl, dying of tuberculosis. At the beginning of the opera she flits about, living for the moment, perhaps because she is aware that she has little time to live. At a party to celebrate her release from the hospital, she encounters Alfredo Germont, who has admired her from afar. Moved by his declaration of love, she falls in love with him and resolves to abandon her former loose lifestyle. They set up house in her country villa. However, their scandalous affair has jeopardized the wedding of Alfredo's sister, so Alfredo's father, Giorgio, visits Violetta while Alfredo is away, to plead with her to renounce Alfredo and preserve the family's honor. She reluctantly but honorably agrees, out of love for Alfredo, and promises Giorgio that she will not reveal the reason for severing their relationship. She pretends to love another, which sends Alfredo into a jealous rage. Later, he discovers the truth and comes to her, only to find her on her deathbed. They declare their love for each other. This momentarily invigorates her, but almost immediately she relapses and dies.

"Dite alla giovine" (roughly, "Say to this child of thine"; see Listen Up!) is the latter half of the pivotal scene in the opera, the moment when Giorgio Germont

LISTEN UP!

Verdi, "Dite alla giovine" and "Morrò! Morrò!" *La traviata* (1853)

TAKEAWAY POINT: Glorious music that softens an old man's hard heart

STYLE: Romantic

FORM: Modified da capo aria; recitative; through-composed

GENRE: Italian opera

INSTRUMENTS: Solo voices and orchestra

CONTEXT: Giorgio Germont begins the scene with nothing but contempt for Violetta; by the end, he has nothing but admiration for her.

MOVEMENT 2: ARIA

A SECTION

0:00   **Violetta**

Ooh, dite alla giovine,   Oh, tell the young girl,

sì bella e pura,   so beautiful and pure,

ch'avvi una vittima della sventura   that an unfortunate woman

cui resta un unico raggio di bene che   crushed by despair,

a lei il sacrifica e che morrà!   makes a sacrifice for her to be happy, and then will die!

B SECTION

1:15   B section: from major to minor and generally much more urgent music

        Germont

Sì, piangi, o misera, supremo il veggo.   Yes, cry, unfortunate lady

È il sacrificio ch'ora io ti chieggo.   It is a great sacrifice that I ask.

Sento nell'anima già le tue pene;   I feel your pain in my soul.

coraggio e il nobile cor vincerà.   Courage and a noble heart will prevail.

A SECTION

2:06   Reprise of A, with commentary from Germont. Orchestral accompaniment becomes richer and more ominous with steady throb in cellos. Verdi extends end of aria by reprising short segments of Germont's contrasting section and adding a cadenza-like duet.

4:30   Recitative-like dialogue

        Violetta

Imponete!   Tell me what to do!

        Germont

Non amarlo ditegli.   Say you no longer love him.

        Violetta

Nol crederà.   He won't believe it.

        Germont

Partite.   Leave him.

        Violetta

Seguirammi.   He'll follow me.

        Germont

Allor . . .   So . . .

(Continued)

MOVEMENT 3

4:51   This brief movement begins almost imperceptibly as Violetta expands accompanied dialogue into a soaring phrase as she asks Germont to embrace her.

Violetta

Qual figlia m'abbracciate forte così sarò.   I've decided; embrace me like a daughter.

5:05   Mood shifts, portending disaster, as she conceives of her plan.

Tra breve ei vi fia reso,	Soon you will have him back,
ma afflitto oltre ogni dire.	but he will be so heartbroken.
A suo conforto di colò volerete.	You must be here to console him.

5:18   **Germont**

Che pensate?   What are thinking?

Violetta

Sapendol, v'opporreste al pensier mio.   If I told you my thoughts, you wouldn't agree.

Germont

Generosa! E per voi che far poss'io?   Generous lady! How can I repay you?

MOVEMENT 4: ARIA

5:39   **Violetta**

Morrò!	I will die!
La mia memoria non fia ch'ei maledica,	My sins cannot be erased from my memory,
se le mie pene orribili	but of my horrible pain
vi sia chi almen gli dica.	let everyone know.

6:00   **Germont**

No, generosa, vivere,	No, generous lady, you must live
e lieta voi dovrete,	and enjoy life.
mercè di queste lagrime	One day Heaven will reward you
dal cielo un giorno avrete.	for these tears you have shed.

6:21   Switch to major and gentler rhythm captures shift in mood, from impending death to a noble deed.

Violetta

Conosca il sacrifizio	One day he should know
ch'io consumai d'amor	the sacrifice that I made for him
che sarà suo fin l'ultimo	and that I loved only him
sospiro del mio cor.	until my last breath.

Germont

Premiato il sacrifizio sarà del vostro amor;	You shall be rewarded for the supreme sacrifice of your love;
d'un opra così nobile sarete fiera allor.	be proud and noble.

7:41   Climax is interrupted with suspenseful music; we learn that Alfredo is returning.

Violetta

Qui giunge alcun. Partite!   Someone is coming. Go!

Germont

Ah, grato v'è il cor mio!   I am grateful with all my heart!

Violetta

Non ci vedrem più forse.   We may never see each other again.

comes to Violetta's country estate while Alfredo is absent, to ask her to terminate her relationship with Alfredo for the sake of his family's honor. At first their confrontation is testy because Giorgio presumes that Violetta is a gold digger as well as a courtesan. But he quickly forms a much more positive impression of her after she responds to his rather brusque introduction and shows him papers that establish that she is selling off her possessions to support Alfredo. He tells her that she must give up Alfredo. After some discussion, she agrees.

This extended excerpt includes three discrete movements, which flow seamlessly from one to the next. In it, we can hear how Verdi modified existing operatic conventions to improve musical flow and dramatic credibility. "Dite alla giovine" is a cleverly disguised da capo aria, with Violetta singing the A section, Giorgio singing the B section, and the two of them singing the reprise of the A section, which Verdi extends by recalling fragments of Giorgio's B section. Through these changes, the aria is no longer dramatically static; instead, we see and hear Violetta and Germont grow closer. Accompanied recitative follows smoothly as the two continue their planning, momentarily retreating from the emotional peak of the aria. The orchestra takes over by abruptly creating a suspenseful mood. This leads to the final movement in the scene, a more active aria that contrasts with the more lyrical "Dite alla giovine." The slow–fast aria sequence was another convention of Italian opera. As before, Verdi modifies it to match the dramatic events—underscoring the growing accord between Violetta and Giorgio and the enormous sacrifice required of her to achieve it. At the beginning of the scene, Giorgio considers her contemptible because of her profession and what he believes her character to be. By the end of it, he has nothing but admiration for her. Through his skillful and innovative handling of form and vivid use of the orchestra, Verdi makes the transformation a continuous process.

15-2D Verdi's Legacy

Verdi's considerable compositional art helped underscore deep feeling by credible characters. Violetta may not have been the next-door neighbor of most audience members, but she and her story were believable in a way that the stories of Orfeo and Dido (who never lived), Cleopatra (who lived long ago and far away), and Don Juan (who is damned through the intervention of the supernatural) are not. *La traviata* is powerful in part because it is so personal: Violetta's transformation through love from a capricious courtesan into a woman of honor has resonated with audiences from Verdi's time to ours because it is a timeless story. That she dies from tuberculosis, a leading cause of death in the nineteenth century, only makes the story more poignant.

Verdi worked within a musical tradition—Romanticism—that encouraged grand gestures and sumptuous sounds; within this tradition, Verdi became a master of conveying even the most emotionally charged moments. The salient features of his style—glorious melodies, evocative orchestral writing, dramatic pacing, and flexibility of form—serve to project deep feelings on a grand scale.

Verdi's mature works from the 1850s and 1860s transformed opera in Europe, Italian opera in particular. They became the new standard against which other operas would be measured, and their focus on realistic characters with real feelings inspired the next generation of Italian opera composers to follow the same path. Some of them adapted *verismo* (realism), an Italian literary movement, to opera: the libretti often portrayed sordid, violent stories. Verdi's most important successor was Giacomo Puccini (1858–1924), who, like Verdi, reshaped the conventions of his time into a personal idiom. Puccini's death brought to an end an era spanning over a century in which Verdi and his countrymen created the heart of the standard operatic repertory.

verismo (realism) Nineteenth-century Italian literary movement adapted to opera; sordid, violent stories often portrayed in the libretti

Georges Bizet
FAST FACTS

- Dates: 1838–1875

- Place: France

- Reason to remember: Composer of Carmen

15-3 Georges Bizet's *Carmen* and Opéra *Comique*

In May 1855, the Paris World's Fair (Exposition Universelle) opened on the Champs-Élysées, then as now one of the most famous streets in the world. At the center of the exposition area was the spectacular Palais d'Industrie. Newly anointed Emperor Napoleon III, a champion of industrial progress, was determined to outdo the English: the structure, which is no longer standing, was France's answer to London's Crystal Palace, which dazzled those who attended the enormously successful Great Exhibition of 1851.

On the periphery of the exposition grounds was a small wooden theater, the Folies-Marigny. To capitalize on the huge crowds attending the exposition, Jacques Offenbach (1819–1880) rented the theater and renamed it Théâtre des Bouffes-Parisiens. Offenbach, a German-born virtuoso cellist, conductor at the Comédie-Française, and aspiring composer, had tried without success for several years to get his witty stage works produced at Parisian theaters. With the opening of the fair, he took matters into his own hands. Although the modest dimensions of the theater limited him to one-act works featuring a handful of performers and a small orchestra, his endeavor was successful enough that he resigned his position with the Comédie-Française and continued his productions through the winter at the Salle Choiseul, which became their permanent home the following year.

In 1856, to recruit other composers for his new enterprise, Offenbach announced a composers' competition. As part of the competition guidelines, he supplied a historical guide to *opéra comique*, which he felt had moved far away from its roots. Among the winners of the competition was a young composer named Georges Bizet (bee-ZAY). ◆ Offenbach's efforts did little to reshape *opéra comique*, as we will discover presently, but it did spawn a new genre, *opéra bouffe*, which took its name from the theater that Offenbach used during the exposition.

Opera lovers are confronted with an array of labels that don't always mean what they seem to mean. *Opéra bouffe* is a cognate of the Italian *opera buffa*, but they are distinct genres; the differences go beyond the language. Similarly, *opéra comique* is a cognate of "comic opera," but there are important *opéras comiques* that lack even a trace of comedy. Distinctions between genres change over time, and they often have more to do with conventions, cultural differences, composers' agendas, and even venue than they do with content. We explore this point in a discussion of Bizet's *Carmen*, the most famous of all *opéras comiques*.

Few operas have sparked more controversy than Georges Bizet's *Carmen*. The rumblings started before the premiere, as several morning papers printed letters denouncing the work. Reviews were generally unfavorable, with critics finding fault on grounds both musical and moral. One provided some historical perspective:

> The stage [in general] is given over more and more to women of dubious morals. It is from this class that people like to recruit the heroines of our dramas, our comedies, and now even our comic operas. But once they have sunk to the sewers of society they have to do so again and again; it is from down there that they have to choose their models.

Others found the opera too "Wagnerian" or too "Chinese." Despite the unfavorable press—or perhaps because of it—the opera ran for forty-eight performances at the Opera Comique and then was a sensation throughout Europe and in New York.

15-3A *Opéra comique*

One reason that audiences found *Carmen* so scandalous was its venue. The Opéra Comique, the company that presented *opéras comiques*, appealed mainly to a middle-class audience—much like the audience for Broadway musicals a century later. And like the Broadway musical of the 1940s and 1950s, *opéra comique* was a genre that featured spoken dialogue alternating with musical numbers.

Opéra comique is a genre that dates from the early eighteenth century. Originally, it mixed humorous spoken dialogue with preexisting melodies. In this respect, it was the French counterpart to the British ballad opera. By the beginning of the nineteenth century, the dialogue remained, but the music was composed specifically for the opera. Plots traded satire for sentimentality; they embodied middle-class virtues. By mid-century, *opéra comique* was wholesome family entertainment, much like the musicals of Rodgers and Hammerstein.

In composing an opera that was neither funny nor sentimental, Bizet hoped to reform and invigorate *opéra comique. Carmen* had the opposite effect; it all but obliterated the genre.

15-3B Exoticism

While central Europe sought to unify, the major western European powers sought to colonize. In particular, both England and France expanded their colonial empires. With this expansion came an interest in other cultures, which was brought home to many through the numerous exhibitions and expositions that were part of late nineteenth-century life. Partly through this contact, exotic settings appeared in opera with increasing frequency toward the end of the nineteenth century and into the twentieth; Bizet's *Carmen*, which premiered in 1875, was among the first.

© iStockPhoto.com/pidjoe

Men saw gypsy women as forbidden fruit.

Bizet based *Carmen* on a novella of the same name by the French author Prosper Mérimée. Mérimée tapped into the nineteenth-century fascination with the exotic. In both novella and opera, the exotic embraced both person and locale. Carmen is a gypsy, an occasional "next-door stranger" for many Europeans. The story takes place in southern Spain: during the nineteenth century and into the twentieth, the Iberian Peninsula and its cultures were a world apart from the rest of Europe, so they counted as "exotic" realms.

Gypsies. Gypsies, now most often called Roma, have been a largely migratory people. Although today the largest concentration of Roma is found in the Balkan region of Eastern Europe, there are Romany populations all over Europe, the Americas, and Africa. The origins of the Roma people are unknown. Linguistic and genetic evidence suggests that they originally migrated from northern India as early as the eleventh century; the cause of their migration remains a mystery. They made their way to Europe by the fourteenth century, and to western Europe, including Spain, by the fifteenth century.

Throughout their history, Roma have been a closed society. They have migrated without regard to national borders; have a culture with distinctly different values from virtually all the settled peoples with whom they share space; and seem to have little regard for non-Roma. They have worked gainfully in nontraditional fields, such as the circus. As a result, the dominant societies have regarded them as outsiders: they have been blamed for numerous evils, banished, persecuted, and murdered.

In the nineteenth century, mainstream European society regarded Roma with a mix of fascination and contempt. It considered them immoral, dishonest, and depraved, and positioned them lower than the lowest class, despite their obvious skills in certain areas. At the same time, people were drawn to what they felt was their hot-blooded, licentious nature. Men saw gypsy women as forbidden fruit: in *Carmen*, the wanton gypsy Carmen seduces Don José, not only severing his relationship with Micaëla, the "girl next door," but also leading him to ruin. For Bizet's audience, the fact that Carmen was a gypsy would have made this course of events all but inevitable.

Spain, an Exotic Part of Europe. For centuries, Spain has been both a part of western Europe and separate from it. In politics and religion, it was a major player for hundreds of years, as evidenced by its vast colonial empire; its marriages with other royal families and dominion over other parts of Europe, such as southern Italy and Sicily; and its staunch support of the Catholic Church—Spain was, after all, home to the Inquisition. However, the prominent place of minority cultures, including Moors, Jews, and Roma, helped produce a culture quite different from that of the rest of Europe. Flamenco music, the most distinctively Spanish musical tradition, has strong roots in gypsy music. Moreover, Spain's relative isolation—the range of mountains known as the Pyrenees forms a natural boundary between France and the Iberian Peninsula that made land travel between the two difficult and treacherous—only increased the perception that Spain was an exotic locale. For Bizet and his audience, the exoticism of the gypsy and of Spain was part of the appeal of *Carmen*.

15-3C *Carmen*

Bizet's masterwork was *Carmen* (1875), his last complete composition and the work that has brought him enduring fame. It was the last of six operas that have survived; none of the others has attracted a fraction of the attention given to *Carmen*. Sadly, Bizet did not live to enjoy the success of Carmen or to compose an even more successful sequel; he died of a heart attack directly after the conclusion of the thirty-third performance in Paris.

This ultra-short plot summary of *Carmen* comes from the writer Jean Henri Dupin. In a remark to Meilhac, one of the librettists, the morning after the premiere, Dupin disparagingly summarized the plot like this: "A man meets a woman. He finds her pretty. That's the first act. He loves her, she loves him. That's the second act. She doesn't love him anymore. That's the third act. He kills her. That's the fourth!"

The story, which also takes place in Seville, a town in the southern part of Spain, revolves around two triangles. One includes Don José, a corporal in the guard; Micaëla, a peasant girl and his hometown sweetheart; and Carmen, a gypsy working in a cigarette factory. Carmen attracts Don José, who soon falls in love with her. Because of her, he does things that turn him from a soldier into an outlaw. In the meantime, Carmen has attracted the interest of Escamillo, a famous toreador. He and Don José compete for Carmen's attention. Carmen ultimately rejects Don José, who murders her in a fit of jealous rage.

Opéra comique, like operetta, alternates spoken dialogue with musical numbers. However, Bizet's decision to compose an *opéra comique* almost certainly had more to do with business than with musical taste: the commission for *Carmen* came from the Opéra Comique (the institution). Throughout the opera, we can hear Bizet straining at the conventions of the genre. The orchestra plays an important role, and the orchestral writing is varied. (Indeed, the importance and independence of the orchestra are demonstrated by two orchestral suites extracted from the opera after the composer's death.) In the same vein, Bizet goes well beyond dialogue that is periodically interrupted by tuneful melody. Although there are set numbers, such as the habanera discussed later, there are more extended numbers with recitative, accompanied dialogue, aria, and numerous gradations in between. Bizet also makes use of a bold and prominent "reminiscence" motive, a musical idea introduced early in the opera that returns with telling effect. Bizet introduces the motive that signals Carmen's ultimate fate in the orchestral prelude to the opera. It occurs right after the high-spirited opening; its message is unmistakable. The motive returns in the final scene between Carmen and Don José. It brutally interrupts the music associated with the bullfight, which is going on in the background, to signal that Don José has lost control and will kill Carmen.

Bizet's decision to use more complex strategies and make the orchestra more important made dramatic sense: it would have been difficult to convey the intense passions of the leading characters in conventional forms. It is in these qualities that we sense the musical dimensions of Bizet's attempt to reform *opéra comique*.

Carmen is a story of passions, in this case uncontrollable ones. Both Don José and Carmen are doomed: Carmen by choice, and Don José because he cannot help himself. The skillful, often transparent orchestral writing, with a prominent role for woodwind instruments (an approach common in French music); the glorious, memorable melodies and motives; and the occasional touches of musical exoticism—all of these qualities musically support this compelling story. Bizet's miracle is music that is evocative, imaginative, dramatically responsive, and—above all—accessible.

15-3D The Habanera

Although the habanera is fundamentally an Afro-Cuban dance genre, the French were the catalysts for its creation. Habanera means "of or related to Havana," the capital city of Cuba. The dance, and the songs built on its distinctive rhythm, acquired its name only after it left Cuba. In Havana, it was known as the contradanza. The *contradanza* (English "country dance", French *contredanse*) came to Cuba with the French colonists who fled Haiti in the wake of the slave insurrection of 1791. It was soon among the most popular dances in Cuba. The orchestras that accompanied the contradanza were typically made up of Afro-Cuban musicians. As in other parts of the New World, African-diaspora musicians interpreted this European dance in terms of their musical heritage. As the dance traveled back to Spain, it acquired the name habanera and a distinctive rhythm, which was a European reinterpretation of the rhythm of the contradanza. From Spain it spread throughout Europe. Bizet borrowed the melody for his habanera from a popular song by Spanish composer Sebastian Iradier, which Bizet assumed was a folk song. (When he learned of his error, he acknowledged Iradier in his score.) Iradier had been to Cuba, where he heard and was intrigued by what was called Creole music, and what we now more precisely term Afro-Cuban music.

The pulsating rhythm of the habanera injected vitality into European concert music via Spanish popular songs, like the one Bizet borrowed. French composers found it irresistible: Bizet, Debussy, and Ravel used the rhythm to give their music a Spanish tinge. The habanera also spread throughout the Americas. It went to Argentina, where it eventually merged with local music to become the tango, and to Mexico, whence it entered the United States via New Orleans to influence ragtime and jazz.

Carmen's famous habanera (see Listen Up!), also identified by the first line of the lyric, "L'amour est

habanera An Afro-Cuban dance genre
contradanza English "country dance"; French *contredanse*

LISTEN UP!

Bizet, "L'amour est un oiseau rebelle," *Carmen* (1875)

TAKEAWAY POINT: Exotic, erotic music for an exotic, erotic leading lady

STYLE: Romantic

FORM: Expanded verse/refrain form

GENRE: Opéra comique

INSTRUMENTS: Soprano and orchestra

CONTEXT: Introduction of Carmen through the habanera, giving a strong first impression of her character

0:00   Instrumental introduction; cellos establish habanera rhythm

VERSE 1

0:06   The melody slithers down a minor chromatic scale over the steady habanera rhythm.

L'amour est un oiseau rebelle	Love is a rebel bird
que nul ne peut apprivoiser,	that no one can ever tame,
et c'est bien en vain qu'on l'appelle,	and you call him in vain
s'il lui convient de refuser.	if it suits him not to come.

0:22
Rien n'y fait, menace ou prière,	Nothing works, threat or prayer,
l'un parle bien, l'autre se tait:	one man speaks well, the other's still:
Et c'est l'autre que je préfère.	And it's the other whom I prefer.
Il n'a rien dit mais il me plaît.	He's said nothing but he pleases me.

0:38   High winds play the major-mode verse melody while Carmen sings "Love! Love!" as an obbligato.

L'amour! L'amour!	Love! Love!
L'amour! L'amour!	Love! Love!

REFRAIN

0:52   Melody of refrain, which stays in major, takes rhythm of habanera.

L'amour est enfant de Bohême,	Love is a gypsy child,
il n'a jamais, jamais connu de loi;	it has never, never known a law;
Si tu ne m'aimes pas, je t'aime:	If you don't love me, I love you;
si je t'aime, prends garde à toi!	if I love you, beware!

1:07   The orchestra plays the first few notes of the melody; Carmen continues.

Si tu ne m'aimes pas, je t'aime:	If you don't love me, I love you;
si je t'aime, prends garde à toi!	if I love you, beware!
Si tu ne m'aimes pas, je t'aime:	If you don't love me, I love you;
si je t'aime, prends garde à toi!	if I love you, beware!

VERSE 2

1:35
L'oiseau que tu croyais surprendre	(The bird that you thought you caught)
battit de l'aile et s'envola . . .	Flaps its wings and flies away . . .
L'amour est loin, tu peux l'attendre;	Love's far away, you wait for it;
tu ne l'attends plus, il est là!	when you don't expect it, it's there!

1:50
Tout autour de toi, vite, vite,	All around you, quickly, quickly,
il vient, s'en va, puis il revient . . .	it comes, it goes, then it returns . . .
Tu crois le tenir, il t'évite,	You think you hold it, it escapes you,
tu crois l'éviter, il te tient.	you think you've escaped it, it holds onto you.

2:06	Once again a vocal obbligato as the winds play the verse melody	
	L'amour! L'amour!	Love! Love!
	L'amour! L'amour!	Love! Love!

REFRAIN

2:22	*L'amour est enfant de Bohême,*	Love is a gypsy child,
	il n'a jamais, jamais connu de loi;	it has never, never known a law;
	Si tu ne m'aimes pas, je t'aime:	If you don't love me, I love you;
	si je t'aime, prends garde à toi!	if I love you, beware!

2:36	Orchestra plays first few notes of melody; Carmen continues.	
	Si tu ne m'aimes pas, je t'aime:	If you don't love me, I love you;
	si je t'aime, prends garde à toi!	if I love you, beware!
	Si tu ne m'aimes pas, je t'aime:	If you don't love me, I love you;
	si je t'aime, prends garde à toi!	if I love you, beware!

🔊)) Listen to this selection streaming or in an Active Listening Guide at CourseMate or in the eBook.

un oiseau rebelle" ("Love Is a Rebel Bird"), is Carmen's first big number. It comes early in the opera, as she returns from lunch with a group of girls who work with her at the cigarette factory across from the guardroom. She uses the song to solicit admiration from the soldiers, especially Don José, who ignores her.

The habanera is one of a small number of Spanish-flavored numbers in the opera, and arguably the most evocative. By introducing Carmen with what he believed to be a familiar Spanish folk song, Bizet immediately establishes place and social class. And by placing her in Spain as a member of an outsider group, Bizet turns the "Latin lover" legend that we encountered in *Don Giovanni* on its head: the sexual aggressor now is not the male, but the female. Carmen's provocative song would have been wildly inappropriate for a noblewoman, or for Micaëla, the innocent peasant girl whom Don José tosses aside for Carmen, but it matches perfectly the nineteenth-century stereotype of the promiscuous gypsy whose sensuality knows no limits.

Bizet turns the "Latin lover" legend on its head: the sexual aggressor now is not the male, but the female.

© Igor Bulgarin/ShutterStock.com

15-3E Carmen and the Diversity of Late Nineteenth-Century Opera

As *Carmen* quickly gained a following, it ascended the operatic social ladder. For a Viennese production in 1875—the year of the French premiere—Bizet's friend and fellow composer Ernest Guiraud converted the spoken dialogue into recitative. It was performed in this manner until the mid-twentieth century, when Bizet's original version was restored.

The sudden upgrade of *Carmen* from *opéra comique* to opera hints at the increasing diversity of opera during the latter part of the nineteenth century. Among the important sources of this diversity were genre and geography. Traditional opera, as exemplified in the music of Verdi, gained company above and below. In the hands of such composers as the British team of Gilbert and Sullivan and the Viennese waltz king Johann Strauss the Younger, operetta, a lighter form of staged musical entertainment, acquired musical sophistication and a sophisticated audience.

Bizet's *Carmen* both popularized *opéra comique* and expanded its range; opera bouffe, best exemplified by the work of Jacques Offenbach, replaced *opéra comique* as the operetta-like family entertainment in France.

Italian opera beginning with Verdi was serious stuff. However, the most high-minded approach was that of the German composer Richard Wagner; his revolutionary reform of opera would produce a new synthesis of words and music.

LEARNING OUTCOME 15-4
Recognize how Richard Wagner changed music and opera.

15-4 Richard Wagner and Music Drama

The 1800s were a century-long quest for bigness. In both North America and Europe, a striving for and fascination with size played out in every arena. Napoleon set the tone for the century as he sought to dominate all of Europe. After his defeat, those countries that were capable vigorously expanded their colonial empires: the British boasted that the sun never set on the British Empire. In the United States, a transcontinental railway was completed in 1869; it linked a country that had spent the preceding decades expanding westward to the Pacific. The first skyscrapers appeared in the 1880s in the United States and then Europe. Around the same time, the Rockefellers, the Vanderbilts, and other enormously wealthy capitalists began building grand mansions in Newport, Rhode Island, and along New York's Fifth Avenue during the Gilded Age, a period that extended from the end of the Civil War to the turn of the twentieth century.

With his expansion of the symphony and the symphony orchestra required to play it, Beethoven had set the same tone in the musical world. But the man who perhaps best exemplified nineteenth-century bigness in thought, word, and deed was Richard Wagner ♪. Wagner had one of the truly colossal egos in recorded history: no other musician thought so highly of his own music that he spent much of his career working to get a theater built in an out-of-the-way town so that audiences could travel, with some difficulty, to experience his music exactly as he wanted it presented. In his theoretical writings, he set out to change opera—the grandest of all genres—so radically that it would become something completely new, even as it echoed the Germanic mythical past. And his fourteen-hour operatic *Ring* cycle, *Der Ring des Nibelungen (The Ring of the Nibelungen)*, extended Beethoven's expansion of musical form and resources on the grandest possible scale.

15-4A Richard Wagner

For those curious about the connection between formative experiences and works of art, the life of Richard Wagner offers a treasure trove of material ripe for speculation. Wagner was born into a humble family in Leipzig; his presumed father was a clerk, who died within a year of Wagner's birth. Even before his death, however, Wagner's mother had moved in with an artist/playwright/actor named Ludwig Geyer, who was probably Wagner's biological father. Young Richard received relatively little formal musical training, and in his reminiscences he downplayed even that, seeking to portray himself as an untutored genius.

He was a true intellectual. He read widely, wrote extensively, and was well acquainted with many of the important ideas of his time. In his writings, he espoused the most high-minded and idealistic values: the nobility of art uncorrupted by commerce and the purity of the soul of the German people. But if you were a man with an attractive wife, you were better off admiring him from afar. He had numerous affairs, including at least two with partners of his supporters and benefactors. The most egregious was one that produced two children with a woman who became his second wife, Cosima. He fathered them while she was still married to Hans von Bülow, the man who had conducted the premieres of two of his operas! And you wouldn't want to lend him money if you expected to get paid back; he repeatedly accumulated debts that he was unable to repay.

Wagner's almost obsessive preoccupation with being German—he considered himself to be the most German of men and propounded the notion of a German Volk, or people—might be linked to his own uncertain roots, as well as the ideas of radical thinkers like Karl Marx and the nationalistic fervor that would soon lead to German unification. His numerous extramarital affairs could also be attributed to his uncertain paternity. His grand lifestyle, often without the means to support it, may have grown out of his humble circumstances growing up.

As a group, composers are hard people to like. Handel reportedly had a devastatingly sharp tongue; Beethoven was, on occasion, boorish; Brahms was often irascible and brusque; Verdi was stubborn and difficult to deal with. Much of this arises from an almost obligatory need to focus on their art. But in his dealings with others, Wagner would seem to be in a league of his own, not only because of the sordid episodes in his personal life but also because of his persistent and especially virulent anti-Semitism, which surfaced after he had sought and received aid from the Jewish opera composer Giacomo Meyerbeer during his time in Paris. His anti-Semitic writings and calls for racial purity have tarnished his reputation, particularly since the rise and fall of the Third Reich.

There is no major composer with a more conflicted legacy than Wagner. This is especially unfortunate, because he was unquestionably the most influential musician of the latter part of the nineteenth century. His innovations set German/Viennese music on its future path—indeed, classical music is still grappling with his legacy—and his musical achievements were monumental.

▶Richard Wagner

FAST FACTS

- Dates: 1813–1883
- Place: Germany
- Reasons to remember: The creator of music dramas and the most influential musician of the latter half of the nineteenth century

15-4B Wagner's Approach to Music Drama

In keeping with his strong literary inclinations—he wrote the librettos for his works—Wagner identified his later works variously as "drama," "dramas of the future," and "stage festival play" as well as opera. Commentators typically refer to the late works, and especially the *Ring* cycle, as music dramas, to distinguish them from more conventional operas. Among the musical features that distinguish his later works from conventional opera are what might be called "endless melody," the use of leitmotifs, and the expansion of the orchestra and its role.

Endless Melody. In Wagner's particular marriage of verse, voice, and orchestra, endless melody replaces the start–stop rhythm of recitative and aria, or even the ebb and flow heard in Verdi. It was important to him that the text be comprehensible, so he set his texts syllabically. The vocal line amplifies the accentuation and inflection of the text; the elaborate melismatic writing heard in more conventional opera is absent.

What makes the melody truly endless is the absence of typical melodic punctuation. In opera, as in so much other vocal music, we are accustomed to hearing regular phrases punctuated by cadences. Wagner's alternative was to string together a series of melodic ideas, some sung and some played, which respond directly to the text. Their function is to amplify the message of the text; as the music unfolds, there is a constant shifting from one idea to the next, without the sense of articulation or conclusion that cadences provide.

This was a truly radical departure from conventional practice. There are no stand-alone arias in the *Ring* cycle, or even

music drama Term for Wagner's later works that distinguishes them from more conventional operas, encompassing such traits as "endless melody," the use of leitmotifs, and expansion of the orchestra and its role

reminiscence motive Theme used to recall a character, mood, or event

leitmotif Motive or theme assigned to a character, object, emotion, or event in a Wagnerian music drama

larger self-contained sections that can be easily extracted. Instead of letting musical conventions—regular phrases, cadences, melodic repetition, and simple variation—dictate the flow of the text, Wagner allows the text to shape the music. His approach presented a challenge both for the audience, because the familiar musical signals are absent, and for Wagner, to find a means of holding these sprawling music dramas together and shaping them into a coherent whole. His solution was the leitmotif.

The Leitmotif. In opera, the idea of using a theme to recall a character, mood, or event dates back to the late eighteenth century; such themes are called reminiscence motives. Typically, a reminiscence motive was a literal repetition of a melodic idea heard earlier in an opera. Wagner transformed this procedure, usually an isolated event, into a key, recurring element of his compositional approach. He saturated his operas with motives, which were assigned to a character, object, emotion, event, or anything else that needed signifying. They were subsequently altered or developed according to the dramatic demands of the passage. Contemporaries who studied his music called these motives leitmotifs. The German word is *Leitmotiv(en)*; its usual English translation is "leading motive."

> Leitmotifs are the glue that holds Wagner's music dramas together.

Leitmotifs occur in both vocal and orchestral lines; indeed, they appear more frequently in the orchestral parts. They often appear in the spotlight, at the beginnings of new sections, where the singers have dropped out and the orchestra takes over, when a singer reenters, and at climactic moments. They range in length from a few notes to a short phrase. Typically, Wagner tries to invest leitmotifs with something of the character of whatever they symbolize. In this sense, the term *leitmotif*, with its strictly melodic implications, is somewhat misleading, especially in reference to instrumental statements, because the choice of instrument or register (high or low) often does more to convey the expressive message than the melodic shape of the motive.

Leitmotifs are the glue that holds Wagner's music dramas together. Collectively, they form a dense network of connections that replace conventional methods of outlining and unifying a piece. In effect, they were Wagner's effective method for reconciling the conflicting demands of words and music. Repetition is not common in literature; it is customary in music. Bringing them into balance has challenged even the greatest composers. Opera initially privileged words, as we heard in the excerpt from Monteverdi's *Orfeo*. By contrast, the da capo aria swings the pendulum to the other extreme, in which music is dominant. With leitmotifs, Wagner can allow the narrative to move forward while still supplying the repetition that helps embed the music in the ear of the audience.

Symphonic Opera. The high concentration of leitmotifs in the orchestra highlights another distinctive feature of Wagner's music dramas: the orchestra plays a much more significant role than in other operatic genres. We might summarize the difference this way: In the works of composers like Verdi, the orchestra supports the voices through accompaniment, changing moods, or commentary. In Wagner, voices and orchestra blend together into a unified whole. Singers are first among equals, but there is not the clear separation between melody and accompaniment that is the rule in other genres. Indeed, Wagner's orchestral writing is often more memorable than his vocal writing. We can sense that the merging of voice and instruments was Wagner's intent from the design of the Festspielhaus, the theater in Bayreuth that he had built to his specifications for the production of his works: the orchestra pit has a hood that directs the sound back to the stage, where it can merge with the voices before going out to the audience.

15-4C *Die Walküre*

We hear all of these features of Wagner's music in an excerpt from Act 1 (see Listen Up!) of *Die Walküre (The Valkyrie)*, the second of the four "stage-festival plays" that make up Wagner's *Der Ring des Nibelungen*. As such, it is an episode in a much longer story, culled from medieval Norse, German, and Icelandic sagas. The story develops a timeless theme: the conflict between power and greed corrupt. Love redeems.

The Valkyries of the title are nine of the chief god Wotan's immortal daughters, who bring slain heroes to Valhalla, the palatial home of the gods, where they are returned to life in order to guard the castle. Wotan's two mortal children, Siegmund and Sieglinde, twins separated shortly after birth and the central characters in *Die Walküre*, appear in this excerpt. As *Die Walküre* begins, Siegmund and Sieglinde have come of age. At the end of the first act, they discover their kinship, which only intensifies their desire for each other. As the act ends, they come together to conceive Siegfried, the hero of the third episode in the *Ring*.

In our excerpt, the vocal lines are an intensified means of expressing the text. They cannot stand alone as independent musical statements. There are striking musical gestures, but these are not developed into phrases punctuated by cadences. Instead, the vocal line responds directly to the narrative.

Wagner surrounds the voices with a lavish orchestral setting that plays a far more prominent role than is customary in opera. The orchestra commands much of the melodic material and the majority of the leitmotifs. Some of the melodic material is shared with the singers, and some of it weaves around the vocal line, sustaining the emotion while the singer reveals more of the narrative. The frequent and sudden shifts in the musical flow and the periodic appearance of the leitmotifs dramatize and give depth to the text.

15-4D The "Music of the Future" and the Future of Music

In 1849, Wagner published an extended essay entitled *Das Kunstwerk der Zukunft (The Artwork of the Future)*. It was the first of several writings on this topic. Although music did not evolve as he had projected, his music would chart the dominant evolutionary path for the late nineteenth century, one that would continue well into the twentieth.

Wagner challenged basic assumptions not only about opera but also about music in general. It was an attack on two fronts: the elements of music and the underlying structure. In Wagner's music, the familiar points of orientation—sound, melody, and rhythm—are less obvious than in most of the music that we have encountered to this point. There are striking sounds and melodic ideas (the leitmotifs), but they repeat only as demanded by the text rather than recur regularly. Moreover, time keeping is more supple and less obvious; the orchestra typically avoids marking the beat with a simple, easily discernible pattern.

Wagner also avoids the conventional harmonic and rhythmic procedures that outline the structure of a composition at all levels, from the phrase to the work as a whole. Regular phrases and cadences to separate them are exceptional. There are in our excerpt no repetition of sections and none of the other cues that normally help listeners grasp the structure of the work. The only decisive cadence comes at the very end of the act.

Wagner's approach represents an attack on the very foundations of musical discourse as it was practiced in the latter half of the nineteenth century. For the better part of two centuries, common practice harmony had provided the structural foundation of musical composition. Wagner uses many familiar chords, but they are often arranged in patterns that deliberately avoid the cadential progressions that articulate the form of a work. This loosening of the rules in the service of the grandest possible gestures would eventually lead to the abandonment of tonality altogether in some works of the twentieth century.

In his music drams, Wagner essentially tore down the structure and built something quite different in its place. His integration of drama and music was a thorough reconception of how the two should be merged.

Wagner, Act I conclusion, *Die Walküre* (1870)

TAKEAWAY POINT: Rich, sensuous music for a sensual couple

STYLE: Late Romantic

FORM: Through-composed

GENRE: Wagnerian music drama

INSTRUMENTS: Solo voices and large orchestra with expanded brass section

CONTEXT: A climactic scene in a long saga

0:00 Wagner's erotic style—gently surging motive, first in violins, then in Sieglinde's line—indicates arousal.

Sieglinde

Wie dir die Stirn so offen steht,	How your forehead stands out,
der Adern Geäst in den Schläfen sich schlingt!	and the veins coil out into your temples!
Mir zagt es vor der Wonne, die mich entzückt!	I tremble with the pleasure that delights me!

0:23 Valhalla leitmotif in horns: Sieglinde is aware of common ancestry.

Ein Wunder will mich gemahnen:	It brings something strange to my mind:
den heut' zuerst ich erschaut,	though I first saw you today,
mein Auge sah dich schon!	My eyes have seen you before!

0:46 Understated erotic style. Rising motive builds toward love leitmotif in Sieglinde's line.

Siegmund

Ein Minnetraum gemahnt auch mich:	A dream of love comes to my mind also:
in heissem Sehnen sah ich dich schon!	In the heat of longing I have seen you before!

1:05 **Sieglinde**

Im Bach erblickt' ich mein eigen Bild	In the stream I've seen my own image
und jetzt gewahr' ich es wieder:	and now I see it again:
Wie einst dem Teich es enttaucht,	As once it appeared in the water,
bietest mein Bild mir nun du!	now you show me my image!

1:29 Music reaches intermediate climax as Siegmund sings love leitmotif. The horn takes it over as Sieglinde also becomes fully aware of their twinship.

Siegmund

Du bist das Bild, das ich in mir barg.	You are the image that I hid in myself.

1:37 **Sieglinde**

O still! Lass mich der Stimme lauschen:	O hush! Let me listen to your voice:
mich dünkt, ihren Klang hört' ich als Kind.	I think I heard its sound as a child.
Doch nein! Ich hörte sie neulich,	But no! I heard it recently,
als meiner Stimme Schall	when the sound of my voice
mir widerhallte der Wald.	echoed back to me from the forest.

2:13 **Siegmund**

O lieblichste Laute, denen ich lausche!	O loveliest sound for me to hear!

2:27 Valhalla leitmotif returns to anticipate discovery that they are Volsungs.

Sieglinde

Deines Auges Glut erglänzte mir schon:	The light in your eyes has shined on me before:
so blickte der Greis grüssend auf mich,	so did the old man look at me in greeting,

als der Traurigen Trost er gab.	when to my sadness he brought comfort.
An dem Blick erkannt' ihn sein Kind	From his look his child recognized him,
schon wollt' ich beim Namen ihn nennen!	I even wanted to call him by name!

3:06   Siegmund previously called himself "Woeful."

Sieglinde

Wehwalt heisst du fürwahr?	Are you really called Woeful?

Siegmund

Nicht heiss' ich so, seit du mich liebst:	I am not called that, since you love me:
nun walt' ich der hehrsten Wonnen.	Now I am filled with the noblest pleasure.

3:23   **Sieglinde**

Und Friedmund darfst du	And "Peaceful" may you,
froh dich nicht nennen?	being happy, not be named?

Siegmund

Nenne mich du, wie du liebst, dass ich heisse:	Name me whatever you love me to be called:
den Namen nehm' ich von dir!	I'll take my name from you!

3:42   **Sieglinde**

Doch nanntest du Wolfe den Vater?	But did you name Wolfe your father?

Siegmund

Ein Wolf war er feigen Füchsen!	A Wolf he was to cowardly foxes!
Doch dem so stolz strahlte das Auge,	But he whose proud eyes shone,
wie, Herrliche, hehr dir es strahlt,	amazingly, just as nobly as yours do,
der war: Wälse genannt.	he was named Volsa.

4:04   Sieglinde gives Siegmund his name.

Sieglinde

War Wälse dein Vater,	If Volsa was your father,
und bist du ein Wälsung,	and you are a "Volsung,"
stiess er für dich sein Schwert in den Stamm,	it was for you he thrust his sword in the tree,
so lass mich dich heissen, wie ich dich liebe:	so let me call you what I love:
Siegmund—so nenn' ich dich!	Siegmund—so I name you!

4:27   **Siegmund**

Siegmund heiss' ich und Siegmund bin ich!	Siegmund I am called and Siegmund I am!
Bezeug' es dies Schwert, das zaglos ich halte!	Let this sword witness, which I fearlessly hold!
Wälse verhiess mir, in höchster Not	Volsa promised me that in deepest distress
fänd' ich es einst. Ich fass' es nun!	I would one day find it. I grasp it now!

4:55   To vibrating chords, Siegmund utters an incantation.

Siegmund

Heiligster Minne höchste Not,	Holiest love's deepest distress,
sehnender Liebe sehrende Not	yearning love's searing need,
brennt mir hell in der Brust,	burn bright in my breast,
drängt zu Tat und Tod:	drive me to deeds and death:
Notung! Notung!	"Needy"! "Needy"!
So nenn' ich dich, Schwert.	So I name you, sword.
Notung! Notung!	Needy! Needy!
Neidlicher Stahl!	Enviable blade!
Zeig' deiner Schärfe schneidenden Zahn:	Show your sharpness, your cutting fang:

(Continued)

heraus aus der Scheide zu mir!	out of your scabbard to me!
Siegmund, den Wälsung, siehst du, Weib!	You see Siegmund, the Volsung, woman!

6:12 Trumpets state sword motive. Brisker statement of Volsung motive is counterpoint.

Siegmund

Als Brautgabe bringt er dies Schwert;	As wedding gift he brings this sword;

6:21 Strings swirl around Siegmund's declaration of love.

so freit er sich die seligste Frau;	so he weds the most blessed woman;
dem Feindeshaus entführt er dich so.	from the enemy's house he takes you away.

6:36 *Fern von hier folge mir nun,*	Far from here follow me now,
fort in des Lenzes lachendes Haus:	away into springtime's smiling house:
dort schützt dich Notung, das Schwert,	there Needy, the sword, will protect you,
wenn Siegmund dir liebend erlag!	even if Siegmund perishes loving you!

7:10 **Sieglinde**

Bist du Siegmund, den ich hier sehe?	Are you Siegmund whom I see here?
Sieglinde bin ich, die dich ersehnt:	I am Sieglinde, who longed for you:
die eigne Schwester gewannst du	your own sister you have won
zu eins mit dem Schwert!	at the same time as the sword!

7:26 Climax of scene, highlighted by Siegmund's high note on first syllable of "Wälsungen."

Siegmund

Braut und Schwester bist du dem Bruder	Wife and sister you'll be to the brother,
so blühe denn, Wälsungen-Blut!	so flower, then, Volsung blood!

 Listen to this selection streaming or in an Active Listening Guide at CourseMate or in the eBook.

In hindsight, it would appear that successful works of this type required Wagner's singular genius. Wagner's strategy of responding in music to the narrative on a moment-to-moment basis would find a more substantial following among film composers, where both words and image tell the story, and musical continuity and coherence are not as much an issue.

Looking Back, Looking Ahead

The music of Wagner and the rapid growth of popular music for home use and onstage led to the stratification of musical life in the latter part of the nineteenth century. In effect, "mainstream" classical music, as represented by such music as the operas of Verdi and Puccini and the orchestral works of Brahms, Tchaikovsky, and Dvořák, became a middle layer in the professional musical world. Wagner's music and the culture that supported it formed the topmost layer: church hymns, band and dance music, the sea of popular songs, and musical entertainment that made use of these genres formed the lower layers.

Even at mid-century, there was a continuum between "classical" and socially acceptable "popular" music. For example, many of Schubert's songs were popular in Europe and North America; simplified versions and piano arrangements of opera arias sold well; dances like the waltz appeared both as music for dancing and as more sophisticated music for listening. Moreover, most of these genres used the same musical language—certainly in widely varying degrees of sophistication, but still with the same foundation.

Musically the stratification occurred because much of the popular music retained a simplified version of the musical language of the early nineteenth century, whereas classical music continued to evolve away from this comfortable common language, and Wagner outright filed for divorce from it. As a result, there emerged a discontinuity between the most elite music and the more mundane middle-class music: Wagner is difficult to dumb down—and trim down—so his music reached larger audiences mainly through short excerpts, such as the famous "Ride of the Valkyries" (from the third act of *Die Walküre*) and performances of the overtures and preludes to the operas. And around the time of Wagner's death, music publishers in the United States began focusing their offerings on songs with (hoped for) popular appeal. This was the beginning of what came to be known as Tin Pan Alley.

These musical changes precipitated realignment within the cultural world. In the eighteenth and early nineteenth centuries, economic (rich versus modest) and social (aristocracy versus commoners) standing influenced musical choices more than strictly musical considerations. However, during the latter part of the nineteenth century, an artistic elite of intellectuals emerged. They were a select group—a minority within a minority—and a prestigious, if not always a financially comfortable one.

By imagining, then creating, a futuristic music, Wagner played a pivotal role in creating this artistic elite. In making explicit in his writings what was implicit in Beethoven's music, he liberated high-minded composers from catering to the marketplace or to the patrons who supported the institutions that provided performance opportunities. Composers could follow their muse wherever it led them, even if it meant (at least in their minds) that their music would be understood fully only by subsequent generations. For some of them, "art for art's sake" was more important than a full stomach.

Moreover, Wagner's music makes musical communication a two-way commitment between musicians and audience. To fully appreciate his operas, listeners needed to know not only the German language and the plot but also the significance of the numerous leitmotifs, which become apparent only with study and repeated hearing—a formidable challenge in the days before recordings. Beginning around the turn of the twentieth century, the most avant-garde composers would transfer the difficult burden of understanding their music from themselves to their audience.

As a result of these developments—the further evolution of classical music, the emergence of a forward-looking mentality and an artistic elite to nurture it, and the growth of a branch of the music industry that catered to mass taste—the musical world in Europe and North America was far more stratified in 1900 than it was in 1850. This trend would continue through much of the twentieth century, as we discover in subsequent chapters.

 study tools 15

Ready to study?
In the book you can:

- Review Learning Outcome answers and Glossary terms with the tear-out Chapter Review card.

Or you can go online to CourseMate, at www.cengagebrain.com, for these resources:

- Chapter Quizzes to prepare for tests

- Interactive flashcards of all Glossary terms

- Active Listening Guides, streaming music, and YouTube playlists

- An eBook with live links to all web resources

16 The Romantic Symphony

Apic/Hutton Archive/Getty Images

LEARNING OUTCOMES

After reading this chapter, you will be able to do the following:

16-1 Describe the evolution of the symphony orchestra and the symphony in the nineteenth century.

16-2 Understand Hector Berlioz's transformation of the orchestra through an exploration of his *Symphonie fantastique*.

16-3 Through an examination of one of Brahms's symphonies, describe how the Romantic symphony expanded on the tradition of Haydn, Mozart, and Beethoven.

study tools

After you read this chapter, go to the Study Tools at the end of the chapter, page 231.

The most oddly named of the major European symphony orchestras is the Gewandhaus Orchestra of Leipzig, Germany. Most orchestras take their name from their host city: the Vienna Philharmonic, the London Symphony, the Orchestre de Paris, and so on. The Gewandhaus Orchestra took its name from the building that housed its first dedicated performance space. In 1781, the mayor of Leipzig ordered the construction of a five-hundred-seat concert hall within a building that housed the clothier's exchange (*gewand*, meaning "clothing" or "garb" in German) to serve as the home for a music society that had been formed in 1775.

In 1835, the composer Felix Mendelssohn (1809–1847) became the conductor of the Gewandhaus Orchestra, a position that he would retain for the rest of his life. Under his direction, the Gewandhaus became one of the finest orchestras in Europe. Among his important contributions were conducting from the podium and using a baton (before Mendelssohn, the concertmaster directed the orchestra from his chair at the front of the first violin section); resurrecting Schubert's last symphony, which had never been performed; reviving the music of Bach in a series of "historical concerts"; and organizing several fund-raising events to secure a firmer financial footing for the orchestra.

16-1 Orchestras and Symphonies in the Nineteenth Century

The rise of the Gewandhaus Orchestra under Mendelssohn and its continued growth after his death reflected the emergence of the symphony orchestra as a major cultural institution in the larger cities of Europe and the Americas during the nineteenth century. At the beginning of the century, most concert orchestras were ad hoc ensembles put together for a particular occasion, such as an evening of music by Beethoven. (Theater orchestras offered more frequent and more reliable employment for orchestral musicians.) By the end of the century, however, cities from Chicago to St. Petersburg, Russia, had resident professional orchestras.

16-1A Orchestras as Cultural Institutions

Many of the major orchestras in Europe and the United States began as concert societies. The London Philharmonic, formed in 1813 by a society of professional musicians, was ahead of its time. A few more formed around mid-century: the Vienna Philharmonic in 1841 and the New York Philharmonic in 1842 are notable instances. Many more in Europe and the United States came together toward the end of the century.

These orchestras became an integral part of the cultural life in their cities, joining opera companies as

The life of nineteenth-century orchestral musicians wasn't always sedate. This centerfold from the British humor magazine *Puck* shows a clash between the Academy of Music and the Metropolitan Opera, with opera singers, conductors, and orchestras all in the fray.

Library of Congress, Prints and Photographs Division [LC-DIG-ppmsca-28438]

221

the most prestigious resident musical institutions. Over time, a natural evolution of supporting enterprises developed around them: performing venues (Amsterdam's symphony also takes its name from its concert hall, the famous Concertgebouw) and conservatories to train musicians for orchestral positions (Mendelssohn founded the Leipzig Conservatory in 1843), as well as administrative support and governmental and private patronage.

As with opera, audiences for symphony orchestras became more diverse. Some orchestras, especially in England and Paris, offered concerts in larger spaces for relatively low prices; others maintained high prices in order to limit the audience to the upper class. Outdoor festivals and concerts, at times with enormous orchestras, attracted large audiences—as many as five thousand listeners. (These were the predecessors of today's pop concerts.) During the course of the century, the prevailing trend was toward larger venues, with ticket prices at several levels and seating to match—from the most exclusive boxes to the nosebleed section in the back.

The Romantic-era orchestra concert was seen by many musicians, critics, and audience members as the most high-minded musical experience available to the general public. They considered such events an aesthetically satisfying and morally uplifting experience, not mere entertainment.

16-1B The Instrumentation of the Nineteenth-Century Orchestra

The dramatic improvement in conventional instruments—woodwinds, brass, and percussion—and the invention of new instruments, most notably the tuba, were a key reason for the expansion of the orchestra. Woodwind, brass, and percussion sections grew larger, and string sections also grew in size, to balance the increased size of the other sections. As a result of this coordinated expansion, the underlying structure of the orchestra did not change. Strings were still the dominant section, although nineteenth-century composers made far more use of the other sections than did their eighteenth-century counterparts.

Despite the proliferation of new instruments, orchestras

Dorling Kindersley/Getty Images

New instruments, such as the ophicleide (soon replaced by the tuba), enriched the sound of the nineteenth-century orchestra.

added no new sections during the nineteenth century; both the tuba and the additional woodwinds were larger or smaller cousins of existing instruments. It wasn't just the orchestra that grew during the nineteenth century. So did its repertoire, in range, if not in quantity.

16-1C The Ever-Diversifying Orchestral Repertoire

One reason for the consistency in instrumentation was the gradual accumulation of standard repertoire—those works that continued to be performed widely in the years and generations after their composition. From the start, the symphonies of Beethoven were at the heart of this standard repertoire. The size of the repertoire continued to grow because it went back in time to the orchestral works of Haydn, Mozart, and (because of Mendelssohn's popularization) Bach, and other eighteenth- and early nineteenth-century composers, and then began to add contemporary works with staying power. Although Mendelssohn's "Italian" and "Scottish" symphonies, concert overtures, and violin concerto were obviously new works during Mendelssohn's lifetime, they had become standard repertoire by the time Brahms completed his first symphony in 1876. As a result, the ratio of classics to new works grew during the latter two-thirds of the century. Works went in and out of fashion, as they have in our own time. However, much of the newly standard repertoire remains central to orchestral programs in our time.

The symphony and the concerto remained at the core of the orchestral repertoire, as they had in the eighteenth century. However, as orchestras became established institutions, their concerts included an increasingly broad range of music. Among the most significant new orchestral genres were programmatic orchestral compositions, such as the tone poems of Liszt, Strauss, and others, and more rhapsodic works for soloist and orchestra. Orchestral concerts might also include works originally intended for another purpose, such as opera overtures, ballet music, and incidental music for theater productions, and orchestral arrangements of music originally written for other instruments, such as the piano. However, the centerpiece of almost every orchestral concert was a symphony.

16-1D The Symphony in the Romantic Era

The symphony was the most prestigious genre in nineteenth-century orchestral music. More than any other genre, the symphony evidenced Beethoven's continuing influence on nineteenth-century music. Its status stemmed most directly from the awe that Beethoven's symphonies inspired. Nineteenth-century composers knew full well that their symphonies would be measured against Beethoven's. All the important symphonies composed during the course of the nineteenth century thus borrowed something from Beethoven's—size, programmatic reference, individuality, or developmental procedures. Even the *number* of Beethoven's symphonies was intimidating; no important composer produced more than nine. Gustav Mahler, the last of the great Romantic symphonists, died with his tenth symphony incomplete.

For Romantic composers, a symphony was a statement. Composers like Brahms and Dvořák may have made much of their money from the sale of songs and dances, but they made their reputation with their symphonies. They intended each work to be a major contribution to the orchestral repertoire; it would have been the product of months—even years—of effort. The numbers tell the story: Haydn composed more symphonies for each of his two visits to London (six for each visit) than many major composers (Brahms, Mendelssohn, Schumann, Franck, and Saint-Saëns) composed during their entire career.

In the nineteenth century, composers expanded on the symphonic tradition of Haydn, Mozart, and Beethoven, whose dominant influence is evident in three of its most distinguishing features: size, originality, and individuality. In general, Romantic symphonies were longer than their late eighteenth-century counterparts. Lengths ranged from around thirty minutes to over an hour, with thirty-eight to forty minutes as a mid-range length. In particular, the symphonies of the late nineteenth-century Austrian composers Anton Bruckner and Gustav Mahler are sprawling works; most of them last at least sixty minutes. The expansion of the symphony was most evident in the final movements. In many nineteenth-century symphonies, the last movement is about as long as or even longer than the opening movement; in Classical symphonies, it is often the shortest.

Composers of symphonies followed one of two paths. The more common by far was a traditional approach. Romantic composers such as Mendelssohn, Schumann, Brahms, Dvořák, and Tchaikovsky adhered almost religiously to the standard four-movement sequence established in the Classical symphony. Typically, they expressed their originality within this well-established plan by modifying such features as the form, tempo, and sequences of keys.

Symphonies that were obviously original—evident in such features as the title of the work and its inspiration, as well as the number, sequence, and tempo of movements—were the rare exception, not the rule. Hector Berlioz stands out in this regard. His program symphonies include not only the five-movement *Symphonie fantastique* but also *Harold in Italy*, a symphony with a viola soloist, and his "symphonie dramatique" on Shakespeare's *Romeo and Juliet*, which requires voices and orchestra and lasts over an hour and a half. In the latter half of the century, composers wishing to depart from the conventional symphonic model typically composed symphonic poems, which were inherently programmatic, rather than program symphonies like those of Berlioz.

We have observed the Romantic predilection for melody in the flowering of art song and the diversification of opera as well as in piano music. So it should not surprise us that the approach to melody was among the most significant differences between the Classical and the Romantic symphony. Romantic composers understood symphonic forms in melodic terms. Typically, they crafted movements around expressive, tuneful melodies rather than around the more instrumentally conceived themes of Classical symphonies; scherzo movements were an occasional exception to this practice. Behind this emphasis on melody was the idea that melody embodied the character of the work. Composers expressed this understanding through the repetition and transformation of earlier melodic ideas, which helps to unify the work and show the development of the character embodied in the original idea.

To suggest the range of the nineteenth-century symphony, we sample movements from two quite different symphonies, by Berlioz and Brahms.

LEARNING OUTCOME 16-2
Understand Hector Berlioz's transformation of the orchestra through an exploration of his *Symphonie fantastique*.

16-2 Berlioz and the Program Symphony

If you were asked to name a phenomenal guitarist who wrote music depicting an artist on a drug-induced trip, being hounded by demons, you'd probably volunteer the names of several prominent rock stars. However, first in line—at least chronologically—would be the French composer

> Berlioz played the guitar expertly, but his real instrument was the orchestra.

FAST FACTS

- Dates: 1803–1869
- Place: France
- Reasons to remember:
A key figure in early
Romantic music who
achieved distinction not
only as a highly original (and misunderstood) com-
poser but also as a conductor, writer, and critic

DEA/G. DAGLI ORTI/De Agostini Picture Library/
Getty Images

Hector Berlioz. The musical evidence? Numerous anecdotal accounts of his guitar playing and the last two
movements of his *Symphonie fantastique* (1830), one of
the most astoundingly original works in a century that
prized originality.

16-2A Berlioz and the Orchestra

Hector Berlioz ♣ was a key figure in early Romantic
music. He achieved distinction not only as a highly
original (and misunderstood) composer but also as a
conductor, writer, and critic.

From contemporary accounts, we learn that Berlioz
played the guitar expertly, but his real instrument was
the orchestra. This is evident in three important ways.
First, Berlioz studied the orchestra more systematically than anyone before him. Second, his performing
"instrument" was the orchestra; he was the first widely
known orchestral conductor. Third, his music typically
requires a large and varied orchestra—sometimes even
with newly invented instruments—and makes unprecedented demands on the musicians, to create effects
never before imagined.

16-2B Berlioz on the Orchestra

In the middle of the eighteenth century, several eminent musicians wrote major treatises on playing
a particular instrument: for example, C. P. E. Bach
wrote one for keyboard, and Mozart's father, Leopold, wrote one for violinists. These were intended for
performers.

Berlioz's *Grand traité d'instrumentation et d'orchestration modernes* (*A Treatise on Modern Instrumentation and Orchestration*) was a tool for composers. In
it, he described the instruments of the orchestra and
assessed their character and how they might best be
used in a composition. He drew examples from his own
music as well as the music of other composers of his
and earlier times, most notably Beethoven and Gluck.
He also included chapters on the ideal disposition of the
orchestra and conducting.

The work was a product of intense study and
vivid imagination. Berlioz spent hours in the library
of the Paris Conservatory studying scores, from which
he drew some of his conclusions about the effective
use of instruments. Other suggestions came from his
own novel ideas about instruments, their character,
and their possibilities. The treatise was published
first in 1843 and again in 1855 in an expanded second
edition.

Berlioz began this work during his student years
so that by the time he set out to compose his grand
work, the *Symphonie fantastique*, he was ready to
demand unusual combinations, timbres, and sounds
from the orchestra. His score study was the compositional counterpart to the rigorous practice regimen
that a serious performer undertakes to achieve mastery of an instrument.

16-2C Berlioz the Conductor

Berlioz became Europe's most visible symbol of a new
kind of virtuoso: the conductor. Instead of performing
on an instrument, he directed an instrument made of
performers—a hundred or more, if he had his way. It
was a demanding task, more so in those days because
both orchestras and much orchestral music—including
Berlioz's own works—were new, and Berlioz's works
asked for many new and difficult musical effects. (By
contrast, the top orchestras of today have performed
works such as the Beethoven symphonies and Berlioz's
Symphonie fantastique dozens, even hundreds of times.)

Berlioz became a conductor out of necessity. After
too many disastrous performances of his own works
conducted by others, he wanted to make sure that his
music was presented as he had imagined it. And he
needed the money, often to help defray the debts he
had incurred producing performances of his works.
Fortunately, there was demand for his services. By
the early 1840s, Berlioz's fame had spread throughout Europe. Among his many tours were several trips
to London, several to Germany, where Liszt also conducted his music on occasion, and two to Russia; the
rigors of a second trip to Russia in 1867–1868 hastened
his death. In an age of stellar virtuosi—Paganini,
Liszt, and others—Berlioz was in this respect also a
virtuoso, of a large and often unwieldy instrument,
the orchestra.

Berlioz's orchestra-related activities—composing
exclusively for the orchestra (no piano music, no chamber music), studying orchestration, and establishing
a conducting career—were firsts. So was the over-
sized orchestra that he required for the *Symphonie
fantastique*.

16-2D Expanding the Orchestra

Fewer than two generations—from 1791 to 1830—
separate Haydn's "Surprise" symphony from Berlioz's

	Haydn, Symphony No. 94	Beethoven, Symphony No. 5	Berlioz, *Symphonie fantastique*
Woodwinds			
Flutes	2	2 + piccolo	2 + piccolo
Oboes	2	2	2 + English horn
Clarinets	0	2	2 + E♭ clarinet (high register)
Bassoons	2	2 + contra-bassoon	4
Brass			
Trumpets	2	2	2 + 2 cornets
Horns	2	2	4
Trombones	0	3	3
Ophicleides	0	0	2
Percussion and harp			
Timpani	2	2	4
Drums	0	0	Snare drum, bass drum, cymbals, bells
Harps	0	0	2

Table 16.1 Expansion of the Symphony Orchestra

Symphonie fantastique. However, the orchestra required for Berlioz's mammoth symphony is more than double the size of Haydn's, and it features an array of new sounds. He utilized additional members of the wood-wind and brass families—including the piccolo, English horn, E♭ clarinet, cornets, and the ophicleide, a newly invented instrument that added a bass voice to the brass section (it would be superseded by the tuba); plus additional percussion instruments and the harp, all of which were in use during Haydn's lifetime but were not part of the orchestras for which he composed. Table 16.1 details this expansion.

Berlioz's enormous orchestral requirements are not just about power but also about sound color. His expanded sound palette, which includes new instruments like the ophicleide and new uses for existing but seldom used instruments like the E♭ clarinet, English horn, and bells, is tangible evidence of his aural sound imagination, as we hear in the last movement of the *Symphonie fantastique*.

16-2E *Symphonie fantastique*

Although Berlioz had been successful enough as a student composer to win the Prix de Rome, the top award for composers at the Paris Conservatory, the work that announced his arrival as an important composer was the *Symphonie fantastique*, first performed in December 1830. It is hard to imagine a grander entrance. The work is quintessentially Romantic. It is intensely subjective, cast on a massive scale, and strikingly original in conception and detail—a thorough embodiment of the new Romantic sensibility.

The seed from which the symphony grew was Berlioz's all-consuming infatuation with Harriet Smithson, an English actress whom he had seen as Ophelia in Shakespeare's *Hamlet*. He fell in love with her on the spot and pursued her so ardently that she spurned him. Rejected, he vowed to immortalize her in his first symphony.

We can gauge the autobiographical impulse that characterizes this symphony by its working title: *Episode in the Life of an Artist*. The artist, of course, was Berlioz, and the episode is his failed pursuit of Harriet Smithson. He made her the focal point of the work by portraying her in melody. He identified this as an idée fixe, a "fixed idea" or melodic representation of the object of the artist's obsession. The melody appears early in the first movement and returns in various forms throughout the work.

And to make sure nobody missed the connection, Berlioz wrote out a program for the symphony that described the events and feelings depicted in each movement. This program was much more detailed—and much more personal—than the brief notes that Beethoven had provided for his Symphony No. 6, the "Pastoral" symphony. It turned Berlioz's symphony into a new genre: the program symphony, a symphony whose movements depict a series of scenes relating to the work's overall program, or theme.

Both the idée fixe and the program dramatize the stunning paradigm shift in cultural life in the early nineteenth century. To be so boldly and baldly personal would have been unimaginable fifty years earlier. It's almost inconceivable that Haydn would compose a "fantastic" symphony at Esterháza in 1780. And even if he had, it's doubtful that his patron would have received it warmly. By Beethoven's time, the shift had certainly begun, in large measure because of him. But Berlioz openly portrays himself as an artist who is pouring out his feelings in music. Composers had, in the space of two generations, moved up the social ladder from servants to citizens with significant social status. The composer may starve, or scuffle to pay the rent, but he is an admired member of society, at least in principle.

Berlioz's extensive and highly personal program is just one of the many original features of the *Symphonie fantastique*. Indeed, there is hardly anything significant about it that is *not* original, or at least a significant departure from convention. Most obvious, perhaps, are the size and sequence of movements. The symphony is a huge piece; it takes almost an hour to perform. Of all the orchestral works from this time and earlier that are still

idée fixe "Fixed idea"; melodic representation of the object of the artist's obsession
program symphony Symphony whose movements depict a series of scenes relating to the work's overall program, or theme

performed regularly, only the ninth symphonies of Beethoven and Schubert are noticeably longer.

There are five movements, not the conventional four. The first is comparable in size and tempo to a standard symphonic first movement. However, the second movement is a scene from a carnival. We hear a lovely waltz, not the slow movement we expect. The third movement is slow—it places the artist out in the country, where time seems to stand still. Only the tempo suggests a connection to a more conventional slow movement. The fourth movement is a march, not the usual minuet and trio: in it, the artist, drugged by opium, sees himself taken to the gallows to be executed rather than to the ballroom to dance a minuet.

All of this is novel enough; still, Berlioz saved the best for last. The opium-induced nightmare continues for the artist in the fifth movement. Here, Berlioz paints in sound the artist's funeral. It features demons and sorcerers swirling around him; his dearly beloved, whom he killed earlier in the dream, returning as a witch; and the booming voice of doom.

> He [the artist] sees himself at the witches' Sabbath, in the midst of a ghastly crowd of spirits, sorcerers and monsters of every kind, assembled for his funeral. There are strange noises, groans, bursts of laughter, far-off shouts to which other shouts seem to reply. The beloved tune appears once more but it has lost its character of refinement and diffidence; it has become nothing but a common dance tune, trivial and grotesque; it is she who has come to the Sabbath. . . . A roar of joy greets her arrival. . . . She joins the diabolical orgy. . . . Funeral knell, ludicrous parody of the Dies irae, the dance of the witches. The dance of the witches and the Dies irae in combination.

16-2F "Dream of a Witches' Sabbath"

The title of the last movement, "Songe d'une nuit de sabbat" ("Dream of a Witches' Sabbath"; see Listen Up!), tells us at once that it's going to be different. Some historical perspective can help us hear exactly how different. Consider the orchestral pieces that we have encountered to this point: in each case, the opening melodic material of a movement has told us what the movement is about. The music that follows has been a coherent argument developed from that opening idea. Moreover, the character of the piece has grown out of this initial melodic material; its pitches, rhythm, and harmonic and textural setting resonate throughout the movement. The opening material is in effect what the movement is about.

Berlioz follows a radically different path, one that has more to do with opera than with symphonic music. The character of the movement comes not so much from the melodies that Berlioz invents as from the sound choices that he makes: what instruments he uses, the special effects that he asks for, the registers in which they operate, the dynamic levels and patterns of dynamic change. In this respect, Berlioz has an aesthetic like that of a rock band. The musical message is as much in the quality of the sound—how much distortion, what special effects—as it is in the riffs.

There is, of course, melodic material, but it serves different functions. Some of it, like the low string growls and the delicate descent in the high strings that follows, is deliberately neutral. This directs attention away from melody to the striking sound qualities the composer requests. Another strategy is to use melody symbolically; it isn't the inherent quality of the melody itself that is paramount but what it stands for. This happens two different times. The first is the parody of the idée fixe; the second is the quotation of the *Dies irae* (Day of Wrath), from the Catholic Mass for the dead. Both would have been familiar to Berlioz's audiences: the first from earlier in the symphony, the second from their prior experience. Both help depict the events in the program by association rather than through their inherent musical qualities. There is original and distinctive melodic material in the movement, but it is a motive that never becomes a full-fledged theme. A conventional melody, with a beginning, clear midpoints, and an end, is not part of the fabric of this movement.

The form is just as innovative. There is a section that Berlioz called "Ronde [rondo] du sabbat," but it is miles away from a typical rondo. Instead, the movement proceeds as a series of episodes or scenes. The musical events are a series of gestures that make sense not so much through a process of internal relationships as through their connection to Berlioz's program. Many would be equally at home in an opera highlighting action onstage. The music starts and stops, and the ideas and sounds tumble over one another until they finally reach the massive climax at the end.

With this approach, Berlioz seems to be asking himself not "How can I put a new spin on existing symphonic forms?" but "How can I tell a story using only instruments as dramatically and vividly as possible?" It is a different point of departure, and it leads to a very different result.

16-2G Berlioz's Legacy

Berlioz's *Symphonie fantastique* is a true original; its novel features are significant and fundamental. They include a design dictated more by a narrative than by formal conventions, a new expressive balance between sound and melody that often leans toward sound, the symbolic use of familiar materials and melodies, and the exploration of new sound possibilities and effects.

 **LISTEN UP!**

Berlioz, "Songe d'une nuit de sabbat," *Symphonie fantastique*, 5th movement (1830)

TAKEAWAY POINT: Quintessentially Romantic orchestral work, with vivid sound images depicting a grotesque program

STYLE: Romantic

FORM: Through-composed "narrative" form

GENRE: Program symphony

INSTRUMENTS: Large symphony orchestra

CONTEXT: A revolutionary and influential work by a visionary composer

0:00   Suspenseful strings, then winds

0:47   Varied repetition of opening material

1:22   Sprightly version of *idée fixe*, played on the clarinet, interrupted by huge commotion

1:40   Mocking version of *idée fixe*, played on a small clarinet

2:09   Transition section, preparing *Dies irae*

2:57   Bells in the midst of suspenseful music

DIES IRAE

3:23   *Dies irae*, played by low brass and bassoon

3:45   Second version, played by brass, twice as fast

3:55   Third version, even faster, played by plucked strings (pizzicato) and high winds

4:01   Another phrase of the chant, in all three versions

4:24   First phrase again, echoed by syncopated lower strings, bells, and drums

4:44   Brass play the phrase twice as fast, then high winds even faster, as before

4:59   Preview of the rondo theme

RONDE DU SABBAT

5:16   *Ronde du sabbat*: rondo theme developed contrapuntally

6:20   Brass flourish signaling disintegration of the dance; fragmentary motive

7:01   *Dies Irae* fragment, beginning in low strings, combined with rondo, building up to a peak

DIES IRAE ET RONDE DU SABBAT

8:01   Full-blown statement of *Dies irae* in brass, layered over rondo material

8:21   More suspenseful music—a special effect (*col legno*): strings use wood part of bow to make skeletal noises

9:07   Final push: *Dies irae* plus frenzied version of rondo

 Listen to this selection streaming or in an Active Listening Guide at CourseMate or in the eBook.

Some of these—such as the expansion of the orchestra—continue trends set in motion by Beethoven, whom Berlioz admired, learned from, and championed. Others are adaptations of operatic orchestral devices and effects for a purely instrumental context. In either case, Berlioz puts his own stamp on them. His idée fixe certainly derives from the idea of a motive that returns throughout a multimovement work, like the opening motive of Beethoven's Fifth Symphony, but it begins with a far different impulse—the portrayal of the artist's beloved—and it returns for programmatic reasons. As such, it unifies the work in a quite different way.

Berlioz's music embodies several of the most compelling features of early Romanticism: an emphasis on performing skill, often to virtuosic levels; acceptance of large musical gestures, whether in miniatures or in grand works; inspired and imaginative settings that open up a new sound world; greater focus on the individual, whether the performer or the subject of a musical program; and a quest for innovation.

His vision was too singular and forward looking to lend itself to imitation by his contemporaries. Berlioz's greatest impact on orchestral music came in the latter half of the nineteenth century. It is most evident in the expansion of the orchestra and the emphasis on tone color, and in new literary-based forms. Musical futurists such as Wagner and Russian composers, such as Tchaikovsky and Rimsky-Korsakov, followed his lead in expanding the orchestra and cultivating a distinctive palette of sounds. (Recall from Chapter 1 how Tchaikovsky's orchestration made Mozart's pitches and rhythms sound Romantic.) Berlioz's music was also a major influence on the tone poem, a programmatic orchestral genre consisting of one movement that emerged during the latter half of the century. Liszt, the inventor of that genre, acknowledged Berlioz's influence; it is also evident in the music of Richard Strauss, the master of the literature-inspired tone poem. Particularly in these areas, Berlioz's influence was substantial if indirect.

tone poem Programmatic, one-movement, Romantic orchestral genre

© iStockPhoto.com/Merrymoonmary

⌐A bust of Beethoven glowered down at Brahms from the wall of his apartment.⌐

Berlioz was one of the original Romantics. In true Romantic fashion, Berlioz conceived his works on a grand scale and with a highly individual character. He seldom repeated genres, preferring instead to invent them, or at least transform them drastically. He demanded large resources, not only for bombastic effects but also for passages of extreme delicacy. Like his major works, he was one of a kind. He has no counterpart in the nineteenth century.

16-3 Brahms and the Romantic Symphony

As the reputation of Johannes Brahms as German-speaking Europe's greatest living composer took shape, he found himself being compared favorably to Beethoven and Bach—together, they had become "the three B's." But for Brahms, acclaim brought pressure as well as prestige. Indeed, a bust of Beethoven glowered down at Brahms from the wall of his apartment. Nowhere was this more evident than in the painfully slow gestation of his first symphony.

Brahms began working on his first symphony in 1862. It would take him fourteen years to complete; in that interval, he composed eight major chamber works, dozens of songs, and numerous other works, in addition to *Ein deutsches Requiem*. The publication of the symphony seemed to lift the burden of composing "Beethoven's tenth symphony" from his shoulders. In the following eleven years, Brahms would compose most of his important orchestral music: three more symphonies; three major concertos for violin and piano, and a double concerto for violin and cello; and two concert overtures.

Brahms's symphonies typify the more traditional form of the Romantic symphony. All have four movements, in the typical sequence. They range in length from around thirty-five minutes (the Third Symphony) to over forty-five minutes (the First Symphony). Brahms's creativity finds expression within this traditional framework. There are no programs, explicit or implicit, although each has a distinct character, and there are no dramatic departures from the norm. Rather, Brahms used conventional forms and materials as a point of departure and transformed them in distinctive, often radical ways. As we listen to his symphonies, we hear both their connection to the rich symphonic tradition of the late eighteenth and nineteenth centuries and the highly individual aspects of his compositional approach.

16-3A Brahms, the Progressive Traditionalist

Following the Vienna premiere of Brahms's First Symphony, the critic (and champion of Brahms's music) Eduard Hanslick compared the work to the symphonies of Beethoven. The conductor Hans von Bülow went a step further, dubbing it Beethoven's tenth. Brahms's more astute contemporaries acknowledged Brahms's strong connection with the past.

Because his innovations use established forms and genres as a familiar point of departure, they do not seem as radical as those of Berlioz, Liszt, and Wagner. Nevertheless, Brahms's thoroughgoing and highly personal transformations of these familiar forms make clear that Brahms viewed his musical heritage as a source of inspiration rather than a model to be imitated.

To illustrate this quality of Brahms's music, we study his Second Symphony (see Listen Up!), with particular focus on the third movement. Brahms composed the symphony in 1877, just a year after completing the First. The symphony is in four movements: an opening movement in an expansive sonata form, a slow movement, a moderately paced third movement, and a brisk finale. The symphony begins innocuously with a simple four-note motive in the lower strings. The horn enters on the fourth note, stating the first theme of the movement; both the instrument and the melody convey the essentially pastoral character of the symphony. However, it is the seemingly generic three-note pattern heard at the outset, not the opening theme, that is the seed from which the symphony grows. The motive returns throughout the first movement, and different versions of it return in the third and fourth movements, in which they submit to further transformation.

A brief refresher course in the form of the minuet and trio: both minuet and trio are typically in rounded binary form, with both sections repeated. The minuet and the trio have different melodies and usually contrast in key or mode, as we heard in the third movement of Beethoven's Fifth Symphony.

Brahms uses the minuet and trio as a point of departure; the opening melody evokes the rhythm and grace of a minuet. The innovative aspects of the movement include these interrelated features:

- Altering the proportions of the form and blurring the formal boundaries so that contrasting sections merge into one another
- Creating contrast between sections through changes in tempo and meter rather than melody
- Deriving virtually all the melodic material from the inversion of the three-note pattern heard at the very beginning of the symphony
- Replacing literal repetition with developmental variation

All of these features extend Beethoven's own modification of the form. They are progressive because they go beyond Beethoven rather than because they chart a new path.

16-3B Brahms, Wagner, and Beethoven

In the German-dominated musical world of the late nineteenth century, Brahms and Wagner were the towering presences and the opposing parties in one of the most vigorously contested musical battles of the nineteenth century. Both were regarded as the heirs apparent to Beethoven, the most prestigious honor that German-speaking culture could bestow on a musician—Wagner by his own reckoning and Brahms by influential critics. Brahms apparently had a high regard for Wagner's music; Wagner apparently resented Brahms's "coronation" as the next Beethoven.

Even the small sampling of music by the two composers that we have encountered highlights key differences. Wagner composed mainly opera, although with an almost symphonic conception; Brahms never composed an opera. Wagner reconceived form and wedded it to words; Brahms adapted well-established forms, often in innovative and individual ways. Wagner's music is the ultimate program music; the musical events amplify the story told in the libretto almost moment by moment. Brahms's music represented what was called absolute music, a term that came into vogue in Germany during the nineteenth century to describe music whose aesthetic value is self-contained; it does not require any extramusical reference, such as lyrics, drama, dance, or a program. Wagner foretold the future of music; Brahms was firmly rooted in the past, in the minds of his contemporaries and subsequent generations.

These pronounced differences may obscure striking similarities in their musical approach. Both are extraordinarily high-minded—Wagner overtly so and Brahms implicitly so in the imagination and craft of his major compositions. More specifically, both unified their compositions by creating complex thematic networks from memorable motives, which in turn enabled them to introduce considerable variety in the setting of the motives and to manipulate form in inventive, even radical ways. That Wagner

> **absolute music** Music whose aesthetic value is self-contained and does not require any extramusical reference, such as lyrics, drama, dance, or a program

 **LISTEN UP!**

Brahms, Symphony No. 2, 3rd movement (1877)

TAKEAWAY POINT: Small but revealing example of Brahms's symphonic strategies

STYLE: Romantic

FORM: Minuet and trio, with modifications

GENRE: Symphony

INSTRUMENTS: Orchestra

CONTEXT: Significant addition to the symphonic repertoire

0:00   The first part of the form: the melody grows out of an inverted and expanded variant of the simple three-note pattern with which the symphony begins.

0:19   The developmental/contrasting part of rounded binary form. The section begins with a two-note stepwise descent, a fragment from the opening phrase of the melody.

0:44   This section includes enough of the opening to mark it as the "rounding" part of the form, but it soon goes off in another direction.

TRIO 1

1:03   Shift to new meter (duple, not triple) and tempo (2 beats = 1 beat in minuet); also uses modified rounded binary form. Melody is more active variant of minuet theme.

1:16   Bold and animated new idea, based initially on the motive heard first in the contrasting section of the minuet

1:35   A "developmental reprise": just enough to convey a sense of return. After that, Brahms goes in a different direction.

BRIEF MINUET

1:51   *Retransition/return:* The first section returns after two 2-note previews, with new harmony.

2:10   New version of opening theme, which quickly winds down

TRIO 2

2:42   Development of contrasting section of first trio, now in compound duple meter (beat equal in length to beat in opening section) and a new, distantly related key

3:04   Varied reprise of first trio, then a more extended transition back to opening that circuitously leads back to opening theme, but in a new, distant key

MINUET

3:23   Still another version of opening melody

3:49   As in the beginning

4:14   A faithful reprise of the final section of the minuet

CODA

4:27   A "new" theme interrupts the reprise.

4:45   Return of opening theme, dissolving gently.

🔊 Listen to this selection streaming or in an Active Listening Guide at CourseMate or in the eBook.

abandoned traditional forms while Brahms reworked them does not alter this underlying affinity. In this respect, both extend Beethoven's practice of unifying a piece by permeating it with material derived from a single melodic kernel.

Brahms and Wagner have retained the stature that they earned during their lifetime: they remain the most important and highly regarded German composers of the latter half of the nineteenth century. One measure of their achievement was their individual and quite different responses to Beethoven's legacy.

Looking Back, Looking Ahead

The composer/conductor Gustav Mahler spent three summers around the turn of the century composing his fourth symphony. He would complete five more; he died at age fifty, leaving a tenth incomplete. His eighth symphony, composed in 1906 and nicknamed "Symphony of a Thousand," required eight vocal soloists, several choirs, and a mammoth orchestra, and requires almost an hour and a half to perform. Mahler envisioned it as a synthesis of orchestral and vocal music: it was his version of a grand *gesamtkunstwerk*. With Beethoven's ninth symphony, it effectively framed the Romantic symphony.

The symphony would retain its prestige as a genre through the first half of the twentieth century. A few major composers, most notably the Russian composer/pianist Sergei Rachmaninoff and the Finnish composer Jean Sibelius, composed in a neo-Romantic style. During the first half of the century, Russian composers—Stravinsky (by now an international figure), Prokofiev, and Shostakovich—took the symphony in a new direction. So did composers from the Americas, including the American Aaron Copland and the Mexican composer Cesar Chavez. However, the heart of the symphony comes from the nineteenth century.

 study tools 16

Ready to study?
In the book you can:

- Review Learning Outcome answers and Glossary terms with the tear-out Chapter Review card.

Or you can go online to CourseMate, at www.cengagebrain.com, for these resources:

- Chapter Quizzes to prepare for tests

- Interactive flashcards of all Glossary terms

- Active Listening Guides, streaming music, and YouTube playlists

- An eBook with live links to all web resources

LEARNING OUTCOMES

After reading this chapter, you will be able to do the following:

17-1 Encounter the more technically difficult, soloist-dominated concerto of the nineteenth century through a movement from Tchaikovsky's violin concerto.

17-2 Grasp the changing role of dance and dance music in the nineteenth century.

17-3 Recognize the conscious nationalism exemplified by Dvořák's music as an important trend in European cultural life during the latter half of the nineteenth century.

 study tools

After you read this chapter, go to the Study Tools at the end of the chapter, page 246.

....

The first concert of the New York Philharmonic took place on December 7, 1842. The Philharmonic would operate as a musicians' cooperative until 1909, when wealthy supporters shored up the orchestra's finances and tripled the number of concerts. Toward the end of the nineteenth century, other major American orchestras formed. Boston was first; it presented its inaugural season in 1881. The Chicago Symphony was formed in 1891; the Philadelphia Orchestra gave its first concert in 1900.

The New York Philharmonic's first concert opened with Beethoven's Symphony No. 5 (a good choice). A musical grab bag followed: chamber music, vocal selections, and more. The concert lasted about three hours; audiences seemed to have more endurance then than now. However, by the end of the century, concert programs began to look more like those in the twenty-first century. By way of example, the Boston Symphony's first concert of 1892 (a half century after the inaugural concert of the New York Philharmonic) included a concert overture by the Hungarian composer Karl Goldmark, Mozart's *Sinfonia Concertante* (effectively a double concerto for violin, viola, and orchestra), incidental music for a play composed by Franz Schubert, and Brahms's Symphony No. 2. This program format—symphony, a work for soloists and orchestra, and shorter orchestral works—would be the rule rather than the exception for the rest of the season, as well as in orchestral concert programming from the late nineteenth century until the present time.

The Boston Symphony program makes clear that there is more to an orchestral concert than a symphony, and more for an orchestra to do than play concerts. Our sampling of Romantic orchestral music includes a concerto, orchestral music to support another expressive art, and music originally composed for another instrumental combination. Collectively, they hint at the breadth of orchestral music in the nineteenth century.

17-1 Tchaikovsky and the Romantic Concerto

In the last third of the nineteenth century, the Hungarian-born Leopold Auer was among the most distinguished violinists in Russia. In 1868, Auer accepted an invitation to become the concertmaster of the orchestra of the St. Petersburg Imperial Theatres, where he would remain for almost half a century. Tchaikovsky was enamored of his playing and dedicated his *Serenade melancolique* (1875) to him. Three years later, he dedicated his newly composed violin concerto to Auer, who refused to play it because he found it too difficult. In 1881, three years after Auer rejected it, Adolph Brodsky, another Russian violinist, championed the work, performing it with great success in Vienna. It quickly became part of the violin repertoire.

The circumstances of their creation and first performance highlight two major changes in the concerto during the nineteenth century. One was that the composer wasn't necessarily creating the concerto for his own use. Although the concerto remained an important outlet for composer-performers from Paganini to Rachmaninoff, many of the most widely performed concertos were composed by musicians such as Robert Schumann and Dvořák, who were not active concert performers, or by composers writing for an instrument they did not play at a concert level, such as the violin concertos of Mendelssohn and Brahms. The other was that concertos became far more challenging technically. Tchaikovsky's concerto is difficult—far

more demanding in certain respects than the concertos of Bach, Vivaldi, and Mozart.

17-1A The Romantic Concerto

Romantics glorified the individual, so it should come as no surprise that Romantic composers transformed the concerto into a vehicle for individual brilliance. Baroque solo concertos like Vivaldi's *Four Seasons* afforded the soloist opportunities to step into the spotlight. In the fast outer movements, the technical demands of the solo part were greater than those of the orchestral parts, and the slow movement often gave the soloist a chance to display the expressive side of his musical personality. In Mozart's concertos, especially those for piano and orchestra, expressiveness and virtuosity served a dramatic purpose. Technical and musical demands increased, particularly in the cadenzas at the ends of the outer movements, which were typically improvised. By the early nineteenth century, virtuosic display had become, for many composers, the raison d'être (reason for being) of the concerto. The orchestra is an almost silent partner in Chopin's concertos when the pianist is playing. Even in those concertos with a more balanced relationship between soloist and orchestra, the soloist tends to be the focal point of the work.

The standard Romantic concerto retained the most general features of the Classical concerto. It was an extended work in three movements, in a fast–slow–fast sequence. The solo part included lyric moments and brilliant passagework, and there was at least one cadenza. The orchestral episodes provided a foil for the soloist. Both the lyric and virtuosic sections offered the opportunity for dialogue and other interactions; the contrast between soloist and orchestra typically highlighted the superior skill of the soloist.

One obvious difference between the Classical concerto and the typical Romantic

> A concise survey of the history of the concerto: in the Baroque era, the soloist came from within the orchestra; in the Classical era, the soloist competed with the orchestra; in the Romantic era, the soloist dominated the orchestra.

▶Pyotr Ilyich Tchaikovsky

FAST FACTS

- Dates: 1840–1893
- Place: Russia
- Reasons to remember: The most popular and versatile composer of the Romantic era

Tchaikovsky's music symbolizes the westward-looking aspect of Russian culture. By birth (his mother was born in Germany), training, and inclination, Tchaikovsky looked to the West more than his peers did. His dominant musical influences were Italian opera and Mozart. His music is not overtly nationalistic, as is the music of many of his important contemporaries, such as Modest Mussorgsky and Nikolai Rimsky-Korsakov. Yet Igor Stravinsky, also Russian and his only peer as a composer for ballet, noted that "Tchaikovsky drew unconsciously from the true, popular sources of our race."

Tchaikovsky was the first Russian composer to attract a substantial following outside Russia. His orchestral music brought him fame and, toward the end of his life, invitations to conduct in Europe and the United States (he attended the inauguration of Carnegie Hall in 1891), and the awarding of an honorary doctorate from Cambridge University in 1893.

Tchaikovsky stands apart from virtually every other Romantic composer in his versatility. He composed significant music in essentially every important genre: symphony, concerto, and other orchestral music; opera; chamber music and song; and especially ballet. Among his most enduring works is his only violin concerto.

concerto was the disappearance of an extended orchestral tutti at the beginning of the work. It was as if neither soloist nor audience could wait the two or three minutes required to perform it. This undermined the drama inherent in the opening movement of a Classical concerto: the progress of the soloist toward equality. In effect, by entering quickly—and usually with a splash—the soloist asserted his dominant position from the outset.

Within the basic three-movement structure, the Romantic concerto was more flexible in design than either the Classical concerto or the Romantic symphony. More often than not, the second movement continued into the third without interruption; cadenzas could appear anywhere in a movement—beginning, middle, or end; dramatic shifts in tempo and character within a movement were more common. We hear many of these features in the last movement of Tchaikovsky's violin concerto.

17-1B Pyotr Ilyich Tchaikovsky

There was a good reason why Pyotr Ilyich Tchaikovsky ♠ initially planned to become a civil servant: it was exceedingly difficult to obtain adequate musical training in Russia during the first half of the nineteenth century. Indeed, Tchaikovsky, at age twenty-one, was a member of the first class admitted to the newly formed St. Petersburg Conservatory.

Then as now, Russia had been both a part of Europe and apart from Europe. It lies on the eastern periphery of the European continent (Europe and Asia are the only continents not separated by an obvious boundary) and for centuries was on the outside culturally as well as geographically. From the time of Peter the Great through the Russian Revolution, Russia looked to the West for culture: French was the preferred language among the aristocracy.

> "Tchaikovsky drew unconsciously from the true, popular sources of our race."
> —Igor Stravinsky

17-1C Tchaikovsky's Violin Concerto

The premiere of Tchaikovsky's violin concerto reminds us how creativity may be damaging to the ego. In his review of its December 1881 premiere, Eduard Hanslick wrote that the concerto "brought us face to face with the revolting thought that music can exist which stinks to the ear." Perhaps Hanslick, one of the most influential critics in Europe and one of Brahms's staunchest supporters, was trying to protect Brahms's reputation; Brahms's violin concerto had received mixed reviews from musicians and critics upon its introduction almost three years previously. Or perhaps the work was not performed well (a constant danger at premieres, especially with a difficult work). Despite Hanslick's scathing review, the concerto quickly caught on; its success vindicated Tchaikovsky while he was still active.

Although he was not a violinist—he relied on the advice of a violin-playing student of his during the composition of the concerto—Tchaikovsky understood the idiomatic qualities and distinctive attributes of the instrument. As a result, the concerto showcases the violin's potential for brilliance and lyricism.

In the hands of a skilled performer, the violin is unmatched in the variety of timbres that can be produced. As a lyric instrument, it can come closer than any other to matching the nuance and expressiveness of a beautiful voice. As a brilliant instrument, it can generate tremendous energy not only because it allows extraordinarily fleet playing but also because performers can give each tone in a fast passage a percussive bite. Moreover, it has a wide range, from the lower notes of a woman's vocal range to the upper threshold of human hearing. The violin can sing, it can dance, and it can soar over the orchestra.

In the last movement of his Violin Concerto in D major (see Listen Up!), Tchaikovsky exploits all of these qualities in a movement that epitomizes characteristic features of the Romantic concerto. Tchaikovsky uses the Classical *rondo* (a form in which a bright and tuneful opening section returns in alternation with contrasting material) as his point of departure and paints the form in bold strokes. Right from the start, the solo violin is in the spotlight, beginning with the brief but bravura cadenza that bridges the second and third movements. The vigorous opening theme gives violinists an opportunity to display their agility. The two themes in the contrasting section show the passionate and lyric possibilities of the instrument. Throughout the movement, the soloist dominates; even when the orchestra takes over, as in the lyric part of the contrasting sections, it's just a matter of time before the soloist "one-ups" the wind instruments.

The dominance of the soloist is one dimension of the Romantic interpretation of the concerto. Others that stand out are the richness of the orchestral accompaniment, the extended sections that maintain and manipulate the same melodic material and texture, and the dramatic contrast in thematic material and tempo. For Tchaikovsky and the audience, it was a winning formula: a brilliant, musically compelling solo part; lavish accompaniment; boldly delineated contrasts between energetic and lyric sections in an easily tracked form; and—as is so often the case with Tchaikovsky—memorable melodic material.

17-1D Tchaikovsky, German Greatness, and a Question of Value

In one of his rock-and-roll–defining songs, Chuck Berry asks Beethoven to roll over and tell Tchaikovsky the news. Berry's catchy lyric seems to imply that in popular culture Beethoven and Tchaikovsky are comparably important: both are (in the vernacular of Berry's era) "longhair" composers. Within the world of classical music, that was not the case.

Wagner and Brahms may be the most esteemed composers of the latter part of the nineteenth century, but Tchaikovsky's music is arguably the most popular. His ballets, concertos, and symphonies have remained audience favorites for over a century, and their appeal shows no signs of diminishing.

By contrast, critical reception of Tchaikovsky's music has been far more mixed. During his lifetime, he received criticism from his fellow Russian composers because his music wasn't fiercely nationalistic enough, whereas central European critics (and those in other parts of the world who followed their lead) felt that his music didn't belong in the exalted company of Beethoven and the other great German-speaking composers because it deviated too much from their compositional approach.

In part because of the dominant presence of German thought in all aspects of musical education—scholarship, performance, composition (in the nineteenth century, aspiring American composers went to Germany for advanced training), German values have held sway over musical aesthetics from the middle of the nineteenth century through much of the twentieth. Indeed, they are still strong. As a result, the aesthetic hierarchy that they propounded has until relatively recently enjoyed almost unquestioned acceptance.

The issue is less the greatness of Bach and Beethoven than it is that the worth of other composers' music should be evaluated according to a set of values derived from the music of Bach and Beethoven. The particular nature of Tchaikovsky's genius, especially his remarkable gift for expansive melody and orchestral color, was not suited to this aesthetic. If Tchaikovsky had adhered to a Beethoven-like approach to melodic and formal development—an approach similar to Brahms's—it would have placed a compromising constraint on his music.

We will encounter this notion of relative worth with increasing frequency in the upcoming chapters. Highly original composers such as Debussy and

> The violin can sing, it can dance, and it can soar over the orchestra.

© iStockPhoto.com/Kativ

 **LISTEN UP!**

Tchaikovsky, Violin Concerto in D major, 3rd movement (1878)

TAKEAWAY POINT: An exemplary Romantic concerto with a brilliant solo part that highlights the particular attributes of the violin

STYLE: Romantic

FORM: Rondo

GENRE: Concerto

INSTRUMENTS: Violin and orchestra

CONTEXT: Orchestral music that showcases the artistry of a skilled violinist

INTRO

0:00   Orchestral transition from the second movement.

0:13   Cadenza, asserting the soloist's dominant position from the outset.

RONDO

0:46   First "theme": it is not a singable melody, but rather virtuosic instrumental writing.

MELODY

1:43   Tuneful and dancelike melody that doesn't finish decisively. Instead, Tchaikovsky uses the scale fragment at the end as the raw material for exchanges between soloist and orchestra. The busy violin obbligato over the orchestra allows the soloist to shine without having to counterbalance the orchestra, as in a piano concerto.

2:28   Orchestra plays a more lyric theme: exchange of melodic fragments among winds.

2:47   Solo first in dialogue with orchestra, then taking over. An opportunity to showcase the expressive side of the violinist's artistry.

RONDO

3:34   First theme returns, which leads to a developmental section.

4:02   Developmental section, using the beginning of the rondo theme.

MELODY

4:41   Return of the dancelike tuneful melody, in a different key. As before, the violinist plays the brilliant obbligaton figuration over the orchestra.

5:27   The lyric theme returns, again played first by the orchestra.

5:49   Violin takes over.

RONDO

6:38   Rondo theme, much like the first statement until the end

CODA

7:18   Coda; rapid exchanges between solo and orchestra leading to a brilliant final flourish

 Listen to this selection streaming or in an Active Listening Guide at CourseMate or in the eBook.

Gershwin found their music relegated to second-class status because it expressed a markedly different aesthetic. Only recently—especially since the rock revolution of the 1960s—have musicians and commentators begun to take a broader view of musical worth, using criteria such as the appropriateness of musical choices to the intended result, instead of an attractive but ultimately arbitrary absolute.

LEARNING OUTCOME 17-2

Grasp the changing role of dance and dance music in the nineteenth century.

17-2 Music and Dance in the Nineteenth Century

During the finale of the first act of Mozart's *Don Giovanni*, Don Giovanni invites Zerlina, Masetto, and the villagers to a festive affair at his residence, an event also attended by Donna Anna, Donna Elvira, and Don Ottavio. There is dancing, with orchestras onstage (as well as in the pit). After Don Giovanni welcomes the villagers, one of the orchestras begins playing a minuet to which Anna, Elvira, and Ottavio dance. Shortly after the dance begins, two other orchestras begin playing distinctly different dances, a *contredanse* in simple duple meter and a *Deutscher*, a peasant dance, in a fast compound meter.

Mozart's compositional tour de force draws class distinctions through dance music. The minuet retained its strong association with the aristocracy throughout the eighteenth century. The *contredanse* (a French version of the English "country dance") had replaced the minuet as the most popular dance in France among the aristocracy and the bourgeoisie. (Recall also that it spread to the French colonies; it was the starting point for the habanera.) Because of its less elite association, Mozart uses it to accompany Don Giovanni as he tries once more to seduce the peasant girl Zerlina on her wedding day; the dance tells us that they have found a social middle ground. The *deutscher* accompanies Leporello as he tries to distract Masetto by dancing with him.

By incorporating dances from three social classes in his opera, Mozart anticipates the most salient aspect of dance in nineteenth-century life: it was the most upwardly mobile of the expressive arts. Ballet, a part of opera since the seventeenth century, would become an independent art form in the 1830s. Social dancing would flourish among all levels of society as more and more people moved into the city. Folk dances scaled the social ladder, offering rhythmic support to popular music and a sense of national identity in art music. Reams of dances were published, from simple pieces for one or two pianists to fiddle tunes, to complex, dance-inspired compositions.

17-2A The Growth of Dance in Industrialized Nations

The rapid growth of the middle class and the Industrial Revolution, which brought working-class people into the cities, triggered an explosion of dance in the nineteenth century. During the course of the century, both wages and working conditions improved, providing people with more money to spend and more time to spend it. Improved transportation made it easier to move around, and—toward the end of the century—electric lights made it safer to go out in the evening.

Ballrooms and dance halls sprang up in major cities throughout Europe, none more so than Vienna. Two large dance halls were opened in consecutive years, in 1807 and 1808; the larger held over six thousand people. These popular venues provided steady employment for musicians. The most popular were two generations of Strausses, who periodically left their Viennese home base to tour throughout Europe.

Dance also became an increasingly important part of theatrical entertainment, either as part of a varied entertainment or, in the case of ballet, as an evening built around dance. The use of dance in musical entertainment cut across class boundaries. Ballet was an important component of opera, especially in Paris; operettas featured dance numbers—Jacques Offenbach's famous "Can-Can," from his 1858 light opera *Orpheus in the Underworld,* brought this working-class dance into a "respectable" venue; dance was also an integral part of more lowbrow entertainment, which included musical comedies and minstrel shows.

Charles Wilda/The Bridgeman Art Library/Getty Images

There was an explosion of dance in the nineteenth century.

Dance-inspired music also entered the home via the thousands of dances composed for pianists. Some were for solo piano; others were for piano duet—duet playing was a popular pastime in the nineteenth century. Franz Schubert was the first important composer to produce a large quantity of dance music for piano, both solo and duet: hundreds of waltzes, galops, *ecossaises*, *Deutscher*, polonaises, and *Ländler*; only some of it—mostly the pieces for piano duet—was published during his lifetime. And Schubert wasn't alone. Virtually every important composer of piano music composed music derived from popular dances.

The rise of dance and social dancing in the nineteenth century parallels the rise of song and amateur singing in several respects. Both had been part of musical life since prehistory among all classes. But not until the nineteenth century did those in the business of music discover how to make substantial amounts of money from them. The profusion of dance pieces, from challenging works suitable for concert performance to simple duets for amateurs, was comparable to the outpouring of song, from the most sophisticated art songs to simple ditties. The more widespread use of dance in theatrical productions, either integrated into some kind of staged vocal work or as a complete entertainment in itself, was one dimension of the explosion in stage entertainment for all classes of society. The sudden popularity of social dancing was analogous to the enthusiasm for amateur choral singing; both were, in essence, group activities that attracted people from all walks of life.

Among the most distinctively nineteenth-century, dance-related genres are music for the ballet and concert music that used dance to express national identity, to be discussed in section 17-3.

17-2B Ballet

For many of us, "ballet" conjures up the sounds and images of *The Nutcracker*, Tchaikovsky's Christmastime favorite: dancers, including ballerinas on their toes, dressed in elaborate costumes, telling a story through elaborately choreographed movement, with the musical support of a full orchestra.

The word *ballet* is French; it is a cognate of the Italian word *balletto*, meaning "little dance." Dance is to the French much as singing is to Italians: not only a basic human activity but also part of their cultural identity. Not surprisingly then, France is the home of ballet, just as Italy is the home of opera.

Dance before Classical Ballet. The godfather of ballet was Louis XIV, an enthusiastic dancer and dance enthusiast himself. During the early years of his reign (b. 1638, r. 1643–1715), he sponsored or supported several important institutions and developments, including the formation of the Académie Royale de Danse, which brought together the leading dancing masters in France; the formation of a professional dance troupe within the Académie Royale de Musique, a training ground for the opera; and the publication of numerous dance treatises.

These developments supported the growth of dance as a virtuosic and expressive art. The formalization of training and the formation of a professional dance troupe expanded the ever-widening gap between skilled amateur and professional dancing; indeed, Louis XIV gave up dancing in public in 1670. In late seventeenth-century French opera, dance became an integral part of the expressive message rather than a diversion, as it had been during the Renaissance. Hybrid genres, such as Lully's opera-ballets, in which dance both animated and complemented vocal numbers, evidence the emergence of professional dancing. Collectively, these developments provided a foundation for ballet as a discipline and a starting point for its evolution into an independent art form.

During the eighteenth century, dance continued to be an important part of opera, in Italy as well as France, and in European centers, such as Stockholm and St. Petersburg, where French cultural influence was prominent. This is reflected in the growth of dance troupes connected with opera companies and the steady employment of choreographers and dancing masters. The use of dance in Italian opera differed from the French approach: typically, it served as an interlude between acts of an *opera seria*. Still, ballet and the music for it played a significant role in opera. Gluck, whose works initiated a thorough reform of opera, was praised for the way in which his music supported the pantomime of the action.

The Ballerina and the Emergence of Classical Ballet. Although the practice of composing and producing ballet as an independent stage work dates from the late eighteenth century, dance historians cite an 1832 production in Paris of *La sylphide*, a work choreographed by Filippo Taglioni, as the beginning of classical, or Romantic, ballet. The star of the production was Marie Taglioni, Filippo's daughter and star pupil, and the first of the great prima ballerinas. The most spectacular feature of her performance was dancing almost exclusively *en pointe* (on the toes). Marie Taglioni's use of pointe was a startling innovation; other dancers had experimented with it, but none before Taglioni had integrated it so fully into her dancing.

Filippo Taglioni's ballet broke new ground in several respects. First, it established the narrative ballet as an independent genre, in which movement and music suffice to tell the story. Second, Marie Taglioni's use of pointe made this practice the norm: it became the defining feature of classical ballet. Third, it completed the gradual shift in dance from masculine to feminine. In seventeenth-century France, the first dance stars were male; men continued to dominate dance through the eighteenth century, although women had become more prominent. However, with the emergence of Marie Taglioni and other prima ballerinas, the spotlight

ballet An independent, expressive dance genre in which movement and music tell the story

Ballerina Marie Taglioni, clearly *en pointe* in *La sylphide*

control of the Imperial Theatres in St. Petersburg in 1881. In 1889, he instructed Marius Petipa to choreograph the fairy tale of the sleeping beauty and commissioned Tchaikovsky to compose the music; Vsevolozhsky designed the costumes and set himself. As was the custom, Petipa provided Tchaikovsky with detailed guidelines; Tchaikovsky collaborated with Petipa in preparing the score. The result was what many commentators regard as the quintessential classical ballet.

Petipa and Tchaikovsky based *The Sleeping Beauty* on a fairy tale first recounted by Charles Perrault in 1697 and later adapted by the Brothers Grimm, whose version the team used as a point of departure. The story is an allegory of good and evil, set in an imaginary kingdom in an unreal world. King Florestan and his queen invite six fairies, who will serve as godmothers, to the christening of their daughter, Aurora. All but one have bestowed their gifts on the infant when Caraboose, an evil fairy who is outraged because she was not invited, puts a curse on Aurora: on her sixteenth birthday, she will prick her finger and die. The Lilac Fairy, who had not presented her gift, mitigates Caraboose's curse by modifying its terms: Aurora and the kingdom will sleep for one hundred years, when a prince will discover Aurora and wake her—and the kingdom— with a kiss. The prince finds the castle, overgrown after the hundred years, overcomes Caraboose, and awakens Aurora. The remainder of the ballet is a celebration of the wedding, in which not only fairies but also a parade of fairy-tale creatures join in the festivities.

Early in Act 1, the dance corps depicts the townspeople celebrating Princess Aurora's birthday. For this scene, Tchaikovsky composed a waltz.

shifted to women. The central character in *La sylphide* is a sylph, a female fairy who falls in love with a mortal.

During the latter part of the nineteenth century, ballet would find a second home in Russia. Much of its success in that country had to do with the three memorable ballets composed by Tchaikovsky.

17-2C Tchaikovsky's *The Sleeping Beauty*

It is ironic that Handel and Tchaikovsky, the most versatile composers of their respective eras, owe their place in the popular imagination to a single work. Just as many know Handel most familiarly from *Messiah*, so do many know Tchaikovsky's music mainly, or even exclusively, through *The Nutcracker*, his most famous ballet. It was the last of three major ballets that he composed.

His first major ballet was *Swan Lake* (1875–1876), which was received poorly, largely because of problems mounting the production. In the thirteen-year interim between *Swan Lake* and *The Sleeping Beauty*, Tchaikovsky's star had risen. During that same period, Ivan Vsevolozhsky, a creative mind with considerable administrative skill and a passion for excellence, had assumed

17-2D The Waltz

In a scathing editorial published in July 1816, a writer for the *London Times* expressed his outrage over the introduction of the waltz at a ball given by the Prince Regent a few nights earlier:

> We remarked with pain that the indecent foreign dance called the Waltz was introduced (we believe for the first time) at the English court on Friday last. . . . It is quite sufficient to cast one's eyes on the voluptuous intertwining of the limbs and close compressure on the bodies in their dance, to see that it is indeed far removed from the modest reserve which has hitherto been considered distinctive of English females.

The editor of the *Times* was not alone in voicing his disapproval of this new dance that was taking Europe

Nineteenth-century illustration for the Charles Perrault fairy tale of "The Sleeping Beauty"

Vienna and ultimately throughout Europe and the United States. As the waltz grew in popularity, composers increased their production of waltzes for home use, for dancing, and as concert music. Because of its popularity and its appeal to all social classes, it was an ideal choice for the celebratory scene in Tchaikovsky's ballet.

17-2E Waltz from *The Sleeping Beauty*

As performed for social dancing, the waltz builds on a rhythmic foundation that features a strong first beat (often called the *downbeat*) followed by two lighter beats: the familiar OOM-pah-pah pattern. The movements of the dancers reflect this pattern of emphasis: they typically consist of a strong step combined with a lift of the bodies on the downbeat, followed by two small steps in alternation. Dancers repeat this pattern of steps endlessly as they twirl around the dance floor, bobbing from one downbeat to the next.

Tchaikovsky's waltz (see Listen Up!) uses the characteristic rhythm of the waltz as a point of departure rather than an essential requirement; this isn't music for social dancing. The beginning of the waltz was enough to communicate the message; this in turn liberated both composer and choreographer from the necessity to adhere strictly to the conventions of the dance. As a result, Tchaikovsky's waltz is not music for social dancing. The most fundamental reasons are rhythmic: the intermittent timekeeping in the accompaniment and the frequent syncopations that regroup beats into pairs. Strict timekeeping is not necessary in ballet, and Petipa's original choreography features elaborate dancing that bears no resemblance to the waltz as danced socially. The dancers make clear what is implicit in the music: Tchaikovsky's waltz is music about waltzing and the occasions at which waltzing takes place, rather than music for waltzing.

Tchaikovsky's rhythmic liberties are characteristic of the rhythmic relationships between dance-inspired art music and the dances that inspired it; the ratio of rhythmic variety and rhythmic play to timekeeping increases when composers are not constrained by the need to mark time for dancers.

17-2F Dance, Class, and Social Status

Those who attended late nineteenth-century performances of *Don Giovanni* would have understood the dance scene described at the beginning of this section as a true period piece. It did not reflect the contemporary

by storm. Religious leaders were virtually unanimous in their condemnation of the waltz, and so were the more priggish members of society. What scandalized them was the fact that in dancing the waltz, particularly at the brisk pace so often used in the nineteenth century, partners typically held each other so closely that there was "compressure" up and down the torso.

Despite (and perhaps also because of) these objections, the waltz became the most popular ballroom dance by far—during the nineteenth century, among all classes. Queen Victoria, the quintessential English female during her sixty-three-year reign, loved to waltz. So apparently did Franz Josef I, the ruler of the Austro-Hungarian Empire; he was the dedicatee of Johann Strauss's *Emperor Waltz*.

The waltz is a social dance in a fast triple meter. It takes its name from the characteristic movement of the dancers. In German, *wälzen* means "to roll or turn"; in the waltz, the dancers twirl around as they glide across the dance floor. The waltz began as a humble peasant dance in the more rural parts of southern Germany, Austria, and Bohemia (now part of the Czech Republic); it was one of many such "German dances." For many, it was a simpler and more appealing dance than the more choreographically complex minuet.

In the 1820s, the waltz enjoyed a surge in popularity, first in Vienna, then throughout Europe. The catalysts were the Viennese composers Joseph Lanner and Johann Strauss the Elder, who delighted Viennese audiences first as a team, then as leaders of their own dance orchestras. Strauss soon toured relentlessly throughout Europe, bringing the Viennese waltz to a much wider audience. Strauss's son (and rival) Johann Strauss the Younger would enjoy even greater success in

waltz Social dance in a fast triple meter

 **LISTEN UP!**

Tchaikovsky, Waltz, from *The Sleeping Beauty* (1889)

TAKEAWAY POINT: A concert waltz for professional dancers

STYLE: Romantic

FORM: Multisectional

GENRE: Ballet

INSTRUMENTS: Orchestra

CONTEXT: The use of a waltz within a ballet as an exuberant sound symbol of celebration

0:00   The introduction serves as a transition from the previous scene.

A

0:33   Brief vamp by accompanying instruments establishes waltz rhythm; violins enter with a long, flowing melody, which leads into the B section with a string of syncopations.

B

1:09   A much more active melody with a decided change in accompaniment: mostly strong downbeats and no afterbeats

A

1:38   The first melody, but with no bass note on the downbeat—just afterbeats, plus an accompanying figure in the flutes that also avoids the downbeat. A longer string of syncopations ends this version of the melody.

INTERLUDE (C)

2:11   Brief contrasting interlude. The melody grows out of a short motive; the waltz pattern returns in the accompaniment, but more subtly.

A

2:41   Brief vamp by accompanying instruments establishes waltz rhythm; violins enter with a long, flowing melody, which leads into the B section with a string of syncopations.

B

3:13   A much more active melody with a decided change in accompaniment: mostly strong downbeats and no afterbeats

A

3:42   The syncopated ending of this section is extended considerably to provide a strong conclusion to the movement.

 Listen to this selection streaming or in an Active Listening Guide at CourseMate or in the eBook.

relationship between dance and class, because gentrified country dances—polka, galop, and above all, the waltz—blurred class boundaries, which were drawn so sharply in the opera. Everyone danced the waltz, from royalty to the working classes. In this way, the waltz and the institutions that sprang up around it—dance halls and ballrooms, the publishing of dance music for concert and domestic use, and touring orchestras—reflected the reluctant but relentless movement toward a more egalitarian society in both Europe and North America.

Ballet represented a different kind of ascendancy: the emergence of dance as an independent expressive art. At the beginning of the nineteenth century, ballet was still largely tied to opera. By the end of the century, ballet as a distinct and self-sufficient art form flourished in France and Russia and was gaining a presence in Europe and the United States. The innovations of Marie Taglioni and others raised the bar, establishing classical ballet in the process. Tchaikovsky's ballets introduced music of comparable quality to the dance.

These and other trends, such as the use of dance rhythms in popular song and the composition of elaborate dance-inspired instrumental works, reflected the increasing importance of dance in cultural life during the course of the nineteenth century. Dance would also be the starting point for another important development in nineteenth-century concert music: the affirmation of cultural identity.

17-3 Nationalism in Nineteenth-Century Music

In June 1891, the Czech composer Antonín Dvořák received a telegram from Jeannette Thurber with the following message: "would you accept position director national conservatory of music New York October 1892 also lead six concerts of your works."

Jeannette Thurber was the daughter of a violinist, the wife of a wealthy businessman, and a musician who had studied at the Paris Conservatory. With the support of fellow philanthropists, she founded the National Conservatory of Music of America in New York in 1885. Her ultimate goal was to create a uniquely American national conservatory along the lines of the Paris Conservatory. She would attract numerous eminent musicians to the faculty. During its first years, the conservatory was open to students of all races, and tuition was free.

One of the most important components of Jeannette Thurber's vision for the conservatory was fostering a national school of classical composition. To increase its prestige and further her vision, she recruited Antonín Dvořák as director. Dvořák was her ideal candidate because he was an ardent nationalist and one of the most highly regarded composers in Europe. He was initially reluctant to leave Prague, but a visit by a National Conservatory faculty member and the offer of an annual salary of $15,000 (over $350,000 today) convinced him to come.

His charge was to guide American composers in the formation of a national school of composition. He accepted enthusiastically, as he indicated in numerous public statements and private correspondence. Shortly after arriving in the United States in late September, he wrote to a friend: "The Americans expect great things of me. I am to show them the way into the Promised Land, the realm of a new, independent art, in short a national style of music!"

The conscious nationalism exemplified by Dvořák's music was an important trend in European cultural life during the latter half of the nineteenth century. In music, it was the second wave of nationalism, a continuation of and a response to the dominant international style that emanated from German-speaking Europe.

nationalism In music, a nineteenth-century movement that sought to portray a uniquely national identity by drawing on the legends, myths, history, and literature of the people; creating vocal music in their own language; and drawing on folk song and dance

century, with the publication of vernacular songs, such as the Italian *frottola* and the French *chanson*. Dances with a regional identity quickly followed songs in print, but the association with their roots tended to dissolve as they moved up the social ladder and from one land to the next. Through the early eighteenth century, composers were more concerned with pleasing patrons and employers than consciously attempting to portray the identity of a people. During the Baroque era, the most identifiably French music was the overture, which was the entrance music of the king.

In the first part of the nineteenth century, the most prominent nationalistic movement involved not a country but a language. After the fall of Napoleon, German-speaking Europe included the Austrian part of the Holy Roman Empire and the thirty-nine states of the German Confederation. With the cultural ascendancy of instrumental music, the widespread veneration of Beethoven, the classicizing of Haydn and Mozart, and the resurrection of Bach's music, German/Viennese music challenged the prestige and influence of Italian opera. The *Lied* added another more specific dimension to the shared culture of German-speaking people. Karl Maria von Weber's *Der Freischütz* (*The Freeshooter*), advertised as a "Romantic opera" and first staged in 1821, tapped into the German fascination with *Volk* (peasants), nature, and the supernatural—themes also evident in *Erlkönig*. It was immediately recognized as a German national opera, in Germany and elsewhere, and exerted a powerful influence on Wagner. Weber's opera would anticipate the unification of Germany by fifty years: the German Empire was formed only in 1871.

German musical nationalism soon became German musical imperialism. By mid-century, the music of German composers dominated the symphonic repertoire, much as the music of Italian composers dominated opera, and German music became the de facto international style in instrumental music. As a result, in the latter part of the century some composers outside German-speaking Europe, particularly in Slavic countries, Scandinavia, and Spain, began to cultivate a national style, to declare cultural independence—at least to some degree—from German and Italian music. To do so, they focused on the folk traditions and history of their cultures.

For nineteenth-century composers, nationalism in music was a means of asserting national identity—a sense of the distinctive cultural characteristics of a nation. Nationalistic composers found three important ways to invest their music with a national identity.

17-3A Music and National Identity

The idea of national styles in music dates from the early sixteenth

- They based works on the legends, myths, history, and literature of the people, particularly in opera and in programmatic instrumental music.
- They created vocal music in their own language and provided folk melodies within sophisticated musical settings, in opera and song.
- And they composed instrumental works based on the folk dances of their cultures.

Nationalistic dance music is in some ways the most accessible, because listeners do not have to know the language to discern its message and because its characteristic rhythms are often immediately recognizable.

17-3B National Dances and Nationalism

Dance music has typically been associated with place, as we noted in our discussion of the Baroque dance suite. However, dances intended as expressions of national identity represent a shift in attitude, in that part of their purpose is to convey not only a particular locale but also the character and spirit of the folk who inhabit it. The emergence of concert and domestic music inspired by national and regional dances can be seen as a reflection of the changing political and social landscape in the nineteenth century. The history of the polonaise is instructive in that regard.

Polonaise is the French name for the *polonez*, a dance from Poland. Like many European dances, the *polonez* first came to light as a folk dance. In the seventeenth century, the Polish aristocracy adapted it for their use; in this setting, it became slower and statelier. Beginning in the late seventeenth century, it began to spread throughout Europe, where it was popular in courts and appeared occasionally in instrumental suites. During this time, the French name for the dance gained currency; it was known even in Poland as a polonaise.

For the polonaise/*polonez* and other folk-derived dances, the seventeenth and eighteenth centuries might be understood as an era of colonization, in the sense that the process of assimilating folk dances into upper-class society stripped away the sense of place and class—in the case of the polonaise, even to the name! That process was reversed to some extent in the nineteenth century. Chopin, a Polish expatriate in the wake of the 1830 uprising and its suppression by Russia, apparently used the dances of his homeland as an expression of solidarity with the Polish people. His later polonaises are grand pieces: many commentators feel that they not only connect to Chopin's homeland but also capture the revolutionary spirit that was suppressed so violently. Similarly, his numerous mazurkas are sophisticated concert pieces and implicit expressions of national identity and pride.

For others, like Robert Schumann and Liszt, the polonaise was simply a characteristic rhythm, without nationalistic overtones. As a result, Polish dances such as the polonaise and mazurka appeared both as social dances or dance-inspired concert music and, for Chopin, as works conveying the spirit of the Polish people.

What was relatively rare in the first half of the century became fashionable toward the end. Increasingly, composers from Spain, Scandinavia, and Slavic regions published collections of piano pieces based on regional folk dances. There were practical as well as political reasons for greater interest in national and regional dance music. In 1869, Brahms's publisher Simrock released the first set of his *Hungarian Dances*. These immensely popular pieces made Simrock and Brahms large sums of money. Much of their appeal came from their distinct regional character. For nineteenth-century Europeans, exoticism was the other side of the nationalism coin, and what was national in Prague, Barcelona, or Oslo was exotic elsewhere—a visit to a foreign land without leaving town.

Among the most popular sets of dances were the *Slavonic Dances* of Antonín Dvořák, a little-known Czech composer at the time of their publication.

17-3C Dvořák's Slavonic Dances: From Village Square to Concert Hall

In July 1874, Antonín Dvořák, newly married and struggling to put food on the table for himself and his bride, applied for a grant from the Austrian government, submitting fifteen of his compositions in support of his application. He received the grant and similar grants during the next four years. The second year, when Brahms was a member of the panel, he learned of Dvořák's music and was particularly drawn to his *Moravian Duets* for two sopranos and piano.

Perhaps Brahms felt kinship on several levels: a common interest in folk music, similar experiences during their formative years (both played extensively in orchestras that performed the popular music of the time and place), a firsthand knowledge of economic hard times. Certainly, he found value in Dvořák's music and offered him musical advice, which Dvořák gratefully accepted. They would establish a close friendship, which lasted until Brahms's death.

Brahms also wrote to his publisher Simrock on Dvořák's behalf, encouraging him to publish some of Dvořák's music. Simrock soon asked Dvořák to compose a set of folk dances for piano duet, in the hope that Dvořák's dances would replicate the success of Brahms's *Hungarian Dances*. He got his wish: the publication of the *Slavonic Dances* in the fall of 1878 brought Simrock healthy sales and brought Dvořák international recognition almost overnight. The choice of title—"Slavonic" rather than "Bohemian"—reflected Dvořák's responsiveness to the Pan-Slavic movement of the late nineteenth century.

Antonín Dvořák ♦ grew up in a village north of Prague in Bohemia, which is now the western and middle third of the Czech Republic. His childhood music-making experiences included playing violin in the village band, which often accompanied local dances. He moved to Prague in 1857, where he received much of his training (at an organ school). During this time, he supported himself by giving piano lessons and playing in theater orchestras, in which he performed under Bedrich Smetana, the ardently nationalistic Czech composer and conductor.

With the success of the *Slavonic Dances*, Dvořák gained the support of leading German musicians and critics. His international renown made him a hero at home and the composer of choice for state occasions. Ten years later he would serve briefly as professor of

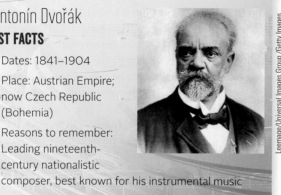

►Antonín Dvořák
FAST FACTS

- Dates: 1841–1904

- Place: Austrian Empire; now Czech Republic (Bohemia)

- Reasons to remember: Leading nineteenth-century nationalistic composer, best known for his instrumental music

composition at Prague Conservatory, before leaving for the United States in 1892. In between came several trips to London, which were gratifying to his spirit and his wallet. His time in the United States was productive for him and the conservatory: he composed his famous "Symphony from the New World" and cello concerto in America. Upon his return to Europe, he devoted himself almost exclusively to opera. However, his reputation as a leading nineteenth-century composer is based mainly on his instrumental music—symphonies, concertos, and other orchestral music, and chamber music for various combinations of strings.

17-3D Slavic Identity

Slavonic is an alternate form of *Slavic*, a term that identifies a family of languages spoken in Eastern Europe, from Poland to Macedonia and from the contemporary Czech Republic to Russia, and those who speak these languages. The underlying connection among these diverse languages has provided a common bond despite differences in alphabet (some languages, such as Czech and Polish, use the Roman alphabet; others, like Russian and Serbian, use the Cyrillic alphabet) and religion (some, such as Poles, Czechs, and Slovenes, are predominantly Catholic; others, such as Russians, Serbians, and Ukrainians, are predominantly Orthodox).

The Austrian (and later, Austro-Hungarian) Empire was the nineteenth-century incarnation of the Habsburg dynasty, which had ruled central Europe since the fifteenth century. The empire was a loose confederation of diverse peoples that stretched from Bohemia (the western two-thirds of the modern Czech Republic) in the northwest and what is now northern Italy in the southwest, to Montenegro in the south and Transylvania in the east. The empire was a checkerboard of peoples whose languages belonged to four different language groups: German, Slavic, Romance (Italian), and Finno-Ugric (Hungarian). German was the official language throughout the empire, much as Russian was the official language of the Soviet Union during its seventy-year history.

In the nineteenth century, a group of Slavic intellectuals and artists who lived in territories governed by the Habsburgs founded a Pan-Slavic movement. Their initial aim was to cultivate an awareness of their common heritage through the study of folk traditions and vernaculars, and promote a sense of Slavic unity despite the geographical separation of the Slavic groups. This quickly led to a drive for the political autonomy of Slavic peoples under Habsburg rule, which did not succeed. However, the movement spread to Russia and other Slavic regions.

As their title implies, Dvořák's *Slavonic Dances* are both a fruit and an expression of this Pan-Slavic movement, which was centered in Prague. The first set of eight dances, published in 1878, features two each of three dances from Bohemia: the *sousedska*, a slow couples dance in triple meter; the *skocná*, a fast duple-meter dance in which the male dancer leaps about; and the *furiant*, a triple-meter dance at a moderate to fast tempo; plus a polka, another Bohemian dance that had already spread through Europe and the Americas, and a *dumka*, a slow song of lament popular throughout the Slavic world, which Dvořák underpinned with a steady dance rhythm. We consider the last of the eight dances, a vigorous *furiant* (see Listen Up!). Following Brahms's example, Dvořák orchestrated the dances; we discuss the orchestral version here.

17-3E The *Furiant*

In Czech, *furiant* means "a proud, swaggering, conceited man." The *furiant* is a couples dance in a moderate to fast triple meter characterized by a specific rhythm in the melody, which Dvořák uses throughout the dance. In his version, each short phrase of the melody in the main section of the work consists of two long notes, each lasting two beats, plus additional shorter values, in a strict rhythm. A common form of this melodic rhythm is shown in Table 17.1. The long notes conflict with the underlying triple meter and are the principal source of the rhythmic excitement that pervades the piece.

In a typical performance of the work, this rhythmic pattern takes about three seconds to perform. It serves as the building block from which melodies, then complete sections grow: the two large sections in the dance consist mostly of this rhythm set to several different melodic shapes and in several different keys. Through Dvořák's skillful manipulation of contour, key, and orchestral setting, this three-second rhythmic pattern spawns a four-minute composition.

In most respects, Dvořák's musical language is very much in the mainstream. However, the distinctive and persistent melodic rhythm, which conflicts with the underlying triple meter, immediately distinguishes the dance from the waltz, polonaise, and other triple-meter dances of the era; the vitality of Dvořák's setting projects the spirit and energy of folk dance music.

Melody rhythm	1	2	1	2	1	2	1	2	&	3	1	2	&	3
Meter	1		2		3		1	2		3	1	2		3

Table 17.1 Rhythm of the Furiant

Dvořák, Slavonic Dance in G minor (1878)

TAKEAWAY POINT: Czech folk dance as brilliant and evocative classical music

STYLE: Romantic

FORM: ABA with coda

GENRE: Nationalistic dance

INSTRUMENTS: Orchestra

CONTEXT: Sophisticated, folk-inspired dance music for concert performance rather than social dancing

SECTION 1

A

0:00   Forte (loud): opening melodic idea, in a question (in minor) and answer (in major) relationship. The idea is repeated literally

0:10   Piano (soft): first variant of the idea, in a new key, with a new harmonic progression, and with an altered melodic contour

0:19   Forte (loud): return of the opening phrases

B

0:29   Piano (soft): new melodic idea with a different, but related rhythm.

A

0:39   Forte, then piano: yet another variant of the opening idea, similar to first variant of A

0:49   Piano, with crescendo: a more contrasting variant—flute and piccolo, plus an active string accompaniment that grows into a woodwind obbligato. The phrase is extended..

1:04   Forte (loud): final restatement of opening idea within this large section

TRANSITION

1:13   Gradual transition to more lyric interlude, with fragmentation of rhythm and a diminuendo

INTERLUDE

1:21   Two statements of a lyric theme. The second has richer orchestration. This interlude serves as a buffer between the more energetic opening section and its restatement.

SECTION 1

A

1:50   Cymbal reinforces grouping of beats by twos. Note contrasting roles of cymbal and triangle in various sections.

2:00   Triangle pings on every downbeat.

2:10   As before

B

2:20   New melodic idea with different rhythm

A

2:29   Cymbal marks the melodic rhythm in the loud part, and the triangle, the downbeats in the soft part.

2:39   Both cymbal and triangle are intermittent in this subsection.

2:53   Cymbal only at the beginning of each phrase

(Continued)

3:03   A developmental-type phrase that implies several keys and shortens the phrase by two measures

3:11   The phrase begins like the previous one but goes in a different direction.

3:19   Further development as the music begins to die away

3:31   Return of the interlude theme, with gradual slowing to a snail's pace

3:51   The last word: the major-mode version of the opening phrase quickly brings the dance to a close.

 Listen to this selection streaming or in an Active Listening Guide at CourseMate or in the eBook.

It may be difficult for us to understand the mind-set of the late nineteenth-century American commentator who remarked disparagingly about Dvořák's "Slav naïveté . . . that degenerates into sheer brainlessness." Dvořák's espousal of nationalism in music was, for him, a double-edged sword. It was his gateway to fame and fortune, but it also relegated his music to second-class status in the musical world of the time, at least in the minds of some critics. Nevertheless, the quest for an identifiably national music was central to his musical identity.

The intriguing question for us is the relationship between folk and art: What is the role of the folk element in concert music? At least in this particular instance, Dvořák's use of the characteristic *furiant* rhythm is far more than a cosmetic overlay. It is the rhythmic seed from which the entire dance springs, and it is the source of the rhythmic vitality that is its essence. It is all but impossible to reconstruct what the *furiant* lost in its journey from village square to concert hall. However, we do know that Dvořák grew up playing this music in its original environment (the village band) and that this kind of rhythmic energy is an organic component of his music. The symphonic setting may give it a gloss that it didn't have in its original home, but it does not enervate the rhythm.

Thirty-five years later, another Slavic composer would turn the world upside down with even more energetic rhythms. We hear excerpts from Igor Stravinsky's *The Rite of Spring* in Chapter 19.

Looking Back, Looking Ahead

At the end of the eighteenth century, the orchestra was an ad hoc ensemble assembled for a particular occasion. At the end of the nineteenth century, it was an institution. Our sampling of nineteenth-century orchestral music highlights the dramatic changes in the orchestra and its place in nineteenth-century culture, and hints at the range of repertoire composed for it. During the course of the century, the orchestra more than doubled in size and consolidated its instrumentation. Permanent orchestras in major cities presented a full season of concerts each year: concert programs included repertoire from the past as well as the present. Certainly by the end of the century, the orchestra had become an institution comparable in prestige to opera.

As we heard during our survey, the range of orchestral music expanded in tandem with the orchestra. Composers continued to write symphonies and concertos, as well as program music of various kinds, including programmatic symphonies and concertos. Additional concert repertoire came from a growing array of sources: music originally composed for opera, ballet, or theater productions as well as music adapted from compositions for other genres. It was a rich mix.

The orchestra would remain the dominant instrumental ensemble in the twentieth century, but the music composed for it would sound strikingly different.

 study tools 17

Ready to study?
In the book you can:

• Review Learning Outcome answers and Glossary terms with the tear-out Chapter Review card.

Or you can go online to CourseMate, at www.cengagebrain.com, for these resources:

• Chapter Quizzes to prepare for tests

• Interactive flashcards of all Glossary terms

• Active Listening Guides, streaming music, and YouTube playlists

• An eBook with live links to all web resources

Romantic Style

 KEY FEATURES

1. **Endless melody.** Much Romantic music, both vocal and instrumental, features long, flowing melodies that develop over the course of a long section, or even an entire work.
2. **Distinctive figuration and accompaniment.** Romantic music replaces Classical music's generic scales and arpeggios with distinctive and evocative figuration and accompaniment.
3. **Expanded sound resources.** In instrumental composition and accompaniments for vocal compositions, composers take advantage of increased ensemble size and instrumental capabilities, as well as greater performer virtuosity, to expand the range and variety of timbral choices.
4. **Dynamic contrasts.** Because of the increased size of ensembles and increased power of many instruments, dynamic contrasts can be more pronounced. Dynamic change can be gradual as well as abrupt, with long crescendos and diminuendos helping to define waves of sound.
5. **Blurred boundaries.** Partly because of the expansion of size and gesture in Romantic music, the boundaries between sections often feature gradual transitions extending over several measures, rather than the decisive cadences of Classical style, which sharply outline sectional divisions.

 KEY CONCEPTS

Telling stories or painting scenes. In much Romantic music, composers tell a story through a series of episodes or scenes. Unlike Baroque music, which developed a single affect, or Classical music, which created and then resolved dramatic tension through well-defined harmonic paths, Romantic music is episodic. It often presents a series of colorful but loosely connected scenes that are more often linked by melodic material than by well-defined formal structures. These features are most evident in many new genres, including art song, ballet, program music, and Wagner's music dramas.

Music Concept Check

To assist you in recognizing their distinctive features, we present an interactive comparison of Classical and Romantic style in CourseMate and the eBook.

 KEY COMPOSERS

Ludwig van Beethoven (1770–1827)
Gioachino Rossini (1792–1868)
Franz Schubert (1797–1828)
Hector Berlioz (1803–1869)
Felix Mendelssohn (1809–1847)
Frédéric Chopin (1810–1849)
Robert Schumann (1810–1856)
Franz Liszt (1811–1886)
Richard Wagner (1813–1883)
Giuseppe Verdi (1813–1901)
Clara Schumann (1819–1896)
Johannes Brahms (1833–1897)
Georges Bizet (1838–1875)
Pyotr Ilyich Tchaikovsky (1840–1893)
Antonín Dvořák (1841–1904)
Giacomo Puccini (1858–1924)
Gustav Mahler (1860–1911)

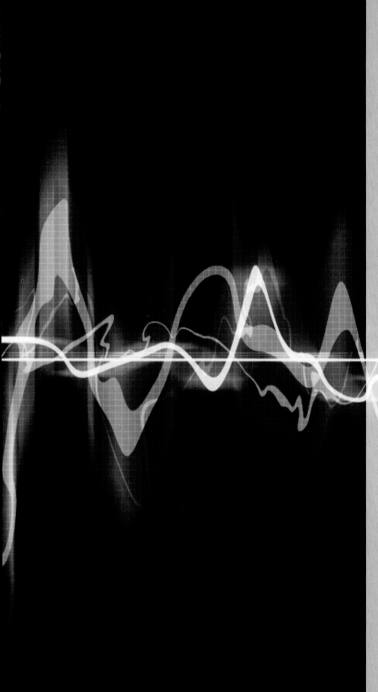

LEARNING OUTCOMES

After reading this chapter, you will be able to do the following:

18-1 Recognize the widespread impact of technology on every aspect of music in the twentieth century.

18-2 Describe the major musical developments during the twentieth century.

18-3 Paint a picture of the fragmented sound world of the twentieth century in terms of changes in the musical elements.

 study tools

After you read this chapter, go to the Study Tools at the end of the chapter, page 257.

The lexicographer who prepared the entry for the first *Oxford English Dictionary*, published between 1884 and 1928, began his definition of music this way:

> That one of the fine arts which is concerned with the combination of sounds with a view to beauty of form and the expression of emotion; also, the science of the laws or principles (of melody, harmony, rhythm, etc.) by which this art is regulated.

Microsoft's *Encarta World English Dictionary*, available online and in a print version published in 1999, first defined music this way:

> Sounds, usually produced by instruments or voices, that are arranged or played in order to create a pleasing or stimulating effect.

The second definition includes no mention of a "fine art," or "beauty of form," or the "science" of music. Instead, music can now be simply "pleasing" or "stimulating." These differences reflect the far broader understanding of what music is at the beginning of the twenty-first century.

The most remarkable fact about musical life in the twentieth century was that the assault on traditional "music" began at the beginning of the century and never let up. Music that was brand-new to twentieth-century audiences covered a wide spectrum, from avant-garde experiments to centuries-old folk styles suddenly preserved on recordings, and it came from every corner of the globe. It received unprecedented support from rapidly evolving technologies, which affected music making, performing, and dissemination in every conceivable way.

18-1 Music and Technology

A century of technological innovation, from sound recording to the Internet, had an impact on every aspect of music: its sounds, creation, performance, dissemination, and the ways people listen to and learn it. For the first time in history, it became possible to preserve musical events exactly—from Appalachian folk songs and African drumming to jazz improvisations, compositions for electronic synthesizer, and The Beatles' *Sgt. Pepper's Lonely Hearts Club Band*—as they were first conceived or performed. Each new generation produced technology so novel that previous generations could barely have imagined it. What we all took for granted at the beginning of the twenty-first century would have been beyond even the most futuristic thinkers' comprehension a century earlier.

On November 2, 1920, KDKA, a Pittsburgh radio station, began broadcasting.

© iStockPhoto.com/Ryan Burke

18-1A Early Sound Recording

Sound recording became a commercial enterprise in the late nineteenth century and grew rapidly after the turn of the century due to improvements in production techniques and playback equipment. At the outset, there were two competing technologies: Thomas Edison's cylinder and Emile Berliner's disc. The two-sided disc eventually won out by the 1910s because it was easier to produce and stock, and included recordings on both sides.

The first recordings were primitive: performers sang, spoke, or played their instruments into a megaphone, which transferred the vibrations to the recording medium. This acoustic process didn't work particularly well, and certain instruments were almost impossible to record. A new, much-improved recording process would supplant it almost overnight in 1925.

18-1B The Electrical Revolution

New electronic technology developed in the first part of the twentieth century sparked a revolution in the production and dissemination of music. Between 1920 and 1927, inventors refined equipment that made possible the conversion of sound into an electrical signal, the transmission of that signal, its conversion back into sound, and its amplification. They applied these new technologies to radio broadcasting, electric recording, amplification of live performance, and talking films. Radio came first.

The first commercial broadcast in the United States took place on November 2, 1920, when KDKA, a Pittsburgh radio station, began broadcasting. By 1925, electrical technology—microphones, amplifiers, and speakers—had replaced the more primitive acoustic technology of early radio. The Radio Corporation of America (RCA) formed the National Broadcasting Corporation (NBC), the first important U.S. radio network, the following year. It was the first audio-based mass medium and made real-time transcontinental communication possible. The technology developed for radio was soon adapted to recording: electrical recordings offered a dramatic improvement in quality over the acoustic recordings from the first part of the century. Microphones and amplifiers also became standard equipment on the bandstand and in larger venues, and the "talking film" became a reality in 1927 with the release of *The Jazz Singer*, starring Al Jolson, one of the top popular singers of the era.

Within only a few years, the sound world of the twentieth century had changed dramatically. Electrical recording offered much-improved fidelity for all kinds of voices and instruments. Network radio made live performances of many kinds of music much more accessible: NBC would create the NBC Symphony Orchestra for conductor Arturo Toscanini in 1937. Dance orchestras routinely broadcast from hotel ballrooms: Benny Goodman's midnight broadcasts from New York found eager listeners in Los Angeles. Early sound systems opened up new venues—Marian Anderson would sing in front of the Lincoln Memorial to a crowd of seventy-five thousand in 1939—and professional opportunities for new kinds of performers. Sound systems made Bing Crosby's career as a crooner possible. Films made musicals available to the masses.

Cumulatively, these developments revolutionized the consumption of music. It was now easier to become acquainted with music, from songs to symphonies, by listening to it rather

theremin The first electronic instrument, which featured two antennae: one to regulate pitch, the other to regulate volume

than reading it. Sheet music sales peaked in the 1910s and have been in decline ever since. No other set of developments has had as transformative an effect on the mode and ease of access to music; that it happened so quickly only added to its impact.

Early Electronic Instruments. Even as radio and recordings were changing the ways music reached its audience, another application of electrical technology was beginning to change the sounds themselves. Three kinds of electronic instruments were developed: purely electronic instruments; instruments that were electronic counterparts, or analogs, to acoustic instruments; and electronic apparatus that amplified acoustic instruments. The first was an all-electronic instrument.

In 1919, Léon Theremin, a young Russian inventor, created the first electronic instrument, which featured two antennae, one to regulate pitch, the other to regulate volume; it bears his name. The theremin is unusual in that performers don't actually touch the instrument; instead, they alter both pitch and volume by moving their hands in relation to the antennae.

Two electric analogs to existing instruments appeared in the 1930s. One was the Hammond organ, designed as a more portable and less expensive alternative to the pipe organ. The first Hammond organ appeared in 1935; it was soon standard equipment not only in churches but also in radio studios, cocktail lounges, and arenas. It would ultimately become a popular instrument in jazz and rock groups and was the first of what would become a flood of electronic keyboard instruments. The other was the Rickenbacker solid-body steel guitar, first introduced in 1931. The instrument was the forerunner of the numerous solid-body instruments that appeared after World War II, most notably Les Paul's electric guitars for Gibson and the electric guitars and basses of Leo Fender.

Electronics were also used to amplify the sound of acoustic instruments. The first amplified instrument to come into common use was the electric guitar, which soon found a home in country music, blues, and rock and roll. Beginning in the late 1950s, companies offered pickups for other string instruments, then wind instruments.

18-1C Mid-Century Technological Innovations

The middle of the century saw technological innovations on several fronts. Among the most far reaching were the development of the magnetic tape recorder, the emergence of commercial television, and electronic sound synthesis.

Magnetic Tape Recording. One of the technologies confiscated by the Allies at the end of World War II was the Magnetophone, an early magnetic tape recorder developed in Germany during the 1930s and kept secret from the rest of the world during the war. It became the prototype for the Ampex tape recorders that revolutionized recording and broadcasting in the postwar decade. Among the significant changes in the recording process eventually made possible by tape recording were much longer recordings, easier on-site recording, record editing, and improved sound quality.

With magnetic tape recorders, the length of a recording jumped from three or four minutes on a 78-rpm disc to thirty minutes or more. This in turn enabled prerecording of radio broadcasts and spurred the development of the long-playing record. Tape recorders were more portable and easier to use than previous generations of recording apparatus, which made live recording in any context considerably easier. Because the recording was preserved on a thin strip of magnetic tape, it became possible to edit the recording simply by splicing: slicing the recordings at appropriate points and taping the ends together. Among the fruits of this new technique were sound collages made up of sounds from a variety of sources, not all of them "musical"; "perfect" recordings by classical performers; and electronic compositions. Sound quality improved rapidly, with the advent of multitrack recording and stereo playback. Multitrack recording made it possible to assemble a recording in stages rather than all at once. Tape recording would remain the preferred method until the 1980s.

Television. Television, which exploded as a commercial enterprise after World War II, brought sound and image into the home. Millions watched Elvis and The Beatles on *The Ed Sullivan Show*, as well as Leonard Bernstein's *Young People's Concerts*. The 1985 broadcast of the Live Aid concert had an estimated global audience of 1.5 billion. Significantly, television replaced radio as the all-purpose mass medium; as a result, radio had to redefine itself as the more important outlet for music of all kinds.

Jack Robinson/Archive Photos/Getty Images

Robert Moog with his massive invention

Synthesizers. In current usage, a synthesizer is an instrument capable of generating sounds electronically. Early synthesizers like the Mark II were huge, cumbersome devices that composers needed to program; they weren't capable of live performance. In the 1960s, transistors replaced vacuum tubes, which reduced the size of the device and made it easier to use. The best known of the synthesizer developers was Robert Moog, whose work became known first through Walter/Wendy Carlos's recording *Switched-on Bach* (1968). Moog soon developed the Minimoog, a portable synthesizer designed for live performance. These early synthesizers were called analog synthesizers, because they generated sound by varying voltage. They would soon be replaced by digital instruments.

18-1D Digital Technology

The digital revolution, which began in the 1970s and continues into our own time, has profoundly reshaped our musical world. In digital technology, an electrical signal from a microphone, input, or playback device is converted into digital information by sampling the waveform at an extremely high rate. Alternatively, computers can generate digital models of the waveform

synthesizer Instrument capable of generating sounds electronically
analog synthesizer Electronic musical synthesizer that generates sound by varying voltage

directly. This in turn enabled the following technological advances:

- Unlimited reproduction of the original sound source without deterioration
- Sampling, the transfer of a recorded sound from its source into another recording
- MIDI (Musical Instrument Digital Interface), the protocol that enables communication between digital instruments and devices
- Audio workstations and computer software capable of manipulating any sound through a wide array of effects

From this have come such new developments as these:

- Sound editing so sophisticated as to be aurally undetectable
- A host of digital instruments—not only keyboards but also drum machines, wind controllers, and the like, each of which can produce an almost unlimited spectrum of sounds: a keyboard can sound like a harp, a flute, or almost any other imaginable sound
- Nondestructive mixing and application of effects, which allow unlimited revision of the musical original
- The ability to adjust one parameter of music without changing others: change pitch without changing tempo or switching timbres
- The ability to deliver audio over the Internet

We are now in a postliterate musical world. Music literacy—the ability to read and write music—was until recently considered an essential qualification for those who created music, or at least music of some sophistication. However, the advances in digital technology have made it possible to completely bypass notation during the creative process. Indeed, contemporary musicians have the best of all worlds because of music notation software that has multiple ways of entering data, plays back compositions, and prints publishable scores; and because of videos that capture musicians in performance.

The advances in electronic music technology over the last half century, especially since the digital revolution, have created an alternative musical world. In this world, the recording is the document; it can be completely detached from live performance. Recordings of this kind are as disparate as electronically generated compositions, like Varese's *Poème électronique*, and pop artists' "perfect" recordings. What they have in common is the fact that the results are impossible to replicate in live performance with acoustic instruments.

At the beginning of the twenty-first century, we are in the enviable position of having all these options for the creation and transmission of musical ideas. The barriers imposed by time and distance have largely dissolved. We have unprecedented access to the music of the past and present.

sampling Transfer of a recorded sound from its source into another recording

MIDI (Musical Instrument Digital Interface) Protocol that enables communication between digital instruments and devices

18-2 Commerce, Culture, and Art

Around the turn of the twenty-first century, a fun-loving academic wrote a revealing parody of a music department search committee's recommendation. In its supposed letter to the dean, the committee argued against hiring Mozart as a colleague, in part because of his prodigious output as a composer (so much quantity must certainly mean poor quality), his lack of familiarity with early music, his inability to obtain foundation support, his frequent appearances as a performer of his own compositions, his irresponsible lifestyle, and—above all—his lack of interest in earning a doctorate.

The parody underscores how different musical life had become two hundred years after Mozart's death. The part of the musical world that keeps Mozart's music alive—academia, established musical institutions, and record companies—might well have seemed stranger to him than the world of high-level pop, rock, and jazz. In both his world and the contemporary world of pop, rock, and jazz, musicians play their own music, improvise, and depend on the marketplace for their living even as they pursue their art. By contrast, those who understand themselves as continuing Mozart's tradition—contemporary "classical" composers and the performers of their music—rely almost exclusively on institutional support: universities, foundations, and governments.

Music grew into a massive business during the twentieth century. The shift in support from church and court to the marketplace, which began in the eighteenth century and gathered steam in the nineteenth, was largely complete by the beginning of World War I. The explosion of mass media in the 1920s and their continuing development through the course of the century confirmed and expanded the commercial basis of much music production and drove the ongoing realignment of the musical world.

The major musical developments during the twentieth century were the emergence of popular music as the dominant commercial force in musical life; the fragmentation of the classical music world and the relentless search in all directions for new sounds and modes of expression; the preservation of folk traditions from around the world; and lively ongoing cross-pollination among music of all types.

18-2A The Growth of Popular Music

To gauge the magnitude of the transformation of popular music, compare these three songs: "The Star-Spangled Banner," "Take Me Out to the Ball Game," and "Thriller." At the turn of the nineteenth century, the melody of "The Star-Spangled Banner" was already familiar as a British drinking song; Francis Scott Key simply put new words to it. "Take Me Out to the Ball Game" (1908) was the work of lyricist Jack Norworth and songwriter Albert von Tilzer. Most of the revenue from the song came from sheet music sales: the most popular arrangement was voice with piano accompaniment. The first popular recording of the song, also from 1908, featured strong-voiced Harvey Hindermyer accompanied by a band. For much of 1982, Michael Jackson collaborated with producer Quincy Jones to produce *Thriller*, the best-selling album of all time (110 million and counting). "Thriller," the title track from the album, was among the music videos that helped Michael Jackson break through MTV's color barrier.

Someone transported from the early nineteenth century to the early twentieth would have had no trouble comprehending "Take Me Out to the Ball Game." It speaks the same musical language as "The Star-Spangled Banner" and reached its audience in much the same way: via sheet music or simply by listening and singing along. The big novelty would have been the recording.

By contrast, "Thriller" would probably have sounded familiar to early twentieth-century listeners only at the most basic level. They might have been aware that the song was on a record. However, the mode of delivery—CD, radio, or music video—would have been completely outside the realm of their experience. For them, films were silent, phonographs were cumbersome contraptions, and recording wasn't yet the primary method of disseminating popular music. None of the key instruments used in the recording—from drum kits to digital synthesizers—had been invented. Moreover, the idea of a rhythm section—a diverse group of chord, bass, and percussion instruments providing consistent rhythmic and harmonic support—would become an essential component of popular music only in the 1920s. The sound system—on video and in live performance—would have been comparably unfamiliar. Even the very identity of the song is fundamentally different. "Thriller" is what is on the recording; no sheet music version can begin to convey what the song is about.

18-2B The Fragmentation of Classical Music

In 1958, an article by the American composer Milton Babbitt, entitled "Who Cares If You Listen?," appeared in *High Fidelity* magazine. In it, he argued passionately for the composer's right to follow his muse no matter where it led, even if he ended up alienating most of his potential audience. Babbitt, a pioneer in electronic music, was a professor at Princeton, so he didn't have to rely on income from performances and sales of his music to survive. Universities and other secular institutions had become the new sponsors of classical music; their support liberated composers from having to please a specific patron or a general audience. Babbitt's attitude was a radical departure from the composer–audience relationship of previous generations and one of the products of the fragmentation of the classical music world in the twentieth century.

From the late seventeenth century through the end of the nineteenth, European music and the music from the Americas that was derived from it had shared a common musical language. There were numerous dialects and levels of sophistication—contrast the songs of Schubert, Schumann, and Brahms with the minstrel-show songs of Stephen Foster, for instance—but there seemed to be a collective understanding regarding what music was and what it should express: from the use of common practice harmony and the organization of rhythm through regular meter to the choice of instruments and how they should be played. Even the then-futuristic music of Wagner and Strauss used these assumptions as a point of departure.

All such assumptions came under assault throughout the twentieth century. The bold departures from conventional practice heard in the music of such early twentieth-century composers as Schoenberg, Debussy, Stravinsky, Bartók, and Ives set the tone for the century. For the "modern" composer, innovation became the overriding virtue; the highest distinction among a composer's peers was membership in the avant-garde.

For much of the century, composers suffered under the burden of novelty. Novelty trumped accessibility, artistry, and other elements of musical appeal as a source of status among peers, although it did not guarantee regular performances in the established concert world. Most of the innovators in early twentieth-century music drew on the world around them, crafting these available materials in strikingly new ways. However, as the century progressed, the most prestigious modes of composition,

At the turn of the twentieth century, most song revenue came from sheet music sales.

at least among the avant-garde, were those completely divorced from vernacular traditions and the language of eighteenth- and nineteenth-century music. Over time, a compositional pecking order took shape. Those who rejected the musical past and present in the interest of moving forward, most notably the Austrian composer Anton Webern and those who built on his legacy, enjoyed the greatest prestige, at least among high-minded artists and intellectuals. More musically "conservative" composers, such as the Finnish composer Jean Sibelius, and early "crossover" classical–popular composers, such as George Gershwin, were much lower down. This trend peaked in the years following World War II, as composers such as Stravinsky embraced new genres like serialism and a new generation of composers created music that was often conceptually stimulating but challenging even to musically sophisticated audiences. The continuous striving for innovation broadened the gap between the avant-garde and the general public. This in turn all but stopped the assimilation of new music into the standard repertoire. Even at the beginning of the twenty-first century, very little of the music composed since 1945 in the most popular genres—operas, choral works, ballets, orchestral music, chamber music, songs, and solo piano music—has received regular performances.

New directions, many inspired by rock, world music, and reclamation of the classical past, have begun to reverse this trend. It is as if those composers who created this music were now saying, "Yes, we do care whether people listen to our music."

18-2C A World of Music: Folk Traditions in the Twentieth Century

Beginning in 1905, the Hungarian composers Béla Bartók and Zoltan Kodály traveled throughout Hungary collecting the songs and dances of peasants in rural areas. They used primitive recording equipment to preserve these folk materials. Eventually, Bartók would travel throughout eastern Europe in search of folk music of diverse cultures. Bartók and Kodály were not alone: throughout the century, musicians and folklorists traveled throughout Europe and the Americas collecting folk music of all kinds. Improvements in travel, mass communication, and sound recording made music from around the world—East India, Africa, the Middle East, and Southeast Asia—increasingly accessible; sound and video recordings preserved this music for future generations. Indeed, ethnomusicology, the study of music within particular cultures, is largely a twentieth-century discipline.

The study and preservation of folk music of the world have shaped musical life in the twentieth century in several important ways. The diligent work of folk researchers has made available a body of music that many have found inherently interesting. Because it often builds on quite different assumptions about the nature and

ethnomusicology The study of music within particular cultures

function of music, it has helped expand our view of what music is. And because it has so often been an integral part of daily life, it can provide insight into different cultures. Collectively, its influence on twentieth-century music has been pervasive, touching all but the most abstruse styles.

The embrace of folk traditions and the music that they helped shape has been the counter point to the cold exclusivity of avant-garde music. Even more than the growth of popular music, it undermined the hierarchy of musical status that Western culture inherited from the nineteenth century. Assumptions of relative musical worth that seemed to be unquestionable at the beginning of the century were scrutinized and challenged during the course of the century: jazz, a music profoundly influenced by a folk tradition, was seen as a corrupting influence in the early years of the twentieth century; by the end of the century, it had become "America's art music." Jazz's dramatic rise in status was a consequence not only of its musical development but also of a shift in cultural attitudes toward musical worth: "art" in music no longer depended on its coming from Europe.

18-2D Beyond Category: Dissolving Musical and Cultural Boundaries

When one considers characteristic sounds and contexts, the distinctions among classical, popular, and folk music during the first few decades of the twentieth century seem as sharply defined as the differences among the three primary colors. The distinctions among audiences seemed just as clear: classical music was upper-class music; popular music served the ever-expanding middle class; and folk music belonged to the rural working classes.

However, such distinctions simply describe tendencies, not mutually exclusive categories; the boundaries between these differing types of music were not impermeable. Guardians of "musical decency and moral rectitude" fought a losing battle against the irrepressible advance of ragtime, then blues and jazz. Indeed, blues singer Bessie Smith became the darling of New York sophisticates during the 1920s. And Scott Joplin would receive a posthumous Pulitzer Prize in 1976 for his opera *Treemonisha*.

The cross-pollination among classical, popular, and folk goes back centuries: our first encounters came in medieval dance music and Josquin's use of "L'homme armé." Two early twentieth-century developments significantly altered the relationship among these traditions. The more pervasive of these was the impact of sound recording. It preserved music of all kinds and, over time, made authentic versions more widely available. This in turn facilitated interactions among musical traditions.

The other development, more specific and particularly American, was the creation of music that effectively dissolved the boundaries between traditions. Gershwin's opera and orchestral music; the musical theater works of Leonard Bernstein and Stephen Sondheim;

and the film music of John Williams: all inhabit their own musical worlds, which draw on multiple traditions but—from a purely musical perspective—do not belong primarily to any one.

If the classical, popular, and folk traditions are analogous to the three primary colors, then the products of their interaction are comparable to the millions of color combinations available on computer displays. The extraordinary diversity of musical life at the end of the century was literally unimaginable at the beginning. This diversity has cultural, geographical, and temporal dimensions—we have music from all over the world, from all strata of society. Moreover, through scrupulous musicological research, we have far better access to the music of the past: we can access more of the music of Bach's time than Bach could.

18-3 What Is Twentieth-Century Music?

It was possible to describe the changes in musical style from the eighteenth to the nineteenth century—from Classical to Romantic—as an evolutionary process: Romantic music proceeded directly from Classical music, although it would soon project a very different set of values. But just as the idea of such musical evolution was gaining widespread acceptance in Western culture (even Wagner's "music of the future" assumed that music evolves), the revolutionary developments of the early twentieth century rendered it invalid. The eighteenth and nineteenth centuries' most basic assumptions about music are overturned; non-European musical traditions blend with the European; and a relentless quest for novelty begins.

Fragmentation, not continuity, is the hallmark of twentieth-century music. To give some sense of the magnitude of the change, we highlight twentieth-century innovations in the elements of music.

18-3A Sound: New Instruments, Sounds, and Sound Combinations

The expanded sound world of the twentieth century came from a host of innovations: new instruments, new vocal and instrumental sounds, new combinations of instruments, even a broader understanding of what constitutes a "musical" sound.

Most of the instruments whose sounds were new to twentieth-century European and American ears came from technological innovations or non-European cultures. The only section of the orchestra that would grow significantly

in the twentieth century was the percussion section, which often incorporated instruments from around the world. However, the most significant new percussion instrument was the drum kit. The instruments were not new, but when assembled into a unit that one person could play, the drum kit enabled a drummer to create rhythms virtually impossible to coordinate among several players.

A host of new vocal sounds also appeared throughout the century. Some involved finding a middle ground between speech and singing: Schoenberg's *Sprechstimme* (speech voice) and rap have this in common. Others evolved in response to new or newly popular genres and new technologies: crooning in popular singing and belting in musical theater; the moaning of the blues singer and the twang of country vocals; nonverbal vocal sounds used in avant-garde music; screaming in heavy metal and punk.

Musicians coaxed new sounds from conventional instruments in a variety of ways. Jazz and popular saxophonists invented new timbres far removed from "classical" models. Jazz trumpeters and trombonists did the same and added even more variety through the use of mutes such as the toilet plunger. John Cage and others produced sounds from the piano by strumming the piano strings directly or altering the sound by putting bolts, erasers, and other objects between the strings. Guitarists created a new, more vocal sound on their instrument by using the neck of a beer bottle. "Found" sounds ranged from the washboards used as a percussion instrument through much of the American South and the cowbells and gourds used in Cuban music to the everyday sounds recorded for some compositions.

18-3B Harmony: New Modes of Pitch Organization

From the beginning of recorded musical history to the beginning of the twentieth century, the most basic assumption about pitch organization was that music is organized around a tonic, or home key. We encountered it first in Hildegard's antiphon and then in every subsequent example. The development of polyphony would eventually lead to an even stronger way to convey a sense of key. For the better part of two centuries, common practice harmony was an almost universal method of pitch organization. However, by the beginning of the twentieth century, traditional expressions of this practice had become the stalest and most conventional of several approaches to pitch organization. Its most common outlets were conservative church music, children's song accompaniments,

© vidguten/ShutterStock.com

"Found" sounds included the cowbells used in Cuban music.

and the blander sort of popular music. Far more exciting were novel modes of pitch organization, which appeared almost simultaneously during the first few decades of the twentieth century.

The most obviously radical new approach was atonality, the principle of avoiding both the tonic and its corollary: organizing harmony and melody so as to move away from and return to the tonic in a coherent fashion. In practice, it took several forms. After two decades of experimentation, Arnold Schoenberg developed serial composition, an approach based on maintaining a strict sequence in presenting the twelve different pitches within the octave.

Less jarring but just as revolutionary were approaches that still focused around a tonic pitch but used differing methods to establish, move away from, and return to the tonic. In some instances, this involved using familiar harmonies in unfamiliar ways, in settings as diverse as the blues and the music of Debussy, Stravinsky, and Bartók. Other approaches included adapting different scales, such as the modal scales of English folk music and the pentatonic scales of African and Chinese music, and building harmonies from them. Even more radical approaches, including dividing the octave into exceedingly small intervals and abandoning pitched sounds entirely, began to appear in the 1920s and 1930s. By mid-century, it was hard to imagine any option for pitch organization that hadn't been explored. More significantly, there was no dominant harmonic practice, as there had been in the previous centuries. An ever-increasing range of possibilities coexisted, sometimes creatively, sometimes uneasily.

18-3C Melody

Melody was at the heart of nineteenth-century music. There were few successful works that didn't have an appealing, singable melody. Even Wagner, who largely avoided tuneful melodies, nevertheless built his works around memorable melodic material. And in vernacular music, popular song was king.

As with the other elements, a proliferation of new or radically altered options emerged in the twentieth century, from simple repetitive motives to angular, wide-ranging melodic lines that were difficult, if not impossible, to sing. Moreover, there was a large body of music that had no discernible melody, from some of the experimental music composed in the middle of the century to techno and rap.

What also changed was the idea that melody should be the expressive focus of a composition. With the development of new rhythmic approaches, especially from Afrocentric cultures and the relentless search for—and delight in—new sounds, it was no longer necessary, or at times even desirable, for melody to be the main focus. Continual improvement in sound

atonality The principle of avoiding both the tonic and its corollary; organizing harmony and melody so as to move away from and return to the tonic in a coherent fashion

recording and playback supported this shift in balance away from melody toward rhythm and sound.

Conventional melodies, in popular song, folk music, and classical compositions, still found a large and receptive audience. But these had become a few among many options.

18-3D Rhythm

The changes in rhythm from the nineteenth to the twentieth century were just as revolutionary and far-reaching as those in pitch and sound, but for a different reason. The most extreme changes, such as the extension of serial procedures to rhythm and the reliance on chance (as in Cage's *4'33"*), completely removed the rhythms of a musical work from its origins in regular movements like those of dancing, marching, or walking. However, the far more pervasive change was the emergence of a new rhythmic paradigm, which blended the metrical structure of European music with an African rhythmic conception. This new rhythmic approach entered the mainstream musical world through ragtime; its gradual accretion of African features would drive the evolution of popular music and also influence classical music. Other rhythmic approaches from outside the central European world typified by Strauss's waltzes also gained traction among classical music composers—for example, the irregular rhythms of eastern Europe inspired Bartók and others.

Characteristic of virtually all of these innovations in rhythmic organization was an increase in complexity. The precisely timed events in electronic music; the improvised interplay of jazz musicians; the pulsing and propulsive rhythms of Stravinsky, Bartók, and Copland; the complex, irregular, and syncopated rhythmic layers of salsa—these and so many other trends in music reflect the rhythmic sophistication of twentieth- century music.

Rhythm, largely subordinate to melody as a source of musical interest in the eighteenth and nineteenth centuries, became more prominent in twentieth-century music; many times, it was the dominant element.

Rhythms in the music of the eighteenth and nineteenth centuries organized musical time hierarchically, much as our system of measuring time organizes it into seconds, minutes, and hours. The emergence of other rhythmic conceptions from Africa, India, eastern Europe, the Americas, and Asia made it clear in retrospect that the comparatively simple metrical hierarchies of European music were the exception among the musics of the world.

18-3E Form: Where Is It?

As they listened to the sonatas and symphonies of Mozart, Haydn, and their contemporaries, eighteenth-century audiences could generally tell where they were in the music. Convention dictated the number and sequence of movements as well as the sequence of events within a movement. Even spontaneous events, such as the cadenza in a concerto movement, occurred within a carefully scripted framework. Performers and listeners expected that a movement or piece would begin and end decisively in the home key, with milestones along the way clearly defined by cadences. It was always easy to keep one's bearings.

The idea that a movement or work should be a coherent, clearly defined musical statement came under attack in the nineteenth century: the spooky beginning of the last movement of Berlioz's *Symphonie fantastique* is a familiar instance of this. More progressive composers expanded the frame and blurred its edges: Wagner's *Tristan and Isolde* begins with a famously ambiguous motive and chord and doesn't resolve to the tonic chord until the very end of the opera, several hours later. Nevertheless, for the most part composers did not abandon the idea that a musical composition meant a coherent narrative developed from a central idea.

By the turn of the century, this formal edifice was riddled with cracks; radically different methods of organizing music soon reduced it to rubble. In classical music, several new conceptions of form emerged in the first two decades of the twentieth century. Some—Ives's collage-like forms, Debussy's cinematic forms, Stravinsky's cubist-inspired forms—challenged the essentially linear progression of events. Atonal music removed the harmonic underpinnings from form, dissolving the framework that had previously been so crucial in shaping form. Afrocentric vernacular music, especially blues and jazz, adapted conventional variation form into a modular, open form.

Even more radical approaches to form emerged during the century, especially after World War II. In the music of some avant-garde composers, form could be predetermined by something as rigorous as a mathematical formula or left largely in the hands of the performer—or the environment. Both options challenged the very idea that a musical work was a self-contained entity with a beginning and an end. A parallel trend developed in vernacular music during the rock era. Fade-out endings, open-ended opening vamps, and internally extensible forms (heard in almost any James Brown live performance) also undermined the idea of a rigid framework.

Post-disco dance tracks went further, breaking down the idea of a song as a discrete entity; typically, they became part of a much longer mix. Some genres still used the closed forms of the eighteenth and nineteenth centuries, but they had become only one option among many.

Looking Back, Looking Ahead

Billboard magazine, founded in 1894, began covering the entertainment industry in 1900. In 1936, it began to chart the popularity of popular songs by noting how frequently the top songs were performed on the three big radio networks. Its first chart for record sales appeared in 1940. By the end of the century, *Billboard* featured over twenty different charts (the number typically varied from issue to issue), including charts for "classical," "classical crossover," and "world" and several Latin music charts. Because these charts consider only genres with relatively substantial sales, they don't even fully represent the diversity of musical life at the end of the century. At the beginning of the twentieth century, only the most forward-seeing thinker could have imagined the variety of today's recordings, their quality, and the ease with which they can be obtained and played back.

It would take an even more prescient individual to predict the major developments of the twentieth century: the pervasive impact of technology, the rise of popular music and the growth of the music business, the new developments from almost every corner of the musical world that challenged the most basic assumptions about music. Those who have grown up in the digital age have inherited a musical world quite different in every respect from that of a century ago. What seems normal today was revolutionary at mid-century and all but unimaginable at the beginning of the twentieth century. The radical developments in thinking about, creating, performing, and listening to music have produced a musical world without precedent.

 study tools 18

Ready to study?
In the book you can:

- Review Learning Outcome answers and Glossary terms with the tear-out Chapter Review card.

Or you can go online to CourseMate, at www.cengagebrain.com, for these resources:

- Chapter Quizzes to prepare for tests

- Interactive flashcards of all Glossary terms

- Active Listening Guides, streaming music, and YouTube playlists

- An eBook with live links to all web resources

what is twentieth-century music? | **257**

LEARNING OUTCOMES

After reading this chapter, you will be able to do the following:

19-1 Describe the traits of expressionist music and atonality through an understanding of the music of Arnold Schoenberg.

19-2 Become familiar with impressionism in the arts, specifically in the music of Claude Debussy.

19-3 Hear how composers such as Igor Stravinsky embedded "primitive" elements in ultramodern settings.

 study tools

After you read this chapter, go to the Study Tools at the end of the chapter, page 273.

I n the nineteenth century, the suffix "-ism" was increasingly used to identify a particular belief system or set of principles: both "Classicism" and "Romanticism" were nineteenth-century terms. So were more focused musical developments, such as nationalism, realism, and even Wagnerism.

Around 1900, a wave of new "isms" rattled the foundations of the classical music world: the expressionism of Schoenberg and Berg, the impressionism of Debussy and Ravel, and the primitivism of Stravinsky developed at more or less the same time. These composers abandoned such fundamental aspects of nineteenth-century music as common practice harmony and regular meter; with the disappearance of those practices, the idea of coherent, comprehensible music based on them also disappeared. These composers spoke different musical languages, and their work challenged long-held ideas about what music could say and how it could say it. Their strongest common bond was what they were not: conventional continuations of what had gone before.

LEARNING OUTCOME 19-1

Describe the traits of expressionist music and atonality through an understanding of the music of Arnold Schoenberg.

19-1 Expressionism

In a letter to the painter Wassily Kandinsky early in 1911, composer Arnold Schoenberg asserted, "Every formal procedure which aspires to traditional effects is not completely free from conscious motivation. But art belongs to the unconscious!" At age thirty, Kandinsky (1866–1944), a Russian by birth, had declined law professorship, moved to Munich, and begun studying art. Over the next fifteen years, Kandinsky's art would become increasingly abstract. By the time he met Schoenberg, his work was almost completely abstract, bearing little relationship to objects in the real world.

> "Art belongs to the unconscious!"
> —Arnold Schoenberg

On January 2, 1911, Kandinsky attended a concert of Schoenberg's music in Munich. The experience sparked two responses. One was an abstract painting entitled *Impression No. 3 (Concert)*. The other was an enthusiastic letter to Schoenberg in which the artist stated, "In your works, you have realized what I . . . have so greatly longed for in music. The independent progress through their own destinies, the independent life of the individual voices in your compositions, is exactly what I am trying to find in my paintings."

Kandinsky's letter sparked a lifelong friendship between the two, which was particularly intense during the three years before World War I. It was a mutual admiration society in which both men crossed artistic boundaries. Kandinsky, the painter, had studied piano and cello and was enthusiastic about new music. Schoenberg, the composer, painted prolifically during this time, studying with the Austrian painter Richard Gerstl (who committed suicide after Schoenberg's wife, Mathilde, broke off an affair with him to return to her husband). Kandinsky, an adept organizer as well as an avant-garde artist, organized Der Blaue Reiter (The Blue Rider), a group of like-minded artists, later in 1911 and invited Schoenberg to show his artwork in the group's first exhibition.

19-1A Arnold Schoenberg, Musical Expressionism, and Atonality

Expressionism was a late nineteenth- and early twentieth-century movement in the arts that sought to convey, to

De Agostini/A. Dagli Orti/Getty Images

A self-portrait: Schoenberg by Schoenberg

express, the deep emotions that lie under the surface of—and are often obscured by—objective reality. Expressionist artists often achieved this by portraying scenes of intense emotion or grotesque images, using distorted and exaggerated gestures. In Kandinsky's painting, there is a suggestion of the lid of a piano and of audience members, but the bold gestures and the strong opposition of colors represent his response to Schoenberg's music. In effect, the painting inverts the relationship between the subject and its representation. In a representational painting, the goal is to represent the subject as accurately and precisely as possible. The elements of art—line, color, texture—are all in the service of this goal. Here, however,

expressionism Late nineteenth- and early twentieth-century movement in the arts that sought to convey the deep emotions that lie under the surface of—and are often obscured by—objective reality

▶Arnold Schoenberg

FAST FACTS

- Dates: 1874–1951
- Place: Vienna, Austria
- Reasons to remember:
  One of the leading
  avant-garde expression-
  ist composers of the
  early twentieth century;
  a pioneering composer of atonal music

Omikron Omikron/Photo Researchers/ Getty Images

> ⌐"It is impossible
> for a person to have
> only one sensa-
> tion at a time. One
> has thousands
> simultaneously."
> –Arnold Schoenberg⌐

the message lies in the elements themselves—most strikingly, in the bold patches of color. The subject is simply a medium for these emotions expressed through these elements.

Color was an important component of Schoenberg's music as well during the years before World War I. Indeed, the third of his five pieces for orchestra, composed in 1909, is entitled "Farben" ("Colors"). Vivid tone colors would become one component of his approach to musical expressionism. Another was atonality, as he mentioned frequently in his correspondence.

Arnold Schoenberg  was born and raised in the Vienna of Brahms and Johann Strauss Jr. His hunger for learning overcame his family's lack of financial resources and background in music; he received much of his training in music from like-minded friends rather than through formal study. In his early years, he moved back and forth between Vienna and Berlin in an effort to find work that would allow him to compose. He managed to scrape by through teaching and various musical odd jobs—orchestrating operettas and working at an avant-garde cabaret; he received far less income than notoriety for his compositions.

Schoenberg's first important compositions show the overwhelming influence of Wagner. As his music evolved, he came to view atonality as an inevitable continuation of Wagner's innovations. Schoenberg proclaimed the "emancipation of dissonance" in theory (in *Harmonielehre*, his 1911 textbook on harmony) and practice, in music that evolved from the lush late Romantic style of his early works to the freely atonal music that he composed just prior to the outbreak of World War I.

19-1B Schoenberg the Musical Expressionist

In a 1909 letter to the Italian composer Ferrucio Busoni, Schoenberg wrote, "It is *impossible* for a person to have only *one* sensation at a time. One has *thousands*

simultaneously." He concludes by saying that his music "should be an expression of feeling, as our feelings, which bring us in contact with our subconscious, really are, and no false child of feelings and 'conscious logic.'"

Schoenberg's letter was in essence a manifesto for musical expressionism. He makes clear that he wants his music to be a gateway to the psyche. His interest in the subconscious was in step with the most advanced thinking of the era. And it was very much part of his world: at the turn of the century, Vienna was home to Sigmund Freud as well as Schoenberg, and Freud's writings had attracted widespread interest.

Three years later, Schoenberg composed *Pierrot lunaire*, a setting of twenty-one poems for voice and small ensemble. Particularly in these works, which feature a solo voice supported by an instrumental ensemble, Schoenberg explored the psychological underpinnings of musical expressionism. He conveyed the "thousands of sensations" mainly through two complementary strategies: the intensification of what had been, in the works of earlier composers, mainly coloristic elements and the abandonment of tonality.

19-1C Schoenberg and Atonality

Atonal music is music that is not tonal in that it does not organize pitches around a tonic, or home key. The first atonal music in Western culture appeared just after the turn of the twentieth century, most notably in the compositions of Schoenberg. In abandoning tonality of any kind, Schoenberg left behind a musical tradition that reached back more than a millennium; his was the most radical change in pitch organization in the history of music. What made it seem even more radical was that it was both a consequence and a negation of the most sophisticated mode of organizing pitch in human history up to that point: common practice harmony.

Common practice harmony has been the most sophisticated method of pitch organization in history because it is the only one that makes syntactic musical organization possible: by the early eighteenth century it had acquired a sense of predictability that parallels syntax in language. So, just as syntax makes it possible for us to organize words into phrases, sentences, paragraphs, chapters, and books, common practice harmony makes it possible to organize music hierarchically into coherent statements. The statements can range in length from a minute or two to more than an hour.

As Schoenberg noted in his letter to Busoni, harmony can be both structural and expressive. The familiar progressions of common practice harmony give musical statements coherence but do not necessarily convey deep feeling. Conventional two- or three-chord accompaniment patterns, such as those used to harmonize simple songs, are easily grasped but emotionally neutral. Expression in harmony comes from defying the expected. Emotionally charged works such as Beethoven's Fifth Symphony use basic structures only as a framework; their power comes in part from elaboration, disruption, and expansion of structural conventions.

During the nineteenth century, even as everyday music (popular song and dance, hymns, parlor music, children's songs, marches) stayed harmonically "scientific," classical composers broke away from these conventions in search of more powerfully and individually expressive music: we heard this particularly in the music of Berlioz and Wagner, who stretched tonality to its limits. However, neither they nor any other significant nineteenth-century composer completely abandoned tonality.

Atonality, as presented in Schoenberg's music, abandons any sense of key, and with it all those conventions associated with tonal music that help orient the listener. As a result, much of the musical meaning arises from more elementally expressive aspects of the music: the shape of the melodic line, the flow of the rhythm, the register within which a voice or instrument operates, and fluctuations in dynamics. This corresponds to the expressionist focus on line, color, texture, and other elements in painting at the expense of realistic depiction of the subject. By closing the door to tonality, Schoenberg opened the door to new, more intense forms of expression.

Given the course of nineteenth-century art music, atonality was, in a way, historically inevitable. Indeed, we will shortly encounter atonal music in works by Debussy, Stravinsky, and Ives. But no composer embraced it as fully as Schoenberg, who came to atonality gradually and painstakingly. That he chose to do so even as he became deeply immersed in painting suggests that atonality was one dimension of a broader

Atonality abandons any sense of key.

effort to adapt the expressionist aesthetic to music. Its complement was the intensification of the most basic musical elements.

19-1D Intense Colors and Expressive Extremes: *Pierrot lunaire*

In his early atonal works for multiple instruments, such as *Pierrot lunaire*, Schoenberg heightens the coloristic qualities of his music through strong timbral contrasts and unusual timbral effects. *Pierrot lunaire* requires six performers: a vocalist and five instrumentalists who play flute or piccolo, clarinet or bass clarinet, violin or viola, cello, and piano. The timbres of the instruments contrast rather than blend; the doubling effectively extends the range of each instrument's particular timbre. The most striking of the timbral effects is the vocal style, which Schoenberg called *Sprechstimme*, "speech voice." Although Schoenberg notated both pitch and rhythm, the vocalist must cultivate a sound that lies somewhere between speech and singing. The instruments, particularly the string instruments, produce unusual sounds: in "Nacht," one of the *Pierrot* poems, the cellist must bow the string virtually at the bridge, which produces an ethereal sound. The strong contrasts in timbre highlight the emphasis on extremes found in virtually every element. That they are compressed into a short time span makes them even more powerful, as we hear in an excerpt from *Pierrot lunaire*.

Pierrot lunaire is a chamber work for voice and instruments. At the time of its premiere in 1912, it was very much in the avant-garde, but its inspiration traces back to a centuries-old theatrical tradition: *commedia dell'arte*.

Sprechstimme "Speechvoice"; vocal style between speech and singing required in Arnold Schoenberg's music

Commedia dell'arte. The Pierrot (French, perhaps derived from the name Peter) of Schoenberg's work is one of the stock characters in *commedia dell'arte*, "comedy of the artists," a type of improvised theater that developed in Italy during the fifteenth century. In *commedia dell'arte*, troupes of professional actors traveled from town to town, portraying stock characters by wearing masks and costumes and acting out familiar story lines. Several of the characters—Harlequin, Columbine, Pulcinella, and Pierrot—became symbols of particular types of behavior. Pierrot is typically either foolish or lovesick, or both. *Lunaire*, like *lunatic*, comes from *luna*, the Latin word for "moon." Both refer to the myth that blames a full moon for moments of temporary insanity or foolishness: those who are "moonstruck" seem to lose their minds momentarily, usually because of romantic infatuation.

Commedia dell'arte soon became popular throughout Europe, and its characters and conventions infiltrated the culture. For example, the word *slapstick* originally referred to slapping two pieces of wood together; it was one of many comedic devices used by *commedia dell'arte* clowns. Over time, it has come to refer to any physical humor based on clumsy actions. Harlequin, the clown who typically slapped the sticks, wore a costume featuring diamond shapes in varying colors; the word *harlequin* can now also refer to an irregular color scheme.

Beginning in the latter part of the nineteenth century, artists, writers, and musicians rediscovered *commedia dell'arte*, not so much as an entertainment per se but as part of a larger movement that used patently unreal characters to explore the disconnect between appearance and reality. Petrushka is a Russian puppet who comes to life in Igor Stravinsky's 1911 ballet of the same name. Ruggero Leoncavallo's 1892 *verismo* opera *Pagliacci* (*pagliacci* means "clowns" in Italian), which involves characters in a *commedia dell'arte* troupe, predates Schoenberg's *Pierrot lunaire* by two decades. In each case, the composition portrays the emotions hidden below the surface—whether the character is a puppet or a clown.

From Poems to Music. The source of the text for *Pierrot lunaire* was a group of fifty poems by the Belgian writer Albert Giraud; Schoenberg encountered them in a translation from French to German by Otto Erich Hartleben. Giraud's poems stimulated Schoenberg's imagination. In his diary, he noted, "read the foreword, looked at the poems, am enthusiastic," and he completed the work in less than three months. From the fifty poems, Schoenberg selected

commedia dell'arte "Comedy of the artists [of improvisation]"; a type of improvised theater that developed in Italy during the fifteenth century

Pierrot, the lovesick clown of *commedia dell'arte*

twenty-one, which he organized into three groups of seven. Schoenberg's subtitle to the work is "Three Times Seven Poems by Albert Giraud."

Giraud subtitled his group of poems *Rondels bergamasques*. A rondel is a strict poetic form. In the rondel "Nacht," for instance, the opening is repeated halfway through and at the end, creating a form similar to musical ABA form:

Sinister, black, giant moths
deadened the sun's radiance.
A closed book of spells,
⸺ the horizon sleeps—in silence.

From the smoke of lost depths
rises a fragrance, memories
murdered!
Sinister, black, giant moths
deadened the sun's radiance.

And from heaven earthward
with heavy leaps descend
invisible monsters
into the human hearts below . . .
Sinister, black, giant moths.

The combination of such strict form with such grotesque imagery seems to have appealed to Schoenberg's compositional aesthetic. Schoenberg knew he was a revolutionary, but he also saw himself as an evolutionary composer. In some of his most revolutionary works—not only *Pierrot* but also his later piano suite—he makes use of traditional forms and genres, as if to counterbalance the more radical elements of his music.

 **LISTEN UP!**

Schoenberg, "Nacht," *Pierrot lunaire* (1912)

TAKEAWAY POINT: Celebrated example of musical expressionism

STYLE: Expressionist

FORM: Passacaglia (variation form)

GENRE: Chamber music

INSTRUMENTS: Voice (using *Sprechstimme*) plus bass clarinet, cello, and piano (work features flute/piccolo, clarinet/bass clarinet, violin/viola, cello, and piano)

CONTEXT: Avant-garde musical work influenced by Freud's psychoanalysis, which portrays the deep emotions that lie below conscious awareness.

0:00   Extended instrumental introduction: darkness of night suggested by extremely slow tempo, plus instruments in low register. First three notes on piano form melodic kernel used throughout the piece.

A

0:23   Dark mood prevails behind vocalist's spoken/sung narration of the first four lines.

Finstre, schwarze Riesenfalter	Sinister, black, giant moths
töteten der Sonne Glanz.	deadened the sun's radiance.

0:39   Notice the ethereal cello sound at the end, behind "verschwiegen."

Ein geschlossnes Zauberbuch,	A closed book of spells,
ruht der Horizont—verschwiegen.	the horizon sleeps—in silence.

B

1:03   Suddenly more active and in a higher register; three-note kernel is used over and over in piano part.

Aus dem Qualm verlorner Tiefen	From the smoke of lost depths
steigt ein Duft, Erinnrung mordend!	rises a fragrance, memories murdered!

1:14   Big crescendo to end of section

Finstre, schwarze Reisenfalter	Sinister, black, giant moths
töteten der Sonne Glanz.	deadened the sun's radiance.

C

1:30   Gradual descent to dark sound of opening underscores descent of monstrous moths described in the poem.

Und vom Himmel erdenwärts	And from heaven earthward
senken sich mit schweren Schwingen	with heavy leaps descend
unsichtbar die Ungetume	invisible monsters
auf die Menschenherzen nieder . . .	into the human hearts below . . .
Finstre, schwarze Riesenfalter.	Sinister, black, giant moths.

END

2:05   Single note from bass clarinet abruptly ends the piece: the aural counterpart to a period at the end of a sentence. Or it might suggest waking abruptly from a nightmare.

 Listen to this selection streaming or in an Active Listening Guide at CourseMate or in the eBook.

"Nacht" is his take on a passacaglia, a centuries-old variation form.

Like the poems themselves, the individual movements of *Pierrot lunaire* are short, because the vocalist declaims the text using Schoenberg's distinctive Sprechstimme. No movement takes more than three minutes to perform, and the entire work amounts to only about thirty-five minutes of music. We consider "Nacht," the first poem in the second group and the eighth movement overall (see Listen Up!).

Schoenberg's emphasis on bold melodic lines, distinctive and sharply contrasting tone colors, and extremes in virtually every element is comparable to expressionist artists' highlighting color and gesture over representation. Similarly, his abandonment of tonality is akin to abandoning language at moments of great intensity: a scream is exactly such a nonverbal sound. In *Pierrot lunaire* and many of his other important works, Schoenberg relies on the text for coherence. In this instance, the text is coherent only in a syntactic sense; what it portrays is nightmarish. Using tonal harmony—even the richly chromatic harmony of Wagner and Schoenberg's earlier works—would have introduced a sense of normalcy that would be at cross purposes with the intent of the poems and with Schoenberg's expressive intent.

Expressionist music, as realized by Schoenberg in *Pierrot lunaire*, seeks to portray the turmoil of a troubled psyche by intensifying the most elemental aspects of music—pulse, tone color, pitch, dynamics—and disorienting the listener by avoiding tonality. Both were radical developments that succeeded in *Pierrot lunaire*. The work was largely successful during and immediately after its premiere, despite the hostility of many critics. It remains one of the most admired and influential works of the early twentieth century.

After composing *Pierrot lunaire* in 1912, Schoenberg went through an eight-year creative crisis brought about by the war (he was in and out of the Imperial Army because of his poor health) and by his need to develop a method of organizing the dissonance that he had recently emancipated. His twelve-tone method, first presented in a series of works composed during the early 1920s, would become the most influential new direction in the avant-garde for the next half-century.

19-2 Impressionism and Beyond

In 1911, the French composer Claude Debussy remarked to his colleague Edgard Varèse, "J'aime presque autant les images que la musique" ("I love pictures almost as much as music"). At the time he made this remark, Debussy was known throughout Europe as one of the most innovative composers of the new century. He had been labeled an "impressionist" composer for almost twenty-five years; members of the Institut de France first used the term in reference to his music in 1887. Debussy himself vacillated between using the term to describe his work and complaining of its inaccuracy. *Impressionism*

> ⌐"I love pictures almost as much as music."
> —Claude Debussy⌐

can succinctly describe some of Debussy's music, but the term limits and misrepresents his output as a whole.

19-2A Claude Debussy, "Musicien parisien"

For a visually oriented composer like Debussy, Paris was the ideal place to be. It was a hotbed of artistic activity and a major center for a newly emerging film industry. Debussy would find inspiration in both.

Born in a town just outside Paris, Claude Debussy ♦ was enrolled at the age of ten in the Paris Conservatoire, where he studied piano and composition. Aside from a two-year stay in Rome (the result of winning the Prix de Rome, the Conservatoire's most prestigious award for young composers), pilgrimages to Bayreuth in his mid-twenties (like many other young composers of the time, he was briefly under the spell of Wagner's music; he would soon move away from it), and occasional trips to England (Debussy and his music were well received in England, and he was an ardent Anglophile), Debussy spent his life in and around Paris.

Turn-of-the-century Paris was an extraordinarily fertile artistic environment, one that embraced all the arts: the music of Debussy and his fellow composers; several new trends in painting; the sculpture of Rodin; the symbolist poetry of Verlaine and Mallarmé; and the first wave of important films, such as George Mèliés's much-viewed 1902 science-fiction fantasy, *A Trip to the Moon*.

Debussy was a regular visitor at the salons of the artistic elite, where he shared ideas with painters and poets alike. He was an avid fan of the cinema. For Debussy, films were not only an exciting new entertainment medium but also a source of national pride. French filmmakers were at the forefront of this new medium until World War I.

Debussy took in the world around him. And likewise, the world came to him, or at least to Paris; three "universal expositions," in 1878, 1889, and 1900, gave him the opportunity to hear Javanese gamelan music and other exotic sounds. He explored cultural life at all levels and brought his experiences into his music.

Although he never exhibited publicly as a visual artist—as Schoenberg did—Debussy was arguably the most visually oriented of the major composers. He channeled these influences into a musical aesthetic that in his mind embodied those qualities that are distinctively French: toward the end of his life, he referred to himself as *musicien français*.

Debussy composed successfully in most genres: opera (*Pelléas et Mélisande*); ballet (*Jeux*); numerous songs; chamber music; orchestral music, including the groundbreaking *Prelude to the Afternoon of a Faun*; and a wide range of piano music.

19-2B Painters in France: Impressionism and Beyond

It isn't unusual for technology to open up new possibilities within an art form. However, it's unusual for technology to establish a new art form that in turn liberates an established art. For visual artists in the latter part of the nineteenth century, the camera was a tool of liberation. Before the camera, the most common way to preserve an image in two dimensions was to draw or paint it. Accordingly, for centuries the first obligation of European artists had been to represent the subject of their artwork with some accuracy.

Like drawings or paintings, the camera could also capture images in two dimensions, and it did so much more quickly and with superior accuracy. Thus, when it emerged as a viable medium during the middle of the nineteenth century, the camera freed painters from the obligation to portray their subjects precisely.

Inspired especially by the English landscape painter J. M. W. Turner, a group of French painters, including Claude Monet, Pierre-Auguste Renoir, and Camille Pissarro, created paintings that focused on representing the perception of light and color rather than forms. Monet's work, for example, includes several series of paintings that show exactly the same scene—a cathedral or a haystack, for example—at different times of day. This revolutionary new direction inverted the relationship between the subject and its portrayal. Previously, painterly techniques had sought to represent the subject as artfully and expressively as possible; the focus was on the subject. For impressionist painters, the subject wasn't so much the focus as the vehicle for exploring elemental aspects of painting, especially light and color. The movement took its name indirectly from a Monet painting, *Impression: Sunrise,* which was part of the group's first exhibition in 1874. A critic reviewing the exhibition used the title of Monet's painting to identify the work of these artists. Although the critic used the term derisively, the group gave it a positive spin by adopting it to refer to their work. They continued to exhibit together until 1886; after that time, the artists elected to pursue different directions.

The impressionists freed all artists from both traditional subjects and conventional ways of representing them. The numerous postimpressionist directions in France (for example, the pointillism of Georges Seurat, the proto-cubism of Paul Cézanne, and Henri Toulouse-Lautrec's vivid portrayals of Parisian decadence) and throughout Europe (the German expressionists, the abstract art of Kandinsky, the Spanish painter Pablo Picasso's numerous shifts in style) all used the new aesthetics of impressionist art as a point of departure.

Claude Debussy was the French musician who was most responsive to these new directions in art. Along with Maurice Ravel, Debussy would create a musical analog to impressionist art. However, for both composers, impressionism was one option among many. In particular, the music of Debussy is extraordinarily varied in inspiration and realization.

Nowhere is this more evident than in his music for the piano. In part because he was a fluent pianist with a real affinity for the instrument, Debussy composed more

▶Claude Debussy
FAST FACTS

- Dates: 1862–1919
- Place: France
- Reasons to remember:
  One of the most innovative composers of the early twentieth century and the leading impressionist composer

Photo Researchers/Getty Images

extensively and more experimentally for the piano than for any other medium. His output for the instrument spans his entire career; it includes several multimovement sets plus two books of twelve preludes and twelve etudes. In keeping with his visual inclination, Debussy gave most works descriptive titles: indeed, two sets are entitled *Images.* In these pieces, Debussy presents an extraordinarily varied range of subjects and moods. There are landscapes and seascapes, personal portraits, musical still lifes, action movies, and much more. Some have slapstick humor; others are emotionally neutral. We sample Debussy's multifaceted musical personality in two of his preludes for piano. In "Voiles," we encounter the musical impressionist; in "Minstrels," the musical cinematographer.

19-2C Debussy the Impressionist

Debussy was still a boy when impressionist painters first exhibited together; he was in Rome when they mounted their last group show. As he matured as a composer, he rejected the oppressive influence of Wagner on French composition. For him, adapting the impressionist aesthetic to music was a way of asserting a distinctively French identity. The composer Erik Satie, who served as a mentor to Debussy early in his career, recalled that he had encouraged Debussy to help develop a music "without any sauerkraut" by following the lead of painters such as Monet, Cézanne, and Toulouse-Lautrec. And just as Monet's painting moved further away from faithful depiction of the subjects, Debussy's impressionist music moved away from the harmonic, rhythmic, and formal conventions of Romanticism toward evocation and color.

Debussy's self-imposed challenge went beyond simply translating image into sound; rather, it involved translating the handling of visual elements into sound. Further complicating this task are two essential differences between art and music. One is that artists use a concrete image—for example, a cathedral, a haystack, or water lilies—as a recognizable point of reference. By contrast, music is almost necessarily evocative rather than depictive. The

impressionism Late nineteenth- and early twentieth-century movement in the arts that favored exploration of elements such as light, color, and sound over literal representation

LISTEN UP!

Debussy, "Voiles," from *Préludes* (1909–1910)

TAKEAWAY POINT: Ideal example of musical impressionism

STYLE: Impressionist

FORM: Free ABA' form

GENRE: Piano prelude

INSTRUMENTS: Piano

CONTEXT: Music for the salon or concert hall

0:00	*First melodic idea:*	Lack of orientation: no accompaniment; no marking of the beat; no sense of tonic: melodic idea formed from whole-tone scale
0:20	*Second melodic idea:*	Another melodic strand, over a pedal point, then combined with the first idea
1:14	*Third melodic idea:*	Still another melodic fragment, combined with rocking accompaniment figure, building to a crest, then receding
1:41	*Second melodic idea:*	The setting is richer, with pedal points above and below
1:57	*Transition:*	Acceleration, then cinematic "dissolve" into the "storm" section
2:05	*"The storm":*	Switch to pentatonic scale; waves of sound, dissipating at the end
2:32	*Second melodic idea:*	Returns again in a new setting: pedal point plus "brushed" whole-tone scale accompaniment
2:59	*First melodic idea:*	Light chords preparing return of first melodic idea
3:11	*Ending:*	Middle register, simply recedes; ending not decisive

 Listen to this selection streaming or in an Active Listening Guide at CourseMate or in the eBook.

other is that art is static, freezing a moment in time, whereas music is dynamic, unfolding in time. Debussy's affinity for the visual made him sensitive to these differences and guided him in creating music that expressed the impressionist aesthetic.

19-2D "Voiles"

"Voiles" (see Listen Up!) is the second of twelve preludes included in Debussy's first book of *Préludes*, which he composed in 1909 and 1910. The title translates into English as "Sails" or "Veils." Debussy's title, placed at the end of the prelude rather than the beginning, leaves the interpretation deliberately ambiguous. The musical evidence suggests sails rather than veils.

Sailboats, particularly a regatta at Argenteuil, a municipality northwest of Paris, were a popular subject for impressionist painters during the 1870s: Claude Monet painted scenes from the regatta twice; Renoir, once. The first series of paintings, by Monet, shows several stages of an Argenteuil regatta. The most familiar shows the sailboats at rest, apparently awaiting the start. At that time, it is a sunny day. The sails reach high into the air and are reflected on the surface of the water. Another painting shows the regatta under way. The day has

whole-tone scale Scale that divides the octave into six equal segments a whole tone apart (A whole tone, or whole step, equals two half-steps.)

become overcast and breezy; the ships are leaning with the wind.

Debussy couldn't depict a sailboat in sound. So, to convey a scene similar to the one painted by Monet, he created a musical setting that captured essential features of such a scene: the lazy, hazy day and—more important—a boat that floats. To imply this requirement Debussy adopted a radical strategy: the pervasive use of a whole-tone scale, a scale that divides the octave into six equal segments a whole tone apart. (A whole tone, or whole step, equals two half-steps.) In this respect, it differs from the other scales we have encountered: major and minor, modal, and pentatonic—all of which feature asymmetrical patterns of whole and half-steps.

In "Voiles," Debussy weaves together short melodic strands drawn from the whole-tone scale at the beginning and end of the prelude; a brief middle section (high winds) makes use of a pentatonic scale. How does the whole-tone scale convey a sense of floating? By avoiding a tonic, and the melodic, harmonic, and rhythmic events that establish and confirm the tonic. Recall that cadences are the musical events that confirm tonics and that the word *cadence* comes from the Latin word *cadere*, "to fall." Because they provide harmonic, rhythmic, and formal orientation, cadences affirm the pull of musical gravity. By avoiding not only cadences but also the scales and chords from which cadences are formed, Debussy defies musical gravity; the music floats from beginning to end. He complements this harmonic floating with rhythms that float over the pulse.

In this prelude, Debussy follows Monet's lead in his approach to melody. During the course of his career, Monet's art moved away from line toward texture. If we view Monet's later paintings at close range, all we see are dabs of various colors; only at some distance does the image come into focus. Similarly, Debussy's musical impressionism evolved away from the longer melodic lines of his earlier works to fragments—even wisps—of melodic material layered to form rich textures of sound.

Monet, *Regatta at Argenteuil* (1872)

19-2E Debussy the Cinematographer

If "Voiles" exemplifies Debussy's musical impressionism, then "Minstrels," the last prelude in Debussy's first book of preludes, shows Debussy creating a film with sound. This prelude is more than a sound track; it is Debussy's attempt to convey in music a filmlike evocation of the minstrel show. This is especially evident in the musical organization, which uses procedures analogous to those used in the first films.

The very first (silent) films were, in essence, animated photographs. A single stationary camera shot the scene as it unfolded; the novelty was simply that the camera captured on film what viewers would experience in real life. However, film editing enabled directors to present an entirely new way of perceiving time and space. Using multiple cameras, directors could show the same scene from different angles, cutting from one to the next as they chose. Through montage, a specifically cinematic process in which discrete sections of film are assembled into a continuously flowing whole, they could compress an extended time span into a few minutes. Specific editing techniques like cuts, fades, and dissolves create a world far different from that of everyday life—a world in which viewers move backward and forward in time and jump from place to place in an instant.

Because we've grown up watching television and films, we readily accept the altered reality that these media provide. But for those living at the turn of the twentieth century, the manipulation of time and space was a startling novelty. For Debussy, the cinema was both an exciting new medium and a source of inspiration. In 1913, he remarked, "There remains but one way of reviving the taste for symphonic music among our contemporaries: to apply to pure music the techniques of cinematography. It is the film—the Ariadne's

thread—that will show us the way out of this disquieting labyrinth."

In this case, practice predated theory: Debussy had applied cinematographic techniques to musical composition in his later piano music years before this pronouncement. "Voiles" features transitions that seem to dissolve and fade in and out of the "storm" section; in "Minstrels," Debussy adapts several different editing techniques.

Debussy's choice of subject—minstrels—was as modern as his compositional technique. The minstrel show was the first distinctively American entertainment to charm European audiences: there, as in the United States, it was a not very respectable mass entertainment that attracted a diverse audience. By portraying such a mundane subject, Debussy followed the lead of both filmmakers and painters such as Toulouse-Lautrec, who blurred the boundary between high and low culture by painting scenes of everyday life.

The minstrel show conjures up vivid images, both visual and aural: the minstrels in blackface, strumming a banjo or scraping a fiddle, spouting nonsense or playing practical jokes on the interlocutor, the minstrel show's straight man. In Debussy's portrayal, there is no consistent musical style; instead, there is a collage of styles that ranges from sprightly fiddle tunes and tambourine taps to spooky music and a cabaret-style popular song. The cinematic inspiration is evident in the frequent shifts from style to style. Everything within the prelude is a fragment; there are no self-contained, closed sections. Its frenetic pace, often featuring abrupt shifts from one sound image to the next, captures the high spirits and improvisatory flow of the minstrel show.

"Minstrels" (see Listen Up!) is a modern work in both its choice of musical materials and the way in which Debussy organizes them. What makes the musical materials modern is their source and Debussy's presentation of them. They don't come from art or folk music; they are inspired by a popular entertainment.

impressionism and beyond | **267**

Debussy, "Minstrels," from *Préludes* (1909–1910)

TAKEAWAY POINT: A cinematic, nonimpressionistic musical composition by the master impressionist

STYLE: Early twentieth century

FORM: Fragmented through-composed form

GENRE: Piano prelude

INSTRUMENTS: Piano

CONTEXT: Piano music for the salon or concert hall

0:00 Simple diatonic melody, in a steady rhythm

0:13 Sudden burst of energy: Debussy's imitation of banjo strumming

0:36 New melody, new key, new cabaret-music style, richer texture; still energetic

0:48 Dissolve, then suspenseful music (series of "mystery" chords; sudden bursts)

0:58 Richer, gentler version of banjo strumming in new key; return of banjo flourish

1:15 New action: tambourine imitation, fades into . . .

1:29 . . . fragment of sentimental pop ballad; banjo figuration suggests shenanigans behind the imagined singer. So does the sudden burst of energy.

1:42 Minstrels, tambourine, banjo: flourishes to a decisive ending: "That's all!"

 Listen to this selection streaming or in an Active Listening Guide at CourseMate or in the eBook.

And Debussy doesn't try to dress them up, as nineteenth-century composers often did with folk melodies; it sounds as if he has simply adapted them for the piano.

Because its materials are familiar sounding and familiar to Debussy and his listeners, "Minstrels" does not sound as radically avant-garde as Schoenberg's "Nacht." Conceptually, however, the prelude *is* radically avant-garde: the adaptation of film-editing techniques to musical composition was not possible until the beginning of the twentieth century, and the collage-like arrangement of the musical fragments anticipates the visual collages of Picasso and Braque, which appeared shortly after Debussy composed the prelude.

19-2F Debussy the Accessible Radical

Throughout much of the twentieth century, it was customary in musical circles to distinguish between "impressionist" composers, such as Debussy and Ravel, and "contemporary," "modern," or "twentieth-century" composers such as Schoenberg, Stravinsky, Ives, and their numerous peers and successors. The implicit message was that musical impressionism was different from Romanticism, but not as relentlessly avant-garde as the other contemporary musical styles, because it was "listenable." However, its accessibility disguised its novelty.

Debussy created radically modern music, not by evolving beyond nineteenth-century music but by branching off in a completely new direction. His use of familiar musical materials in works such as "Minstrels" helped make his music accessible, and even the musical materials in his atonal music, such as the whole tone–based "Voiles," sound familiar because the scale is presented mainly through stepwise motion. In this respect, he was not as defiantly avant-garde as other important early twentieth-century composers.

What was most radical about his music, though, was his reconception of the relationship between composer and style. Increasingly, through the nineteenth century and into the twentieth, composers cultivated a personal style through characteristic ways of handling the musical elements: Brahms sounds like Brahms, not like Wagner or Verdi. However, Debussy avoided developing such an individualistic style. In the two books of preludes, there is not a characteristic Debussy sound—that is, music that is the product of certain predilections for harmony, texture, rhythm, or form. Instead, Debussy often employs existing styles much as an actor would don a costume: he dresses his music in familiar styles to portray such diverse characters as a minstrel troupe, a failed Latin lover, and an English gentleman.

What is novel about Debussy's compositional approach is not the programmatic aspect per se, but the extent to which Debussy carries it through. In creating individual sound worlds in each of the preludes, Debussy goes beyond earlier composers of program music in suppressing his musical personality in order to portray the subjects of the preludes more vividly.

Debussy could be an impressionist, as we heard in "Voiles." But he was also capable of far more. The two preludes discussed here hint at the larger picture: taken as a whole, the two books of preludes are the musical counterpart to walking through a gallery containing a cross section of French art from around the turn of the twentieth century: not only Monet and Renoir but also Cezanne, Seurat, Gauguin, and Van Gogh.

In his stylistic adaptability, Debussy anticipated the work of late twentieth-century film composers like John Williams and Danny Elfman. Despite his keen interest in the cinema and his application of film-editing techniques to music, Debussy did not leave an actual film score. Nevertheless, he merits consideration as the godfather of film composers.

19-3 Primitivism

On May 29, 1913, a riot broke out in Paris's Théâtre des Champs-Élysées. The occasion was an evening of ballet presented by Ballets Russes, a Russian dance company based in Paris. The evening began innocently enough with a performance of *Les Sylphides*, a traditional ballet choreographed to the music of Chopin. It was the second ballet of the evening, the premiere of Igor Stravinsky's *The Rite of Spring*, that provoked hisses, boos, and catcalls from displeased members of the audience and an equally strong opposing reaction from Stravinsky's supporters. Before the first act had finished, fistfights had broken out among audience members. The police were called in to restore order, but the tumult in the audience drowned out the rest of the performance.

The riot at the premiere devastated Stravinsky, but Sergei Diaghilev, the impresario who ran Ballets Russes, was reportedly delighted with the audience's reaction: the scandal would be free publicity for his company. Reviews suggest that the most provocative aspect of the work was Nijinsky's choreography. A triumphant concert performance of the work a year later, also in Paris, supports the view that it was the dance, more than the music, that sparked the riot.

Still, Stravinsky's ballet was revolutionary, even for a revolutionary time. It challenged the relationship of contemporary audiences with primitive and exotic cultures and introduced vibrant new sounds, rhythms, and harmonies into musical life.

19-3A Russia, France, and Stravinsky

The presence of a Russian ballet company in Paris highlights the continuing cultural connection between France and Russia. Ballets Russes, formed in 1909 with

► **Igor Stravinsky**

FAST FACTS

- Dates: 1882–1971
- Place: Russia
- Reasons to remember: A composer of great imagination and one of the dominant figures in twentieth-century music

John P Taylor/Photo Researchers/Getty Images

dancers brought to France from the Russian Imperial Ballet, was an immediate sensation in Paris. The enthusiastic reaction of the French to the Russian dancers was akin to American Beatlemania in the sense that the Russian dancers brought a welcome new energy and skill to an art that had originated in France, much as The Beatles reinvigorated popular music in the country that had given birth to rock and roll.

The prominent place of ballet in Russian cultural life was in turn a reflection of the widespread impact of French culture on upper-class Russian society, which was still more focused on the West than on its own homeland. Although nineteenth-century reform efforts had resulted in modest improvements for the rural working class, Russian society remained rigidly stratified through the early twentieth century, with a small elite at the top and an enormous, painfully poor, and largely uneducated peasant class at the bottom. Rich and poor typically coexisted side by side: although peasants worked as servants or farmers for the rich, they inhabited worlds that were, for the most part, mutually exclusive. The economic and social circumstances of Tsarist Russia and the Deep South after the Civil War are parallel in many respects.

Nevertheless, nationalism in music was particularly strong in Russia, where composers such as Mussorgsky, Borodin, and Rimsky-Korsakov (Stravinsky's teacher and mentor) cultivated a national style in reaction to the dominant presence of French culture among the Russian elite. However, with the singular exception of Mussorgsky, Russian nationalist composers presented folk materials using conventional resources. Igor Stravinsky ◆ would go well beyond this: he made his reputation by drawing on age-old Russian folk culture and presenting it in increasingly modern settings.

19-3B Igor Stravinsky

Igor Stravinsky was the son of a leading bass singer in the Imperial Opera, based in St. Petersburg. He grew up hearing the music performed at the Mariinsky Theater, which was home to both opera and ballet. His early musical education was typical for the Russian middle and upper class; more intense piano study during his teens would serve him well later in his career, when he toured as a pianist. His calling as a composer came relatively late: he studied law in desultory fashion instead of attending the still-young conservatory in St. Petersburg. Most of his training in composition came from Nikolai Rimsky-Korsakov, with whom he studied privately and who became a mentor and father figure, especially after the death of Stravinsky's father in 1902.

Stravinsky encountered peasant life and culture most directly at his family's summer home in Ustilug, a small village on the border between Poland and the Ukraine (the Ukraine was part of the Russian Empire at the time). The sounds and images of the villagers' songs and dances would be a major inspiration for the first, Russian phase of his career, which peaked with *The Rite of Spring*.

In 1909, Diaghilev heard a performance of Stravinsky's *Fireworks*, a short orchestral piece, and was sufficiently impressed to commission a ballet from the still relatively unknown composer. Stravinsky's first ballet for Diaghilev was *The Firebird* (1910), which was based on Russian folk tales about a mythical phoenix-like creature. *The Firebird* was Stravinsky's breakthrough work; its success prompted a second commission for the following season: *Petrushka*. Petrushka was a popular stock character in Russian puppet shows; in the ballet, the puppet made of straw comes to life.

Stravinsky left St. Petersburg to attend the premiere of *The Firebird*. By the time he composed *The Rite of Spring*, Stravinsky's wife and child had joined him in Paris. They settled in Switzerland during the 1910s, where two other children were born. He returned to Russia briefly in 1914, just before the onset of World War I; because of the Bolshevik Revolution, he would not return for another fifty years. Ironically, his fascination with the primitive and Russian folk culture enabled him to become the first important cosmopolitan composer, a true musician of and for the world.

19-3C Primitivism and Folk Culture

The Rite of Spring tapped into Europe's fascination with the primitive. The roots of this interest extend back at least to the discovery of the Americas and the subsequent colonization of much of Africa, North America, and South America. The majority of Europeans regarded those whom they colonized as savage, even subhuman: this enabled them to justify the slave trade and still profess their Christian faith. The French Enlightenment philosopher Voltaire, who championed social reform in other areas, articulated the prevailing view by describing blacks as inferior to whites and born to be slaves; not coincidentally, perhaps, he reputedly made a substantial fortune investing in the slave trade.

However, around 1750, Voltaire's contemporary Jean-Jacques Rousseau advanced the idea that humans were inherently good (rather than burdened with original sin) and that civilization had evolved into a corrupting influence because it had lost touch with nature and natural emotions. This was a seed from which the Romantic notion of living in harmony with nature grew.

With the publication of *Robinson Crusoe* in 1719, the English writer Daniel Defoe introduced into literature the idea of the "noble savage" in the person of Crusoe's companion, Friday. Romantics also expanded on this idea. American writers found it especially compelling because of the frontier and the ongoing contact with Native Americans: it is evident in writings by Cooper, Thoreau, Poe, Whitman, and above all Longfellow, whose poem *The Song of Hiawatha* was extremely popular in the United States and abroad. Underlying the image of the "noble savage" was the assumption that savages become noble by allying themselves with European culture: Friday converts to Christianity. The "noble savage" has remained a popular notion in mass entertainment: Tonto, the Lone Ranger's Native American sidekick, was a familiar example to those growing up around 1950, and Chewbacca, Han Solo's barely articulate copilot in the Star Wars saga, is a more recent extraterrestrial extension of the idea.

The quest for national identity in folk culture was a homegrown corollary to the "noble savage" idea. Both were concerned with the inferior other: the uneducated, illiterate peasant classes of the homeland vis-à-vis the "savage" but educable members of other races. And in both cases, the "other" was made acceptable by embedding it in the dominant culture. In the nineteenth century, just as savages assumed the trappings of European culture, artifacts of folk culture—stories, songs, dances—were polished for presentation to a sophisticated and literate audience.

In *The Rite of Spring*, Stravinsky and his collaborators took a radically different approach.

19-3D *The Rite of Spring*

After the success of *The Firebird* and *Petrushka*, Stravinsky received a third commission from Diaghilev. For inspiration, he drew on a vision, which he later described in this way:

> There arose a picture of a sacred pagan ritual: the wise elders are seated in a circle and are observing the dance before death of the girl whom they are offering as a sacrifice to the god of Spring in order to gain his benevolence. This became the subject of *The Rite of Spring*.

In this work, the Russian folk elements seemed to offer a conduit back to a past before recorded time. He would adapt these sounds to orchestral instruments and weave them into a musical fabric that featured innovative, complex harmonies and rhythms. Working closely with Nicholas Roerich, an artist, folklorist, and spiritual teacher—and the designer of the sets for several Ballets Russes productions, including *The Rite of Spring*—and drawing on his familiarity with the music and dance of Russian peasants, Stravinsky and choreographer Nijinsky created a work that challenged every important convention of ballet: the story, the scenery, the dancing, and the music.

By envisioning a prehistoric Russian ritual, Stravinsky merged the primitive with the folklore of his own culture. What made the work revolutionary in its conception was the willingness of Stravinsky and his collaborators to remove the filter of civilization. The plot of the ballet suggests that they understood how differently prehistoric people valued something as fundamental as life itself. The "wise elders" understand that the sacrifice of the young girl is necessary for the preservation of the tribe. She, in turn, is willing to give up her life for the greater good. This idea was completely incomprehensible to early twentieth-century audiences.

19-3E *The Rite of Spring*: Rhythm and the Assault on Musical Civilization

The Rite of Spring (see Listen Up!) was conceived as a radically different kind of dance music. It became a frontal assault on musical civilization as Europeans in the early twentieth century understood it. At the heart of this assault is an approach to rhythm that is both timeless and radically innovative. It would undercut a practice that had evolved slowly but steadily over the previous three centuries.

The most obvious rhythmic innovation in *The Rite of Spring* is the very prominence of rhythm. Percussion instruments and percussive sounds on pitched instruments are pervasive. Moreover, there are passages where an insistent rhythm, made unpredictable by syncopations and irregular metrical groupings, provides the main musical interest. This alone would set it apart from much nineteenth-century music. However, it is the nature of Stravinsky's rhythmic conception that enables the work to overturn established practice. His use of a repetitive rhythm in which each attack gets the same emphasis connects back to the kind of drumming that one might hear at a Native American ceremony. In this respect, the rhythm is much more "primitive" than the rhythms of eighteenth- and nineteenth-century music.

However, every other aspect of the rhythm is more modern than in conventional practice. Instead of the regular grouping and division of beats, there are strong syncopations and measures of varying length and grouping. Both undermine the predictability of regular meters. Moreover, he abandons the regular phrase rhythm of nineteenth-century dance music, thus extending the unpredictability into a larger dimension.

To musically sophisticated Europeans, the rhythmic organization in art music had come to be understood as an expression of natural laws, like the beating of one's heart or breathing in and out. However, because he framed conventional practice temporally by including both primitive and modern elements in his rhythmic approach, Stravinsky effectively isolated this purportedly universal rhythmic practice in time and place: it is, in retrospect, the product of a particular culture at a particular time in history.

By going beyond a civilized form of musical discourse, Stravinsky undercut both its supposed universality and its status as the most sophisticated mode of rhythmic organization. Through the rhythms of *The*

	Old/New	Completely New
Rhythm	"Drumming" chords (complex chords in an ancient repetitive rhythm)	Complex rhythmic textures; irregular meters
Melody	Slavic folk songs are borrowed or serve as models and are fragmented and rearranged in asymmetrical patterns	Figuration constructed from atonal materials
Instrumentation	Emphasis on percussion instruments and sounds (string players are asked to play col legno, tapping the wood part of the bow on the string); evocation of folk vocal styles in instrumental writing	Expanded orchestra, highlighting of unusual instruments (contrabassoon) and unusual timbres (high bassoon opening)

Table 19.1 Stravinsky's New Paths in *The Rite of Spring*

Rite of Spring, Stravinsky opened the door in art music to greater rhythmic complexity, founded on completely different rhythmic assumptions.

19-3F Stravinsky's Revolutionary "Primitivism"

Stravinsky's radically old/new approach to rhythm underpinned a new conception of form. Unlike most nineteenth-century composers, who organized form mainly around melody, Stravinsky built his large sections from a series of what might be called "sound panels." As used here, "sound panels" refer to sections of music with a characteristic mix of melodic material, timbres, rhythm, and texture. They are often active, but they are nondirectional and fragmentary. Unlike melodic material in conventional phrases, melodic ideas do not progress toward cadences, nor do they form coherent elements in a hierarchical structure. Instead, Stravinsky arranged the sound panels, which are of varying length, in a sequence. One may follow directly after another, with an abrupt shift, or material from the sound panels may overlap so that one seems to bleed into the next. In conception and implementation, this was radically different from eighteenth- and nineteenth-century practice.

In *The Rite of Spring*, Stravinsky synthesized the ancient and the avant-garde. He embedded the primitive elements in ultramodern settings: dissonant harmonies, irregular patterns and rhythms, melodies without cadences, densely layered textures, and instrumentation that exploited new orchestral timbres. In several elements, there is a two-pronged approach to modernity. One path is a new take on existing material, whereas the other is an approach that is completely new. Table 19.1 offers examples of these two paths.

col legno Violin technique that involves tapping the wooden part of the bow on the strings

 **LISTEN UP!**

Stravinsky, "Introduction," "The Augurs of Spring," and "Mock Abduction," from *The Rite of Spring* (1913)

TAKEAWAY POINT: Revolutionary rhythms that embed the primitive in an ultramodern setting

STYLE: Twentieth-century primitivism

FORM: Through-composed

GENRE: Orchestral work for ballet

INSTRUMENTS: Orchestra

CONTEXT: Music for a dance that evokes prehistory time in a radically new way

INTRODUCTION

0:00   Several varied repetitions of six-note melodic fragment, moving mainly by step or small skip in narrow range. Played first in highest register of bassoon, then briefly taken over by clarinet. Meandering counterpoint by bass clarinets.

0:37   English horn plays different melodic fragment, similar to bassoon line. Other parts enter, including meandering counterpoint now played by bassoons. The gradual accumulation of lines suggests earth awakening from winter.

1:05   Increase in activity and textural density—several competing melodic fragments plus sustained chords. Stravinsky moves abruptly through several "sound panels" before stabilizing briefly on an oscillating pattern played by the flutes.

1:42   Return to more active texture, with frequent oscillations between competing sound panels. Transitions are abrupt and decisive.

2:04   Another distinctive melodic fragment, played by oboe, is supported by busy flute line and joined later by other high winds.

2:14   Collage of melodic fragments, with more joining in. Brighter sound of trumpet and low-register rumbling suggest that spring has advanced considerably.

2:34   Return to opening bassoon solo. This leads to a clarinet trill and a four-note pattern played by plucked (pizzicato) violins, at first intermittently, then insistently, after a suspenseful moment.

AUGURS OF SPRING

3:08   Harmonized "drumming": relentlessly repetitive rhythm akin to shamanic/Native American drumming; percussive string sound

3:16   Complex chord replaces indefinite pitch of drumming. Syncopated chords in horns. Four-note pattern, with more active accompaniment, interrupts briefly.

3:21   "Drumming" chord continues; melodic fragments layered in

3:31   Abrupt switch to melodic fragments in winds darting around over pizzicato strings

3:44   Equally abrupt return to "drumming" chord

3:53   Simple, stepwise melodic idea (bassoons, trombones, oboes) layered over "drumming" chord

4:21   Sudden interruption, then back to four-note pattern

4:34   New version of four-note pattern, with other active layers; a brief hint of horn melody that soon follows

4:46   New melody, played by horn, over an insistent rhythm

4:51   Flute answers; they come together.

4:58   Other melodic fragments (oboe and muted trumpet stand out) come next.

5:06   Horn melody, played by flutes, returns; there are two settings of this melody, after which trumpets play another simple tune.

5:35   A more agitated rising pattern, followed by still another setting of the horn melody, with contrabassoon counterpoint. A big crescendo and increasingly dense texture build to the abduction scene.

MOCK ABDUCTION

6:18   Steady rhythm disappears; instead, sustained chords and scurrying lines from brass and winds, then strings

6:31   Strident horn call echoes through the din.

6:51   Entire orchestra plays simple melodic material in a steady rhythm, arranged in asymmetrical patterns.

7:00   Horn call returns.

7:12   Two new melodies with irregular rhythm. Ending trill leads to next scene.

 Listen to this selection streaming or in an Active Listening Guide at CourseMate or in the eBook.

19-3G The *Rite of Spring* and Stravinsky's Career

The Rite of Spring was Stravinsky's musical declaration of independence: it served as the catalyst for his musical transformation from Russian to international composer. When he first conceived of the work, he was a Russian. He drew both inspiration and musical ideas from his homeland—not the imported culture of the elite, but the Slavic folk traditions found throughout the Russian Empire. However, in the wake of the success of *The Rite of Spring*, Stravinsky increasingly distanced himself from the roots of the music. Almost immediately, he encouraged concert performances of the work. Always a shrewd businessman, he realized that *The Rite of Spring* would receive many more performances as a concert work than as a ballet. And he certainly recognized that it was self-sufficient musically. Musicians soon recognized its stunning originality.

Looking Back, Looking Ahead

The "isms" music of Schoenberg, Debussy, and Stravinsky represents the cutting edge of the transition from the relatively unified musical world of the nineteenth century to the fragmented musical landscape of the early twentieth. All three began their careers as late Romantic composers. However, by the beginning of World War I, each had moved far beyond this tradition. The impact of their music on fellow musicians and sympathetic listeners made it impossible to suppress their innovations.

What made the new music of the early twentieth century different in kind from the music that appeared during earlier periods of revolutionary change was the fact that the "old practice" was replaced by not one, but several, new practices, each quite different from the other. Although these composers knew and admired each other's work, neither they nor their peers worked collectively toward a new common style that would replace Romanticism. Rather, they expressed their individuality not by making individual statements within an established style, but by making their style individual or even masking it altogether.

Schoenberg and Stravinsky would become the two most influential composers of the first half of the twentieth century. Their esteem would have two far-reaching consequences for twentieth-century music. First, it established novelty as a primary measure of prestige among composers: to earn the highest respect of one's peers, a composer had to create work that featured concepts and sounds without precedent. This quest for novelty in turn skewed the relationship between avant-garde composers and their audience: their need to, as Schoenberg said, "write what my destiny orders me to write" outweighed the need for acceptance beyond a small circle of the knowledgeable. Inspired by Beethoven's rapid stylistic evolution and Bach's resurrection from obscurity, they comforted themselves that the more sophisticated audiences of the future would eventually appreciate their music. This idea would reach its peak in the decades after World War II.

In America, new kinds of popular music, as notorious in their own way as the avant-garde music of Stravinsky and Schoenberg, also took shape in the early years of the twentieth century. They would become a far more pervasive presence in musical life. We examine their early manifestations and encounter the music of America's first modern composer in the next chapter.

 study tools 19

Ready to study?
In the book you can:

- Review Learning Outcome answers and Glossary terms with the tear-out Chapter Review card.

Or you can go online to CourseMate, at www.cengagebrain.com, for these resources:

- Chapter Quizzes to prepare for tests

- Interactive flashcards of all Glossary terms

- Active Listening Guides, streaming music, and YouTube playlists

- An eBook with live links to all web resources

© iStockPhoto.com/Susaro

LEARNING OUTCOMES

After reading this chapter, you will be able to do the following:

20-1 Describe Arnold Schoenberg's and Anton Webern's approach to serial composition.

20-2 Recognize the substantial differences between Igor Stravinsky's early compositions and his later neoclassical works.

study tools

After you read this chapter, go to the Study Tools at the end of the chapter, page 283.

The journal *Modern Music*, published by the League of Composers from 1924 to 1946, gave composers and scholars a forum for discussing the compositions and compositional procedures of their peers—American and European. The journal was remarkably inclusive, embracing virtually the entire spectrum of cutting-edge compositional styles, from avant-garde sound experiments to serialism.

Modern music was a term widely used in the first half of the twentieth century to identify the works of forward-looking composers. *Modern* does not represent a common stylistic approach; the works of modern composers were extraordinarily diverse. What linked them—and what made them "modern"—was a rejection of the past and a quest for novelty. The most forward-looking composers of the era sought distinctive identities. Collectively, their innovations touched every musical element and continued the stylistic fragmentation of concert music during the early twentieth century. Among the most important and influential trends were serialism, as practiced by Schoenberg and his disciples, and neoclassicism, whose most radical exponent was a remade Stravinsky.

20-1 Serialism, Schoenberg, and Webern

In 2000, Brilliant Classics, a budget record label based in the Netherlands, began work on a massive project: to issue recordings of all of J. S. Bach's known works in celebration of the 250th anniversary of Bach's death. The boxed set, finally released six years later, contains 155 CDs. By contrast, the CD set that contains the thirty-one works to which Anton Webern (1883–1945) gave opus numbers contains only three CDs, a little more than three hours of music—only about half an hour longer than Bach's *St. Matthew Passion.*

Webern's modest output over a compositional career that spanned almost forty years shows not only the high standards he held for his own music but also the extreme brevity of most of his compositions. The works are short because they are so concentrated; they distill conventional musical gestures into drastically compressed time spans. This sense of compressed energy is one of several innovative aspects of Webern's music. Another is his wholesale adoption and imaginative application of the serialist procedures that he learned from his mentor Arnold Schoenberg.

20-1A Serialism

If you sit down with a guitar, electric bass, or other fretted string instrument, play an open string, then move up the fingerboard one fret at a time, you will reach the note an octave above the open string at the twelfth fret. This activity can confirm experientially the fact that the octave is divided into twelve equidistant half-steps. This consistent division of the octave, known as equal temperament, was known and advocated before Bach's time and has been the customary way to arrange the available pitches within the octave since the nineteenth century.

However, in the common practice harmony of the eighteenth and nineteenth centuries, equal distance did not correlate with equal importance. Among the twelve notes within an octave, there is a three-level hierarchy: the tonic pitch, the six other notes of the diatonic scale, and the five chromatic pitches, those not in the scale of a particular key.

In Baroque and Classical music, chromatic pitches are most often simply fleeting decorative elaborations. However, they typically played a prominent role in music intended to convey tragic emotions, as we heard in "Dido's Lament" ("When I Am Laid in Earth"). Romantic composers in search of greater expression used chromatic pitches more liberally, as we heard in Chopin's mournful E minor prelude. By the end of the nineteenth century, forward-looking composers such as Wagner composed highly chromatic music. Schoenberg took the inevitable next step, liberating the twelve notes of the octave from the organization around a tonic pitch.

In emancipating dissonance, Schoenberg discarded the hierarchical arrangement of the twelve pitches. To gain freedom from tonality, he sacrificed order—the well-established framework for organizing pitch that common practice harmony provided. After a flurry of atonal compositions, including *Pierrot lunaire,* Schoenberg struggled for the better part of a decade with the organizational difficulties that his embrace of atonality had caused. However, in the years around 1920, he and composer Joseph Hauer independently developed a system of atonal pitch organization.

In Schoenberg's method, usually called serialism, or twelve-tone composition, the composer begins by arranging all twelve pitches within the octave in a particular sequence. (The series is often called a tone row.) The key relationship in the row is the sequence of intervals—the number of half-steps—between pitches. So long as these remain constant, the composer can alter the starting pitch of any statement of the series to begin with any of the other eleven notes, reverse the direction of the series (the series in reverse order is called a retrograde), or invert the series (known as inversion) by reversing the direction of the interval (for instance, the second note is three half-steps lower than the first note rather than three half-steps higher). Collectively, these transformations yield forty-eight possible versions of the original series.

The tone row and its various permutations are the composer's raw material. They are specific to each particular work, rather than patterns

equal temperament Consistent division of the octave into twelve equidistant half-steps

chromatic pitch Pitch not in the scale of a particular key

serialism (twelve-tone composition) System of pitch organization in which all twelve pitches within the octave are organized in a series rather than organized hierarchically

tone row In serial composition, the arrangement of all twelve pitches within the octave in a particular sequence

retrograde Reversal of the original sequence of twelve pitches in a serial composition (backward)

inversion In serial composition, reversing the direction of the intervals between pitches of the tone row

Anton Webern
FAST FACTS

- Dates: 1883–1945
- Place: Vienna, Austria
- Reasons to remember: A student of Schoenberg; the primary influence on the mid-century avant-garde

Imagno/Hulton Archive/Getty Images

common to multiple musical works. We can describe the relationship between common practice harmony and serialism in this way: in a tonal work, the composer invents a statement in an established and familiar language; in a serial work, the composer invents both the statement *and* the language.

It is possible to create a series in which the intervals form familiar patterns. But more typically, tone rows are formed from dissonant intervals that do not resemble triads, scales, or any other conventional patterns. Indeed, Schoenberg's goal was to distance his music as much as possible from the trappings of tonality.

20-1B Webern and Schoenberg: Tradition and Evolution in Austro-German Music

Anton Webern ♣ was born in Vienna; his family was on the fringes of the nobility, and his father was a high-ranking civil servant in the Austrian government. Webern obtained a well-rounded musical education, mainly at the University of Vienna, where he earned a doctorate in musicology. However, the decisive event in his musical life was studying composition with Schoenberg. Their association began in 1904, when Webern became one of Schoenberg's first private students. Formal training ended in 1908, but their work together would continue throughout most of Webern's life. Although he was less than a decade older than Webern, Schoenberg became for Webern a mentor, friend, and model. They would maintain a close working relationship until Schoenberg's flight to the United States.

Schoenberg, Webern, and Alban Berg, also a student of Schoenberg, formed the Second Viennese School. (Haydn, Mozart, and Beethoven were the first Viennese school.) The three composers were determined to follow their musical destiny from expressionism through serial composition. Schoenberg led the way, but all three composers developed distinctly different compositional approaches. With the support of a small circle of like-minded associates, they worked largely independent of public opinion, which was generally far from enthusiastic.

To that end, Schoenberg formed the Society for Private Musical Performances in 1918, which sponsored frequent concerts of contemporary music; only those who subscribed to the society could attend. Webern was on the board of directors. The following year, Webern moved to Mödling, a Vienna suburb, in order to be near Schoenberg, and they spent considerable time together during the period in the early 1920s when Schoenberg was developing his twelve-tone method.

Schoenberg's group viewed their compositions as the most important continuation of the Austro-German musical tradition, which they valued more than any other. They saw their radical rejection of tonality as the almost inevitable conclusion of the evolutionary path that had begun in the eighteenth century, continued through Beethoven and Wagner, and reached a crisis point early in the twentieth century. They acknowledged their heritage by embracing established genres—suite, string quartet, symphony, concerto—and using traditional forms as a point of reference. Nevertheless, adapting these forms to twelve-tone composition radically altered them, because the structural goals defined by the familiar harmonic progressions of tonal music were no longer present.

Of the three composers, Webern was the most deeply involved, as a performer, with the music of the Austro-German tradition. He derived most of his income from his work as a conductor; his programs focused almost exclusively on this repertoire. Nevertheless, his music moved the farthest away from this tradition. Unlike Webern, Berg never completely abandoned tonality, and Schoenberg reincorporated tonal elements in his later works. It was Webern who committed most fully to serial composition and worked through its implications for other elements: rhythm, texture, dynamics, and timbre. This is particularly evident in his later works, such as the Concerto for Nine Instruments.

20-1C Concerto for Nine Instruments

Webern began work on his Concerto for Nine Instruments (see Listen Up!), Op. 24, in 1931 and completed it in 1934. The concerto is a work for large chamber ensemble, not the usual soloist and orchestra. The ensemble is comprised of three wind instruments (flute, oboe, clarinet), three brass instruments (trumpet, horn, trombone), two strings (violin, viola), and piano. Webern's concerto has three movements, in a traditional fast–slow–fast sequence. The form of the second movement, which is discussed later, is also derived from a traditional model: it resembles the rounded binary form used in so much tonal music.

In this movement, Webern's connection to the Austro-German tradition is specifically evident in his method of creating the tone row. Recall that the practice of building a movement or composition from a simple melodic kernel had been part of Austro-German music since the early eighteenth century and that the melodic material became progressively more individual: Bach

LISTEN UP!

Webern, Concerto for Nine Instruments, 2nd movement (1934)

TAKEAWAY POINT: Exquisite example of color-rich abstract music

STYLE: Serial atonal music

FORM: Rounded binary

GENRE: Chamber music

INSTRUMENTS: Flute, oboe, clarinet, trumpet, horn, trombone, violin, viola, piano

CONTEXT: Music directed toward a knowledgeable elite made up mainly of avant-garde composers and their supporters

0:00　Steady rhythmic flow enlivened by constantly changing instrumental colors; one or two notes per entrance

0:20　New phrase begins after drastic deceleration in tempo. Dynamic contrasts reinforce changes in instrumental color.

0:54　Developmental material begins quietly, then sharper contrasts and quicker exchanges between instruments, rise in dynamics

1:23　A highpoint in the movement: loud, bright (with oboe, muted trumpet timbres), then gradually receding

1:45　Return to opening two cells occurs at a low point in momentum; the entire section through the drop in tempo is more subdued.

2:12　Sharp piano chord signals the beginning of a coda-like section; the movement ends by winding down.

 Listen to this selection streaming or in an Active Listening Guide at CourseMate or in the eBook.

built the Brandenburg Concerto movement from a generic three-note motive; Beethoven used a distinctive motive crafted from generic material as the building block for both melodic material and figuration; Wagner saturated his music drama with leitmotifs.

With Webern, the progression from generic to specific reached one logical conclusion. In this movement, Webern constructs his row from permutations of a three-note cell. Thus, every note in the movement—harmony as well as melody—derives from the three notes heard at the outset: the trumpet note and the two-note piano chord. Pitch choices belong specifically and uniquely to this work. There is no apparent connection to the familiar scales and chords of common practice harmony; indeed, the complementary relationship of melody and harmony dissolves in this movement.

The absence of familiar reference points in pitch organization that common practice harmony typically provides brings other elements to the forefront. There is virtually no variation in the rhythmic flow, but there are extreme and frequent fluctuations in tempo—like rubber being stretched and released. The most pronounced tempo changes help articulate the form.

Among the most immediately striking features of the movement are the frequent contrasts in timbre, a procedure that Schoenberg called *Klangfarbenmelodie* (tone color melody). The piano plays continuously throughout. The other instruments typically play only a note or two at a time, like sparkles of different colors against the more neutral background of the piano.

20-1D Webern and Abstract Music

Among the major currents in the visual arts during the first part of the twentieth century was abstract art. Abstract artists eschewed representation in favor of work that concentrated on such painterly elements as form, line, color, and texture in and of themselves. The works of abstract artists range from the almost improvisatory paintings of Jackson Pollock to Mark Rothko's studies in color and the geometric compositions of Piet Mondrian, which feature patterns of black, white, and vivid colors.

The familiar rhythmic patterns, melodic procedures, and harmonic progressions of tonal music are like representation in the visual arts, in the sense that both depict "reality" as encountered in day-to-day life. By taking virtually every element to its extreme and divorcing pitch organization from tonality in any form, Webern skewed musical "reality" to the point of abstraction. The musical materials are so far removed from their source that the sense of connection with the tradition that inspired them is obscured by the radical differences. They may be inspired by traditional models, but their transformation by Webern gives them a completely different cast.

Webern's music opened a new sound world and introduced a new aesthetic. His wholehearted embrace of serialism and his extreme approach to composition effectively severed the connection with the Austro-German tradition. The signals on which generations of musicians and listeners had relied for meaning were largely absent or distorted beyond easy recognition. In their stead came music with a new kind of beauty: sound objects linked by the consistency of pitch, seemingly floating in space. Despite its debt to the past, Webern's music looked squarely to the future.

Webern's music would prove to be especially influential. Many of the composers active in the two decades after World War II embraced serialism; some applied serial procedures to other elements, such as rhythm and dynamics. Schoenberg may have been the architect of this new method, but Webern's music was, for the more forward-thinking composers, the more widely used model.

The "mainstreaming" of serialism among the classical avant-garde was a decisive moment in the history of music. For the first time since the advent of widespread commercial publishing in the seventeenth century, there was clear discontinuity between everyday music and the music of the most prestigious composers of the day. Twelve-tone composition is a method of pitch

Abstract artists eschewed representation in favor of work that concentrated on such painterly elements as form, line, color, and texture in and of themselves.

In particular, the use of serial procedures has the effect of "ungrounding" the music. The tonic note and tonic chord on a downbeat anchor tonal music: they provide a point of departure and a point of arrival. Melodies may soar, but they come to earth at cadences. By contrast, Webern's music seems to float. The effect is analogous to a mobile by Alexander Calder, made up of abstract shapes in contrasting colors, suspended almost invisibly by a thin wire.

Webern's music seems to float.

organization that is different in kind from tonal music. Listeners unfamiliar with the method would find virtually no common harmonic or melodic ground between serial compositions and other music that they might encounter, such as tonal classical music, popular and folk music, or music for religious services. As a result, avant-garde classical composition became detached from virtually every other kind of music making.

20-2 Stravinsky and Neoclassicism

As 1914 began, Igor Stravinsky's professional fortunes seemed on the upswing: *The Rite of Spring* received two concert performances in Paris in April 1914. This time there were no riots as at the premiere, just adulation. However, his wife was diagnosed with tuberculosis, so Stravinsky and his family relocated to Switzerland, where they lived until 1920. He visited the Ukraine in July 1914, just before the outbreak of World War I. It was his last visit there. The war and the Russian Revolution that followed cut him off from his homeland; he did not return to Russia until 1962. Stravinsky returned to France in 1920 and used the country as his home base until 1939, when he emigrated to the United States as World War II broke out in Europe.

Given the instability of his professional and personal circumstances, one might reasonably expect Stravinsky to have taken the safe course: composing music that mined much the same vein as the three ballets that had established his reputation. In fact, the opposite happened: Stravinsky would never again compose a work similar in style to *The Rite of Spring*. Instead, he brought his unique vision to neoclassicism.

20-2A Neoclassicism

Neoclassicism is any trend in the arts characterized by the revival or reinterpretation of classical values of harmony, clarity, restraint, and adherence to established practices. In architecture and the visual arts, neoclassicism meant embracing these values as embodied in the artworks of Greek and Roman civilization: the Greek Revival buildings on many college campuses exemplify this trend. Neoclassicism emerged as a trend in the visual arts during the Renaissance as one response to reawakened interest in classical civilization. It flourished during

neoclassicism Any trend in the arts characterized by the revival or reinterpretation of classical values of harmony, clarity, restraint, and adherence to established practices, as embodied in the artworks of Greek and Roman civilization; in music, an umbrella term identifying a body of twentieth-century music that has in common a rejection of Romantic and post-Romantic musical values and a return to, or reworking of, many of the musical features characteristic of eighteenth-century music

The U.S. Supreme Court building, completed in the 1920s, is another example of neoclassicism in architecture.

the eighteenth century as an expression of Enlightenment values. For nineteenth-century commentators, the music of the late eighteenth century also embodied these values; hence its designation as the Classical period in music.

In music, *neoclassicism* (as opposed to classicism) serves as an umbrella term identifying a body of twentieth-century music that has in common a rejection of Romantic and post-Romantic musical values and a return to, or reworking of, many of the musical features characteristic of eighteenth-century music. Neoclassical compositions are generally characterized by clear tonal orientation, straightforward rhythms, easily understood forms inspired by traditional models, and modest dimensions. They tend to be emotionally reserved, in contrast with the hyperexpressiveness of late Romantic and expressionist music and the sensuousness of impressionism and primitivism.

The first neoclassical musical works appeared toward the end of World War I. During the 1920s and 1930s, neoclassicism flourished in France: for a decided majority of significant French composers, *this* was the sound of modern music. One reason was the close correspondence between neoclassical values and aesthetic features that they felt were distinctively French. During his years of residence in France, Stravinsky was also among the neoclassical adherents.

20-2B Neoclassicism and Stravinsky's Stylistic Transformation

Between 1913 and 1930, the year in which he completed his Symphony of Psalms, Stravinsky composed an astonishing amount of music: ballets, operas, choral music, works for large instrumental ensemble, chamber works, songs, works for solo instruments (especially piano), and works that are a genre unto themselves. These new works were remarkably varied in both genre and style. Their most obvious common ground was only that Stravinsky had composed them and that they were unlike the earlier ballets.

His first two important works of the 1920s were *Symphonies of Wind Instruments* and the ballet *Pulcinella*. The two works are radically different. *Symphonies of Wind Instruments* is an austere, modernist work, with irregularly formed panels of sound performed by a twenty-four-member wind band. *Pulcinella* is, by contrast, a reworking of eighteenth-century music. Stravinsky adapted music attributed to the eighteenth-century composer Giovanni Pergolesi so skillfully that it is often impossible to detect where the original music ends and Stravinsky begins.

For Stravinsky, neoclassicism wasn't merely a matter of musical style: important works, such as his opera *Oedipus Rex* and his ballet *Apollon musagète*, derive directly from classical Greece. Cumulatively, Stravinsky's neoclassical works are at once deeply indebted to the past and clearly removed from it. No other composer of the era embraced both the old and new dimensions of

neoclassicism so fully. The *Symphony of Psalms* continues Stravinsky's neoclassical style but adds a new element: his religious faith.

20-2C Stravinsky, Religion, and the *Symphony of Psalms*

On Easter 1926, Stravinsky once again became a communicant in the Orthodox faith. His return to the organized religion of his youth was inspired in part by the Catholic philosopher Jacques Maritain, who was responsible for reviving the philosophy of the thirteenth-century Dominican priest Saint Thomas Aquinas. Through Maritain, Stravinsky embraced the idea of an orderly world in which the artist suppresses his ego in the service of God and the greater good. As he remarked in an interview given two months after the Paris premiere of *Symphony of Psalms*, "Individualism in art, philosophy, and religion implies a state of revolt against God. Look at Nietzsche's Antichrist. The principle of individualism, and of atheism, is contrary to the principle of personality and subordination before God: in the former we find the supermen, in the latter we recognize men."

This remark suggests that Stravinsky's return to organized religion was the spiritual counterpart to the essentially conservative impulse that influenced the music of his neoclassical period. And both reflect not only an important dimension of Stravinsky's personality but also the tenuous life of a composer in a turbulent time. With the success of *The Rite of Spring*, Stravinsky was arguably the most celebrated living composer in the world. However, fame and acclaim did not automatically convert into cash. Commissions and royalties provided only part of his income; more came from his numerous concert appearances as a conductor and pianist. Further, the unsettled circumstances of his personal life—a life divided almost equally between family in the south of France and Paris, and touring with his mistress; the forced separation from his homeland; the poor health of his wife and daughter—may also have motivated Stravinsky to ground himself in a medieval conception of Christianity.

20-2D *Symphony of Psalms*

Stravinsky expressed his recently renewed faith most directly through *Symphony of Psalms* (see Listen Up!), a three-movement work for chorus and orchestra. He composed the work in 1930 to fulfill a commission from Serge Koussevitsky, the conductor of the Boston Symphony. The dedication reads, "This Symphony was composed for the glory of God and dedicated to the Boston Symphony Orchestra on the occasion of its 50th anniversary."

Stravinsky's commission was for a traditional symphony. However, Stravinsky used the commission as an opportunity to compose a work that realized an idea apparently germinating for a while: a symphonic setting of Psalm texts. Stravinsky described the work this way: "It is not a symphony in which I have included

 **LISTEN UP!**

Stravinsky, *Symphony of Psalms*, 1st movement (1930)

TAKEAWAY POINT: Modern setting of ancient texts

STYLE: Neoclassical

FORM: Through-composed

GENRE: Choral

INSTRUMENT: Mixed choir with orchestral accompaniment

CONTEXT: Sacred texts performed in a secular setting

0:00	Neoclassical Stravinsky in a nutshell: conventional chord orchestrated so distinctively that it's immediately recognizable, followed by contrasting material with no functional connection to the chord and based on a completely different scale
0:18	Distinctive piano figuration based on modal scale becomes accompaniment to . . .
0:22	. . . cello solo, which previews vocal line.
0:34	Choir begins singing barely moving melodic line in unison (evoking chant).

Exaudi orationem meam, Domine,	Hear my prayer, O Lord,

0:53	Sudden shift to homophonic choral texture. Steady, repetitive patterns underneath choral parts.

Et deprecationem meam.	And my supplication.

1:03	Section ends with short, cadenza-like passage for solo oboe.
1:10	Repetition of opening melodic material

Auribus percipe lacrimas meas.	Give ear to my tears.

1:30	Vocal line on one pitch with piano accompaniment from introduction. Opening chord punctuates end of section.

Ne sileas, ne sileas	Be not silent, be not silent

1:40	Sudden change in melodic style: big skips, wide-ranging melody. Voices enter in stages. Accompaniment continues in steady rhythm; brasses predominate.

Quoniam advena ego sum apud te	For I am a stranger with Thee
et peregrinus, sicut omnes patres mei.	and a sojourner, as all my fathers were.

2:27	Strong declamation of "forgive me," with brass playing piano accompaniment at half speed.

Remitte mihi	Forgive me

2:32	Sudden drop in dynamics, return to opening choral material, set contrapuntally. Movement concludes on conventional chord.

Remitte mihi,	O forgive me,
rius quam abeam et amplius non ero.	that I may be refreshed, before I go hence and be no more.

 Listen to this selection streaming or in an Active Listening Guide at CourseMate or in the eBook.

Psalms to be sung. On the contrary, it is the singing of the *Psalms* that I am symphonizing."

Stravinsky set verses from Psalms 38 and 39 and all of Psalm 150; he drew the texts from the Vulgate, the Latin-language Bible used by the Catholic Church. The title "Symphony" is used in its more general sense of "instruments (including voices) sounding together" rather than in the more restricted meaning

of a four-movement work. The work has three distinct movements, each of which is about twice as long as the preceding movement; in concert they are performed without break. The first movement includes verses 13 and 14 from Psalm 38.

In keeping with the idea that the work symphonizes psalm singing, Stravinsky avoids conventional forms. There is repetition of melodic material, in both vocal and instrumental parts, but the repetition does not resolve into a standard formal pattern.

20-2E Stravinsky, "Neo" and "Classical"

It is a measure of Stravinsky's art that it can be both "classical" and "neo" in a single sound. The chord with which Symphony of Psalms begins is a minor triad, which has been used countless times in tonal music. But Stravinsky's instrumentation and voicing of the chord are unique, and the chord is so distinctive that it immediately identifies the work and presages the particular mix of old and new that permeates it.

For Stravinsky, the past is a vast resource that he can cherry-pick for his immediate needs and then transform and embed in a setting that is thoroughly modern. For example, the chorus enters singing in unison a melodic line that barely moves from the opening pitch. Particularly in conjunction with the Latin text that it sets, Stravinsky's melody evokes chant. But unlike chant, the melody has a measured rhythm and is supported by an active accompaniment. The instrumental writing recalls the rhythms of Baroque music (the "classic" in neoclassical embraces *all* the past, not just the Classical style), and much of the accompanying figuration moves in sequential patterns. But the passages do not sound Baroque because the figuration, although consonant, doesn't resemble the patterns used by Bach and other Baroque masters.

> It is a measure of Stravinsky's art that it can be both "classical" and "neo" in a single sound.

One of the most individualistic features of the work is its instrumentation. Stravinsky scored the work for a mixed-voice choir (with the upper two parts sung by a children's choir, if available) and an unusual orchestra: there are no violins, violas, or clarinets, but two pianos. Violins and violas add warmth to the sound of the orchestra in the middle and upper registers. Their absence coupled with the drier sound of the pianos gives the work an austere sound, a kind of instrumental analog to the Latin text and its vocal setting. In turn, the austere sound, along with the unison or homophonic vocal writing and the syllabic setting of the psalm, suggests Stravinsky's hierarchy of importance: words, voices, and instruments, in that order. The melody amplifies the text; the instrumental accompaniment supports and colors the melody.

20-2F Stravinsky's Approach to Musical Style

The two samples of Stravinsky's music encountered in our survey contrast strikingly in numerous ways: one depicts a pagan ritual, and the other, a medieval-style homage to God; one is vivid, colorful, and programmatic, and the other is austere, somewhat dry, and detached; one is rich in complex rhythms and textures, shifts of tempo and mood, and tuneful snippets, whereas the other maintains a steady pulse and is more transparent, and its most memorable melodic material is almost irreducibly simple. There are common features: irregular blocks of sound, active ostinato patterns. However, there is virtually no sense that the *Symphony of Psalms* is the product of the ongoing evolution of Stravinsky's musical approach. Rather, it seems like an abrupt change of direction.

It is possible to view these apparent discontinuities and contrasts as aspects of a consistent musical personality. We know that Stravinsky was an avid consumer of culture during his expatriate years in western Europe. He mingled with artists in all fields and collaborated with several, including Pablo Picasso and the writer Jean Cocteau. He attended concerts, films, and exhibitions and sampled Parisian nightlife. He absorbed new ideas and sounds. His encounter with ragtime in the 1910s led to three rag-inspired compositions. At the same time, Stravinsky had an intense interest in the past. His three early ballets are based on centuries-old material, and almost all his neoclassical works connect back to pre-nineteenth-century sources, both musical and extramusical.

The musical evidence suggests that Stravinsky is a chameleon-like composer: the point of departure for his compositions comes from the world around him. His early works draw heavily on his Russian heritage; several of his works from the 1910s draw on novel and popular vernacular styles; and his post-1920 works reflect musical life in Paris: neoclassicism was primarily a French movement. Stravinsky's extreme responsiveness to outside influences led to radically different approaches to musical style.

In our experience, musical style has typically been the product of musical choices made by a composer (or performer) or a group of composers. For example, we identify a composition as Romantic when we hear a long, flowing melody with distinctive accompaniment. Stravinsky's strategy is fundamentally different. He often uses or adapts established style features not to identify his personal vision but to connect the composition to its inspiration: the parody of chantlike unison singing and the use of medieval modes offer a musical counterpart to the Latin version of the psalm, which dates from the fifth century.

These borrowed style elements disguise the innovative and individual elements of Stravinsky's musical vision, at times to the point of obscuring it. More often, however, Stravinsky's musical personality emerges in his distinctive way of adapting and interpreting these diverse style elements. It is manifest in his highly individual (and difficult to emulate) approach to rhythm, orchestration, tonal organization, and form. These characteristic features continued to influence his music despite the striking surface contrasts from composition to composition.

Stravinsky did not return to Europe until 1951. During his visit, he was disturbed to discover that younger European composers were more interested in the music of Schoenberg and his disciples than they were in his. At the urging of Robert Craft, a conductor, writer, advocate of contemporary music, and Stravinsky's longtime collaborator, Stravinsky gradually adopted serialism. It was the third and final phase of his compositional career.

Looking Back, Looking Ahead

The trajectory of Stravinsky's career follows that of modern music in the first half of the twentieth century. The premiere of *The Rite of Spring* was far more sensational than the premiere of Schoenberg's *Pierrot Lunaire*, and it would enter popular culture in 1940 via Walt Disney's *Fantasia*. The music that Stravinsky composed between the wars would cement his reputation as one of the important composers of the century, but it would not achieve the popularity of his three early ballets. The music of the second Viennese school would never become popular, but increasingly it gained mindshare as the most advanced music of the time among composers. Webern's music effectively completed the divorce of the avant-garde not only from a mass audience but also from most of their fellow composers. However, after World War II, serialism became the dominant method of pitch organization among avant-garde composers, as even Stravinsky hopped on the bandwagon.

Serialism was a truly international compositional approach. Because serial compositions typically had no connection with everyday music, there was no evident influence of folk or popular styles in the music. That was not the case with the music of other composers in the first part of the century. We consider the music of four composers whose music projects a strong national identity in the next chapter.

 study tools 20

Ready to study?
In the book you can:

- Review Learning Outcome answers and Glossary terms with the tear-out Chapter Review card.

Or you can go online to CourseMate, at www.cengagebrain.com, for these resources:

- Chapter Quizzes to prepare for tests

- Interactive flashcards of all Glossary terms

- Active Listening Guides, streaming music, and YouTube playlists

- An eBook with live links to all web resources

stravinsky and neoclassicism | **283**

LEARNING OUTCOMES

After reading this chapter, you will be able to do the following:

21-1 Describe how Charles Ives embodied a new American approach to musical nationalism.

21-2 Understand how Aaron Copland became a major player in a new kind of musical nationalism that peaked during the 1930s and 1940s.

21-3 Recognize how Béla Bartók expressed musical nationalism in the language of Hungarian folk music.

21-4 Describe the challenging musical path that Sergei Prokofiev traced in finding artistic expression within a restrictive, government-imposed framework.

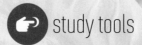 study tools

After you read this chapter, go to the Study Tools at the end of the chapter, page 299.

While staying at a resort in what was then northern Hungary, Béla Bartók heard a maid named Lidi Dósa sing a song whose title translates as "Red Apple." He learned that it was a folk song from her native Transylvania. He wrote it down and published a setting of it the following year. In 1904, the year of his stay, Bartók was a promising young Hungarian composer and pianist. His compositions to that point were derivative, based on the influence of Richard Strauss, Brahms, and what passed for authentic Hungarian music in urban centers. Bartók recognized that his music needed a more distinctive voice, and he wanted to make it sound Hungarian but was unsure how to achieve this.

The encounter with Lidi precipitated a decisive shift in Bartók's compositional focus. He gradually became aware that the path to a recognizably Hungarian personal style lay through the folk music of the peasants who lived in isolated rural areas. He began modestly. As he wrote to his sister at the end of 1904, "Now I have a new plan: to collect the finest Hungarian folksongs and to raise them, adding the best possible piano accompaniments, to the level of art-song." As he deepened his involvement with this folk music, he imbued all his concert music—not only songs but also operas and instrumental music—with the melodies and rhythms that he recorded and transcribed during his field trips.

Bartók was one of several important composers active in the first half of the twentieth century who took a new approach to communicating their national identity through their music, and he would become one of the major players in a new kind of musical nationalism that peaked during the 1930s. Like their nineteenth-century predecessors, this new generation of nationalist composers wished to infuse their music with the character of their homeland. However, the musical results were substantially different because the world in which they worked was changing so drastically and at such a rapid pace.

Among the changes that had a significant impact on their music were these:

1. *The growing political, social, and cultural presence of the working classes.* This presence was manifest in numerous ways, including revolutions that toppled monarchies; the decline of colonialism; the rise of labor unions; migration from rural to urban areas; and increased visibility of minorities in public life.
2. *A deepened interest in folk traditions and a desire to preserve them against the encroachment of mainstream culture.* In pursuit of this goal, collectors took advantage of new technologies. Sound recording was the most significant.
3. *The emergence of a new kind of commercial music.* The African-influenced popular music of the early twentieth century represented the beginning of a new musical tradition. The continuum between art and commercial music that had been part of nineteenth-century musical life all but disappeared.
4. *The fragmentation of style in concert music.* By World War I, Romantic music was an anachronism; in its place was a host of styles, substantially different from one another.

These nationalist composers did not embed folk and vernacular elements in common practice. Rather, they blended vernacular elements from their homeland with innovative elements drawn from concert music to produce works that sounded modern and that acquired over time a national identity. The fact that none of them made use of common practice (even familiar chords are completely restructured) only sharpened the sense of national identity.

21-1 Charles Ives: Toward an American Art Music

In 1910, a year after he formed the Ives and Myrick Insurance Agency with his longtime friend Julian Myrick, Charles Ives published a how-to pamphlet for his agents. The pamphlet would eventually grow into a substantial publication entitled *The Amount to Carry—Measuring the Prospect*. The publication came to be recognized as one of the first practical guides to estate planning.

Charles Ives led two lives. By day, he was a prominent and innovative insurance executive. By the time he retired from business in 1930, he was a wealthy man. At night and on weekends, he composed feverishly—until one day in early 1927, when he painfully acknowledged that he had exhausted his inspiration.

Unlike most other turn-of-the-century American composers, Ives did not go to Europe for further training and did not pursue a career in music. Instead, by opting for a career in business, Ives provided financial security for himself and his family and liberated himself from the necessity to please the tastemakers in the classical music world. What he sacrificed in time, he gained in artistic freedom. This fiercely independent path was characteristic of the man and his music, and of the environment in which he lived.

21-1A A Connecticut Yankee

New England lives up to its name: it's the region of the United States that is most like England, and it was the center of the movement that would enable the colonies to create a new country, independent of England. It is home to the Handel and Haydn Society, which honors the two most esteemed eighteenth-century composers connected to England. The vast majority of the nation's elite prep schools are in New England. Many of its smaller towns cover a lot of land and consist of groups of villages a few miles apart—all reminiscent of the English countryside.

In cities and towns throughout the six states, one finds memorials to Revolutionary War heroes; in Danbury, Connecticut, there is a monument to David Wooster, who lost his life trying to repel the British. Nearby is the camp where troops under the command of Israel Putnam, one of the heroes of the Battle of Bunker Hill, spent the winter of 1778–1779.

▸Charles Ives
FAST FACTS

- Dates: 1874–1954
- Place: United States
- Reasons to remember: A truly American musical innovator

Concord, Massachusetts, would later become the home of the transcendentalists. Charles Ives celebrated them in his *Concord Sonata*: he named the four movements after Emerson, Hawthorne, the Alcotts, and Thoreau. Litchfield, Connecticut, was home to the Beechers, including Henry Ward Beecher and Harriet Beecher Stowe, author of *Uncle Tom's Cabin*. Both were among the prominent abolitionists in the North; so were their not-too-distant neighbors, George and Sarah Ives, Charles Ives's grandparents.

New Englanders project seemingly contradictory values. They can be pragmatic, philosophical, or preposterous—P. T. Barnum grew up in Connecticut and lived in Danbury; Ives's uncle Isaac was a snake-oil salesman. They value tradition, yet their institutions are also hotbeds of innovation; ideas and inventions have poured forth from their universities.

Few New Englanders embodied these diverse values more fully than Charles Ives ♠. In business, he was pragmatic and populist: his goal was to provide security for as many Americans as possible. Yet these pragmatic objectives were shaped by deep philosophical convictions, which he expressed not only in his writings about his music but also in a long preamble to the nuts-and-bolts aspects of selling insurance in *The Amount to Carry*. His business innovations grew out of traditional New England values: they made money through hard work and did good at the same time. His musical innovations were another matter entirely.

Ives is arguably America's most original composer. His determination to survey uncharted musical territory grew out of his strong sense of time and place, of family going back generations, and of the particular attitudes toward learning and ideas that were characteristic of New England during his formative years.

Ives's forebears were among the first Europeans to settle in the colonies: William Ives captained a ship from England in 1637, arrived in Boston, and then made his way to New Haven. His descendants settled in Wallingford, about fifteen miles north of New Haven; Ives's great-grandfather Isaac was the first Ives in Danbury, arriving there in 1785. The family prospered and acquired a reputation for unconventional, even eccentric behavior. Ives's father, George, was the most unconventional of the Iveses. The youngest Union bandmaster during the Civil War, George Ives returned home and assumed direction of the municipal band. Music was sometimes his only work, but he ran a store early in his career and worked at a family bank later.

Many of the most central elements of Ives's musical life respond directly to his father's attitudes and his career as a town musician. Like his son, George had a curious and open mind and remarkable industry. He delighted in unusual sound combinations: on one occasion, he had two bands cross paths to see what they would sound like. He valued substance over style and in amateur music making gave far more weight to the intent than the result. Ives recalled his father's comment about a stonemason's off-key hymn singing: "Look into his face and hear the music of the ages. Don't pay too much attention to the sounds—for if you do, you may miss the music. You won't get a wild, heroic ride to heaven on pretty little sounds." He preferred band music to Mozart, and the fervor of camp meetings to more traditional church services. From this came Ives's familiarity with and delight in the full range of vernacular traditions: marches, gospel hymns, ragtime, popular songs, and the like.

Ives's father, the youngest Union bandmaster during the Civil War, returned home and directed the municipal band.

Putnam's Camp was Connecticut's Valley Forge.

Although Danbury claimed to be "the most musical city in Connecticut" largely on the strength of George Ives's work, many of its influential citizens regarded a musical career as an unworthy profession. Charles Ives detested the more genteel sorts of ladies who gathered in stuffy parlors to listen to sentimental songs and tamer varieties of classical music—these were the same ladies who looked down their noses at George Ives and his music.

Like many of his forebears—but not his father—Charles Ives went to Yale, where he studied under Horatio Parker, one of the most highly esteemed members of the New England school of composers. Ives came to Yale knowing mostly the vernacular music with which he had grown up. Parker led him through more traditional classical literature; Ives's understanding of the Romantic tradition, musically and philosophically, came much more from Parker than from his father. By the time he graduated, he had composed a draft of his first symphony and a string quartet.

Although he was prepared academically for a career in music and had been a professional church organist since he was fourteen, Ives disdained music as a profession. At the same time, his music was Beethoven-like in its boldness and grandness, and it featured a wholesale infusion of vernacular elements. What makes his music even more remarkable is that he heard so little of it performed by anyone other than himself around the time he composed it. The American avant-garde began to perform his music only after he stopped composing new work. The performance history of his orchestral set *Three Places in New England* is all too typical: composition completed around 1914, a first performance as a work for chamber orchestra in 1929, publication in 1935, a full orchestral performance only in 1948. It is now Ives's most popular orchestral work.

21-1B The Music of Charles Ives: *Three Places in New England*

Ives's *Three Places in New England* is true to its title: it depicts the Boston Common, a Revolutionary War site near Ives's home, and a place along a river running through the Berkshires. The three pieces are also about time: in his program notes, he describes the experiences that inspired the works.

In the second movement, entitled "Putnam's Camp, Redding, Connecticut" (see Listen Up!), time and place are specific and close to home: Putnam's Camp is only

a few miles from Danbury and even closer to Ives's home in West Redding, which he had built shortly before composing *Three Places in New England*. The movement begins in the present, then drifts back in time. The "present" in this work is a typical Independence Day celebration, circa 1912. The past recalls the winter of 1778–1779. Putnam's Camp was Connecticut's Valley Forge; the winter that year was especially hard. The dream section recounts an incident well known to many Connecticut citizens: some soldiers are thinking of deserting, but Putnam returns to the encampment and gives a stirring speech that persuades them to stay, endure hardship, and fight.

Ives uses these events that are so specific in time and place in order to universalize their meaning. The trip back in time serves as a vivid reminder of the underlying purpose of the holiday. It is a tribute to the virtues that made independence possible: courage, perseverance, and altruism. It's clear from his writing and his music that these larger themes are central to his outlook on life. Indeed, like the transcendentalists that he so admired, Ives felt the connectedness to all life and the world of the spirit. His most characteristic work may well have been one that he never completed: his proposed "Universe" symphony. Ives's sense of connectedness radiates from his immediate environment: from family, Danbury, New England, and America, to the world. Thus, even as he reaches out to the world, he conveys where he is from and what it stands for.

Ives's self-imposed challenge was to communicate his vision musically. For someone with such a keen sense of place and such deeply rooted populist values, looking to Europe was out of the question, despite Parker's strong influence. European influence is evident only on the most basic level: the use of a symphony orchestra and the intent to present the music in an art-music setting. To achieve this, Ives charted a radically new approach to music composition.

"Putnam's Camp" is a sprawling musical collage. Among its most striking features are the snippets

Ives, "Putnam's Camp, Redding, Connecticut," from *Three Places in New England* (1914)

TAKEAWAY POINT: Sprawling orchestral collage that embodies a particular kind of American spirit

STYLE: Twentieth century

FORM: Free ABA'

GENRE: Programmatic orchestral work

INSTRUMENTS: Orchestra

CONTEXT: Highly individual orchestral music that rebels against the stuffiness of the "cultivated" music of nineteenth-century New England

A: PRESENT

0:00   After a raucous opening, the orchestra settles into . . .

0:09   . . . a stirring march.

0:19   Competing melodic material—flurries of notes, fragments of familiar tunes—intrudes on main melody. Melody and bass go out of phase, suggesting that the "band" is made up of amateurs.

0:47   Brass take over; quotation from Sousa march in low brass; texture remains complicated, with several musical events happening at once. This leads to a string of melodic fragments, including "Yankee Doodle."

1:05   Simpler texture, with several children's songs following each other; gradual drop in dynamics suggests the boy moving away from the center of activity.

1:20   Piano chord begins gradual slowing of activity.

1:37   Low strings swirling about, fading away to silence

B: PAST

2:02   Misty "mystical" chords in strings, piano, and flute flash back to 1776.

2:15   Oboe melody is plea of Goddess Liberty.

2:35   Another familiar-sounding but altered melody takes over. Gradual increase in activity; drum rhythm "out of step" with other rhythms.

2:58   Drum rhythm becomes regular—the march out of camp begins.

3:04   Brass sound the "new national note"; more patriotic melodies filter into the texture.

3:27   Brass blare out a simple tune, leading to a huge climax.

A: PRESENT

3:47   Return of children's song suggests that the boy has awakened and returned to the present.

3:57   Other melodic ideas interrupt the song, implying a return to the July 4th activity.

4:20   It is as if more than one band is playing at the same time, and the sounds blend together.

4:46   Chaotic finish ends on a clashing final chord.

 Listen to this selection streaming or in an Active Listening Guide at CourseMate or in the eBook.

of familiar (and familiar-sounding) melodies. Ives "samples" patriotic songs, folk tunes, minstrel show songs, Sousa marches, children's songs, and more. He seldom includes more than a fragment of each song. These are songs that Ives heard growing up in Danbury, and he correctly expected that his audience would also know them. Here, Ives uses these familiar melodies not as the raw material for a larger composition, as Mozart did in his variation sets, but rather for their associative value, much like Berlioz's quotation of the "Dies irae." However, Ives's approach is much more pervasive.

As a result, the simple large-scale ternary form is not defined mainly by melodic material, but by the ebb and flow of activity and changes in dynamics. This simple formal model outlines the shift from present to past and back to the present that Ives describes in his program for the work:

A: (present) Once upon a "4 July," some time ago, so the story goes, a child went here on a picnic, held under the auspices of the first Church and the Village Cornet Band. Wandering away from the rest of the children past the camp ground into the woods, he hopes to catch a glimpse of some of the old soldiers. As he rests on the hillside of laurels and hickories the tunes of the band and the songs of the children grow fainter and fainter;

B: (past)—when—"mirabile dictu"—over the trees on the crest of the hill he sees a tall woman standing. She reminds him of a picture he has of the Goddess Liberty—but the face is sorrowful—she is pleading with the soldiers not to forget their "cause" and the great sacrifices they have made for it. But they march out of camp with fife and drum to a popular tune of the day. Suddenly, a new national note is heard. Putnam is coming over the hills from the center—the soldiers turn back and cheer.

A: (present) The little boy awakes, he hears the children's songs and runs down past the monument to "listen to the band" and join in the games and dances.

21-1C Ives: An All-American Art Music

Among the most productive new ideas in mathematics and physics advanced in the latter part of the twentieth century was chaos theory. Chaos theory describes dynamic systems with multiple variables, in which seemingly random events resolve on a larger scale into patterns determined by the initial conditions. In Ives's music, exemplified here by "Putnam's Camp," the seemingly random sequence of musical events resolves into a meaningful larger structure. The impression is that Ives is expressing an idea so powerful that it cannot be realized in conventional musical terms.

Ives's unkempt grandeur—a big statement emerging from apparent disorder—is just one aspect of his compositional art. There are exquisite moments, such as the harmonic haze that ushers in the flashback to 1778 and the haunting oboe melody that follows, and there is the dizzying and dazzling complexity of the work, with so many competing melodies, rhythms, and instruments. Above all, there is the imagination to conceive of something so different from anything that had come before. It is unquestionably important art, although in its sources and in their presentation, it rejects many of the conventions of the established art tradition.

Ives's art serves his vision of America: it is populist, patriotic, and particular to New England and its long history. Although he composed "Putnam's Camp" for symphony orchestra and derived his sense of grandeur from the European symphonic tradition, he wanted his music to sound homegrown, not imported. He achieved this not only by drawing on the music that was well known to ordinary folk but also by weaving it into a musical fabric that expressed values that he found particularly American—bigness, humor, energy, wildness, honor, enthusiasm—and that rejected those that were in his view not intrinsic to the American character—refinement and sentimentality.

In works like *Three Places in New England*, Ives created an all-American musical tradition, a tradition that was American in concept as well as musical substance. He achieved his implicit objective: to create a uniquely innovative new kind of art music. It is music that is both populist and elite, and a music that far transcended the more conventional musical styles enjoyed by the cultivated members of American society, in Danbury and elsewhere. No other composer discussed in this book conveyed such a specific cultural identity.

Ives's music would not become known until years, even decades, after its composition. As it did, it would inspire a particularly American openness to new sounds. Out of it would come music from composers like Henry Cowell, Lou Harrison, and John Cage.

21-2 Aaron Copland: An American Composer

In 1936, Davidson Taylor, the head of the Music Division at CBS radio, arranged for the commission of orchestral works by six American composers for radio broadcast. Not yet thirty, Taylor was nevertheless knowledgeable enough about music to write for the journal *Modern Music* and make critical suggestions to several of the composers. Among those commissioned was Aaron Copland.

Copland was enthusiastic about the opportunity. For him, "Radio was an exciting new medium—the very idea of reaching so many people with a single performance." He finished the work in the summer of 1937 and submitted it as "Radio Serenade." However, just before the work's radio premiere, CBS radio announced that Copland's new composition would temporarily be identified by the even blander title "Music for Radio" but that it "had a program, or scenario, that not even its composer ... ventured to interpret." The network and Copland invited listeners to suggest titles, and they received over one thousand suggestions. Copland selected *Saga of the Prairie*; he would change the name of the work to *Prairie Journal* in 1968. For Ruth Leonhardt, the woman who suggested the title that Copland chose,

Ballet dancers Agnes de Mille and Frederic Franklin in *Rodeo*, a ballet scored by Aaron Copland and choreographed by de Mille, New York City, 1942

Constance Bannister Corp/Hulton Archive/Getty Images

21-2A "Americanness" and the West during the Depression

For many Americans, sagebrush replaced the skyscraper as the defining image of America during the Depression years. The stock market crash took some of the luster off the fast-living lifestyle glamorized in the media during the 1920s. The progress toward wealth and material success that seemed inevitable before the crash became a pipe dream for too many Americans in the 1930s. In response, defining images of America seemed to shift from tall buildings, fast cars, busy streets, and full theaters to open spaces, horses, and cowboys with guitars.

In popular culture, the most pervasive expression of this shift was the western. Although western films date from the early silent film era, the genre really took off in the 1930s. Two acclaimed westerns framed the decade: *Cimarron* (1931) won an Academy Award for Best Picture, and *Stagecoach* (1939), featuring a young John Wayne, received several Academy Award nominations, including one for best musical score: the sound track included numerous folk tunes. In between came hundreds of films, including dozens featuring Gene Autry and other singing cowboys.

Westerns presented a simpler view of life: good guys wore white hats; bad guys wore black hats or headdresses. Frontier justice prevailed: problems were resolved with six-shooters. They glorified the lone hero, even when he flouted the law. Westerns were one manifestation of America's fascination with its frontier heritage. Collections of cowboy songs also became increasingly popular during the 1930s, in large part because of the rise of radio shows that featured country-and-western music, such as the National Barn Dance. Rodgers and Hammerstein's landmark 1943 musical *Oklahoma!* brought the frontier to Broadway. This romanticized view of life in the West contrasted sharply with the brutal present: the Dust Bowl, a decade-long drought that would devastate farmers and ranchers in the Plains and the Southwest, would leave half a million people homeless.

During this same time, folklorists, most notably John Lomax (who published one of the first collections of cowboy songs in 1910) and his son Alan, traveled throughout the South and Southwest, recording folk musicians. Their work received support from the Library of Congress; it was eventually added to the Archive of Folk Culture.

Although the Archive included songs of blacks and Native Americans as well as whites, Americans' sense of musical folk roots resided mainly in the songs of whites preserved in collections and presented through the media, and in the recordings and performances of contemporary "folk" performers, most notably Woody Guthrie. This was a retreat from the "melting-pot" ethos that was so much a part of American life through the first quarter of the century. Both the music and the cultures from which it emerged inspired Aaron Copland's cultivation of a distinctively American style.

> "I visualize a music which is profound in content, simple in expression and understandable to all."
>
> —Aaron Copland

"The music seemed typically American and it reminded me of the intense courage—the struggles and final triumphs—of the early settlers, the real pioneers."

Copland never "interpreted" the program of *Prairie Journal* directly, but he did acknowledge that he had used a "cowboy tune" (which researchers have not been able to identify), "so the western titles seemed most appropriate." In fact, the work evokes a range of styles heard on radio during the 1930s. Some of this music looks back to Copland's jazz-influenced music of the 1920s, but the "cowboy" and "prairie" elements are the first inkling of Copland's new populist style. In 1940, by which time he had already written the western-themed ballet *Billy the Kid* and two film scores, Copland said, "I visualize a music which is profound in content, simple in expression and understandable to all." This vision would continue to inform his music through the 1940s and, in the process, give America a third regional musical style, one that evoked the West rather than Ives's New England or Gershwin's New York.

21-2B Copland and Vernacular Music

The early careers of Aaron Copland  and George Gershwin were remarkably similar in several respects. Gershwin, born two years before Copland, was the Brooklyn-born son of Russian Jewish immigrants; Copland was the last of five children of Lithuanian Jewish immigrants. Both grew up with a keen interest in vernacular music, developed into fluent pianists, and briefly studied classical composition with Rubin Goldmark in the 1910s. Both were great admirers of French music and traveled to Paris to study composition with Nadia Boulanger. Copland stayed three years, from 1921 to 1924. Gershwin traveled to France in 1928 and introduced himself to Boulanger with a letter from Ravel, whom he admired greatly and had met earlier in the decade. She did not accept him because she felt that he had already found his compositional voice. Both Gershwin and Copland composed "jazz" piano concertos in their mid-twenties.

Virtually from the start of his career, Copland had wanted his music to sound American. In his earlier works, such as the piano concerto, he sought this sound by fusing contemporary classical music with jazz. However, by 1930, the American qualities in his most modern-sounding music had assumed a more abstract character. The *Piano Variations* of 1930 features jagged rhythms, dissonant harmonies, clangorous sounds, and sparse textures, all of which support the development of a four-note motive. The work placed Copland in the forefront of modern American composers. During this same period, he had been a tireless advocate of music by composers of the Americas.

With the *Piano Variations*, Copland had found the essential features of his personal style. Beginning in mid-decade, he composed a series of works, mainly for orchestra, that presented these features in a more accessible form. Copland called this approach "imposed simplicity." He achieved this by replacing the strident dissonances of the *Piano Variations* with the familiar chords and scales of common practice harmony, and incorporating folk material and familiar melodies.

Copland had altruistic and pragmatic reasons for simplifying his style. Creating art music for the people was his way of supporting the working class with whom he identified. Moreover, it meant more professional opportunities: commissions for ballets and orchestral music, contracts for film scores, performances, lectures, and the like.

The folk materials that Copland employed in his post–*Prairie Journal* music were one dimension of his "frontier" sound. He frequently quoted cowboy songs, folk melodies, and other thematically appropriate material in his "American" music, most explicitly in his use of a transcription by composer-folklorist Ruth Crawford Seeger of a Kentucky fiddle song called "Bonypart's Retreat" in the ballet *Rodeo*.

However, Copland's music evokes the vast expanses of frontier America mainly through musical choices that are, at best, tangentially related to the use of folk materials. Among the most striking features of his music is the

▶ Aaron Copland
FAST FACTS

- Dates: 1900–1990
- Place: United States
- Reasons to remember: America's best-known classical composer; created an accessible style with a distinct American identity

predilection for musical space. He achieves this mainly through his handling of texture, melody, and rhythm: he favors single lines, or widely separated multiple lines, writes melodies with wide intervals, and makes extensive use of silence. We hear Copland's spacious-sounding music in two excerpts from *Appalachian Spring*.

21-2c *Appalachian Spring*

In 1942, Copland received a commission from Elizabeth Sprague Coolidge to compose a ballet for the dancer-choreographer Martha Graham, to be performed at the Library of Congress. Originally titled merely *Ballet for Martha*, it acquired its title through a suggestion from Graham. His score for the ballet, which premiered in 1944 and won the Pulitzer Prize in music the following year, included only thirteen instruments, due to the small size of the orchestra pit in Coolidge Auditorium. Also in 1945, Copland would rework *Appalachian Spring* as an orchestral suite that included eight of the fourteen numbers in the ballet. It is this version that is most often performed (see Listen Up!).

If much of Copland's American music tapped into one enduring American image by evoking the old West and the frontier, his career tapped into another. Copland was a "melting-pot" success story: the Brooklyn-born son of immigrants who rose to fame and fortune. So there is a delicious irony in the fact that Copland would find his American voice not in the new vernacular music that he heard growing up in New York but in music far removed from his early experience.

By the time Copland found his American sound, there were several recognizably American musical styles in the air: among them the music of Ives (which Copland helped promote during the 1920s and 1930s); the numerous black-inspired styles of the early twentieth century—ragtime, jazz, blues, popular song; and the vernacular/classical fusions of Gershwin and others.

That Copland took the particular musical direction he did seems largely the serendipitous confluence of several developments:

- Fascination with life on the frontier—in the West and elsewhere—expressed in popular culture

LISTEN UP!

Copland, *Appalachian Spring*, Sections 1 and 2 (1945)

TAKEAWAY POINT: A fine example of Copland's populist style

STYLE: Twentieth-century nationalism

FORM: Both movements through-composed, but with intermittent repetition

GENRE: Orchestral suite

INSTRUMENTS: Symphony orchestra

CONTEXT: Copland composing accessible modern music

SECTION 1

0:00　Copland's open sound: a tonic (I) chord, played slowly by clarinet, then strings, supported by tonic pitch in middle, then low register. Dominant (V) chord is briefly superimposed over tonic pedal. Everything unfolds slowly.

0:53　Bassoon and low strings present IV chord. Strings take over, mixing IV and I chords.

1:20　Back to I and V, with clarinet returning

1:39　Horn enters after a moment; clarinet and trumpet, then flute follow.

2:06　Oboe enters with melodic figure made up of skips derived from I and IV chords.

2:34　Strings and oboe continue with another skip-filled melodic idea made from the tones of the three basic chords.

3:00　Brief return to opening, then continuing into second section

SECTION 2

3:12　Two short motives, again derived from tonic chord and based on skips. The rhythm of the motive will pervade first part of section. Answering figure formed from triads in other keys.

3:30　Opening motive returns but continues along a different path.

3:41　Flute plays opening figure in different key.

3:48　Brass enter with new motive, also built around a triad. Texture thickens; original melody returns amid sustained hymn-like brass chords.

4:24　Woodwinds return to main melody, then triads, then suddenly loud, with new motive formed from rising skips. Developmental writing with alternation among previously presented motives.

4:56　The dominant short–short–long rhythm, this time on a series of repeated notes; this is compressed; then the rising-skip motive again.

5:20　Quiet section: gentler presentation of the opening melody over hymnlike strings. "Fade-out" ending built from a string of triads.

 Listen to this selection streaming or in an Active Listening Guide at CourseMate or in the eBook.

- Heightened awareness of the "common man," prompted in part by the hardships of the depression
- The urgent drive to preserve the folk heritage of the United States before it was lost
- Copland's musical evolution
- The composer's commitment to a "people's music"

Copland's populist style carried over into other works: his film scores, his famous *Fanfare for the Common Man*, the patriotic *Lincoln Portrait,* and his *Symphony No. 3*, composed in 1945. Although his populist style certainly evokes "spacious skies," "amber waves of grain," and "purple mountain majesties," his works from the late 1930s and early 1940s makes clear that the American sound of Copland's music transcends an exclusively regional identity.

LEARNING OUTCOME 21-3
Recognize how Béla Bartók expressed musical nationalism in the language of Hungarian folk music.

21-3 Bartók and a New Kind of Musical Nationalism

Despite growing up some distance from Budapest, Béla Bartók's ◗ interest in authentic Hungarian folk music remained latent until his chance encounter with Lidi Dósa. It blossomed almost overnight. The following year he met Zoltan Kodály, a fellow Hungarian composer whose enthusiasm for folk music matched his own and whose training complemented Bartók's. His field trips with and without Kodály over the next several years

292 | CHAPTER 21 : national identity in early twentieth-century concert music took him to remote regions of Hungary, into what is now Slovakia, Romania, Bulgaria, and eventually even to Turkey. "Bulgarian" rhythm would become Bartók's term for the asymmetrical rhythms that occur in the folk music of the Balkans, which he would adapt to his own music.

Bartók's fieldwork represented a breakthrough in the collection, preservation, and transformation of folk music. His goal was to locate national identity in this music, so his objective was to distinguish it from more mainstream urban music. He brought to this task his own remarkable musical abilities and a brand-new technology—sound recording. As a result, he was able to transcribe the music he collected with an unprecedented accuracy. It would become the essential tool for defining his music apart from the international style whose base was in German-speaking Europe.

21-3A Bartók and Hungarian Identity

During Bartók's childhood, what would become Hungary was part of the Austro-Hungarian Empire—the diminished descendant of the Holy Roman Empire, which had encompassed virtually all of central Europe from the tenth through the eighteenth centuries. The empire had always been a relatively loose confederation of small political entities ruled by kings, princes, dukes, and other royalty. By the late nineteenth century, the empire was a patchwork of numerous ethnic groups, with two governments—one for Austria and the western part of the empire; the other for Hungary and the east. The emperor ruled over both in theory, but not always in practice. Like the division of the empire into two largely independent entities, the emergence of "official" languages throughout the empire as alternatives to German was a further indication of the erosion of central authority.

Nevertheless, Vienna remained the capital, politically and culturally. Its influence was evident throughout the empire, especially in urban centers such as Prague and Budapest. Just as Russians looked to France for cultural guidance, so did the middle and upper classes in provincial capitals follow Vienna's lead. In Budapest, German and Jewish musicians were prominent in

© Andranik7/ShutterStock.com

▶ Béla Bartók
FAST FACTS

- Dates: 1881–1945
- Place: Hungary/Romania
- Reasons to remember: The greatest Hungarian composer in the first half of the twentieth century and a pioneer ethnomusicologist

musical life; so were the gypsy bands that purported to play authentic Hungarian music.

Bartók was raised on the outskirts of the empire. He was born in a small town that is now part of Romania. After his father's death in 1888, his family moved several times, finally settling in Pozsony—now Bratislava, the capital of Slovakia—where he gave his first public recital. He went to Budapest at eighteen to receive formal training in piano and composition. Musically, he was at first drawn to the works of German composers, particularly the modernist Richard Strauss. The developmental procedures found in eighteenth- and nineteenth-century Austro-German music would remain a prominent feature of his large-scale compositions throughout his career, but they would be transformed by the use of folk materials.

21-3B Bartók, Folk Music, and Art Composition

The composer's deep immersion in folk music had idealistic, personal, and practical implications. Like other folklorists active in the first part of the century, he felt that by collecting this music, he was preserving a heritage that would soon be lost and providing a firm foundation for a national art music. Sorting through the music that he had collected was an intellectual problem that intrigued him throughout his life and was a task left incomplete at his death. Most significantly, Bartók fully absorbed the music that he studied. From the 1910s to the end of his career, virtually all of his music showed qualities that identified it as the work of an eastern European composer.

No major composer left a more comprehensive record of involvement with the folk music of his homeland than Bartók. His legacy includes field recordings and transcriptions of folk music throughout the eastern part of the empire; compositions that show the full spectrum of possibility when blending folk and art music—from simple settings to abstract compositions; essays on the connection between the two; and his recordings of his own music.

© iStockPhoto.com/Günay Mutlu

 **LISTEN UP!**

Bartók, *Music for Strings, Percussion, and Celesta,* 2nd movement (1936)

TAKEAWAY POINT: Vigorous music with deep folk roots and a modern sound

STYLE: Twentieth-century nationalism

FORM: Modified sonata form

GENRE: Orchestral music

INSTRUMENTS: String orchestra, plus percussion and keyboard instruments

CONTEXT: Original, imaginative concert music expressing a Hungarian identity

EXPOSITION

0:00   Brief introduction (pizzicato strings), then vigorous opening theme. Note continuing development of the material and the dialogue between string sections.

0:25   A brief lull, then active development of a short motive, with an increasingly contrapuntal texture and fragmentation of the melodic material

0:54   Contrasting theme: a folklike melody, developed only slightly, then repeated by the lower strings

1:09   A new melodic fragment in the violins initiates another round of developmental writing, this time reaching a moment of relative stasis on sustained trills throughout the strings.

1:31   Another new motive, again subject to immediate development; activity under a repeated note; gradual fading away

2:03   Piano enters with altered version of its first entrance; further fragmentation, rhythmic excitement, leading to syncopated chords in strings; timpani solo marks end of exposition.

DEVELOPMENT

2:27   Return and expansion of pizzicato introduction signals the beginning of development. First section consists of piano chords and percussion over steady, active pizzicato strings.

3:09   A long section with contrapuntal lines played by pizzicato strings and—later—harp

3:59   Percussion-only interlude marks beginning of third part of development, here featuring bowed strings with mutes treating a motive contrapuntally. After entering, each part spins off into scale passages, eventually creating a pulsing sound mass.

4:31   The simple two-note motive heard throughout the movement emerges.

RECAPITULATION

5:01   Return of opening theme, but in a new, compound meter. Its development is somewhat shorter.

5:35   The contrasting theme, significantly altered by the new meter and varied instrumentation

5:59   Climactic section, which develops simple motives over repeated notes/trills

6:30   Final restatement of the opening theme, in the original meter and at a faster tempo leads to final flurry; the movement ends with the scale fragment from the piano's first entrance, played backwards—to end on the tonic note.

 Listen to this selection streaming or in an Active Listening Guide at CourseMate or in the eBook.

In a 1941 lecture entitled "The Relation between Contemporary Hungarian Art Music and Folk Music," Bartók enumerated five levels of folk influence on art music, which reflect varying degrees of the balance between folk and art elements. The most folklike was presenting the folk melody with a simple, unobtrusive accompaniment. The more artful end of the spectrum involved imitating specific features—such as particular scales or rhythms—or evoking the spirit of the music without referencing folk materials directly. We hear an example of Bartók's individual fusion of folk and contemporary art elements in the second movement from *Music for Strings, Percussion, and Celesta* (see Listen Up!).

21-3C *Music for Strings, Percussion, and Celesta*

Bartók's *Music for Strings, Percussion, and Celesta* was commissioned by Paul Sacher, the conductor of the Basel Chamber Orchestra and an immensely wealthy man who would commission works from several leading European composers, including Stravinsky. Bartók completed the work in 1936; the premiere took place in January 1937. There are four movements, in a slow–fast–slow–fast sequence. The work has an unusual scoring: full string orchestra, divided into two sections that answer back and forth, plus a large array of percussion instruments, harp, piano, and celesta (a keyboard instrument that produces a bell-like sound). There are no winds or brass.

21-3D The Spirit of Hungarian Music

What's remarkable about works like the *Music for Strings, Percussion, and Celesta*, where the national element is present in spirit only, is how seamlessly the folk elements are integrated into the fabric of the piece. The energetic rhythms, the percussive sound world that enhances them, the catchy motive-based themes, the novel effects, and the frequent—if incessantly varied—repetition invest the music with accessible and interesting points of entry. All reflect the inspiration, if not the direct imitation, of folk music. The music sounds modern, Hungarian, and personal, in large part because Bartók did not have to embed the folk elements into common practice. Rather, he was able to use them as a springboard for a unique sound: one with an eastern European identity.

As a result, Bartók *was* Hungarian music to the concertgoing world between the wars, and even more so in the two decades after his death. His music was far better known than his colleague Kodály's and that of every other non-Russian composer from eastern Europe. It remains a stellar example of a nationalistic music from the first part of the twentieth century.

Bartók's search for national identity came from within. In the Soviet Union, national identity was imposed from above: the guardians of socialist realism required that works of art be accessible to the proletariat so that they could be used as propaganda tools.

> **LEARNING OUTCOME 21-4**
> Describe the challenging musical path that Sergei Prokofiev traced in finding artistic expression within a restrictive, government-imposed framework.

21-4 Prokofiev, Totalitarianism, and Music for Film

For musicians living in central and eastern Europe during the 1930s, the overriding facts of life were the rise of totalitarian governments and the military aggression of

‣Sergei Prokofiev
FAST FACTS

- Dates: 1891–1953
- Place: Ukraine
- Reasons to remember: One of the two greatest Soviet composers during the Stalinist era

© Igor Golovniov/ShutterStock.com

Nazi Germany, the Soviet Union, and Italy, which would lead to all-out war by 1939. Some, especially those of Jewish descent, fled Europe; several ultimately settled in the United States. Schoenberg was teaching in Berlin when the Nazis came to power. He left in 1933 and in 1936 joined the music faculty at UCLA. Among the other Jewish musicians affected by the Nazis were two who ended up near Schoenberg; they were among the European-born film composers working for Hollywood studios. Franz Waxman arrived in the United States in 1935; he would immediately become a top film composer and single-handedly defined music for horror films with his score for *The Bride of Frankenstein* (1935). After shuttling back and forth between the United States and Austria during the 1930s, Erich Korngold returned to the United States in 1938 to compose the film score for *The Adventures of Robin Hood*, just before the Anschluss, which annexed Austria to Germany. He did not return home again.

The Hungarian composer Béla Bartók contemplated leaving his homeland through the latter half of the 1930s but could not leave his mother behind. He left Hungary only in 1940, less than a year after she passed away. By contrast, the Russian composer Sergei Prokofiev (1891–1953) jumped from the frying pan into the fire: he returned to the Soviet Union in 1936 after living abroad for almost twenty years, then had to deal with the Soviet authorities, from Stalin on, for the rest of his life.

21-4A Sergei Prokofiev

Josef Stalin died on March 5, 1953, after almost thirty years of increasingly brutal rule of the Soviet Union. On that same day, the composer Sergei Prokofiev ‣ also passed away. It was the ultimate irony in the life of a composer whose career, like his music, was laced with irony. Among the composers of his time, Prokofiev stands apart, because of the complex crosscurrents among personal ambition, patriotism, and political circumstances that shaped his career decisions.

Prokofiev was born in the Ukraine, at that time part of the Russian Empire, and grew up in a relatively privileged environment. He received his musical education in St. Petersburg during a time of political and artistic ferment. Almost from the start of his career, he sought to pursue his own provocative path as a composer and pianist: among his early piano works are his first concerto, a work entitled "Diabolic Suggestion," which established him as a major talent, and a series of several small solo piano pieces called "Sarcasms."

Shortly after the Russian Revolution in 1917, Prokofiev decided to leave Russia, as his initial enthusiasm for the uprising gave way to the realization that the new Russia would not be a congenial place for artists. Accordingly, he left for the United States the following year, where he met his Spanish-born wife, an opera singer. They moved to Europe in 1922, where they used Paris as a home base, and married the following year. Prokofiev toured frequently as a pianist and composed prolifically in virtually all genres, including opera, ballet, orchestral music, and piano music.

Prokofiev was dissatisfied with his situation in the West. During his time away from his homeland, he saw himself as professionally overshadowed by the Russian pianist-composer Sergei Rachmaninoff in the United States and Stravinsky in Paris. Reciprocal contact with the Soviet Union, which began around the time of his move to Paris, led to an invitation to perform in 1927, and eventually to his return in 1936.

Prokofiev was aware of the political changes in the Soviet Union, particularly as they affected artists: around the time of his return, he publicly declared that he was simplifying his compositional approach, which would bring it in line with "socialist realism." Patriotic sentiments and homesickness were apparently other factors in his decision. He wrote to friends that he needed to "hear the Russian language in my ears." Perhaps he also saw what he thought was an opportunity to be top dog: Dmitri Shostakovich, the most esteemed Soviet composer during the 1930s, had just fallen out of favor with the cultural bureaucrats.

Whatever his motivation for returning, it is clear in retrospect that Prokofiev's decision to return to his homeland made the last years of his life increasingly difficult. The praise and support given his music during his years abroad diminished dramatically once he returned. He soon relinquished his passport, had performances canceled, and received critical reviews in official publications. After World War II, he lived a nightmare: he had works banned, had to write a public "apology" for straying from the goals of socialist realism, and learned from his sons that Lina, his first wife, whom he had left in 1941, had been sentenced to twenty years in a labor camp. It was a dismal end to a career that had seemed so promising earlier in the century.

Aside from *Peter and the Wolf*, which he composed in 1936, the work of the late 1930s that attracted the most favorable reviews both in and outside the Soviet Union was his film score to *Alexander Nevsky*. It involved a new kind of collaboration between composer and film director, in a medium that was still taking shape.

21-4B Music and Film in the Early Twentieth Century

Music *inspired by* cinema developed more rapidly than music *for* cinema. Although Debussy had predicted in 1913 that "apply[ing] to pure music the techniques of cinematography" would be the "one way of reviving the taste for symphonic music" and clearly followed his own advice in his compositions, he never composed a film score.

During Debussy's lifetime, original film scores by established composers were rare. Far more common were printed anthologies filled with stock musical snippets—either original or borrowed from classical compositions—for common dramatic situations: a villain doing a dastardly deed, a hero riding to the rescue, the romantic moment between the hero and the fair maiden he saved. These were often based on or influenced by music used for melodrama. During the silent film era, theaters engaged pianists, organists, and even orchestras to supply this music; typically, they played continuously throughout the film.

Musical backgrounds often disappeared during the action in the first talking films; film musicals were the major exception. One reason was the relatively primitive state of the technology. Initially, music had to be recorded while the scene was being shot, which presented severe logistical difficulties and constrained film editing because everything had to be planned in advance.

Only in the early 1930s did it become possible to dub in sound after filming. Composers quickly took advantage of the new technology. In Hollywood, the trend-setter was Max Steiner. Steiner had emigrated from his native Austria to Hollywood by way of London and New York, where he acquired considerable experience as a conductor and orchestra-tor-arranger of musical stage productions. Shortly after his arrival in Hollywood, he composed the score to the 1933 film *King Kong*. It was novel and stunningly successful, and almost overnight it became the model for Hollywood sound tracks. Steiner and other European-trained film composers adapted Romanticism—complete with Wagnerian leitmotifs—and impressionism to film scoring.

Film composers in Europe often charted a different, more experimental path. Among the most significant was Prokofiev, whose collaborations with Eisenstein would prove to be among the most influential film scores of the 1930s and 1940s.

> Music inspired by cinema developed more rapidly than music for cinema.

Walt Disney's work was extraordinarily popular in Russia during the 1930s: he was the only American filmmaker honored at the first Moscow Film Festival in 1935. Two Russian artists were among those who had visited the Disney Studios in Hollywood to witness the production process firsthand. The film director Sergei Eisenstein spent time there in 1930. Eight years later, the composer-pianist Sergei Prokofiev also visited and spent a day with Disney at his home.

Eisenstein's and Prokofiev's direct contact with the working methods at the Disney Studios would have a profound influence on their first collaboration on a sound film, the 1938 epic *Alexander Nevsky*.

21-4D *Alexander Nevsky*

In the face of Hitler's rise to power in 1933 and his escalating hostile threats, the Soviet government commissioned a propaganda film disguised as a historical drama.

Alexander Nevsky celebrates the achievements of Prince Alexander, who saved Novgorod, a city in northwest Russia, by reaching an agreement with the Mongols (who had swept through much of Russia from the east) and defeating two invaders from the West (the Swedes and a crusading band of Teutonic Knights).

The climax of the film is the 1242 "Battle on the Ice," in which an army of foot soldiers defeated the mounted crusaders. The scene, which lasts about thirty minutes, is a thinly disguised allegory. Almost seven centuries after the 1242 encounter, Russians again faced the threat of invasion by a technologically

mickey mousing The close synchronization of music with on-screen action

Max Steiner composed the score to the 1933 film *King Kong.*

21-4C Sergei Prokofiev and the Art of Composing for Film

In the film industry, mickey mousing refers to the close synchronization of music with on-screen action. The term came into use because the Walt Disney Studios were the first to coordinate film and sound track with great precision. As early as "The Skeleton Dance" (1929), Disney's first *Silly Symphony*, there was almost flawless integration between the music—which in this instance featured an adaptation of nineteenth-century Norwegian composer Edvard Grieg's "March of the Trolls"—and the movements of the characters. In this respect, Disney was far ahead of conventional filmmakers.

New York Philharmonic performing Sergei Prokofiev's *Alexander Nevsky* to the film by Sergei Eisenstein

prokofiev, totalitarianism, and music for film | **297**

Prokofiev, "Peregrinus expectavi" ("The Foreigners Are Expected"), from *Alexander Nevsky* (1938)

TAKEAWAY POINT: An early example of film music that is integral to the message of the film

FORM: Through-composed

GENRE: Voices and orchestra

INSTRUMENTS: Voices and orchestra

CONTEXT: Compelling music that sets the mood for the beginning of a battle

0:00   Ominous opening—high sustained strings, abrasive lower strings

0:44   Similar material in new key, with strings occasionally swirling around

1:24   Muted horn plays chantlike melody over sustained strings

1:51   Chantlike melody now sung and played

2:12   The Teutonic army is seen from a distance as they begin their attack. Prokofiev portrays white knights as evil through dark sounds—motives in low brass and relentless rhythm supporting them.

3:02   High and mid-range strings and winds enter as cavalry draws closer. Biting two-note fragments underscore the anxiety of the Russian infantry.

3:27   The chantlike melody blared out by the brass, as mounted knights stream across the screen

3:45   Biting strings/muted trumpet figures return; then they are combined with ponderous melodic fragment in low brass. New ideas based on simple materials follow.

4:20   Choir sings a folk song–like melody as Russians prepare to meet invaders; folk tune is combined with earlier material, notably the dark motives first played by low brass, now played in higher register.

5:20   Return of earlier material, but presented at a quicker pace as the battle is about to be joined

 Listen to this selection streaming or in an Active Listening Guide at CourseMate or in the eBook.

more advanced German enemy. Its message to the Russian people was, in effect, "We did it before, and we can do it again."

The film was released in 1938 and received favorable press within the Soviet Union and in the West. However, when Germany and the Soviet Union signed a nonaggression pact in August 1939, the film was abruptly withdrawn from circulation. It would be re-released about two years later, when Germany invaded the Soviet Union.

In creating the film, Eisenstein and Prokofiev enjoyed an extremely close working relationship, which resulted in unprecedented integration of film and music. Each admired the other's work. Prokofiev stated that Eisenstein was Russia's finest film director, and Eisenstein, who was knowledgeable about music, commented on how quickly and easily Prokofiev supplied music for recently shot scenes. Prokofiev composed to rough cuts—footage with only preliminary editing—during the shooting of the film, and Eisenstein often synchronized his edits with Prokofiev's music. One product of this working method was a fusion of image and sound,

where they combine to largely replace dialogue as the narrative element. This innovative approach is used to great effect in the battle on the ice.

The musical excerpt presented here (Listen Up!) is the music that underscores the opening of the battle, from the time when the Russian lookouts spy the Teutonic enemy in the distance to the moment they engage. This first part of the battle scene lasts over six minutes. There is virtually no dialogue. Instead, Eisenstein uses Prokofiev's music and his own montage technique (in montage, fragmentary clips are edited together to form a continuous whole) to build almost unbearable tension that is released only with the shouts of the combatants. Prokofiev's music begins ominously with sustained chords spread from extremely high to extremely low. As the camera shifts from the Russians to the Teutonic Knights, Prokofiev parodies medieval chant, first played by horns made to sound ancient, then sung. A relentless rhythm that carries through the final part of the scene accompanies the cavalry as they begin their advance. Several motives, mostly in a low range, add to the suspense: as the forces draw closer, the cuts between shots become faster, and the motives pile on top of each other, until the music gives way to the thunder of hooves and the sounds of the battle.

This scene dramatically highlights the way in which music and on-screen action work synergistically to convey the emotional impact of the scene. Despite Eisenstein's use of montage to create opposition and tension, the scene falls flat without sound. Although Prokofiev soon arranged the music for *Alexander Nevsky* into a cantata for concert performance, his music has considerably more impact when heard as part of the film. This functional concept has influenced several generations of film composers.

Eisenstein and Prokofiev would collaborate once again during the 1940s on a trilogy about Ivan the Terrible. The first film won the Stalin Prize, and the second film was banned. Eisenstein died in 1948, before he finished the third and final film; most of it was confiscated and destroyed.

Looking Back, Looking Ahead

The four musical examples of nationalism considered in this unit highlight both their composers' common ground and differences in approach with each other and with nineteenth-century nationalism. The works connect to each other and to earlier nationalistic music in that all were grounded in some way in the music of peoples within their homeland and concerned with reaching out to those who inspired the music. Yet the composers were also in tune with current developments in modern music, and their music bears evidence of that. All four composers found a balance between modernity and accessibility. The music is innovative, but it contains familiar and appealing features: vigorous rhythms, tuneful motives, restructured common practice chords, and a variety of percussion instruments. In this way, these composers turned back to the people, even as many of their peers seemed to be turning their back on a larger audience in the pursuit of their art.

The progressive nationalism of these and other like-minded composers represented an important new direction in concert music during the 1930s and into the 1940s. However, this trend largely disappeared after World War II, with the increasing influence of serial composition—both Stravinsky and Copland would adopt serial techniques during the 1950s—and the continuing expansion of musical frontiers by members of the avant-garde. We explore several of these new developments in Chapter 23.

 study tools 21

LEARNING OUTCOMES

After reading this chapter, you will be able to do the following:

22-1 List the most significant aspects of ragtime's legacy.

22-2 Be familiar with the role of jazz in the evolution of American music.

22-3 Describe the place of classic blues as the first "first-person" music in American culture.

22-4 Describe the blossoming of the modern age in popular music.

22-5 Discover the sound of 1920s American popular song and its use in Broadway musicals.

22-6 Appreciate how George Gershwin's "symphonic jazz" contributed to the new classics of the modern era.

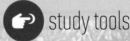 study tools

After you read this chapter, go to the Study Tools at the end of the chapter, page 317.

Among the bigger hits of 1896 was a song entitled "All Coons Look Alike to Me." In our own time, a song with that title would seem to be the work of a first-class bigot. However, the end of the nineteenth century was a low point in post–Civil War race relations; in the same year that the song appeared, the Supreme Court's decision in *Plessy* v. *Ferguson* ratified the "separate but equal" policy that became the law of the land until the 1950s. In this environment, most mainstream Americans seemed not to find derogatory racial terms particularly offensive.

As it happened, the composer of "All Coons Look Alike to Me" was not a bigot, but a black man. Ernest Hogan was one of the leading black entertainers of the time. He had begun his career as a minstrel, performed extensively in black vaudeville, and was among the first wave of black stars on Broadway.

Hogan's title was an unfortunate choice. It offended many blacks, to the extent that some black performers replaced "coon" with another term when they sang the song. It also created a vogue for "coon songs," which white performers sang without apparent embarrassment. And it offered little clue to the content of the lyric. Hogan's song is romantic: it describes a young man who has eyes for only one girl; other girls "look alike" to him. However, in a climate where the majority of Americans assumed that blacks were inferior, a love song between blacks was not socially acceptable outside the black community. So Hogan found himself with a bitter choice: buy into the stereotypes of the time—even as he tried to undermine them somewhat in the lyric—or fail to get the song published.

Hogan's music is the good news that balances the bad news of the title. In the published version of "All Coons Look Alike to Me," the repetition of the chorus features a "Negro 'rag' accompaniment." This was the first published example of raglike piano style. The first published piano rags, including Scott Joplin's "Original Rags," appeared a year later.

Ragtime was the first of several African American vernacular musical styles that would transform American music in the first three decades of the twentieth century. Blues and jazz would follow in the teens and flourish in the twenties. All three were important musical genres in their own right, and they would dramatically reshape popular song and attract the interest of important composers. Our examples highlight all of these trends.

LEARNING OUTCOME 22-1
List the most significant aspects of ragtime's legacy.

22-1 Ragtime

Ragtime first surfaced as an obscure folk-dance music played throughout the Mississippi valley in the last quarter of the nineteenth century. Soon black pianists were playing it in bars and bordellos in the Midwest and along the East Coast.

Toward the end of the century, the terms rag and ragtime came into use to identify this new style. They were applied to any music with even a hint of syncopation, or "ragged" rhythm. Authenticity was not an issue: it seemed to matter little whether whites or blacks performed it, how much syncopation it contained, or whether it was vocal or instrumental. Among the entertainers most responsible for its popularity was Ben Harney, a white singer-pianist-comedian who was a vaudeville headliner around the turn of the century. Harney's *Ragtime Instructor*, published in 1897, showed aspiring pianists how to "rag" (that is, syncopate) popular songs, classical compositions, and other well-known

Wolcott/Library of Congress, Prints and Photographs Division [LC-USF351-113]

Black pianists began playing ragtime in bars.

works. Sousa's band would introduce these syncopated rhythms in Europe: their performance of Fred Stone's 1898 dance, "Ma Ragtime Baby," won a prize at the Paris Exposition in 1900. Only with the publication of the rags of Joplin and others, most notably Joplin's "Maple Leaf Rag" (1899), did "rag" come to refer primarily to the piano music with which we now associate the term.

The sudden popularity of ragtime provoked a powerful backlash from virtually every corner of the establishment, musical and otherwise. In their view, ragtime was immoral, fit only for the saloons and brothels where it was played, and musically inferior, the product of an inferior race incapable of the musical sophistication that Europeans had achieved. Ragtime was also seen as a cause of moral decay. The "Ragtime Evil" should not be found in Christian homes, according to one writer. It is in this environment that Scott Joplin sought to elevate ragtime from a popular style into art.

22-1A Scott Joplin and the Piano Rag

The most enduring music of the ragtime era has been the classic piano rags of Scott Joplin ♪. These have remained familiar, especially since the ragtime revival of the 1970s. Joplin's "Maple Leaf Rag" was the first commercially successful piano rag, and his output of piano rags remains the core of the ragtime repertoire.

A professional musician from his teenage years, Joplin played in saloons and clubs, at first along the Mississippi valley and eventually in Sedalia, Missouri. The "Maple Leaf Rag" is named after the Maple Leaf

ragtime, rag Syncopated American musical style of the late nineteenth and early twentieth centuries that began as dance music in the bordello districts of New Orleans

301

Arkady Mazor/Shutterstock.com

►Scott Joplin
FAST FACTS

- Dates: 1868–1917
- Place: United States
- Reasons to remember: Through ragtime, introduced African American elements into American popular music

Club in Sedalia, his place of employment from 1894 until the turn of the century. He also received formal musical training in the European tradition, principally through study at George R. Smith College in Sedalia, and was a fluent composer and arranger in the white popular styles of the day.

In the wake of his success with "Maple Leaf Rag," Joplin devoted most of his efforts as a composer and musician to legitimizing ragtime. This is evident in his and his publisher's insistence on referring to Joplin's rags as "classic" and in his excursions into large-scale classical genres: he composed a ballet, *The Ragtime Dance*, and two operas, *Treemonisha* and the now-lost *A Guest of Honor*.

The rags that followed "Maple Leaf Rag" are typically more melodious and less syncopated. The syncopated figurations that characterize ragtime are present, but they do not permeate the rags and are somewhat toned down from those found in Joplin's first rags. Moreover, in both his tempo indications for rags and written commentary on the correct performance of ragtime, Joplin constantly admonishes pianists against playing ragtime too fast: for him, ragtime played at a slower tempo gains in dignity.

A Joplin piano rag is, in essence, a march that has been "ragged," played on the piano. Virtually all of its musical features come from the European tradition; only the syncopations hint at its African heritage. We hear this in one of Joplin's best-known rags, "The Entertainer" (see Listen Up!).

22-1B The Legacy of Ragtime

Ragtime would have a profound impact on the African American community, on musical life in the United States, on the appeal of American music abroad, and on the relationship between classical and vernacular

jazz A genre consisting of a group of popular styles primarily for listening; usually distinguished from the other popular music of an era by greater rhythmic freedom (more syncopation and/or less insistent beat keeping), extensive improvisation, and more-adventurous harmony

traditions. These are among the most significant aspects of ragtime's legacy:

1. *The music itself.* The classic piano rags of Scott Joplin and other distinguished composers constitute a repertoire of real artistic worth and individuality.
2. *The introduction of an authentic black music to white America.* Because it could be notated, ragtime was the first authentically black music to enter the mainstream.
3. *The blurring of boundaries between classical and vernacular.* Joplin aspired to art; the new syncopated music intrigued important composers of art music, including the American composer Charles Ives, as well as Debussy and Stravinsky.
4. *The transformation of popular music.* Ragtime would play a crucial role in introducing African American elements into popular music.

In all these ways, ragtime was, by example and influence, a catalyst for change—within the world of music and within American society.

In his rags, Joplin strives to elevate the vernacular dance music of an oppressed minority into art by following European practice. Nevertheless, its outstanding feature is the characteristic syncopation. This infused his rags with a particularly American vitality, and the fusion of African-inspired rhythms with European practice invested the music with a particularly African American elegance.

22-2 Jazz in the Early Modern Era

Like ragtime, jazz began as an obscure regional black music. It exploded on the music scene in the United States and abroad during the 1910s and early 1920s. It would be recognized as a vibrant and distinctive music by the end of the decade. In its purest form, it stood apart from popular music. Yet it was notorious and influential enough to embody the spirit of a decade and give it its name.

22-2A The Roots of Jazz

We do know that New Orleans was the birthplace of jazz and that contemporary accounts date its beginnings sometime around the turn of the century. It flourished in the rich cultural mix that was New Orleans: whites of English and French descent, blacks, immigrants from the Caribbean and Europe, plus many citizens of mixed race. Then as now, New Orleans liked to let the good times roll, and music was part of this mix: brass bands for parades; pianists and small groups for the bars, honky-tonks, and houses of prostitution. (From 1897 to 1917, prostitution was legal in New Orleans; it was confined to Storyville, a small area near the French Quarter.)

 **LISTEN UP!**

Joplin, "The Entertainer" (1902)

TAKEAWAY POINT: An elegant example of the classic piano rag

STYLE: Ragtime

FORM: Multisection

GENRE: Piano rag

INSTRUMENT: Piano

CONTEXT: Joplin working to dignify "saloon music"

INTRO

0:00   The first hint of syncopation

STRAIN 1

0:06   A question-and-answer pair of melodic ideas. Both are syncopated, and both focus on the syncopation by repeating the same pitches.

0:29   The syncopations occur over the steady OOM-pah accompaniment, borrowed from the march.

STRAIN 2

0:51   Here the question and answer opposes a syncopated repeated pattern with more running, unsyncopated figuration.

1:14   Joplin requests that the melody be played an octave higher.

1:36   Question-and-answer pair, as before

STRAIN 3: TRIO

1:59   A series of short phrases, with a hint of syncopation and more of the question and answer exchanges

2:21   Literal repetition of the previous section

INTERLUDE

2:43   Interlude

STRAIN 4

2:49   The opening melodic idea again focuses on the syncopation by repeating the same two notes.

3:11   As before

 Listen to this selection streaming or in an Active Listening Guide at CourseMate or in the eBook.

Throughout much of the nineteenth century, New Orleans had been a relatively hospitable environment for blacks. During the period of slavery, Congo Square (now Louis Armstrong Park) was the only part of the South where people of African descent could legally gather and play drums and other percussion instruments. Over time, New Orleans developed a complex social structure in which the proportion of European and African blood was the main determinant of social status. "Creoles of color," those with ancestors from France and Africa, enjoyed a higher social standing than ex-slaves. They lived in better neighborhoods, were better educated, and had more freedom. An aspiring Creole musician received traditional classical training, whereas black musicians typically learned to play by ear. Creoles of color tended to look down on the ex-slaves. They emulated white culture rather than black. That changed with the passage of "Jim Crow" legislation, most notably the *Plessy* v. *Ferguson* decision that made "separate but equal" legal and reduced race in New Orleans to simply "white" and "colored."

© iStockPhoto.com/jtgriffin07

Nevertheless, contact among the musicians who created jazz remained relatively open: jazz would develop from the interaction of blacks, Creoles, and whites. Several lighter-skinned blacks worked not only in black bands but also in the mostly white band of "Papa Jack" Laine, the top white bandleader in New Orleans around the turn of the century. Among the alumni of Laine's band were the five original members of the Original Dixieland Jazz Band. This all-white group was the first jazz band to record; their first discs appeared in 1917, at a time when many white bands in the North refused to play the new syncopated music because of its low-life association. The group's recordings were a novelty success. They put the word *jazz* on people's lips, and a jazzlike sound in people's ears.

22-2B The Sound of Jazz in the 1920s

The first jazz bands, black and white, were small groups of five to eight musicians. The standard New Orleans jazz band blended the instrumentation of three key popular music genres. From the marching band came the clarinet, cornet or trumpet, trombone, sousaphone, and drum line, now consolidated into a set that could be played by a single musician. From the minstrel show came the banjo, and from the saloons and bordellos came the piano.

These instruments were grouped into two distinct units, the front line and the rhythm section. The front line (so called because the musicians stood at the front of the bandstand) typically featured three of the band instruments: clarinet, trumpet or cornet, and trombone. A complete rhythm section consisted of banjo, piano, brass bass (sousaphone), and drums; many early jazz recordings (including the Armstrong recording discussed later) feature partial rhythm sections. The front line instruments played melody-like lines. The rhythm section had two jobs: to mark the beat and to supply the harmony.

Precedents for the rhythm section date from the Renaissance; the Baroque continuo is similar in many respects. However, the novel features in the jazz rhythm section that distinguished it from earlier practice were the emphasis on percussive sounds, most obviously in the drums, but also in the bass and chord instruments, and the rhythmic conception of the musicians, which was fundamentally different from most European music. This new rhythmic approach was called "swing."

front line The wind and brass instruments (or other melody-line instruments) in a jazz combo; from the position of the players on the bandstand, standing in a line in front of the rhythm instruments

rhythm section The part of a musical group that supplies the rhythmic and harmonic foundation of a performance; usually includes at least one chord instrument (guitar, piano, or keyboard), a bass instrument, and a percussion instrument (typically the drum set)

swing Rhythmic play over a four-beat rhythm

improvisation Creating music spontaneously rather than performing a previously learned song the same way every time; one of the key elements of jazz

22-2C Swing

Swing is the essence of jazz, as Duke Ellington asserted in the title of his 1932 song "It Don't Mean a Thing (If It Ain't Got That Swing)." Here is a succinct definition of swing: rhythmic play over a four-beat rhythm. Both the four-beat rhythm and the rhythmic play over it were paradigm-shifting innovations. They were the clearest indications that jazz—and the popular music that it influenced—had embraced a new rhythmic approach, which was the product of an African-derived reinterpretation of European rhythm. The term *four-beat rhythm* is a numerical way of identifying the particular nature of the steady timekeeping that underpins all other rhythmic activity. "Four-beat" refers to the equal emphasis on each beat of a measure with four beats. In Armstrong's "Hotter Than That," which we hear next, the pianist and guitarist typically play chords on each beat; each receives the same amount of emphasis. This is the typical rhythmic foundation of jazz, although it can be expressed in varied ways.

The black musicians who created jazz kept the metrical structure of European music but interpreted it through an African sensibility. Instead of accenting the first beat of each measure, jazz musicians who marked the beat typically stressed all beats equally. The unvarying emphasis on each beat in jazz was a fundamental departure from nineteenth-century practice in concert music, even in dance-influenced music: recall the pronounced differentiation among beats in Tchaikovsky's waltz. So was the rhythmic play over this relentless rhythm.

In isolation, the undifferentiated beats of the rhythm instruments do not produce swing. Swing results from the interplay between the beat and the syncopated accents and irregular patterns that conflict with the steady timekeeping of the rhythm instruments. It is this interplay that makes the rhythm so irresistible and differentiates jazz from all other music of the 1920s and before.

The ease and daring with which a jazz musician played over time was one measure of artistry. Often it was especially infectious because it happened spontaneously, during an improvisation.

22-2D Improvisation

Jazz restored improvisation to mainstream musical practice in Western culture. In music, to improvise means to create new music in the moment—as one is singing or playing—rather than re-creating someone else's composition. Improvisation in music is comparable to a comedy troupe's creating a skit on the spot from an audience suggestion rather than performing a well-rehearsed and fully scripted routine.

The first generation of jazz musicians began with a melody and supporting harmony, then improvised a series of variations that consisted of new melodies over the underlying harmony. In this respect, they are similar in approach to the Mozart variation sets, which began as improvisations. However, unlike Mozart's variation sets, improvised variations in jazz flow continuously; there is no break between variations.

Improvisation was part of classical music through the early nineteenth century: Bach, Mozart, Beethoven, Clara Schumann, and Franz Liszt were all gifted improvisers. However, by 1850 it had largely disappeared from concert music. It returned with jazz, but in a radically different form, because of the interplay among musicians, instrumentation of the jazz band, the jazz rhythm, and the overall feel of the music. Still, the formal organization (theme and variations) and improvisational approach (new melodies over the same harmony) of early jazz are remarkably similar to European practice.

It is likely that improvisation was customary in popular entertainments, especially those involving black musicians: ragtime and blues can be improvised music. But only with jazz does a sophisticated form of improvisation become an integral component of a new genre. We hear this new approach to improvisation in "Hotter Than That," a recording by Louis Armstrong's Hot Five.

22-2E Louis Armstrong

In 1922, Louis Armstrong received an invitation from fellow cornetist Joe Oliver to join him in Chicago. During the late 1910s, Oliver led the top black jazz band in New Orleans. He moved them north in 1919, leaving Armstrong behind. Armstrong accepted Oliver's invitation and married Lil Hardin, the pianist with Oliver's band, early in 1924. Soon after, they moved to New York, where Armstrong joined Fletcher Henderson's hot dance orchestra. In New York, Armstrong was a regular in the studio as well as the bandstand, recording with Henderson, a host of blues singers (including Bessie Smith), and the pianist Clarence Williams. Williams, who doubled as Okeh Records' A&R (artists and repertoire) man, noticed that the recordings on which he used Armstrong sold better than others. So in 1925, he offered Armstrong the chance to record as a leader rather than as a sideman. Armstrong, who had returned to Chicago, proceeded to record with what amounted to a studio band of his New Orleans friends, plus Hardin (and, somewhat later, the pianist Earl Hines). Okeh billed them as Louis Armstrong's Hot Five or Hot Seven (depending on the number of players). Armstrong's groups made dozens of recordings over the next four years and made jazz—and music—history in the process.

Louis Armstrong recorded "Hotter Than That" with the Hot Five combo in December 1927. The other band members included clarinetist Johnny Dodds and trombonist Kid Ory—both of whom Armstrong knew from New Orleans—pianist Hardin, and guitarist Lonnie Johnson, an able blues and jazz musician. This recording is unusual in that it features a scat vocal solo from Armstrong in addition to his trumpet playing at the beginning and end. (Scat singing is an improvised instrumental-style vocal with no words.)

The harmonic framework for "Hotter Than That" (see Listen Up!) consists of two 16-measure harmonic progressions. Songs containing two 16-measure phrases were

scat singing Improvised instrumental-style vocal with no words

Joe "King" Oliver's Creole Jazz Band in 1923. From left to right: Honore Dutrey, trombone; Baby Dodds, drums; Joe Oliver, lead cornet; Louis Armstrong, slide trumpet; Lil Hardin, piano; Bill Johnson, banjo; and Johnny Dodds, clarinet

Frank Driggs Collection/Hulton Archive/Getty Images

 **LISTEN UP!**

Lil Hardin Armstrong, "Hotter Than That" (1927), performed by Louis Armstrong and his Hot Five

TAKEAWAY POINT: Hot jazz performed by the first great jazz soloist and his group

STYLE: 1920s jazz

FORM: Theme and variations

GENRE: Small-group jazz

INSTRUMENTS: Trumpet, clarinet, trombone, banjo, guitar, piano

CONTEXT: Skilled and swinging musicians at play in the recording studio

INTRODUCTION

0:00   Short introduction features entire band, with Armstrong in forefront.

CHORUS 1

0:09   Statement of melody by Armstrong, with steady timekeeping from Lil Armstrong on piano and Johnson on guitar. Melody is almost certainly improvised, at least in part; virtually none of repetition that typically occurs in pop-song melodies.

CHORUS 2

0:44   Clarinetist Johnny Dodds. Throughout much of solo, he outlines the underlying harmony with arpeggio-based figuration. There are also several bent notes—bluesy alterations of standard pitches.

CHORUS 3

1:19   Armstrong scat-sings over Johnson's steady guitar accompaniment. Armstrong's conception remains much the same whether he's playing or singing.

1:40   Armstrong begins second half of solo with a marvelous stretch in which he repeats a long/short rhythm lasting three beats—out of phase with the underlying harmonic progression.

INTERLUDE

1:55   Armstrong and Johnson extend vocal chorus with blues-influenced call-and-response exchanges. Hardin leads the group to the final chorus.

CHORUS 4

2:19   Trombonist Kid Ory plays first half of final chorus.

2:34   Second half features collective improvisation: all front line players improvising at same time. Armstrong's repeated high notes, on and off the beat, distill swing to its essence: rhythmic play over a four-beat rhythm chunking away underneath.

TAG

2:52   Short tag featuring Armstrong and Johnson ends performance with musical question.

 Listen to this selection streaming or in an Active Listening Guide at CourseMate or in the eBook.

common in popular music in the 1910s and early 1920s. The performance consists of four variations over the harmonic progressions; each variation is considered a chorus, the term used by jazz musicians to indicate one statement of the form.

Louis Armstrong was the first great soloist in jazz. Every aspect of his playing—his beautiful sound; the bent notes, slides, shakes, and other expressive gestures; his melodic inventiveness; and above all, his incomparable sense of swing—inspired jazz and popular musicians of the era. His playing became the standard by which other jazz musicians measured themselves.

Recordings like "Hotter Than That" captured an exuberance that is unique to early jazz, and especially in the playing of Louis Armstrong. It comes from the interaction of the relentlessly pulsing beat, the ebb and flow of harmonic tension, and Armstrong's extraordinarily varied and subtle rhythmic play, with its note-to-note variation in accent, timing, and expressive gesture. It got musicians and listeners moving in time to the music: feet tapping, heads bobbing, fingers snapping.

There is no known precedent for the swing heard in early jazz. No earlier music that has come down to us, not even ragtime, creates a comparably infectious rhythm. Its defining features are far too subtle to commit to notation and seem to elude precise definition. Indeed, when asked to explain swing, Armstrong responded with something like "If you have to ask, you'll never know." Armstrong's influence was pervasive: swing became common currency in the 1930s, when the musicians who followed him absorbed his lessons on how to swing, and audiences responded to this vital new rhythm.

Jazz provided mainstream audiences with an instrumental introduction to the blues. Many of the first jazz recordings were blues in title and form, and captured key elements of the style and feeling. And when blues singers began to record in the 1920s, jazz musicians usually accompanied them.

Wolcott/Library of Congress, Prints and Photographs Division [LC-DIG-fsac-1a34367]

Folk blues flourished in the rural South, especially in the Mississippi Delta.

22-3 Classic Blues

Among the hottest releases of 1920 was Mamie Smith's recording of "Crazy Blues." The record sold 75,000 copies within a month and reputedly sold around 1 million copies. By the time she recorded the song, Smith was a veteran performer who had starred in Perry Bradford's 1918 production *Maid in Harlem*. Bradford—a key figure in black music in the 1910s and 1920s, and a successful songwriter, arranger, singer, pianist, bandleader, and entrepreneur—was sure that there was a market for a black female singer. He had tried to persuade Columbia and Victor, two of the biggest record companies of the era, to record her. Okeh Records, a branch of the German record company Odeon, which was more open to recording music for smaller markets, finally agreed. Her first session did well enough that she returned later to record Bradford's "Crazy Blues." The sensational success of Smith's record got the attention of record companies, who soon began to release race records, recordings by black artists aimed primarily at an African American audience.

But Mamie Smith wasn't really a blues singer, and despite its title, "Crazy Blues" wasn't really blues. Rather, it was a blues-influenced popular song that Smith sung in a bluesy, distinctively black singing style. Still, it was a dramatic departure from other kinds of pop singing of the time, and it opened the door for a wave of other female blues singers. They would give America its first taste of real blues style.

22-3A Blues

The blues is quintessentially African American music. It has roots in African music, most directly in the stories of griots. Griots were the historians and shamans of African tribes, who often sang and spoke their stories while accompanying themselves on a plucked string instrument. Blues also has roots in European music, in its customary use of chords and regular meter. But it is far different from both, and far different from Afrocentric musical traditions in other parts of the Americas. There is no other music that resembles it, although there is much music that has been shaped by it—from early jazz, country, and popular song to hard rock and heavy metal.

We know virtually nothing about the earliest history of the blues. We surmise that it took shape as a folk music created by Southern blacks sometime after the Civil War. The field hollers and work songs of slaves and sharecroppers are the most recent ancestors of the blues, although they differ from blues in both musical style and social function. Early anecdotal accounts of blues and blues singing date from shortly after the turn of the century. Down-home folk blues—what Paramount Records would call "real old-fashioned blues by an old-fashioned blues singer"—flourished in the rural South, especially in the Mississippi Delta. Shortly after the turn of the century, female blues singers like Ma Rainey began performing blues commercially on the black vaudeville circuit, in tent shows, and in other forms of entertainment.

W. C. Handy's raglike "Memphis Blues" (1912) was among the first of the printed blues; his "St. Louis Blues" (1914) was the most enduring. These typically used the most conventional form of the

> What ragtime and jazz did for the feet, blues did for the heart and soul.

race records Recordings by black artists aimed primarily at an African American audience

blues Quintessentially African American music with its roots in Africa and the Mississippi Delta; created by Southern blacks sometime after the Civil War; characterized by twelve-bar form, call and response between voice and instrument, bent or "blue" notes, and phrases that start high and end low

griot Historian and shaman of an African tribe, who often sang and spoke his stories while accompanying himself on a plucked string instrument

folk blues Down-home blues that flourished in the post–Civil War rural South, especially in the Mississippi Delta

blues but only hinted at many essential features of blues style. During the 1910s, both black and white bands performed and recorded these songs; almost all were some distance stylistically from the folk blues of the Mississippi Delta. In the late 1910s, jazz bands often recorded instrumental blues; a few featured horn playing that emulated blues singing. However, not until the aftershock of Mamie Smith's "Crazy Blues" did authentic blues style find its way onto recordings.

22-3B Bessie Smith and the Sound of Classic Blues

The most popular and artistically acclaimed of the female blues singers was Bessie Smith (1894–1937). The passion and power of her singing earned her the nickname of "the empress of the blues." By the early 1920s, she had a large following, which prompted Columbia Records to sign her to a recording contract in 1923. Her first record sold over 2 million copies, an enormous number for that time. She would continue to record for Columbia during the 1920s; almost all of the recordings were blues.

Smith's recordings epitomize classic blues. They feature Smith's rough, full-voiced singing supported by jazz musicians. The accompaniment varies, from just a pianist to a full jazz band. Most of her recordings are conventional twelve-bar blues, a strophic form with well-established conventions for the lyrics, harmony, texture, and form.

Each complete statement of the twelve-bar blues form—typically called a chorus—has three 4-measure phrases. The lyric is a rhymed couplet (two lines of text), with the first line repeated. In "Empty Bed Blues" (see Listen Up!), each phrase begins with Smith singing a line of the lyric to a mournful melody. And in each phrase her singing is answered by trombonist Charlie Green. Regular exchanges between contrasting voices is typically identified as call and response; it is a common feature of African music. Pianist Porter Grainger supports the voice and trombone with a somewhat elaborated form of a basic blues progression. A blues progression uses the three basic chords of common practice harmony as its foundation: each phrase begins with a different chord and returns to the tonic chord halfway through the phrase. The song as a whole is strophic, with much the same melody setting a series of rhymed couplets.

Table 22.1 uses the opening chorus of "Empty Bed Blues" to illustrate the form and harmonic plan of a conventional twelve-bar blues.

classic blues Commercially recorded blues

twelve-bar blues A strophic form with well-established conventions for the lyrics, harmony, texture, and form

chorus Each complete statement of the twelve-bar blues form, consisting of three 4-measure phrases

call and response Regular exchanges between contrasting voices, common in African music

blues progression Series using the three basic chords of common practice harmony as its foundation, with each phrase beginning with a different chord and returning to the tonic chord halfway through the phrase

Frank Driggs Collection/Hulton Archive/Getty Images

This photo, shot when Bessie Smith was about thirty, shows her at her most elegant and vulnerable. Smith was a big woman with a big voice; other publicity shots show a more rambunctious side of her personality.

Smith's classic blues were the first first-person music in American culture. When Smith sings, "I woke up this morning with a awful aching head," we sense that she is talking about herself; the events in the song could literally have happened the night before. The lyric swings back and forth between the joys of love and the pains of love lost and love betrayed. For most of the song, she describes lovemaking, sometimes in metaphor ("coffee grinder," "deep-sea diver") and sometimes directly. All of this makes her partner's infidelity even more painful. This emotional range and the intimacy of the subject suggest to us that Smith is singing from the heart, that she is using the blues to talk about *her own* good and bad times—not the feelings of a character in a musical.

	Vocal	Instrumental response
Phrase 1	I woke up this morning . . .	Trombone
	I chord	I chord
Phrase 2	I woke up this morning . . .	Trombone
	IV chord	I chord
Phrase 3	My new man . . .	Trombone
	V chord	I chord

Table 22.1 Twelve-Bar Blues Form

 **LISTEN UP!**

"Empty Bed Blues," performed by Bessie Smith (1928)

TAKEAWAY POINT: Classic 1920s commercial blues, sung by the "empress of the blues"

STYLE: Blues

FORM: Strophic, with each chorus a twelve-bar blues form

GENRE: Classic blues

INSTRUMENTS: Voice, trombone, and piano

CONTEXT: Authentic blues as commercial music during the 1920s

INTRODUCTION

0:00 Brief introduction showcases accompanying instruments: piano and trombone. Piano supplies rhythm and harmony, while trombone answers Smith's voice.

CHORUS 1

0:11 Form of twelve-bar blues: rhymed couplet with first line repeated, sung to three phrases, each lasting four bars

I woke up this mornin'. . .

CHORUS 2

0:44 In this and the next chorus, Smith describes her lovemaking through oblique metaphor. This was a clever way to skirt the censors.

Bought me a coffee grinder . . .

CHORUS 3

1:18 Trombonist Charlie Green growls to match Smith's singing.

He's a deep sea diver . . .

CHORUS 4

1:52 Smith's singing is much like intensified speech in its free rhythm over a steady beat, narrow melodic range, and rough, gravelly timbre.

He knows how to thrill me . . .

CHORUS 5

2:26 As in many blues songs, voice and instrument alternate in a call-response pattern: vocalist sings first half of phrase, and instrumentalist answers.

Lord, he's got that sweet somethin' . . .

 Listen to this selection streaming or in an Active Listening Guide at CourseMate or in the eBook.

What makes "Empty Bed Blues" classic? Three features stand out: the earthy, direct lyrics; Smith's singing; and the use of several blues conventions—the twelve-bar form, call and response between voice and instrument, blue notes ("bent," expressive notes outside the major scale), and phrases that start high and end low. The expressive power resides in the words and Smith's singing; the blues conventions are the familiar packaging.

22-3C The Legacy of Classic Blues

Commercial blues by Smith and other female blues singers were a phenomenon of the 1920s. At the end of the decade, the Great Depression hit America hard, and blacks especially hard. Too few could afford to buy records or attend the theaters and clubs where these blues singers performed. As a result, the core market for this kind of commercial blues singing had all but dried up by the early 1930s. Despite her earlier popularity, Smith's career nose-dived; mismanagement and her heavy drinking were also contributing causes. She died in 1937 in a Clarksdale, Mississippi, hospital from injuries sustained in an automobile accident.

blue note "Bent," expressive note outside the major scale

© iStockPhoto.com/AdShooter

Nevertheless, through performers like Smith and Ma Rainey and those they influenced, both the idea and the sound of the blues entered the popular mainstream in the 1920s. It reshaped popular song, jazz, musical theater, and even pop-based concert music. What ragtime and jazz did for the feet, blues did for the heart and soul.

22-4 The Modern Era in Popular Music

In November 1931, the American writer F. Scott Fitzgerald wrote the obituary of the decade he had named. In his essay "Echoes of the Jazz Age," he declared the Jazz Age "the ten-year period that, as if reluctant to die outmoded in its bed, leaped to a spectacular death in October, 1929." For him, "it was an age of miracles, it was an age of art, it was an age of excess, and it was an age of satire." He saw "a whole race going hedonistic, deciding on pleasure," although in fact over 70 percent of Americans lived below the poverty line during the 1920s.

The sound track for the decade was what Fitzgerald called jazz, which "in its progress toward respectability has meant first sex, then dancing, then music." For him, "it is associated with a state of nervous stimulation, not unlike that of big cities behind the lines of war. . . . Wherefore eat, drink and be merry, for tomorrow we die."

For Fitzgerald and most others of his generation, "jazz" meant all the new black and black-influenced music. In retrospect, much of what was called jazz in the 1920s wasn't what we now consider to be jazz. Al Jolson, who played the lead role in *The Jazz Singer*, the first talking film, was never really a jazz singer. The "symphonic jazz" presented in Paul Whiteman's 1924 Aeolian Hall concert, which featured the premiere of George Gershwin's *Rhapsody in Blue*, was neither "symphonic" nor "jazz" in their most limited meanings. But there was plenty of real jazz, by black musicians and by whites who emulated them, and it helped usher in a new, more modern era in American life.

By the 1920s, America had entered a modern era. To be "modern" in America during the 1920s meant moving and living at a faster pace. It meant believing in progress, especially material progress. It meant moving out of the country and into the city. It meant taking advantage of new technologies, from automobiles and air conditioning to the zippers that were now used on clothing, luggage, and a host of other products. It meant buying into fashionable intellectual ideas and artistic trends. And it meant listening—and dancing—to a new kind of music.

During the first part of the century, cities swelled with a flood of immigrants and the migration of Americans from country to city. Large ethnic and minority populations in cities like New York and Chicago helped support their resident musicians and entertainers. Many of the top jazz and popular musicians were black or Jewish: trumpeter-vocalist Louis Armstrong and pianist-composer George Gershwin are two among many. During the 1920s, they found audiences for their music within and beyond their communities, despite rampant and overt prejudice.

> "Does Jazz Put the Sin in Syncopation?"
> —*Ladies Home Journal*, 1921

The 1920s was a decade of contradictions. Prohibition banned alcohol; speakeasies served it anyway. Suffragettes fought for and gained rights for women: in 1920, the Nineteenth Amendment, giving women the right to vote, became law. Flappers, fast-living young ladies who smoked, drank, "petted," and danced the Charleston throughout the night, seemed to abuse their newfound freedom. Parents were worried over the financially frivolous activities of their daughters and sons, but many invested their savings in the stock market, then watched it all disappear in the stock market crash of 1929. The decade saw real advances in black music: on Broadway, on records, in clubs, and even on film. But bandstands were still segregated, and many regarded the music and the musicians as primitive and immoral: an article that appeared in a 1921 issue of *The Ladies Home Journal* asked, "Does Jazz Put the Sin in Syncopation?"

The most popular music of the era was a new, more modern popular song. The influence of the new

African American vernacular styles was evident in both its composition and its performance. Ragtime was the primary source of the fox trot rhythm that underpinned the songs. Blues helped shape the more conversational rhythm of lyric and melody. The jazz band was the nucleus of the dance orchestras that proliferated in the 1920s. All three—ragtime, blues, and especially jazz—brought syncopation into popular song, and some of the expressiveness of blues and jazz gradually filtered into popular song performance. These new songs were both singable *and* danceable, whether performed by a dance orchestra, a small group, or even around the piano at home, on stage, over the air, or in the studio.

During the first quarter of the century, popular songs reached their audience through several paths. However, the surest strategy for songwriting success was getting it on stage.

22-5 *Show Boat* and Stage Entertainment in the 1920s

The 1920s were the heyday of stage entertainment in the United States: there was more activity and variety than any time before or since. There were four main types of stage entertainment: vaudeville, revues, musical comedy, and operetta. Vaudeville was simply a succession of acts, some of which featured singing or acting. Still, because vaudeville was so surpassingly popular, it was an effective way to introduce a new song. The revue was a series of song and dance numbers held loosely together by a topical story line. The most famous of the revues were the *Ziegfeld Follies*, presented annually from 1907 to 1927, but there were other annual revues, some of which featured black performers. The two stage entertainments constructed around a story line were operetta and musical comedy.

22-5A Operetta and Musical Comedy

In the early years of the twentieth century, operetta and musical comedy were largely independent forms of stage entertainment. Operettas, composed mainly by Europeans, typically featured long-ago-and-far-away plots, often involving royalty of nonexistent European nations; the most popular were simply lighthearted entertainment, without Gilbert and Sullivan's sophisticated brand of satire. The music drew almost exclusively on European practice; there was little evidence of the new sounds and rhythms that were emerging in popular music.

Musical comedy, with music by American composers such as George M. Cohan, Gershwin, Irving Berlin, and Jerome Kern, was more up to date in story and music and less concerned with dramatic integrity. The plots for musical comedies were lighthearted, comparable in

dramatic depth to today's average sitcom. There was a lot of singing, a lot of dancing, and a lot of comedy. These productions were fun—designed to entertain and occasionally to titillate. But they usually didn't go much deeper than that. That would change in 1927 with *Show Boat*, a musical based on a novel by Edna Ferber.

22-5B *Show Boat*

In 1926, Edna Ferber published the novel *Show Boat*. Ferber was one of America's most prominent writers; a year earlier, she won the Pulitzer Prize in 1925 for her novel *So Big*. *Show Boat* tells the bittersweet story of Magnolia, the daughter of Cap'n Andy and Parthy Ann Hawks. In Ferber's novel, the Hawks run the *Cotton Blossom*, a showboat that travels up and down the Mississippi River putting on theatrical productions. At a stop in Natchez, Mississippi, Magnolia meets and eventually marries Gaylord Ravenal, a gambler who leaves her when his luck runs out. They are reunited at the end of the musical after several years apart; their long separation and Magnolia's hard times in the interim drains much of the happiness from the ending.

Among the most enthusiastic readers of Ferber's new novel was the songwriter Jerome Kern, who by 1926 was already a twenty-year Broadway veteran. He had just scored a success with *Sunny*, his first collaboration with lyricist Oscar Hammerstein II, and was looking for a more substantial story. He was convinced that *Show Boat* could be adapted to the Broadway stage.

To get *Show Boat* on Broadway, he first had to convince two people: Ferber and Florenz Ziegfeld. Ferber was concerned that Kern would trivialize her novel. She agreed only after Kern convinced her that he would remain largely true to her novel.

Ziegfeld, Broadway's top producer, was an even harder sell. After producing his *Follies* for two decades, he had recently branched out into musical comedy. As the person responsible for the finances of such a production, he was reluctant to produce a show that would depart too dramatically from other kinds of stage entertainment. Only when Kern and Hammerstein convinced Ziegfeld to bill the production as an "American musical play" did Ziegfeld agree to throw his considerable resources behind its production.

So, sometime after eight o'clock on the evening of December 27, 1927, Paul Robeson, a young African American actor-singer, stepped into the spotlight of the Ziegfeld Theater in New York to sing a song about a river.

22-5C The Innovations of Kern and Hammerstein

In *Show Boat*, Kern and Hammerstein effectively Americanized operetta and made musical comedy more significant in the process. Their "musical play" featured an

revue A series of song and dance numbers held loosely together by a topical story line

musical comedy Lighthearted stage entertainment born in the early twentieth century, featuring a great deal of singing, dancing, and comedy

Jerome Kern
FAST FACTS

- Dates: 1885–1945
- Place: United States
- Reason to remember:
  The first important
  American songwriter to
  concern himself seriously
  with the integration of
  music and drama

American take on the typical long-ago-far-away operetta plot: "long ago," for instance, was the turn of the century. To help convey this, Kern incorporated still-popular hits from that time. And the Mississippi River was, for 1920s New Yorkers, far enough away.

Kern and Hammerstein presented Ferber's controversial interracial story and complex characters with relatively little sugarcoating. Compared to the typical stage entertainment of the era, *Show Boat* was more serious and substantial; dramatically it was closer to opera than it was to conventional Broadway entertainment. However, it relied musically on the conventions of popular song. The team's challenge was to find a dramatically effective way to use this highly conventional genre. By training and experience, Kern was well equipped to meet the challenge.

Jerome Kern ► was the elder statesman of the great songwriters active in the 1920s and 1930s: he had his first hit song in 1905, the year Harold Arlen (the composer of "Over the Rainbow") was born. Moreover, Kern received traditional musical training in New York and Germany and spent much of the 1900s and 1910s traveling between New York and London, where he supplied dozens of songs

for shows. And perhaps because of his extensive experience writing songs for the shows of others, he was the first important American songwriter to concern himself seriously with the integration of music and drama. Between 1915 and 1918, he collaborated with Guy Bolton on a series of operetta-influenced musicals for the Princess Theater, a small venue in New York City.

By training, experience, and inclination, Kern, of the major songwriters, was, ironically, the least in touch with the sounds and rhythms of the new black-influenced popular music. Many of the songs from late in his career ("The Way You Look Tonight," "All the Things You Are") favor European values: flowing melodies, surprising harmonies, and rhythms with little or no syncopation. However, when the occasion demanded it, he was able to tap into a broad range of vernacular styles. In *Show Boat*, this is most evident in two songs that feature black performers.

The first is Robeson's unusual opening number, "Old Man River." The song was a jarring departure from the parade of chorus girls that usually opened Broadway productions. To convey the dignity of the black workers, Kern evoked the African American spiritual, which was familiar to a broad audience mainly through the publication of art song-like settings of the melodies by the brothers James Weldon and J. Rosamund Johnson in 1925 and 1926. It was ideally suited to Robeson's sonorous bass voice. The other song clearly influenced by black music came shortly after.

22-5D "Can't Help Lovin' Dat Man": Popular Song within Drama

The main actors on the Hawks's showboat, as well as in a subplot, are Steve and Julie Baker. Julie is part black but light enough to pass for white. However, in Mississippi (where mixed marriages were illegal at the time) her racial heritage is exposed, and she and Steve must leave the *Cotton Blossom*.

To alert the audience that Julie has is of mixed race, Kern composed "Can't Help Lovin' Dat Man" (see Listen Up!). Julie sings the song prior to the scene where she and Steve have to leave the showboat. When Queenie, the black cook, hears her singing "Can't Help Lovin' Dat Man," she asks Julie how she knows the song, because "Ah didn't ever hear anybody but colored folks sing dat song." In 1927, the most familiar "colored-only" songs were the classic blues of Bessie Smith and others. For numerous reasons—among them the racial climate at the time, the jarring musical contrast it would have created, and Kern's own musical predilections—Kern chose instead to compose a blues-*influenced* popular song, rather than an authentic blues song. "Can't Help Lovin' Dat Man" is an up-to-date song for 1927, in the style of its lyrics, its melodic construction, its use of dance rhythms, and its form. Although their awkward imitation of black speech (downplayed in Morgan's performance) derives from the minstrel show, the lyrics are typical of the modern era in popular song. The diction, with a preponderance of one-syllable words, is close to everyday speech, and the song is a gentrified blues lament.

 **LISTEN UP!**

Kern and Hammerstein, "Can't Help Lovin' Dat Man," *Show Boat* (1927)

TAKEAWAY POINT: Characteristic and dramatically effective popular song from the early modern era

STYLE: Modern popular song

FORM: AABA

GENRE: Musical theater song

INSTRUMENTS: Voice and theater orchestra

CONTEXT: Julie sings this song, inadvertently revealing her African American heritage.

INTRODUCTION

0:00   Instrumental version of a fragment from a song that appears later in the show

INTERPOLATION

0:14   Part of another song, sung just before the point in the musical when Julie is discovered to be part black.

       Let me lay . . .

REFRAIN

0:42   Black-influenced features include short phrases (riffs), frequent syncopations, especially on "man," also a blue note.

       Fish got to swim . . .

0:59   Tell me he's lazy . . .

INTERLUDE

1:12   Complete instrumental statement of verse

VERSE

1:35   Syncopated melody shifts between two- and four-beat rhythms.

       Oh, listen . . .

REFRAIN

1:58   Post-1925 popular song form: 8-bar opening phrase, repeated; contrasting eight-bar phrase (bridge); final restatement of opening phrase

2:14   Fish got to swim . . .

       Opening phrase grows out of riff: here, a 4-note motive that ends in a syncopation.

2:30   Tell me he's lazy . . .

       When he goes away . . .

 Listen to this selection streaming or in an Active Listening Guide at CourseMate or in the eBook.

Our recording begins with an excerpt from another song in the musical; it is sung just before the point in the musical when Julie is discovered to be part black. It continues with half of the chorus, the verse, then the full chorus.

22-5E *Show Boat:* A New Kind of Musical Theater

Show Boat was the first of the great modern musicals. It elevated the level of discourse in musical theater, dramatically and musically. Through the example of *Show Boat*, musical theater became a more elite entertainment, even as vaudeville and the revue disappeared from the stage, casualties of the onset of the Depression and the rise of talking films. Many of the top songwriters on Broadway, including Kern and Gershwin, moved to Hollywood, where they composed memorable songs for film musicals. Those who stayed behind, most notably the team of Richard Rodgers and Lorenz Hart, created musicals that followed the lead of *Show Boat* in musical sophistication and dramatic substance. However, their musicals enjoyed relatively modest success, and they are seldom revived. Only

►George Gershwin

FAST FACTS

- Dates: 1898–1937
- Place: United States
- Reasons to remember: Composer-pianist who brought together classical and modern popular music

with the Rodgers and Hammerstein musicals, beginning with *Oklahoma!* (1943) and extending through *The Sound of Music* (1959), did the musical enjoy critical acclaim and commercial success comparable to that of *Show Boat*.

LEARNING OUTCOME 22-6

Comprehend George Gershwin's "symphonic jazz" as one of the new classics of the modern era.

22-6 George Gershwin and "Symphonic Jazz"

On January 4, 1924, George Gershwin was shooting pool with his brother, Ira, and Buddy DeSylva, Gershwin's lyricist at the time, when Ira happened to read an article in the *New York Tribune* about an upcoming concert to be presented by bandleader Paul Whiteman, who billed it as an "Experiment in Modern Music."

Paul Whiteman (1890–1967) had begun his professional career as a classical violist, then formed his own dance orchestra in 1919. Within a year, the band had two million-selling recordings; it would become the most popular and most admired dance orchestra of the 1920s. In 1924, Whiteman attempted to elevate jazz to the stature of classical music by offering a concert of "symphonic jazz" in New York's Aeolian Hall. Among the featured pieces on the program would be a "jazz concerto" by George Gershwin.

The announcement in the *Tribune* threw Gershwin into a panic. George had had an informal and rather vague conversation with Whiteman about the project but hadn't imagined that Whiteman took the discussion as a commitment. Working feverishly, he finished the piece, by then entitled *Rhapsody in Blue*, in time for the premiere on February 12. Gershwin's jazz concerto was the highlight of the concert and a critical success.

22-6A Vernacular Music and Modern Composers

However, not all approved. For people like Anne Shaw Faulkner, the author of the *Ladies Home Journal* article, National Music Chairman of the General Federation of Women's Clubs, and subsequently the author of one of the first music appreciation books, there was "good" music:

operas and orchestral music, songs and sonatas, as well as popular songs and dances stylistically aligned with it. And there was also "evil" music: Faulkner notes that in surveys that seek to account for the "immoral conditions among our young people . . . the blame is laid on jazz music and its evil influence on the young people of to-day."

For many members of the upper and middle classes, Whiteman's "symphonic jazz" and "jazz concerto" were oxymorons, culturally if not musically. Jazz, blues, and ragtime were several rungs down the social ladder, in large part because of their African American roots, and the popular music that they influenced was not much higher. Indeed, throughout most of the teens, dance orchestras playing the new syncopated music were black because white dance orchestras did not want to sully their reputations by performing it. Only at the end of the decade did white musicians begin to perform this music.

However, many of the leading composers of the early twentieth century did not share their prejudice. Debussy, who died before jazz became known, was fascinated with American vernacular music (as we heard in "Minstrels") and wrote several rag-inspired compositions. Ives seasoned his music liberally with quotations from rags and ragtime-inspired fragments. Stravinsky composed three ragtime-inspired works during the teens; the French composer Maurice Ravel worked jazz and blues into his music; and the American composer Aaron Copland composed a jazz-inspired piano concerto in 1926. However, the composer who most successfully fused these new sounds and rhythms with classical practice was George Gershwin.

22-6B George Gershwin

Like several top songwriters, George Gershwin ◖ began his musical career as a *song plugger*: a pianist who would play (and sing) a publisher's sheet music for prospective buyers. He discovered his passion for music and the piano in 1910, when his family bought a piano. Although his training was brief, Gershwin quickly developed into an excellent pianist—he and Fats Waller would be the most skilled pianists among the top songwriters of the era. He also received extensive training in classical composition, beginning in 1915. Both skills would serve him well. By the early 1920s, Gershwin was an up-and-coming songwriter. "Swanee," his first big hit, appeared in 1919 and became a best-selling record for Al Jolson the following year. Gershwin was also a well-known performer—he accompanied the singer Eva Gauthier in concert in November 1923 in a program that mixed classical and popular vocal music. Gershwin's obvious skills as a composer and pianist and his openness to bringing together classical music with the new modern popular music made him an ideal choice to compose the central work for Whiteman's grand experiment.

22-6C *Rhapsody in Blue*

Rhapsody in Blue (see Listen Up!) certainly approaches the symphonic in its scale, length, and sound. A complete performance of the piece typically lasts about fifteen

George Gershwin, *Rhapsody in Blue* (1924)

TAKEAWAY POINT: A unique and popular fusion of classical and popular music

STYLE: Pop/classical fusion

FORM: Multisectional

GENRE: Rhapsody

INSTRUMENTS: Piano and augmented dance orchestra

CONTEXT: A work composed for a concert to make jazz more upscale

A

0:00   Clarinet cadenza, then the "blues" melodic idea

B

0:37   Horn plays second, jazzy melodic idea.

A

0:47   A section returns, played on muted trumpet

C

0:52   Piano interlude

A

0:57   A again, with full orchestra

C

1:05   Gershwin (the pianist), and then the orchestra, elaborates on C.

1:21   Big cadenza for piano follows.

A

1:42   Piano solo version of A, answered by **C** (played on bass clarinet)

D

2:02   Interlude

C

2:17   More development of C, leading to another virtuosic cadenza

A

2:48   A returns in orchestra.

C

2:52   C response, played on oboe

D

3:01   Interlude connects to . . .

3:06   . . . new, different statement of **A**.

E

3:15   New theme in pop song form (aaba), each with a distinctive piano obbligato, dissolves into . . .

(Continued)

B

3:38   Different section: Orchestra plays B, pianist shows off.

3:50   B in orchestra, answered in piano by a fragment of A. This grows into what seems like another aaba-type section, except that it dissolves as members of the orchestra toss around fragments of B.

4:22   Another piano cadenza, leading to. . . .

B

4:41   The pianist's aaba version of B, complete with answering fragment of A. It dissolves into a transition to a new section.

F

5:19   A new, more romantic theme (F), complete with syncopated obbligato answer (**G**), first in the horns, then in other instruments

G

6:39   Improvised-sounding musings on G by Gershwin, then solo piano version of F, which dissolves into yet another cadenza

H

7:24   The "Latin" section (H)—in this recording it is abbreviated.

F

7:38   F returns, but much more up-tempo and with a Latin piano accompaniment. It ends with a dramatic chord.

C

8:06   A frantic version of C in the piano (here covered by the accompaniment), which leads to . . .

B

8:25   A grand version of a fragment of B in the piano

A

8:31   An even grander version of A, with the answer C in the piano

🔊)) Listen to this selection streaming or in an Active Listening Guide at CourseMate or in the eBook.

minutes, the approximate length of the first movement of a standard piano concerto. (The performance heard here, by Gershwin and Whiteman's orchestra, is an abridged version of the original.) Similarly, Whiteman's good-sized orchestra approaches the sound of a symphony orchestra, but with a popular twist. The string section is, by classical standards, quite small, and Whiteman's orchestra includes three saxophones and a banjo. (A revised orchestration of the work for piano and full symphony orchestra appeared soon after the 1924 premiere.) All this is very much in the classical style, in intent and result.

It's what Gershwin did within this framework that was so remarkable. The piece bubbles over with fresh musical ideas. Almost all of them are stylized reworkings of the sounds, rhythms, and melodies of the ragtime, jazz, blues, and dance music that African Americans had contributed over the prior twenty-five years. Gershwin

rhapsody Piece of music that moves from section to section as if cutting or fading between scenes in a film

created rich, distinctive harmonies by blending twentieth-century French harmony with commercial blues sounds. The virtuosic piano writing, however, is Gershwin's own. There are no real precedents for it in classical, ragtime, or jazz piano playing.

Rhapsody in Blue is a rhapsody in the way it moves from section to section, as if it were cutting or fading between scenes in a film. And it is blue from the first notes—the famous clarinet solo that begins the work takes off from blues-influenced New Orleans jazz clarinet playing.

Rhapsody in Blue was absolutely unique. It created a new language for concert music, one based on the progressive popular music of the early twentieth century. It inspired many other jazz concert pieces, including several by Gershwin. But none has challenged *Rhapsody in Blue* as the most successful and popular work of its kind. Its premiere was a defining moment in the history of popular music and in the history of twentieth-century music of all kinds.

More than eighty years after its premiere, *Rhapsody in Blue* remains the single most popular work written by an American composer. Given its success, one might expect that its "formula" would have been widely copied. That is not the case. No one, not even Gershwin, has created a work of comparable popularity. Many critics, especially from the traditional classical side, have commented on *Rhapsody in Blue*'s alleged shortcomings; they have pointed out what it is not—another Beethoven symphony or Mozart concerto. In the process, they have failed to recognize it for what it is: an extraordinarily original, successful, and inimitable piece of music.

Looking Back, Looking Ahead

Although they differ in style, genre, and performance context, the five examples presented in this chapter share several common features.

1. *They were exemplars of their particular genre.* To this day they remain among the finest examples of ragtime, early commercial blues, early jazz, musical theater, and "crossover classical" from their era.
2. *They broke new musical ground.* Joplin's rag invested ragtime with elegance; Smith's blues brought deep feeling into vernacular music; Armstrong's recordings remain the most valued early examples of jazz as a solo art; Kern and Hammerstein's "musical play" transformed musical theater; Gershwin's jazz concerto had no significant precedent.
3. *They drew on African and European sources for their innovations.* Joplin's rag is effectively a syncopated march played on the piano; Smith's blues features harmony and harmony instruments supporting the melody; Armstrong's jazz shows its indirectly acquired European provenance in its harmonic and melodic invention and stunning virtuosity, and its African roots in the irresistible swing and expressive nuance; Gershwin fused classical concepts with the new rhythms and sounds of the 1920s.
4. *They remain among the most enduring American music of the early twentieth century.* Joplin's classic rags got new life through the ragtime revival of the 1970s and are still familiar. Smith's recordings are exemplars of "classic blues." Scholars, musicians, and enthusiasts agree that Armstrong was the first great soloist in jazz and a seminal influence on its development. *Show Boat* was filmed multiple times and has enjoyed several major revivals on stage. Gershwin's rhapsody is arguably the most widely performed twentieth-century classical composition (as of this writing, there are almost two hundred recordings of the work currently available).

The judgment of history belies Ms. Faulkner's harsh judgment: jazz, sinful in 1921, is now "America's art music." For all of this music, and the genres that they exemplify, it is not a question of whether "good music" is good (it is), but rather whether it is the only good music. Collectively, this music helped set in motion a more expanded understanding of art in music. It would take several generations and another revolution in popular music, but it is now widely accepted that musical art does not require a European provenance, that expressive communication through music can come in multiple forms, and that accessibility and art are compatible virtues.

 study tools 22

Ready to study?
In the book you can:

- Review Learning Outcome answers and Glossary terms with the tear-out Chapter Review card.

Or you can go online to CourseMate, at www.cengagebrain.com, for these resources:

- Chapter Quizzes to prepare for tests
- Interactive flashcards of all Glossary terms
- Active Listening Guides, streaming music, and YouTube playlists
- An eBook with live links to all web resources

New York Times Co./Getty Images

In an article in the February 1958 issue of *High Fidelity*, Milton Babbitt, a leading avant-garde composer and professor at Princeton University, bemoaned the cultural isolation of those who created what he called "'serious,' 'advanced,' contemporary music" and suggested that avant-garde composers return the favor by withdrawing to a more private world where they could follow their muse without concern for public acceptance. He compared the composer of "advanced" music (of which he was a leading exemplar) to pure mathematicians or theoretical physicists, who explore the frontiers of knowledge without much regard for its practical application. He called on universities to support such composers, just as they support other specialized and advanced areas of inquiry.

Babbitt was part of a musical avant-garde that was extremely active in the generation after World War II. His position is extreme, even for the avant-garde, but there is no question that the thrill of discovery—of exploring uncharted musical territory—was far more important to Babbitt and his peers than public acceptance.

23-1 The Postwar Avant-Garde

In the *Crystal Reference Encyclopedia*, a 1911 publication that comprised the basic entries for the *Cambridge Encyclopedia*, the definition of music begins like this: "An orderly succession of sounds of definite pitch, whose constituents are melody, harmony, and rhythm." This definition is typical of those found in dictionaries and encyclopedias from the first part of the twentieth century. It would be obsolete a half-century later, principally because of the efforts of the postwar avant-garde.

23-1A The Range of the Avant-Garde

The avant-garde movement began almost immediately after the war ended, as if the cease fire set off a nuclear explosion of creativity that would annihilate traditional conceptions of music. Its epicenter of the postwar avant-garde movement was Darmstadt, a small city in central West Germany, in the northern part of the United States occupation zone. In 1946, German music critic Wolfgang Steinecke founded what came to be called the Darmstadt summer courses. They soon became a leading center for avant-garde music, attracting composers, performers, scholars, and critics from both sides of the Atlantic.

Although the lecturers who presented at the summer courses over the next two decades represented widely divergent trends, the dominant figures were four Europeans: the Italian composers Bruno Maderna and Luigi Nono, the German composer Karlheinz Stockhausen, and the French composer Pierre Boulez. Known as the "Darmstadt School" (of composition) after a 1957 lecture by Nono, they saw their music as the continuation of the Second Viennese School and were determined to extend serial techniques in inventive ways, including serializing not just pitch but also other parameters, including duration and dynamics.

Serialism, although dominant, was just one of several new directions among the mid-century avant-garde. Avant-garde music exploded in all directions, testing the limits and expanding the possibilities of virtually every musical parameter and creating novel combinations of features. Most fundamentally, this meant exploring the extremes of compositional control, from the elimination of the performer (via electronic sound synthesis) to the virtual elimination of

the composer, as in Cage's "silent piece" introduced in Chapter 1. However, as varied as they were in methodology, the avant-garde shared a common purpose: to explore and expand the boundaries of musical practice.

In this chapter, we sample these new directions in three works composed between 1946 and 1964. These works convey some sense of the range of innovation—in sound, pitch, rhythm, texture, and every other musical parameter—produced by the avant-garde during the years after World War II.

23-1B New Resources, New Sounds

The most immediately apparent innovations of the postwar avant-garde were an array of new sounds that came from four principal sources:

1. *Innovative performance techniques on conventional instruments.* Some examples of these techniques are multiphonics for wind players (playing more than one pitch simultaneously on an instrument designed to play one note at a time); and tone clusters produced by striking the piano keys with a fist or other objects, or guitar-like chords produced by strumming the piano strings. Some of these techniques were not new; composers had made use of them before 1945. However, they became far more common and far more varied in the decades after World War II.

2. *Radical modifications of conventional instruments.* A more extreme version of the previous practice was altering an instrument so drastically that it produced a completely different range of timbres. No instrument underwent more drastic alternation than the grand piano: composers like Cage "prepared" the instrument by inserting various everyday materials, such as nuts, bolts, and spoons, between the strings.

3. *The invention of new instruments.* The most innovative new instrument of the postwar era was the programmable synthesizer, a fully electronic instrument. The first was the RCA Mark II sound synthesizer, which came into use in 1957; it filled an entire room. Rapid technological improvements resulted in a modest-sized instrument that could be used for performance in real time by the early 1970s. No other sound source developed in the twentieth century has had such a widespread impact.

multiphonics For wind players, playing more than one pitch simultaneously on an instrument designed to play one note at a time

tone cluster Effect produced by striking the piano keys with a fist or other objects

4. *The use of "found" sounds.* Almost as soon as the tape recorder became a commercially viable product, composers began recording sounds not produced by musical instruments, extracting sound snippets, sometimes subjecting them to various modifications, and combining them. Pierre Schaeffer, the French radio broadcaster who assumed a leading role in developing these procedures, called this process *musique concrète*.

The new sounds that composers asked for or produced themselves represented only one dimension of their exploration of virgin musical territory. They went hand in hand with innovations in pitch, rhythm, and other musical parameters.

23-1C Innovations in Pitch and Rhythm

Avant-garde composers continued to move away from the mainstream in their handling of pitch and rhythm, to the point that they often severed any sense of connection between traditional practice and their work. Here are some of the more radical departures in pitch and rhythm:

1. Dissolving conventional pitch organization through a variety of procedures that included these elements:

    -   The use of white noise (a broad band of multiple frequencies sounding simultaneously)
    -   The production of sounds with a sense of high and low, but without definite pitch
    -   Tone clusters that fill in the gaps between half-steps
    -   Continuous pitch change, ranging from rapid glissandi to slow, almost imperceptible movement up or down

2. The use of wide intervals and extreme registral contrast (moving quickly between pitches in a low register and pitches in a high register) to weaken or eliminate any sense of melodic continuity
3. Rhythms so rapid that it is all but impossible to distinguish discrete pitches
4. Rhythms so slow that no underlying pulse is evident
5. Rhythms so varied and nonrepetitive that no underlying metrical organization is apparent
6. Harmonies that are simply the coincidences of pitches sounded simultaneously rather than chords selected from a preexisting or predetermined harmonic language

musique concrète Music created by recording sounds not produced by musical instruments, extracting sound snippets, and subjecting them to various modifications

white noise A broad band of multiple frequencies sounding simultaneously

prepared piano John Cage's technique of changing the piano's timbre by inserting objects among its strings

Other elements also underwent considerable expansion of possibilities: textures ranged from single lines to dense clusters of sound or free interpretation of parts played by performers at their discretion; dynamic change ranged from virtually unchanging to extremely rapid change.

Because of these radical extensions of every musical parameter and because repetition, especially regular repetition, was the infrequent exception rather than the rule, the forms of avant-garde compositions seldom resolve

White noise—a broad band of multiple frequencies sounding simultaneously

into familiar patterns. Instead, the majority of works seem to be through-composed: music that continuously evolves or changes from beginning to end.

The avant-garde was an international movement. Regional styles were the product of peer-group interaction, not connection with a folk or popular tradition. Accordingly, our sample of this music includes works by an American composer, a Polish composer, and a French-born composer who spent much of his career in the United States and was at home on both sides of the Atlantic.

LEARNING OUTCOME 23-2
Explain the place of John Cage in the postwar American avant-garde.

23-2 John Cage and the Prepared Piano

It isn't often that one begins preparing a new piano work for performance with a trip to the hardware store. However, the score to John Cage's *Sonatas and Interludes* lists the materials required to "prepare" a piano: an assortment of bolts of varying sizes and lengths, screws, plastic, and rubber, to be inserted among the strings. The score also details precisely where these materials are to be placed inside the piano. With this preparation, the sound of the piano was modified so radically by the prepared piano technique that it became in effect a different instrument.

(The image at this chapter's opening shows Cage in the process of preparing a piano.)

In a conversation with Peter Yates, a patron of both Arnold Schoenberg and John Cage ◗, Schoenberg described Cage as "not a composer, but an inventor—of genius." Cage had studied with Schoenberg during the mid-1930s, mostly in classes but also privately on a few occasions. He revered the man as the greatest living composer but realized that his abilities did not align well with Schoenberg's expectations for his students. Cage acknowledged to Schoenberg that he had "no feeling for harmony," a self-assessment with which Schoenberg concurred. Although he continued to admire him personally, Cage found himself increasingly at odds philosophically with Schoenberg and left rather abruptly to take work in Seattle as an accompanist for dance classes at the Cornish School. There he met Merce Cunningham, a dancer and choreographer, and one of the pioneers in modern dance. They quickly formed a close professional and personal relationship that would last until Cage's death.

Cage's work with dancers, and with Cunningham in particular, stimulated his already active interest in sound and time. Among his early experiments with sound were a percussion ensemble that played "found" instruments like a brake drum; a work for radio broadcast scored for piano, cymbals, and record players playing test tones at varying speeds; and his first experiments at preparing a piano.

In these early compositions, Cage was, in effect, inventing new sounds and new sound combinations—or at the very least, incorporating them into a musical experience. His sonic explorations follow the lead of Henry Cowell, the great American experimentalist whom Cage would describe as "the open sesame for new music in America." Cage had worked with Cowell in the early 1930s; it was Cowell who had suggested that he seek out Schoenberg.

23-2A *Sonatas and Interludes*

Cage had encountered non-Western music in Cowell's classes; contact with an East Indian musician in 1946 rekindled his interest, which would soon lead to an embrace of Eastern aesthetics and spirituality. This experience introduced him to an ancient idea in both West and East: the purpose of music is to induce a state of tranquility, thus opening the door to the divine. His major work from the late 1940s, the *Sonatas and Interludes* for prepared piano, expresses this goal. It is a large group of short pieces; a full performance lasts about an hour. We hear Sonata V next (see Listen Up!).

Cage composed *Sonatas and Interludes* over a three-year period between 1946 and 1948. The entire work consists of sixteen short sonatas, grouped into sets of four and separated by interludes. Although the individual movements are short, the work as a whole lasts over

◗ John Cage
FAST FACTS

- Dates: 1912–1992
- Place: United States
- Reasons to remember: A profound and influential musical thinker who challenged the most basic assumptions about what music is

an hour. *Sonatas and Interludes* was Cage's first work to reflect an alternative conception of the function of music: to quiet and sober the mind.

The piano requires extensive preparation: forty-five notes are prepared, with screws and bolts, plus fifteen pieces of rubber, four pieces of plastic, six nuts, and one eraser. The sounds produced by the prepared piano are more like those of Eastern percussion instruments than like those of a piano.

In its novel timbres, shifting rhythms, absence of harmony, and static forms, Cage's piece represents a radical reconception of music and musical organization. In these respects, it bears more resemblance to a contemporary dance track than it does to the music of most of Cage's contemporaries or predecessors.

⌈The purpose of music is to induce a state of tranquility, thus opening the door to the divine.⌋

 **LISTEN UP!**

Cage, Sonata V, from *Sonatas and Interludes* (1946–1948)

TAKEAWAY POINT: A piano that doesn't sound like a piano

STYLE: Avant-garde

FORM: AABB

GENRE: Short piano piece

INSTRUMENT: Prepared piano

CONTEXT: Cage stretching the sound frontiers of the avant-garde

A

0:00   A distinctive melodic gesture over steadily moving percussive sounds gradually becomes more active, then quiets down.

A

0:18   A distinctive melodic gesture over steadily moving percussive sounds gradually becomes more active, then quiets down.

B

0:37   This section flows directly from the first. It begins quietly, with long notes supported by a less regular accompaniment. The rhythm becomes more erratic, then relaxes at the end.

B

0:58   Begins quietly, with long notes supported by a less regular accompaniment. The rhythm becomes more erratic, then relaxes at the end.

 Listen to this selection streaming or in an Active Listening Guide at CourseMate or in the eBook.

23-2B Cage and Contemporary Music

Many commentators regard *Sonatas and Interludes* as Cage's first mature work. It also signaled the beginning of Cage's passionate interest in Far Eastern culture, which would in turn directly influence his music. Around the time of the premiere of *Sonatas and Interludes*, Cage began studying Zen Buddhism and immersing himself in Japanese culture. In 1950, he received a copy of the *I Ching*, a classic Chinese text, which inspired him to introduce chance into the performance of his music, which he called chance music: he would compose segments, but the order in which the segments were performed depended on coin tossing, according to the method prescribed in the *I Ching*.

Cage's subsequent works and his writings, which were even more influential than his music, challenged the most basic assumptions about music and art. They compelled listeners and readers who took them seriously

Cage would compose segments, but the order in which the segments were performed depended on coin tossing.

chance music Twentieth-century avant-garde music that introduced the element of chance into composition and performance, such as determining the order of performance through the toss of a coin

to expand their minds as well as their ears. Few twentieth-century artists in any field of activity have had a more pervasive impact on American culture than Cage.

LEARNING OUTCOME 23-3
Appreciate the contributions of Edgard Varèse and electronic music to the avant-garde.

23-3 Edgard Varèse and Electronic Music

If dedicated clubbers could be transported back to 1958 and find their way into the Phillips Pavilion at the Brussels World's Fair, they would encounter a dazzling spectacle, on the inside as well as the outside. They would see and hear hundreds of speakers stationed throughout the pavilion, driven by a battery of amplifiers. Complementing this soundscape were images, photographs, film montages, and color projections, all intended to be symbolic rather than storytelling. Sound and image created a completely immersive experience.

The all-encompassing multimedia nature of the event and electronic sound generation would have been familiar, but the music would have been well outside most clubbers' experience. Instead of a DJ mixing a long series of tracks, there was an eight-minute composition played on three synchronized tape recorders that was repeated while the pavilion was open; another two-minute electronic composition by the Greek composer-architect-mathematician Iannis Xenakis, who assisted the esteemed architect Le Corbusier in designing and constructing the pavilion, filled the interval between presentations of the eight-minute work. And instead of the relentless thump of a synthesized bass drum and endlessly repeated loops, there was an assortment of electronically generated and "found" sounds coming from speakers throughout the pavilion in a seemingly random sequence.

The music was Edgard Varèse's *Poème électronique*, one of the first important electronic music compositions. Varèse was commissioned to create the piece and was given free rein regarding its substance. He organized the sonic events to take advantage of the unusual shape of the pavilion and the hundreds of sound sources; the spatial interrelation of the musical events was a key element. For those who heard it, it was a once-in-a-lifetime experience, because the pavilion was torn down in January 1959, shortly after the fair concluded. Although a fully realized experience of Varèse's work is no longer possible, both the music and the setting provided a glimpse into the future.

23-3A Edgard Varèse

Poème électronique was Varèse's last completed work. Varèse was not a prolific composer: in a career that spanned over four decades, he completed only thirteen mature works. The paucity of his output is attributable to several factors: the grandness of his vision (he left several mammoth projects incomplete); difficulty in

▸ Edgard Varèse
FAST FACTS

- Dates: 1883–1965
- Place: France
- Reasons to remember: Pioneering avant-garde composer with a particular interest in sounds of all kinds and cutting-edge technology.

Katherine Young/Hulton Archive/Getty Images

finding resources and audience support for his music; the radical nature of his musical aesthetic, even by the standards of the avant-garde; and a profound depression that lasted over a decade.

Edgard Varèse ▲ was perhaps the most international of twentieth-century composers. He was born in France; lived in Berlin for seven years; left just as World War I began; relocated to the United States the following year, where he would remain for most of the rest of his life and where he would compose the music that earned him his reputation; and received recognition on both sides of the Atlantic after World War II. He played a major role in the founding and promotion of two organizations to support modern composers: the International Composers' Guild (1921–1927) and the Pan American Association of Composers (1928–1934). And wherever he went, he gravitated toward like-minded composers and their supporters: for someone who pursued such an independent course, he seemed especially adept at networking.

Beginning with *Amériques*, his first major work and the composition that celebrated his move to the United States, Varèse outlined the path of his radical musical evolution. The Second Viennese School abandoned tonality, but pitch organization remained central: the role of the twelve-tone row was to provide a systematic alternative to tonality. Varèse was prepared to abandon pitch—or at least definite pitch—as necessary to musical organization, or even necessary at all. *Amériques*, although radical for its time, seems tame in comparison with his subsequent compositions. It is scored for full orchestra with a dramatically expanded percussion section. In addition to the conventional percussion instruments, Varèse also requires such unconventional sound sources as a whip, wind machine, and siren.

In his subsequent compositions, Varèse continued to favor unconventional sound sources, and especially those that did not produce definite pitch. They include early electronic instruments (theremin, ondes martenot), sound-producing devices not typically associated with musical composition, and percussion instruments. The boldest of these compositions, at least in terms of resources, was *Ionisation* (1929–1931), the first major work for percussion ensemble.

Varèse, *Poème électronique*, excerpt (1957–1958)

TAKEAWAY POINT: Seminal composition for electronic tape

FORM: Through-composed

GENRE: Electronic music

INSTRUMENTS: Tape recorder/sound system

CONTEXT: Composition that stretches the boundaries of what music is in multiple ways. This excerpt begins at 5:47 into the original recording.

0:00   A single pitch gradually surrounded by an electronic halo

0:13   A string of percussion sounds (produced mainly by conventional instruments) with electronically generated tones interpolated throughout, then taking over

0:47   After silence, jet takeoff, then assorted percussion sounds (gong-like sounds, rattles, etc.)

1:01   Operatic voice (no words) seems to come from nowhere and then take over.

1:14   Male chorus takes over as female voice floats away; jarring noise interrupts; more percussion, then organ sounds. Rapid tapping (on a bottle?), followed by more organ sounds.

1:42   Repetition of gradual ascent of a siren—this motive-like pattern is heard prominently earlier in the work. Jet plane sounds fade in, followed by more indefinite-pitched sounds, including **glissandos** (continuous sliding changes of pitch) up and down that bring the work to an abrupt end.

 Listen to this selection streaming or in an Active Listening Guide at CourseMate or in the eBook.

From the 1920s, Varèse was especially intrigued by the potential of electronic instruments, as is evidenced by his use of them in his compositions. Two disappointments in the 1930s put his enthusiasm on hold for two decades. In 1933, he applied for two grants to construct an electronic music studio. Both were turned down. And in 1939, Léon Theremin, the inventor of the device that bears his name, returned to Russia; Varèse had hoped to work with him. He composed very little after the grant rejection.

However, in 1953, an anonymous donor gave him an Ampex tape recorder, which he used to create his last three major works. *Poème électronique* would be his second fully electronic composition; the first was a soundtrack for a film.

23-3B *Poème électronique*

Stereophonic recordings went mainstream in 1958. A series of stereophonic recordings issued by small audiophile labels and a dramatic drop in the cost of manufacturing stereophonic record players compelled the major labels to begin releasing their recordings in both monaural and stereophonic formats.

The technology for simulating the ambience of a live performance space in commercial media had been available since the 1930s. Walt Disney's animated feature *Fantasia* (1940) was originally presented

glissando Continuous, sliding change in pitch

with a stereophonic soundtrack; the success of widescreen Cinerama films, which also featured early surround-sound audio, whetted the public's appetite for this new sonic experience.

Even as this new technology became a mass-market phenomenon, Edgard Varèse was preparing an electronic composition that offered stereophonic sound on steroids. Whereas stereophonic sound on commercial recordings was mainly an effort to more closely approximate the sound of music in performance, Varèse's approach was to sculpt sound in space. The Philips Pavilion was in this sense an ideal venue. With so many speakers mounted throughout the unusually shaped structure, visitors would hear *Poème électronique* (see Listen Up!) coming at them from all directions; the location of the sounds was part of the experience in a way it almost never is in traditional performances of art music.

23-3C The Aesthetics of Electronic Music

We live in a time when the innovations of digital technology have democratized the creation of electronic music. For less than a thousand dollars, one can buy an iPad or PC; install an inexpensive but high-quality audio workstation; buy a microphone, maybe a MIDI keyboard, and a few loops; and produce a professional-sounding recording.

Further, most of us consume most of our music through recordings of some kind, rather than in live performance. In many popular genres, the recording is most often the referential version; live performances replicate the recording, not the other way around; and recordings that contain electronically generated sound are the rule, not the exception. So although Varèse's electronic composition may contain musical surprises, the fact that it is an electronic composition is business as usual for today's audiences.

However, at the time that Varèse composed it, music created on and "performed by" a tape recorder was a novelty, and a dramatic departure from tradition. Much of the excitement of a live performance comes from the connection between performer and audience, and with it, the sense that the audience is hearing a unique musical event. A concert-like performance of an electronic work through speakers cannot replicate either the performer–audience connection or the sense of uniqueness. As a result, successful performances of electronic music often involve other appealing elements, such as dancing (as in a club), multimedia display, or a distinctive venue. In this sense, Varèse's work, presented in a structure through which people walked, with film and images coordinated with the music, and with the additional novelty of spatially decentralized sound sources, was a foretaste of the future.

Varèse clearly was ahead of his time, by several generations. He envisioned a musical future much different from his own time and much like ours in several respects, especially in its reliance on technology and the prominence of percussion. He would influence musicians in many domains, from academic composers to rock stars: Frank Zappa, the most important experimentalist among 1960s rock musicians, was a devoted admirer. One wonders what Varèse would have been able to create with today's technology.

LEARNING OUTCOME 23-4
Describe Krzysztof Penderecki's work in the avant-garde's exploration of alternative pitch constructs.

23-4 The Avant-Garde in Eastern Europe

While audiences were filing through the Philips Pavilion in August and September 1958, Van Cliburn's recording of Tchaikovsky's Piano Concerto No. 1, recorded with Kiril Kondrashin and the Moscow Philharmonic Orchestra, climbed to the upper reaches of the album charts. The previous spring, Cliburn had won first prize in the piano division of the first International Tchaikovsky Competition, held in Moscow and sponsored by the Soviet government. The Soviets were so confident that a Russian pianist would win again that the judges asked Nikita Khrushchev, the Soviet premier at the time, whether they could name Cliburn the winner. Khrushchev asked them whether Cliburn was the best. When they affirmed that he was, Khrushchev said, "Then give him the prize." Cliburn returned to the

United States a hero, receiving a ticker-tape parade in New York. *Time* magazine put him on its cover, an unprecedented honor for a young classical musician.

Cliburn's victory came at the height of the Cold War, when tensions between the United States and the Soviet Union were at their peak. With the detonation of the first hydrogen bomb in 1952 by the United States and the subsequent development of the bomb in the Soviet Union, the threat of nuclear annihilation hung over the world like a giant mushroom cloud. Perhaps to channel their aggression into less destructive outlets, the two sides competed in virtually every domain, including the arts.

23-4A Culture and the Cold War

Even before the surrender of Germany in May 1945, the wartime alliance between the United States and Western European countries and the Soviet Union had begun to deteriorate. After the war, the Soviet government quickly expanded its sphere of influence over much of Eastern Europe: Poland, Czechoslovakia, Hungary, Romania, and Bulgaria, and the Soviet Zone in Germany, which became East Germany in 1949.

After the Korean War (1950–1953), the Cold War was fought everywhere except the battlefield. The East and West competed in numerous arenas. In technology, the biggest contest was the race to space, and beyond. The Russians won that with their 1957 launch of *Sputnik*, the first satellite to orbit the earth. Beginning in 1952,

Sputnik

FAST FACTS

- Dates: b. 1933
- Place: Poland
- Reasons to remember: Avant-garde composer noted for his use of innovative and expressive string sonorities

Erich Auerbach/Hulton Archive/Getty Images

when the Soviet Union first fielded a team, the Olympic Games were a quadrennial competition for world sports supremacy. The Soviet Union won the medal count in both winter and summer in 1956, 1960, and 1964.

Culture, especially high culture, was another battleground. Almost as soon as the war ended in Europe, OMGUS—the Office of the Military Government of the United States—took control of German musical life. They restored music by composers whose works had been banned under the Nazis, suppressed composers sympathetic to the Nazis, promoted American music, and helped underwrite the Darmstadt summer courses in new music, initiated in 1946 by Wolfgang Steinecke to foster the teaching of modern composition and promote premieres of new works. The CIA played an even bigger role in the promotion of avant-garde music in the 1950s and 1960s, funding or helping to fund numerous organizations that promoted avant-garde music. As Alex Ross, music critic and contributor to the *New Yorker* magazine has noted, "'Advanced' styles symbolized the freedom to do what one wanted . . . the liberty to experiment . . . to be esoteric or familiar." The most prominent of the CIA-supported organizations was the Congress for Cultural Freedom, which sponsored activity in all the arts. The CIA formed the organization in 1950 as a covert operation to counteract the impression among left-leaning intellectuals and artists that socialism and communism provided better opportunities for artists and thinkers. The involvement of the CIA was revealed only in 1967.

In practice, freedom of expression within the communist bloc in Europe depended to a large extent on distance from Soviet control. Among the most artistically liberated countries was Poland, whose cultural policies adhered to Stalin's socialist realism policy in the early 1950s but opened up after Stalin's death, particularly after the "Polish thaw" of October 1956, which led to a less hard-line government and a loosening of the ties with the Soviet Union. That same month, the Union of Polish Composers presented the first Warsaw Autumn, an international festival of contemporary music, with substantial support from the government. Poland assumed a leading role in promoting artistic freedom in the Eastern Bloc, partly in response to the

avant-garde activities in Western Europe. Among the beneficiaries of the more open policies of the Polish government was the composer Krzysztof Penderecki (pen-de-ret-sky).

23-4B Krzysztof Penderecki

According to his friend and benefactor Peter Yates, John Cage complained that "he could see no reason why Schoenberg, having freed music from tonality, should not have gone the entire way and freed music from its twelve notes. If every tone is equal to every other, then any controllable sound is equal to any other or to any tone."

Although Schoenberg and Webern never went that far, some composers who assimilated their ideas did. Among them was the Polish composer Krzysztof Penderecki ◀, one of a wave of composers active after World War II who expanded the range of pitched sounds beyond the discrete twelve notes within the octave. The practice dated from the early part of the century but became far more widespread after World War II, in large part because of Cage's influence. Indeed the original title of the Penderecki work discussed later is an homage of sorts to Cage. By contrast, its second and final title hints at the influence of politics in the world of the avant-garde, a group that prided themselves on their independence.

Like many composers of his generation, Krzysztof Penderecki initially modeled his music after that of Stravinsky and Webern, then Pierre Boulez, a prominent avant-gardist who, like Babbitt, used Webern's music as a point of departure for the development of more advanced and comprehensive serial techniques. He quickly found a more personal direction, which involved the extensive use of innovative string techniques. The first was *Emanations*, a work for two string orchestras tuned a quarter tone apart (a further subdivision of the standard twelve half-steps within an octave to twenty-four quarter-steps within an octave). Other works for strings, sometimes with other instruments, followed soon after. Among them was a one-movement work for fifty-two stringed instruments, originally entitled *8'37"* but soon retitled *Tren (Threnody for the Victims of Hiroshima)*.

23-4C What's in a Name? The Avant-Garde and Cold War Politics

Almost thirty-five years after composing *Tren*, Penderecki recounted why he changed the name: "I had written this piece, and I named it, much as in Cage's manner, *8'37"*. . . . But . . . in the end, I decided to dedicate it to the Hiroshima victims."

That's one version. A few years later, in a *New York Times* interview, Penderecki commented about the renaming more offhandedly: "Oh, I don't know . . . you know in those days we were surrounded with all this

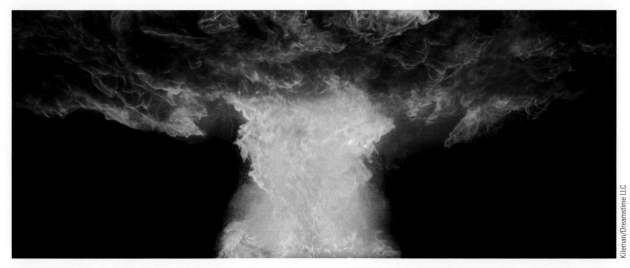

"Oh, I don't know . . . you know in those days we were surrounded with all this propaganda about the American bomb." —Krzysztof Penderecki

propaganda about the American bomb." Other accounts mention that the director of Polish radio had recommended the change to Penderecki before he submitted the work for the UNESCO prize, a fact that Penderecki does not mention.

Penderecki's work appeared during the height of the Cold War. Partly in response to the avant-garde activities in Western Europe, governments in Eastern Europe encouraged avant-garde composition and supported composers with publication. Penderecki was one of the beneficiaries of this more open policy.

Tren is a work of truly expressive power. A major source of its impact is Penderecki's handling of pitch. His innovations were part of a larger movement to develop alternatives to equal temperament.

23-4D Alternative Pitch Constructs

At the time of Schoenberg's twelve-tone revolution during the early 1920s, the division of the octave into twelve equal half-steps was, for most musicians and their audience, the closest thing to an immutable law of music. It seemed as permanent and unvarying as the piano keyboards on which one could play all twelve tones. Musicians played "in tune" when the pitches that they played matched precisely the twelve tones within the octave; they played "out of tune" when the pitches did not match one of the twelve tones.

However, as early as the eighteenth century, a few musicians had experimented with other divisions of the octave, particularly on fretted and keyboard instruments. This practice remained a curiosity until the twentieth century, when composers such as Ives composed works requiring quarter tones (twenty-four notes per octave). Ives, Cowell, Bartók, and several other composers also made use of tone clusters: groups of adjacent or nearly adjacent tones struck at the same time. These

experiments in fragmenting or blurring the twelve tones appeared in the 1920s, around the time that the first electronic instruments—the theremin and the Ondes Martenot—were invented, and composers, most notably Edgard Varèse, composed works mainly or exclusively for percussion instruments. Collectively, these developments represented a far-reaching assault on equal temperament.

The exploration of alternative pitch constructs and the use of sounds with indefinite pitch became more frequent and more varied in the 1930s and 1940s—Cage's prepared piano piece is a now familiar example. However, challenges to the twelve-tone division of the octave gained even more momentum among avant-garde composers, not only through the use of "concrète" and electronic sounds but also through innovative demands made on conventional instruments. Strings were the instrument family best suited to explore subtle gradations of definite pitch. Because the fingerboard has no frets, it is possible to play the twelve tones within the octave as well as any pitch between adjacent half-steps.

23-4E *Tren* and Avant-Garde Expressionism

Among the compositions that exploited these novel sonorities were three works by Penderecki that date from around 1960. The most widely performed is *Tren (Threnody for the Victims of Hiroshima)*. In the excerpt from the work presented here (see Listen Up!), Penderecki uses an array of devices to blur pitch; among them are quarter tones, glissandos, and blocks of pitches so dense that it is virtually impossible to identify individual pitches.

Recall that much of the expressive power in Schoenberg's *Pierrot lunaire* came from three pitch-related elements: atonality, *Sprechstimme* (which makes pitch less definite), and the use of extreme registers. By

 **LISTEN UP!**

 TOTAL TIME: 2:06

Penderecki, *Tren (Threnody for the Victims of Hiroshima)*, excerpt (1960)

TAKEAWAY POINT: Innovative string sounds to depict the horrors of war

FORM: Through-composed

GENRE: Orchestral work

INSTRUMENTS: Fifty-two strings

CONTEXT: Avant-garde music with a political message

0:00   Static blocks of pitched sound, first low- to mid-range, then clusters in several registers, piling in, one after the other, gradually tapering away with glissandos down and up

0:43   Low note in cello, quickly surrounded by quarter tones, then welling up into another massive block of sound, then slowly tapering away to another single note

 Listen to this selection streaming or in an Active Listening Guide at CourseMate or in the eBook.

---

moving away from, then back to, definite pitch and eliminating all rhythms except the entrances and exits of the string players, Penderecki considerably extends Schoenberg's innovations. There is virtually no conventional musical information to process: no distinctive rhythms, no motives, no recurrent patterns. As a result, Penderecki's work provides a direct path to the subconscious. Although it is unlikely that the composer conceived the work programmatically, *Tren* would make a compelling sound track for a documentary of the bombing: the sounds seem to evoke the buzz of the airplanes flying overhead, the explosions, the inarticulate cries of the victims, and desolation in the wake of the bombing.

Looking Back, Looking Ahead

It is a measure of the extent to which avant-garde composers distanced themselves from the larger music-making world that none of the works discussed in this chapter would have been considered "music" as it was defined in the first part of the century. None has melody or harmony in any conventional sense, and only the Cage piece has a perceptible pulse. After World War II, a definition of music inclusive enough to account for these works would have to be more Cage-like: "music is controlled sound."

As is evident from even this small sample of works, composers bought into the idea that music must evolve: the quest for novelty was the predominant characteristic of this musical generation. For most, the music of the Second Viennese School—Schoenberg, Berg, then Webern—represented the immediately prior stage. As they continued to extend the frontiers of music, avant-garde composers closed ranks, as Babbitt intimated in

his article. Their main audience was each other—at festivals, new music concerts, and the like. They sought to please and impress themselves rather than cater to a larger audience.

In their small world, there was a sense of urgency—the excitement of discovery, the pleasure of innovation. But there was a kind of tyranny from within: whereas composers from the Eastern Bloc faced tyranny from without—the state ministries of culture—composers who aligned themselves with the avant-garde faced enormous peer pressure. Serialism was the new orthodoxy, and composers such as Babbitt, Boulez, and Karlheinz Stockhausen were truly the vanguard. Their influence is evident in the widespread adoption of serialism, in varying degrees, not only by a younger generation of composers but also even esteemed composers of the prior generation, such as Stravinsky and Copland, who had previously rejected it.

The widespread adoption of serial procedures had the advantage of providing something approaching a common practice for contemporary composition; it remained in force through the early 1970s. However, it had the disadvantage of being a practice that even attentive lay listeners found largely impenetrable. Serial works are inherently difficult to aurally process in real time: the musical information is, by design, unfamiliar, and the amount that listeners must assimilate can be overwhelming. A row contains twelve tones, not seven, in a unique intervallic relationship (which makes it far more difficult to recall, even after several hearings); and the tones do not coalesce via well-established practice into larger units, in a manner similar to the scales, chords, and progressions of tonal harmony.

As a result, little of this music has received broader acceptance. There are, for example, virtually no serial orchestral compositions from the postwar era that have

> "Well, perhaps we did not take sufficiently into account the way music is perceived by the listener."
>
> —Pierre Boulez

entered the standard repertoire, the way Stravinsky's ballets, Shostakovich's symphonies, or Copland's orchestral music has. In 1999, in explaining the dearth of avant-garde serial works crossing over to a more mainstream audience, Boulez said, "Well, perhaps we did not take sufficiently into account the way music is perceived by the listener."

Serial composition represented increasing amounts of precompositional control over the content of a composition. Those who moved in opposite directions—transferring the result in performance to performers, or even to chance (as Cage did)—enjoyed somewhat more success, particularly if the work had an appealing point of entry or readily imagined expressive intent. Penderecki's *Tren* still receives regular performances. However, here too the endless search for new sounds worked against broader acceptance because the unfamiliarity of the innovations and the absence of common ground with established styles made assimilation a challenge.

Despite the seeming gulf between the avant-garde and the rest of the musical world—classical, popular, folk, and ethnic—and the relatively small audience for their music, the postwar avant-garde has had a substantial influence on the course of music during the latter part of the twentieth century, because many of their innovations were adapted for use in other contexts. For example, Varèse's pioneering work in electronic composition led to the now normative practice of bypassing the performer completely: almost any dance track is evidence of this.

Musique concrète–inspired "found" sounds were used in concept albums of the 1960s and 1970s, such as The Beatles' *Sgt. Pepper's Lonely Hearts Club Band*, Frank Zappa's *We're Only in It for the Money*, and Pink Floyd's *The Dark Side of the Moon*. Film composers have mined the music of the avant-garde in an effort to expand their sound palette: almost any horror film makes use of avant-garde–derived effects.

Even as their innovations began to filter into other kinds of music, avant-garde composers faced a dilemma: they couldn't go forward or back. Collectively, their work in the 1950s seemed to explore virtually every musical frontier: it is difficult to imagine music that could evolve much beyond the complexity of Babbitt's synthesizer compositions, and it is even more difficult to imagine anything simpler than Cage's *4'33"*. Further evolution seemed impractical, if not impossible. However, if they turned away from cutting-edge approaches and novel concepts, they risked censure from many of their peers.

In retrospect, the postwar avant-garde has functioned within the larger musical world much as Babbitt envisioned. Like pure mathematicians and theoretical physicists, avant-garde composers have explored new frontiers, seemingly without much regard for their wider application. Their work is understood and appreciated almost exclusively by a small group of like-minded specialists. And as with their scientific counterparts, their cutting-edge innovations eventually found application beyond the laboratory: without the ideas and compositions of the avant-garde, the sound world of the late twentieth century would have been considerably poorer and far less interesting.

 study tools 23

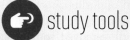 study tools

After you read this chapter, go to the Study Tools at the end of the chapter, page 337.

To create the cover of The Beatles' 1967 album *Sgt. Pepper's Lonely Hearts Club Band*, designer Peter Blake cut out and arranged more than sixty life-size cardboard images of the band's current heroes. It's a provocative assemblage of famous, once-famous, and not-so-famous personalities: geniuses and gurus; athletes, artists, and actors; writers and comics; and many more. The Beatles appear twice: as wax-museum like-nesses (left of center) from their Beatlemania period and "live," dressed in bright band uniforms.

By conflating high and popular culture, past and present, and musicians and nonmusicians—except for The Beatles and ex-Beatle Stuart Sutcliffe, the only musicians on the cover are Fred Astaire, better known for his dancing than his singing, avant-garde composer Karlheinz Stockhausen, and Bob Dylan—Blake's collage signals a new understanding of culture and society. In the post-modern world of the last part of the twentieth century, class distinctions diminished, cultural hierarchies crumbled, and boundaries dissolved. Rock was not only the sound track for these developments but also an agent of change. No other aspect of culture played as significant a role as rock did in reshaping values in Western society. With their openness to new ideas, their unparalleled imagination in integrating the most disparate elements into coherent statements, and their unprecedented popularity, The Beatles played a leading role in a movement that transformed both musical life and Western culture in the last third of the twentieth century.

In this chapter, we focus on rock's meteoric ascent from a teen-themed tangent of postwar rhythm and blues to music of significance and influence. We highlight key stages in its transformation through four examples, by Chuck Berry, the Beach Boys, Bob Dylan, and The Beatles, then summarize its impact on musical life in the latter part of the twentieth century. We begin with rock and roll.

Michael Ochs Archives/Getty Images

The *Sgt. Pepper* album cover conflates high and popular culture, past and present, and musicians and nonmusicians.

24-1 From Rock and Roll to Rock

In the excellent documentary *Rock and Roll: The Early Years,* there's a clip of a white preacher ranting and raving about the evils of rock and roll. He asks his congregation what it is about rock and roll that makes it so seductive to young people, then immediately answers his own question by shouting, "The BEAT! The BEAT! The BEAT!" thumping the pulpit with each "beat." It was the beat that drew teens to rock and roll during the 1950s.

24-1A Rock Rhythm

The "beat"—the distinctive rhythmic organization of rock and roll—wasn't entirely new. Boogie-woogie pianists had been pounding it out in bars and barrelhouses since the late 1920s. But delivered on an amplified guitar with backing from bass and drums, it became invasive and, to some listeners, abrasive. Rock and roll had a rhythm and a sound that many teens found irresistibly appealing and their parents found simply appalling.

What made rock rhythm so attractive to teens and so repellent to many of their parents was the fundamental level of activity. Adults had grown up listening to the rhythms of swing, in which the defining rhythms moved at beat speed—the walking bass of jazz—or slower. By contrast, the defining feature of rock is its insistent rhythm that moves twice as fast as the beat. It was this doubling of activity, delivered relentlessly and at what was then considered to be a loud volume, that stimulated teens in the early years of rock. The architect of this sound was Chuck Berry.

24-1B Chuck Berry, Architect of Rock and Roll

Sometime early in 1955, Chuck Berry "motorvated" (to use a Chuck Berry coinage) from St. Louis to Chicago to hear Muddy Waters, for years his idol, perform at the Palladium Theater. After the concert, Berry went backstage and asked Waters how he could get a record deal. Waters suggested that he contact Leonard Chess. Two weeks later, Berry was back in Chicago, handing Leonard Chess a demo tape containing four songs. Among them was Berry's remake of a song called "Ida Red," which he entitled "Maybellene." Chess liked the song, Berry recorded it, and Chess released it on August 20, 1955.

"Maybellene" caught the ear of DJ Alan Freed, who promoted the song by playing it frequently on his radio show after negotiating a share of the songwriting credits—and the royalties that went with them. With Freed's considerable help—Freed reportedly played the song for two hours straight on one broadcast—"Maybellene" quickly jumped to number 5 on the *Billboard* "Best Seller" chart.

Berry would have to wait almost a year for his next hit, "Roll Over, Beethoven," to reach the charts in the fall of 1956. In the hits from "Roll Over, Beethoven" to "Johnny B. Goode," Berry assembled the distinctive sound of rock and roll, step by step.

The heart of Berry's new conception was an intensified adaptation of the repetitive accompaniment patterns of boogie woogie, a two-fisted blues piano style popular in the 1930s and 1940s. Berry learned the sound of **boogie woogie** during his long association with pianist Johnny Johnson. He transferred Johnson's patterns to his guitar, gave it an edgy sound, and surrounded himself with piano, bass, and drums. Simultaneously, he developed a lead guitar style that built on the same active rhythm, with frequent double notes and lots of syncopation.

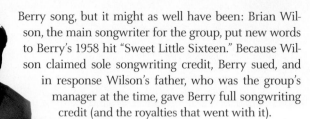

© Pictorial Press Ltd/Alamy

Chuck Berry, the architect of rock and roll

On his classic recordings, Berry advanced this new conception by himself, most notably on "Johnny B. Goode," where he apparently plays both lead and rhythm guitar through **overdubbing**, the process of recording additional sounds on an existing recording. But the other band members—Johnson and the best of Chess Records' house musicians—were still locked into the less active rhythms of swing and country.

24-1C Rock and Roll Evolves

However, it didn't take long for Berry's innovation to catch on. Aspiring rock and rollers on both sides of the Atlantic tuned in to Berry's new rhythmic conception. The list of acts that covered Berry's music reads like a Who's Who of late 1950s and early 1960s rock: Buddy Holly, the Beach Boys, The Beatles, the Rolling Stones, the Hollies, and the Kinks. These and other acts covered far more Chuck Berry songs than the songs of any other rock-and-roll artist.

Among the first Beach Boys hits was "Surfin' U.S.A." The song was released in March 1963 and quickly climbed the charts, peaking at number 3. The song wasn't a cover of a Chuck

boogie woogie Blues piano style characterized by repetitive accompaniment patterns in a low register

overdubbing Process of recording additional sounds on an existing recording

Berry song, but it might as well have been: Brian Wilson, the main songwriter for the group, put new words to Berry's 1958 hit "Sweet Little Sixteen." Because Wilson claimed sole songwriting credit, Berry sued, and in response Wilson's father, who was the group's manager at the time, gave Berry full songwriting credit (and the royalties that went with it).

A comparison of the two versions highlights key features of the transformation of rock and roll into rock. One key difference is the Beach Boys' use of electric bass instead of the acoustic bass of pre-rock pop. In 1963, the electric bass was still a relatively new instrument. Leo Fender invented it in 1950, but it was not widely used until the early 1960s. However, it soon became the standard bass instrument in rock because with amplification, it could match the power of the electric guitar.

The other significant change was the use of Berry's innovative rock rhythm by the entire band. Every part in the song—vocal line, rhythm guitar, organ solo, bass line, and drum part—either reinforces this more active rhythm or lines up with it. This development harnessed the energy of rock rhythm so that listeners felt its full impact.

More than any other developments, these two changes transformed rock and roll into rock. The pervasive use of rock rhythm and the replacement of the acoustic bass with the electric bass made this still-new music louder, more active, and more intrusive. We can hear this transformation in a side-by-side comparison of Berry's "Sweet Little Sixteen" and the Beach Boys' "Surfin' U.S.A."

By the time British bands invaded the United States in early 1964, rock had become impossible to ignore. Beatlemania reinvigorated rock, which had lost much of its momentum in part due to Elvis's induction into the army and Buddy Holly's death in a plane crash on February 3, 1959.

But it was still possible to dismiss rock as mindless music for teens: the original cast album of the musical *Hello, Dolly!* replaced The Beatles' second album at the top of the album charts in June 1964. That would soon change in the wake of a fateful meeting two months later.

LEARNING OUTCOME 24-2

Describe how rock grew up, in the music of Bob Dylan and The Beatles.

24-2 Rock of Significance: Dylan and The Beatles

On August 28, 1964, Bob Dylan and The Beatles met face-to-face for the first time. The Beatles were on tour in the United States and staying at the Delmonico

LISTEN UP!

Berry, "Sweet Little Sixteen" (1958)/Wilson, "Surfin' U.S.A." (1963)

TAKEAWAY POINT: The Beach Boys' remake of Berry's hit demonstrating the transformation of rock 'n' roll into rock

STYLE: Rock 'n' roll/early 1960s rock

FORM: Modified blues form in melody; strophic/variation form in song as a whole

GENRE: Rock 'n' roll/early 1960s rock

INSTRUMENTS: Voice, electric guitar, piano, bass, drums, lead and backup vocals, electric guitar, electric bass, organ, drums

CONTEXT: Both songs directed toward young audience

BERRY

0:00   Notice Berry's rhythm guitar, which moves twice as fast as the beat, underneath his vocal. This is the defining feature of rock rhythm.

       They're really rockin' in Boston . . .

0:23   Nice stop-time effect, as rhythm instruments (guitar, bass, piano, drums) are silent under vocal phrase and play in the breaks.

       Sweet Little Sixteen . . .

0:45   Bandmates don't get Berry's new rhythm. Bass walks—one note per beat. Drummer plays swing rhythm with heavy backbeat. Pianist plays triplets now and then. Berry is the only one playing with a rock rhythmic conception.

       Oh mommy mommy . . .

1:07   Bassist downshifts to two-beat rhythm: notes on every other beat. However, groups like Beach Boys and Beatles listened to Berry. Soon everyone was thinking in and playing rock rhythm.

       'Cause they'll be rockin' on bandstand . . .

BEACH BOYS

0:00   By early 1960s, the entire band played or meshed with rock rhythm: rhythms that moved twice as fast as the beat. Here, both bass and drums move at rock beat speed.

       Surfin' U.S.A. . . .

0:26   The rock rhythm is even clearer during the organ and guitar solos. Note also the electric bass, which replaced the string bass as the standard bass instrument in rock around 1960.

       Everybody's gone surfin' . . .

 Listen to this selection streaming or in an Active Listening Guide at CourseMate or in the eBook.

Hotel in New York. They had acquired the album *The Freewheelin' Bob Dylan* while in Paris in January 1964; according to George Harrison, they wore the record out, listening to it over and over. John Lennon in particular seemed drawn to Dylan's gritty sound and rebellious attitude. Somewhat later during that same year, Dylan was driving through Colorado when he heard The Beatles for the first time over the radio. Later he would say, "I knew they were pointing the direction where music had to go." Each had something that the other wanted, and perhaps found intimidating. The Beatles, especially Lennon, envied Dylan's forthrightness; Dylan responded to the power of their kind of rock and envied their commercial success. It was Lennon who requested the meeting, through Al Aronowitz, a columnist for the *New York Post*; Aronowitz brought Dylan down from Woodstock to meet The Beatles.

Whatever initial uneasiness they may have felt with one another quickly went up in smoke. Upon learning that none of The Beatles had tried marijuana, Dylan promptly rolled a couple of joints and passed them around. As Paul McCartney later recalled, "Till then, we'd been hard Scotch and Coke men. It sort of changed that evening."

However, there was more to this meeting than turning The Beatles on. It seemed to further motivate both parties to learn from the other. In explaining their musical breakthrough in the mid-1960s, McCartney said, "We were only trying to please Dylan." As for Dylan, the experience gave him additional motivation to go electric, which he did on one side of his next album, *Bringing It All Back Home*, recorded in January 1965. After that, he never looked back. In retrospect, his years as a folksinger, as important as they were to his career, were simply a prelude to his more substantial career as a rock musician.

We encounter both acts through music from the most significant period in their careers—from the date of their meeting through the release of *Sgt. Pepper's Lonely Hearts Club Band.*

24-2A Bob Dylan

Highway 61 Revisited and *Blonde on Blonde*, Dylan's first two all-electric albums, brought into full flower the rock-fueled power promised on the electric side of *Bringing It All Back Home.* However, none of his early electric music is typical rock fare. There are no recurrent stylistic conventions, such as a basic beat, harmonic approach, or formal plan. Instead, Dylan invests rock with a freewheeling, anything-goes attitude. Despite their deep roots in rock and roll, blues, folk, country, and Beat poetry, the songs are shockingly original. They juxtapose the sublime and the ridiculous and package elusive and challenging ideas in images that brand themselves in your memory.

Dylan's most far-reaching musical innovation was the evocative use of musical style. He used beats, instruments, harmonies, forms, and the like to create an atmosphere. No one before Dylan had let it penetrate so deeply into the fabric of the music. The varied settings continually recontextualized Dylan's voice. When he sings, it isn't pretty by conventional pop standards, and much of the time his vocalizing is closer to speech than to conventional singing. But it is the ideal vehicle for the trenchant commentary in his lyrics.

Among the most provocative examples of this new approach on *Bringing It All Back Home* was "Subterranean Homesick Blues" (see Listen Up!). The lyric was a stream of obscure references, inside jokes, and stinging social commentary—all delivered much too fast to understand in a single hearing. The density of the lyric and the speed of Dylan's delivery challenged listeners to become engaged; one could not listen to him casually and expect to get much out of the experience.

Dylan embedded his challenging lyrics in a blue-jeans musical setting. His backup band included a full rhythm section behind his acoustic guitar and harmonica. They supported Dylan with a clear two-beat rhythm with a strong backbeat, which derived most directly from honky-tonk, the post–World War II country style popularized by

honky-tonk Post–World War II country style popularized by such artists as Hank Williams

such artists as Hank Williams. The ornery mood it set up right at

Bob Dylan in 1964, just before going electric

the start was an ideal backdrop for Dylan's words and voice. Dylan delivered his proto-rap lyric as a talking blues, a genre created by Southern rural bluesmen and adapted by Dylan's hero Woody Guthrie.

Dylan's music inverted the traditional pop approach to artistry. Before him, those who wanted to create artistic popular music emulated classical models: George Gershwin's *Rhapsody in Blue* or musical theater productions like *West Side Story.* Dylan's music sent a quite different message: one can be sophisticated without being "sophisticated"— that is, without borrowing the conventional indicators of musical sophistication, such as symphonic strings.

With Dylan, rock grew up. It was no longer possible to mock rock—or at least Dylan's music—as mindless music for teens. His music and the music of those inspired by him not only gave rock artistic credibility and significance but also redefined what credibility was. It democratized popular music while elevating its message in a way that had never been done before: with Dylan, high art did not have to assume high-class trappings.

Dylan's early electric work quickly became the standard by which those who followed him were measured. He inspired others not so much by providing a model that others would copy as by showing through example what could be said in rock. In this way, his influence was profound and pervasive.

For The Beatles, the reverberation from their encounter with Dylan bore fruit about ten months later, when they began work on *Rubber Soul*; the album would be released in December 1965. *Rubber Soul*, the "Dylan album," would make clear the dramatic evolution of their music. The evolution would continue in *Revolver*, released the following year, and most remarkably in *Sgt. Pepper's Lonely Hearts Club Band.*

24-2B The Beatles

By the time The Beatles got together with Dylan, they were riding the crest of Beatlemania. Their first three American albums topped the charts; so did numerous singles. Their first appearance on *The Ed Sullivan Show*, on February 9, 1964, drew 73 million viewers, and their first film, *A Hard Day's Night*, had just opened in American theaters.

In 1964, The Beatles (John Lennon, Paul McCartney, George Harrison, and Ringo Starr) were young but experienced and versatile, the result of long hours spent performing in Liverpool clubs and strip joints in Hamburg, Germany. In 1962, they auditioned for producer George Martin, who would become their irreplaceable collaborator, and had their first hit later that year. The year 1963 saw a string of hits and growing international recognition, which led to the release of their recordings in the United States and their first American tour.

Their early work built mainly on the work of important American rock-and-roll acts. They typically used the two guitar/bass/drums instrumentation popularized by Buddy Holly, and their first hits were teen-themed songs like "I Want to Hold Your Hand." Before their encounter with Dylan, they had begun searching for qualities that would set them apart: the clangorous chord that begins "A Hard Day's Night" is evidence of that. But even this striking sound hardly prepared their fans for the dramatic evolution of their music over the next three years.

The Beatles' musical growth was unparalleled in popular music; the suddenness with which their music matured remains an astounding development. Like Dylan, they were expanding their sound world, but in a more adventurous, all-encompassing way. Dylan drew mainly on existing popular styles and used them evocatively. By contrast, The Beatles reached further afield, into musical traditions far removed from rock and its roots, such as classical Indian music and string playing reminiscent of classical music. Moreover, they synthesized these nonrock sounds seamlessly into their music; they became part of the fabric of sound behind the vocals.

As their music matured, it became bolder and more individual. The songs are more clearly the work of The Beatles—no one else could have made them—and less like each other. The contrast from song to song had clearly deepened. One can almost reach into a bag filled with song titles, pull out any five, and marvel at the distinctive identity in meaning and sound of each song and the pronounced differences from song to song. These differences reached a peak in *Sgt. Pepper's Lonely Hearts Club Band*, released in June 1967. The most remarkable track on this extraordinary album is "A Day in the Life."

LISTEN UP!

TOTAL TIME: 2:23

Dylan, "Subterranean Homesick Blues" (1965)

TAKEAWAY POINT: Complex, sophisticated lyrics in a down-home musical setting

STYLE: Rock

FORM: Expanded blues form

GENRE: Significant rock

INSTRUMENTS: Voice, harmonica, acoustic guitar, electric guitars, electric bass, drums

CONTEXT: Dylan using working-class music as a background for a significant social statement

INTRO

0:00   Rhythm section sets up a honky-tonk style two-beat rhythm.

CHORUS 1

0:09   Blues-derived harmonic progression is shown with the lyric.

      (I) Johnny's in the basement . . .

0:20   (IV) Look out kid . . .

      (I) God knows when ..

      (V) The man . . .

      (I) Wants eleven . . .

0:34   Instrumental break

CHORUS 2

0:39   (I) Maggie comes fleet . . .

0:50   (IV) Look out kid . . .

      (I) Walk on your tiptoes . . .

      (V) Keep a clean nose . . .

      (I) You don't need . . .

1:03   Instrumental break

CHORUS 3

1:09   (I) Oh get sick. . .

      (IV) Look out kid . . .

      (I) But losers . . .

      (V) Girl by the . . .

1:20   (I) Don't follow leaders . . .

1:33   Instrumental break

1:40   (I) Oh get born . . .

1:52   (IV) Look out kid . . .

      (I) Better jump . . .

      (V) Don't wanna be a bum . . .

      (I) The pump don't work . . .

🔊 Listen to this selection streaming or in an Active Listening Guide at CourseMate or in the eBook.

An early group portrait of The Beatles (1962). Left to right: Paul, John, George, and Ringo

24-2C The Sound World of The Beatles: "A Day in the Life"

The Beatles' "style" was an approach to musical choices more than a particular set of musical choices. Their music is almost always tuneful, regardless of its message: McCartney, Lennon, and Harrison were great melodists. More important, The Beatles were among the first important rock-era musicians to write melody-oriented songs that were in step with the changes in rhythm, form, and other elements that were transforming the sound of popular music.

They complemented their memorable melodies with distinctive sound worlds. Settings—instruments, textures, rhythms, even form—were purposeful; their function was to amplify and illuminate the message of the lyrics. Strong contrasts from song to song, and occasionally within a song, as in "Lucy in the Sky with Diamonds" and "A Day in the Life," both from *Sgt. Pepper's Lonely Hearts Club Band*, show the extent of their imagination and musical range. Both imagination and range are clearly evident in "A Day in the Life."

In "A Day in the Life" (see Listen Up!), Lennon creates sound worlds that highlight the contrast between the mundane, everyday world and the elevated consciousness that results from tripping on LSD. They are projected by the most fundamental opposition in music itself, other than sound and silence: music with words versus music without words. The parts of the song with lyrics are everyday life, while the strictly instrumental sections depict tripping—they follow "I'd love to turn you on" or a reference to a dream.

This contrast is made even more striking by the nature of the words and

concept album Album unified by a particular creative theme

music. The lyric features four vignettes. The first involves a gruesome automobile accident; the second is about a film—perhaps an allusion to the film *How I Won the War*, in which Lennon had acted. The third depicts someone in the workaday-world rat race, and the last one is a commentary on a news article about counting potholes. In Lennon's view, this is news reporting—and by extension, daily life—at its most trivial: who would bother counting potholes anyway?

The music that underscores this text is, in its most obvious features, as everyday as the text. It begins with just a man and his guitar. The other instruments layer in, but none of them makes a spectacular contribution. This everyday background is opposed to the massive orchestral blob of sound that depicts, in its gradual ascent, the elevation of consciousness. The dense sound, masterfully scored by George Martin, belongs to the world of avant-garde classical music—it recalls Penderecki's *Threnody for the Victims of Hiroshima* and other works of that type, works familiar to forward-thinking classical music devotees but not well known generally. This creates another strong opposition: well-known versus obscure, and by implication, the unenlightened (not turned on) masses versus those few who are enlightened.

The final chord is an instrumental *om*, suggesting the clarity of enlightenment after the transition, via the orchestral section, from mundane life in the "normal" world. It is a striking ending to a beautifully conceived and exquisitely crafted song, a song that is one of the most powerful metaphors for the LSD experience ever created.

"A Day in the Life" encapsulates the art and achievement of The Beatles as well as any single track can. It highlights key features of their music: the sound imagination, the persistence of tuneful melody, and the close coordination between words and music. It represents a new category of song: more sophisticated than pop; more accessible and down to earth than pop; and uniquely innovative. There literally had never been a song—classical or vernacular—that had blended so many disparate elements so imaginatively. Critics searched for a way to describe the song and the album: they labeled it a concept album (an album unified by a particular creative theme) and declared it the rock-era counterpart to the song cycles of nineteenth- and twentieth-century art music.

"A Day in the Life" is less than four years removed from "She Loves You" and the other teen-themed singles of their early years. The Beatles had begun their career by affirming what rock was, in comparison to rock and roll and pop. As they reached the zenith of their career, they showed what rock could be.

The Beatles remains rock's classic act in the fullest sense of the term. Their music has spoken not only to its own time but also to every generation since. Their songs are still in the air; they remain more widely known than any other music of the rock era. The Beatles' music is a cultural artifact of surpassing importance. No single source—of any kind—tells us more about the rock revolution of the 1960s than the music of The Beatles.

Looking Back, Looking Ahead

The rock revolution was sudden and far reaching. In 1959, rock and roll seemed dead. However, less than a decade later, it had captured both market share and mind share: it had become *the* commercially dominant popular music and had begun to redefine both artistic merit and cultural values.

Rock was revolutionary because it changed both the sound of popular music and the messages it communicated. The generational difference might be summarized like this: pre-rock pop typically sought an escape from reality; rock intensified reality. During the Depression and World War II, momentary escape was a welcome, if occasional, antidote to the often harsh reality of daily life. In the more prosperous postwar era it became as artificial as the lives portrayed in the popular situation comedies that filled TV screens.

By contrast, the best rock was real in a way that earlier generations of pop seldom were. The message of the song reached its audience directly because rock-era songwriters usually performed their own songs. Songs were not written *for* something—a musical or a film—so much as to say something. Rock's concern with the present, combined with its direct and often personal communication between song, singer, and audience, elevated the role of the music for many members of that audience from simple entertainment to (quoting noted rock critic Geoffrey Stokes) "a way of life."

Moreover, the rock revolution occurred during the 1960s, a decade of tumultuous social change. Civil rights, protests against the Vietnam War, free love, the gradual empowerment of women, the environmental movement, and a huge generation gap—all challenged the established social order. Rock was the sound track for these developments as well as an agent of change. The messages embodied in the music and the example of its musicians helped shape attitudes toward minority rights and multiculturalism.

Rock soon gained a presence that the larger musical world could no longer ignore. It influenced virtually all established popular and vernacular genres: soft rock and pop rock, rock musicals, and jazz fusion were important new directions in the late 1960s and early 1970s. Even classical music wasn't above rock's influence. Among the important new trends in the latter part of the twentieth century that were at least tangentially influenced by the openness of rock were more eclectic compositional styles, a return to more accessible concert music, and minimalism. We sample these new directions in the next chapter.

LISTEN UP!

The Beatles, "A Day in the Life" (1967)

TAKEAWAY POINT: The greatest song of a great rock band

STYLE: Rock

FORM: Multisectional

GENRE: Early art rock

INSTRUMENTS: Voices, rhythm instruments, strings

CONTEXT: The defining track on one of the first concept albums

 Listen to this selection on iTunes or YouTube.

 study tools 24

Ready to study?
In the book you can:

- Review Learning Outcome answers and Glossary terms with the tear-out Chapter Review card.

Or you can go online to CourseMate, at www.cengagebrain.com, for these resources:

- Chapter Quizzes to prepare for tests

- Interactive flashcards of all Glossary terms

- Active Listening Guides, streaming music, and YouTube playlists

- An eBook with live links to all web resources

LEARNING OUTCOMES

After reading this chapter, you will be able to do the following:

25-1 Explain the place of minimalism in late twentieth-century music.

25-2 Become aware of the first generation of women composers who have enjoyed status comparable to that of their male counterparts, through the work of Joan Tower and Ellen Taaffe Zwilich.

25-3 Describe the world of the late twentieth-century film composer through an exploration of the music of John Williams.

 study tools

After you read this chapter, go to the Study Tools at the end of the chapter, page 352.

O n December 31, 1999, the BBC's television program "2000 Today" broadcast the dawn of the new millennium around the world. Over a period of twenty-eight hours, almost a billion viewers worldwide saw the sun rise in country after country. The sound track for the program was the Chinese composer Tan Dun's *A World Symphony for the Millennium*, which merged symphony orchestra and choir with sounds from around the world, from low-pitched throat singing in the chanting of Tibetan Buddhist monks to the steel drums of Caribbean calypso. The music shifted in step with the shift from location to location.

Tan's score suggests how radically musical life had changed in just half a century. The insularity of the 1950s—when the avant-garde kept largely to itself and more familiar music was valued according to a widely accepted pecking order, with classical music at the top and rock and roll toward the bottom—gave way to a more open and inclusive attitude. In his *World Symphony*, Tan embraced literally a world of music by drawing on musical traditions from almost every continent. In the process, he dissolved the temporal, geographical, cultural, and stylistic boundaries that seemed immutable only a few decades earlier.

A new generation of composers of concert music working in the last third of the twentieth century shared the attitude exemplified by Tan's work. They challenged long-held assumptions about musical worth and saw the serial music of the midcentury avant-garde as an evolutionary dead end. They opened themselves up to music from other cultures, as well as to all the music of their own. They drew their cue from the rock revolution. The Beatles' *Sgt. Pepper* was a seminal expression of this attitude.

The music presented in this chapter exemplifies two of the dominant trends in late twentieth-century concert music: minimalism and eclecticism. Both signal in quite different ways the greater openness of post-serial contemporary composers.

LEARNING OUTCOME 25-1
Explain the place of minimalism in late twentieth-century music.

© Shutterstock.com

25-1 Minimalism

Manhattan is an island borough of New York City. It's just under twenty-three square miles: about thirteen miles north to south and just over two miles east to west at its widest point. It has a small area: more than twenty Manhattans would fit inside the Los Angeles city limits, with room to spare. And it's densely populated: almost 2 million people live in the borough.

Partly because it's such a compact and populous area, it has supported a dazzling range of musical activity, which is associated not just with the city or the borough but also with particular places (and times) within the borough itself. A stretch of Broadway, between 53rd and 42nd Streets, has been home to musical theater for more than a century. Adventurous New Yorkers during the late 1920s and 1930s traveled uptown to hear Duke Ellington at the Cotton Club, on 142nd Street in Harlem. Modern jazz fans frequented the clubs along 52nd Street in the postwar years. If they wanted to mambo, they could go up a street and up a flight of stairs to the Palladium Ballroom, located on 53rd Street. Milton Babbitt composed electronic music at the Columbia-Princeton Electronic Music Center, located on the Columbia University campus at 125th Street.

"Uptown" Manhattan is the part of the borough above 59th Street, the southern boundary of Central Park. Columbia University and the Juilliard School are situated in the uptown part of Manhattan. "Midtown" Manhattan includes the area between 59th Street and 14th Street. "Downtown" Manhattan reaches from 14th Street to the southern tip of the island. The north end of downtown includes the more bohemian areas of the borough: Greenwich Village, Soho, the Lower East Side.

In *The Rest Is Noise*, Alex Ross uses geography to demarcate a sharp division—philosophical and musical—between two groups of composers who were active during the 1960s and 1970s. "Uptown" composers were those who taught at major universities and conservatories, in New York and elsewhere. Because they were the apostles of atonality, they did not attract large audiences. However, on campus, they were the tastemakers: there was enormous pressure on their students to conform to the composers' nonconformist orthodoxy. Not all of their students did: a few turned their back on the training they received, in search of a decidedly different direction. Many of them gravitated to the art scene downtown.

25-1A Minimalism and the "Classical Music" Counterculture

During the rock revolution, when university composers were at the height of their influence, a small group of American composers, most notably LaMonte Young, Terry Riley, Steve Reich, and Philip Glass, created a new kind of contemporary music. Their new style, soon called "minimalism," was a comprehensive rejection of serialism and the European tradition from which it came. As Glass said some years later, the avant-garde was "a wasteland, dominated by these maniacs, these creeps, who were trying to make everyone write this crazy, creepy music." Instead, the minimalists sought inspiration in non-Western music and in jazz and rock: Reich

► Steve Reich

FAST FACTS

- Dates: b. 1936
- Place: United States
- Reason to remember: Pioneer of minimalism

Craig Barritt/Getty Images Entertainment/ Getty Images

> "[The avant-garde was] a wasteland, dominated by these maniacs ... who were trying to make everyone write this crazy, creepy music."
> —Philip Glass

would later become the mastermind of U2's expansive sound) were in attendance at a London performance of Glass's *Music with Changing Parts;* it would lead to several collaborations. John Cale worked with LaMonte Young before forming the Velvet Underground with Lou Reed.

Minimalist composers represented the "classical music" branch of the 1960s counterculture. Reich and Glass lived in downtown Manhattan, below 14th Street. Rather than seek out university teaching positions, they

> Minimalist composers represented the "classical music" branch of the 1960s counterculture.

worked odd jobs outside the music field. Like rock and jazz composer-performers, both eventually led their own groups: both the Philip Glass Ensemble and Steve Reich and Musicians were touring ensembles. They performed in a variety of venues—wherever they might attract a crowd. Composer David Schiff recalls attending a Steve

immersed himself in African music; Glass and Riley studied with East Indian musical masters. Both Riley and Reich had a strong connection to jazz—especially bebop and the post-bop music of John Coltrane—and, later, rock. The interest was reciprocal. David Bowie and Brian Eno (who worked with Bowie in the 1970s and

Reich concert in 1974 at a dreary auditorium on the Columbia University campus. At the outset, there were only a few people there,

minimalism Umbrella term used to describe a diverse body of music with little activity or little change in activity; a comprehensive rejection of serialism and the European tradition from which it came

and several of them left. However, many of those who left returned with friends; by the end, the hall was full, of students and other like-minded listeners.

Drugs played a central role in the composers' creative and personal lives: marijuana and mescaline were the drugs of choice. In these and other respects, minimalist composers had much more in common with rock and jazz musicians of the 1960s and 1970s than they did with the classical avant-garde.

25-1B Roots of Minimalism

Minimalism is an umbrella term used to describe a diverse body of music with little activity or little change in activity. Commentators borrowed the term from the visual arts: it had come into use to describe the work of visual artists such as Frank Stella, Sol LeWitt, and Richard Serra. Minimalism began as an American music. Its two main sources were the American experimentalist composers of the 1930s, 1940s, and 1950s, as well as music from the vernacular countercultures, especially bebop and rock.

The American experimentalists were a diverse group. They shared an interest in new sounds, especially percussive sounds, and they typically looked to the Far East, rather than Europe, for new ideas. Among the most influential were Henry Cowell, Lou Harrison, and John Cage (whose *4'33"* is the ultimate minimalist work). An even stronger influence was Morton Feldman, whose quiet, spare works often left pitch choice up to the performers. The San Francisco Bay Area and downtown New York were the two main nodes of activity for the minimalist movement.

The composer who served as the bridge between Cage and Feldman and the minimalists was LaMonte Young. Young was a superb jazz saxophonist during his high school and college years; he received much of his training as a composer at UCLA, working with an assistant of Schoenberg, before moving to the Bay Area for graduate study. He relocated to New York in 1960, where he became active in the art scene, ingested and dealt drugs, and revamped his compositional approach, often stripping it down to cryptic sets of directions. The entire score of his *Composition 1960 #10* asks the performer simply to "draw a straight line and follow it." Another consists of two notes "to be held for a long time." Young and Terry Riley, whose 1964 composition *In C* put minimalism on the cultural map, never developed a following. Glass and Reich did.

25-1C Steve Reich and American Minimalism

In 1969, the German bassist Manfred Eicher started ECM Records to make available the music of Keith Jarrett, Chick Corea, and other important contemporary jazz musicians: Jarrett's ECM recording of a 1975 solo piano concert in Köln, Germany (released as *The Köln Concert*), remains one of the best-selling jazz recordings of all time. In 1978, Eicher expanded the musical range of his label by adding to ECM's catalog Steve Reich's ◀ recording of *Music for 18 Musicians*, a work that Reich composed between 1974 and 1976.

Reich's recording was an extension of Eicher's catalog, rather than a departure from it, because of the affinity between Reich's music and that of ECM jazz artists. *Music for 18 Musicians* features motoric rhythms, slowly changing harmonies that were consonant but not commonplace, percussive sounds, and syncopated riff-like figures that are repeated relentlessly. For jazz fans, the materials were familiar, but Reich's handling of them opened up a completely new sound world.

Steve Reich's musical affinity with ECM artists was a consequence of experiences gained during the latter part of his traditional training. Reich majored in philosophy at Cornell but took several music courses. After graduation, he studied composition, first with classical composer–jazz pianist Hall Overton, then at Juilliard, and finally at Mills College in Oakland, California, where he worked with the Italian avant-garde composer Luciano Berio. After graduating from Mills, he remained in the Bay Area, where he listened to jazz intently—he was particularly drawn to the music of John Coltrane—studied African drumming, and worked at the San Francisco Tape Music Center, where he accidentally happened on a process that would point his music in a new direction. While manipulating a recording of a black street preacher, he discovered that two identical tape loops would go out of phase, creating a unique echoing effect. He soon applied this technique—playing the same phrase on two musical instruments, in slightly different tempos (called, appropriately enough, phasing)—to live performance, then adapted features of it, notably the extensive repetition of short melodic ideas, to a richer instrumental setting.

The work that epitomizes this phase of Reich's career is his *Music for 18 Musicians* (see Listen Up!). He began composing the work in 1974 and finished it two years later; the official premiere was in 1976 in New York's Town Hall. Like many important early minimalist compositions, *Music for 18 Musicians* is a long work: there is an opening section that presents eleven chords; eleven sections, each built on one of the chords; and a reprise of the opening. A complete performance lasts about an hour. Moreover, the music is continuous, with no pauses between sections.

LISTEN UP!

TOTAL TIME: 3:31

Reich, *Music for 18 Musicians*, Section IIIA (1974–1976)

TAKEAWAY POINT: Kaleidoscopic, hypnotic musical minimalism

STYLE: Minimalism

FORM: Multisectional

GENRE: Large chamber ensemble

INSTRUMENTS: Piano, pitched percussion instruments, violin, clarinets

CONTEXT: One section of a nonstop minimalist work lasting more than an hour

A

0:00   Bell-like sound signals transition to Section IIIA. Riff A begins faintly; other instruments join in.

0:18   Descending bell-like sound announces riff B.

B

0:22   Riff B, a modified and expanded form of riff A

C

0:42   Riff C, further expansion through repetition of riff B rhythm

D

1:09   Riff D = riff C at a higher pitch

1:32   Repeated notes in voices, clarinets underneath riff D. Irregular oscillation between two chords. Repeated notes fade out. As before, bell signals shift back to riff C.

C

2:24   Riff C: steady oscillation in marimbas continues underneath riff.

B

2:50   Riff B

A

3:11   Riff A; several instruments drop out.

3:27   Bell-like sound signals beginning of Section IIIB.

🔊 Listen to this selection streaming or in an Active Listening Guide at CourseMate or in the eBook.

The scoring of the work is idiosyncratic: four female singers, a violinist and cellist, two clarinetists doubling on bass clarinet, and ten instrumentalists who move between piano, pitched percussion instruments, and maracas. It bears no resemblance to traditional ensembles in either classical music or jazz. Moreover, the singers perform without words, as if they are instruments.

phasing Technique, popularized by Steve Reich, of playing the same phrase on two musical instruments, in slightly different tempos, to achieve a unique echoing effect

◆Arvo Pärt
FAST FACTS

- Dates: b. 1935
- Place: Estonia
- Reason to remember:
  A leading proponent of
  "sacred" minimalism

The instrumentation is one of several innovative features. Most prominent is the rhythmic approach that simultaneously connects to the most basic rhythms in human history even as it rejects the more recent rhythmic approaches within the classical tradition. We get some sense of this from the excerpt here.

Reich built his music on the undifferentiated marking of time heard in African music, Afrocentric music, and "primitive" music and was able to recontextualize European-derived elements to enrich the sound world. His music includes familiar sounds that connect to the vernacular tradition—rich chords, percussive sounds, rifflike melodic material. But they are embedded in a musical fabric in which change happens at an extremely slow pace, despite the incessant activity. As a result, his music seems expansive: we are not so concerned with measuring time as with immersing ourselves in the moment-to-moment experience of the familiar, yet different, sounds. In this way, Reich at once reconnected "concert music" with the vernacular tradition and helped chart a distinctly different musical direction.

The music of Reich and Glass inspired younger American composers, most notably John Adams, to follow a similar path. It also influenced a small but important group of European composers whose music took a related but distinctively different form.

25-1D Arvo Pärt and "Sacred Minimalism"

Among the more surprising platinum recordings of the 1990s were a 1994 recording of Gregorian chant by the Benedictine monks of Santo Domingo de Silos and a recording by the London Sinfonietta, featuring soprano Dawn Upshaw and conducted by David Zinman, of the Polish composer Henryk Gorecki's *Symphony No. 3*. At the turn of the twenty-first century, best-selling classical recordings were rare enough; what was even more surprising was that this music was not only classical but among the most unfamiliar classical music genres: chant and contemporary composition—Gorecki composed the symphony in 1977. The common ground

holy (sacred) minimalism
European school of minimalist music, different from the music of Reich, Glass, and Adams most obviously because of its sacred subject matter and slow tempos and halting rhythms

between the two recordings begins with their spirituality and the enthusiastic response to it. As Gorecki remarked, "Perhaps people find something they need in this piece of music... . Somehow I hit the right note, something they were missing. Something, somewhere had been lost to them. I feel that I instinctively knew what they needed." The statement could as easily apply to chant.

Sacred Minimalism. Gorecki, the English composer John Tavener, and the Estonian composer Arvo Pärt are the most prominent of a small group of European composers who have sought to express their religious faith through music. Pärt, Gorecki, and Tavener have enjoyed success far beyond that of most contemporary composers. Manfred Eicher recorded Pärt's music on ECM; Tavener's *Celtic Requiem* caught the attention of The Beatles, who arranged to have it recorded on their label, Apple Records; and all have had several of their works receive multiple recordings and frequent performances.

Although the three composers have distinctive, and distinct, styles, they share several common characteristics. Among the most significant are these:

- They often set sacred texts, drawn from scripture or the liturgy of a particular religious denomination, and even music that does not use sacred texts may have a spiritual dimension: two of the three texts in Gorecki's symphony are songs to the Virgin Mary.
- They compose extensively for chorus, both a cappella and with accompaniment.
- They have turned to the music of the past, especially the distant past, for inspiration and musical material.
- Their music is mostly consonant, with freshly reconceived modal and tonal harmonies.
- Their works typically unfold expansively, with slow tempos and understated rhythmic activity.

Because of the similarities in intent, resources, and musical practice, some commentators have described their music as holy, or sacred, minimalism. It is strikingly different from the music of Reich, Glass, and Adams, most obviously because of its sacred subject matter and a radically different approach to rhythm: the rapid, motoric rhythms of the American minimalists versus the slow tempos and halting rhythms of the Europeans. We hear a beautiful example of sacred minimalism in the Kyrie from Arvo Pärt's *Berlin Mass*.

Arvo Pärt. Estonia is the northernmost of the three Baltic republics. For most of its history, it has been under the dominion of foreign powers: Sweden; imperial, then Soviet Russia; Germany during World War II; and the Soviet Union after the fall of East Germany. In its recent history, it has been an independent nation only twice: a brief period between the two world wars and since 1991.

Estonia's most distinguished composer is Arvo Pärt ◆. Like most composers active after World War II, Pärt explored serialism. Unlike most composers outside the Soviet bloc, he faced official criticism from the Soviet cultural authorities for his serial compositions. Even more provocative was his undisguised profession of faith in *Credo* (1968), a work for chorus, piano, and orchestra. Pärt's work was, in the context of the Soviet Union's active suppression of religious expression, a defiant act. After *Credo*, Pärt immersed himself in early music, including Gregorian chant. From this study he developed an approach to harmony that mixed centuries-old practice with modern dissonance. Pärt calls this harmonic approach tintinnabuli (from *tintinnabulation*, "the ringing of bells"). This characteristic technique involves grouping two or more voices, one singing a modal melody and the others singing the pitches of a chord. The interplay between the voices produces harmonies that vary from completely consonant to slightly dissonant. We hear it throughout the Kyrie from his *Berlin Mass* (see Listen Up!).

Pärt's *Berlin Mass* relates more directly to the music of Hildegard and Josquin than it does to any other music that we have encountered. There are obvious reasons: like Hildegard's antiphon and Josquin's mass movement, it is liturgical music, to be used to celebrate the Mass. But Pärt goes well beyond that: his style seems to recapture the rapture that the earlier music conveys. It is a world that evokes the past yet is unmistakably modern.

LISTEN UP!

TOTAL TIME: 2:40

Pärt, Kyrie, from *Berlin Mass* (1992)

TAKEAWAY POINT: Serene, sublime sacred music

STYLE: Sacred minimalism

FORM: ABC (corresponds to three-part prayer)

GENRE: Mass

INSTRUMENTS: Chorus and string orchestra

CONTEXT: Music for a liturgical service

KYRIE ELEISON

0:00   Open sound: voices over pedal tone. The two-voice writing introduces *tintinnabuli*. Both orchestral interludes and richer choral sections make use of this technique.

CHRISTE ELEISON

0:56   Bolder choral sound at beginning of section; the music recedes, then gives way to a string interlude and thinning of the texture to a single line.

KYRIE ELEISON

1:45   Second statement of "Kyrie eleison" reprises texture but not melody of opening line. The setting maintains delicate, open texture of previous sections.

🔊 Listen to this selection streaming or in an Active Listening Guide at CourseMate or in the eBook.

25-1E Minimalism, the Past, and the Twentieth Century

Three qualities of minimalism evident in the music of Reich and Pärt reconnected the past with a vibrant present: consonance, an expansive conception of time, and a return to spirituality.

Like many of their peers working in other directions, minimalist composers restored consonant harmony without turning back the clock. There are, of course, connections with the past. Reich's static, vibrating chords are pleasing sound objects in themselves. In this respect, Reich is following the lead of Debussy, Stravinsky, and generations of jazz musicians. Pärt mixes familiar chords in unfamiliar progressions with his "tintinnabulized" harmonies; the effect is simultaneously old and new. Both bring a fresh perspective to familiar sounds.

Minimalists also reconceived the way music presents time. Among the significant achievements of eighteenth-century musicians was the hierarchical organization of musical time. Their accomplishments in this domain are comparable to those of clockmakers, whose products enabled people to perceive the passage of time with unprecedented precision. In minimalism, the intent is just the opposite: to free listeners from marking the passage of time at comfortable intervals. Reich achieves this goal by laying fast, undifferentiated rhythms over musical events that change slowly; in Pärt's music, *everything* moves slowly.

The slowly changing harmony, open-ended rhythm, and anonymity of the performing resources—there are no soloists in either work, just choirs of voices and strings in Pärt's work and teams of musicians keeping time or playing riffs or oscillating chords in Reich's—help project a sense of connection to something beyond the self that is essentially spiritual. The spiritual dimension of Reich's music is nondenominational; Pärt's *Berlin Mass* universalizes a specifically Catholic expression of the mystical. Each in its own way connects to the spiritual impulse that inspired much earlier music: shamanic drumming and chanting; the liturgical music of the Middle Ages and Renaissance; the *santería* music of Afro-Cubans seeking to communicate with their *orishas*. In the two examples considered here, minimalism has restored the spiritual dimension of music in a decidedly innovative way.

tintinnabuli Arvo Pärt's characteristic technique that involves grouping two or more voices, one singing a modal melody and the others singing the pitches of a chord, to produce harmonies that vary from completely consonant to slightly dissonant

More than any other development in concert music during the latter part of the twentieth century, minimalism reconnected concert music with the larger musical world. One can hear both works discussed in this chapter as part of a contemporary soundscape that also includes music as diverse as electronica, rap, punk, and New Age music. Indeed, one can argue that a DJ's mix at a dance club, with the endless and undifferentiated thump of a digital bass drum, is different only in degree, not in kind, from the motoric rhythms in Steve Reich's music.

As the numerous interactions between contemporary pop artists and minimalist composers exemplify, minimalism holds the promise of restoring a sense of continuum between diverse levels of musical discourse that existed in the eighteenth and nineteenth centuries but that largely disappeared during the first two-thirds of the twentieth century.

LEARNING OUTCOME 25-2

Become aware of the first generation of women composers who have enjoyed status comparable to that of their male counterparts, through the work of Joan Tower and Ellen Taaffe Zwilich.

25-2 Uncommon Women and Musical Eclecticism

In 1902, Otto Ebel published *Women Composers: A Biographical Handbook of Women's Work in Music*. Ebel's pioneering survey included entries for more than 750 composers. *The Norton/Grove Dictionary of Women Composers*, compiled by Julie Anne Sadie and Rhian Samuel and published in 1996, discusses almost 900 composers, all born before 1955. More inclusive musical dictionaries, such as Johann Walther's *Musicalisches Lexicon* and Grove's *Dictionary of Music and Musicians*, have also mentioned numerous women composers.

However, despite abundant sources and opportunities for research, many music scholars have until recently given women composers short shrift. Scholars' low opinion of women composers was often implicitly instilled from the start of their training. A case in point: through its first several editions, one leading music history textbook cited more than 450 composers; none was a woman. So it isn't surprising that in the preface of their dictionary, Samuel notes: "The move to unearth women artists, in music as in any other art, is not a neutral act, any more than is their previous neglect."

eclecticism Widely used twentieth-century compositional strategy that derives from diverse sources

Today, women composers no longer work in obscurity. During the last part of the twentieth century, women composers past and present began to receive greater recognition. Several have won prestigious awards for their works, served as composers-in-residence for major orchestras, received substantial commissions for orchestral music and operas, and increasingly populate composition departments at major universities. The playing field in contemporary classical composition may not yet be level, but equal opportunity is much closer than it was a century ago.

Within a larger discussion of such matters as a distinctive "woman's voice" in composition, Samuel identifies "musical eclecticism"—a reconciliation of conflicting styles and cultures—as potentially a defining characteristic of the music of women composers. According to the *Oxford American Dictionary*, *eclectic* means "deriving ideas, style, or taste from a broad and diverse range of sources." In music, eclecticism can be a vice or a virtue. Commentators discussing music composed before 1900 often used the term disparagingly to describe composers who simply imitated existing styles rather than found their own creative paths. However, in the twentieth century eclecticism has become a widely used compositional strategy, in both classical and vernacular music. Important composers have combined diverse styles evocatively, as we have heard in music by Debussy, Stravinsky, Ives, Gershwin, Prokofiev, and Copland. For film composers, it is an almost indispensable tool, and it has been used increasingly in musical theater since Bernstein's *West Side Story*. Rock, because of its diverse genealogy and inclusive nature, is inherently eclectic.

In this section, we discuss two works: Joan Tower's *Fanfare for the Uncommon Woman* (1986) and Ellen Taaffe Zwilich's *Concerto Grosso 1985*. Their common ground goes beyond the fact that both are works by women composers and that both were composed only a year apart. Both demonstrate in varying degrees the musical eclecticism noted by Samuel, chart new approaches to tonality, and pay homage to Aaron Copland. In these ways, the works highlight noteworthy developments in late twentieth-century concert music.

"The move to unearth women artists, in music as in any other art, is not a neutral act, any more than is their previous neglect."
—Rhian Samuel, 1996

© Nikolais/Dreamstime.com

25-2A Reconceiving Tonality

Among the more active participants in the Darmstadt School during the 1950s was the young German composer Hans Werner Henze (b. 1926). In the late 1940s, Henze embraced serial composition but turned away from it during the mid-1950s. His defection from serial orthodoxy was not well received by his some of his peers. In 1957, Henze's *Nachtstucke und Arien*, a work for soprano and orchestra, was performed at the Donaueschingener Musiktage, a long-running German new music festival. In the audience were three Darmstadt colleagues, Pierre Boulez, Karlheinz Stockhausen, and Luigi Nono. According to several accounts, all three walked out of the performance as soon as they heard a consonant horn melody.

It is possible to write atonal—even twelve-tone—music that retains elements commonly associated with tonal music, such as stepwise motion and consonant intervals. But the most avant-garde of composers disdained the use of these more familiar sounds in the quest for novelty and difference, as we heard previously. Accordingly, in the postwar years, cutting-edge music traded the trappings of tonality for bold new sound worlds that were compelling, but not always easy on listeners.

For those contemporary classical composers who turned away from the extremes of serialism to return to more tonal, consonant, and "listenable" music, it was all but impossible to simply turn back the clock. The pressure for novelty was still there, and composers needed to find new modes of expression but use familiar materials. They had as resources the new approaches to tonality in jazz and rock, in addition to alternative approaches to tonality from the first half of the century. Mixing tonal music with atonal music, or even mixing it with sounds without specific pitch, was also an option.

Among the most widely used features of this neotonal music composed since the mid-1960s are these:

1. Orientation around a tonic, which is affirmed by a method other than common practice harmony
2. Heavy reliance on consonant intervals
3. Motives or musical cells created mainly or exclusively from consonant intervals, including scale fragments and triads

We will hear these more consonant approaches to pitch organization in works by Tower and Zwilich—in fact, in all the works discussed in this chapter.

25-2B Beyond Ceremony: Music for Brass and Percussion

George Lucas's *Star Wars* series begins not with the famous main theme heard in later in the chapter, but with an eighteen-second fanfare. The famous film composer Alfred Newman composed it in 1933, and for many years all films from 20th Century Fox began with searchlights scanning the sky around the famous art-deco logo while the fanfare was playing. This film opener fell out of favor during the 1970s, until George Lucas reclaimed it for the Star Wars films. It has since been used in most 20th Century Fox films, occasionally in parody: the film *White Men Can't Jump* begins with a funk/disco version of the fanfare.

Fanfares date back to the Middle Ages. Originally, they were short, often improvised pieces performed by trumpets and drums to present royalty during a ceremony or state occasion. Such fanfares were more about noise than music. In his musical dictionary, Johann Walther described its effect in this way: "[a fanfare] indeed makes enough noise and strutting, but otherwise hardly smacks of art."

Toward the end of the nineteenth century and into the twentieth, composers began producing short, ceremonial works for brass instruments—and occasionally with percussion—which they entitled fanfares. The most famous is Aaron Copland's *Fanfare for the Common Man*, composed in 1942. Copland's composition is stately and spacious sounding. Its title pointedly democratizes the fanfare: it is for the "common man" instead of a king or queen.

In 1986, Joan Tower composed the first of five fanfares "for the uncommon woman." She conceived of the work as a tribute and a response to Copland's fanfare. Both the Copland and the Tower works are scored for eleven brass and three percussion instruments. Both fanfares are more than ceremonial flourishes; they are short but substantial musical statements. As such, they exemplify a relatively recent trend in musical life: concert music for large ensembles featuring winds and percussion.

© iStockphoto.com/mijpan

25-2C Concert Music for Winds

Among the major ensembles found in almost every good-sized university music program and many

neotonal music Music composed since the mid-1960s that shares the qualities of (1) orientation around a tonic, (2) heavy reliance on consonant intervals, and (3) motives created mainly or exclusively from consonant intervals, including scale fragments and triads

fanfare Short, ceremonial work for brass instruments and occasionally percussion

► Joan Tower

FAST FACTS

- Dates: b. 1938

- Place: United States

- Reasons to remember: Renowned twentieth-century woman composer who abandoned serialism in favor of more accessible music

Hiroyuki Ito/Hulton Archive/Getty Images

music conservatories is a group composed almost exclusively of woodwinds, brass, and percussion. These groups are typically identified by some combination of the terms *symphonic*, *wind(s)*, and *ensemble*: for example, wind ensemble, symphonic winds, and symphonic wind ensemble. These are more prestigious terms for ensembles that evolved from the concert and military bands of the late nineteenth and early twentieth centuries.

The idea of a large ensemble whose repertoire consists almost exclusively of original concert music for winds and percussion took hold only in the latter half of the twentieth century. The driving force in this movement was Frederic Fennell, who formed the Eastman Wind Ensemble in 1952. The name of the group—wind ensemble, not band—reflected Fennell's high-minded approach. This approach distinguished them from the concert bands of the turn of the century, which performed marches, popular music, and transcriptions of the orchestral literature.

In 1952, there weren't many concert works for wind ensemble. The staples of the repertoire were early twentieth-century works by British composers, most notably Gustav Holst and Ralph Vaughan Williams, and individual works for large wind bands by Stravinsky, Schoenberg, and Hindemith. However, a series of innovative recordings by the Eastman Wind Ensemble helped popularize this repertoire, and the wind ensemble quickly became the high-minded counterpart to the concert band in university music programs.

Although there are no full-time resident wind ensembles comparable to symphony orchestras, there are numerous high-level amateur and part-time professional organizations throughout the world, including the Netherlands Wind Ensemble, a part-time professional ensemble made up of musicians from the three major Dutch orchestras, and wind symphonies in Tokyo and Dallas. As a result of commissions and the increased likelihood of performance and recording opportunities, late twentieth-century composers have considerably enriched the wind ensemble literature: the Eastman Wind Ensemble alone has premiered over 150 works.

More generally, the outpouring of music for large groups of wind and percussion instruments brings what used to be "outdoor" music into the concert hall. Much of the wind music composed in the eighteenth century was intended for performance outdoors. For instance, Mozart's works for large wind groups are called "serenades"; according to Walther, a serenade was "an evening piece; because such works are usually performed on quiet and pleasant nights."

In the nineteenth century, band concerts by amateur and professional groups often took place outside: many town squares have bandstands where municipal bands would perform in the summer. Sousa's band performed before thousands at the Chicago World's Fair. By contrast, there are only a handful of nineteenth-century concert works for wind groups, and most are large chamber works mainly for woodwinds, horns, and perhaps double bass.

In the twentieth century, composers have written concert works not only for band and wind ensemble but also for orchestral winds, brass, and/or percussion. The fanfares of Copland and Tower were among the numerous works of this type commissioned by symphony orchestras. These works could just as easily be performed by wind ensembles because they don't require strings; they also contribute to the growing body of music for larger ensembles of winds and percussion.

25-2D Joan Tower's *Fanfare for the Uncommon Woman*

Like many composers of her generation, Joan Tower ◆ (b. 1938) began her compositional career as a serialist, and like many of her peers, she abandoned serialism for a more accessible style during the mid-1970s. As she said in a 1993 interview, "I don't trust systems at all. . . . I composed serial music for 10 years, but I've gone totally the other way."

Tower has composed almost exclusively for instruments, which reflects her long-standing commitment to performing. A skilled pianist, she was a founding member of the Da Capo Chamber Players, which remains one of the leading contemporary-music ensembles in the United States. Since the mid-1970s, she has been a prolific and popular composer. Her music has received frequent performances, and much of it has been recorded. During the time she composed the fanfare, she was serving as the composer-in-residence of the St. Louis Symphony, and she has been honored with fellowships, commissions, and awards, including three Grammy Awards for *Made in America*.

> "I don't trust systems at all. . . . I composed serial music for 10 years, but I've gone totally the other way."
> —Joan Tower

The character of her music reflects her early exposure to the sounds and rhythms of ethnic musical traditions. Tower's father was a mining engineer, and she spent much of her childhood in South America. She credits that experience with stimulating her interest in rhythm and percussion instruments; much of her mature music is characterized by complex, active rhythms and bold tonal colors.

Among Tower's most widely performed works is the first *Fanfare for the Uncommon Woman* (see Listen Up!). The work was one of more than twenty fanfares commissioned by the Houston Symphony to celebrate the 150th anniversary of the independence of Texas.

> Knowing Copland's *Fanfare for the Common Man* and being a great admirer of his music, I decided not only to write a tribute to him, but to balance things out a little by writing something for women—in this case, for women who are adventurous and take risks. —Joan Tower

Like many contemporary composers who have written works for large ensembles of winds and percussion, Tower builds harmonies from intervals that are consonant but do not form the triads of common practice harmony. The result is music that sounds largely consonant but defines its own tonality through harmonies that frame the heart of the work: the piled-up harmony that concludes the first brass flourish also serves as the final chord.

Tower's fanfare is an exuberant work. Although there are moments of relative quiet, the prevailing impression is of great energy in the numerous brass flourishes and percussion barrages. It is also a tightly organized work built from a series of rhythmically active melodic kernels. It is noisy, as a fanfare should be, and it does "smack of art."

LISTEN UP!

TOTAL TIME: 2:34

Tower, *Fanfare for the Uncommon Woman* (1986)

TAKEAWAY POINT: Brief, brilliant work for brass and percussion

STYLE: Late twentieth-century neotonal music

FORM: Through-composed

GENRE: Fanfare

INSTRUMENTS: Full brass (trumpets, horns, trombones, tuba) and percussion

CONTEXT: Artful realization of a celebratory musical genre

0:00	Gong and snare drum: percussion instruments without a beat
0:10	A pyramid of brass sound, all derived from the five-note motive first played by the trumpet
0:28	Another gong blast, used as a bridge to connect to energetic music featuring low brass
0:54	Horns play an active line full of small leaps in a triplet rhythm.
1:08	A passage of relative quiet: trumpets play sustained harmonies over trombones, which play a varied version of their earlier music
1:18	Return of opening trumpet motive; all then develop the energetic material first presented by the trombones.
1:48	Fragments of earlier brass music answer the timpani. The active triplet figuration introduced previously by the horns returns, building to a climax.
2:09	An abrupt return to the five-note motive leads to the final push to the end, which spotlights percussion before a sustained final chord.

Listen to this selection streaming or in an Active Listening Guide at CourseMate or in the eBook.

25-2E Ellen Taaffe Zwilich

Often a composer's eclectic bent is evident in contrast from work to work, as exemplified by the two Debussy preludes. Less common but more dramatic are works in which the diverse sources commingle. Ives's "Putnam's Camp" and The Beatles' "A Day in the Life" are spectacular instances of this approach. Ellen Taaffe Zwilich's *Concerto Grosso 1985* offers an even more obvious and focused kind of eclecticism, one that collapses time.

Ellen Taaffe Zwilich 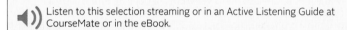 was born in Miami and grew up in Florida. She graduated in 1960 from Florida State University, where in addition to composing, she played violin in the orchestra and trumpet in the jazz band, and sang in an early-music group. After graduation, she came to New York to study violin at Juilliard but switched to composition, where she became the first woman to receive a doctorate in composition from the school. It was a 1975 performance of her orchestral work *Symbolon*, conducted by Pierre Boulez, that

brought her work to a wider audience. Since receiving the Pulitzer in 1983, Zwilich has earned a steady stream of awards and commissions, including the first Composer's Chair at Carnegie Hall; performances of her works by most major American orchestras and leading chamber ensembles; and numerous recordings, four of which have received Grammy nominations. Her success has enabled her to focus exclusively on composing.

In 1984, Zwilich received a commission from the Washington Friends of Handel to compose a work commemorating the three-hundredth anniversary of Handel's birth. To fulfill the commission, Zwilich composed *Concerto Grosso 1985*.

25-2F *Concerto Grosso 1985*

Concerto Grosso 1985 (see Listen Up!) is a five-movement work that lasts about fifteen minutes. The five movements form an arch: the outer movements are comparable in tempo and musical material; the second and fourth movements are fast and rhythmically active; and the third movement, marked "Largo," is the emotional heart of the work. The outstanding feature of the work is Zwilich's quotation of fragments from the first

♦ Ellen Taaffe Zwilich

FAST FACTS

- Dates: b. 1939
- Place: United States
- Reasons to remember: One of America's most honored composers and among the most distinguished women composers of her time

Mark Kauffman/Time & Life Pictures/Getty Images

Because there are musical connections between the music of Handel and Zwilich, the work brings the past into the present. It is as if Handel's sonata is an old and familiar film, and Zwilich's original music portrays a viewer watching the film, pausing it periodically as she engages in a kind of free association with the earlier music.

This merging of past and present is clearest in the outer movements because they contain direct quotations of Handel. However, throughout the work, Zwilich filters characteristic sounds, textures, and rhythms of Baroque music through a contemporary sensibility. Zwilich's musical language recalls the pre-1950 music of such composers as Stravinsky and Copland, so that the Handel is clearly anachronistic: the sonata is integral to the work yet clearly apart from Zwilich's music. It is a stunning effect.

🎧 LISTEN UP!

TOTAL TIME: 2:45

Zwilich, *Concerto Grosso 1985* (1985)

TAKEAWAY POINT: Contemporary take on Baroque music

STYLE: Late twentieth-century neoclassical

FORM: Through-composed

GENRE: Orchestral concerto

INSTRUMENTS: Orchestra with harpsichord

CONTEXT: Innovative, accessible orchestral music

0:00	Sustained pedal tone that is also the first note of Handel's sonata
0:17	Motive spun out Baroque-style into a long phrase. The three pitches of the motive are also borrowed from the opening of the sonata. Phrase is repeated more softly.
0:34	Orchestral version of beginning of Handel's sonata. Note harpsichord in orchestra to strengthen connection with Baroque style. Pedal tone continues underneath.
0:55	Return to present as opening motive generates another long phrase, which also ends abruptly
1:15	Flashback to sonata, with melody now played by oboe
1:32	Strings resume developing three-note motive underneath oboe's high note, which leads to rapid exchanges between strings and winds.
1:52	Rich orchestral continuation of the sonata flows seamlessly from Zwilich's original music.
2:03	Phrase from original motive continues after midpoint cadence in sonata. This time, high sustained chords in winds combine with low pedal tone to frame phrase spun out by strings. Sustained chords become more dominant as phrase becomes more fragmentary.

🔊 Listen to this selection streaming or in an Active Listening Guide at CourseMate or in the eBook.

---

movement of Handel's *Sonata for Violin and Continuo* in D. Handel's work is among the most familiar Baroque solo sonatas, and Zwilich played it in her student days. Zwilich commented, "My concerto is both inspired by Handel's sonata and, I hope, imbued with his spirit."

25-2G Women Composers in Contemporary Culture

Tower and Zwilich belong to the first generation of women composers who have enjoyed status comparable to that of their male counterparts, as evidenced by the number and quality of commissions, prizes, recordings, and publications. They are not alone. The Israeli-American composer Shulamit Ran (b. 1949) became the second woman to win the Pulitzer Prize for music, in 1990, and has served as composer-in-residence for the Chicago Symphony. Composer-performers such as Meredith Monk (b. 1942) and Laurie Anderson (b. 1947) have been important innovators. Monk has introduced a wide range of vocal styles; Anderson is known in part for replacing the hair of the violin bow with magnetic tape. Barbara Kolb (b. 1939) and Pauline Oliveros (b. 1932) are among the leading composers of electronic music.

However, they don't have much company. The achievements of Tower, Zwilich, and other twentieth-century women composers are exceptional. Despite greater activity, greater awareness, and greater professional support, women still lag well behind men in the customary measures of acceptance—performances, awards, teaching positions in composition. As several commentators have noted, parity in the profession is still a work in progress. Still, the door has been opened; the successes of Tower, Zwilich, and others should be a prelude to greater opportunities and recognition for women composers.

Eclecticism may well be the common bond of this generation of women composers. It is certainly the trademark of many important late twentieth-century film composers, most notably John Williams.

25-3 Music and Film in the Late Twentieth Century

In explaining why film biographies of classical composers so often present a distorted view of their lives, actor Simon Callow, who portrayed Handel in the acclaimed 1985 film *Honor, Profit and Pleasure*, wrote:

> The reason for this is pretty simple: composing as such, like most artistic activities, is drudgery, and—unlike painting—one that is hard to represent on the screen or stage. To watch even a genius compose is like watching paint dry—with the difference that once the paint has dried, one has something to look at.*

Callow's acid observation about what he calls the "Great Dead" underscores the central issue of filming a biography of a composer: composing, the least interesting aspect of composers' lives from a dramatic perspective, is the very reason we most remember them—and why they are central characters in films in the first place.

To address this issue, filmmakers often seek out a dramatic hook and build their narrative around it. Those who approach the task conscientiously research the composer's life and times. Still, in the interest of telling a good story, they often opt for historical plausibility—what *could* have been—rather than historical probability. A case in point is the 1994 film *Immortal Beloved*, which uses the great unsolved mystery of Beethoven's life as a focal point. In a famous unsent letter found among his effects, Beethoven pours out his heart to an "immortal beloved," whose identity cannot be established with absolute certainty. The resulting biographical portrait of Beethoven gives far more weight to the composer's relationship with this mystery woman than is warranted by the historical account.

> One problem that filmmakers *don't* have when filming composer biopics is music for the sound track.

One problem that filmmakers *don't* have when filming composer biopics is music for the sound track. They draw freely on the composer's works, not only in scenes where the composer performs and conducts but also as background music.

However, for most other films, they must engage a composer to create music for the sound track.

The life of the film composer is far different from a composer's life on film. Beethoven would likely have found the rules and requirements of film composition maddeningly restrictive.

25-3A So You Want to Be a Film Composer . . .

Composing for films presents a unique set of challenges. They begin with the most fundamental: artistic control. In every other genre that we have studied, the creator has had the final say on the musical work. There may be patrons to please, librettos to set, or choreography to accompany, but the composition typically reflects the composer's artistic vision.

Not so with film. In most cases, the film composer's conception must be subordinated to the person who has artistic responsibility for the project. Typically, this is the director, but it may be the producer or even the executive producer. Indeed, the composer must work with a large team of decision makers; the ability to work well with others is an essential requirement for any successful film composer. And this is only the first of several constraints within which composers must work. In *On the Track*, their definitive guide to film composition, Fred Karlin and Rayburn Wright describe in exhaustive detail nine stages in the process of creating music for a film: composing doesn't arrive until the sixth stage!

The process of creating music for a film begins with a first encounter with the film and those responsible for it, sometime after the film has been shot and editing has begun. As a rule, the composer typically meets with the director and other parties, mainly to ascertain the director's vision for the film, and then views a preliminary version of the film. In subsequent meetings, the director may make his vision more specific by providing musical excerpts, often culled from his own music collection, called "role models." If a role model is cued into the film, it becomes a "temp" (for temporary) track. From these initial experiences, the composer begins to form his musical response to the director's conception.

The next stage in the process is spotting, which involves viewing the film and determining—"spotting"—those scenes where music will enhance the on-screen events. This is typically a collective decision on which the composer consults with the director and others. In the process, the composer learns how much music must be composed: the team provisionally decides the "in" and "out" points of each musical segment. Music rarely runs throughout a film. More commonly, music accompanies anywhere from 30 to 70 percent of on-screen action. With these decisions made and a budget from the studio, the composer then schedules the recording sessions: the composer

spotting Process during composing for film that involves viewing the film and determining those scenes where music will enhance the on-screen events

---

*Simon Callow, Foreword, in John C. Tibbetts, *Composers in the Movies: Studies in Musical Biography* (New Haven, CT: Yale University Press, 2005), p. xi.

▶John Williams
FAST FACTS

- Dates: b. 1932
- Place: United States
- Reason to remember: Preeminent film composer of the late twentieth and early twenty-first centuries

must determine the number of musicians required for each musical segment of the film and the number of hours needed to record the music.

At this point, composers often begin formulating a concept that will carry through the entire film. It may reflect the dominant idea of the film, a main character, or perhaps a location. It may be expressed in a melody, a sound, or a rhythm, or some combination of these: the main theme of *Star Wars*, discussed later, is a memorable instance of defining the message of the film from the outset. At this point, composers begin to work out the math, matching the speed of a click track, which will set the tempo for the segment, to frame-by-frame events in the film. This is a tedious process, but when it's complete, the composer has the time framework within which he must express his musical support for the onscreen drama. Only then does he actually begin to compose, and he will have only a few weeks to prepare the finished score.

The successful film composer must be an imaginative and skilled musician, a diplomat, and an effective communicator and collaborator. The composer must be able to work under extreme pressure, massage egos and calm anxious directors, and subordinate his musical personality to the requirements of the film with great specificity: for example, "This cue lasts 1 minute and 35 seconds." It's about as far from the Romantic idea of the composer as solitary genius as a composer can get. In the late twentieth century, no one has been better at composing for film than John Williams ◆.

25-3B John Williams and *Star Wars*

In 1941, science fiction writer Bob Tucker coined this definition of space opera:

> Westerns are called "horse operas," the morning housewife tear-jerkers are called "soap operas." For the hacky, grinding, stinking outworn space-ship yarn, or world-saving for that matter, we offer "space opera."[†]

For several decades, "space opera" retained its pejorative connotation. However, around the time that the first *Star Wars* episode was released, the term began to identify a subgenre of science fiction. Its rise to respectability was

---

[†]Bob Tucker, "Depths of the Interior," *Le Zombie* 4 (January 1941), 36.

helped significantly by the popularity of the Star Wars films, which incorporated a number of its conventions.

Star Wars is the grandest of all space operas. The saga unfolds over seven films, released between 1977 and 2005. In its scope and size, it invites comparison with the grandest opera, Richard Wagner's *Der Ring des Nibelungen*. Both are based on a mythical story spanning several generations: one takes place in an indeterminate future, while the other is set in an indeterminate past; and both require about fourteen hours for a complete presentation.

Although the characters speak, rather than sing, in *Star Wars*, the films owe a large musical debt to Wagner. John Williams, who composed the music for the Star Wars films, adapts two of the most distinctive features of Wagner's music: lavish and varied orchestration, and the leitmotif.

Williams's use of Wagnerian devices, particularly the leitmotif, was all but inevitable. During the 1930s and 1940s, film composers, especially European émigrés like Max Steiner and Erich Korngold, composed sumptuous scores strongly influenced by Wagner's orchestration, harmony, and use of leitmotifs. Williams's scoring of Star Wars is at once a throwback to Wagnerian-influenced film scoring and a modern adaptation of it.

John Williams is the great emulator. He is at home in a dazzling array of compositional styles: his music may evoke Wagner, Schoenberg, Debussy, Stravinsky, Prokofiev—even Duke Ellington. Williams came by this facility by talent, inclination, and experience. During the 1950s, he led a triple life as a student of classical music in composition and piano, including study at Juilliard; working as a commercial and jazz pianist in clubs and on numerous recordings; and orchestrating and arranging for film, television, and the air force during his military service in the early 1950s. His first major success as a film composer came in 1967, when he received an Academy Award nomination for his score to the film *Valley of the Dolls*. In 1974, he began his long association with director Stephen Spielberg; this led to his work for George Lucas and the Star Wars films. For his score to *Star Wars: A New Hope*, the first of the films to be released, he received an Academy Award in 1977.

The opening music for the film provides a glimpse of Williams's compositional modus operandi. After the 20th Century Fox fanfare, there is silence as a message on the screen reads, "A long time ago in a galaxy far, far away . . ." Fanfarelike music sounds as the *Star Wars* logo appears on the screen; the triumphant main theme follows as scrolling text sets the stage for the opening action in the film. This segment lasts just over a minute. As the on-screen narrative recedes, the music turns suspenseful by becoming delicate and tonally ambiguous; a piccolo plays a whole-tone melody after Wagnerian strings. Shortly before two spacecraft appear on-screen, the music abruptly shifts to an ominous, warlike character. The rapidly shifting brass chords clash with the pedal tone that runs throughout this section. The dissonances mix with martial rhythms and sounds to create a sense of impending disaster even before the spacecraft come into view.

In the space of just over two minutes, Williams establishes three distinct and stylistically unrelated sound worlds, connecting the first two with a skillful transition and moving abruptly into the third. As this excerpt (see Listen Up!) demonstrates, Williams doesn't project a consistent individual compositional personality, as Prokofiev did in *Alexander Nevsky* and as we'll see that Tan Dun does in his music for *Crouching Tiger, Hidden Dragon*. Instead, he calls on his vast knowledge of musical styles to cherry-pick those that can anticipate and amplify the on-screen events, then tweaks them to make them specific to the film.

The main theme shows how Williams imbues an existing style with a distinct identity. The stirring melody and richly orchestrated, brass-dominated accompaniment evoke the heroic music of the nineteenth century. But Williams places it squarely in the twentieth century through such features as the rhythmic organization of the theme: instead of presenting a four-measure phrase in a conventional quadruple meter, Williams creates measures of 5, 4, 4, and 3 beats. This asymmetry gives the theme a more modern sound while still retaining its connection with the heroic music of the past.

Williams's score for the rest of the film follows much the same path: astonishing stylistic variety, with modifications that elevate the music above mere imitation. It has been a winning formula, for Williams and for the many successful films that he has scored. More generally, film composing became more eclectic in the 1970s, and it was arguably the most eclectic musical genre even in a time when eclecticism was a significant new direction in both vernacular and classical music.

Looking Back, Looking Ahead

The five musical examples in this chapter signal in quite different ways a return to accessibility in contemporary classical music, through reconnecting to the larger musical world in some way. For Reich, it began with a

LISTEN UP!

TOTAL TIME: 2:14

Williams, "Main Title/Rebel Blockade Runner," from *Star Wars Episode IV* (1977)

TAKEAWAY POINT: Memorable music by a masterful film composer

STYLE: Eclectic

FORM: Through-composed

GENRE: Film music

INSTRUMENTS: Full orchestra

CONTEXT: Music amplifies on-screen events: scrolling text, chase scene

0:00	Brief fanfare featuring brass instruments
0:06	The famous main theme of *Star Wars*
0:26	A contrasting phrase, played by the violins. It is heard twice; the restatement is extended to set up the return of the main melody.
0:48	Return of main melody
1:09	Beginning of transition to more mysterious music as the on-screen "crawl" recedes into the background and the screen grows dark
1:23	Suspenseful music, featuring piccolo melody, to shift mood from the hopeful message on the crawl to the chase with which action begins. Frantic strings interrupt as a planet and two moons come into view.
1:36	Ominous, ponderous music, with brass and percussion dominant. It slows down as the chase scene develops.
1:55	Chase continues, as a martial melody, again with brass prominent, reinforces sense of foreboding.

 Listen to this selection streaming or in an Active Listening Guide at CourseMate or in the eBook.

connection to jazz and African music. For Pärt, it was a connection to chant and pre-common practice liturgical music. For Tower, it was connecting to Copland—more specifically one of his best-known compositions. And more broadly, it was also connecting to the wind band, and the evocation of outdoor music; the brass/percussion combination is effectively an indoor counterpart to a drum and bugle corps. For Zwilich, it was the smooth juxtaposition of old and familiar with new and freshly composed. For Williams, it was seamlessly evoking multiple sound worlds in response to onscreen events.

For the last half-century, a key question for concert music composers and their adherents has been whether this reconnection to other musical styles would help effect a return to relevance. So far it has not happened, at least with regard to the most established institutions in classical music: opera and symphony. No opera or orchestral music composed since 1945 has become standard repertoire—compositions regularly performed and recorded by most of the major opera companies or symphony orchestras. By contrast, a significant body of early twentieth-century music has. Among the frequently heard twentieth-century compositions are Puccini's operas; Gershwin's *Porgy and Bess;* Stravinsky's three early ballets; all of Ravel's orchestral music; several works by Debussy, Prokofiev, Copland, and Bartók; and even Ives's *Three Places in New England*.

It isn't a question of the excellence of individual composers. Even our small sample suggests that fresh and appealing new directions in concert music emerged in the latter third of the twentieth century. Still, it is unlikely that any current or future composer of "classical" music will create major operatic or orchestral works that become standard repertoire, much less attain Beethoven-like stature, for at least two reasons.

First, standard repertoire requires a widely recognized standard of greatness. In Beethoven's time, it was relatively easy for musicians and audiences to compare his music to not only the music of his compositional predecessors and contemporaries, but also all of the published music of the day: hymns, songs, dance music, and other everyday music. Beethoven's greatness was measured in relation to that body of music. Moreover, it depended on that body of music for its expressive impact: consider again how shocking contemporary audiences must have found of the opening seconds of both the *Pathétique* sonata and the Fifth Symphony. Two centuries ago, audiences could, with Beethoven (and Rossini and Schubert), compare apples to apples, because there was a relatively small range of musical styles, and they differed more in degree than in kind.

By contrast, the fragmented musical landscape of the latter half of the twentieth century makes it all but impossible to establish a "greatness standard." The progressive individualization of musical style within classical music from the early nineteenth century through the middle of the twentieth century—from the stratification of musical discourse within Romanticism through the "isms" of the early twentieth century to styles unique to a composer, or even a specific work—has worked against the establishment of a common reference point. Further, the gradual disconnect between classical music and music directed at a mass market that began in the nineteenth century and accelerated with the rise of African-influenced popular music in the twentieth century has further fragmented musical life. As recently as the late 1960s/early 1970s, there was at least a cultural connection between the more high-minded rock musicians and classical music of all

kinds: recall concept albums by the Beatles and others and the art rock movement. That connection seems to have dissolved. So assessing greatness is no longer a matter of apples to apples, but rather apples to a huge basket filled with common and exotic fruits.

It isn't just the music but also the audience that has been fragmented. The number of people who could encounter Beethoven's music during his lifetime was limited mainly to those who were able to attend performances of his music in salons or public concerts, those who could read music well enough to play or sing his compositions, and those who might hear these musically literate performers perform. Today, anyone with a decent Internet connection can access all of Beethoven's music—and millions of other tracks—by opening a browser, Spotify, or iTunes. The Internet has broken the distribution bottleneck and unleashed a flood of music in the process. This in turn has motivated music lovers to explore the "long tail" of music—less commercially successful recordings that are now as easily and inexpensively accessed as hits—and they do: in digitally delivered music, videos, and more, someone will buy or try almost everything that's available. In 2005, Apple reported that every track in iTunes—at the time around 1 million—had been downloaded at least once.

Moreover, with the Internet, music evaluation has become almost as democratic as distribution. Peer-to-peer sites, social networks like Facebook, customer recommendations on subscription services like Spotify and digital download services like iTunes recommend tracks based on your previous choices. If you have a strong opinion about a particular musical work, you can share it with the world, and others will at least consider your opinion.

The challenge for twenty-first-century composers who want to create a work with the enduring appeal and popularity of Beethoven's Fifth or *Rhapsody in Blue* is to find the right mix of art and accessibility, innovation and convention. If they are successful, it will be due in part to the global reach of the Internet. Meanwhile, music lovers have literally a world of music to sample. We briefly introduce this world in our next and final chapter.

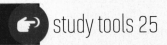 study tools 25

Twentieth-Century Music

 KEY CONCEPTS

Stylistic fragmentation. The relentless quest for novelty in concert music, the continuing evolution of popular music, and the embrace of new music-related technologies resulted in stunning stylistic diversity that increased dramatically during the course of the century.

 KEY FEATURES

Despite the stylistic diversity of twentieth-century music, there are trends and developments that cut across stylistic boundaries. Among the features that distinguish twentieth-century music are these:

1. **New sounds.** Among the most distinctive new sounds of the twentieth century were an array of percussion instruments; electronic sounds of various kinds and electronically amplified instruments; "found" sounds—natural and human-made sounds not associated with traditional music making; and extended techniques on conventional instruments.
2. **Novel sound combinations.** In both concert music and vernacular styles, three trends stand out: the small mixed-timbre ensemble; an emphasis on percussion instruments; and the use of electronic sounds, alone and in combination with acoustic instruments.
3. **New modes of pitch organization.** New approaches to pitch organization included dialects of common practice; harmony and melody based on modes and pentatonic scales; tonal music that eschewed common practice; free and serial atonality; and in extreme cases, the abandonment of the twelve discrete pitches within the octave.
4. **Diverse rhythms.** New rhythmic approaches included rhythms that immersed listeners in rhythms with a compelling, undifferentiated beat; irregular meters; and rhythms so complex, unpredictable, or slow to unfold that a consistent pulse was not apparent.
5. **Nonlinear forms.** Nonlinear forms, including music for or inspired by film, through-composed forms in concert music, and extensible forms in popular styles from blues and jazz to techno, became common alternatives to the closed forms inherited from nineteenth-century music.

 KEY TERMS

1. **Serialism.** A structured approach to atonality in which the twelve pitches within the octave are presented according to a predetermined order
2. **Rhythm section.** Providing the rhythmic and harmonic foundation in popular music since the 1920s
3. **Musique concréte.** Music composed from recordings of natural or human-made sounds not associated with traditional music
4. **Avant-garde.** Those who depart most radically from tradition
5. **Modern music.** Umbrella term widely used in the first two-thirds of the twentieth century to identify music that rejected the values and materials of nineteenth-century music

 KEY COMPOSERS

Claude Debussy (1862–1919)
Scott Joplin (1868–1917)
Arnold Schoenberg (1874–1951)
Charles Ives (1874–1954)
Béla Bartók (1881–1945)
Igor Stravinsky (1882–1971)
Anton Webern (1883–1945)
Edgard Varèse (1883-1965)
Jerome Kern (1885–1945)
Sergei Prokofiev (1891–1953)

George Gershwin (1898–1937)
Aaron Copland (1900–1990)
John Cage (1912–1992)
John Williams (b. 1932)
Krzysztof Penderecki (b. 1933)
Arvo Pärt (b. 1935)
Steve Reich (b. 1936)
Joan Tower (b. 1938)
Ellen Taaffe Zwilich (b. 1939)

Music Concept Check

To assist you in recognizing their distinctive features, we present an interactive comparison of Romantic and twentieth-century style in CourseMate and the eBook.

World Music

© Mats/ShutterStock.com

LEARNING OUTCOMES

After reading this chapter, you will be able to do the following:

26-1 Outline the gradual emergence of the world music movement.

26-2 Recognize authentic Celtic regional folk music replicated in as pure a state as possible.

26-3 Understand the nature of popular African-international fusion.

26-4 Appreciate Tan Dun's East–West art fusion.

study tools

After you read this chapter, go to the Study Tools at the end of the chapter, page 367.

WOMAD (World of Music, Arts, and Dance), the organization that brings performers from around the world to international audiences, was formed in 1980 and presented its first festival in the United Kingdom in 1982. Since that time, WOMAD has grown into a multifaceted organization. Its festivals are huge events that take place around the world: In the *2001 Guinness World Records*, it was cited as the biggest International Music Festival. It has provided a platform for numerous world music performers. Since its inception, its mission has been to use the arts to open minds and hearts to the world around us. As it states on its website (http://womad.org), "at festivals, performance events, through recorded releases and through educational projects, we aim to excite, to inform, and to create awareness of the worth and potential of a multicultural society."

WOMAD's main festival takes place in Charlton Park, a grand estate west of London in the United Kingdom. In 2013, it featured four days of entertainment. There were seventy-six acts from dozens of countries located on every continent except Antarctica: from Algeria, Armenia, and Argentina to Zimbabwe. The goal of this chapter is not to emulate WOMAD in breadth of coverage of native musics: that's a task best attempted in a course devoted to world music or ethnomusicology. Rather, the goal is to provide some context on the emergence of interest in world music and to hint at its geographical and musical range, through three examples.

26-1 The Study of World Music

In its most widely used connotation, world music refers to music from anywhere in the world that is not part of the established art and commercial music traditions of Europe and North America. Most obviously, world music embraces folk traditions from every inhabited corner of the globe. However, it also includes regional fusions (hybrid styles that draw on both the traditional music of a region and internationally known popular music styles), such as zydeco and tribal rock in the United States; Afropop styles such as *juju* from Nigeria and *mbalax* from Senegal; and art traditions from other cultures, such as the classical music of India and Chinese opera.

What we now know as the world music movement began as an effort by Europeans and North Americans to collect, preserve, and share music different from the music that they encountered in daily life, and to incorporate elements of these "outsider" sounds into their own music. Its roots go back to colonial times.

26-1A Exploring the Exotic

Our first accounts of music making in the Americas and Africa come from missionaries. Several kept detailed journals about their experiences. Girolamo Merolla, writing in 1682, noted that the Africans they observed used drums in religious ceremonies, such as the one that sent the dead to the next world, and for long-distance communication, especially in wartime. Merolla's work took him only to the Congo and southwest Africa— what is now Angola. However, percussion instruments were apparently used extensively all along the west coast of sub-Saharan Africa at that time. Drawings by Giovanni Cavazzi, another missionary, as well as written accounts by other Europeans, show Africans from Senegal to the Congo playing drums, rattles, marimba-like instruments, and other percussion.

Most commentators found it strange, or at least different from the music that they knew. Still, intermingling of musical traditions apparently took place almost immediately. The first slaves arrived in Cuba in 1513; the first mention of the sarabande, a Spanish dance with Latin American roots, occurred in 1539. Colonists then brought the dance back to Spain, where it was promptly banned because the authorities found it obscene. The sarabande would eventually morph into the most dignified of the Baroque dances (see section 6-4).

The use or evocation of exotic sounds increased dramatically during the latter half of the nineteenth century. We've already noted Bizet's use of the habanera in *Carmen* (section 15-3). A series of world's fairs beginning with the Crystal Palace Exhibition, which took place in London in 1851, brought musicians from other parts of the world to Europe. This enabled Europeans to encounter exotic music directly from the source. Debussy was among the many who heard gamelan music (the traditional music of Indonesia) performed at the 1889 Paris Universal Exposition; he would draw on this experience in several of his compositions.

26-1B Canvassing the Countryside: Folk Music Collection

A complement to exploring the exotic was a collection of folk materials from the countryside. We experienced this in Dvořák's folk dance–based compositions (section 17-3), but the first significant efforts predate his work by two centuries. England was a center for this activity at least from the middle of the seventeenth century.

In 1651, John Playford published the first edition of *The English Dancing Master*, a collection of country dances and a step-by-step manual for performing them. It launched a career that would soon make him the dominant music publisher in England. His company would publish six more editions before his death, and eleven more after that, the last appearing in 1728. The novel features of Playford's anthology were not the dances themselves. Playford's anthology simply presented dances that were well known at the time and likely dated back decades, if not centuries. What was significant was the publication of them in musical notation and the identification of them as "exotic" curiosities called *country dances*.

An enthusiasm for regional folk songs from the British Isles developed just before the turn of the nineteenth century. Both Haydn and Beethoven were commissioned to compose song settings; settings of Irish folk songs by Thomas Moore and Scottish folk songs by Robert Burns were among the most popular English-language songs of the nineteenth century. We still sing one of them every New Year's Eve—"Auld Lang Syne."

world music Music from anywhere in the world that is not part of the established art and commercial music traditions of Europe and North America

fusion Hybrid style that draws on both the traditional music of a region and internationally known popular music styles

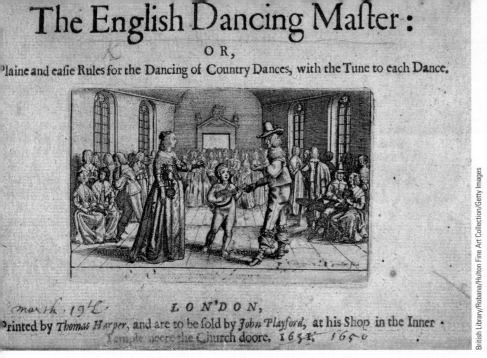

The English Dancing Master:

OR,

Plaine and easie Rules for the Dancing of Country Dances, with the Tune to each Dance.

march 19 C.   LONDON,
Printed by *Thomas Harper*, and are to be sold by *John Playford*, at his Shop in the Inner Temple neere the Church doore. 1651. 1650

British Library/Robana/Hulton Fine Art Collection/Getty Images

The publication of Playford's country dances and the numerous folk song settings around 1800 were commercial enterprises. *Slave Songs of the United States*, a collection of African American spirituals prepared by four abolitionists and published in 1867, represented a different emphasis in folk song collection. It was the first published attempt to transcribe any African American music; its primary purpose was to preserve and disseminate what was at the time a largely unfamiliar musical tradition. (Jubilee choirs, which were African American vocal groups, would bring this music directly to white audiences in the years after the Civil War.)

26-1C The Foundations of the World Music Movement

A true world music movement would require three important developments, in technology, musical style, and culture. They were parallel but largely independent, and they all took shape during the first part of the twentieth century and gained momentum after World War II.

The *technological* breakthrough that enabled a true world music movement was sound recording. Bartók's recordings of folk music throughout eastern Europe, as primitive as they are, are different in kind from the notated version of a folk song or dance because they preserve the actual sound of the music. For all its capabilities, musical notation is inadequate for representing defining features of a wide range of music.

As the portability and quality of the sound recording equipment improved, field recordings became more common. The English folklorist Cecil Sharp traveled through southern Appalachia during the 1910s, notating folk music performed by the inhabitants of the region. Two decades later, the American folklorists John and Alan Lomax revisited the territory and recorded them performing their

music. A comparison of printed and recorded versions reveals how much of the essence of the style cannot be notated.

The crucial *musical* breakthrough for development of world music was the emergence of alternatives to common practice tonality. As we have noted, common practice tonality is the only widely used musical syntax. It is also the product of urban European culture; in their original settings, folk songs and dances from the countryside of the British Isles do not have harmony-based accompaniments. Indeed, most indigenous musical traditions from other parts of the world—such as the Americas, Africa, and Asia—do not include a harmonic practice of any kind.

Reducing common practice tonality from the only "correct" way to harmonize to one option among many was liberating at all levels of discourse. The reason? Tonality acted as a filter between an authentic folk tradition and an audience of outsiders. Providing a folk song or dance with a conventional chordal accompaniment (performed by a symphony orchestra or pianist) effectively gentrified it, making it more familiar-sounding to European and North American audiences but making it less authentic in the process.

So when we listen to Dvořák's Slavonic dance, we can hear the folk influence in the characteristic rhythm. But we are not hearing an authentic folk music, and we can only wonder what the music that influenced Dvořák actually sounded like. By contrast, Bartók's music seems more connected to its folk roots not only because of the composer's extensive fieldwork but also because he developed a personal harmonic language saturated with folk elements, rather than employing conventional harmony.

Tonal harmony would become one option among many in folk-classical and folk-popular fusions, and the chords that make up its raw material would often be recontextualized, as was the case in rural blues styles before World War II.

The third crucial development was a shift in attitude toward the "other." Even with the gradual abolition of slavery throughout most of the European colonies and the United States during the course of the nineteenth century, there was still the presumption of the inferiority of non-whites among Europeans and North Americans at the dawn of the twentieth century. This presumption manifested itself in countless ways: for example, in the "separate-but-equal" Supreme Court decision; in pseudo-scientific research proving the inferiority of Africans; and in the persistence of colonial empires. "The White Man's Burden," the title of a poem by Rudyard Kipling published in 1899, seems to summarize the prevailing attitude: at best, a duty to help the less fortunate; at worst, blatant racism.

However, during the first part of the twentieth century, that attitude began to shift, albeit reluctantly. Music played a key role in this shift: less than two decades after jazz was accused of corrupting a generation, Carnegie Hall hosted two "Spirituals to Swing" concerts in 1938 and 1939. Each offered a brief survey of African American music. Among the highlights were jam sessions featuring black and white musicians performing jazz before an integrated audience—almost a decade before Jackie Robinson integrated baseball. Although it would never be considered a world music, jazz was the first musical genre created by a minority culture to be considered artistically significant by some whose opinion mattered in the musical world, not only in the United States but even more in Europe. This interest was an important intermediate step in changing the perception regarding the relative worth of musical traditions.

26-1D Ethnomusicology

The study of what was sometimes called "primitive music" had taken shape in Germany and England during the late nineteenth century. German musicologists referred to the discipline as "comparative musicology"; the stated goal was to collect and compare folk songs from around the world. Much of comparative musicologists' early work was informed by evolutionary theory, then much in vogue in scientific circles. Many assumed that the art music of the time was unquestionably the most evolutionarily advanced music, and none seemed ready to challenge that assumption.

During the first part of the twentieth century, researchers recorded folk musicians in many locales, including among Native Americans, African Americans, and rural white Americans in North America, and throughout Eastern Europe. To compare the results, they developed classification systems for pitch and instruments. In the United States, musicologist Charles Seeger, husband of composer/folklorist Ruth Crawford Seeger and father of folksinger Pete Seeger, formed the American Society for Comparative Musicology in 1935 to support not only American researchers but also those who were fleeing Europe to

escape the Nazis. In 1955, the Society for Ethnomusicology was formed at a meeting of the American Anthropological Association. The change of name from "comparative musicology" to ethnomusicology went hand in hand with a broadening of focus, to study not only the music itself but also the cultural context that shaped it. The emphasis on hearing the music as an expression of the culture that produced it was a decided shift in perspective, and it opened the door for appreciating a musical tradition on its own terms rather than comparing it to the established cultural hierarchy.

26-1E Popular Music and the World

In popular music, the roots of the world music movement that took shape in the early 1980s go back to the late 1940s, to the music of the Weavers. Among their biggest hits were songs from Israel ("Tzena, Tzena, Tzena") and South Africa ("Wimoweh"). In the latter part of the 1950s, Harry Belafonte would enjoy comparable success with his versions of calypso songs like "Banana Boat (Day O)." Although their music doesn't sound much like authentic versions of the songs, their advocacy of folk music from then-exotic locales and their effort to capture something of its spirit played a large role in creating the open-minded attitude that has characterized rock-era music. Belafonte also played a key role in introducing South African singer Miriam Makeba to United States audiences. She would enjoy a long run in the 1960s, but her success did not lead to widespread interest in South African music.

During the 1960s, Dylan and the Beatles played key roles in encouraging a more inclusive musical approach. Dylan came back to rock via folk music, and his music combined verbal sophistication with clear folk and blues roots. The Beatles were not afraid to try anything or use music from any source. By their example, they nurtured the open-mindedness of rock and folk artists: George Harrison's flirtation with the sitar and his use of it in songs like "Norwegian Wood" helped build a Western audience for Indian musicians like Ravi Shankar.

The 1970s were the prelude to the world music explosion of the 1980s. The most significant development was the emergence of reggae. Reggae was an international-regional fusion with distinctive, easily recognizable sounds and rhythms. Its popularity and influence outside of Jamaica inspired artists and industry members in other Afrocentric styles, such as juju and calypso, to promote their music to a wider audience. Moreover, reggae's role as the conscience of popular music in the 1970s

George Harrison's use of the sitar in songs like "Norwegian Wood" helped build an audience for Indian music.

ethnomusicology The study of music within particular cultures

demonstrated once again that music could go beyond mere entertainment to be a force for social change. Artists in other Afrocentric styles also embraced this concept.

All of this laid the groundwork for the world music movement that flowered during the 1980s. The key ingredients were in place: the use of music as an expression of national or cultural identity, the growing international recognition of regional popular styles, deep interest from a few mainstream popular musicians, and the drive to reclaim folk heritages around the world.

26-1F Regional Styles

Reggae's popularity during the 1970s helped spark interest in other Afrocentric music. Among the regional styles to gain a toehold in the international market were calypso and *soca* (soul calypso, a regional/international hybrid that had emerged during the 1970s) from Trinidad, *zouk* and cadence from the French Caribbean, samba from Brazil, and Afropop styles like *juju* from Nigeria (King Sunny Ade was the best-known Nigerian musician).

None of these styles has succeeded on the same scale as reggae—many, especially the West African styles, must overcome a language barrier—but all have an international presence. Most were already in existence well before the 1980s (calypso, for one, dates back to the 1910s). Their emergence in the 1980s reflects both changes in the music—a more updated sound, through the addition of electronic instruments and the incorporation of elements from the international style—and the growing interest of musicians and audience from other parts of the world in new sounds.

26-1G Rock: A Musical Dialogue

The complement to regional musicians' blending elements of the international style with their local music was mainstream musicians bringing these regional styles into their music. Three musicians stand out: Paul Simon, David Byrne of Talking Heads, and Peter Gabriel. All played an active role in promoting world music by using ethnic musicians on their recording dates (such as Youssou N'Dour with Peter Gabriel), and by seeking out and promoting regional music.

Like the nationalistic art music and the folk-inspired commercial song and dance of the nineteenth century, the rock-regional fusions of the late twentieth century mixed a local musical tradition with the dominant style. But these late twentieth-century fusions were different in kind from those in the previous century, for several reasons. First and foremost is the fact that the rock- and blues-based international style was already a syncretic music: it has African and European roots, which in their purest form are so profoundly dissimilar as to be incompatible. Second, rock and R&B were egalitarian: the work of major acts from the 1960s dissolved class boundaries, as we heard most explicitly in the Beatles track we discussed in Chapter 24. Third, the formation of regional fusions was a two-way process:

even as international stars sought out regional musicians, local musicians were listening to music from the United States and United Kingdom: reggae's roots are partly in late 1950s and early 1960s R&B, and African musicians were big fans of James Brown's music. With the British Invasion of the 1960s, rock became an international music. By the 1980s, the core rock/R&B style had become a global phenomenon: the first living musical language to reach around the world. It was different from playing Mozart in China, or even Bach in Brazil; the music of those composers is part of an established and non-evolving tradition. Instead, musicians in almost every part of the world were taking a contemporary musical language and effectively creating their own dialect by blending it with their own traditional music.

26-1H National Identity

In many cases, the revival and promotion of traditional music had a political dimension. This was particularly the case in Africa and the Caribbean. Almost all of the countries had formerly been colonies of England or France, and most had gained their independence only in the 1960s and 1970s. As the countries shook off colonial rule, traditional music became an expression of cultural identity and national pride, especially in Africa. For example, Kwame Nkrumah, Ghana's first president, made the restoration of traditional music a matter of governmental policy.

After independence, both England and France had liberal policies regarding immigration from former colonies. Indeed, the Caribbean islands Guadeloupe and Martinique are *départements* of France. As a result, London and Paris became the centers of the "world beat" movement in part because of the large expatriate colonies in both cities. These European capitals were homes away from home for both musicians and audience.

26-1I The Range of World Music Today

The 1980s also saw intense interest in folk traditions around the world: WOMAD was both benefactor and beneficiary of this interest. Chief among these traditions was Celtic music, but other regional folk and folk/international styles found enthusiastic international audiences—among them, music from Bulgaria (*Le Mystère des Voix Bulgares* and clarinetist Ivo Papasov), flamenco (the Gipsy Kings), contemporary Native American music, indigenous Australian music, and the chanting of Tibetan monks. Technology played a crucial role in creating access to this music, as affordable and portable recording equipment made it possible to record music almost anywhere in the world.

The world music movement includes a broad spectrum of musical styles and traditions. At one end of the spectrum is the preservation or replication of folk and regional traditions in as pure a state as possible. Covering a broad middle band are international-regional syntheses that feature collaborations among musicians from different cultures. Folk-connected concert music, so prominent in the first part of the century, largely disappeared in the decades after World War II, as was previously noted. That trend was reversed in the last third of the century, particularly among minimalists and eclectics.

In the remainder of this chapter, we sample three very different kinds of music. They come from three widely separated regions: North America, West Africa, and China/New York. And they exemplify three broad musical families: folk, commercial fusion, and art fusion.

26-2 A Folk Dance from Newfoundland

Newfoundland is the fifteenth largest island in the world. It is northeast of Maine and east of the Canadian mainland. On the outskirts of St. John's, the capital city, is Cape Spear, the easternmost point in North America. Newfoundland has the longest documented connection with Europe of any region in the Americas. Viking explorers landed on the island five centuries before Columbus. John Cabot founded St. John's in 1497; the city is the site of the oldest European settlement in North America. Fishermen, first from Portugal and England and then from Ireland, fished the waters off the Newfoundland coast. Eventually, emigrants from the southeast part of Ireland and the southwest part of England established permanent settlements on the island. From the mid-seventeenth century through much of the eighteenth century, England and France fought over Newfoundland and its fishing grounds. Eventually the English prevailed, but not before the French devastated English settlements. Today, most Newfoundlanders are of Irish and English heritage; however, there is a small pocket of French-speaking citizens in the southwest corner of the island.

England discouraged colonization because it was to its advantage to retain the fishing rights, rather than to cede them to a colony. In part because of its fishing grounds, Newfoundland remained under British control after Canada gained its independence; it joined the Canadian confederation only in 1945.

Climate and geography have also kept Newfoundland isolated from the rest of Canada. For much of the year, the waters around the island are frozen; ice creates a barrier between Newfoundland and the rest of Canada almost as formidable as the Appalachians did between its residents and the eastern seaboard. As a result, the settlers retained much of their culture—this was especially so outside of St. John's. The similarity between the accents of

Climate and geography have kept Newfoundland isolated . . .

LISTEN UP!

TOTAL TIME: 1:42

Traditional, "Boston Laddie"

TAKEAWAY POINT: Vigorous, fast-moving rhythm at a brisk tempo

STYLE: Anglo-Celtic folk dance

FORM: Two strains in alternation

GENRE: Jig

INSTRUMENTS: Fiddle and foot (for timekeeping)

CONTEXT: Good-time music: tunes for vigorous folk dancing

0:00   Spoken introduction

A

0:05   First strain and repetition. Brisk tempo encourages lively dancing.

B

0:17   Second strain and repetition. Each beat contains either three fast notes or two notes in long-short rhythm.

A

0:26   First strain and repetition. This strain contains two short phrases that begin the same and end differently.

B

0:38   Second strain, twice. This strain begins differently but ends like first strain.

A

0:47   The first phrase yet again. Notice long–short rhythm that Guinchard keeps with his feet.

B

0:58   Second phrase

A

1:07   First phrase

B

1:19   Second phrase

A

1:42   First strain and its repetition, for the last time

🔊)) Listen to this selection streaming or in an Active Listening Guide at CourseMate or in the eBook.

Irish living in southeastern counties like Kilkenny and the accent of Newfoundlanders is evidence of this. So is the apparent similarity between their folk dances and those preserved in Playford's collections.

26-2A The Jig

About two-thirds of the dances in Playford's anthology are in duple compound meter (two beats to the measure, with each beat typically divided into three equal parts). In our time, we associate this meter most often

jig Sprightly dance popular throughout the British Isles

with the jig, a sprightly dance popular throughout the British Isles. The jig dates back to the fifteenth century; Ireland is, to the best of our knowledge, its home. The jig became a staple in English stage entertainment during the sixteenth century— it was a dance commonly used in a jigg, an often bawdy burlesque, with acting, singing, and dancing, and elsewhere. A century later, it became a more aristocratic and somewhat more sedate dance in France, Italy, and Germany. In France, it was the *gigue*; in Italy it was the *giga*. On the continent, it became part of a suite made up of several dances, as Bach's gigue in section 6-4 exemplified.

Few of the dances in compound duple meter are actually called jigs; some instead have fanciful names, like "An Old Man Is a Bed Full of Bones." However, the meter and the rhythm of the melody often match the rhythm we associate with the jig in other contexts. These musical features and the occasional title tell us that the jig was very much a part of musical life in seventeenth-century England, both in the country and in the city.

Most of the dances consist of a single strain, usually between eight and sixteen measures in length; some have two slightly contrasting strains. Playford's anthology shows only the melody, to be played by a treble instrument, preferably the violin (as Playford noted on the title page of the second edition). We can infer that accompaniment was optional, and typically improvised. The dances are short; they last less than a minute. Fiddlers extended these dance tunes into longer numbers by repeating the strain or combining two or more similar melodies.

The similarity between Playford's dances and contemporary recordings of jigs suggest that the culture in such isolated areas often seems almost unchanged for generations. We get some sense of this when we hear a performance of "Boston Laddie," an original jig by Rufus Guinchard similar to those found in Playford's anthology.

26-2B "Boston Laddie": A Jig from Newfoundland

Especially during the latter part his life, Rufus Guinchard was one of the most popular fiddlers in Newfoundland. He was born in 1899; at the time of this recording (see Listen Up!) he was eighty-three. "Boston Laddie" is Guinchard's tune, but it is also very much in the style of a traditional jig. Newfoundland is heavily Irish, so he would have heard dance tunes in this style growing up. Guinchard's style of playing seems deeply rooted in the past; it's similar to the fiddle playing one hears on the earliest recordings of American old-time music, which date from the 1920s.

"Boston Laddie" consists of two short strains. Each strain is constructed from short phrases of fast-moving notes; the melody typically contains rhythmic patterns of three equal notes to a beat, or two notes per beat in a long/short pattern. The complete jig consists of the two strains (A and B) played in alternation four times; the first strain comes back at the end for a fifth time.

In Canada, and especially in Newfoundland, recording of old-time fiddlers like Guinchard was an important dimension of the late twentieth-century revival of Celtic music—the Celtic music scene in Newfoundland was one branch of a movement on both sides of the Atlantic to reclaim this centuries-old music and bring it into the present.

LEARNING OUTCOME 26-3
Understand the nature of popular African-international fusion.

26-3 Afropop: An African-International Fusion

All along the upper west coast of sub-Saharan Africa, from Senegal to Zaire, native popular musics have flourished. Each country has its own popular style; indeed, many "national" styles actually emerge from a people within a country, such as the Wolof in Senegal. Nigeria is home to Afrobeat; Ghana has highlife. *Makossa* is a popular local dance music in Cameroon; so is *soukous* in Zaire. *Gbegbe* grew up alongside other African popular styles in the Ivory Coast; *mbalax* is native to Senegal.

Some styles are updated versions of older popular styles. Highlife, for example, dates back to mid-century but was modernized with the addition of electric guitars and other changes. Other styles are transformations of traditional music: in the 1970s, Nigerian musicians created *gbegbe* to give their traditional music a modern sound.

National styles have moved freely from country to country. *Juju* has flourished in Ghana and Sierra Leone as well as Nigeria. Not surprisingly, perhaps, the colonial language has had some effect on the dissemination of a style. Highlife is more popular in English-speaking countries; *soukous,* more popular in French-speaking nations.

But cross-fertilization transcends tribal, national, and linguistic barriers. In Africa and within expatriate communities in Europe and the United States, musicians listen to and learn from each other. As a result, there are common elements in much West African commercial music. Some of them distinguish it not only from U.S. and U.K. rock-era music but also from Afrocentric Caribbean styles.

We hear the fruits of an African-international fusion in a track featuring two of Africa's most distinguished musical ambassadors.

26-3A Youssou N'Dour and Angelique Kidjo

In 1991, Senegalese singer Youssou N'Dour (b. 1959) was appointed a Goodwill Ambassador for UNICEF. Eleven years later, Angélique Kidjo (b. 1960), a native of Benin, also became a UNICEF Goodwill Ambassador. Senegal and Benin are former French colonies in sub-Saharan Africa. Senegal is along the west coast: Dakar, the capital city and N'Dour's hometown, is the westernmost city on the African continent. Benin is a small country directly west of Nigeria and southeast of Senegal.

Kidjo and N'Dour are, respectively, the best-known African female and male singers. They have earned widespread critical acclaim: both have won Grammys, and the *New York Times* labeled N'Dour "one of the world's greatest singers." Both have been extraordinarily active on behalf of causes that they believe to be important. Kidjo founded the Batonga foundation to provide young African girls with upper-level education to prepare them for leadership positions, and N'Dour helped organize the 2006 Africa Live: The Roll Back Malaria Concert, which was given in Dakar.

Youssou N'Dour and Angelique Kidjo

CRIS BOURONCLE/AFP/Getty Images

Kidjo moved to Paris in 1983, where she obtained work as a backup vocalist. By 1989, she had a recording contract and a career in Europe. Within a few years, she had become the best-known African female vocalist since Miriam Makeba. N'Dour's international career also took off in the 1980s after Peter Gabriel recruited him for his first WOMAD concert.

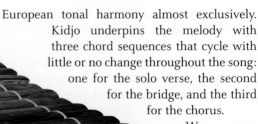

© ermess/ShutterStock.com

In 2005, N'Dour's *Egypt* won a Grammy for Best Contemporary World Music Album; three years later, Kidjo received the same honor for *Djin Djin*. For Kidjo, *Djin Djin* was a conscious effort to return to her roots, to recapture and integrate into her music the rhythms and sounds of her home country. She had grown up listening to native musicians as well as rock, funk, and pop from abroad; the album is an expression of that rich heritage. The album features an impressive list of guest artists, including Peter Gabriel, Alicia Keys, saxophonist Branford Marsalis, Josh Groban, and Carlos Santana.

26-3B "Ae Ae"

"Ae Ae" (see Listen Up!) features three of the most common features of African-international fusions. One feature is the extensive and prominent use of traditional African instruments. In addition to a large array of unpitched percussion instruments, "Ae Ae" uses a balafon, a xylophone-like instrument, and a kora, a harp-lute made from a calabash. Both play moving lines behind the vocal throughout the song.

Another characteristic of fusion is a complete Western rhythm section. The rhythm section on "Ae Ae" includes drum set, electric bass, guitars, and organ, in addition to the African percussion instruments. The musicians lay down a vibrant groove with busy background rhythms, an active bass line, and a dense, percussive texture. The particular timbre of the electric guitar on this recording is distinctive to much West African music, and the African instruments, both pitched and unpitched, color the sound to give it a specifically African flavor. Still, it is a version of the international groove so popular around the turn of the new century.

© Clive Chilvers/ShutterStock.com

Balafon and kora

balafon Xylophone-like African instrument
kora African harp-lute made from a calabash

The third is the approach to harmony. The song uses the three core chords of European tonal harmony almost exclusively. Kidjo underpins the melody with three chord sequences that cycle with little or no change throughout the song: one for the solo verse, the second for the bridge, and the third for the chorus.

We sense an African adaptation of this unquestionably European harmony in what *doesn't* happen: using chord progressions to create a hierarchical structure with such features as different kinds of cadences and changes of key, which are found not only in classical music but also in commercial songs and dance music intended for a broad market. This approach to harmony may have been derived from the hymns and other religious music brought to Africa by missionaries—but it has more in common with early blues, country, and folk music. It recalls Woody Guthrie's maxim about three chords: "Anything more than three chords is just showing off." This oscillating approach to harmony—familiar chords, but no larger architecture—is common in much African popular music.

Weaving through the buoyant rhythms are the voices of Kidjo and N'Dour. Kidjo's lyric is part commentary on the plight of Africans who emigrate to Europe to escape the poverty, poor health, and political turmoil back home, and part exhortation to Africans to become self-sufficient. In this respect, the song continues the practice among members of the African diaspora of sending a powerful message over a compelling groove. As Kidjo said in the video about *Djin Djin*, she wants to "entertain each other but learn at the same time."

In "Ae Ae," as in much of the music by African artists who have enjoyed international success, there is something of the atmosphere of a family reunion. It isn't so much a coming together of people as of styles and cultures—music from the mother continent meeting up with its offspring in the Americas. What Africa had sent to the Americas via the slave trade came back to Africa transmuted but still compatible, so that old and new could be easily blended. A second wave of African music, mixed from traditional sounds and their

 **LISTEN UP!**

Angelique Kidjo with Youssou N'Dour, "Ae Ae"

TAKEAWAY POINT: Exuberant exhortation

STYLE: Afropop

FORM: Verse/bridge/chorus

GENRE: Afropop

INSTRUMENTS: Two solo voices, backup singers, full rhythm section, African pitched and percussion instruments

CONTEXT: Music to move the body and send a message

0:00   Instrumental introduction; hear the balafon just before Kidjo enters.

1ST STATEMENT OF VERSE/BRIDGE/CHORUS FORM

0:11   *Verse:* Verse twice, first with Kidjo, then N'Dour, with responses from the backup vocalists

0:29   *Bridge:* Notice how the sustained line sung by the backup singers helps build to the title phrase by making the texture richer.

0:39   *Chorus:* Backup singers sing the chorus; busy instruments in the background; both Kidjo and N'Dour sing comments. The interaction helps create a festive mood.

0:56   Intro becomes an interlude.

2ND STATEMENT OF FORM

1:06   *Verse:* N'Dour sings second verse; no verse by Kidjo

1:15   *Bridge:* As before

1:24   *Chorus:* As before, but now mostly chorus to the end, with jamming by Kidjo and N'Dour

1:42   Interlude, shift to a higher key after one false start

2:00   Chorus returns.

2:18   Duet between balafon player and N'Dour, who seems to improvise his vocal line

2:35   The joyous chorus again and again, with commentary from the stars. An extraordinarily rich and exuberant texture, featuring lots of percussion, an active bass line, a balafon line, the backup singers repeating the title phrase, and Kidjo and N'Dour adding commentary.

 Listen to this selection streaming or in an Active Listening Guide at CourseMate or in the eBook.

---

evolutionary mutations among the diaspora, has found a welcome audience in America and around the world.

For most of the world, world music means some kind of commercial-traditional synthesis. In an age where communication is global and instantaneous, musical encounters are bidirectional. Among those enjoying a special perspective on the integration of different musical traditions are those who have grown up in one culture and trained in another. Among those composers who have drawn on such an experience is the Chinese composer Tan Dun.

LEARNING OUTCOME 26-4

Appreciate Tan Dun's East–West art fusion.

26-4 Tan Dun and East– West Fusions

The film *Crouching Tiger, Hidden Dragon* (2000) grew out of a collaboration among director Ang Lee, composer Tan Dun, and cellist Yo-Yo Ma. The three had been friends for about a decade when they began working on the film in 1996. All three exemplify the synthesis of East and West. Ma, the son of Chinese musicians, was born in Paris and

▶Tan Dun
FAST FACTS
- Dates: b. 1957
- Place: China/United States
- Reasons to remember: Distinguished and popular Chinese composer whose music often fuses East and West

LEE CELANO/AFP/Getty Images

came to the United States when he was five. After establishing himself in the top rank of classical cellists, he began to branch out in numerous directions; among the most far reaching has been his Silk Road project, a musical collective that nurtures interactions among the cultures along the venerable Silk Road from Eastern Europe to China.

Originally from Taiwan, Ang Lee received his film training in the United States: at New York University, he was a classmate of fellow director Spike Lee. He has established himself as one of the leading contemporary directors, winning an Academy Award in 2005 for his direction of *Brokeback Mountain*. *Crouching Tiger, Hidden Dragon* was his "roots" project, an opportunity to connect with the classical Chinese culture he had studied so deeply as a child.

26-4A Tan Dun

Tan Dun ◆ grew up in southern China, and as a young man he spent several years planting rice on a commune. After joining a Beijing Opera troupe and relocating to Beijing, he enrolled at the Central Conservatory of Music. After occasional conflict with the government, Tan came to the United States to pursue doctoral studies in composition at Columbia University. Since completing his studies, he has accumulated a steady stream of honors and commissions, and his major works—operas, orchestral compositions, and chamber works—have been recorded and performed widely. Among them are a commission for a symphony celebrating the return of Hong Kong to China in 1997 and a setting of the *St. Matthew Passion* to honor the 250th anniversary of Bach's death.

Tan's formative musical experiences range from observing shamanic rituals and learning traditional Chinese instruments in the village where he worked, to encounters with leading classical composers such as Hans Werner Henze and Toru Takemitsu and study with Mario Davidovsky, a leading composer of electronic music. He drew deeply

erhu Chinese stringed instrument | on these experiences

for his score for *Crouching Tiger, Hidden Dragon*, for which he won an Academy Award.

26-4B *Wuxia*

The Chinese counterpart of the westerns of American fantasy fiction and European tales of chivalric knights is a genre known as *wuxia* (pronounced "woo-shya"). The main characters in all of these genres are lone warriors who adhere to a code of honor and fight for right. In *wuxia* novels, martial arts weapons are the counterpart to the six-shooter of the gunslinger and the lance and sword of medieval knights.

Although the themes of *wuxia* novels date back hundreds of years, the genre flourished only in the early twentieth century. The Chinese Communist Party suppressed *wuxia*, beginning shortly after they took control of the government after World War II until the 1980s, but the genre remained popular in Hong Kong and Taiwan. Wuxia novels typically blend martial arts and romance. Among the best-known examples is the five-novel *Iron-Crane* series by Wang Du Lu. *Crouching Tiger, Hidden Dragon*, the fourth novel in the series, served as the basis for the screenplay for Lee's film.

Lee turned to Wang's novel in an effort to produce a martial arts film with what Tan called a "human touch." The story intermingles stunning fight scenes, including one high in the trees of a bamboo forest, with two bittersweet romances.

26-4C *Crouching Tiger, Hidden Dragon*: Film and Film Score

Tan, Lee, and Ma began working on the film four years before its release. The relationship between Lee and Tan was similar to that between Eisenstein and Prokofiev, in that the music influenced the shooting of the film. As Tan noted, "The musical idea, if you can set it up at the beginning of the film process, benefits the director when he's shooting the film. It helps set up the contrast between the characters, and bridge elements together."

Tan is the quintessential East–West eclectic. For his score for the film, he employed four kinds of sounds: Chinese percussion instruments; traditional Chinese pitched instruments, including the **erhu** (a stringed instrument) and flutes; the symphony orchestra; and the cello playing of Yo-Yo Ma. Tan blends these elements seamlessly: indeed, both Ma and the orchestral strings emulate Chinese performance styles. He took a similar approach to pitch organization by building the most memorable melodic material around the pentatonic scale, which is frequently used in Chinese music, and supporting it with modal harmony. Thus, the music is often not only tonal but also diatonic—a far cry from the unrelenting dissonance of much twentieth-century concert music.

Tan Dun, "Farewell," from *Crouching Tiger, Hidden Dragon* (sound track version; 2000)

TAKEAWAY POINT: Expressive fusion of Chinese and Western musical traditions

STYLE: East–West fusion

FORM: Varied repetition of a short phrase

GENRE: Film music

INSTRUMENTS: Cello, erhu, Chinese percussion, orchestra

CONTEXT: The final statement of the love music in the film

0:00   Main melody, played by Yo-Yo Ma. Accompaniment includes orchestral strings and Chinese percussion. Erhu enters unobtrusively in a higher range.

0:17   Slight variant; erhu now a full-fledged partner

0:33   Restated. Each phrase of melody is a five-note descending scale with slightly different elaboration.

0:49   Like the second version of the phrase, but an octave higher

1:05   The first version of the phrase, an octave higher. The higher register lends greater intensity to the repetition.

1:21   Another restatement of the melody, as orchestral strings and drums become somewhat more prominent

1:37   The third version of the phrase, again an octave higher and with a somewhat richer accompaniment

1:53   Like the opening statement at first, but gradually dissolving

2:08   A slow trill ends the track enigmatically, while credits are rolling, as if it were receding into the background.

 Listen to this selection streaming or in an Active Listening Guide at CourseMate or in the eBook.

Because of his extensive experience in classical composition, Tan was, in his words, "exercising the power of the structure" in conceiving the score. Accordingly, the music is economical melodically and harmonically: most of the music is in one of two keys, and melodic motives, which are fully realized in the love music that ends the work, appear in various forms and fragments throughout the film. This gives Tan's score a consistency that emphasizes the broad themes in the film rather than moment-to-moment events. Ma's role is central: his solo line lends a personal touch, especially in the love music.

Tan's music for *Crouching Tiger, Hidden Dragon* is both an integral part of the film and apart from it. Since the release of the film, the music has gained a life of its own. The sound track includes versions of the music that are different from those in the film. The love theme was recast in a pop song version: "A Love before Time," released in both Mandarin and English versions. Tan also created a concert version of the score, which was published as the Crouching Tiger Concerto for cello and chamber orchestra.

26-4D "Farewell"

In the sound track version of "Farewell" (see Listen Up!), the music that underscores the hero's profession of love as he is dying, Tan brings together the four sound groups. Ma states the melody, accompanied by drums and orchestral strings. An erhu (not heard in the film version) plays an achingly beautiful obbligato above Ma's cello melody: it is the feminine counterpoint to Ma's masculine voice. The track ends (while the credits are rolling) as enigmatically as the film, with a slow trill that dissolves over a sustained note that is not the tonic.

The beauty of Tan's music is in large part the product of the seamless blending of the different sounds and the sophisticated use of simple musical materials. It is a superb example of the work of a composer with a truly global vision.

26-4E Philosophies of Film Composition

In his foreword to Karlin and Wright's *On the Track*, John Williams writes, "I wish this book had been

An erhu plays an achingly beautiful obbligato above Ma's cello melody—the feminine counterpoint to Ma's masculine voice.

© Hung Chung Chih/ShutterStock.com

Boston Globe/Getty Images

available when I started in the film industry in the 1950s." Karlin and Wright's book represents the most widely used approach to film scoring—applying music from a palette onto the canvas of film—which Williams's music consistently exemplifies.

Tan opposes this method. He says, "Typically, the director will shoot a script and then during the tight post-production period, they will come up with musical ideas and see what they can develop. I really don't like that. The music can't be just attached to the picture." Williams would probably disagree.

The three excerpts from film scores presented in this survey represent two sharply contrasting approaches to film scoring. Williams's is the more common by far, given the structure of the Hollywood-based film industry and the relatively slight importance given to film music by the industry as a whole, despite its substantial impact on the final product. Because of their long-standing friendship and shared vision, Lee, Tan, and Ma could conceive of their film organically so that Tan's music was a *component of* the film rather than a *response to* it. The same is true of the collaboration between Prokofiev and Eisenstein. The difference in approach is evident in the excerpts: there is considerable stylistic contrast in Williams's music and stylistic consistency in excerpts from Tan and Prokofiev. Each is characteristic of the score as a whole.

The contrasting approaches reflect the professional lives of Williams and Tan. Williams has made his compositional reputation as a film composer; his music in other genres has been less successful. As we listen to his music, we do not sense a personal style so much as his ability to personalize existing styles in the service of the story. By contrast, Tan is a composer who has composed film scores. Although he simplified his compositional approach to make his music more accessible and appropriate to the narrative, the music has the clear imprint of his personal style.

Looking Back, Looking Ahead

When heard in relation to the other music that we have encountered in this survey, our minuscule sampling of world music hints at some of the qualities that distinguish world music fusions from folk-inspired classical and popular music. First and foremost are the sounds: the singing styles, and the choice of instruments and the way they are played. Guinchard's fiddle playing is so different from the violin playing heard in classical music that it almost sounds as if this is a different instrument. In "Ae Ae," Kijdo and N'Dour have non-pop voices (whose differences are accentuated by the unfamiliar language); the balafon is the main instrumental responder to the voice; and percussive instruments enrich the texture. In "Farewell," cello and erhu share the spotlight, with drums and strings in the background. Moreover, Yo-Yo Ma periodically emulates the slow slides between notes characteristic of erhu performance.

Another difference is the harmony: "Boston Laddie" has none; "Ae Ae" uses basic chords in a way different from traditional practice; "Farewell" supports the solo parts with strings that collectively form complete chords on occasion, but without a sense of progression. The use of a modal scale, rather than the familiar major or minor scale, further distances the harmony from conventional practice.

A third distinguishing feature is the rhythm. The rhythmic approaches in the three examples are strikingly different. However, a key common feature is an undifferentiated beat: Guinchard's heel–toe rhythm is constant throughout; so are the percussion parts in the music of Kidjo and Tan Dun. This is fundamentally different from the hierarchical rhythmic organization that is characteristic of eighteenth- and nineteenth-century classical music.

What this brief summary highlights is the balance between traditions found in both the Kidjo and Tan examples. The African and Chinese elements—especially in sounds and rhythms—are prominent enough and the international elements different enough from conventional practice that we hear both tracks as fusions. In particular, the sounds are integral to the work, rather than a cosmetic overlay. World music fusions typically feature a successful balance between international and local traditions.

The three examples discussed here might be considered analogous to a trailer for a movie: a brief tease to explore the bigger picture. You might take up Peter Gabriel's invitation: "I challenge anyone to come to a WOMAD festival and not be really excited or inspired by at least one thing"; and/or you might consider enrolling in a world music course if your school offers one. Or you might simply follow the lead of musicians with open ears and open minds, who are listening more widely than ever before and then acting upon the experience. To cite just one relevant example: Yo-Yo Ma formed the Silk Road Ensemble to promote collaboration among artists and others for the music and culture along the Silk Road, the old trade routes between Europe and Asia.

Final Words

If you are a student using this text, chances are that most of the music that you've heard during this survey has been unfamiliar, either because it goes back almost a thousand years, before returning to the present, or because it comes from unfamiliar locales. Our goal has been not only to introduce you to music that has stood the test of time—these are "classics" for a reason!—but also to give you varied listening experiences that will sharpen your perception of all the music that you listen to. We hope that you will use this course as a springboard for exploring music from many eras and many more places.

 study tools 26

Ready to study?
In the book you can:

• Review Learning Outcome answers and Glossary terms with the tear-out Chapter Review card.

Or you can go online to CourseMate, at www.cengagebrain.com, for these resources:

• Chapter Quizzes to prepare for tests

• Interactive flashcards of all Glossary terms

• Active Listening Guides, streaming music, and YouTube playlists

• An eBook with live links to all web resources

THE IN-CROWD

Share your 4LTR Press story on Facebook at
www.facebook.com/4ltrpress for a chance to win.

To learn more about the
In-Crowd opportunity 'like'
us on Facebook.

Note: Key terms are bolded. Figures are indicated by an f.

ONE APPROACH.
70 UNIQUE SOLUTIONS.

CHAPTER IN REVIEW

1-1 Describe and recognize the basic properties of musical sound, relating them to the elements of music. The four basic properties of musical sound are loudness, or dynamics; duration, the length of time a musical sound lasts; pitch, highness or lowness based on the speed at which a sound wave vibrates; and timbre, the distinctive tonal properties of a sound. These properties relate to the elements of music that grow out of them: loudness to dynamics, timbre to instrumentation, duration to rhythm, pitch to melody and harmony, and all of these properties to texture and form.

1-2 Define *dynamics* in detail. Dynamics is simply the relative loudness or softness of musical sound, from the very quietest pianissimo to the very loudest fortissimo.

1-3 In the context of understanding timbre and instrumentation, compare the tone color of a piano with that of an orchestra. Instrumentation encompasses the instruments and voices used in the performance of a musical work. Today's symphony orchestra is built around four major sections, or families, of instruments: strings, woodwinds, brass, and percussion. Orchestration is the technique and artistry of assigning musical parts for instruments in various combinations. One purpose of orchestration is to add timbral variety, or tone color, to a work. If we compare the timbre of a work for a single instrument, such as the piano, with a black-and-white film, then arranging that work for an orchestra, with its dozens of timbres and countless timbral combinations, is like "colorizing" it.

1-4 Learn the musical meanings of *rhythm*, *beat*, *tempo*, and *meter*. Rhythm is the pattern or patterns of musical movement in time. Beat is the regularly recurring pulse associated with music. Tempo is the speed of the beat, from largo to presto. Meter is the framework for rhythmic organization, created by the grouping and division of beats.

GLOSSARY TERMS

music Organization of sound in time (p. 3)

1-1 **dynamics** Relative loudness or softness of musical sound (p. 3)

decibel (dB) Unit that measures the volume of sound (p. 3)

duration The length of time that a musical sound or silence lasts (p. 4)

pitch The relative highness or lowness of a sound (p. 4)

timbre The distinctive tonal properties of a sound (p. 4)

elements of music Dynamics, rhythm, timbre, melody, harmony, texture, and form (p. 4)

1-2 **fortissimo, *ff*** Very loud (p. 6)

forte, *f* Loud (p. 6)

mezzo forte, *mf* Medium loud (p. 6)

mezzo piano, *mp* Medium soft (p. 6)

piano, *p* Soft (p. 6)

pianissimo, *pp* Very soft (p. 6)

crescendo, ＜ Growing louder (p. 6)

decrescendo (diminuendo), ＞ Growing softer (p. 6)

sforzando, *sf* Strong accent on a single note or chord (p. 6)

1-3 **instrumentation** Selection and combination of instruments and voices used in the performance of a musical work (p. 5)

THINKING CRITICALLY ABOUT MUSIC

1. Replicate David Tudor's performance of John Cage's *4'33"* or create your own "silent" piece of a given duration.

2. Find one or more cover versions of a classic 1960s or early 1970s rock or soul song. Compare instrumentation and dynamics in the various versions. To this end, make a chart listing the instruments used. Also consider the vocal or instrumental style of the lead singer or of the main instruments. Then comment on the impact of dynamics, instrumentation, and performing style on your interpretation of the musical message in each case. What kinds of signals are you picking up from instrument choice, loudness, and so on?

3. Find a song in your music collection in which part of the song does not have a beat and part of the song does have a steady beat. As you listen to the transition from no beat to steady beat (or vice versa), ask yourself where in the music you find the musical cues that tell you where the beat is and how fast it moves.

4. Find in your collection three songs in quite different tempos. Using the lyrics as a guide, decide what the mood of the song is. Then ask yourself if you find any correlation between tempo and mood.

continued

GLOSSARY TERMS

symphony orchestra Large (often 100 musicians or more) musical ensemble containing strings, woodwinds, brass, and percussion (p. 5)

strings Musical instruments that produce sound when the musician draws a bow across or plucks the strings (p. 5)

double Having the same line of music played by more than one instrument simultaneously (p. 7)

pizzicato Technique of plucking a string instead of bowing it (p. 8)

woodwind Musical instrument that produces sound by blowing air through a reed or across an open hole, causing air to vibrate within a tube (p. 8)

brass Musical instrument that produces sound when the musician's lips vibrate against a mouthpiece that has been inserted into a coiled tube ending in a flared bell (p. 9)

mute Device that can change the timbre of an instrument when it is inserted in or applied to the instrument; instruments that most frequently use mutes are those of the brass and string families (p. 9)

percussion instrument Musical instrument that produces sound by striking one object against another (p. 10)

orchestration The craft and artistry of assigning musical parts for instruments in various combinations (p. 11)

tone color A distinctive timbre (p. 11)

1-4 **rhythm** Pattern or patterns of musical movement in time (p. 11)

beat Regularly recurring pulse associated with music (p. 12)

tempo Speed of the beat in a piece of music (p. 12)

meter Framework for rhythmic organization, created by the grouping and division of beats (p. 12)

duple meter Meter whose beats are grouped by two (p. 12)

triple meter Meter whose beats are grouped by three (p. 12)

quadruple meter Meter whose beats are grouped by four (p. 12)

measure (bar) Consistent grouping of beats in a work (p. 12)

accent *More* of some musical element (p. 12)

time (meter) signature Notational device indicating number of beats per measure and note value that is assigned to represent the beat (p. 14)

syncopation Accent that conflicts with the beat or meter instead of confirming it (p. 15)

CHAPTER IN REVIEW

2-1 Define *melody* and describe how melodies are constructed of pitches and intervals. A melody is an organized succession of pitches that presents a complete musical idea. Melodies are constructed of pitches at intervals ranging from a half-step (two adjacent pitches) to a leap (any interval larger than a step).

2-2 Understand the terms *scale*, *key*, and *tonality*. Melodies are constructed from scales, consistent arrangements of pitches in order from lowest to highest, within an octave. Major scales are considered "happy," whereas minor scales are considered "sad." Music that uses one note of a scale as a reference pitch is said to be "tonal."

2-3 Understand harmony as the complement of melody; describe a chord progression; and discuss the meaning and function of a cadence. Harmony is the study of chords, several notes sounding together. A chord progression is chords that proceed toward a harmonic goal. A cadence is a short series of chords that marks the end of a chord progression.

2-4 Define *texture* and the roles of part, line, and voice in texture; and distinguish between density and independence in texture. Texture is the fabric of sound created by the interaction of all parts of a piece of music. The terms *part, line,* or *voice* refer to a single layer of activity in the texture Density emerges from the interaction of performers, spacing between lines, and the register. Independence describes the degree to which a part stands out from those around it: monophonic, homophonic, or polyphonic.

2-5 Define *musical form*; describe how we recognize musical form through musical punctuation (cadences) and pattern; and differentiate some basic musical forms. Form is the overall organization of music in time. The musical punctuation of a cadence is a decisive change in the musical flow that marks a boundary between two sections of music, and pattern results from the recognizable return after change of previously presented musical material.

Repetition, contrast, and variation represent points on a continuum of possible musical change.

A vocal form in which different lyrics are sung to each repetition of the same melody is called strophic. Variation form typically begins with a theme, with the rest of the work being variations based on it. Binary form is a two-part form in which both the first and the second parts are typically repeated. Rounded binary form is a two-part form in which the opening material returns in the second part. Ternary form is a three-part form in which the outer sections are typically identical or similar.

2-6 Describe what we mean by musical style and important considerations in identifying it. Musical style is a consistent and comprehensive set of choices that define a body of music from a time, place, culture, or creative entity.

THINKING CRITICALLY ABOUT MUSIC

1. Find three songs of your own choosing, and describe their contours in terms of steps and leaps.
2. Listen to three songs of your own choosing and try to describe their form. Can you identify a recurring theme? Can you identify the punctuation? If so, how?

GLOSSARY TERMS

2-1 **melody** Organized succession of pitches that presents a complete musical idea (p. 17)

contour Pattern of rise and fall in a melody (p. 17)

interval Distance between two pitches (p. 17)

octave Relationship between two pitches that vibrate in a 2:1 ratio, with the higher pitch vibrating twice as fast as the lower; notes that are an octave apart share the same note name (p. 17)

step A small interval between two pitches (p. 17)

leap Any interval larger than a step (p. 17)

2-2 **half-step** The smallest interval possible between any two pitches (immediately adjacent keys) on a piano (p. 18)

scale Unique arrangement of whole and half-steps within an octave (p. 19)

tonic (keynote) Focal pitch of a scale, to which the other pitches are related (p. 19)

Chapter 2 in Review

GLOSSARY TERMS

diatonic scale Specific sequence of seven pitches per octave (p. 19)

major scale A diatonic scale with half-steps between the third and fourth notes and seventh and eighth notes of the scale (p. 19)

minor scale A family of three diatonic scales, all of which have a half-step between the second and third notes of the scale (p. 19)

mode (modal scale) A diatonic scale that predates major and minor scales (p. 19)

pentatonic scale Scale containing five pitches per octave (p. 19)

chromatic scale Scale containing all twelve possible pitches within the octave (p. 19)

sharp (♯) Musical symbol that raises a pitch by a half-step (p. 20)

flat (♭)Musical symbol that lowers a pitch by a half-step (p. 20)

staff Set of five horizontal lines used for music notation (p. 20)

key The pitch that serves as the central reference point for pitch organization in a scale (p. 20)

tonal Used to describe music that uses one note of the scale as a reference pitch (p. 20)

atonal Used to describe music that does not use one pitch as a reference point (p. 20)

clef Symbol placed on a staff to indicate specific pitches; treble and bass clefs are the two most common (p. 21)

2-3 **chord** Several notes sounding together (p. 21)

arpeggio (broken chord) Chord whose notes are presented separately, in a series (p. 21)

block chord Chord whose notes are sounded simultaneously (p. 21)

harmony A synonym for *chord*; also an umbrella term that encompasses all aspects of chords (p. 22)

chord progression Series of chords that proceed toward a harmonic goal (p. 22)

tonic chord The single chord that represents the definite center or "home" in relationship to other chords that are used in the composition (p. 22)

cadence A short series of chords (typically two or three) that defines and achieves a harmonic goal (p. 22)

2-4 **texture** The fabric of sound created by the interaction of all the parts of a piece of music (p. 23)

part (line; voice) Music that an individual performer sings or plays (p. 23)

doubling Two or more instruments sharing the same line or part (p. 23)

density A measure of the thickness of texture (p. 23)

textural independence Degree to which a musical line stands apart from those around it (p. 24)

monophonic (n. monophony) Used to describe texture with a single line, or voice (p. 24)

polyphonic (n. polyphony), **contrapuntal** (n. counterpoint) Used to describe multipart texture in which every part is of comparable interest and moves with distinct rhythm and contour (p. 24)

round Staggered entrances of a melody by different voices or instruments at predetermined points in a composition (p. 24)

homophonic (melody and accompaniment; n. homophony) Used to describe a wide range of textures that includes more than one part, with one part a clearly dominant melody and the others subordinate (p. 24)

2-5 **form** Organization of musical elements in time; concerned principally with the structure and coherence of a musical work (p. 25)

repetition Literal restatement of something heard earlier in a work (p. 25)

contrast Substantial change in a work, usually in more than one element (p. 25)

variation The compositional technique of applying changes to one or more elements of a musical work (p. 26)

phrase Short musical unit of varying length (p. 26)

motive Short musical idea used as a building block (p. 26)

period Complete musical statement made up of two or more phrases (p. 26)

parallel periods Complete musical statements made up of two or more phrases that begin identically (p. 26)

strophic form A vocal form in which different lyrics are sung to each repetition of the same melody (p. 27)

variation form (theme and variations) Form that typically begins with a theme; the rest of the work is some number of variations on the theme (p. 27)

binary form Two-part form in which both parts are usually repeated (p. 28)

ternary (ABA) form Three-part form in which the outer sections are typically identical or similar, while the middle section contrasts (p. 28)

rounded binary form Two-part form in which the opening material returns in the second part (p. 28)

2-6 **style** A consistent and comprehensive set of characteristics that define a body of music from a time, place, culture, or creative entity (a composer, performer, or group) (p. 29)

USE THE TOOLS.

- Rip out the Review Cards in the back of your book to study.

Or Visit CourseMate to:

- Read, search, and interact with live media in the Interactive eBook
- Review Flashcards (Print or Online) to master key terms
- Test yourself with Auto-Graded Quizzes
- Bring concepts to life with Games, streaming music, Active Listening Guides, and YouTube playlists

Go to CourseMate for **MUSIC** to begin using these tools. Access at **www.cengagebrain.com**

Complete the Speak Up survey in CourseMate at **www.cengagebrain.com**

f Follow us at **www.facebook.com/4ltrpress**

©iStockphoto.com/A-Digit | © Cengage Learning 2011

WHY CHOOSE?

Every 4LTR Press solution comes complete with a visually engaging textbook in addition to an interactive eBook. Go to CourseMate for **MUSIC** to begin using the eBook. Access at **www.cengagebrain.com**

CHAPTER IN REVIEW

3-1 **Describe monastic life in the Middle Ages.** Members of a monastery or convent during the Middle Ages followed a particular rule, or set of guidelines for living, working, and praying. Life centered on God, and the daily routine revolved around prayer (the Divine Office and Mass) and work. Both prayer and work involved song.

3-2 **Define *chant* and its three forms of text setting.** Chant, or plainchant, began between the eighth and eleventh centuries. It is pure melody, most often unaccompanied, with a free rhythm. Chant may be syllabic, neumatic, or melismatic.

3-3 **Recognize the style of an antiphon through Hildegard of Bingen's "Nunc aperuit nobis."** An antiphon is a chant with prose text, sung before and sometimes after a psalm. It is pure melody, with no pulse or steady beat; has mostly stepwise movement; and can be melismatic. The drone, or sustained tone, used in a chant acts as a home base for the melody.

3-4 **Become familiar with the emergence of secular culture in France during the late Middle Ages.** The emergence of secular culture in France during the late Middle Ages reflected changes in feudal society. The nature of love and marriage changed, and the vernacular began to be used more as a common language.

3-5 **Understand more about minstrels and troubadours, the most important secular musicians of the time.** The musicians most responsible for the new secular music of the late Middle Ages were minstrels and troubadours. Minstrels served the court as instrumentalists and entertainers; troubadours wrote music and poems about courtly love.

3-6 **Describe the life, poetry, and music of Guillaume de Machaut, an important fourteenth-century composer.** Equally renowned as a poet and a composer, Machaut revised the rondeau to become a multipart song with a recurrent refrain. These songs had vernacular texts with love as a theme.

3-7 **Analyze an example of the earliest dance music that has come down to us.** Almost all early dance pieces made use of mensural notation, that is, notation that indicates rhythmic relationships as well as pitch. The estampie, a lively dance in fast triple meter, was popular in France and Italy from the twelfth through the fourteenth centuries. The estampie's clear, simple rhythms contrast with the suppleness of chant.

GLOSSARY TERMS

secular Nonsacred (p. 33)

3-1 **Divine Office** Periods of daily prayer in monasteries, which occurred at regular intervals in the day, from sunrise to after sunset (p. 36)

3-2 **chant (plainchant)** Monophonic vocal music in a free rhythm, used in both the Mass and the Divine Office (p. 36)

continued

THINKING CRITICALLY ABOUT MUSIC

1. Chart a history of melisma in twentieth-century popular music. Start with blues and black gospel music; then trace it through postwar R&B, Motown, and soul, through the 1970s and 1980s to the turn-of-the-century divas and the present day. Are you able to detect an evolutionary pattern?

continued

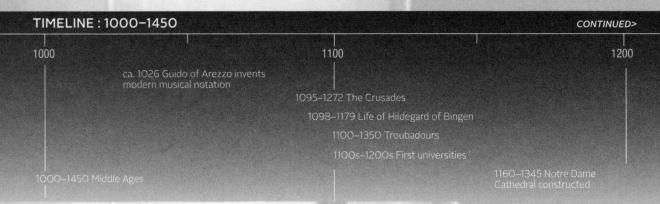

TIMELINE : 1000–1450   CONTINUED>

1000   1100   1200

ca. 1026 Guido of Arezzo invents
modern musical notation

1095–1272 The Crusades

1098–1179 Life of Hildegard of Bingen

1100–1350 Troubadours

1100s–1200s First universities

1000–1450 Middle Ages

1160–1345 Notre Dame
Cathedral constructed

GLOSSARY TERMS

Gregorian chant The most widely used chant in western Europe (p. 36)

syllabic Used to describe chant text setting that has one note per syllable of text (p. 36)

neumatic Used to describe chant text setting that generally has two to four notes per syllable (p. 36)

melismatic Used to describe the most elaborate form of text setting, in which a single syllable may be sustained for many notes (p. 36)

3-3 **antiphon** Chant with prose (not poetic) text, sung before and sometimes after a psalm (p. 37)

drone Note continuously sounding throughout a piece or a large section of a piece (p. 37)

3-4 **chivalry** Code of behavior expected of the medieval noble class (p. 38)

courtly love Rigid medieval social protocol in which a man could think of having an adulterous relationship with a woman but could not consummate it (p. 39)

vernacular Everyday language of a particular region (p. 39)

3-5 **minstrel** Multifaceted entertainer who, by the thirteenth century, was typically an instrumentalist attached to a court (p. 40)

troubadour Poet-musician who wrote and sang about courtly love (p. 40)

3-6 **rondeau** Multipart song with a recurrent refrain (p. 41)

3-7 **mensural notation** Notation developed in the mid-thirteenth century that, for the first time, indicated specific rhythmic relationships as well as pitch (p. 43)

estampie Dance for couples, popular in France and Italy from the twelfth through the fourteenth centuries (p. 43)

THINKING CRITICALLY ABOUT MUSIC

2. The overriding purpose of chant is to connect the human with the divine. To further explore music as a spiritual practice, take the recording of Hildegard's chant to a quiet place—an isolated part of campus, a church, a room away from it all. Listen to the music several times and reflect on your response to it.

3. Explore the similarities between the estampie and contemporary dance tracks by comparing the estampie to a dance mix of your choice. Outline the form of the dance mix; then compare it to the estampie. Note underlying similarities (and differences) in the instruments used. Compare the textures. Is melody more dominant in one or the other?

TIMELINE : 1000–1450 *CONTINUED*

1300   1400   1500

1300s Black Death

ca. 1300–1377 Life of Guillaume de Machaut

1308–1321 Italian secular literature: *Divine Comedy*

1350–1353 Italian secular literature: *Decameron*

1000–1450 Middle Ages

CHAPTER IN REVIEW

4-1 Understand the significance of "L'homme armé," a popular song from the fifteenth century. "L'homme armé" was an exceedingly popular song for over a century. Several composers, among them Josquin des Prez, incorporated the song into sacred polyphonic compositions.

4-2 Recognize the main features and functions of Renaissance polyphony, and hear a Catholic Mass movement set by Josquin des Prez. Renaissance polyphony is characterized by several parts of comparable melodic interest weaving together in a seamless musical flow, as well as by the frequent use of imitation. The music that we can hear echoes the cosmic music that we cannot hear but that is more sublime than any that humans can produce. The presumed existence of music of the spheres earned music its lofty place in university curricula. The ordinary (unchanging) parts of the Catholic Mass that are set to music, such as Josquin's Mass movement, include the Kyrie, Gloria, Credo, Sanctus, and Agnus Dei.

4-3 Describe the madrigal, its history in Italy and England, its sound, and its social function. The madrigal is a polyphonic secular song, most often unaccompanied. It was developed in Italy in the early part of the sixteenth century and became popular throughout Europe, especially England. John Wilbye was one of several English composers who made a lasting contribution to the genre.

4-4 Understand Elizabethan solo song, the instrument that typically accompanied it, and the use of song in theatrical productions. The Elizabethan solo song features a simple melody, mostly chordal accompaniment on the lute, and strophic form

4-5 Identify the sounds of Renaissance instruments and their roles within a chamber ensemble. The Elizabethan consort included viols, lutes and other strummed instruments, and flutes.

GLOSSARY TERMS

4-1 **Renaissance** Era between roughly 1450 and 1600 in which there were a rediscovery of classical Greek and Roman civilization, a rebirth of humanistic values, and more widespread use of vernacular languages. In music, the era was characterized by such features as seamless, imitative polyphony; rapid growth in quantity and quality of secular music; and the increasing use of instruments. (p. 46)

chanson Secular French song of the fifteenth and sixteenth centuries (p. 47)

continued

THINKING CRITICALLY ABOUT MUSIC

1. To explore the various ways in which music can be used to connect to the spirit, find two or three different versions of "Amazing Grace." One should be a simple harmonized hymn setting. Then compare the versions with each other and to the Josquin Kyrie. In particular, listen to the difference between the homophonic hymn setting and Josquin's polyphony, and relate the texture to your perception of the spiritual message.

continued

TIMELINE : 1450–1600

CONTINUED>

1450

1500

1400s "L'homme armé" is popular

1517 Protestant Reformation begins in Germany

1445?–1521 Life of Josquin des Prez

1483–1546 Life of Martin Luther

1520s Madrigals first emerge in Italy

1450–1600 Renaissance

GLOSSARY TERMS

cantus firmus Preexisting melody that serves as the starting point for a polyphonic composition (p. 47)

ABA form Three-part form featuring an opening section, a contrasting middle section, and the repetition of the opening section (p. 48)

4-2 **imitation** Polyphonic technique in which other parts restate—imitate—a melodic idea soon after its first presentation (p. 51)

proper Parts of the Mass that change from day to day (p. 51)

ordinary Unchanging parts of the Mass (p. 51)

ABC form Three-part form in which each section is different (p. 52)

4-3 **ayre (air)** Elizabethan solo song with lute accompaniment (p. 53)

madrigal Polyphonic setting of a secular poem, composed in the sixteenth and early seventeenth centuries (p. 53)

a cappella Without instrumental accompaniment (p. 53)

text painting (word painting) Strategy to highlight meaning in a text with striking musical gestures: a melodic inflection, a bold harmony, or a quick change of rhythmic pace (p. 54)

4-4 **course** On a lute, a pair of strings tuned to the same pitch (p. 56)

strophic song Song in which the same melody sets two or more stanzas of text (p. 56)

obbligato Second melody playing under a main melody (p. 56)

4-5 **consort** Small group of diverse instruments in Elizabethan England (p. 58)

idiomatic composition Composing in a way that makes use of an instrument's distinctive sounds and capabilities (p. 59)

THINKING CRITICALLY ABOUT MUSIC

2. Proceeding from Hildegard to Josquin is a bit like moving from one city to another without experiencing the trip in between. If you're interested in tracing the evolution of polyphony, try listening to at least one polyphonic Kyrie per century from 1100 to 1500. (If necessary, your instructor can help you locate recordings.) Describe the relationship between parts. Are they comparably active? Are they comparably interesting melodically?

3. In much twentieth-century popular music, we hear in effect a combination of the two versions of the same melody: several iterations of a melody, featuring vocal and instrumental versions of the melody in alternation—or at least one instrumental statement of the melody sandwiched between several vocal versions. Find two examples of this from different eras or styles, and ask yourself these questions:

   a. How do the statements of the melody compare? Are they all the same? Is there any difference between vocal versions? Does the instrumental version depart from the vocal version? If so, how much?

   b. Describe the supporting instruments and their roles. Consider in particular how melody-like their parts are. How do the textures compare with those of the madrigal, the accompanied solo song, and the instrumental setting of the melody?

TIMELINE : 1450–1600 *CONTINUED*

1550

1557/8?–1602 Life of Thomas Morley

1558–1603 Elizabeth I reigns in England

1574–1638 Life of John Wilbye

1600

1601 Morley publishes
The Triumphes of Oriana

1450–1600 Renaissance

CHAPTER 4 IN REVIEW

CHAPTER IN REVIEW

5-1 Describe the characteristics of the Baroque era in music. The Baroque era in music spans the century and a half between 1600 and 1750, encompassing almost all of the concert music of the seventeenth and early eighteenth century. Paid public performance was a new commercial enterprise of the Baroque era, part of a substantial expansion of the music industry. Music publishing of all genres—sacred music, opera and secular song, instrumental music, and much more—catered to church, court, and a growing middle class. Writing about music was directed to professionals and amateurs. Instrument making reached new heights of craftsmanship.

5-2 Understand what opera is and the revolutionary impact of the first operas in Europe. Opera is drama in which all of the dialogue is sung; therefore, the pace of the drama is much slower. To address this, composers developed musical gestures that could convey deeply felt emotion. Opera revolutionized virtually every aspect of musical life in Europe. It became a public entertainment; it produced a shift in attitude—music could mean more, and could mean more specifically; it made stars of its singers; it added resources, especially the orchestra, and used them in new ways; it integrated song and dance.

5-3 Recognize the importance of Claudio Monteverdi and the sound and vocal style of his opera *Orfeo*. Monteverdi was a major composer who served as the bridge between Renaissance and Baroque. Many of opera's revolutionary changes were already in the air, but *Orfeo* helped bring them together, harness them, and provide a springboard for further change—more than any other single development of the period. Those changes included (1) integration of drama and music; (2) transformation of opera into a grand spectacle; (3) formation of an orchestra, use of orchestral effects, and attention to idiomatic instrumental writing; (4) attention focused on the star; (5) integration of song and dance in a musical drama; and (6) development of a language that could convey expressive meaning through musical gesture.

5-4 Understand the growth of opera, including musical and dramatic changes, during the seventeenth century. During the seventeenth century, opera became a business and a major cultural export. Its performers were stars. The plots, adapted mainly from mythology, epics, and ancient history, quickly assumed a conventional structure featuring noble lovers, with comic servants providing intermittent relief from the tragedy that almost invariably ensued. Operatic plots typically revealed themselves over three acts. The basic unit of discourse in opera became the recitative and the aria.

5-5 Recognize an early example of the use of recitative and aria, as well as the expressive capabilities of common practice harmony, in Henry Purcell's "Dido's Lament." In *Dido and Aeneas*, Purcell exploited the expressive capabilities of common practice harmony, as well as the recitative-aria combination.

5-6 Understand the changes in Baroque opera from Monteverdi to Handel, through an examination of Handel's *Giulio Cesare*. Typically, Baroque operas would unfold in recitative. When they reached an emotional crest, the action would stop while one of the characters pondered the moment in aria form. This pattern is revealed in *Giulio Cesare* by one of the great composers of the late Baroque era, George Frideric Handel.

    Giulio Cesare demonstrates how opera was basically turned on its head during the Baroque era. At first the function of the music was to enhance the drama, but Baroque *opera seria* later came to place the music first.

TIMELINE : 1600–1750

CONTINUED>

1600

1650

1567–1643 Life of Claudio Monteverdi

ca. 1650–1700 Middle Baroque era

ca. 1600–1650 Early Baroque era

1658/9?–1695 Life of Henry Purcell

1601 Caccini publishes *Le nuove musiche*

1689 Purcell's *Dido and Aeneas* first performed

1607 Monteverdi's *Orfeo*

1640s Public opera performances in Venice and other Italian cities

Chapter 5 in Review

GLOSSARY TERMS

5-1   **Baroque** Era in music spanning the century and a half between 1600 and 1750 (p. 63)

5-2   **opera** Drama, either tragic or comic, in which all dialogue is sung (p. 64)

     recitative Section of an opera that generally contains dialogue to further the action; features text delivered in a rhythm approximating speech, often with strings of repeated notes (p. 64)

     aria Accompanied solo operatic melody (p. 64)

5-3   **score** Notated musical document that contains every part to be performed (p. 67)

     basso continuo Continuous bass line, as well as harmony built on the bass, in support of the melody (p. 68)

     continuo An innovation of Baroque music, a group of both bass and chord-producing instruments, providing a strong bass line and continuous harmonic support (p. 68)

5-4   **libretto** Text to be sung in an opera (p. 70)

5-5   **semi-opera** Work in which the main characters speak and minor characters sing and dance (p. 71)

     ground Continuous bass line that is recycled without interruption throughout a work; also called **ground bass** or **basso ostinato** (p. 72)

5-6   *opera seria* Form of more serious dramatic opera, based mainly on classical mythology, historical figures, and classic literature, that thrived during most of the eighteenth century (p. 74)

     da capo aria Aria with three sections: an opening section (A), a contrasting section (B), and a reprise of the opening section (A) in which singers were expected to embellish the opening melody (p. 74)

     castrato Male singer castrated prior to puberty to preserve the singer's voice in the female range (p. 75)

THINKING CRITICALLY ABOUT MUSIC

1. Insofar as it often integrates story, song, and dance, the music video (from Michael Jackson's genre-defining videos such as *Thriller*) can be understood as a mini- (or even micro-) opera. With Monteverdi's music firmly in mind, find an extended music video (at least five minutes long) and evaluate it from an operatic point of view: What is the dramatic element in the story? To what extent does the music help convey this? What aspects of the music seem to help express the flow of the story?

2. Compare recitative to rap, a more contemporary musical style in which words are also the focus. There are interesting parallels and contrasts between them. Both focus on the words, delivering them at a rapid speed (relative to song). Both have sparse accompaniment: drum and bass; harpsichord and cello. An obvious difference between the two is the way each presents rhythm and pitch: rap has definite rhythm and indefinite pitch; recitative has definite pitch and indefinite rhythm.

TIMELINE : 1600–1750 *CONTINUED*

1700   1750

1700-1750 Late Baroque era

1711 Handel arrives in England

1724 Handel's *Giulio Cesare in Egitto* is first staged

CHAPTER IN REVIEW

6-1   **Understand the fugue and fugal composition through an early Bach fugue.** A fugue is a contrapuntal composition in which several parts enter one by one and continue until the end. Sonatas and other independent instrumental works may have fugal passages—sections that feature imitative counterpoint as is heard in a fugue. Fugues consist of an opening section, called an exposition, containing subject, answer, a series of episodes, and sequences.

6-2   **Understand Baroque instruments, ensembles, and orchestra.** The most important instruments in the Baroque era were the violin family and the harpsichord. The preferred small-group ensembles were those for the solo sonata (one melody instrument plus continuo) and trio sonata (two melody instruments plus continuo). The orchestra evolved during the Baroque era. The string section, the core of the modern orchestra, became standardized in the late seventeenth and early eighteenth centuries.

6-3   **Recognize the sound of the Baroque sonata through the music of Arcangelo Corelli.** Corelli's music served as a model for eighteenth-century Baroque composers. In his sonata, we hear the standard instrumentation, texture (melody plus continuo), and melodic style. We also hear idiomatic, virtuosic writing for the violin.

6-4   **Become familiar with the Baroque suite through the music of J. S. Bach.** A suite is a collection of dances. In one of these dances, the gigue, we hear how Bach transforms the simple texture and form of the jig into a more complex and contrapuntal work.

6-5   **Review the prevailing Baroque musical aesthetic and style.** By the early eighteenth century, composers felt that their music—even instrumental—could communicate quite specific emotional states. Writers on music described such moods as "affects" or "affections." This aesthetic principle thus became known as the Doctrine of Affections. Corelli's sonata and Bach's gigue sustain the same mood throughout. This is consistent with the Baroque idea of maintaining one mood, or affect, throughout a movement.

6-6   **Become acquainted with the Baroque concerto through Vivaldi's *The Four Seasons* and Bach's Brandenburg Concertos.** The Baroque concerto pitted large against small to express the affect of a movement even more forcefully. Vivaldi created a program for "Spring," along with the other seasons in *The Four Seasons*, which he expressed musically with bold effects and virtuosic demands on the soloist. Bach's third Brandenburg Concerto shows key elements of his musical style: interest in instruments and a tendency to generate an entire movement from the opening idea.

THINKING CRITICALLY ABOUT MUSIC

1. Bach's gigue is dance-based music that has become listening music. Find an example of twentieth-century dance music (rock 'n' roll, disco) and compare it to a song or composition that is no longer dance music but whose rhythm was derived from the dance beat. What differences and similarities do you find?
2. Vivaldi's *The Four Seasons* demonstrates how musicians can evoke images and moods. Review the episodes where Vivaldi evokes the sounds of nature. Then locate a copy of The Beatles' *Sgt. Pepper's Lonely Hearts Club Band*. Pick a song or two and identify instrumental sounds and melodic gestures that you feel are evocative. How does Vivaldi's approach compare to that used by The Beatles?

TIMELINE : 1650–1770 CONTINUED>

1650

1700

1643–1715 Louis XIV is king of France

1685–1741 Life of Antonio Vivaldi

1700–1750 Late Baroque era

1703-1707 Bach serves at Arnstadt

1717–1723 Bach serves at Cöthen

1721 Bach presents the Brandenburg Concertos to Margrave of Brandenburg

1723 Vivaldi composes *The Four Seasons*

1723–1750 Bach serves at Leipzig

GLOSSARY TERMS

6-1   **stop** Row of pipes in an organ (p. 81)

manual Organ keyboard (p. 81)

fugue Composition in which several parts enter one by one and continue until the end (p. 81)

fugal passage Section that features imitative counterpoint, much as is heard in a fugue (p. 81)

fugal exposition Opening section of a fugue, in which the subject is presented in all voices through a series of entries (p. 81)

subject Opening melodic idea in a fugue (p. 81)

answer A version of the fugue subject that has been altered or moved to a different pitch level (p. 81)

sequence Fugue passage consisting of several short segments that repeat the same melodic material at higher or lower pitches (p. 82)

episode Fugue section that states neither the fugue subject nor the fugue answer (p. 82)

6-2   **harpsichord** Keyboard instrument in which depressing a key causes a plectrum to pluck one or more strings (p. 83)

plectrum Harpsichord plucking device originally made from a quill (the hard shaft of a bird feather) (p. 83)

continuo Instrumental combination playing chords and a bass line: typically a bass instrument and a chord-producing instrument (p. 83)

chamber music ensemble A group of several musicians, at least two and usually no more than ten, with each musician playing a different part (p. 84)

6-3   **canzona** Italian instrumental genre derived from polyphonic vocal music (p. 84)

sonata Solo and small-group instrumental composition; a three- or four-movement work (p. 84)

movement Self-contained section of larger work (p. 84)

church sonata (*sonata da chiesa*) Four-movement sonata, often music for the Mass (p. 85)

chamber sonata (*sonata da camera*) Secular sonata in three or more movements (p. 85)

solo sonata Instrumental composition that requires three players: one playing a melodic instrument, plus continuo (chord-producing and bass instruments) (p. 85)

trio sonata Instrumental composition that typically calls for four performers: two playing melodic instruments and two others playing the continuo (p. 85)

ritornello Melodic idea introduced at the beginning of a movement and returning periodically; form that uses this device (p. 85)

opus Term usually followed by a number, used to identify a musical composition (p. 86)

figured bass Bass line and numerical symbols used as an abbreviated system indicating specific notes and chords for a keyboard player (p. 86)

cadenza Virtuosic solo passage (p. 87)

6-4   **suite** Collection of dances (p. 87)

allemande German dance, typically in quadruple meter with a moderate tempo (p. 88)

courante French dance in triple meter (p. 88)

sarabande Slow, stately dance of Spanish origin, in triple meter (p. 88)

gigue Dance, typically in compound duple meter, inspired by the jig (p. 88)

6-5   **Doctrine of Affections** Baroque aesthetic principle holding that music could communicate quite specific emotional states, such as joy, languor, or melancholy, through entire movements or complete works (p. 89)

6-6   **concerto** Dominant orchestral genre of the late Baroque, featuring contrast between large and small; orchestra made up of strings along with one or more spotlighted instruments (p. 90)

solo concerto Concerto that features a single solo instrument, such as a violin or flute (p. 90)

concertino Small group of soloists featured in a concerto grosso (p. 90)

concerto grosso Concerto that features a small group of soloists (the concertino) (p. 90)

tutti Passages in which everyone plays (p. 90)

program music Instrumental music in which a composer depicts an extramusical inspiration, such as a scene, story, or idea, or the experience or feeling that the inspiration arouses (p. 91)

TIMELINE : 1650–1770 CONTINUED

1750

1770 Corelli publishes Sonata in C major

early 1770s Violin-family instruments assume their modern form

CHAPTER IN REVIEW

7-1 Understand the Lutheran chorale as the point of departure for Bach's sacred vocal music. Luther sought to close the distance between those who said or sang the Mass and those who heard it. He did so by encouraging monophonic hymn singing in the vernacular and by composing hymns and hymn tunes himself. Luther's "Ein' feste Burg" is a chorale, a Lutheran hymn designed for congregational singing. Bach, the most esteemed contrapuntal composer in the history of music, composed a homophonic setting of this same chorale. However, for Bach, the chorale was one component of a large multimovement composition.

7-2 Recognize the relationship between the chorale and the cantata through an exploration of Bach's Cantata No. 80. Bach's cantatas were an integral component of Sunday services. The overall design of the most common cantata included a setting of a chorale for congregational singing, a series of recitative/aria pairs, and one or more choruses. All were connected to the scripture readings of the day. The chorale derived directly from scripture. The recitative/aria pairs set contemporary commentaries on the scripture readings. Choruses were large-scale works for chorus and orchestra. In them, Bach surrounded the chorale melody with a rich polyphonic texture performed by the orchestra.

In his cantata choruses, Bach often used the chorale melody as the cantus firmus. Because both words and melody were so familiar to the congregations in Leipzig, they served as the Bible passages on which Bach would sermonize. The use of familiar chorales gave Bach's congregation a head start in understanding the message in his music. By surrounding the chorale melody with much richer music that has a clear affect, Bach could convey his interpretation of the message expressed in the lyrics of the chorale.

7-3 Get acquainted with the Baroque oratorio, its importance to Handel's career, and Handel's most successful oratorio, *Messiah*. In Handel's time, opera and oratorio were cousins. Both told a story through music, using recitative, arias, and ensemble numbers (duets, choruses, and the like). In Handel's vocal music, there are two major differences: the subject and its presentation. His operas took their plots from history, as was the case with *Giulio Cesare*. By contrast, almost all of Handel's oratorios are based on religious subjects. Moreover, unlike opera, oratorio is not staged; it is simply presented in concert. There is no action or scenery; words and music carry the story, without visual aids.

TIMELINE : 1700–1750

CONTINUED>

1685	1700
1685–1750 Life of J. S. Bach	1703–1707 Bach serves at Arnstadt
1685–1759 Life of George Frideric Handel	1711 Handel arrives in England
1687 Isaac Newton publishes Mathematical Principles	

Chapter 7 in Review

GLOSSARY TERMS

7-1   *Meistersinger* German lyric poet of the fourteenth
through sixteenth centuries (p. 97)

chorale Lutheran hymn designed for congregational
singing (p. 97)

7-2   cantata Church or secular vocal composition (p. 99)

church cantata Cantata written for church use. Bach's
church cantatas typically include one or more choruses, a series of recitative/aria pairs, and a setting of a
chorale. (p. 99)

chorus In a Bach cantata, a large-scale work for
chorus (choir) and orchestra that is built around the
chorale for a church service (p. 99)

7-3   oratorio A genre performed in a concert setting that
tells a story through music, using various forms of
recitative, arias, and ensemble numbers (p. 101)

THINKING CRITICALLY ABOUT MUSIC

1. Explore the sacred/secular relationship in contemporary sacred music of your choice. Find
out where you are most likely to hear it, and
determine to what extent its style is related to or
distinct from secular musical styles.

TIMELINE : 1700–1750 *CONTINUED*

1715   1730   1745

1717–1723 Bach serves at Cöthen

1723–1750 Bach serves at Leipzig

1742 Handel's
Messiah
premieres in
London

CHAPTER IN REVIEW

8-1 **Understand key developments in late eighteenth-century music.** As the audience for music expanded beyond church and court to include a rapidly growing middle class, public performance, publishing royalties, and private instruction supplemented—and in some cases replaced—patronage as sources of income for musicians. Music making in the home, both vocal and instrumental, and by both professionals and amateurs, grew significantly during the latter half of the century. During the last quarter of the century, Vienna became the main center of musical activity and influence. Haydn, Mozart, and Beethoven all settled there.

8-2 **Contrast the two main styles of eighteenth-century music: Baroque and Classical.** By the 1770s, the new style that we now call the Classical style had taken shape. The music featured stronger and more frequent contrasts within movements, and greater length. The contrasts touched every element: for example, dramatic shifts between loud and soft, varied melodic material, homophonic versus contrapuntal textures, and slow versus fast rhythms. The consistent, comfortable rhythm of the continuo was now an anachronism. Moreover, these contrasts almost demanded greater length, to present and ultimately reconcile more diverse material. As a result, movements in genres inherited from the Baroque era, such as the concerto, were up to four times longer.

8-3 **Outline sonata form and see it as an expression of Classical style.** To shape varied materials into more expansive and coherent statements, Classical composers gradually developed a set of procedures that were consistent in principle yet remarkably varied in their realizations. Typically, these procedures were used most extensively and expansively in the first movements of instrumental compositions: sonatas, quartets, symphonies, concertos, and the like. The organizational principle that informs these procedures in these movements came to be known as "sonata form."

Movements written in sonata form contain at least three large sections: exposition, development, and recapitulation. An introduction in a slow tempo occasionally precedes the exposition, to convey a greater sense of importance. And a concluding coda may follow the recapitulation, to bring the movement to an even more emphatic close. Within these broad, large-scale guidelines, there is virtually unlimited flexibility, in thematic content, connections and contrasts, and proportions.

8-4 **Explore a movement from a Mozart piano sonata as an example of Classical sonata form.** The first movement of Mozart's piano sonata offers a clear outline of sonata form, with main sections clearly delineated and themes marking important milestones in the form. The frequent contrast and movement toward goals that characterize Classical style occur throughout the movement. The sonata also introduces a new keyboard instrument, the piano.

8-5 **Discover the sound of the string quartet, the main chamber ensemble of the Classical era, through a string quartet by Franz Joseph Haydn.** The first movement of Haydn's quartet introduces the sound of the string quartet, a chamber ensemble with a homogenous sonority. It also enhances our understanding of sonata form because of its similarity in general outline to the Mozart sonata movement, as well as the significant differences in the basic musical material and the ways in which they are developed.

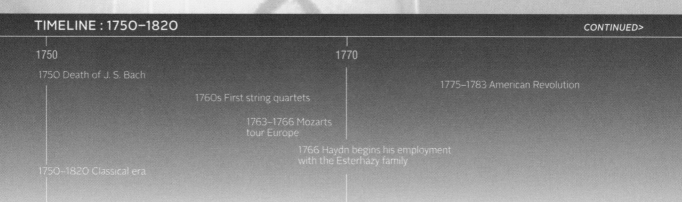

TIMELINE : 1750–1820

CONTINUED>

1750

1750 Death of J. S. Bach

1760s First string quartets

1763–1766 Mozarts tour Europe

1766 Haydn begins his employment with the Esterhazy family

1750–1820 Classical era

1770

1775–1783 American Revolution

GLOSSARY TERMS

8-2   **Enlightenment** Eighteenth-century period in Western culture when reason and the scientific method replaced heredity as the main sources of legitimacy for authority (p. 109)

Classical style In music, a term that identifies the concert music of the late eighteenth century; Classical composers sought to create musical tension, typically through contrasts, then to resolve the tension. (p. 110)

8-3   **sonata form** The most characteristic form of first movements (and occasionally other movements) in instrumental compositions of the Classical era; contains three major sections: exposition, development, and recapitulation, and sometimes an introduction and coda; an expansion of rounded binary form (p. 110)

introduction Optional introductory section of sonata form in slow tempo; common in Classical symphonies (p. 110)

exposition Section of sonata form that serves two main purposes: to establish the basic character of the movement and to present the musical ideas that are to be worked out in the rest of the movement (p. 111)

transition Portion of the exposition in sonata form that moves decisively to a new key and highlights the move; in the recapitulation, the transition is modified so that the second theme enters in the tonic. (p. 111)

development Section of sonata form where material from the exposition (and occasionally new material) is developed, or manipulated through fragmentation and alteration, to project great instability (p. 111)

modulation Harmonic procedure that produces a smooth change from one key to another (p. 112)

recapitulation Mostly literal restatement of sonata form's exposition, but with all the material in the contrasting key restated in the home key (p. 112)

coda Optional section of sonata form that follows the recapitulation (p. 112)

8-4   **K.** Abbreviation in the titles of Mozart compositions that stands for **Köchel**, the man who attempted to arrange all of Mozart's known works in chronological order (p. 114)

string quartet Chamber ensemble consisting of two violinists, a violist, and a cellist; also, a work composed for this ensemble (p. 114)

THINKING CRITICALLY ABOUT MUSIC

1. One of the most distinctive features of sonata form is the transition section, which typically builds to a climax to prepare the presentation of a contrasting theme. Many rock-era songs feature a "bridge," a section that serves as a transition between verse and chorus. Like the sonata-form transition section, it also typically builds to a climax. Find two songs in your music collection that use verse/chorus form with a defined bridge section but do not add instruments in the transition from verse to chorus. To better understand the similarities and differences between the bridge in rock-era song and the transition sections in the sonata and string quartet, consider the following, then consider the differences and similarities between bridge and transition in relation to their respective roles in the overall form: verse/chorus or sonata.

   a. How do the bridge sections build up to the chorus? What changes in dynamics, melody, rhythm, texture, and harmony do you hear?

   b. Where in the songs does the climax arrive? How does that compare to the high point in a sonata-form transition section?

TIMELINE : 1750–1820 *CONTINUED*

1790	1810	1830

1789–1799 French Revolution

1790 Haydn first visits London

CHAPTER IN REVIEW

9-1 Describe the instruments and orchestration of the Classical orchestra. The Classical orchestra includes not only a full string section but also the permanent addition of woodwinds, brasses, and percussion. The major difference between early and late eighteenth-century orchestras was that these new instruments were no longer optional. Compositions that required an orchestra were scored for strings and most or all of the woodwind, brass, and percussion instruments, and occasionally even more. Woodwinds became permanent parts of the orchestra in stages: first oboes, then flutes and bassoons, and finally clarinets. Horns were the first brass instrument to become a permanent part of the orchestra. Trumpets and timpani were used intermittently during the last quarter of the century but did not become fixtures in the symphonic orchestra until the 1790s.

The addition of winds, brass, and percussion added a wealth of tone color and greatly expanded the opportunity for timbral, dynamic, and textural contrast. Frequent and vivid contrasts in timbre, dynamics, and texture are one quality that distinguishes the Classical symphony from earlier orchestral music.

9-2 Be familiar with the Classical symphony, as exemplified by Haydn's Symphony No. 94. Typically, a Classical symphony had four movements. The first movement might begin at a fast tempo, or it might have a slow introduction. In either event, the fast part would be cast in sonata form. The second movement was slow. It could take almost any form, from a trimmed-down sonata form to simple theme and variations, as in Haydn's symphony. The third movement was either a minuet, a popular eighteenth-century dance in triple meter, or a scherzo, a playful, more high-spirited alternative. Although both minuet and scherzo derived from dance music, neither was music for dancing. Haydn's minuet begins as a heavy-footed peasant dance rather than an elegant accompaniment for aristocrats. The gentler continuation and the flourish that ends the first part move the music up both the social and the musical scale. The last movement was typically a rondo, a form in which a tuneful and simple opening theme returns again and again.

9-3 Understand the form and style of the Classical piano concerto. Recall that concerto movements by Vivaldi and Bach open with an orchestral ritornello. Solo passages, no matter how brilliant, expanded on the character of the ritornello. In the sense that the music played by the orchestra determined the fundamental character of the movement, the orchestra was in charge. By contrast, in the Classical concerto, the "star" soloist is heard *in opposition to* the orchestra rather than as an extension of it. The idea of opposition and its harmonious resolution is inherent in the Classical style.

The concerto, Mozart's piano concertos in particular, adds another element to the opposition of contrasting materials that is integral to the Classical style: the conflict between soloist and orchestra. Piano concertos are different in kind from all other solo concertos because the piano is a self-sufficient solo instrument. That is, pianists can play both melody and harmony, with as many parts as necessary to create a complete texture.

9-4 Explore the first movement of a Mozart piano concerto in detail. Mozart expanded and modified the sonata-form model found in sonatas, chamber music, and symphonies. First movements in the later Mozart piano concertos typically follow this sequence of events: (1) a long orchestral exposition; (2) a soloist exposition; (3) a development section that includes the central tutti, an extended statement by the orchestra, rapid dialogue between soloist and orchestra, and a long preparation for the return of the opening theme; (4) a recapitulation that merges the orchestral and solo exposition; and (5) a coda, including a cadenza, a rhapsodic and virtuosic improvisation of variable length.

TIMELINE : 1750–1820

CONTINUED>

1750

1750 Death of J. S. Bach

1750–1820 Classical era

1763–1766 Mozarts tour Europe

1766 Haydn begins his employment with the Esterhazy family

1770

1775–1783 American Revolution

1786 Mozart's Concerto in C minor first performed

Chapter 9 in Review

GLOSSARY TERMS

9-2 **symphony** An extended work for orchestra that typically contains four movements: a first movement in sonata form, a slow movement, a minuet or scherzo, and a finale (p. 122)

scherzo Playful, high-spirited third movement of a four-movement instrumental composition, such as a symphony or string quartet (p. 122)

minuet Dance in triple meter, the most popular dance of the eighteenth century among the aristocracy; often the third movement of a four-movement instrumental composition (p. 124)

rondo Form in which a tuneful and simple opening theme returns again and again, but only after alternating with one or more contrasting themes (p. 126)

concerto In the Classical era, a work for solo instrument and orchestra in which the soloist counterbalances the greater numbers of the orchestra through virtuosity, harmonic ingenuity, and lyricism (p. 126)

9-4 **cadenza** Virtuosic and rhapsodic improvisation of variable length that typically occurs close to the end of each of the outer movements of a concerto (p. 132)

THINKING CRITICALLY ABOUT MUSIC

1. In the discussion of the Haydn symphony, it was noted that all four movements contain humorous elements and that good humor is common in much music of the Classical period. To explore this point further, listen to three works: Mozart's *Eine kleine Nachtmusik*, P.D.Q. Bach's *Eine kleine Nichtmusik*, and Mozart's *Musical Joke*, K. 522.
   a. Do you hear any humor in Mozart's *Eine kleine Nachtmusik*? If yes, can you describe its character? Do you find P.D.Q. Bach's parody of Mozart's piece funny? If so, why? Can you hear differences between the two Mozart works that make Mozart's joke obvious? If so, what are they? If not, why not?
   b. Finally, go to a classical concert where a symphony or string quartet of Haydn is being performed. Do you hear any passages that strike you as humorous? What do you think would happen if you were to laugh out loud at a funny passage; how do you think your fellow audience members would react?
2. One of the hallmarks of the Classical style is frequent and comprehensive contrast. It is also a common feature in much of the alternative music of the 1990s, especially the work of groups like Radiohead. Compare one of the Haydn symphony movements with a track like Radiohead's "Paranoid Android," considering:
   a. What elements are being contrasted (dynamics, melody, texture) and what kinds of differences there are within an element (for rhythm, contrast in meter, tempo, amount of syncopation, and activity). How do they compare with the contrasts in the Haydn symphony?
   b. What is the expressive function of the contrast in the Radiohead track that you chose? How do the contrasts coordinate with the lyrics? How do the musical differences match up with the differences (or similarities) in expressive purpose?

TIMELINE : 1750–1820 *CONTINUED*

1790	1810	1830

1789–1799 French Revolution

1790 Haydn first visits London

1794 Haydn's Symphony No. 94 first performe

CHAPTER IN REVIEW

10-1 Describe the changes in opera during the late eighteenth century. One can use opera as a barometer of social change in eighteenth-century Europe. At the beginning of the century, *opera seria* reigned supreme. However, after mid-century, "lighter" forms of music and theatrical entertainment became popular. Their rise in popularity coincided with drastic changes in the social order.

    The radical transformation of opera during the latter part of the eighteenth century grew out of three interrelated developments: the growing popularity and sophistication of new, lighter forms of stage entertainment; the reform of serious opera; and the dramatic change in musical style. Collectively, they reshaped opera into a more flexible and more dramatically credible genre.

10-2 Recognize Mozart's opera *Don Giovanni* as an example of a successful eighteenth century opera that also reflected the significant weakening of aristocratic control of culture and society. The premiere of *Don Giovanni* came about a decade after the American Revolution and two years before the start of the French Revolution. In *Don Giovanni*, it is quite clear that the aristocracy is no longer being viewed through rose-colored glasses.

10-3 Understand the dramatic power of Mozart's music and opera through a comparison of two scenes from *Don Giovanni*. The two excerpts from *Don Giovanni* give some insight into the dramatic potential of Classical style. The action moves forward during each selection because of Mozart's ability to depict the characters and context musically, and regulate musical tension. They also show the dramatic power of strong contrast: the disarming duet and the death scene employ radically different musical resources.

TIMELINE : 1750–1820
CONTINUED>

1750

1770

1750 Death of J. S. Bach

1750–1820 Classical era

1763–1766 Mozarts tour Europe

1775–1783 American Revolution

1786 Mozart's *Marriage of Figaro* premieres

GLOSSARY TERMS

10-1   **ballad opera** British stage entertainment, popular through most of the eighteenth century, that mixed spoken dialogue with popular and traditional songs (p. 135)

opéra comique Humorous French stage entertainment that blends spoken dialogue with song (p. 135)

opera buffa In the 1700s, Italian comic opera, often with contemporary everyday characters instead of gods and historical heroes (p. 135)

Singspiel Literally "song/play"; lighthearted stage entertainment in German that, like *opéra comique*, combines spoken dialogue with song (p. 135)

THINKING CRITICALLY ABOUT MUSIC

1. Music may often be romantic, but it's rare to actually see and hear the seduction progress through the music, as in "Là ci darem la mano." More contemporary cases of music as the agent of romance occur in 1930s films featuring Ginger Rogers and Fred Astaire. Among them is the scene from *Top Hat* where Fred sings "Cheek to Cheek" to Ginger as they dance and she falls under his spell. As you view and listen to the scene (which is almost certainly on YouTube), consider these questions:

    a. Does Irving Berlin's melody help depict Fred's romancing of Ginger, and if so, what features of the melody serve that function?

    b. A key difference between the Mozart scene and the film scene is the central role of dance. How does the social dancing in this scene compare to the social dancing that you do? Which do you consider more "romantic"? Why? What is the role of the music in creating and developing a romantic mood? Do you think that the dancing in the film adds an element that is missing in the Mozart?

TIMELINE : 1750–1820 *CONTINUED*

1790	1810	1830

1787 Mozart's *Don Giovanni* written

1789–1799 French Revolution

CHAPTER IN REVIEW

11-1   **Understand the revolutionary qualities in Beethoven's music that set it apart from the music of other composers.** The cultural climate of Vienna, coupled with the political and social changes that occurred during Beethoven's lifetime, made it possible for Beethoven to earn unprecedented recognition for his achievements. His achievements and influence are unmatched by any other composer's. He played the leading role in the transformation from Classical to Romantic and in elevating instrumental music to a status higher than that of vocal music.

11-2   **Describe Beethoven's radically different approach to the piano and the piano sonata.** We can sense in his sonatas Beethoven's almost symbiotic relationship with the piano. First, he composed far more piano sonatas than symphonies, string quartets, or any other major genre. Second, he single-handedly elevated its status from an amusement for young women to serious music for public performance. Third, his piano sonatas document his unparalleled growth as a composer more fully than any other genre in which he worked. And most compellingly, the sonatas were his laboratory—the place where he experimented with bold new approaches and ideas, which he often used subsequently in other genres, such as the string quartets and symphonies.

11-3   **Understand Beethoven's conception of a four-movement symphony as an integrated musical statement.** Like the Classical symphonies of Haydn, Mozart, and others, Beethoven's Fifth Symphony has four movements in the typical sequence. However, Beethoven expands, integrates, and individualizes these procedures in ways that stamp the work as a product of the nineteenth century. The Fifth Symphony is remarkable for its integration and distinct identity. Not only the first movement but the entire work reverberates with the famous opening motive.

11-4   **Grasp the impact of Beethoven and his music.** We sense in Beethoven's music that he is almost compelled to follow his own path rather than write on demand. No other composer has gone through such a dramatic evolution in style. That he continued to develop as a composer despite the seemingly insurmountable obstacle that his deafness imposed makes his achievement even more compelling. His innovations would have a decisive influence on most of the important composers of the 1800s.

TIMELINE : 1750–1830   *CONTINUED>*

1750   1770

1750–1820 Classical era

1775–1783 American Revolution

1769–1830 Industrial Revolution

1770 Birth of Beethoven

Chapter 11 in Review

GLOSSARY TERMS

11-3   **scherzo and trio** More modern version of the minuet and trio, typically the third movement in a four-movement instrumental work. In the Classical style, scherzo (minuet) and trio movements almost always have three major sections, in an ABA pattern: the scherzo (or minuet); the trio, which is in a different key; and a repetition of the scherzo. Each major section is most often in rounded binary form. Scherzo originally designated a composition or movement with a playful, high-spirited character. However, with Beethoven, the term came to refer more to the form of the work than the character. (p. 154)

THINKING CRITICALLY ABOUT MUSIC

1. Compare Beethoven's original version of the Fifth Symphony's first movement with Walter Murphy's 1976 disco hit "A Fifth of Beethoven." Assess the effect of the added (and subtracted) elements on the emotional impact of the movement.

2. In both the "Pathétique" sonata and the Fifth Symphony, Beethoven uses strong contrasts in several parameters—tempo, dynamics, timbre—to help convey his expressive message. Compare Beethoven's use of contrast with strong contrasts in rock-era classics, such as The Beatles' "Lucy in the Sky with Diamonds" or "A Day in the Life," or Nirvana's "Smells Like Teen Spirit." Do you think that the use of strong contrasts in these tracks coordinates with their expressive intent? In what ways are the experiences similar to your experiences with Beethoven? In what ways are they different?

TIMELINE : 1750–1830 *CONTINUED*

1790   1810   1830

1789–1799 French Revolution

1793–1822 Beethoven composes piano sonatas

1804–1815 Napoleon emperor of France

1806–1807 Beethoven composes Fifth Symphony

1820–1900 Romantic era

1824 Beethoven completes Ninth Symphony

1827 Death of Beethoven

1830 Nationalist revolutions in Europe

CHAPTER IN REVIEW

12-1   Chart the development of diverse trends in nineteenth-century musical life: music publishing, music education, musical instruments and technologies, and entertainment.

12-2   Describe the characteristics of Romanticism.

12-3   Discuss the increasing stratification of musical life, particularly in the latter part of the nineteenth century.

TIMELINE : 1820–1900   *CONTINUED>*

1820

1820–1900 Romantic era

    1825 Alpheus Babcock creates one-piece metal piano frame

    1826 Birth of Stephen Foster

    1827 Death of Beethoven

    1829 Mendelssohn launches Bach revival

    1830 Nationalist revolutions in Europe

1840

1853–1876 Richard Wagner writes *Der Ring des Nibelungen*

1857 First American music conservatory is founded

GLOSSARY TERMS

12-1 **musicologist** Scholar who researches the history of music (p. 164)

12-2 **Romanticism** Cultural movement of the nineteenth century that valued subjectivity, feeling, and inspiration and venerated individuals whose work expressed those values; a Romantic sensibility that had a focus on individuality, an obsession with size, and a fascination with the exotic (p. 167)

    virtuosity Performance skills far beyond the norm; extraordinary technical abilities (p. 167)

    etude Musical work designed to develop a particular technical skill (p. 167)

    atonality System of tonal organization in which pitches do not focus around a tonic (p. 170)

    Gesamtkunstwerk Total work of art, or work that synthesizes all the arts; associated with Richard Wagner (p. 171)

THINKING CRITICALLY ABOUT MUSIC

1. In the nineteenth century, music publishing brought a wide range of music to a mass audience. To get a sense of its impact, trace some aspect of the history of music dissemination—radio, recording, television, film—in your grandparents' era, your parents' era, and your experience since 2000. Consider in particular these two aspects: How has ease of access improved, and how has the quality of the original musical source document improved?

2. The stylistic fragmentation of contemporary life parallels in certain respects the stratification of musical life in the latter part of the nineteenth century. Using your music collection (and perhaps those of your family and friends) as a point of departure, consider the diversity of your collection(s) from three perspectives:
   a. What is the function of a particular track (listening only, dancing, and so on)?
   b. To what extent do the tracks represent different eras?
   c. To what extent do the different styles and genres reflect differences in social status?

TIMELINE : 1820–1900 *CONTINUED*

1860   1880   1900

1859 Darwin publishes *On the Origin of Species*

1861–1865 American Civil War

1877 Edison invents first phonograph

1894 First "records" are issued

CHAPTER IN REVIEW

13-1 **Describe the flowering of song in the nineteenth century.** Song held a central place in nineteenth-century musical life. Song with piano accompaniment flourished as never before, in all strata of society. Choral music ranged from simple hymn settings to grand works for chorus and orchestra. Music for stage entertainment was often disseminated via sheet music in arrangements for voice and piano.

13-2 **Recognize the art song, through the *Lieder* of Franz Schubert.** The goal of the art song was to set poetry with music of comparable quality. This practice took shape first in German-speaking Europe, most decisively and importantly in the *Lieder* of Schubert. Schubert established the art song as a significant Romantic musical genre. Schubert's early songs are harbingers of Romanticism. Both the genre and Schubert's realizations of it helped usher in a new era and turn the page on the Classical style. Schubert's *Lieder* manifest the Romantic ascendancy of feeling over thought.

13-3 **Encounter the song cycle through Robert Schumann's *Dichterliebe*.** Beginning in the late eighteenth century, *Lieder* with piano accompaniment were often published in collections, rather than individually. Early composers of *Lieder* composed song cycles, groups of thematically connected poems set as songs that are compiled into a single large-scale work. Schubert played the key role in establishing the song cycle as the large-scale counterpart to the *Lied*. However, his two major cycles represent only a small fraction of his total *Lieder* output. That was not the case with Robert Schumann, who composed four song cycles in a single year.

13-4 **Reexamine the musical and social boundaries between sacred and secular, and religious and spiritual, through an exploration of Brahms's *Requiem*.** In disassociating his requiem not only from its Catholic context but also from a Christian orientation, Brahms divorced spiritual from religious. His *Requiem* blurs boundaries between religious and spiritual, sacred and secular, personal and universal.

TIMELINE : 1815–1900

CONTINUED>

1815

1815 Schubert publishes *Erlkönig*

1820-1900 Romantic era

1821 The first Schubertiade

1822 Handel and Haydn Society in Boston publishes Mason's first hymnal

1827 Death of Beethoven

1830 Nationalist revolutions in Europe

1835

1846–1864 Stephen Foster composes popular songs in America

GLOSSARY TERMS

13-2 *Lied* (plural, *Lieder*) In art music, a song for voice and piano in which both melody and accompaniment amplify dominant themes and images in the text (p. 174)

art song Nineteenth- and early twentieth-century song that set poetry to music of comparable quality (p. 174)

Schubertiade An evening of music composed by Franz Schubert, often with Schubert as accompanist (p. 175)

through-composed form Form in which there is no large-scale formal repetition (p. 176)

13-3 **song cycle** Group of thematically connected poems set as songs that are compiled into a single large-scale work (p. 180)

13-4 **deism** A belief originating in the seventeenth century that asserted that the divine could be understood through reason alone (p. 183)

requiem A mass offered to honor the dead (p. 183)

Dies irae A section of the Requiem Mass that deals with the day of judgment (p. 184)

THINKING CRITICALLY ABOUT MUSIC

1. Find a significant singer-songwriter recording that features voice and a single accompanying instrument, such as a guitar or piano. Go back as far as an early song by Bob Dylan or a track from one of Joni Mitchell's early albums, or stay more recent with a song by an artist such as Ani Di Franco or Tracy Chapman. Listen carefully to the lyrics and consider the message. Then listen to melody and accompaniment, and consider in what ways they amplify or modify the message of the lyrics. Do you hear any common ground between the approach of the singer-songwriter and Schubert in his *Lieder*?

TIMELINE : 1815–1900 *CONTINUED*

| 1855 | 1875 | 1895 |

1861–1865 American Civil War

1869 First performance of Brahms's *Ein deutsches Requiem*

1820-1900 Romantic era

CHAPTER IN REVIEW

14-1 Explain how the piano became the most common vehicle for the first generation of star soloists during the nineteenth century. Beginning in the 1830s, Romantic pianist-composers brought a Romantic sensibility to eighteenth-century forms, such as the prelude, sonata, and variation set, and to dances. They invented a host of new forms, some literary, some visual, and some free forms.

14-2 Describe the conservative approach of early Romantic piano composers Robert and Clara Schumann, and Felix and Fanny Mendelssohn. The more conservative early Romantics were German: the Schumanns and the Mendelssohns. Their conservative approach is evident in their approach to the piano; in closer adherence to established forms; in steadier and less contrasting rhythms; in thicker textures; and in more predictable harmony.

14-3 Contrast the conservative approach with the more progressive approach of Paris-based piano composers Frédéric Chopin and Franz Liszt. The most important of these Romantics were Paris-based expatriates: Chopin from Poland and Liszt from Hungary. Their piano music featured more elaborate figuration and accompaniment, more open textures, greater dynamic range, more flexibility in tempo, and more adventurous forms and harmonies.

TIMELINE : 1820–1900   *CONTINUED>*

1820   1840

1820–1900 Romantic era

1827 Death of
Beethoven

1830 Nationalist
revolutions in Europe

1830s Decade of virtuoso
composer-pianists

GLOSSARY TERMS

14-2   **romance**   Short, lyrical piano piece (p. 191)

14-3   **prelude**   Originally a brief introduction to a longer work; a short work for piano (p. 195)

       two-phrase parallel period   Two phrases that begin the same way and end differently, the first phrase typically ending with a comma-style cadence and the second with a period-style cadence (p. 195)

THINKING CRITICALLY ABOUT MUSIC

To experience the growth of virtuosity, compare the Tchaikovsky violin concerto with Vivaldi's "Spring," compare the Chopin etude with the Mozart sonata, and trace the development of virtuosic rock guitar playing by noting the progression from the 1950s (Chuck Berry) through the 1960s (Jimi Hendrix) into the 1970s (Eddie Van Halen) and beyond.

TIMELINE : 1820–1900 *CONTINUED*

1860	1880	1900

1820–1900
Romantic era

CHAPTER IN REVIEW

15-1 **Understand how Gioachino Rossini inspired a renaissance of Italian opera through his innovative approach to integrating music and drama.** Rossini's success was the result of a fresh and appealing approach to the use of music in drama. He understood better than any composer before him how to shape familiar musical materials for dramatic effect. His operas would inspire a renaissance of Italian opera. His operas and those of his successors, most notably Giuseppe Verdi and Giacomo Puccini, have retained their appeal and remained at the heart of the operatic repertory into the twenty-first century.

15-2 **Describe how Giuseppe Verdi reformed Italian opera.** The glory years of Italian opera began around the middle of the nineteenth century, mainly in the mature operas of Giuseppe Verdi, who reformed Italian opera by making it more real.

15-3 **Differentiate *opéra comique* from other types of nineteenth-century opera through an understanding of Bizet's *Carmen*.** Originally, *opéra comique* mixed humorous dialogue with preexisting melodies. By mid-century, *opéra comique* was wholesome family entertainment. In composing an opera that was neither funny nor sentimental, Bizet hoped to reform and invigorate *opéra comique*.

15-4 **Recognize how Richard Wagner changed music and opera.** Wagner challenged basic assumptions about opera and music in general. Striking sounds and melodic ideas (leitmotifs) repeat only as demanded by the text rather than recurring regularly.

TIMELINE : 1815–1900

CONTINUED>

1815

1835

1816 Premiere of Rossini's *The Barber of Seville*

1820–1900
Romantic era

1827 Death of
Beethoven

1830 Nationalist
revolutions in
Europe

Chapter 15 in Review

GLOSSARY TERMS

15-2 **bel canto** Literally, "beautiful singing" in Italian; a vocal style that prizes evenness of sound, vocal agility, and sweetness (p. 203)

verismo (realism) Nineteenth-century Italian literary movement adapted to opera; sordid, violent stories often portrayed in the libretti (p. 207)

15-3 **habanera** An Afro-Cuban dance genre (p. 210)

contradanza English "country dance"; French *contredanse* (p. 210)

15-4 **music drama** Term for Wagner's later works that distinguishes them from more conventional operas, encompassing such traits as "endless melody," the use of leitmotifs, and expansion of the orchestra and its role (p. 214)

reminiscence motive Theme used to recall a character, mood, or event (p. 214)

leitmotif Motive or theme assigned to a character, object, emotion, or event in a Wagnerian music drama (p. 214)

THINKING CRITICALLY ABOUT MUSIC

1. To explore Wagner's concept of a *Gesamtkunstwerk*— a total artwork—in a more contemporary setting, compare a contemporary track that also exists as a music video and consider these questions:
   a. What additional art forms are represented?
   b. To what extent are these additional art forms integral to the expression of the video?
   c. After viewing the video, does the audio-only version of the track seem incomplete?

TIMELINE : 1815–1900 *CONTINUED*

1855

1875

1895

1853 Premiere of Verdi's *La traviata*

1875 Bizet's *Carmen*

1853–1876 Richard Wagner writes *Der Ring des Nibelungen*

1820–1900 Romantic era

1861–1865 American Civil War

1871 German unification

CHAPTER IN REVIEW

16-1 **Describe the evolution of the symphony orchestra and the symphony in the nineteenth century.** Nineteenth-century symphony orchestras became an integral part of the cultural life in their cities, joining opera companies as the most prestigious resident musical institutions. The dramatic improvement in conventional instruments—woodwinds, brass, and percussion—and the invention of new instruments, most notably the tuba, were a key reason for the expansion of the nineteenth-century orchestra. The symphony was the most prestigious genre in nineteenth-century orchestral music.

16-2 **Understand Hector Berlioz's transformation of the orchestra through an exploration of his *Symphonie fantastique*.** Berlioz's *Symphonie fantastique* is a true original, featuring a design dictated more by a narrative than by formal conventions; a new expressive balance between sound and melody, which often leans toward sound; the symbolic use of familiar materials and melodies; and the exploration of new sound possibilities.

16-3 **Through an examination of one of Brahms's symphonies, describe how the Romantic symphony expanded on the tradition of Haydn, Mozart, and Beethoven.** Among the most popular and prestigious genres in nineteenth-century orchestral music was the symphony. Inherited from the eighteenth century, it reflected Beethoven's continuing influence on nineteenth-century orchestral music.

TIMELINE : 1815–1900

CONTINUED>

1815

1835

1820–1900 Romantic era

1827 Death of Beethoven

1830 Nationalist revolutions in Europe

1830 Berlioz's *Symphonie fantastique* is first performed in December

GLOSSARY TERMS

16-2   **idée fixe** "Fixed idea"; melodic representation of the object of the artist's obsession (p. 225)

      program symphony Symphony whose movements depict a series of scenes relating to the work's overall program, or theme (p. 225)

      tone poem Programmatic, one-movement, Romantic orchestral genre (p. 228)

16-3   **absolute music** Music whose aesthetic value is self-contained and does not require any extramusical reference, such as lyrics, drama, dance, or a program (p. 229)

THINKING CRITICALLY ABOUT MUSIC

1. Among the new sounds of the last part of the twentieth century were those produced by digital synthesis. These included sounds that were similar to existing timbres (synthesized sounds) as well as completely novel sounds. To explore once again the impact of timbral choices on sound identity, revisit Haydn's symphony and Tchaikovsky's orchestration of the Mozart variations. Then find a contemporary (post-1980) cover version of a rock song from the 1950s or 1960s, and compare the timbres.

TIMELINE : 1815–1900 *CONTINUED*

1855   1875   1895

1877 Brahms composes Second Symphony

1861–1865 American Civil War

1862–1876 Brahms works on his First Symphony

1820–1900 Romantic era

1871 German unification

CHAPTER IN REVIEW

17-1 **Encounter the more technically difficult, soloist-dominated concerto of the nineteenth century through a movement from Tchaikovsky's violin concerto.** In the Baroque era, the soloist came from within the orchestra; in the Classical era, the soloist competed with the orchestra; in the Romantic era, the soloist dominated the orchestra.

17-2 **Grasp the changing role of dance and dance music in the nineteenth century.** The waltz reflected the reluctant but relentless movement toward a more egalitarian society in Europe and North America. Ballet represented the emergence of dance as an independent expressive art. These and other trends, such as the use of dance rhythms in popular song, evidenced the increasing importance of dance.

17-3 **Recognize the conscious nationalism exemplified by Dvořák's music as an important trend in European cultural life during the latter half of the nineteenth century.** The conscious nationalism in Dvořák's music was a continuation of the dominant international style.

TIMELINE : 1815–1900

CONTINUED>

1815

1816 A new dance, the waltz, scandalizes the English court

1820–1900 Romantic era

1827 Death of Beethoven

1835

1830 Nationalist revolutions in Europe

1830 Berlioz's *Symphonie fantastique* is first performed in December

1830s Ballet becomes independent art form

1848 First Pan-Slavic Congress in Prague, Bohemia

GLOSSARY TERMS

17-2 **ballet** An independent, expressive dance genre in which movement and music tell the story (p. 238)

waltz Social dance in a fast triple meter (p. 240)

17-3 **nationalism** In music, a nineteenth-century movement that sought to portray a uniquely national identity by drawing on the legends, myths, history, and literature of the people; creating vocal music in their own language; and drawing on folk song and dance (p. 242)

THINKING CRITICALLY ABOUT MUSIC

1. To experience the growth of virtuosity, compare the Tchaikovsky violin concerto with Vivaldi's "Spring"; compare the Chopin etude with the Mozart sonata; and trace the development of virtuosic rock guitar playing by noting the progression from the 1950s (Chuck Berry) through the 1960s (Jimi Hendrix), into the 1970s (Eddie Van Halen) and beyond.

2. *White Nights* (1985) stars dancers Mikhail Baryshnikov and Gregory Hines. Compare three scenes: the opening ballet in which Baryshnikov dances with death, personified by a ballerina; the dance done to the song by Vladimir Vysotsky; and the dance number he performs with Gregory Hines. (All three scenes are on YouTube.) In what ways is the dancing expressive, and how does the mode of expression change with the situation?

3. To explore a more contemporary connection between dance rhythms and national identity, find two contrasting Bob Marley songs, one that deals with topical matters (such as "Get Up, Stand Up") and one that doesn't (such as "Is This Love"). Consider to what extent you associate the reggae rhythm with Jamaica and what images it brings to mind. Then find non-Jamaican music that uses a reggae rhythm (The Clash and The Police are good sources). Do the other features of the track you chose affect your sense of association between reggae rhythm and national identity?

TIMELINE : 1815–1900 *CONTINUED*

1855	1875	1895

1861–1865 American Civil War

1871 German unification

1878 First set of Dvořák's Slavonic Dances published

1820–1900 Romantic era

CHAPTER IN REVIEW

18-1 **Recognize the widespread impact of technology on every aspect of music in the twentieth century.** A century of technological innovation, from sound recording to new modes of transmission such as radio, to new instruments, to developments in digital technology, had a comprehensive impact on every aspect of music: its sounds, creation, performance, dissemination, and ways people listen to and learn it.

18-2 **Describe the major musical developments during the twentieth century.** Popular music emerged as the dominant commercial force in musical life and continued to evolve during the century. The classical music world became fragmented amid a relentless search in all directions for new sounds and modes of expression. Folk traditions from around the world were reclaimed and preserved. And there was lively ongoing cross-pollination among music of all types.

18-3 **Paint a picture of the fragmented sound world of the twentieth century in terms of changes in the musical elements.** The expanded sound world of the twentieth century came from a host of innovations: new instruments, new vocal and instrumental sounds, new combinations of instruments, and even a broader understanding of what constitutes a "musical" sound. Novel modes of pitch organization, including atonality, appeared during the first few decades of the twentieth century. A large body of music developed that had no discernible melody, from some of the experimental music composed in the middle of the century to techno and rap. No longer was it assumed that melody should be the expressive focus of a composition. Rhythm, largely subordinate to melody as a source of musical interest in the eighteenth and nineteenth centuries, became more prominent in twentieth-century music. Finally, several new conceptions of form emerged in the first two decades of the twentieth century.

TIMELINE : 1875–1960

CONTINUED>

1875

1877 Thomas Edison invents cylinder phonograph recorder

1892 First commercial disc records produced

1900

1908 Bartók and Kodály begin collecting folk recordings in eastern Europe

1910s Two-sided phonograph discs predominate

1919 The first electronic instrument, the theremin, is invented

1920 KDKA transmits first commercial radio broadcast

GLOSSARY TERMS

18-1   **theremin** The first electronic instrument, which featured two antennae: one to regulate pitch, the other to regulate volume (p. 250)

     synthesizer Instrument capable of generating sounds electronically (p. 251)

     analog synthesizer Electronic musical synthesizer that generates sound by varying voltage (p. 251)

     sampling Transfer of a recorded sound from its source into another recording (p. 252)

     MIDI (Musical Instrument Digital Interface) Protocol that enables communication between digital instruments and devices (p. 252)

18-2   **ethnomusicology** The study of music within particular cultures (p. 254)

18-3   **atonality** The principle of avoiding both the tonic and its corollary; organizing harmony and melody so as to move away from and return to the tonic in a coherent fashion (p. 256)

THINKING CRITICALLY ABOUT MUSIC

1. Bring the discussion of the impact of technology on music into the present by surveying innovations and changes in the creation, production, and dissemination of music since 2000. Which ones have had the biggest impact on your experience of music?

TIMELINE : 1875–1960 *CONTINUED*

1925	1950	1975
1925 Electrical technology replaces acoustic technology of early radio	1950s Television explodes as commercial enterprise	
1927 The first "talking" movie	Early 1950s Moog synthesizer is commercially produced	
1930s Magnetic tape recorder is developed in Germany		

CHAPTER IN REVIEW

19-1   **Describe the traits of expressionist music and atonality through an understanding of the music of Arnold Schoenberg.** The first Western atonal music appeared after the turn of the twentieth century, most notably in the compositions of Schoenberg. In abandoning tonality, he left behind a musical tradition that reached back more than a millennium; his was the most radical change in pitch organization in the history of music. It was both a consequence and a negation of the most sophisticated method of organizing pitch up to that point: common practice harmony. Schoenberg's emphasis on bold melodic lines, distinctive and sharply contrasting tone colors, and extremes is comparable to expressionist artists' favoring color and gesture over representation.

19-2   **Become familiar with impressionism in the arts, specifically in the music of Claude Debussy.** Debussy was arguably the most visually oriented of the major composers. He channeled these influences into a musical aesthetic that embodied the influence of impressionism in the visual arts as well as the new cinematography.

19-3   **Hear how composers such as Igor Stravinsky embedded "primitive" elements in ultramodern settings.** In *The Rite of Spring*, Stravinsky synthesized the ancient and the avant-garde. He embedded "primitive" elements in ultramodern settings: dissonant harmonies, irregular patterns and rhythms, melodies without cadences, densely layered textures, and instrumentation that exploited new orchestral timbres.

TIMELINE : 1870S–1920

CONTINUED>

1870

1870s–1880s Impressionism begins to flourish in the arts

1885

1894 Debussy composes *Prelude to the Afternoon of a Faun*

GLOSSARY TERMS

19-1 **expressionism** Late nineteenth- and early twentieth-century movement in the arts that sought to convey the deep emotions that lie under the surface of—and are often obscured by—objective reality (p. 259)

Sprechstimme "Speech voice"; vocal style between speech and singing required in Arnold Schoenberg's music (p. 261)

commedia dell'arte "Comedy of the artists [of improvisation]"; a type of improvised theater that developed in Italy during the fifteenth century (p. 262)

19-2 **impressionism** Late nineteenth- and early twentieth-century movement in the arts that favored exploration of elements such as light, color, and sound over literal representation (p. 265)

whole-tone scale Scale that divides the octave into six equal segments a whole tone apart (A whole tone, or whole step, equals two half-steps.) (p. 266)

19-3 *col legno* Violin technique that involves tapping the wooden part of the bow on the strings (p. 271)

THINKING CRITICALLY ABOUT MUSIC

1. *Sprechstimme* was the first of several instances in the twentieth century of a vocal technique that was more than speech but less than singing. Compare the relationship between vocal technique and expressive impact in Schoenberg's music with another "in-between" vocal approach, such as the "talking blues" of Woody Guthrie and Bob Dylan, or Lou Reed's sort-of-spoken, sort-of-sung vocal style with the Velvet Underground. In your judgment, does the avoidance of singing in each case enhance or detract from the impact? Why?

2. Compare impressionism in music and art. First, listen to a recording of one of Debussy's *Images*—there are two sets for piano and one for orchestra—and select one that appeals to you. Then find a detailed reproduction of a painting by Monet or another impressionist. Consider in particular these two questions: What common ground, if any, do you find between impressionism in art and in music? How does the fact that Debussy is working with sound in time affect his efforts to translate images into music?

3. Visit YouTube to see two visual interpretations of the opening movements of *The Rite of Spring*: the ballet (if available, view the re-creation of Nijinsky's original choreography by the Joffrey Ballet) and the opening of Walt Disney's *Fantasia*. Which version seems to you to be more effective? Why?

TIMELINE : 1870S–1920 *CONTINUED*

1900	1915	1930

1899 Sigmund Freud publishes *Interpretation of Dreams*

1909 Ballets Russes formed

1910 Kandinsky organizes Der Blaue Reiter, which Schoenberg joins

1911 Schoenberg's *Harmonielehre* proclaims "emancipation of dissonance"

1912 Schoenberg composes *Pierrot lunaire*

1913 Riot breaks out at premiere of Stravinsky's *Rite of Spring*

1914–1918 World War I

CHAPTER IN REVIEW

20-1 **Describe Arnold Schoenberg's and Anton Webern's approach to serial composition.** Schoenberg and Webern committed fully to serial composition and worked through its implications for other elements. By taking virtually every element to its extreme and divorcing pitch organization from tonality in any form, Webern skewed musical "reality" to the point of abstraction.

20-2 **Recognize the substantial differences between Igor Stravinsky's early compositions and his later neoclassical works.** Between 1913 and 1930, Stravinsky composed an astonishing amount of music. These new works were remarkably varied in genre and style. From the 1920s to early 1950s, many of Stravinsky's works were heavily influenced by neoclassicism. Cumulatively, Stravinsky's neoclassical works are at once deeply indebted to the past and clearly removed from it.

TIMELINE : 1900–1945

CONTINUED>

1900

1912

ca. 1920 Schoenberg and Hauer develop serialism

1920s Stravinsky embraces neoclassicism

1920s–1930s Neoclassicism flourishes

GLOSSARY TERMS

20-1   **equal temperament** Consistent division of the octave into twelve equidistant half-steps (p. 275)

chromatic pitch Pitch not in the scale of a particular key (p. 275)

serialism (twelve-tone composition) System of pitch organization in which all twelve pitches within the octave are organized in a series rather than organized hierarchically (p. 275)

tone row In serial composition, the arrangement of all twelve pitches within the octave in a particular sequence (p. 275)

retrograde Reversal of the original sequence of twelve pitches in a serial composition (backward) (p. 275)

inversion In serial composition, reversing the direction of the intervals between pitches of the tone row (p. 275)

20-2   **neoclassicism** Any trend in the arts characterized by the revival or reinterpretation of classical values of harmony, clarity, restraint, and adherence to established practices, as embodied in the artworks of Greek and Roman civilization; in music, an umbrella term identifying a body of twentieth-century music that has in common a rejection of Romantic and post-Romantic musical values and a return to, or reworking of, many of the musical features characteristic of eighteenth-century music (p. 279)

THINKING CRITICALLY ABOUT MUSIC

1. Consider the idea of neoclassicism in popular music by listening carefully to The Beatles' "Yesterday" and relating it to the music of yesterday—that is, the popular songs of the modern era. In what ways are the form, harmony, melodic construction, and melody-oriented texture reminiscent of this earlier songwriting style? What features place the song in the 1960s? Then listen to a cover of the song by Frank Sinatra (or other pre-rock pop singer). In what ways, if any, does this pop version remove the "neo" dimension of this song?

TIMELINE : 1900–1945 CONTINUED

1924   1936   1948

1931–1934 Webern composes serialist Concerto for Nine Instruments

1935–1936 Chavez composes Sinfonia India

1939–1945 World War II

CHAPTER IN REVIEW

21-1 **Describe how Charles Ives embodied a new American approach to musical nationalism.** Ives's art serves his vision of America: it is populist, patriotic, and particular to New England and its long history. In works like *Three Places in New England*, Ives created an all-American musical tradition. He achieved his implicit objective: to create a uniquely innovative new kind of art music. It is music that is both populist and elite, and a music that far transcended the more conventional musical styles enjoyed by the cultivated members of American society. No other composer discussed in this book conveyed such a specific cultural identity. Ives's music would not become known until years, even decades, after its composition. As it did, it would inspire a particularly American openness to new sounds.

21-2 **Understand how Aaron Copland became a major player in a new kind of musical nationalism that peaked during the 1930s and 1940s.** Copland's vision gave America a third regional musical style, one that evoked the West rather than Ives's New England or Gershwin's New York. But although Copland's populist style certainly evokes his nation, other work from the late 1930s and early 1940s makes clear that the American sound of Copland's music transcends an exclusively regional identity.

21-3 **Recognize how Béla Bartók expressed musical nationalism in the language of Hungarian folk music.** Bartók's fieldwork represented a breakthrough in the preservation and transformation of folk music. No major composer left a more comprehensive record of involvement with the folk music of his homeland than Bartók.

21-4 **Describe the challenging musical path that Sergei Prokofiev traced in finding artistic expression within a restrictive, government-imposed framework.** Bartók's search for national identity came from within. In Prokofiev's Soviet Union, national identity was imposed from above: the guardians of socialist realism required that works of art be accessible to the proletariat so that they could be used as propaganda tools. Prokofiev stands apart, given the complex crosscurrents among personal ambition, patriotism, and political circumstances that shaped his career decisions.

TIMELINE : 1900–1945
CONTINUED>

1900

1912

1904 Bartók begins field-work collecting folk songs

1914 Charles Ives composes
Three Places in New England

1914–1918 World War I

CHAPTER 21 IN REVIEW

GLOSSARY TERMS

21-4   **mickey mousing** The close synchronization of music
with on-screen action (p. 297)

THINKING CRITICALLY ABOUT MUSIC

1.   In our discussion, it was suggested that Ives created an American sound. Explore the idea that the
influence of folk and country music gives rock
an American sound by comparing the music of
acts like the Allman Brothers, Alabama, or John
Mellencamp, with rock from the same time frame
by acts from outside the United States.

TIMELINE : 1900–1945 *CONTINUED*

1924	1936	1948

1927 The first "talking" movie

1936 Bartók composes *Music for
Strings, Percussion, and Celesta*

1944 Copland's
Appalachian Spring

1938 Prokofiev composes
Peter and the Wolf

1938 The film *Alexander Nevsky*
premieres

1939–1945 World War II

CHAPTER IN REVIEW

22-1 List the most significant aspects of ragtime's legacy. (1) The syncopated music itself; (2) the introduction of an authentic black music to white America; (3) Scott Joplin's blurring of boundaries between classical and vernacular; and (4) the transformation of popular music with African American elements.

22-2 Be familiar with the role of jazz in the evolution of American music. Recordings like "Hotter Than That" captured an exuberance that is unique to early jazz. Its rhythmic improvisations got musicians and listeners moving in time to the music: feet tapping, heads bobbing, fingers snapping. There is no known precedent for the swing heard in early jazz. No earlier music that has come down to us, not even ragtime, creates a comparably infectious rhythm. Jazz provided mainstream audiences with an instrumental introduction to the blues. Many of the first jazz recordings were blues in title and form, and captured key elements of the style and feeling. And when blues singers began to record in the 1920s, jazz musicians usually accompanied them.

22-3 Describe the place of classic blues as the first "first-person" music in American culture. Three features of this essentially African American music stand out: earthy, direct lyrics; the style of singing; and the use of blues conventions, including twelve-bar blues form, call and response, and a basic blues progression. Through performers like Bessie Smith and Ma Rainey and those they influenced, both the idea and the sound of the blues entered the popular mainstream in the 1920s.

22-4 Describe the blossoming of the modern age in popular music. The most popular music of the 1920s was a new, more modern popular song. The influence of African American vernacular styles was evident in both its composition and its performance. Ragtime was the primary source of the fox trot rhythm that underpinned the songs. Blues helped shape the more conversational rhythm of lyric and melody. The jazz band was the nucleus of the dance orchestras that proliferated in the 1920s. All three—ragtime, blues, and especially jazz—brought syncopation into popular song, and some of the expressiveness of blues and jazz gradually filtered into popular song performance.

22-5 Discover the sound of 1920s American popular song and its use in Broadway musicals. *Show Boat* was the first of the great modern musicals. Through the example of *Show Boat*, musical theater became a more elite entertainment, even as vaudeville and the revue disappeared from the stage.

22-6 Appreciate how George Gershwin's "symphonic jazz" contributed to the new classics of the modern era. The composer who most successfully fused the vernacular sounds and rhythms of ragtime, jazz, and the blues with classical practice was George Gershwin. Gershwin's *Rhapsody in Blue* was unique in creating a new language for concert music, one based on the progressive popular music of the early twentieth century. More than eighty years after its premiere, *Rhapsody in Blue* remains the single most popular work written by an American composer.

TIMELINE : 1899–1930

CONTINUED>

1899

1899 Joplin, "Maple
Leaf Rag"

1900

GLOSSARY TERMS

22-1 **ragtime, rag** Syncopated American musical style of the late nineteenth and early twentieth centuries that began as dance music in the bordello districts of New Orleans (p. 301)

22-2 **jazz** A genre consisting of a group of popular styles primarily for listening; usually distinguished from the other popular music of an era by greater rhythmic freedom (more syncopation and/or less insistent beat keeping), extensive improvisation, and more-adventurous harmony (p. 302)

front line The wind and brass instruments (or other melody-line instruments) in a jazz combo; from the position of the players on the bandstand, standing in a line in front of the rhythm instruments (p. 304)

rhythm section The part of a musical group that supplies the rhythmic and harmonic foundation of a performance; usually includes at least one chord instrument (guitar, piano, or keyboard), a bass instrument, and a percussion instrument (typically the drum set) (p. 304)

swing Rhythmic play over a four-beat rhythm (p. 304)

improvisation Creating music spontaneously rather than performing a previously learned song the same way every time; one of the key elements of jazz (p. 304)

scat singing Improvised instrumental-style vocal with no words (p. 305)

22-3 **race records** Recordings by black artists aimed primarily at an African American audience (p. 307)

blues Quintessentially African American music with its roots in Africa and the Mississippi Delta; created by Southern blacks sometime after the Civil War; characterized by twelve-bar form, call and response between voice and instrument, bent (or "blue") notes, and phrases that start high and end low (p. 307)

griot Historian and shaman of an African tribe, who often sang and spoke his stories while accompanying himself on a plucked string instrument (p. 307)

folk blues Down-home blues from the post–Civil War rural South, especially in the Mississippi Delta (p. 307)

classic blues Commercially recorded blues (p. 308)

twelve-bar blues A strophic form with well-established conventions (p. 308)

chorus Each complete statement of the twelve-bar blues form (p. 308)

call and response Regular exchanges between contrasting voices, common in African music (p. 308)

blues progression Series using the three basic chords of common practice harmony as its foundation (p. 308)

blue note "Bent," expressive note (p. 309)

22-4 **revue** A series of song and dance numbers held loosely together by a topical story line (p. 311)

22-5 **musical comedy** Lighthearted stage entertainment born in the early twentieth century (p. 311)

22-6 **rhapsody** Piece that moves from section to section as if cutting or fading between scenes in a film (p. 316)

THINKING CRITICALLY ABOUT MUSIC

1. "Rap is the final stage in the rhythmic evolution of American popular music that began with the introduction of African-influenced syncopations via ragtime." Test the accuracy of this by first comparing rhythms in "The Entertainer" to rap tracks, then comparing the rap tracks to today's music.

2. Armstrong's jazz is exuberant and high-spirited. Find a track in your music collection that you think approaches its upbeat mood. What common features do you find? What differences?

3. In his "folk opera" *Porgy and Bess*, Gershwin portrays African Americans in a genre associated with classical music. Select a number from his opera, and compare his methods of suggesting black identity with Jerome Kern's in *Show Boat*.

TIMELINE : 1899–1930 *CONTINUED*

1911	1922	1933
1914–1918 World War I	1924 Gershwin's *Rhapsody in Blue* composed and performed	
1917 Original Dixieland Jazz Band first records	1925 F. Scott Fitzgerald publishes *The Great Gatsby*	
1920 Nineteenth Amendment gives women the vote	December 27, 1927 *Show Boat* premieres on Broadway	
1920s Harlem Renaissance; the Jazz Age	1928 Bessie Smith records "Empty Bed Blues"	
	1929 Stock market crash; beginning of Great Depression	

CHAPTER IN REVIEW

23-1 Outline the range, sources, and innovations of the postwar avant-garde in music. The most immediately apparent innovations of the postwar avant-garde were an array of new sounds. They came from four principal sources: (1) innovative performance techniques on conventional instruments; (2) radical modifications of conventional instruments, such as Cage's prepared piano; (3) the invention of new instruments; and (4) the use of "found" sounds, as in *musique concrète*.

23-2 Explain the place of John Cage in the postwar American avant-garde. In his early compositions, Cage was, in effect, inventing new sounds and new sound combinations—or at the very least, incorporating them into a musical experience. His sonic explorations follow the lead of Henry Cowell, the great American experimentalist whom Cage would describe as "the open sesame for new music in America."

23-3 Appreciate the contributions of Edgard Varèse and electronic music to the avant-garde. Beginning with *Amériques*, his first major work, Varèse made a radical musical evolution. Varèse was prepared to abandon pitch as necessary. Varèse favored unconventional sound sources, especially those that did not produce definite pitch. They include early electronic instruments, sound-producing devices not typically associated with musical composition, and percussion instruments. Varèse was especially intrigued by the potential of electronic instruments. At the time that Varèse composed *Poème électronique*, music created on and "performed by" a tape recorder was a novelty, and a dramatic departure from tradition.

23-4 Describe Krzysztof Penderecki's work in the avant-garde's exploration of alternative pitch constructs. Penderecki was part of a wave of composers active after World War II who expanded the range of pitched sounds beyond the discrete twelve notes within the octave. By moving away from, then back to, definite pitch and eliminating all rhythms except the entrances and exits of the players, Penderecki considerably extends Schoenberg's innovations. There is virtually no conventional musical information to hear: no distinctive rhythms, no motives, no recurrent patterns. As a result, Penderecki's work provides a direct path to the subconscious.

TIMELINE : 1945–1965

CONTINUED>

1945

1950

1945 Atomic bomb dropped on Hiroshima

1946 Darmstadt summer courses

1946–1948 John Cage composes *Sonatas and Interludes*

1947 Cold War begins

GLOSSARY TERMS

23-1   **multiphonics**   For wind players, playing more than one pitch simultaneously on an instrument designed to play one note at a time (p. 319)

tone cluster   Effect produced by striking the piano keys with a fist or other objects (p. 319)

musique concrète   Music created by recording sounds not produced by musical instruments, extracting sound snippets, and subjecting them to various modifications (p. 320)

white noise   A broad band of multiple frequencies sounding simultaneously   (p. 320)

23-2   **prepared piano**   John Cage's technique of changing the piano's timbre by inserting objects among its strings (p. 320)

chance music   Twentieth-century avant-garde music that introduced the element of chance into composition and performance, such as determining the order of performance through the toss of a coin (p. 322)

23-3   **glissando**   Continuous, sliding change in pitch (p. 324)

THINKING CRITICALLY ABOUT MUSIC

1. Cage's preparation of the piano effectively turned the piano into a different instrument. Consider the role of Jimi Hendrix in creating a new sound world for the electric guitar, by comparing his early recordings to jazz and rock guitar playing from the 1950s and early 1960s. Do you think that the changes evident in Hendrix's music are as transformative as those of Cage?

2. Locate one or more recordings of completely synthesized electronica: no vocals or acoustic instruments. Compare the examples you chose with the excerpt from Varèse's *Poème électronique*. Do you find any common ground? Use your comparison to support or refute the idea.

3. Extreme distortion, as heard in post-1980 heavy metal, has the effect of blurring pitch. Consider the expressive impact of distortion in heavy metal (and by extension, in rock) by comparing early recordings by Black Sabbath with the 1980s recordings of acts such as Metallica, Slayer, Pantera, or Megadeth. Do you find any parallels between Penderecki's tone clusters and distortion so severe that pitch is all but indistinguishable?

TIMELINE : 1945–1965 *CONTINUED*

1955

1960

1965

1957 RCA Mark II synthesizer comes into use

1957 Launch of Sputnik

1957–1958 Edgard Varèse composes *Poème electronique*

1960 Krzysztof Penderecki composes *Tren*

CHAPTER IN REVIEW

24-1   **Trace the evolution of rock and roll into 1960s rock through an overview of Chuck Berry and the Beach Boys.** Rock ascended, through the 1960s, from a teen-themed tangent of postwar rhythm and blues. The pervasive use of rock rhythm and the replacement of the acoustic bass with the electric bass made rock music louder, more active, and more intrusive.

24-2   **Describe how rock grew up, in the music of Bob Dylan and The Beatles.** Rock became music of significance and influence in the hands of Bob Dylan and The Beatles. Rock became revolutionary because it changed both the sound of popular music and the messages it communicated. The generational difference might be summarized like this: pre-rock pop typically sought an escape from reality; rock intensified reality.

TIMELINE : 1955–1970

CONTINUED>

1955

1960

1955 Chuck Berry's "Maybellene" is released

1957 Launch of Sputnik

1963 "Surfin' U.S.A." is released

1964 Bob Dylan meets The Beatles

GLOSSARY TERMS

24-1 **boogie woogie** Blues piano style characterized by repetitive accompaniment patterns in a low register (p. 332)

overdubbing Process of recording additional sounds on an existing recording (p. 332)

24-2 **honky-tonk** Post–World War II country style popularized by such artists as Hank Williams (p. 334)

concept album Album unified by a particular creative theme (p. 336)

THINKING CRITICALLY ABOUT MUSIC

1. Neither the Dylan nor The Beatles track exemplifies the "core rock style" shaped by such acts as the Rolling Stones and The Who. Select a famous track by one of these bands, such as the Rolling Stones' "Jumpin' Jack Flash," and consider the trade-off between creating a great groove and making a significant statement. In your opinion, could tracks like "A Day in the Life" have conveyed their message with the same impact if they had used the kind of rock rhythm heard in the great Stones' tracks? Why or why not?

TIMELINE : 1955–1970 CONTINUED

1965   1970   1975

1967 The Beatles release *Sgt. Pepper*

1968 *Hair* opens on Broadway

CHAPTER IN REVIEW

25-1 Explain the place of minimalism in late twentieth-century music. Minimalist composers restored consonant harmony without turning back the clock. There are, of course, connections with the past. Reich's static, vibrating chords are pleasing sound objects in themselves. Pärt mixes familiar chords in unfamiliar progressions with his "tintinnabulized" harmonies; the effect is simultaneously old and new. Both bring a fresh perspective to familiar sounds. Minimalists also reconceived the way music presents time. Among the significant achievements of eighteenth-century musicians was the hierarchical organization of musical time. In minimalism, the intent is just the opposite: to free listeners from marking the passage of time at comfortable intervals. Reich achieves this goal by laying fast, undifferentiated rhythms over musical events that change slowly; in Pärt's music, *everything* moves slowly. The slowly changing harmony, open-ended rhythm, and anonymity of the performing resources—there are no soloists in either work, just choirs of voices and strings in Pärt's work and teams of musicians keeping time or playing riffs or oscillating chords in Reich's—help project a sense of connection to something beyond the self that is essentially spiritual. The spiritual dimension of Reich's music is nondenominational; Pärt's *Berlin Mass* universalizes a specifically Catholic expression of the mystical. Each in its own way connects to the spiritual impulse that inspired much earlier music.

25-2 Become aware of the first generation of women composers who have enjoyed status comparable to that of their male counterparts, through the work of Joan Tower and Ellen Taaffe Zwilich. Tower and Zwilich belong to the first generation of women composers who have enjoyed status comparable to that of their male counterparts, as evidenced by the number and quality of commissions, prizes, recordings, and publications. However, their achievements are exceptional. Despite greater activity, greater awareness, and greater professional support, women still lag well behind men in the customary measures of acceptance—performances, awards, teaching positions in composition. As several commentators have noted, parity in the profession is still a work in progress. Still, the door has been opened.

25-3 Describe the world of the late twentieth-century film composer through an exploration of the music of John Williams. Film composing became more eclectic in the 1970s, and it was arguably the most eclectic musical genre even in a time when eclecticism was a significant new direction in both vernacular and classical music. Williams has made his compositional reputation as a film composer; his music in other genres has been less successful. As we listen to his music, we do not sense a personal style so much as his ability to personalize existing styles in the service of the story.

TIMELINE : 1960–2000

CONTINUED>

1960
1960s–1970s Minimalism flourishes

1970

1977 John Williams receives Academy Award for *Star Wars*

Chapter 25 in Review

GLOSSARY TERMS

25-1 **minimalism** Umbrella term used to describe a diverse body of music with little activity or little change in activity; a comprehensive rejection of serialism and the European tradition from which it came (p. 340)

phasing Technique, popularized by Steve Reich, of playing the same phrase on two musical instruments, in slightly different tempos, to achieve a unique echoing effect (p. 341)

holy (sacred) minimalism European school of minimalist music, different from the music of Reich, Glass, and Adams most obviously because of its sacred subject matter and slow tempos and halting rhythms (p. 342)

tintinnabuli Arvo Pärt's characteristic technique that involves grouping two or more voices, one singing a modal melody and the others singing the pitches of a chord, to produce harmonies that vary from completely consonant to slightly dissonant (p. 343)

25-2 **eclecticism** Widely used twentieth-century compositional strategy that derives from diverse sources (p. 344)

neotonal music Music composed since the mid-1960s that shares the qualities of (1) orientation around a tonic, (2) heavy reliance on consonant intervals, and (3) motives created mainly or exclusively from consonant intervals, including scale fragments and triads (p. 345)

fanfare Short, ceremonial work for brass instruments and occasionally percussion (p. 345)

25-3 **spotting** Process during composing for film that involves viewing the film and determining those scenes where music will enhance the on-screen events (p. 349)

THINKING CRITICALLY ABOUT MUSIC

1. Brian Eno, a multitalented composer, performer, and producer, has been connected with minimalism and also important rock-era artists such as David Bowie and U2. Listen to a track from his *Music for Airports*, the recording that helped initiate the ambient music trend in rock, and compare it to the two minimalist works discussed in this chapter. What are common features? What are the most obvious differences?

2. To explore a feminine perspective in rock-era popular music, compare a song by a female singer-songwriter—from Joni Mitchell to Ani Di Franco—with a song recorded by a pop singer such as Mariah Carey or Christina Aguilera, who seldom writes her own material. Focus not only on the lyrics but also on the instrumental support: What aspects (if any) of the accompaniment are *not* gender neutral, in your opinion?

3. Get to know and evaluate the music in a favorite film of yours through this process. First, note the beginning and end points of each musical segment in the sound track. Then, add up the total time of the segments and compare it to the overall length of the film. Finally, pick two scenes where you find the music to be particularly effective, and for each scene list three aspects of the music that seem to coordinate with the on-screen action.

TIMELINE : 1960–2000 *CONTINUED*

1980

1990

2000

1985 Ellen Zwilich composes *Concerto Grosso 1985*

1986 Joan Tower composes first of five "fanfares"

CHAPTER IN REVIEW

26-1 Outline the gradual emergence of the world music movement. What we now know as the world music movement began as an effort by Europeans and North Americans to collect, preserve, and share music different from the music that they encountered in daily life, and to incorporate elements of these "outsider" sounds into their own music. Its roots go back to colonial times.

A true world music movement would require three important developments in the technology of sound recording; acceptance of alternatives to common practice tonality; and cultural shifts in attitudes toward the "other." In many cases, the revival and promotion of traditional music had a political dimension.

In popular music, the roots of the world music movement that took shape in the early 1980s go back to the late 1940s, and developed through interactions with rock in the 1960s and 1970s.

The world music movement includes a broad spectrum of musical styles and traditions. At one end of the spectrum is the preservation or replication of folk and regional traditions in as pure a state as possible. Covering a broad middle band are international-regional syntheses that feature collaborations among musicians from different cultures. Folk-connected concert music, so prominent in the first part of the century, largely disappeared in the decades after World War II.

26-2 Recognize authentic Celtic regional folk music replicated in as pure a state as possible. The jig has been a popular folk dance in the British Isles for over four centuries, and in North America for almost as long. The jig and other folk dances have also inspired popular songs and dances as well as aristocratic social dance music and dance-derived art music.

26-3 Understand the nature of popular African-international fusion. All along the upper west coast of sub-Saharan Africa, from Senegal to Zaire, native popular musics have flourished, with each country having its own popular style. Some styles are updated versions of older popular styles. Other styles are transformations of traditional music. National styles have moved freely from country to country.

"Ae Ae" features three of the most common features of African-international fusions: use of traditional African instruments; a complete Western rhythm section; and the approach to harmony, using the three core chords of European tonal harmony almost exclusively.

26-4 Appreciate Tan Dun's East–West art fusion. For most of the world, world music means some kind of commercial-traditional synthesis. But among those enjoying a special perspective on the integration of different musical traditions are those who have grown up in one culture and trained in another. Among those composers who have drawn on such an experience is the Chinese composer Tan Dun.

TIMELINE : 1539–2010 CONTINUED>

1539
1539 First mention of the sarabande

1657
1651 John Playford publishes The *English Dancing Master*

1682 Merolla notes use of drums in African religious ceremonies

GLOSSARY TERMS

26-1 **world music** Music from anywhere in the world that is not part of the established art and commercial music traditions of Europe and North America (p. 355)

fusion Hybrid style that draws on both the traditional music of a region and internationally known popular music styles (p. 355)

ethnomusicology The study of music within particular cultures (p. 357)

26-2 **jig** Sprightly dance popular throughout the British Isles (p. 360)

26-3 **balafon** Xylophone-like African instrument (p. 362)

kora African harp-lute made from a calabash (p. 362)

26-4 **erhu** Chinese stringed instrument (p. 364)

THINKING CRITICALLY ABOUT MUSIC

1. To further explore regional–international fusions, do either or both of the following activities:
   a. Listen to a recording of Ravi Shankar playing traditional Indian music. Then view one or two Bollywood dance scenes. (There are plenty on YouTube.)
   b. Find a recording or video of a traditional music from a country or region in the Middle East. Then try to find a regional–international fusion in a genre or style with which you're familiar—for example, Turkish techno. Then consider the extent to which the regional influence shapes the final result. Based on what you heard in the traditional music, what regional influences (if any) are most prominent? What elements are featured? In what ways does the track you chose differ from the music in the style that you typically listen to?

TIMELINE : 1539–2010 *CONTINUED*

1775   1893   2010

1851 Crystal Palace Exhibition brings world musicians to Europe

1867 *Slave Songs of the United States* published

1889 Debussy hears gamelan music at Paris Universal Exposition

1906 Bartók and Kodály begin recording Hungarian folk music

1910s Cecil Sharp notates folk music in Appalachia

1930s Lomaxes record folk music in Appalachia

1935 Pete Seeger forms American Society for Comparative Musicology

1955 Society for Ethnomusicology is formed

1960s–1970s Many African and Caribbean nations achieve independence

1970s Reggae becomes popular

1980 WOMAD (World of Music, Arts, and Dance) formed

2005 N'Dour's *Egypt* wins Grammy for Best Contemporary World Music Album

2008 Kidjo's *Djin Djin* receives the same honor

2001 Tan Dun wins Academy Award for score of *Crouching Tiger, Hidden Dragon*

4LTR Press solutions are designed for today's learners through the continuous feedback of students like you. Tell us what you think about **MUSIC** and help us improve the learning experience for future students.

YOUR FEEDBACK MATTERS.

Complete the Speak Up survey in CourseMate at www.cengagebrain.com

 Follow us at www.facebook.com/4ltrpress